psychometric theory

McGRAW-HILL SERIES IN PSYCHOLOGY

Consulting Editors

NORMAN GARMEZY

HARRY F. HARLOW

LYLE V. JONES

HAROLD W. STEVENSON

psychometric theory

JUM C. NUNNALLY
Professor of Psychology
Vanderbilt University

McGRAW-HILL
BOOK COMPANY
NEW YORK
ST. LOUIS
SAN FRANCISCO
TORONTO
LONDON
SYDNEY

to my parents

PREFACE

This book is intended to serve as a comprehensive text for graduate-level courses in psychology designated Psychological Measurement, Test Theory or in courses designated by names that imply the same subject matter. In addition, it is hoped that the book will be useful to psychologists and other behavioral scientists.

This book is written for the general student in psychology rather than for any special group. It is intended to present an understandable account of what every good psychologist should know about psychometric theory. The book is slanted mainly toward those graduate students who plan to make a career of basic research in one of the subfields of psychology. In writing the book, I tried to keep in mind the needs of students interested in physiological psychology, learning, perception, personality, and other areas of investigation. Because measurement theory is particularly important to those who plan to perform basic research in differential psychology, the book contains much that is of direct interest in that area.

The emphasis on the general student and on problems of measurement in basic research guided the selection of topics and the selection of examples. This resulted in the exclusion of topics that would be of interest to psychologists in particular specialities. For example, the book does not go into the technical details of validating predictor tests, which is a topic of great interest to applied psychometricians but of slight interest to the general student. As another example, some esoteric models for psychological scaling (such as latent-structure analysis and nonmetric factoring) are not discussed. Such models are of direct interest mainly to basic researchers in psychological measurement, but they are not of much interest to the general student.

As the title implies, the book is concerned mainly with the theory of psychological measurement rather than with a summary of empirical findings. If, for example, the reader is seeking an acquaintance with existing tests of intelligence or personality, he is looking in the wrong book. If instead the reader would like to learn the principles that underlie the development and use of all psychological measurement methods, it is hoped that he is looking in the right book.

Since much of psychometric theory is intimately related to mathematical models of one kind or another, particular care has been given to the choice of mathematical language for discussing each topic. Much of the book could have been written more concisely if it were safe to assume that the average reader has a respectable acquaintance with mathematics and statistics, but that is not a safe assumption. In particular, if it were safe to assume that most readers have an acquaintance with elementary principles of matrix algebra, many of the topics could have been presented both more concisely and more elegantly. It was decided to assume slight mathematical background on the part of the average reader, and consequently the important mathematical developments are talked out and explained in detail. I believe that this approach will be beneficial to the average reader, but those readers who are gifted in mathematics and statistics may find themselves yawning at the slow pace of some mathematical arguments.

Since this book is written for the general student rather than only for future specialists in psychological measurement, care has been taken to list references to other sources only where (1) the points are controversial, (2) the sources are readily available, and (3) the material is understandable to the average reader. Whenever possible, readers are referred to comprehensive summaries of research in an area (e.g., research on response styles) rather than to multitudes of reports of separate studies. At the end of each chapter, additional readings are listed for the reader who wants to explore topics in greater depth.

In the final paragraph of the preface, it is customary to say that the author is indebted to many persons, and I truly am. I am indebted to Drs. Andrew Baggaley, Richard Gorsuch, and Lyle Jones for critical comments on the manuscript, but also as is customary to say, they certainly are not to blame for any inadequacies of this book. I am indebted to Drs. J. P. Guilford, Thelma Gwinn Thurstone, and W. C. Torgerson for permission to borrow extensively from their writings. I also appreciate permission to reproduce these materials granted by their publishers, these being, respectively, The American Psychological Association, *Educational and Psychological Measurement,* and John Wiley & Sons, Inc. In Chapter Twelve (on human abilities) I took the unusual step of quoting whole journal articles from the writings of J. P. Guilford and Thelma Gwinn Thurstone. I had intended to summarize their articles as part of my chapter, but my efforts to summarize did little justice to the richness and historical significance of their own writings. Drs. Guilford and Thurstone were very kind to permit me to reproduce their articles. Finally, I am deeply indebted to Miss Dorothy Timberlake and Mrs. Jacqueline Caldwell for their skillful, patient assistance in preparation of the manuscript for this book.   **JUM C. NUNNALLY**

CONTENTS

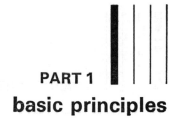

PART 1

basic principles

CHAPTER ONE
INTRODUCTION

measurement in science

Although tomes have been written on the nature of measurement, in the end it boils down to something rather simple: *measurement* consists of *rules for assigning numbers to objects to represent quantities of attributes*. The term "rules" indicates that the procedures for assigning numbers must be explicitly formulated. In some instances the rules are so obvious that detailed formulations are not required. This is the case when a yardstick is employed to measure lengths of lumber. What should be done is intuitively obvious, and consequently it is not necessary to study a thick manual of rules before undertaking the measurement. Such examples are, however, the exception rather than the usual in science. For instance, to measure the amounts of various components in chemical compounds often requires complex procedures that are not intuitively obvious. Certainly the rules for measuring most psychological attributes are not intuitively obvious. Examples are the measurement of intelligence in schoolchildren, the measurement of the amount of retention in a study of paired-associate learning, the measurement of "drive level" in the study of rats, the measurement of attitudes toward Negroes, and many others.

Frequently in this book reference will be made to the "standardization" of measures of psychological attributes. Essentially, a measure is said to be "well standardized" if different people who employ the measure obtain very similar results. Thus a measure of the surface temperature of planets in the solar system is well standardized if different astronomers who employ the methods obtain very similar numerical results for particular planets on particular occasions. Similarly, an intelligence test is well standardized if different examiners give approximately the same scores to the same children. Formulating explicit rules for the assignment of numbers is a major aspect of the standardization of measures. Other aspects of standardization will be discussed throughout this book.

basic principles

In the definition of measurement given above, the term "attribute" indicates that measurement always concerns some particular feature of objects. Strictly speaking, one does not measure objects—one measures their attributes. Thus one measures not the child, but rather the intelligence of the child. Although the distinction may sound like mere hairsplitting, it is important. First, it demonstrates that measurement requires a process of abstraction. An attribute concerns relations among objects on a particular dimension, e.g., weight and intelligence. A red rock and a white rock may weigh the same, and two white rocks may have different weights. Thus the attribute of weight is an abstraction which must not be confounded with all the particular features of objects. The point will be quite obvious to the sophisticated reader of this book, but it is not obvious, for example, to children or to adults in many primitive societies. With the latter there sometimes is confusion between a particular attribute of objects and all the recognizable attributes of objects. The failure to abstract a particular attribute makes concepts of measurement difficult to grasp. To some extent this confusion resides in the minds of civilized adults. For example, it is difficult for some people to understand that a criminal and a well-behaved member of society can have the same level of intelligence (as measured by intelligence tests).

A second reason for emphasizing that measurement always concerns a particular attribute is that it forces us to carefully consider the nature of the attribute before attempting to measure it. One possibility is that the attribute does not exist. For example, the many negative results obtained in the efforts to measure an attribute of "rigidity" in people make it doubtful that there is such an attribute. It is not necessarily the case that all the terms used to describe people are matched by measurable attributes, e.g., ego strength, extrasensory perception, and dogmatism. Another possibility is that a measure may concern a mixture of attributes rather than only one attribute. This frequently occurs in questionnaire measures of "adjustment," which tend to contain items relating to a number of separable attributes. Although such conglomerate measures sometimes are partly justifiable on practical grounds, the use of such conglomerate measures offers a poor foundation for psychological science. As this book will show in detail, each measure should concern some one *thing*, some isolatable, unitary attribute. To the extent to which unitary attributes should be combined to form an overall appraisal, e.g., of adjustment, they should be rationally combined from different measures rather than haphazardly combined within one measure.

Still looking at the definition of measurement, it is emphasized that *numbers* are used to represent *quantities*. Quantification concerns *how much* of an attribute is present in an object; numbers are used to communicate the amount. Quantification is so intimately interwoven with the concept of measurement that the two terms are often used interchangeably.

In the definition it is said that numbers are assigned to *objects*. The objects in psychology are usually people or lower animals. In some instances, however, the objects are material objects. For example, when people rate the pleasantness of each word in a list, the words are measured and the people act as part of the measurement process.

Although the definition emphasizes that *rules* for quantification are at the heart of measurement, it does not specify the nature of such rules or place any limit on the "allowable" kinds of rules. This is because a clear distinction should be made between the standards of measurement, qua the measurement process, and standards for validating measures, or determining their usefulness, once they are in existence. Initially, any particular set of rules, or any class of rules, is only a hypothesis. The hypothesis must be tested with respect to standards that are external to the measurement process per se. In other words, the proof of the usefulness of any measure is determined by the extent to which it enhances scientific explanation. Thus one psychologist might establish a set of rules for the measurement of dogmatism which seems quite illogical to his colleagues, but the usefulness of the measure could not be dismissed a priori. The usefulness of the measure would be determined by empirical investigations, where it would be determined to what extent the measure had functional relationships with important variables.

In establishing rules for the employment of a particular measure, the crucial consideration is that there must be a set of rules that is unambiguous. The rules may be developed from an elaborate deductive model, they may be based on much previous experience, they may flow from common sense, or they may spring from only hunches, but the proof of the pudding is in how well the measure serves to explain important phenomena. Consequently *any* set of rules that unambiguously quantifies properties of objects constitutes a *legitimate* measure and has a right to compete with other measures for scientific usefulness. (How scientific usefulness is determined will be discussed in Chapter Three.) The importance of this point is that it indicates a way of settling disputes about the correctness of different methods of *scaling* psychological attributes (different classes of rules for their measurement).

advantages of standardized measures

Although the reader probably has a healthy respect for the importance of measurement in science, it might be useful to look at some of the particular advantages which measurement provides. To note the advantages of standardized measures, It is necessary to compare them with what would be left if they were not available—for example, if there were no measures of temperature or intelligence. What would be left would be subjective appraisals, personal judgments, or whatever one would want to call the intuitive processes involved. Some of the advantages of standardized measures over personal judgments are as follows:

OBJECTIVITY   The major advantage of measurement is that it takes the guesswork out of scientific observation. A key principle of science is that any statement of fact made by one scientist should be independently verifiable by other scientists. The principle is violated if there is room for disagreement among scientists about the observation of empirical events. For example, since we have no standardized measure of "ego strength," two psychologists could disagree widely about the ego strength of a particular person. Obviously, then, it is not possible to make scientific tests of theories concerning ego strength. Thus theories concerning atomic particles, temperature of stars, intelligence of children, drive level in rats, and so on are testable to the extent to which there are unambiguous procedures for documenting empirical events. Standardized measures provide such procedures.

A case could be made that the major problem in psychology is that of measurement. There is no end of theories, but the theories are populated with terms (hypothesized attributes) which presently cannot be adequately measured; consequently the theories go untested. This is the problem with Freudian theory. There are no agreed-on procedures for observing and quantifying such attributes as ego strength, libidinal energy, narcissism, and others. In fact it seems that major advances in psychology, and probably in all sciences, are preceded by breakthroughs in measurement methods. This is attested to by the flood of research following the development of intelligence tests. Recent advances in techniques for measuring the electrical activity of individual nerve cells provide another example of how the development of measurement methods spurs research. Scientific results inevitably are reported in terms of functional relations among measured variables, and the science of psychology will progress neither slower nor faster than it becomes possible to measure important variables.

QUANTIFICATION   The numerical results provided by standardized measures have two advantages. First, numerical indices make it possible to report results in finer detail than would be the case with personal judgments. Thus the availability of thermometers makes it possible to report the exact increase in temperature when two chemicals are mixed, rather than only that "the temperature increases." Similarly, whereas teachers may be able to reliably assign children to broad categories of intelligence such as "bright," "average," and "below normal," intelligence tests provide finer differentiations.

A second advantage of quantification is that it permits the use of powerful methods of mathematical analysis. This is essential in the elaboration of theories and in the analysis of experiments. Although it may be a long time off for psychology, it is reasonable to believe that all theories eventually will be expressed in mathematical form. Only when theories are in mathematical form is it possible to make precise deductions for experimental investigation. Without powerful methods of analysis, such as factor analysis and analysis of variance, it would be all but impossible to assess the results of research.

COMMUNICATION   Science is a highly public enterprise in which efficient communication among scientists is essential. Each scientist builds on what has been learned in the past, and day by day he must compare his findings with those of other scientists working on the same types of problems. Communication is greatly facilitated when standardized measures are available. Suppose, for example, in an experiment concerning the effects of stress on anxiety reaction, it is reported that a particular treatment made the subjects "appear anxious." This would leave many questions as to what the experimenter meant by "appear anxious," and consequently it would be very difficult for other experimenters to investigate the same effects. Much better communication would be achieved if standardized measures of anxiety were available. If the means and standard deviations of scores for the different treatment groups were reported, very efficient and precise communication with other scientists would be possible. Even if subjective evaluations of experimental results are very carefully done, they are much more difficult to communicate than are statistical analyses of standardized measures. The rate of scientific progress in a particular area is limited by the efficiency and fidelity with which scientists can communicate their results to one another.

ECONOMY   Although it frequently requires a great deal of work to develop standardized measures, once developed they frequently are much more economical of time and money than are subjective evaluations. For example, even if a teacher were a good judge of intelligence, he probably would need to observe a child for some months to make a good judgment. A better appraisal usually could be obtained from one of the group measures of intelligence, which would take no more than an hour to administer and might cost less than 25 cents per child. Rather than have clinical psychologists individually interview each recruit for the armed services, a large group of recruits can be administered a printed test. In a study of the effect of a particular drug on amount of activity of white rats, it would be far more economical to employ standardized measures (e.g., the activity wheel) than to have trained observers sit for hours noting the amount of activity.

Besides saving time and money, standardized measures often free highly trained professionals for more important work. Physicists, psychologists, and many other types of professional people are in short supply, and the shortages apparently will grow worse in the years ahead. Consequently, a great saving is obtained in many instances when time-consuming observations by professionals are replaced by standardized measures. Of course, sometimes it is difficult to disentangle the scientist from the measurement process, which, for example, is the case in employing individually administered tests of intelligence. Although some individual tests of intelligence are highly standardized, they still require much time for administration and scoring. The direction of progress, however, is always toward developing measures that either require very little effort to employ or are so simple to administer and score that semi-skilled workers can do the job. Standardized measures are in most cases, although not all, more economical of the scientist's time than is subjective observation; consequently they give scientists more time for the scholarly and creative aspects of their work.

measurement and mathematics

It is important to make a clear distinction between measurement, which is directly concerned with the real world, and mathematics, which is purely an abstract enterprise that need have nothing to do with the real world. Perhaps the two would not be so readily confused if they did not both frequently involve quantification. Mathematical systems are purely deductive, being sets of rules for the manipulation of symbols. Symbols for quantities constitute only one type of symbol found in mathematics, and much of modern mathematics concerns deductive systems whose symbols do not relate to numbers. Any set of rules for manipulating a group of symbols can be a legitimate branch of mathematics as long as the rules are internally consistent. Thus the statement *"iggle wug drang flous"* could be a legitimate mathematical statement in a set of rules stating that when any *iggle* is *wugged* it *drang* a *flous.* An elaborate mathematical system could be constructed in which both the objects and the operations were symbolized by nonsense words. Of course, the system might not be of any use, but the legitimacy of the system would depend entirely on the internal consistency of the rules. Thus if the system of rules left it in doubt whether the *iggle drang* a *flous* or *drang* a *squiegle,* there would be a flaw in the system.

In contrast to mathematics, measurement always concerns numbers, and the legitimacy of any system of measurement is determined by empirical data. Measurement always concerns *how much* of an attribute is present, which requires a numerical statement of the amount. (The only exception to this principle would be in those cases where detecting the presence or absence of an attribute was thought of as measurement, e.g., the detection of brain damage. In such instances it might be more appropriate to speak of "identification" rather than "measurement.")

Measurement concerns the real world in terms of purposes, operations, and validity. The purpose is to quantify the attributes of real objects and persons; the operations concern doing something (according to a set of rules) to obtain measurements. The validity, or usefulness, of a measure always depends on the character of empirical data. If a measure is intended to fit a set of axioms for measurement (a model), the closeness of the fit can be determined only by the extent to which relations in empirical data meet the requirements of the model. Regardless of the character of the model or even if there is no formal model, the eventual and crucial test of any measure is the extent to which it has explanatory power in its relations with other variables.

Scientists *develop* measures by stating rules for the quantification of attributes of real objects; they *borrow* mathematical systems for examining the internal relations of the data obtained with a measure and for relating different measures to one another. Although past experience, common sense, and rational argument may make a good case for one method of measurement or mathematical analysis over another, the final justification requires finding a rich set of lawful relations among variables in the real world.

MEASUREMENT AND STATISTICS Because the term "statistics" is used so broadly, one could argue that the theory of psychological measurement has either a great deal or little to do with statistics. First, it is important to make a distinction between *inferential statistics* and other mathematical methods of analysis. Inferential statistics concern probability statements relating observed sample values to population parameters. Thus obtaining the arithmetic mean of the scores on one test or the correlation between scores on two tests would constitute mathematical analyses which need not involve inferential statistics. Since the purpose of performing mathematical analyses of central tendency, dispersion, and correlation is to describe various aspects of empirical data, these and related methods of analysis are said to form *descriptive statistics* in contrast to inferential statistics. Employment of inferential statistics, as in setting confidence zones or in "testing for significance," would constitute additional steps. Because very little will be said in this book about probability statements relating sample values to population parameters, the quantitative methods would be better spoken of as methods of analysis or descriptive statistics rather than as inferential statistics. Thus correlational analysis, factor analysis, discriminatory analysis, and others can be discussed and employed without necessarily resorting to inferential statistics, which is not meant to imply that inferential statistics per se are not useful adjuncts to the development and use of psychological measures.

A second important distinction is that between statistics concerning the sampling of people and statistics concerning the sampling of content (test items). After measures are developed and then employed in empirical investigations, it is important to employ inferential statistics concerning the sampling of people. Before measures are developed, however, the theory that guides such measurement is much more related to the sampling of content than to the sampling of people. As will be described in detail later, it is useful to think of the items on a particular test as being a sample from a hypothetical infinite population or universe of items measuring the same trait. Thus a spelling test for fourth-grade students can be thought of as a sample of all possible words that would be appropriate. Measurement theory then would concern statistical relations between the scores actually made on the test and the hypothetical scores that would be made if all items in the universe had been administered.

Thus there is a two-way sampling problem in psychology, one concerned with the sampling of people and the other with the sampling of content. The former concerns the generality of findings over populations of persons, and the latter concerns the generality of findings over populations of test items. It proves all but impossible to simultaneously take account of both dimensions of sampling when performing statistical analyses. One dimension of sampling is difficult enough to consider in any particular analysis. What typically is done in practice is to explicitly take account of one dimension of sampling and simply keep the other dimension in mind as a possible influence on the results of the experiment. Thus in a study of the influence of a particular type of training on achievement in mathematics, explicit account would be taken of the sampling of subjects, but it would be kept in mind that somewhat different results might have been obtained with a different measure of achievement. Similarly, in a study of reliability, where the major concern would be with the sampling of content, it would be kept in mind that the results might have been somewhat different in a larger sample of persons or in a sample drawn from another source.

The practical necessity in particular studies of making explicit statistical analyses of only one of two dimensions of sampling does not spoil the game. What is required is that the generality of findings, either over people or over content, be investigated in subsequent studies. An even safer approach, if feasible, is to sample so extensively on one dimension that only sampling error with respect to the other dimension need be a serious concern. This is the recommended approach in the development of psychological measures. Enough subjects should be used in developing psychological measures that sampling error with respect to persons is a minor consideration. At least hundreds, and where possible, thousands of subjects should be used in the development of a new measure. In the remainder of this book it will be assumed that all mathematical analyses are based on large numbers of subjects; consequently the text will be left free to consider only the sampling of content. Even if it were feasible to work with statistics that simultaneously considered both dimensions of sampling, studies conducted on relatively small numbers of subjects would not be sufficient. For example, in a study of the reliability of a new measure, the need is to determine what the reliability *is*; a statement only that the reliability coefficient is significantly different from zero is nearly worthless.

Apparently it is difficult for some persons to comprehend that in the development of psychological measures the major concern is with the sampling of content rather than with the sampling of people. For example, graduate students in psychology frequently fall into the trap of assuming that the reliability of a test increases with the number of people used in the study of reliability. Any reader who does not already know will learn later that the reliability estimate obtained in any particular study is independent of the number of persons in the study, but in any study the reliability is directly related to the number of items on the test.

measurement scales

During recent years in psychology there has been much talk about the different possible types of measurement scales, and there has been much soul-searching about the types of scales characterized by different types of psychological measures. Although these discussions represent a healthy self-consciousness about scientific methods, they have, the author thinks, led to some unfortunate confusions. Essentially the issues concern what sorts of "interpretations" can be made of the numbers obtained from psychological measures. More precisely, the issues concern the legitimacy of employing particular classes of mathematical procedures with measures of psychological attributes. Does a measure of intelligence have the same mathematical status as does a yardstick? Does a measure of learning rate in paired-associate learning have the same mathematical status as does a measure of electrical resistance? In this section will be presented a simplified, conventional classification of measurement scales. The next section will contain a more probing discussion about the nature of psychological measurement.

Measurement scales concern different uses made of numbers. Following is a classification of some of these uses.

LABELS Numbers are frequently used as a way of keeping track of things, without any suggestion that the numbers can be subjected to mathematical analyses. For example, a geologist working in the field might choose to number his specimens of rocks 1, 2, 3, etc., in which case the numbers would be used purely as labels and would have no implications for mathematical analyses. It would make no sense to add the numbers representing the first and second rock and equate that in any way with the 3 relating to the third rock. Other examples of numbers used as labels are the numbers on the backs of football players, numbers on highway signs, and the numbers of atomic elements.

It must be emphasized that any measurement scale concerns an *intended use* of numbers. One intended use of numbers is for labeling. In this instance there is no intention of performing mathematical analyses of the numbers, and the numbers are not considered to represent quantities of attributes. It may be the case, however, that numbers used as labels happen to correlate with quantities of attributes. Thus in the example of the geologist and his rocks it may be that, as his sack of rocks grows heavier, he discerningly picks smaller and smaller specimens; consequently the numbers used as labels would incidentally relate to the weights of the rocks. Similarly, high-numbered highways may in some way be quantitatively different from low-numbered highways, and atomic elements further along in the numbering scheme may be quantitatively different from earlier-positioned elements. The crucial point is that, in discussing the nature of measurement scales in particular instances, one must justify the *use* of the numbers. Whether or not there are incidental quantitative correlates of a particular set of numbers is not relevant to a discussion of the legitimacy of the intended use of the numbers. Since labels are not intended to imply quantities of attributes, no justification is required for employing numbers as labels.

CATEGORIES Closely related to the use of numbers as labels is their use to represent groups of objects. For example, the geologist might classify each of his rocks into one of the categories of sedimentary, igneous, or metamorphic, and refer to these categories as 1, 2, and 3. Other classification schemes include different professions, the two sexes, and brain-damaged and normal people. The only differences between employing numbers as labels and employing them to represent categories are that in the latter use (1) more than one object goes with each number and (2) all the objects assigned to the same number are alike with respect to some attribute. As is true of numbers used as labels, numbers used to represent categories in a classification scheme have no quantitative implications. Similarly, numbers used to represent categories may have many incidental correlates with quantities of attributes. Thus, on the average, males and females differ in height, athletic ability, and a host of other attributes; but that is entirely unrelated to justifying the use of the numbers 1 and 2 to stand for males and females, respectively. Since numbers used to represent categories are not intended to have quantitative implications, no justification is required for using numbers for that purpose.

Some would speak of categorization as representing the lowest form of measurement. Earlier it was stated that categorization might better be spoken of as identification rather than measurement. As used in this book, "measurement" will always refer to some type of quantification of an attribute rather than to the use of numbers as labels or to represent categories.

In discussing categorization, a distinction should be made between using numbers to represent categories and using them to signify the frequency with which objects appear in different categories. Thus the geologist might categorize 22 of his specimens as being igneous rocks. In such instances it is sometimes said that one "measures" the number of cases in different categories, but according to the definition of "measurement" given earlier, this would be an improper use of the term. It would be more proper to say that one "enumerates," or counts, the objects in categories.

ORDINAL SCALES An ordinal scale is one in which (1) a set of objects or people is ordered from "most" to "least" with respect to an attribute, (2) there is no indication of "how much" in an absolute sense any of the objects possess the attribute, and (3) there is no indication of how far apart the objects are with respect to the attribute. Rank ordering is the most primitive form of measurement (excluding labels and categories as constituting measurement)—primitive in that it is basic to all higher forms of measurement and it conveys only meager information.

An ordinal scale is obtained, for example, when a group of boys is ordered from tallest to shortest. This scale would give no indication of the average height: as a group the boys might be relatively tall or relatively short. The scale would supply no information about how much the boys varied in terms of height. With respect to methods of analysis, it is meaningless to compute the mean and the standard deviation of a set of ranks. These indices are the cornerstones of most of the powerful methods of mathematics and statistics needed in psychology, methods without which it would be all but impossible to advance the science.

What is frequently not understood is that the numbers employed with ordinal scales provide only a convenient shorthand for designating relative positions of objects. A rank-order scale is obtained when, for any N persons (S's), it is known that $S_i > S_j > S_k > S_n$ with respect to an attribute.

Some have claimed that most psychological scales, e.g., intelligence tests, should be considered as providing only a rank ordering of people rather than any higher form of measurement. In a later section issue will be taken with that point of view.

INTERVAL SCALES An interval scale is one in which (1) the rank ordering of objects is known with respect to an attribute and (2) it is known how far apart the objects are from one another with respect to the attribute, but (3) no information is available about the *absolute* magnitude of the attribute for any object. An interval scale would be obtained for the heights of a group of boys if, instead of being measured directly, the height of each boy were measured with respect to the shortest boy in the group. Thus the shortest boy would obtain a score of 0, a boy 2 inches taller than the shortest boy would obtain a score of 2, and a boy 3 inches taller would obtain a score of 3, and so on. More directly related to what is done with most psychological measures would be to specify intervals in terms of the distance of each boy from the arithmetic mean of heights of the boys. Thus a boy whose height is 2 inches above the mean would receive a score of $+2$, and a boy who is 2 inches below the mean would receive a score of -2. Intervals about the mean height, or such intervals for any other attribute, can be calculated without actually knowing how far any of the persons are from the zero point (for example, zero height or zero intelligence).

A potentially important item of information not supplied by interval scales is the absolute magnitude of the attribute for any particular person or object. Thus even though the tallest boy may have an interval score above the mean of $+6$ (6 inches above the average), this would not tell us how tall he is in an absolute sense. He might be the tallest boy in a group of pygmies.

Because interval scales are sometimes spoken of as "equal interval" scales, it is easy to make the mistake of assuming that such scales require an equal number of persons or objects at each point on the continuum—a rectangular distribution of scores. What actually is meant by "equal" is that intervals on the scale are equal regardless of the number of persons or objects at different points on the scale. Thus on an interval scale for the measurement of intelligence, the *difference* between IQs of 100 and 105 would be assumed equal to the *difference* between IQs of 120 and 125. Of course, the practical implications of such equal differences on the scale might be most unequal, but strictly speaking that has nothing to do with the interval character of the scale.

Similarly, if three automobiles are traveling 30, 60, and 90 miles per hour, respectively, the interval between the first two is equal to the interval between the second and third, but of course, these two intervals might have very different implications for traffic safety, gas mileage, and wear and tear on the automobiles. Thus it is necessary to draw a careful distinction between the character of a measurement scale, interval scale or otherwise, and the practical implications of the scale points.

RATIO SCALES   A ratio scale is obtained when (1) the rank order of persons with respect to an attribute is known, (2) the intervals between persons are known, and (3) in addition, the distance from a rational zero is known for at least one of the persons. In other words, a ratio scale is a particular type of interval scale in which distances are stated with respect to a rational zero rather than with respect to, for example, the height of the tallest boy or the shortest boy or the mean height. Obviously, if an interval scale of height is available and in addition the absolute height (distance from zero) of any boy in the group is known, the absolute heights of all the other boys can be calculated.

OTHER SCALES   Ordinal, interval, and ratio scales are the basic scales of measurement. There are, however, many possible variants and combinations of these (see Coombs, 1960, for a discussion of some of the possibilities). For example, one could have an *ordered metric* scale in which (1) the rank order of persons is known, (2) the rank order of intervals is known, but (3) the magnitudes of the intervals are not known. In such a scale it would be possible to say that the largest interval is between persons A and B and the smallest interval is between persons C and D, but it would not be possible to say that the former interval is twice as large as the latter.

Stevens (1958) has proposed a *logarithmic interval scale*, where if the successive points on the scale are designated a, b, c, etc., the successive ratios of magnitudes corresponding to those points would be $a/b = b/c = c/d$, etc. Then

$$\log a - \log b = \log b - \log c = \log c - \log d$$

etc. Many other variants of the three basic types of measurement scales can be postulated, but they have been of little importance in psychometric theory or application.

PERMISSIBLE OPERATIONS   The relative importance of discussing different measurement scales is that some types of scales are open to many more forms of mathematical treatments than are others. The ratio scale is susceptible to the fundamental operations of algebra: addition, subtraction, division, and multiplication. Thus it makes sense to apply these operations to the height of boys, e.g., to say that Tom is three-fourths as tall as Bob. With these operations come all the power of mathematics, including algebra, analytic geometry, calculus and all the more powerful statistical methods. Without such mathematical tools the scientist is almost out of business.

An important consideration with regard to measurement scales is that of the circumstances over which a particular type of scale remains *invariant*. Thus any ratio scale remains invariant over all transformations where the scale is multiplied by a constant:

$$X' = cX$$

If X symbolizes all possible points on a ratio scale, and all such points are multiplied by a constant c, the resulting scale X' is a ratio scale. The resulting scale will meet all the requirements of a ratio scale, because (1) the rank order of points will remain the same, (2) the ratios of points will remain the same, and (3) the zero point will remain the same. An example of such a transformation is when one changes a scale of inches to a scale of feet—by dividing all the points in the scale of inches by 12.

Two examples of invariant transformations of a ratio scale are shown in Figure 1-1. An invariant transformation is represented by any straight line passing through the origin. If the line curves or does not go through the origin, the transformation is not invariant. In those cases if X is a ratio scale, X' is not a ratio scale.

The importance of invariance is that it determines the generality of scientific statements regarding a scale. It is easy to imagine the chaos that would result if some measures of physical quantities lacked the invariance of ratio scales. Without invariance, it might be found that one stick is twice as long as another when measured in feet but three times as long when measured in inches. The range of invariance of a scale determines the extent to which natural laws remain essentially the same when the scale is expressed in different units, e.g., feet rather than inches. Suppose that a natural law has the following form:

$$X = 2Y^2 + 4Y + 6$$

Let Y be any variable of scientific interest—monthly rainfall, speed of atomic particles, reaction of humans to stress, or whatever. Let X be any other variables that it would be of scientific interest to relate to Y. If X is a ratio scale, any invariant transformation of a ratio scale will produce another scale which will preserve the general form of the relationship with Y. Thus if $X' = cX$ and $c = 2$, the above relation with Y would be

$$X' = 4Y^2 + 8Y + 12$$

An invariant transformation of a ratio scale alters proportionally the coefficients of any equation relating that measure to any other measure, but otherwise has no effect on the form of the relationship, e.g., it does not alter any of the exponents. Thus, for all practical purposes, any invariant transformation of a scale produces the *same* scale—same in the sense that it will manifest the same general form of relationship with any other variable.

The potential disadvantage of having only an interval scale of measurement rather than a ratio scale is that with the former some limitations are placed on application of the fundamental operations of algebra.

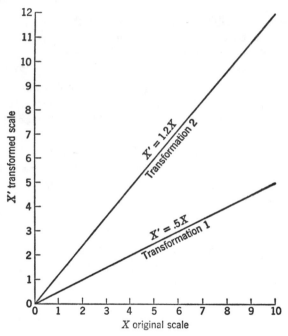

figure 1-1 *Two invariant transformations of a ratio scale (X) to a new ratio scale (X').*

For example, if on an intelligence test John gets 80 items correct and Bill gets 40 items correct, it makes no sense to say that John is twice as intelligent as Bill. Multiplication and division with interval scales are permissible only with respect to the *intervals* and not with respect to the scale values. With interval scales, it is permissible to employ addition and subtraction on the scale values as well as on the intervals.

If $a, b, c, \ldots, k$ are points on a scale, an interval scale is defined by two statements:

(1) $a > b > c \ldots k$ and (2) $a - b = b - c = c - d = \ldots = j - k$

basic principles

Since an interval scale is defined in terms of algebraic differences between points, it follows that subtraction and addition of the scale points are permissible operations. Thus since $a - b = b - c$, the sum of the two intervals equals $(a - b) + (b - c) = a - c$, which it logically should. The difference of the two intervals should equal zero:

$$(a - b) - (b - c) = a - 2b + c$$

The expression equals zero because $a + c = 2b$:

$$a - b = b - c$$

$$a + c = 2b$$

These calculations demonstrate the reason for permitting addition and subtraction of the scale values on interval scales.

Since by definition the points are assumed to be equidistant on an interval scale, it follows that

$$\frac{a - b}{b - c} = 1$$

which illustrates the legitimacy of forming ratios of *intervals* on interval scales. As another example of the legitimate employment of multiplication and division with the intervals, the distance from a to c should equal twice the distance from a to b when calculated from the equalities stated in the definition of the scale, which, of course, it does.

The permissible mathematical operations with interval scales relate to the circumstances under which invariance is obtained. Whereas a ratio scale is invariant under transformations of the form

$$X' = cX$$

an interval scale is invariant under any linear transformation:

$$X' = cX + b$$

In transforming one interval scale for measuring an attribute to any other interval scale for measuring the same attribute, invariance will be obtained not only if the points on the first scale are multiplied by any constant, but also if a constant amount b is added to each point. This is because the absolute magnitudes on an interval scale are irrelevant. Adding such a constant will not change the ordinal positions of points or the equality of intervals. After the transformation is made, intervals separating persons at different points on the scale will be a constant proportion of the same intervals on the original scale. Take the case where on the original scale person S_1 is at 20 (a point on the interval scale), S_2 is 30, S_3 is 40, and S_4 is 45. The interval between the first two persons is 10, and the interval between the latter two persons is 5—the first interval is twice as large as the second. Any transformation that maintains such proportions is invariant. Suppose that we transform the scale by multiplying all the points by 2 and then adding 10 to each of the resulting points. Now S_1 and S_2 are 50 and 70, respectively, and S_3 and S_4 are 90 and 100, respectively. The proportionality of intervals is maintained, and thus the transformation is invariant. Because the b term is the same for all points, it "falls out" when the intervals are calculated and consequently the proportionality is maintained regardless of what b is.

Whereas the conditions of invariance demonstrate why it is permissible to form ratios of the *intervals* (multiply and divide by one another), they also demonstrate why it is not permissible to form ratios among the *scale points* on an interval scale. Conditions of invariance permit the addition of an arbitrary constant to each of the scale points on an interval scale, but the arbitrary constant could markedly change the ratios among the scale points. Consider the invariant transformation

$$X' = X + 50$$

and consider persons at points 2 and 4 on X. The ratio of the second person to the first person is 2, but the ratio of the transformed scores is 54:52. This illustrates why it is not permissible to multiply scale points by one another or divide them into one another.

As is true of invariant transformations of ratio scales, invariant transformations of any interval scale do not change the general form of the relationship of that scale with any other variable. Thus if there is a linear relationship between X and Y and an invariant (linear) transformation is made of X, X' will also have a linear relationship with Y. The importance of this point is that any natural laws stated with respect to an interval scale will remain essentially the same when invariant transformations are made of the scale. Some invariant transformations of an interval scale are shown in Figure 1-2.

With ordinal scales, none of the fundamental operations of algebra may be applied. In the use of descriptive statistics, it makes no sense to add, subtract, divide, or multiply ranks. Since an ordinal scale is defined entirely in terms of inequalities, only the algebra of inequalities can be used to analyze measures made on such scales—which is awkward, weak algebra. Ordinal scales are invariant over any *monotonic* transformation. Some invariant transformations of an ordinal scale are shown in Figure 1-3. In the figure, X is either an interval or ratio scale on which the scores of individuals are to be ranked; X' is any monotonic transformation of X, on which individuals also are to be ranked. It might be helpful to think of X as a measure of the height of boys in inches and X' as any monotonic transformation of the scale of inches. If boys are ranked on X, the order will be preserved when they are ranked on X'.

Functional relations among ordinal scales provide only meager in-

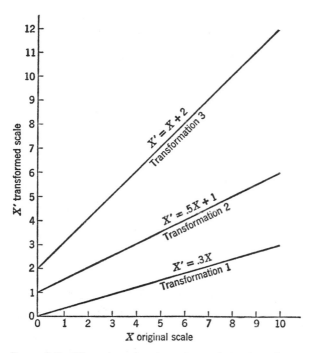

figure 1-2 *Three invariant transformations of an interval scale (X) to a new interval scale (X').*

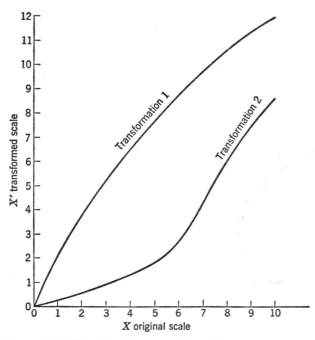

figure 1-3 *Two invariant transformations that preserve the rank order of points from X to points on X'.*

formation about what the relations would be if interval or ratio scales were available. Suppose that with ratio scales the following monotonic relations are known between positive values of X and positive values of two other variables, Y and Z:

$$Y = aX + b$$
$$Z = X^3 + X^2 + X + b$$

If all three scales were transformed to ordinal scales, the expressions would change to

$$Y = X$$
$$Z = X$$

Since both Y and Z are monotonic functions of X, the ordinal scales are unable to "detect" the very different forms of relationship, which illustrates the amount of information that is lost when only ordinal scales are available.

decisions about measurement scales

The previous section presented the "fundamentalist" point of view about measurement scales, which, to summarize, holds that (1) there are distinct types of measurement scales into which all possible measures of attributes can be classified, (2) each measure has some "real" characteristics that permit its proper classification, and (3) once a measure is classified, the classification specifies the types of mathematical analyses that can be employed with the measure. In this section it will be argued that this is a narrow point of view that needs to be severely modified before it can meet the actualities of scientific inquiry.

The fundamentalist point of view has caused much consternation among psychologists about proper methods of analysis. Take, for example, the psychologist who wants to study the relations among tests involving a variety of human abilities. What type of scales does he have? He does not need to claim that they are ratio scales, because the powerful methods of analysis needed in this situation, such as factor analysis, require only interval scales. But how does he know if he has interval scales? Maybe they are only ordinal scales, or maybe they are not legitimate scales of any kind. Although the fundamentalist point of view forces these questions upon the investigator, it does not provide methods for answering the questions. One result of this dilemma was a flight into nonparametric statistics (those appropriate to ordinal scales and categories) during the early 1950s. In many cases these methods are so weak that they simply cannot do the job at hand. Partly as a consequence, psychologists apparently have mainly gone back to those powerful methods of analysis that take the interval seriously; but still there is a lingering feeling of guilt among some that such methods of analysis are not really justified. Here it will be argued that it is only the guilt, rather than the use of methods of analysis, that is unjustified.

Those who accept the fundamentalist point of view hold that (1) measurement scales have empirical reality in addition to being theoretical constructions and (2) the investigator must show evidence of the scale properties of particular measures before employing certain methods of analysis. The first will be severely questioned in a later section. Even if one accepts the first point, no one has made it clear what types of evidence would justify the assumption of a particular type of scale. The following sections will attempt an answer.

OSTENSIVE CHARACTERISTICS   One way to judge the scale characteristics of a particular measure is in terms of the physical characteristics of the measurement operations. The best example of this, and perhaps the only pure one, is the measurement of length with a yardstick. To prove that the attribute in question is measured on a ratio scale requires (1) a proof of equal intervals and (2) the demonstration of an axiomatically unquestionable zero point. Anyone can see the zero point—it is where the yardstick starts. Back of that point is open space; in front of it is the wooden beginning of the measuring instrument. Who could argue that a more meaningful zero point could be located elsewhere on the yardstick? The equality of intervals is also easy to demonstrate. One way would be to saw the yardstick inch by inch and then compare the pieces two at a time to ensure that they are all equal. (Actually, one could make science fiction–type arguments that there are alternative zero points and alternative ways of establishing equal intervals in the measurement of length, but for the sake of the discussion here it will be assumed that the scale properties of yardsticks are intuitively obvious.)

The yardstick exemplifies the two ostensive characteristics supposedly required for a ratio scale: visually (or palpably otherwise) discernible zero and fractionation into visually equal intervals. No other measure so obviously passes the tests. The closest is the measurement of weight with a balance. If two objects keep the scale in balance even when the right-left placements on the scale are alternated, it is intuitively obvious that they are of the same weight. Then either of the two weights can be compared with other weights to find one that is equal to the first two. Continuing in this way, a collection of equal units can be obtained, e.g., of 1-pound size, to form an interval scale for the measurement of weight. This would provide an obvious physical fractionation into equal intervals of weight. The rational zero also is intuitively obvious—nothing on the scale.

No other measures have the palpable qualities that allow the scale properties to be determined by ostensive characteristics. To a lesser or greater extent, all other measures consist of inspecting the physical states of variables that correlate (perfectly or only in a statistical sense) with the variable to be measured. In other words, all other measures are indirect. When measuring length, one is actually seeing the attribute directly rather than seeing some correlate of length. Any two pieces of twine can be directly compared in length; thus one sees length itself and not just a correlate of length. With the measuring of weight, this is only partially so, because the attribute itself is the pull of gravity on the object, which is correlated with the influence of the object on the balance (or other devices for the measurement of weight). Thus one cannot see weight directly. Though it may be argued that one can *feel* weight directly (by lifting), such judgments are not nearly reliable enough to serve as evidence that weight has the ostensive characteristics required for a ratio scale.

When measures of length and weight are set aside, it becomes obvious that almost all attributes are measured indirectly, and consequently one cannot look to the ostensive characteristics of the *correlate* to determine the scale characteristics by which the attribute itself is manifested in the correlate. Even the measurement of such a basic attribute as time is done quite indirectly. Time has no ostensive characteristics that specify the equality of intervals as measured by clocks and other devices. Intervals of time are *defined* in terms of the regularity of certain events. Thus the clock ticks, the pendulum swings, and the earth turns, and these are defined as measures of time (which, of course, is not completely in keeping with the Einsteinian concept of time).

For other measures of physical attributes, it is even more obvious that the measure itself is only a correlate of the actual attribute. Thus to observe the height of the column of mercury in a thermometer is to observe not temperature itself, but a correlate of temperature. In all sciences, and certainly in psychology, the observations required in the operations of measurement usually are not the same as observations of the attributes themselves. Thus in a measure of intelligence, one is observing not intelligence directly, but rather Its supposed by-products. A body-sway test of suggestibility is, of course, only an indirect measure of the attribute.

Although perhaps none have said it directly, those who take the fundamentalist point of view imply that scale properties can be judged only by ostensive characteristics. Since, for example, there are no ostensive properties to guarantee the equality of intervals in the measurement of intelligence, it has been argued that tests of intelligence constitute at best ordinal scales. It is hoped the previous paragraphs have shown that by the same standards there would be few measures in all science that could be considered more than ordinal scales; it is hoped the following sections will show that proper standards for judging the scale properties of a measure are not dependent on observing the ostensive characteristics of the attribute to be measured.

SCALING MODELS   Another approach to the discussion of scale characteristics concerns the use of various models for the construction of measures. Each such model constitutes a set of axioms concerning how the data should appear when the measure is put to use. For example, a sensible axiom in any model for the development of interval scales is that of *transitivity*. If a model leads to independent scorings of intervals among persons on a scale of measurement and it is found that the score for person A is 5 points above that for person B and the score for person B is 5 points above that for person C, it should also be found that the score for person A is 10 points above that for person C. This extremely simple and commonsense assumption is mentioned only to illustrate the axioms that appear in different measurement models. The details of some of the most prominent different measurement models will be described in Chapter Two.

If the data obtained from applying a measurement scale fit the axioms of the particular model under consideration and the axioms (assumptions) of the model are correct, the measure has scale properties specified by the model. An example may help to clarify this important point. In Chapter Two will be described a model proposed by Louis Guttman for the construction of ordinal scales. It makes a set of assumptions about patterns of responses of people to test items. After the items are administered to samples of persons, mathematical analyses can be made to determine how well the actual patterns of scores fit the patterns of scores predicted by the model. If the fit is good, the model stipulates that an ordinal scale of measurement has been obtained; if the fit is poor, the hypothesis of an ordinal scale is rejected.

There are two important points to be made about the place of scaling models in discussions of scale properties. First, this type of standard is based on empirical data, in contrast to standards concerning ostensive characteristics. In the former, one studies the results from applying a measure to objects in the real world; in the latter, one "studies" the observable characteristics of the measurement tool itself. For example, instead of determining the scale properties of yardsticks merely by looking at them, one could establish a model concerning the properties of ratio scales and then see if the data obtained from employing the yardstick to measure many objects fit the model. One could derive the scale properties of the yardstick from the model even if one had never seen a yardstick. (Actually, data obtained from applying the yardstick to, say, sticks of different lengths would beautifully fit a number of the models that have been proposed for the scaling of psychological attributes. The data would, for example, fit the assumption of transitivity mentioned previously.) This is what psychological scaling is about: it is an attempt to work backward from empirical data to test the fit to a model. In this way an attempt is made to develop ratio, interval, and ordinal scales for psychological attributes, many of which attributes cannot be seen directly.

A second important point to make about the place of scaling models in discussing the properties of measurement scales is that a model is no better and no worse than its assumptions (axioms). There is ample room for disagreement, and there is plenty of it, about the *fruitfulness* of different models. For example, later it will be argued that certain measures should be analyzed with methods that assume interval scales even though data obtained with the measures would not even fit the assumptions of one of the models for ordinal scaling. If psychologists are "allowed" to disagree about the correctness of different scaling models, how then are the scale characteristics of measures ever determined? If, for example, models for the development of interval scales are being tried on a particular type of data, e.g., responses to statements concerning attitudes toward Negroes, the failure of the data to fit one model does not automatically prevent the measure from being considered as an interval scale; and if the data fit all the models under consideration, this does not automatically indicate that the measure should be considered as an interval scale. The final decision in this matter should be made with respect to standards that will be discussed in the following sections.

CONSEQUENCES OF ASSUMPTIONS Even if one believes that there is a "real" scale for each attribute, which is either mirrored directly in a particular measure or mirrored as some monotonic transformation, an important question is, "What difference does it make if the measure does not have the same zero point or proportionally equal intervals as the 'real' scale?" Since so much importance is attached to characteristics of measurement scales, if the scientist assumes, for example, that his scale is an interval scale when it really is not, something should go badly wrong in the daily work of the scientist. What would go wrong? How would the difficulty be detected? All that could go wrong would be that the scientist would make misstatements about the specific form of the relationship between the attribute and other variables. For example, using an imperfect interval scale, the scientist might report a linear relationship between the attribute and some other variable, whereas if he had employed the "real" interval scale, he would have found a power function instead.

How seriously are such misassumptions about scale properties likely to influence the reported results of scientific experiments? In psychology at the present time, the answer in most cases is "very little." The results of most studies are reported in the form of either (1) correlations between scores of individuals on different measures or (2) mean differences between differently treated groups. Regarding the former, correlations are affected very little by monotonic transformations of variables. Suppose that (1) a product-moment correlation is computed between a measure and another variable, (2) the measure is only an imperfect representation of the "real" scale, the intervals on the "real" scale being obtainable by a square-root transformation of the measure, and (3) the correlation is found to be .50. Would the correlation have been very different if the "real" scale rather than the imperfect scale had been correlated with the other variable? The correlation would change very little. It might, for example, go down to .48 or up to .52.

Within very broad limits, the correlation between two variables is affected very little by monotonic transformations of the variables. Product-moment correlation mainly is sensitive to the rank order of individuals on two measures. As long as that rank order is not disturbed, changes in the shapes of distributions make only very small changes in the correlation. Since the correlation coefficient is basic to all more complex methods of multivariate analysis, e.g., factor analysis, it follows that these more complex methods also are affected very little by transformations of measures. Consequently a strong argument can be made that the analysis of results would be very much the same whether the "real" scales had been employed or only approximate ones had been used. Then even if one accepted the fundamentalist point of view about measurement scales, what sense would it make to sacrifice powerful methods of analysis just because there is no way of proving the claimed scale properties of the measures?

In analyzing differences between means in differently treated groups, of major concern are ratios of variances among different sources of variation. For example, an important ratio is the variance among treatment means divided by the pooled variance within treatment groups. This and other important ratios among sources of variation are affected very little by monotonic transformations of the dependent measure. Then if it is granted that the measure used in the experiment is at least monotonically related to the "real" scale, it usually will make little difference which is used in the analysis.

After analyzing the results of investigations (obtaining correlations and ratios of variance components), it often is important to make probability statements about the results—in other words, to apply inferential statistics. Thus it may be important to set confidence zones for a correlation coefficient or to test the "significance" of a particular ratio among components of variance. Such statistical methods are completely indifferent to the zero point on a scale, and consequently ratio scales are not required. However, since such methods are based on ratios of variation and covariation, they operate directly on the interval properties of the measures. Following from this it has been mistakenly assumed by some that such methods of analysis, e.g., analysis of variance, can be performed only on interval scales of measurement. Statistical methods are completely blind to any meaning in the real world of the numbers involved. All that is required for the use of such methods is a definable population of numbers that meet the assumptions in the particular statistical method, e.g., normality of the population distribution. It would be, for example, perfectly permissible to employ analysis of variance to test hypotheses about the average size of the numbers on the backs of football players on different teams. Taking a more extreme example, if one suspected that different methods of obtaining tables of random numbers led to different results, analysis of variance could be used to compare different tables.

The important question in relation to inferential statistics concerns whether or not the indices of relationship, e.g., ratio of variance, should be computed and whether or not they can be meaningfully interpreted. After it is decided that such indices should be computed, there is no question of whether or not it is permissible to take the next step and apply inferential statistics. When dealing with measures of attributes, the computation of such indices requires assumptions about the interval character of the data; however, as was said above, violations of the assumptions usually have very little effect on the indices or on inferential statistics applied to the indices.

CONVENTION   So far in this section it has been necessary to take seriously the fundamentalist point of view that it is meaningful to think in terms of "real" scales and to think of actual measures as approximations of such "real" scales. These assumptions were tolerated up to this point to show that (1) they lead to unanswerable questions and (2) even if they were good assumptions, violations of them usually would not be harmful. As must be clear by this point, the author opposes the concept of "real" scales and deplores the confusion which this conception has wrought. It is much more appropriate to think of any measurement scale as a convention—an agreement among scientists that a particular scaling of an attribute is a "good" scaling.

In saying that scales are established by convention (rather than God-given), it is not meant to imply that such conventions should be arbitrary. Before measures of particular attributes are constructed, all manner of wisdom should be brought to bear on the nature of the attribute. With some types of measures, the nature of a "good" scaling is so readily agreed on by all that a convention is easily established. Thus it is with length and weight: no one opposes the ways of setting the zero point and the establishment of intervals. In exasperation about the confusion in theories of measurement, it is tempting to wish that there were no yardsticks and no balances for the measurement of weight. Then all scientists might more readily see that measurement is a matter of convention rather than of discovering the "real" measure.

In some instances a convention of measurement is established by one man, and since many scientists do not realize that they do, or should, participate in establishing such conventions, the particular scale is accepted by the scientific community as *the* scale. Thus for some time the Fahrenheit thermometer was taken as *the* scale for measuring temperature. Later, with the discovery of "absolute zero," a new scaling was developed, one which scientists in general will agree is a more proper scale for the assertion of natural laws. Another example is that of the use of "age scales" for intelligence tests, in which the IQ is a ratio of mental age to chronological age. This convention was established for many years, until it gradually became apparent that the approach to scaling had enormous practical difficulties. Now the convention is changing to the use of "normative scores," in which IQs are expressed normatively within each age group. In both these instances it would be wrong to think that the "real" scales had been discovered. It would be more proper to say that conventions changed, and in both examples it may be that better conventions will be established in the future.

After all manner of wisdom has been applied to the problem, in the actual construction of measurement scales it is good to apply some type of formal model. Although any set of rules for the assignment of numbers constitutes measurement, if the rules seem silly and/or *ad hoc*, they probably will not result in a measure that will eventually be agreed on as a good scaling of the attribute in question. It might be useful to think of a model as an internally consistent plan for seeking a good scaling of an attribute. When the plan is put to use, it may result in a measure that eventually proves unsatisfactory to the scientific community, but having a plan increases the probability of finding an acceptable measure. The situation is much like that in which two persons are searching for gold—one has a definite plan based on known facts about the location of gold, and the other person simply wanders around aimlessly hoping to discover the stuff. If the first man finds no gold and the second stumbles onto a bonanza, there is no question which obtained the best result *in that particular instance*. Most persons will agree, however, that plans based on common sense and past experience improve the probabilities of finding gold or finding a measurement scale that eventually will be accepted as a useful convention.

Even if some of the models disagree with one another about the scaling of particular attributes, those who advocate and deal with formal models for the scaling of attributes are to be praised. Even if the data fit a number of the models for forming a particular scale, however, this does not guarantee that the obtained measure will serve as a useful convention. It may be that a relatively planless scale will win out in the end, but the odds are in favor of the more systematic approaches.

A convention establishes the scale properties of a measure. If it is established as a ratio scale, then the zero point can be taken seriously and the intervals may be treated as equal in any forms of analysis. If it is established as an interval scale, the intervals may be treated as equal in all forms of analysis. This is not meant to imply that such conventions are, or should be, established quickly or until much evidence is in, but in the end they are conventions, not discoveries of "real" scales.

Certain conventions are not established because they make no sense to scientists. For example, it made no sense to scientists to adopt the zero point on the Fahrenheit thermometer as a rational zero. Similarly, it makes little sense to establish zero points on scales for many, but not all, psychological attributes. What would be zero intelligence? Only that of a dead person or a stone would qualify, and compared to either, all living persons could be scored only as infinitely intelligent. Psychologists do seek to develop interval scales for many attributes, because it is reasonable to think not only in terms of the ordering of persons, but also in terms of how far apart they are on the scale.

Even those scaling procedures that do make sense to scientists may not produce scales that *work well in practice*. The last four words are the key to establishing a measurement convention—a good measure is one that mathematically fits well in a system of lawful relationships. In Chapter Three it will be emphasized that the usefulness (validity) of a measure is in the extent to which it relates to other variables in a domain of interest. The "best" scaling of any particular attribute is that which will produce the *simplest* forms of relationship with other variables. In an ascending scale of simplicity would be (1) a random relationship, which is the most complex of all possible relationships, (2) a nonrandom pattern, but one which fits no particular line of relationship, (3) an unevenly ascending or descending monotonic relationship, (4) a smooth monotonic relationship, (5) a straight line, and (6) a straight line passing through the origin. Whereas the only way to completely describe a random relationship is to describe every point on the graph, a straight line passing through the origin is completely described by $Y = aX$. Since the task of the scientist is to translate the complexity of events in the universe into a relative simplicity of lawful relationships, the simpler those relationships, the better.

basic principles

One way to make relationships simpler is to change the scaling of one or more of the variables. Thus a nonsmooth monotonic relationship can be smoothed by stretching some of the intervals. A monotonic curve can be transformed to a straight line with the proper equation. A straight line can be made to pass through the origin by changing the origin (zero point) on one of the scales. Of course, the conventions regarding a particular attribute should not be altered because of the relationships found with only one or two other measures; but in the long run if it is found that many relationships would be simplified by a particular transformation of that scale, logically the new scale would be a better scale. Such transformations actually are made quite frequently. For example, logarithmic transformations have been made of many scales to simplify relations with other variables.

Following this point of view to the extreme, there is no reason that all the variables known to science could not be rescaled so as to simplify all natural laws. If this could be done, it would be a wise move. The new scales would be as "real" as the old ones, and there would be every reason to take seriously the zero points and the intervals on the new scales.

There are two major problems with considering scaling as a matter of convention. First, it is disquieting to those who think in terms of "real" scales and who wish for, but cannot find, some infallible test for the relationship between a particular measure and the "real" scale. Also, looking at measurement scaling as a matter of convention seems to make the problem "messy." How well a particular scaling of an attribute "fits in" with other variables is an open-ended question. Which variables? How good is a particular "fit"? To avoid such questions, however, is to blind one's self to the realities of scientific enterprise. To seek shelter in the apparent neatness of conceptions regarding "real" scales is not to provide answers about the properties of measurement scales but to ask logically unanswerable questions.

A second, and more serious, problem with considering scaling as a matter of convention is that there often are two or more conventions strongly competing with one another. For example, there has been much dispute about which of two methods of scaling certain dimensions of sensation—Thurstone's law of comparative judgment or the magnitude-estimation methods—is *the* correct method. (The methods are described in Chapter Two.) When these methods are used to scale judgments about the loudness of tones, different scales are obtained: one is logarithmically related to the other. More appropriate than asking which is "correct" would be asking which in the long run will "fit" in better in a system of natural laws. For example, there already is evidence that scalings based on methods of magnitude estimation have a broad generality over different modalities of sensation—which is the kind of evidence required to establish a convention for the employment of one method rather than others.

For two reasons, having competing conventions regarding the scaling of attributes is not as bad as it may sound. First, if the two scalings are monotonically related to each other, as is usually the case, then if one has a monotonic relationship with a third variable, so will the other. Thus the laws established with one scaling will show the same variables functionally related as would be found with employing the alternative scaling, albeit the specific forms of the relationships could differ. Actually, at the present time in psychology, there are few problems in which the *specific form* of a relationship is the major issue. In correlational analysis, the major issue is the regression of one variable on another. Correlations greater than .60 are the exception rather than the rule, and as was said previously, such correlations are insensitive to transformations of the variables involved. Consequently if there are two competing conventions for scaling which are monotonically related, both would correlate much the same with any other variable. In analyzing the results of experiments, the major considerations are (1) whether there are mean differences among treatment groups and (2) whether, in some problems, the means are monotonically or nonmonotonically related to levels of a treatment parameter. In these problems, transformations of the scale of the dependent measure make little difference in the findings. Consequently it would make little difference which of two monotonically related scalings of the dependent measure were employed.

There are some problems in which the specific form of a relationship is very important: (1) the previously mentioned problem of determining the specific form of relationship for judging the loudness of tones, (2) determining the shape of a learning curve, and (3) determining the shape of the curve relating intelligence to age. The specific forms of relationship in such studies can be settled only when there are firm conventions for scaling the variables involved. The specific form of a relationship is relative to the measurement convention; to hope to find *the* relationship is to either (1) continue to search in vain for "real" scales or (2) assume that one measurement convention eventually will win out over others.

SUGGESTED ADDITIONAL READINGS

Coombs, C. H. A theory of data. *Psychol. Rev.,* 1960, **67,** 143–159.

Stevens, S. S. (Ed.) *Handbook of experimental psychology.* New York: Wiley, 1951, chap. 1.

Stevens, S. S. Problems and methods of psychophysics. *Psychol. Bull.,* 1958, **55,** 177–196.

Torgerson, W. *Theory and methods of scaling.* New York: Wiley, 1958, chaps. 1, 2.

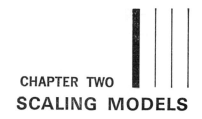

CHAPTER TWO

SCALING MODELS

In the previous chapter it was said that measurement concerns the assignment of numbers to objects to represent quantities of attributes. Although any system of operations that will so assign numbers can be spoken of as measurement, it helps to have some internally consistent plan for the development of a new measure. The plan is spoken of as a *scaling model,* and the measure which results from exercising the plan is spoken of as a *scale* ("scale" being another word for "measure"). The simplest example is that of the ruler as a scale of length. The methods for constructing and applying rulers constitute the scaling model in that case. The purpose of any scaling model is to generate a continuum on which persons or objects are located. In the following example, persons P_1, P_2, P_3, and P_4 are located on such a continuum:

The attribute could be thought of as anxiety or as spelling ability. Because it is an interval scale, the distances between persons are taken seriously. Thus P_1 is considerably higher in the attribute than the other persons, P_2 and P_3 are close together, and P_4 is far below the others.

In any particular measurement problem, scaling concerns a data matrix (table) such as that in Figure 2-1. On the front face of the cube, rows represent stimuli and columns represent responses to the stimuli. The "slices" of the cube going from front to back represent the responses of each person to each of the stimuli. The words "stimuli" and "responses" represent anything that the experimenter does to the subject and anything the subject does in return. Typical things (stimuli) the experimenter does to the subject are to have him lift weights, to present him with spelling words, or to show him a list of foods. Typical responses required for these types of stimuli would be judging which of two weights is heavier, indicating whether or not each word is correctly spelled, and rating how much each food is liked.

The data matrix illustrated in Figure 2-1 presents a very complex problem for scaling. The problem is much simpler when there is only a two-dimensional table, as when only one person is studied at a time. This also would be the case if only one type of response were made to each stimulus, e.g., agreeing or disagreeing with each of a list of statements (stimuli). Also, there would be a two-dimensional table of data if each person made a number of different types of responses to the same stimulus, e.g., rating the United Nations on different rating scales anchored by pairs of adjectives such as "effective-ineffective," "valuable-worthless," and "strong-weak." If in the problem there are

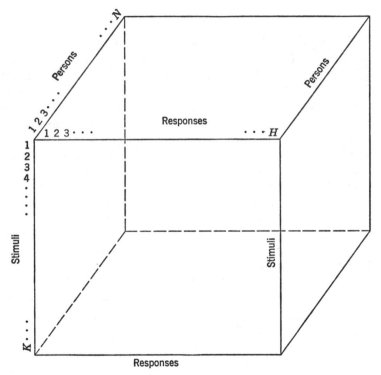

figure 2-1 *A data matrix for H responses of N persons to K stimuli.*

more than one person, more than one stimulus, and more than one type of response required for each stimulus, there are many, many ways in which one of the three could be scaled. Usually an effort is made to simplify the problem by making the elements in one dimension "replicates" of one another, or at least assuming them to be so.

Some methods of scaling assume that persons are replicates of one another. For example, the percentage of persons in a *group* that says one weight is heavier than another is assumed to be the same as the percentage of times an ideal *modal individual* would say that one weight is heavier than another on different occasions. The assump-

basic principles

tion that individuals are replicates is frequently made in scaling stimuli. In scaling persons, it frequently is assumed that responses are replicates of one another. Thus in the previous example of rating stimuli on scales anchored by bipolar adjectives, an overall "favorableness" rating can be obtained by adding responses over the separate rating scales.

When one looks carefully at the different methods for scaling, he will see that in most cases either one of the dimensions of the data matrix is not present (e.g., only one person, or one stimulus, or one type of response made to each stimulus) or an assumption is made that allows him to do away with at least one of the dimensions. When the latter is the case, there usually are ways of testing the correctness of the assumption. For example, if a different scale concerning the judgment of weights is constructed for each person and it is found that there are systematic differences in those scales, this would violate the assumption that persons are replicates in that particular situation. If it is found that the bipolar rating scales either do not correlate with one another or evolve into a number of different factors, it would be wrong to assume that the scales are replicates. When such assumptions are found to be incorrect, however, it often makes the problem of measurement very messy indeed.

Starting with a two-dimensional table of data, the usual strategy in the development of a measurement method is to test for the presence of a unidimensional scale. Essentially this consists of trying to do away with one of the two dimensions. An example would be that in which each individual has been required to rank a number of weights from heaviest to lightest. The data matrix would then consist of the ranks of weights for each person—a two-dimensional table of data. One way to do away with the person dimension would be to average the ranks over persons, which would provide a scaling of the weights. The average ranking could be considered an ordering of the weights, and one might also want to take the intervals between average ranks seriously. Another example would be in having individuals either agree or disagree with statements concerning the United Nations. Agreement with each statement is thought to represent a positive attitude; disagreement, a negative attitude. Since there is only one object being rated, a two-dimensional table of data is obtained. By summing the number of agreements for each person, one collapses the response dimension of the table. Then sums of agreements would constitute an ordering of the persons with respect to their attitudes, and one might want to take the intervals between persons seriously.

Before one turns a two-dimensional table of data into a one-dimensional scale, he should first state a set of assumptions regarding how the attribute in question is manifested in actual data. Then he must test how well the assumptions hold in the data. Each set of assumptions is a model. This chapter is primarily concerned with the models that are most frequently employed for turning two-dimensional tables of data into unidimensional scales. If the data do not fit the assumptions of a particular model for unidimensional scaling, the investigator has three choices: (1) try one of the other models for unidimensional scaling, (2) try methods of multivariate analysis, or (3) try some other problem. If methods of multivariate analysis are applied, it might be found that more than one unidimensional scale is required to account for the data. For example, with statements concerning attitudes toward the United Nations, factor analysis might indicate that the statements relate to two different dimensions of attitude. It might be found that some statements relate to a factor concerning the effectiveness of the United Nations in settling diplomatic disputes among nations and other statements relate to a factor concerning activities of the United Nations in economic matters. Then two scales of attitudes rather than only one would be developed. Such methods of multivariate analysis will be treated in Chapters Nine to Eleven. This chapter will be concerned only with models that are used for developing unidimensional scales.

EVALUATION OF MODELS   There often are different models that can be used for the development of particular scales, and sometimes the models lead to different conclusions about the scale properties of the data. One model might lead to a scale that failed to have a linear relationship with a scale derived from another model applied to the same data. One model might reject the data as conforming to an ordinal scale, whereas another model would accept the data as conforming to an interval scale. How then does one know which model is appropriate for a particular problem? As was said in the previous chapter, there is no sure way to know this in advance. The ultimate test is how well the scales which are derived fit in a nexus of lawful relations with other variables. Before time and effort are spent on such investigations, however, there are some criteria of "good sense" that can be applied.

Part of "good sense" concerns the intuitive appeal of a scaling model. Although the data of science must be objective, the scientist must rely on his intuition for research ideas. Looked at in one way, a measurement model is nothing more than an explicitly defined hunch, a hunch that particular operations on data will lead to an important measure. If the author's observations are correct, psychologists tend to find intuitively appealing those measurement models that relate to the measurement of simple physical attributes such as length and weight.

Another aspect of "good sense" in selecting scaling models concerns the evaluation of assumptions in the models in terms of what is already known about the type of data involved. For example, one of the models that will be discussed below assumes that responses to individual test items are highly reliable, yet there is a wealth of evidence to show that such items usually are not highly reliable.

After a model is used to derive a scale and before strenuous efforts are made to find lawful relations with other variables, there are some preliminary forms of evidence regarding the usefulness of the scale. If the scale values for objects or persons are markedly affected by slightly different ways of gathering data, the scale probably will not work well in practice. There are, for example, numerous ways in which one can have subjects make judgments of weight. If two approaches that seem much the same lead to very different intervals of judged weight, one would be quite suspicious of the interval scales obtained by both approaches. An even more important type of preliminary evidence concerns the amount of measurement error involved in using a particular type of scale, a matter which will be discussed in detail in Chapters Six and Seven. A scale that occasions a great deal of measurement error cannot possibly be useful for any purpose. Beyond the standards of "good sense," however, the ultimate test of any model is the extent to which it produces scales with a high degree of explanatory power for natural phenomena.

STIMULI AND PEOPLE   Previously it was stated that scaling problems concern a three-dimensional matrix of persons, stimuli, and types of responses. In unidimensional scaling, usually each person makes only one type of response to each stimulus; or if he makes more than one type of response, it is sensible to combine responses in some manner. (If there is doubt about the sensibility of combining responses, methods of multi-variate analysis can be employed.) In either situation, a scaling model is applied to a two-dimensional matrix of data. What has not been made explicit so far is that usually methods of scaling employed for scaling stimuli are different from those for scaling people. Also, which of the two is to be scaled has a strong influence on the way responses are obtained.

It is probably easier to think of measurement problems in terms of the scaling of people. In a simple example, the data matrix is bordered by spelling words on the side and by people on the top. The required response is to indicate whether or not each word is correctly spelled (a single response to each stimulus). With the use of a 1 for correct spellings and a zero for incorrect spellings, the data matrix would be filled with 1s and zeros. The dimension concerning stimuli (spelling words) would be collapsed by summing the number of 1s for each person. If it were not thought necessary to apply a more elaborate model to the data, the simple sums of correct responses would serve to scale people on the attribute of spelling ability.

Something more subtle is at issue when the object is to scale stimuli rather than people. For example, when subjects are asked to judge the loudness of tones by one method or another, the object is to generate a continuum of perceived loudness. In this instance the tones are quantified with respect to the attribute, and people are part of the measurement process. In another example of scaling stimuli, preferences for foods can be scaled by having a group of people rate each food on a like-dislike rating scale. One method of scaling in this instance would be to let the average rating of each food be its scale value.

When one seeks a unidimensional scale of stimuli, the hope is to find a scaling that fits the modal individual. Thus a scale developed in this way would be typical of persons as a group, even though it might not perfectly represent the scale that would be obtained by an intensive investigation of any one person. The long-range research pur· pose in scaling stimuli (rather than persons) is to relate scalings of the same stimuli with respect to different attributes. Thus after a unidimensional scale is developed for the perceived loudness of tones, another scaling of the same tones could be made against a background of noise. Another scaling could be made when each tone is accompanied by a light whose intensity is correlated with the intensity of the tone. Scaling of the tones could be made in various applied problems, such as in employing the tones as communication signals. At issue would be mathematical relations between the different scalings of the tones. The same would be true of scaling foods in terms of preferences. Rated preferences could be compared with what men in the armed forces chose to eat or with what housewives would purchase. In each instance the object is to relate a scaling of stimuli on one attribute with the scaling of stimuli on another attribute.

Important as it is to scale stimuli, this is not nearly so large an issue in psychology as is the scaling of people with respect to attributes. It is probably true that if one searched through numerous journal articles and textbooks in psychology, one would find that most of the studies are primarily concerned with variables involving the scaling of people (or lower organisms) rather than the scaling of stimuli. Prominently appearing in the literature are studies of learning rate, anxiety, decision time, intelligence, and strength of conditioned responses—all definitely concerned with the scaling of people. The issue is the same regardless of whether the scaling of people is for studies of individual differences or for controlled experiments. Although, for example, approaches to measurement employed for studies of individual differences concerning typical levels of anxiety might be different than those for controlled experiments on anxiety, it would be necessary in both types of studies to scale persons with respect to the attribute of anxiety.

It is important to make a distinction between the scaling of stimuli and the scaling of persons, because there are more severe problems with the former. In the scaling of stimuli, research issues frequently concern the exact nature of functional relations between scalings of the stimuli in different circumstances. Thus in the scaling of tones under different conditions, a careful study would be made of the exact "curves" between different scalings. Then it would make quite a difference if a particular relation was linear rather than logarithmic. As was stated in Chapter One, in most studies concerning the scaling of people, exact forms of relationship between different scalings are not important—at least, not at the present stage of development of psychological science. The major requirement is that different scalings of people be monotonically related to one another, i.e., that they rank-order people in the same way. Thus if there are two different methods for scaling people for the attribute of anxiety and the two are monotonically related, research results will be much the same regardless of which scale is employed.

Because there are more serious problems with the scaling of stimuli than with the scaling of persons, most of the issues concerning scaling, and most of the models for scaling, have arisen in the context of problems concerning the scaling of stimuli. This can be seen, for example, in the comprehensive treatments of scaling methods by Guilford (1954) and by Torgerson (1958). In both books, most of the scaling models are illustrated with the scaling of stimuli (tones, weights, foods), and most of the models are more appropriate for the scaling of stimuli than for the scaling of persons. This difference has had an influence on the language used to describe psychological research. When one speaks of "scaling" and "scaling methods," he usually is discussing a problem concerning the scaling of stimuli. When one is discussing a problem concerning the scaling of persons with respect to an attribute, he is more likely to use terms like "measurement" and "test construction."

types of responses required of subjects

Before scaling models are discussed, it is necessary to review some of the different types of responses required of subjects. The type of response tends to correlate with the type of stimuli being studied, e.g., one would require that types of responses to tones and to the names of foods be different. Different types of responses usually are required for the scaling of stimuli and for the scaling of persons. Also, different scaling models often require different types of responses. There is no end to the distinctions that one could make regarding all the kinds of responses that are possible in different studies. The three most important types of distinctions are discussed in the following sections.

JUDGMENTS AND SENTIMENTS   Although there are no two words that perfectly symbolize the distinction, one of the most important distinctions in measurement theory is that between responses concerning *judgments* and those concerning *sentiments*. The word "judgment" is used to cover all those types of responses where there is a *correct* response. This would be the case, for example, when a child is asked, "How much is two plus two?" This would also be the case when subjects are required to judge which of two tones is louder or which of two weights is heavier. In all these instances there is some *veridical comparison* for the subject's response, and it is possible to determine whether each response is correct or incorrect. With some types of judgments, it also is possible to determine the degree of correctness and thus the relative accuracy. For example, when a subject is required to adjust one light to the apparent brightness of another light, it is possible to measure how accurate the subject is in units of illumination.

The word "sentiment" is used to cover all responses concerning personal reactions, preferences, interests, attitudes, and likes and dislikes. An individual makes responses concerning sentiments when he (1) rates boiled cabbage on a seven-step, like-dislike rating scale, (2) answers the question, "Which would you rather do, organize a club or work on a stamp collection?" and (3) rank-orders 10 actors in terms of his sentiments. The important difference between judgments and sentiments is that with sentiments there is no veridical comparison. Thus if an individual says, "I like chocolate ice cream better than vanilla ice cream," it makes no sense to tell him, "You are incorrect." We may abhor another person's tastes for food or sentiments in any other sphere, but sentiments do not require veridical justification. Of course, it may be that the subject is incorrect in the sense that he lies or that he actually behaves in daily life in a manner different from that implied by his stated sentiments. The important point, however, concerns *what the subject is asked to do* in the experimental setting. When expressing a sentiment, the subject is asked to give a personal reaction to a stimulus, and there is no external standard of "accuracy" that makes sense.

In the study of judgments, an important problem is to relate *perceived* intensity of some attribute to the *physical* intensity of the attribute. For example, in a study where subjects are asked to adjust one light so that it appears twice as bright as another light, the ratio of perceived brightness can be compared with the ratio of physical magnitudes of illumination. Whenever subjects make judgments, there is a veridical comparison either actually available or at least potentially so. The latter possibility is illustrated in the problem where astronomers are asked to estimate the temperature of a number of stars. At the present there might be considerable controversy about the correct answers, but *conceivably* there are correct answers that one day can be used to determine the accuracy of present judgments. Such veridical comparisons are not conceivable with sentiments.

In the scaling of stimuli, the logic for validating models for the scaling of judgments is clearer than that for the scaling of sentiments. This is because the scale of judgments, after it is developed, can be compared with the scale of physical magnitudes. Then, intuitively, one would expect certain types of relations between the scale of judgments and the scale of physical magnitudes. If, for example, an interval scale of the judged loudness of tones does not have a smooth, monotonic relationship with the scale of physical magnitudes, one would probably reject the model used for developing the scale. One probably would expect not a straight line of relationship, but some type of smooth, monotonic curve. If this expectation is borne out, it provides no guarantee that the model is correct, but it does provide intuitive support for continued use of the model. Since with sentiments there is no physical scale, there is no way of comparing a scale of sentiments with "actuality." What typically is done then is to explore new scaling models on data concerning judgments, and if they apparently work well there, to extend them to studies of sentiments. It is even more apparent with sentiments than with judgments that the usefulness of any scale is determined in the long run by how well it fits in a system of lawful relations with other variables in a particular area of scientific interest.

In the scaling of people, all tests of ability concern judgments, in a broad sense of the term. This is true in tests of mathematics, vocabulary, and reasoning ability. Either the subject exercises his judgment in supplying a correct answer for each item or he judges which of a number of alternative responses is most correct. Tests of interests concern sentiments: the subject indicates the activities that he likes and those that he dislikes. Measures of attitudes and personality can require either judgments or expressions of sentiment, and it is with these types of measures that the distinction frequently is obscure. On a personality inventory, when responding to the item, "Do you like to be the center of attention at parties?" the subject is asked to express a sentiment. When responding to the item, "Do you usually lead the discussion in group situations?" the subject is asked to make a judgment about his actual behavior in group situations. When responding to the item, "Do most people like you?" he is asked to make a judgment about other peoples' sentiments. Of course, with such items, subjects frequently get sentiments mixed up with judgments, whether by intention or out of sheer confusion, and this is one reason why it is difficult to develop valid inventories for measuring personality.

COMPARATIVE AND ABSOLUTE RESPONSES   Another important distinction concerns whether the subject is required to make an absolute response to each stimulus separately or required to make comparative judgments or expressions of sentiment among the stimuli. An example of an absolute response would be to the question, "How long is this line in inches?" Another example is when the subject is required to rate boiled cabbage on a seven-step, like-dislike scale. In both instances the subject responds to each stimulus separately, and he indicates the amount of the attribute in an absolute sense.

With comparative judgments and sentiments, stimuli are presented in groups of two or more, and the subject responds to the "more" and "less" of some property. A comparative response is required when the subject is asked to indicate which he likes more, boiled cabbage or boiled turnips, or when he is asked to indicate which of two weights is heavier.

There are few instances in which it makes sense to require absolute responses of subjects. For example, there is little interest in having people judge the physical magnitude of stimuli, e.g., "How long is this line in inches?" People are notoriously poor at making absolute judgments of length, weight, and other physical properties of stimuli. In many cases the subject has no way of communicating his absolute judgment of such physical properties. How would the subject respond if he were asked simply, "How bright is this light?" or "How loud is this tone?"

People simply are not accustomed to making absolute judgments in daily life, since most judgments are inherently comparative. Thus subjects can respond with a high degree of confidence when asked which of two lights is brighter or which of two tones is louder. Whereas people are notoriously inaccurate when judging the absolute magnitudes of stimuli, e.g., the length of a line in inches, they are notoriously accurate in making comparative judgments. If the subject is within 20 feet of the stimuli and is asked to judge which of two lines is longer, he will be accurate almost every time unless the lines differ by less than ½ inch.

As is true of most judgments in daily life, most sentiments are inherently comparative. The individual has some feeling regarding the absolute liking for an object or activity, but such sentiments are strongly influenced by the range of objects or activities available. Thus an individual required to rate boiled cabbage on a like-dislike rating scale (supposedly an absolute response) must surely say to himself, "What else would there be to eat?" If girls are required to rate the photograph of a man on a rating scale anchored by the adjectives "handsome" and "ugly," how can they make such responses unless they subjectively compare the features of the man with those of the many men that they have seen previously?

Even when subjects are requested to make absolute responses to each stimulus in a set, there is considerable evidence that their responses are largely comparative. This would be found when weights are to be rated on a scale ranging from "very heavy" to "very light." If subjects actually were responding to each weight separately, the rating given any weight would remain the same regardless of the sizes of the other weights in the set. But as anyone would guess, the rating of a particular weight shifts markedly when it is placed in the context of heavier or lighter weights. The same is true of sentiments. If girls are asked to make ratings of the handsomeness of men shown in 20 photographs, the rating of the man in any particular photograph can be shifted markedly by placing it in the context of all relatively ugly men. When giving absolute judgments and expressions of sentiment, subjects tend to anchor their responses in terms of (1) stimuli of the same kinds that they have experienced in the past and (2) the range of stimuli in the set which is presented.

Potentially, the major advantage of absolute responses is with sentiments rather than with judgments. The comparative methods are sufficient for most studies of judgments, but in some studies of sentiments, it is important to learn the absolute level of responses to stimuli. This is the case in most studies of attitudes, e.g., in studies of attitudes toward different national groups. This Information could not be obtained from comparative responses, as where the subject is required to rank the names of 10 national groups from "most prefer" to "least prefer." The individual may dislike all of the national groups or like them all, but there would be no hint of that from the rankings (comparative responses). Absolute responses are important In those studies of sentiments where it is necessary to obtain an approximate indication of the "neutral" point either for the scaling of persons or for the scaling of stimuli. For example, in studies of attitudes, it has been hypothesized that people near the neutral point (e.g., of attitudes toward the United Nations) are more susceptible to change than are people who are far from the neutral point in either direction. By requiring absolute responses from subjects, one would be able to approximately determine the neutral point.

Even when absolute responses are required of subjects, the experimenter usually makes comparative analyses and interpretations of those responses. This is done because absolute responses frequently are much easier and faster to obtain than comparative responses. For example, in a study of preferences for 50 foods, the investigator probably would be interested mainly in which foods are liked more and which are liked less. A direct way to obtain this information would be to have each subject rank all the foods from "most prefer" to "least prefer," but that probably would take each subject an hour or more. Approximately the same information could be obtained in a much shorter time from absolute responses. Each subject would rate each food on a like-dislike scale. An average rating of each food over subjects would be obtained.

Then the experimenter could rank the foods in terms of average ratings, and some of the comparative models for scaling could be used to estimate intervals between foods on the continuum of sentiment. Thus in many cases where subjects are asked to make absolute responses, the experimenter takes seriously only the comparative information in those responses.

To summarize, absolute responses are useful in some situations for (1) providing a shortcut method of obtaining comparative information and/or (2) obtaining an approximate indication of the neutral point on a continuum of sentiment. In all other situations, comparative methods clearly are more appropriate.

SCALE FOR RESPONSE   Another important distinction among types of responses concerns the scale on which the subject is required to respond. In most types of responses, subjects are required to respond to stimuli in terms of an ordinal, interval, or ratio scale; that is, each subject is required to generate a scale having the properties of one of these three basic types of scales. There are many ways in which responses can be obtained with respect to the three types of scales, each way being referred to as a *psychophysical method*.

Most frequently, subjects are required to operate on an ordinal scale. All the particular methods that can be applied for that purpose are called methods of *ordinal estimation*. The most straightforward way to do this is by the method of *rank order*, which, as the name implies, requires the subject to rank stimuli from "most" to "least" with respect to some attribute of judgment or sentiment. A more thorough approach is with the method of *pair comparisons*, in which the subject is required to rank stimuli two at a time in all possible pairs. For example, eight weights would be presented two at a time in all possible pairs, and for each comparison, the subject would be required to indicate which is heavier. Even though on each response a comparison is made between only two stimuli, in essence the subject is required to rank the stimuli "one" and "two" on each comparison. From these responses, the experimenter deduces ordinal and interval scales for the full set of stimuli, by methods which will be described in a later section.

Another ordinal method is the method of *constant stimuli*. This method is similar to pair comparisons, except that a standard stimulus is successively paired with each member of a constant set of stimuli. An example would be in a study of lifted weights where the standard stimulus is a weight of 200 grams and the six constant comparisons are weights of 185, 190, 195, 205, 210, and 215 grams, respectively. Constant stimuli would be paired in a random order with the standard stimulus, and on each comparison the subject would be required to indicate which is heavier. (Of course, on each comparison only the experimenter would know which is the standard stimulus.) To obtain reliable data, it usually is necessary to present numerous random orderings of the constant stimuli in comparison with the standard stimulus. Typical results obtained from applying the method of constant stimuli are shown in Figure 2-2.

Another ordinal method is that of *successive categories*, in which the subject is asked to sort a collection of stimuli into a number of distinct "piles," or categories, which are ordered with respect to a specified attribute. For example, subjects could be required to sort 100 statements concerning their favorableness toward the United Nations. The subject would be given 10 categories, with the first category defined

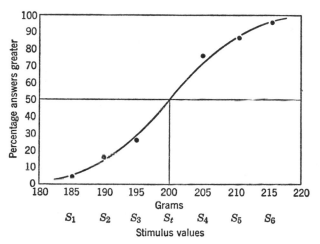

figure 2-2 *Psychometric function for the application of the method of constant stimuli to a study of lifted weights.*

as "very favorable," the tenth category defined as "very unfavorable," and categories between being anchored with verbal labels representing intermediate levels of favorableness. There are many variants of the method of successive categories, depending on the type of information that the experimenter hopes to obtain. When the experimenter is seeking only ordinal information, the subject usually is allowed to operate in any way he chooses in assigning stimuli to categories. A variant is to require subjects to place an equal number of stimuli in each category, e.g., the top 10 stimuli in category 1 and the bottom 10 stimuli in category 10. Another variant is to require subjects to sort the stimuli into an approximate normal distribution, with it being specified how many stimuli are to be placed in each category (this variant is called the "Q sort").

These three approaches to the method of successive categories can be used to obtain ordinal information about the stimuli. The method can be thought of as requiring the subject to rank a set of stimuli in a situation where tied ranks are mandatory. Thus if it is required to place 10 stimuli in each of 10 categories, those placed in category 1 can be thought of as tied for the top rank, and those placed in category 10 as tied for the bottom rank. Then, by averaging the tied ranks over subjects, one can obtain a rather complete ranking of the stimuli, in which there would be few tied ranks. Although there are numerous variants of these methods, the basic approaches to obtaining ordinal judgments and expressions of sentiment are with rank order, pair comparisons, constant stimuli, and successive categories.

One of the most frequently used methods for obtaining *interval* responses from subjects is the method of *equal-appearing intervals*. Superficially, the method is very similar to that of successive categories—in both, a set of stimuli must be sorted into a number of ordered categories. The difference is in the instructions. In the method of equal-appearing intervals, the subject is instructed to sort the stimuli in such a way as to make the intervals between categories subjectively equal. Thus if the individual is sorting 100 shades of gray paper from darkest to lightest, he would be instructed to work so that the perceived differences between adjacent categories are equal. Although it is rather difficult to instruct subjects in this task and hard to know how well the experimenter's intention is communicated, the method seeks to obtain equal-appearing intervals.

More useful than the method of equal-appearing intervals for obtaining interval responses is a broad category of methods which will be referred to as methods of *interval estimation*. The most frequently used particular method in this group is the method of *bisection*. For example, the subject is given two lights of different intensity and asked to adjust a third light to the point where it is halfway between the other two lights in terms of apparent brightness. Or the subject is given two statements differing in favorableness toward the United Nations and asked to select a statement that is halfway between the two in favorableness. Rather than having the distance between two stimuli bisected, another approach has intervals estimated in terms of some other ratio. For example, with two fixed stimuli, the subject can be asked to select a third stimulus such that the interval between one of the fixed stimuli and the third is twice as great as the distance between the other fixed stimulus and the third. Another approach presents the subject with two stimuli that are extreme with respect to the attribute and has him judge the ratio of intervals formed when each of a number of stimuli are inserted between.

It must be kept in mind that with all the methods of interval estimation, the subject responds in terms of *intervals* of judgment or sentiment. Though the subject may be forming ratios, e.g., a 1:1 ratio in the method of bisection, responses are with respect to intervals among the stimuli and not with respect to the absolute intensities of the stimuli. The experimenter might seek to deduce absolute intensities for the stimuli according to a model, but it is important to make a clear distinction between what the subject is required to do and interpretations that the experimenter makes of what is done. With the interval-estimation methods, the subject is required to estimate the comparative sizes of intervals among stimuli.

The *ratio-estimation* methods require subjects to respond to the absolute magnitudes of stimuli. As is true of the interval-estimation methods, there are numerous particular forms of ratio estimation. In a simple example, the subject is given a light at one intensity and asked to adjust another light until it appears twice as bright as the first. Or a subject is given the name of a food that is thought to be liked moderately well by most persons and asked to rate each food in a list on a scale ranging from "like only one-tenth as much" to "like ten times as much."

Superficially, some of the methods of interval estimation appear similar to some of the methods of ratio estimation. For example, choosing a stimulus that is halfway between two others is apparently similar to choosing a stimulus that is twice as great as another with respect to some attribute. There are, however, very important differences between methods of interval estimation and methods of ratio estimation. In both the examples above, the subject forms two equal-appearing intervals. When a stimulus halfway between two others is chosen, two equal-appearing intervals are formed. When a stimulus that is twice as intense as another with respect to an attribute is chosen, again two equal-appearing intervals are formed. The important difference is that in the latter case the lower interval is bounded by a *phenomenal zero*. In that case the subject essentially is required to form an interval between two stimuli that is equal to the interval between the less intense stimulus and zero. Whether or not the subject can perform the task, this must be what the experimenter wants the subject to do. In other words, in methods of ratio estimation, the experimenter seeks to obtain responses from subjects with respect to a ratio scale of judgment or sentiment.

The purpose of this section has been to discuss three broad categories of methods depending on the scaling tasks required of subjects: ordinal estimation, interval estimation, and ratio estimation. There are many variants of each of these, many of which have their own names and many of which are called by different names. These are the so-called psychophysical methods, and if one wants to give a different name to each shade and hue of difference in procedure, there are literally hundreds of psychophysical methods. The reader who has a special interest in these methods should consult the excellent books by Guilford (1954) and by Torgerson (1958). More important for most readers, however, is to understand the three major classes of scaling tasks described in this section.

SPECIFICATION OF AN ATTRIBUTE With all the methods discussed so far in this section, judgments or sentiments are expressed with respect to a *stated attribute*. Thus weights are judged with respect to heaviness, and men are rated with respect to handsomeness. In most studies it is possible for the experimenter to specify the attribute involved, but in some studies this is not the case. The latter occurs when it is known in advance, or suspected, that the stimuli differ with respect to more than one dimension or attribute. This would be the case where responses are made to colored chips that vary in terms of hue, saturation, and brightness. It would occur when subjects respond to the names of United States senators, the senators varying on a number of dimensions of political belief and practice. When the attribute cannot be stated in advance and/or the stimuli vary with respect to a number of attributes, the methods discussed so far cannot be used. The experimenter must obtain *similarity estimates* from the subjects. A frequently used method is to present the subject with three stimuli at a time and ask him which two are more similar. In this way, the experimenter does not have to specify the attribute(s), but relies instead on the rather global notion of similarity. Although similarity estimates can be used in place of some of the methods discussed in this chapter for obtaining unidimensional scales, they are mainly useful in multidimensional scaling, which will be discussed in some detail in Chapter Eleven.

methods for scaling stimuli

After responses have been obtained by one of the methods discussed above, the next step is to generate an ordinal, interval, or ratio scale. In the scaling of stimuli, complex models usually are not required for deriving ordinal scales, and the different models used for that purpose usually arrive at the same ordering of stimuli. Some examples will serve to show how ordinal scales are obtained. With the method of rank order, the average ranks would be obtained over subjects, and these would be converted to ranks. The final set of ranks would constitute an ordinal scaling of the stimuli for the typical subject. In a study where men in photographs are rated for handsomeness, the average ratings would be obtained over subjects, and these would be converted to ranks. So it is with all the methods discussed in the previous section—methods for obtaining ordinal scales usually are intuitively obvious.

Scaling models become important when the effort is to construct either an interval or ratio scale for stimuli. Usually the effort is to construct an interval scale; in only a few special cases are efforts made to construct ratio scales. The remainder of this section will consider models that are used for these purposes. Computational procedures are described by Guilford (1954) and by Torgerson (1958).

SCALES BASED ON SUBJECTIVE ESTIMATES In the previous section psychophysical methods were discussed in terms of the *scale of responses*. It was said that each method requires the subject to respond in terms of an ordinal, interval, or ratio scale. Even though the subject might be instructed to respond in terms of one type of scale, the experimenter might take the responses as representing another type of scale; e.g., although the subject responded in terms of interval estimates, the experimenter might take seriously only the ordinal information obtained.

With some models for scaling stimuli, the experimenter *does* take seriously the scaling task required of the subject. In those instances it is easy to obtain ratio or interval scales. Some examples of how this is done follow. The subject is required to sort 100 shades of gray paper into 10 categories ranging from "darkest" to "lightest." Either the more general method of successive categories is employed or the special instructions are used that result in the method of equal-appearing intervals. The experimenter assumes that the subjective processes of the individual are capable of generating an interval scale of perceived brightness. It is admitted that there is some error in the judgments made by one person on one occasion, but efforts are made to reduce the error by averaging judgments over subjects. Thus if a particular shade of gray is rated 9, 9, 8, and 8 by four subjects, the average rating of 8.5 is considered the measurement of that shade of gray on an interval scale. In the same way, measurements would be obtained for all the shades of gray. The scale then would be used in other investigations concerning discrimination of shades of gray.

In another example of a scale based on subjective estimates, methods of interval estimation are applied to statements concerning attitudes toward the United Nations. First, a number of subjects would be employed to determine the most positive and the most negative statements in the set. If there were good agreement at this stage, approximately 100 subjects would then be asked to select a statement that is halfway between the two extreme statements. The statement receiving the most choices would constitute the center of the scale. Next, subjects would be required to select a statement that is halfway between the most negative statement and the center statement. Continued fractionation in this way would arrive at an interval scale for the stimuli.

The example above concerning attitude statements can be extended to demonstrate how subjective estimates can be used to approximate a ratio scale. Let us assume that an interval scale of 20 items has been obtained by the method described above. Next, methods of ratio estimation would be required of subjects. To obtain a preliminary indication of the zero (neutral) point, each statement would be rated on a seven-step scale anchored by the terms "highly favorable" for a rating of 7, "highly unfavorable" for a rating of 1, and "neutral" for a rating of 4. The statement having an average rating (over subjects) closest to 4.0 could be used to represent the neutral point on the interval scale, or more refined methods could be employed.

One refinement would be to choose three statements that are rated as moderately favorable, say, with average ratings on the seven-step scale from 5.0 to 6.0. For each of these, each subject would be required to pick an unfavorable statement that is as unfavorable as the other is favorable. In other words, for each favorable statement, the subject would be asked to go across the neutral point an equal distance on the unfavorable side of the continuum. With this information, one could derive a zero (neutral) point for the interval scale which was obtained from the method of interval estimation (the scale discussed in the previous paragraph, not the seven-step scale used to obtain preliminary information about the zero point). Some simple arithmetic could be used to locate the zero point. For example, if the average score on the interval scale for the three negative statements is 2.6 and the average score for the positive statements is 7.4, the zero point should be halfway between, which is 5.0. Then, by subtracting 5.0 from each of the scores of the 20 stimuli on the interval scale, one would arrive at a ratio scale for the stimuli.

In developing scales from models based on subjective estimation, it sometimes is assumed (rightly or wrongly) that the subject was employing a higher form of scale than he was asked to employ. This is best illustrated with the method of rank order, where, for example, subjects are asked to rank-order the photographs of 50 men in terms of handsomeness. Although subjects are asked to operate with respect to an ordinal scale, the experimenter might assume that each subject has an interval scale "in his head." If this were so, each subject would have to convert interval information about the pictures into an ordinal scale. Each subject might feel that most of the men in the photographs ranged from slightly ugly to slightly handsome and that there were only a few men at each tail of the distribution. Thus the subject might have "in his head" an approximately normal distribution on at least an interval scale. Then the experimenter would require the subject to flatten out the distribution to a complete rank order.

A set of assumptions (a model) can be employed in the situation above to recover the interval scale "in the head" of the subject. First, if the individual really possesses an interval scaling of the stimuli and the distribution of stimuli is approximately normal, converting this distribution to a rank order will require many difficult, if not impossible, discriminations. This is because in a normal distribution the majority of the stimuli are bunched together in the middle of the scale. Consequently the subject will have to make numerous errors in ranking the stimuli. If the subject repeats the rank ordering on two occasions and there is some way of erasing the memory of the first ordering, there will be some disagreement between the two orderings. If the amount of agreement is not high, e.g., a correlation no higher than .5, the average of the two rankings will regress from a rank order back toward a normal distribution. The average (over stimuli) of 100 independent rankings of the same stimuli will resemble the approximately normal distribution on the subject's interval scale "in the head."

Although it usually is not possible to require one subject to rank-order stimuli on numerous occasions, an assumption allows one to get around this difficulty. If it is assumed that people are replicates of one another (i.e., they differ in their rankings only because of random errors), one can obtain a single ranking from each subject and average the rankings. According to the assumptions in this model, the average ranks could be considered an interval scaling of the stimuli.

There are numerous other models for developing interval and ratio scales based on subjective estimates. The essence of them all is that subjects are assumed capable of producing such scales directly. After this fundamental assumption is made and appropriate methods of gathering responses (particularly those of interval estimation and ratio estimation) are employed, special sets of additional assumptions allow the derivations of interval scales and sometimes ratio scales. The actual models and computational procedures for this purpose tend to be simpler than models based on other fundamental assumptions.

DISCRIMINANT MODELS   The second major class of models (there are only two that have achieved prominence so far) differs in a number of important ways from the class based on subjective estimates. In discriminant models, one does not take very seriously the subject's ability to generate interval and ratio scales directly; rather, one assumes that this is something the scientist has to do after the data are collected. Discriminant models place primary emphasis on the variability of response to each stimulus—the variability of responses by different persons to the same stimulus and the potential variability of responses by the same person to the same stimulus on different occasions. Although with models based on subjective estimates it is admitted that such variability is present, most models take no formal account of the variability. Whereas models based on subjective estimates typically require responses by various methods of interval estimation and ratio estimation, discriminant models typically require responses by methods of ordinal estimation, e.g., rank order and pair comparisons.

The foundation for all discriminant models for scaling stimuli was laid by L. L. Thurstone. For any individual confronted with any stimulus, there is assumed to be a *discriminal process* with respect to a specified attribute. A discriminal process is simply a broadly defined *reaction* of some kind which correlates with the intensity of the stimulus on an interval scale for an attribute. Because of fluctuations of many different kinds within the individual, there is a *discriminal distribution* for each stimulus. That is, if the individual responds to the same stimulus on numerous occasions, the discriminal processes will be somewhat different. Since these differences are thought to represent random errors, it is expected that reactions would be normally distributed. Such distributions for three stimuli are illustrated in Figure 2-3.

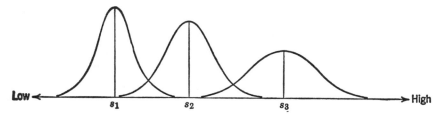

Low s_1 s_2 s_3 High

figure 2-3 *Discriminal distributions with respect to three stimuli.*

The mean discriminal process (reaction) to each stimulus is the best estimate of the scale value for that stimulus (best in the sense of least squares). If the means were known for all stimuli, an interval scale would be obtained and the scaling problem would be complete. According to the discriminant class of models, there is no way to obtain these means directly; they must be deduced from the subject's responses. In doing this, each of the different models makes somewhat different assumptions about the nature of the discriminal distributions. In the general model, it is not assumed that the standard deviations are equal (unequal standard deviations are illustrated in Figure 2-3). This allows for the possibility that a subject would vary more in responses to some stimuli than in responses to others.

Crucial to all discriminant models is that there be overlapping distributions of discriminal processes. If, for example, the discriminal distribution of one stimulus is so high on the attribute that the lower tail of the distribution does not overlap somewhat with the distribution of the stimulus immediately below, there is no way to determine the position of that stimulus on an interval scale. Because it is crucial to have overlapping discriminal distributions, it is said that discriminant models are based on *confusions*.

A series of brilliant simplifying assumptions and deductions **by** Thurstone (1927) led to the now-famous law of comparative judgment. Actually there are numerous forms of the "law," depending on the assumptions made in particular cases. Complete discussions of numerous models and research techniques following from the law of comparative judgment are given by Guilford (1954) and by Torgerson (1958). Here, we shall consider only the basic ideas and the particular model which has been used most widely. The major assumptions and deductions are as follows:

1   Let covert discriminal responses to stimulus j be denoted r_j and covert discriminal responses to stimulus k be denoted r_k.

2   Let the mean discriminal responses to two stimuli, $\bar{r}_j$ and $\bar{r}_k$, be the best estimates of scale positions for those stimuli.

3   If the discriminal distributions overlap, on some occasions the difference in response to the two stimuli $r_j - r_k$ will be positive and on other occasions negative, i.e., the subject will "change his mind" from one occasion to another about which is higher on the attribute.

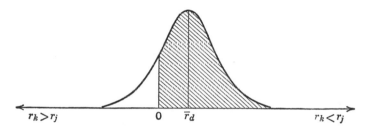

figure 2-4 *Distribution of discriminal differences for two stimuli.*

4   If the discriminal processes for two stimuli are normally distributed, the distribution of differences in discriminal processes will be normally distributed. That is, on each occasion, if r_k were subtracted from r_j, the distribution of such differences over many occasions would be normal. A distribution of discriminal differences is illustrated in Figure 2-4. The shaded area is proportional to the percentage of times stimulus j is judged greater than stimulus k, and vice versa for the unshaded area.

5   The mean of the differences between responses to the two stimuli on numerous occasions $\bar{r}_d$ equals the best estimate of the interval separating the two stimuli on an interval scale. This would be equal to $\bar{r}_j - \bar{r}_k$. Although there is no way to obtain this quantity directly, it can be estimated through the following steps.

6   On numerous occasions have a subject state whether stimulus j is greater or less than stimulus k with respect to an attribute. (For the sake of exploring this model, assume at this point that such an approach is feasible.) This proportion is denoted $p_{j>k}$.

7   Next, make the preliminary assumption that discriminal differences are normally distributed with a standard deviation of 1.0. The mean of the distribution would

scaling models   **5 1**

be $\bar{r}_d$ rather than zero. The zero point would be either to the left or to the right of the mean, depending on which of the two stimuli is more frequently judged to be greater with respect to the attribute. Then the zero point could be expressed in terms of the number of standard deviations it is below or above the mean $\bar{r}_d$(or $\bar{r}_j - \bar{r}_k$). This is done by looking in a table of areas under the normal curve for the normal deviate corresponding to $p_{j>k}$. If, for example, j is judged greater than k 92 percent of the time, this corresponds to a normal deviate z_{jk} of approximately 1.4. Thus the zero point on the scale of discriminal differences is 1.4 standard deviations below the mean. More importantly, *the mean is 1.4 standard deviations above the zero point* (and this is the fact that gets us close to a solution).

8   With the size of $\bar{r}_d$(or $\bar{r}_j - \bar{r}_k$) found in terms of standard deviations on the unit normal curve z_{jk}, all that is left is to express $\bar{r}_d$ in terms of the actual standard deviation of the dispersion of discriminal differences. This is necessary to account for the possibility that the standard deviations of discriminal differences might be different for different pairs of stimuli. This would tend to be the case if the discriminal dispersions for two stimuli were larger than those for two other stimuli. If that occurred, even if two pairs of stimuli were separated by a function of the same normal deviate, they could be separated by very different intervals on an interval scale. Thus even if z_{fl} and z_{jk} are the same, when account is taken of the standard deviations of distributions of discriminal differences in the two cases, the two intervals might be very different. Account needs to be taken of these standard deviations to place intervals back on the same unit of measurement as that of the discriminal continuum.

9   The standard deviation of the dispersion of discriminal differences can be expressed as follows:

(2-1)
$$\sigma_d = \sqrt{\sigma_j{}^2 + \sigma_k{}^2 - 2r_{jk}\sigma_j\sigma_k}$$

where σ_d = standard deviation of discriminal differences

$\sigma_j + \sigma_k$ = sum of standard deviations of discriminal distributions for stimuli j and k

r_{jk} = correlation between discriminal processes for the two stimuli

The standard deviation of the distribution of discriminal differences involves the standard deviations of the two discriminal distributions and the correlation between them. If the correlation is different from zero, it means that there are correlated "errors" in the fluctuations in discriminal processes from one occasion to another.

10   If the standard deviation of the distribution of discriminal differences is known, the interval separating two stimuli is obtained as follows:

$$\bar{r}_d = \bar{r}_j - \bar{r}_k = z_{jk}\sigma_d$$

(2-2)
$$\bar{r}_j - \bar{r}_k = z_{jk}\sqrt{\sigma_j{}^2 + \sigma_k{}^2 - 2r_{jk}\sigma_j\sigma_k}$$

Equation (2-2) is called the "complete law of comparative judgment." To use it requires knowledge of (1) the proportion of times each stimulus is judged greater than another with respect to an attribute, (2) the standard deviations of discriminal distributions for the two stimuli, and (3) the correlation between the two discriminal distributions. Rarely is information obtained about all three of these statistics; consequently some simplifying assumptions usually are made. (See Guilford, 1954, and Torgerson, 1958, for some methods of learning about these statistics.) Most frequently, two assumptions are made: (1) that the correlations between discriminal distributions are zero (responses are independent) and (2) that standard deviations of discriminal distributions are all equal. Then Eq. (2-2) reduces to the following:

(2-3) $\quad \bar{r}_j - \bar{r}_k = z_{jk} \sqrt{\sigma_j{}^2 + \sigma_k{}^2}$

(2-4) $\quad \bar{r}_j - \bar{r}_k = z_{jk}\sigma \sqrt{2}$

Since all dispersions (standard deviations) of discriminal processes are assumed to be the same, the term under the radical can be reduced to the square root of 2 multiplied by any of the standard deviations. Since that term would be constant for all pairs of stimuli and since the intervals on an interval scale remain proportionately the same when all scale values are multiplied by a constant, the formula can be reduced to

(2-5) $\quad \bar{r}_j - \bar{r}_k = z_{jk}$

Thus, with these assumptions, the normal deviate itself serves as the interval separating two stimuli. By far the most frequent use of the law of comparative judgment has been with this formula.

To actually apply the law of comparative judgment, further simplifying assumptions are made. In its most general form, the model is based on the distributions of responses for one subject on numerous occasions. For three reasons, this is only a handy fiction. First, with most types of judgments and sentiments it would be totally impractical to have the same subject respond to the same stimuli on numerous occasions. It would be hard to find subjects who would devote the time. Second, with most types of stimuli it would not be possible to obtain independent responses. Subjects would remember some of their responses on previous occasions and would tend to repeat them. Third, even if it were not for these difficulties, the usual purpose in scaling stimuli is to obtain a scale that applies to people in general or at least to some definable class of persons. It would be chaotic if a different scale had to be developed for each person. For these reasons, the law of comparative judgment is almost always applied to the responses of a group of persons rather than to numerous responses by only one person.

Although any method of ordinal estimation can be employed with the law of comparative judgment, the method of pair comparisons is the most obvious approach. Each subject is given all possible pairs of stimuli in a set (the number of stimuli in the set usually ranges from 10 to 20). For each pair, the subject indicates which is greater along a stated dimension of judgment or sentiment. A table is formed showing the proportion of persons in a group who indicate that each

table 2-1 *Proportions of subjects that preferred each vegetable in comparison to each of the other vegetables*

	VEGETABLE	1	2	3	4	5	6	7	8	9
1	turnips	.500	.818	.770	.811	.878	.892	.899	.892	.926
2	cabbage	.182	.500	.601	.723	.743	.736	.811	.845	.858
3	beets	.230	.399	.500	.561	.736	.676	.845	.797	.818
4	asparagus	.189	.277	.439	.500	.561	.588	.676	.601	.730
5	carrots	.122	.257	.264	.439	.500	.493	.574	.709	.764
6	spinach	.108	.264	.324	.412	.507	.500	.628	.682	.628
7	string beans	.101	.189	.155	.324	.426	.372	.500	.527	.642
8	peas	.108	.155	.203	.399	.291	.318	.473	.500	.628
9	corn	.074	.142	.182	.270	.236	.372	.358	.372	.500

SOURCE: Adapted from Guilford, 1954, by permission of the author and publisher.

table 2-2 *Derivations of an interval scale from normal deviates among stimuli*

	VEGETABLE	1	2	3	4	5	6	7	8	9
1	turnips	.000	.908	.739	.882	1.165	1.237	1.276	1.237	1.447
2	cabbage	−.908	.000	.256	.592	.653	.631	.882	1.015	1.071
3	beets	−.739	−.256	.000	.154	.631	.456	1.015	.831	.908
4	asparagus	−.882	−.592	−.154	.000	.154	.222	.456	.256	.613
5	carrots	−1.165	−.653	−.631	−.154	.000	−.018	.187	.550	.719
6	spinach	−1.237	−.631	−.456	−.222	.018	.000	.327	.473	.327
7	string beans	−1.276	−.882	−1.015	−.456	−.187	−.327	.000	.068	.364
8	peas	−1.237	−1.015	−.831	−.256	−.550	−.473	−.068	.000	.327
9	corn	−1.447	−1.071	−.908	−.613	−.719	−.327	−.364	−.327	.000
	sum	−8.891	−4.192	−3.000	−.073	1.165	1.401	3.711	4.103	5.776
	average	−.988	−.465	−.333	−.008	+.129	+.156	+.412	+.456	+.642
	final scale	.000	.523	.655	.980	1.117	1.144	1.400	1.444	1.630

SOURCE: Adapted from Guilford, 1954, by permission of the author and publisher.

stimulus is greater than the others. Typical results from a study of food preferences are shown in Table 2-1. It is assumed that each stimulus would be judged greater than itself half of the time, so .5 goes in each diagonal of the table. The next step is to convert each proportion into a normal deviate z_{jk}, which is done in Table 2-2.

If the assumptions are correct for Eq. (2-5), each of the normal deviates in Table 2-2 can be considered an interval between the two stimuli involved. However, since there is likely to be some error in the normal deviate between any two stimuli, the error can be reduced as follows. The sum of normal deviates in each column is obtained,

basic principles

and these are averaged. These are then normal deviates expressed about the average stimulus in the set. To prevent having negative values on the final scale, the positive amount of the largest negative value is added to each of the values. This produces the final scale, which, in the example in Table 2-2, is presumed to be an interval scale of preference for the foods involved.

CHECKS AND BALANCES   So far in this section numerous assumptions have been made in employing different models. How does one know if the assumptions are correct? First, for any model, there are standards of *internal consistency* that the data must meet. (See Torgerson, 1958, for a detailed discussion of these standards.) Some examples will serve to show how such standards are applied. If a rank-order scale is developed by averaging the ranks given to the same stimuli by different people, the data are internally consistent to the extent that subjects give much the same ranks to the stimuli. Internal consistency for the method of bisection can be tested as follows. First, the subject is required to adjust a light to the point where it is halfway between two others in perceived brightness. Second, the subject obtains two intensities that bisect the two intervals obtained in the first step. Finally, the subject bisects the intensities obtained in the second step. If the data are internally consistent, the subject should arrive back at the first intensity used to bisect the first two stimuli. Data obtained from pair comparisons can be tested for internal consistency by examining the transitivity of scale values. If, for example, stimulus j is found to be 1.0 greater than stimulus k, and stimulus k is .5 greater than stimulus i, and if the data are internally consistent, stimulus j should be 1.5 greater than stimulus i. For all the scaling models, there are standards of internal consistency that apply. If the internal consistency is low, one would be very suspicious of the scale.

In addition to internal consistency, another important standard concerns the extent to which scale values can be replicated in studies that differ slightly in procedures. This applies when a new study is undertaken using only some of the stimuli employed in an earlier study. If, for example, the study of vegetables illustrated in Table 2-2 were redone and five new vegetables were added, the relative sizes of the intervals between turnips, cabbage, and beets should remain much the same. If the relative sizes of these intervals change markedly, it would provide little confidence in any scaling of vegetables by that method. Previously it was described how an approximate zero point on a scale regarding attitudes could be developed by having subjects balance positive statements with negative statements equidistant across the zero point. In that case there would be a choice as to whether the experimenter would give the subject negative or positive statements to be balanced across the zero point. Also, there would be some choice as to which statements would be used in either case. To the extent that such different approaches would lead to *different* zero points, the method would be suspect with respect to the particular problem of scaling. In all other uses of scaling models, it is expected to find essentially the same rank order, intervals, and ratios when methods of gathering responses or methods of analysis are slightly different.

models for scaling people

Early in the chapter it was stated that problems of scaling potentially concern a three-dimensional table of data, with the dimensions representing persons, stimuli, and responses. (This was illustrated in Figure 2-1.) In the development of unidimensional scales for either persons or stimuli, it is usually possible to "collapse" the dimension concerning different types of responses. Either it is known from previous studies that all the types of responses concern the same attribute, e.g., by a factor analysis of rating scales bounded by different pairs of adjectives, or only one type of response is required to each stimulus. The latter would be the case, for example, if the subject were required only to agree or disagree with each statement in a list or to indicate whether each statement in a list is correct or incorrect. After the three-dimensional table is reduced to a two-dimensional table, models for developing unidimensional scales concern ways for collapsing one of the two remaining dimensions. The previous section discussed ways of collapsing the person dimension to scale stimuli. This section will treat ways of collapsing the stimulus dimension to scale persons.

MULTI-ITEM MEASURES Prior to a discussion of models for collapsing the stimulus dimension of a two-dimensional table of data, it might be wise to reflect on the need for more than one stimulus in psychological measures. The word "items" will be used in a broad sense to stand for any stimuli used in measurement methods. Thus items may be words on a spelling test, comparisons between weights, statements concerning attitudes toward the United Nations, correct choices of a rat in a maze, and reactions in a study of reaction time. What is presented the subject is the item (stimulus), and in each of the examples above, the subject is required to make only one type of response to each item.

There are a number of important reasons for requiring more than one item in nearly all measures of psychological attributes. First, individual items usually have considerable *specificity* (a term which will become more meaningful after Chapter Nine on factor analysis is read). That is, each item tends to have only a low correlation with the attribute being measured and tends to relate to other attributes. On a spelling test, for example, whether or not a child could correctly spell "umpire" would depend in part on his interest in baseball. A boy who spent much time reading baseball stories might correctly spell the word even though he was a poor speller in general. Another example of the specificity of individual items is in rating the following statement on a seven-step scale of agreement-disagreement: "We give more to the United Nations than we get in return." Supposedly that is a negative statement about the United Nations, and people who agree with the statement *tend* to have negative attitudes. Even though a person might have an overall positive attitude, however, he might agree with the statement because he is not happy with the share of financing borne by our country.

In both examples above, it can be seen that each item relates only in a statistical sense with the attribute being measured. Each item tends to correlate with the attribute in question, but also correlates with attributes other than the one being measured.

Even if individual items had no specificity, there are other reasons why measures require more than one item. One reason is that most items attempt to categorize people into either two groups or only a relatively small number of groups. Thus an item requiring dichotomous responses (e.g., pass or fail) can at most distinguish between two levels of the attribute. A seven-step rating scale can at most distinguish between seven levels of an attribute. In most measurement problems it is desirable to make fine differentiations among people, and this can seldom be done with a one-item measure.

Even if there were no specificity in items and items were capable of making very fine distinctions among people, there still would be an important reason why one-item measures would not suffice. Individual items have considerable measurement error; in other words, they are unreliable. Each item, in addition to its specificity, occasions a considerable amount of random error. This is seen when people are required to repeat a set of ratings after a period of time. The person who gave a rating of 3 on one occasion is likely to give a rating of 5 on another, and many other changes of this kind are expected. Another example would be in the solving of arithmetic problems on two occasions. The child who got the correct answer on one occasion might not get the correct answer to the same problem on another occasion, and vice versa. Thus there is some randomness related to any item, and consequently the individual item cannot be trusted to give reliable measurement of an attribute.

All three difficulties that have been discussed can be diminished by the use of multi-item measures. The specificity of items can be averaged out when they are combined. By combining items, one can make relatively fine distinctions among people. For reasons which will be discussed in Chapters Six and Seven, the reliability tends to increase (measurement error reduces) as the number of items in a combination increases. Thus nearly all measures of psychological attributes are multi-item measures. This is true both for measures used in studies of individual differences and for measures used in controlled experiments. The problem of scaling people with respect to attributes is then one of collapsing responses to a number of items so as to obtain one score (measurement) for each person.

THE TRACE LINE   Nearly all models for scaling people can be depicted by different types of curves relating an attribute to the probability of responding in one way rather than another to items. Four different types of trace lines are depicted in Figures 2-5 to 2-8. Dichotomous items are depicted in these figures. For each item, it will be said that there are two types of responses, alpha and beta. Alpha would variously consist of passing rather than failing an item, agreeing rather than disagreeing with a statement, and a rat making the correct rather then the incorrect turn in a maze.

In Figures 2-5 to 2-8, the attribute is the particular thing being measured. In this connection, it is important to make a distinction between the particular attribute being measured and some more general attribute of interest. Thus the responses of a rat in a maze constitute a particular attribute. It is hoped that this attribute relates to the more general attribute of habit strength. On vocabulary tests, identifying correct synonyms for words is a particular attribute, and it is hoped that this particular attribute relates to the general attribute of intelligence. The particular attribute will be referred to as an "attribute." More general attributes will be referred to as "constructs." (The measurement of constructs is discussed in Chapter Three.) The measurement problem itself concerns the relations between particular attributes and the probability of responding in one way rather than another. It is only after measures of particular attributes are constructed that they can be combined to measure more general attributes (constructs).

In the remainder of this chapter, the abscissa for models concerning trace lines will concern particular attributes. Attributes are defined in a circular sense in terms of whatever a number of items tends to measure in common. Thus a list of spelling words would tend to measure spelling ability, and the number of correct turns of a rat in a maze would tend to measure amount learned. The word "tend" is used because it must be recognized that no attribute is perfectly mirrored in any set of items. Perfect measurement would be available, for example, if children were administered a spelling test containing all words in the English language or if rats were capable of running an infinitely long maze. When there is a limited number of items, as there always

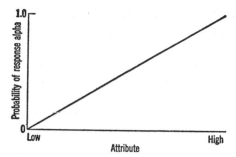

figure 2-5   *An ascending linear trace line for an item.*

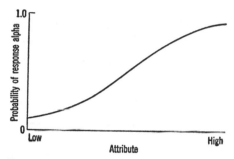

figure 2-6   *An ascending monotonic trace line for an item.*

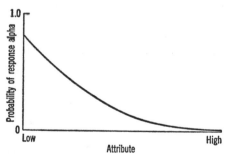

figure 2-7   *A descending monotonic trace line for an item.*

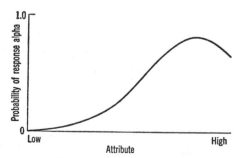

figure 2-8   *A nonmonotonic trace line for an item.*

scaling models

is, there is some unreliability of measuring the particular attribute. Completely reliable measures of the attribute are called *true scores*, and the approximations to true scores obtained from any collection of items are called *fallible scores*. In all the figures showing item trace lines, the abscissa concerns true scores on the particular attribute. Of course, one does not know exactly what the true scores are, but they can be approximated by scores obtained from some combination of the available items. For this reason, after some way has been formulated for combining items, an approximate test can be made for the actual trace line of any particular item; e.g., the trace line for a spelling item can be computed as a function of the number of words correctly spelled on the test.

The concept of trace lines also applies to multipoint items (items that are scorable on more than two points), an example of which is shown in Figure 2-9. Instead of depicting the probability of response alpha, the ordinate depicts the average score on the item. In Figure 2-9 are shown the average scores on a seven-step rating scale for persons at different levels of an attribute. Other multipoint items whose trace lines could be depicted in that way are scores on essay questions in a classroom examination, number of words correctly recalled in a study of memory, and amount of time in responding to a signal in studies of reaction time. It should be recalled that an average score is an *expected score*, and consequently Figure 2-9 depicts the expected score as a function of levels of an attribute.

In discussing trace lines, it is useful to think of the attribute as being completely continuous—i.e., it is theoretically possible to make

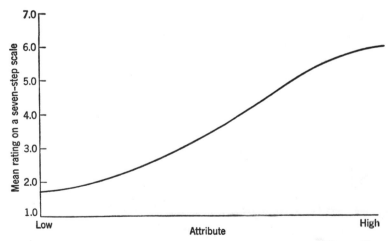

figure 2-9 *Trace line of average scores on a seven-step rating scale.*

basic principles

infinitely fine discriminations among people. Also, it is useful to think of there being a large number of persons at each of the infinite number of points on the attribute. In this hypothetical circumstance, the trace line shows the expected response for people at each level of the attribute, the expectation being expressed either as a probability of response alpha for dichotomous items or as an average score for multipoint items. By their nature, expectations are accompanied by some error. On dichotomous items, there is a probability of response alpha at each point, but there is no certainty as to *which* persons at a point will make response alpha and which persons will make response beta. On multipoint items, there is a band of error surrounding the expected average score. Thus although the expected score for a particular point on an attribute might be 3.0, the actual scores of people at that point might range from 1.5 to 4.5.

deterministic models for scaling people

Deterministic models are so called because they assume that there is *no error* in item trace lines. For dichotomous items, at each point of the attribute it is assumed that the probability of response alpha is either 1.0 or zero. The particular deterministic model employed most frequently is one which assumes that up to a point on the attribute the probability of response alpha is zero (probability of responses beta is 1.0) and beyond that point the probability of response alpha is 1.0. An item of this type is shown in Figure 2-10, and a family of such

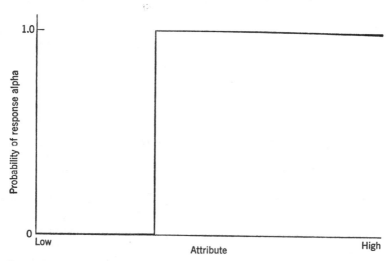

figure 2-10 *Trace line of an item that discriminates perfectly at one point on an attribute.*

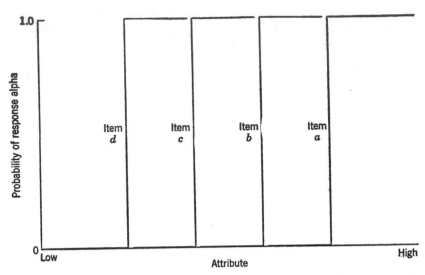

figure 2-11 *Family of trace lines for four items that meet the requirements of a monotone deterministic model.*

items is shown in Figure 2-11. Each item has a biserial correlation (see Chapter Four) of 1.0 with the attribute, and consequently each item perfectly discriminates at a particular point of the attribute. Intuitively, this is a very appealing model, because it is exactly what one expects to obtain in measurements of length. Thus one would expect to obtain a family of trace lines like that in Figure 2-11 for the following items.

		YES	NO
a	Are you above 6 feet 6 inches in height?	————	————
b	Are you above 6 feet 3 inches in height?	————	————
c	Are you above 6 feet in height?	————	————
d	Are you above 5 feet 9 inches in height?	————	————
e	Are you above 5 feet 6 inches in height?	————	————

Answering "yes" can be considered response alpha. Any person who answered yes to question (item) a would answer yes to the others. Any person who did not answer yes to a but did answer yes to b would also answer yes to questions c through e. For five people with different patterns of responses, a triangular pattern of data would be found like that in Table 2-3. An X symbolizes an answer of yes (response alpha).

basic principles

table 2-3 *Triangular pattern of responses that would fit requirements of a monontone, deterministic scaling model*

ITEM	PERSON				
	1	2	3	4	5
a	X				
b	X	X			
c	X	X	X		
d	X	X	X	X	
e	X	X	X	X	X

GUTTMAN SCALE   Although one never knows the exact nature of trace lines, one can look at data and see if they evolve into a triangular pattern like that in Table 2-3. (In so doing, however, one is making a subtle logical assumption—a point which will be discussed later.) Some types of items tend to produce a pattern of data like that in Table 2-3. The following is an example.

		YES	NO
a	The United Nations is the savior of mankind.	___	___
b	The United Nations is our best hope for peace.	___	___
c	The United Nations is a constructive force in the world.	___	___
d	We should continue to participate in the United Nations.	___	___

For any person who answers yes to *a*, there is a high probability that he will answer yes to the other items. Any person who does not answer yes to *a* but does answer yes to *b* has a high probability of answering yes to the other items.

Any set of items that produces a pattern of responses approximately like that in Table 2-3 is called a "Guttman scale." In developing such a scale, what one does is administer a collection of items to a group of people and then attempt to arrange the responses so as to produce the required triangular pattern. (Since in actual data there would be more than one person at each level of the attribute, the data would appear in the form of a solid staircase, with the width of each step being proportional to the number of persons at each level.) There are numerous cut-and-try methods for doing this (see Torgerson, 1958). Of course, obtaining the triangular pattern exactly is very unlikely, and therefore it is necessary (1) to discard some items and (2) to find the best possible ordering of items and people. Regarding the latter consideration, of primary concern is the *reproducibility* of score patterns.

If the triangular pattern is perfectly obtained, a knowledge of the *number* of responses of yes allows one to reproduce all the person's responses. When the triangular pattern is approximately obtained, a knowledge of the number of yeses by a person allows one to approximately reproduce all that person's responses. For all people and all items, one can investigate the percentage of reproducibility, and it is this percentage which is all important in the development of Guttman scales.

Conceivably, Guttman scales could be developed for all types of items requiring dichotomous responses. This can be illustrated with a spelling test where there are 40 items. For each item, the subject indicates whether or not the word is correctly spelled. If the items had trace lines like those in Figure 2-11, a triangular pattern of data would be obtained. In this instance an x would stand for a correct response to the spelling of the word. If one person has a score of 35 and another a score of 34, this would necessarily mean that the former person got the *same* 34 items correct as the latter person, plus one additional item. If one knew how many words an individual passed, he would know exactly which items that person passed.

EVALUATION OF THE GUTTMAN SCALE   In spite of the intuitive appeal of the Guttman scale, it is highly impractical. First, it is highly unrealistic to think that items could have trace lines like those in Figure 2-11. No item correlates perfectly with any attribute. Although there is no way to obtain the trace lines directly, some good approximations are available. For example, with items concerning spelling, the number of words correctly spelled can be used as an approximation of the attribute (true scores in spelling). When the trace line is obtained in such instances, not only is it not perpendicular at a point, but it typically tends to have a relatively flat, approximately linear form. Typically, individual items correlate no higher than .40 with total scores. Consequently it is very unreasonable to work with a model that assumes perfect biserial correlations between items and an attribute.

Second, having the triangular pattern of data is no guarantee that items have trace lines like those in Figure 2-11. If items are spaced far enough apart in difficulty (popularity on nonability items), the triangular pattern can be obtained even if the trace lines are very flat rather than vertical. This is illustrated with the following four items.

a   Solve for x: $x^2 + 2x + 9 = 16$.

b   What is the meaning of the word "severe"?

c   How much is 10×38?

d   When do you use an umbrella? (given orally)

Although the author has not performed the experiment, the above four items administered to persons ranging in age from six to sixteen probably

basic principles

would form an excellent Guttman scale. Any person who got the first item correct probably could get the others correct. Any person who failed the first item but got the second correct would probably get the other two correct. Those four items would produce the required triangular pattern of data even though there is good evidence that they do not all belong to the same attribute ("factor," in the language of factor analysis). The reason they apparently fit the model for a unidimensional scale is that they are administered to an extremely diverse population. They would not fit the model if they were investigated within one age group only. Consequently, as was suggested earlier, it is not entirely logical to assume that having a triangular pattern of data like that in Table 2-3 is *sufficient* evidence for the presence of a unidimensional scale.

Because the triangular pattern of data can be approximated in any study where items vary greatly in difficulty, in practice this results in scales with very few items (seldom more than eight). To take an extreme case, if there are three items that respectively are passed by 10 percent, 50 percent, and 90 percent of the people, the triangular pattern will be obtained almost perfectly regardless of what the items concern. The difficulties of items can be dispersed in this way only if the final scale contains only a small number of items. This usually is done by starting with a relatively large number of items (say, 20) and discarding all items but a few that vary widely in difficulty. This is only a way of fooling one's self into believing that a unidimensional scale has been obtained when it really has not. Also, since such scales seldom have more than eight items, they can make only rather gross distinctions among people.

A third criticism of the Guttman scale is that it seeks to obtain only an ordinal measurement of human attributes. As was argued in the previous chapter, there are good reasons for believing that it is possible to measure human attributes on interval scales, if not usually on ratio scales. If psychology were to settle only for ordinal measurement, it would so limit the usable methods of mathematics that the science would be nearly crippled.

A fourth criticism of the Guttman scale concerns its intuitive appeal. It would be more appropriate to think of items not as yardsticks being applied to the heights of people, but rather as rubber yardsticks applied by half-blind investigators. Also, to complete the analogy, one should think of each item as a different rubber yardstick which has been copied from a real yardstick by a five-year-old boy. On some of the yardsticks, the zero point starts at 4 inches, and the boy has made numerous, large random errors in copying intervals (widths of 1 inch). If 20 such rubber yardsticks were applied to a group of people, any yardstick (item) would have only a rather flat trace line with respect to the actual heights. By methods which will be discussed in subsequent sections, one could combine the different measurements for each person to obtain an approximately linear relationship with the real scale of heights, and thus in this way one could obtain an interval scale.

In summary, the deterministic model underlying the Guttman scale is thoroughly illogical for most psychological measurement because (1) almost no items exist that fit the model, (2) the presence of a triangular pattern is a necessary but not sufficient condition for the fit of the model in particular instances, (3) the triangular pattern can be (and usually is) artificially forced by dealing with a small number of items that vary greatly in difficulty, (4) the model aspires only to develop ordinal scales, and (5) there are better intuitive bases for developing models for psychological attributes. Considering this heavy weight of criticism, it is surprising that some people still consider this deterministic model a good basis for developing measures of psychological attributes.

NONMONOTONE DETERMINISTIC MODELS There are other deterministic models in addition to the Guttman scale (Torgerson, 1958). One of these makes the following assumptions. Each item is responded to in manner alpha by all the people at one level, and each person responds in manner alpha to only one item. Trace lines for three such items are shown in Figure 2-12. The pattern of data produced by such a model is shown in Table 2-4. In contrast to the Guttman scale, in this deterministic model each item has a nonmonotone trace line; i.e., the

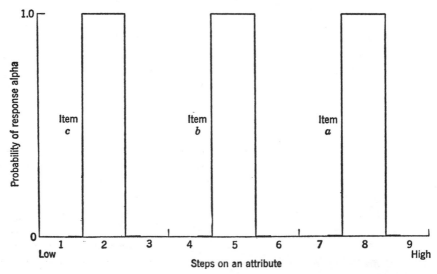

figure 2-12 *Trace lines for three items that meet the requirements of a nonmonotone, deterministic scaling model.*

table 2-4 *Pattern of responses to four items that meets requirements of a monontone, deterministic scaling model*

ITEM	PERSON			
	1	2	3	4
a	X			
b		X		
c			X	
d				X

line goes up and then comes down. The following four items would fit this model.

		YES	NO
a	Are you between 6 feet 3 inches tall and 6 feet 6?	_____	_____
b	Are you between 6 feet tall and 6 feet 3 inches?	_____	_____
c	Are you between 5 feet 9 inches tall and 6 feet?	_____	_____
d	Are you between 5 feet 6 inches tall and 5 feet 9?	_____	_____

Using the word "items" in the broadest sense, it would be very rare to find any items on psychological measures that would fit this model. All the criticisms that apply to the Guttman scale apply with added force to this nonmonotone deterministic model.

Deterministic models are of use mainly to specialists in the theory of psychological measurement. Such models frequently represent "limiting cases" of models that are actually used to develop measures of psychological attributes. Other than for this use, they are only interesting museum pieces. Only by working with some type of nondeterministic probability model can one develop the measures that are needed in research.

probability models for scaling people

If trace lines are not assumed to have perpendicular ascents and descents, one is working with some type of probability model. There are numerous types of probability models, depending on the type of curve assumed for the trace lines. The most prominent models are discussed in the following sections.

NONMONOTONE MODELS   Analogous to nonmonotone deterministic models such as the one discussed above, there are nonmonotone probability models. Any type of curve that changes slope at some point from positive to negative or vice versa is nonmonotone. Some examples are shown in

Figure 2-13. The only nonmonotone model that has been used frequently assumes that (1) the attribute is continuous and (2) each item has a trace line that approximates the normal distribution. The probability of responding in manner alpha is highest at a particular point on the attribute, and from that point the probability of responding in manner alpha falls off in both directions in general resemblance to the normal curve. Three such items are shown in Figure 2-14.

Trace lines need not be exactly normal, and standard deviations of trace lines need not be identical. This model has been used for only one purpose: the development of certain types of attitude scales. Since the scaling procedure was developed by Thurstone, the type of

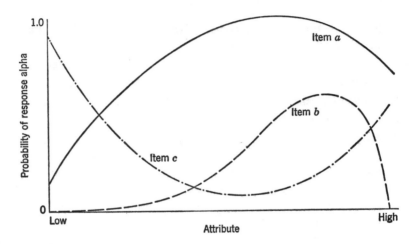

figure 2-13   *Three items with nonmonotone trace lines.*

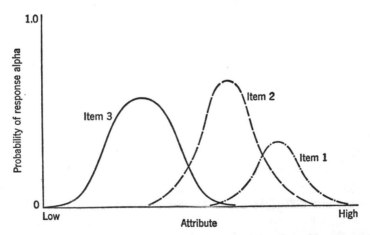

figure 2-14   *Nonmonotone, normal trace lines for three items.*

basic principles

scale is referred to as a "Thurstone scale of attitudes." Items at three points on such a scale are as follows.

AGREE   DISAGREE

1 I believe that the church is the greatest institution in America today.   _____   _____

2 When I go to church I enjoy a fine ritual service with good music.   _____   _____

3 The paternal and benevolent attitude of the church is quite distasteful to me.   _____   _____

The first step in obtaining a Thurstone scale is to have a large number of attitude statements rated by about 100 judges (see Edwards, 1957a, for a complete discussion of procedures). Each statement is usually rated on an 11-step scale ranging from "strongly favorable statement" to "strongly unfavorable statement." From 10 to 20 items are selected from the larger collection of items according to the following two standards: (1) items that have small standard deviations of ratings over judges, i.e., agreement is good among judges about where the items belong on the scale, and (2) items that range evenly from one extreme to the other.

The essence of the Thurstone nonmonotone model is that each item should tend to receive agreement (response alpha) at only one zone of the attribute. To assume an approximately normal distribution for the trace line is to admit that each item occasions some error.

The major fault of the Thurstone scale and of other nonmonotone probability models is that it is very difficult to find any items that fit. The model obviously would not fit most types of items. For example, how could one find spelling words such that each would be correctly spelled only by persons in a narrow band of the attribute of spelling ability? An item that "peaked" at the lower end of the scale would be one that is spelled correctly only by rather poor spellers. For an item that peaked in the middle of the scale, very few people with superior ability in spelling would give a correct response. This type of scale clearly does not apply to any items requiring judgments.

Even with responses concerning sentiments, the Thurstone model would seem to apply only to certain types of statements relating to attitudes, and even there the model is in logical trouble. Attitude statements tend to fit this model only if they are "double-barreled": only if they say two things, one of which is good and the other bad. This can be seen by a careful analysis of the three attitude statements given earlier. In item 2, the subject is asked to agree simultaneously with two hidden statements:

I sometimes go to church.

I probably would not go to church if it were not for a fine ritual service with good music.

Item 3 is "triple-barreled." To agree with it, the subject must agree that the church is paternal, benevolent, and distasteful. The three modifiers add up to a moderately negative attitude toward the church. It is possible to construct such items only by subtly building two or more statements into what is ostensibly one statement. This type of item not only is very difficult to construct, but tends to be ambiguous to subjects. Some subjects respond to one of the hidden statements and some subjects to another. In a more exaggerated form, this ambiguity is evidenced in the following double-barreled statement:

The church is a wonderful, horrible institution.

Another important criticism of nonmonotone probability models is that it is very difficult to think of items for the ends of the scale that would fit. This is illustrated with item 1 in the previous example. Who could have so positive an attitude toward the church that he would *disagree* with the statement, "I believe the church is the greatest institution in America today"? Such items necessarily are monotone, continuing to rise as one reaches higher and higher levels of the attribute.

In summary, nonmonotone probability models conceivably apply to only certain types of items for the measurement of attitudes, and there are better ways to construct attitude scales (see Chapter Fourteen).

MONOTONE MODELS WITH SPECIFIED DISTRIBUTION FORMS   In some of the models that assume monotone trace lines, it is assumed that the trace lines fit a particular statistical function. Most frequently it has been assumed that the function is a *normal ogive*. (A normal ogive is a cumulative normal distribution.) In Figure 2-15 are shown three items having

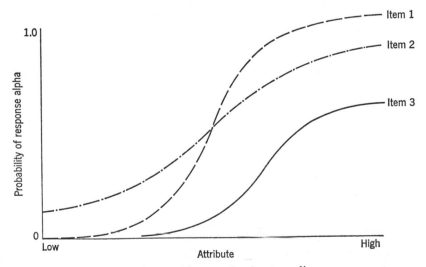

figure 2-15   *Three items with normal-ogive trace lines.*

normal-ogive trace lines. The important feature of a normal-ogive trace line is that it is much more discriminating at certain levels of the attribute than it is at neighboring levels. The zone where discrimination is good is that below the steeply ascending part of the curve. The steeper that section of the curve, the higher is the biserial correlation of that item with the attribute. If that section were vertical, the "tails" would disappear, the item would correlate perfectly with the attribute, and a collection of such items would form a Guttman scale. As items correlate less and less with the attribute, the S shape tends to flatten toward a straight line and the slope approaches the horizontal.

The normal-ogive model is appealing for two reasons. First, it makes good sense intuitively. Thus, for each item, one can think of a critical zone on the attribute where there is considerable uncertainty concerning how people will respond. As one moves away from that zone in either direction, the uncertainty is markedly reduced. Persons below that zone will predominately fail the item, and persons above it will predominately pass. An increasing slope of the trace line over some zone is more to be expected than, say, a straight line. Other intuitive support for the normal ogive comes from studies concerning the scaling of stimuli. There it is found, for example, that judgments of weights by the method of constant stimuli usually fit a normal ogive (see Figure 2-2).

The second reason for the appeal of this model is that it has very useful mathematical properties that permit the deduction of many important principles (Lord, 1952b). For example, the sum of any number of normal ogives is also a normal ogive, and the exact shape and slope of the latter can be predicted from the ogives which are summed. Then if one obtains a scale by summing scores on individual items (e.g., enumerating the number correct), the average scores or sums of scores form a normal-ogive relationship with the attribute. (The sum of probabilities for any number of normal ogives over a point on an attribute would be the expected sum of scores on the test as a whole for persons at that point.) This means that summing scores on items to obtain total scores (which is the usual approach) produces a scale that is *not* linearly related to the attribute. However, in practice this is a very slight danger, because even if trace lines do form normal ogives, the curves are so flat that they are hard to distinguish from straight lines. Also, when items are combined that vary considerably in difficulty, combined normal ogives look less S shaped than if all items are equally difficult. For these two reasons, even if one accepts the normal-ogive model, it is reasonable to assume that total test scores have an approximately linear relationship with the attribute.

There are many other interesting deductions from the normal-ogive model. The most discriminating collection of items for any particular point on the attribute would be those items whose sum of ogives is as steep as possible over that point. This fact permits some interesting deductions about the relations among discrimination at a point, difficulty of items, and correlations of items with total scores (Lord, 1952b). Other interesting deductions from this model concern the amount of measurement error (unreliability) for a test corresponding to different points on the attribute (discussed in Chapter Eight).

In addition to the normal ogive, other statistical functions have been proposed for trace lines. The function which has achieved most use in this respect is the logistic curve. To the naked eye the logistic curve and the normal ogive are very much the same. The advantage of the logistic curve is that it is much easier to work with mathematically. Very much the same deductions are made from both types of curves.

An important point to grasp in discussing monotone models with specified distribution forms is that these models have not led to ways of scaling persons other than by the conventional approach, which is to sum scores on items. Thus if one is scaling spelling ability, these models do not argue against the conventional method of scaling, which is to count the number of words correctly spelled. The situation is the same with all other attributes. What these models do is to permit some important deductions about the psychometric characteristics of measures that are obtained by summing item scores, and for that purpose, they have proved very useful.

MONOTONE MODELS WITH UNSPECIFIED DISTRIBUTION FORMS Finally we arrive at the model that underlies most efforts to scale people (and lower animals). The model makes three major assumptions. First, it is assumed only that each item has a monotonic trace line. It is not assumed that all items have the same type of monotonic curve. Second, it is assumed that the sum of the trace lines for a particular set of items (the trace line for total test scores) is approximately linear. That is, even if items do not all have the same type of monotonic trace line, it is assumed that departures from linearity tend to average out as items are combined. A family of such trace lines is shown in Figure 2-16. The sum of these trace lines is shown in Figure 2-17, which is the trace line of expected scores on a four-item test.

The third assumption is that the items as a whole tend to measure only the attribute in question. This is the same as saying that the items have only one factor in common, a point which will be discussed in detail in later chapters. The implication is that total scores on the particular collection of items summarize all of the information about psychological attributes that is inherent in the item scores.

The three assumptions discussed above constitute the *linear model*, or, as it is frequently called, the *summative model*. It is said to be "linear" for two reasons. First, it is assumed that the sum of item

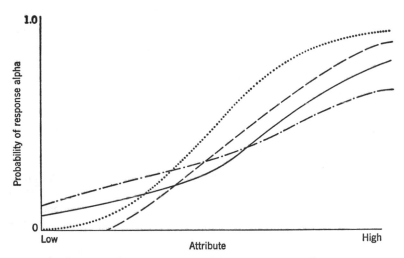

figure 2-16 *A family of four items with monotone trace lines.*

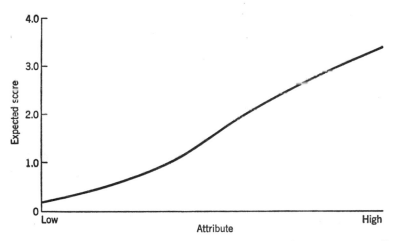

figure 2-17 *Expected scores on a four-item test—the sum of trace lines in Figure 2-16.*

scores has an approximately linear relationship with the attribute in question. Second, and more important for the sake of the name, the model leads to a *linear combination* of items. A simple sum of variables is a linear combination of variables, and a simple sum of item scores is a linear combination of those scores.

If one looks carefully at psychological measures, he will see that in nearly all cases they consist of summing scores over items. Spelling ability is measured by summing scores over items, i.e., by simply counting the number of words correctly spelled. In paired-associate learning, the amount learned by each person is measured by counting the number of pairs correctly recalled. In a study of rat learning in a T maze, the level of learning is measured by the number of correct choices in a block of trials. In a measure of attitudes toward the United Nations, a total score is obtained by summing the number of agreements to positive statements and the number of disagreements with negative statements.

The linear model applies to multipoint items as well as to items which are scored dichotomously. Reaction time in a particular experiment would be determined by averaging the reaction times for a subject in a block of trials. Total scores on an essay examination in history would be obtained by summing scores on individual questions. Attitudes toward the United Nations would be obtained by summing the ratings of 10 statements on a seven-step scale of agreement-disagreement.

It is not difficult to think of psychological measures that fit the linear model—rather, it is difficult to think of measures that do not fit the model. In this chapter we have come a long way around to the conclusion that the most sensible way to measure psychological attributes of people is to sum scores on items. The essence of the linear model is that it does not take individual items very seriously. It recognizes that the individual item has considerable specificity and measurement error. It does not make stringent assumptions about the trace line. The only assumption made is that each item has some form of monotonic trace line, and even that is not a strict assumption, since some of the items could have slightly curvilinear trace lines and a linear relationship of total scores with the attribute would still be obtainable.

The remainder of the book is mostly based on the linear model. This model makes sense and works well in practice. At the present time there is no serious challenge on the scene for the scaling of people with respect to psychological attributes.

SUGGESTED ADDITIONAL READINGS

Coombs, C. H. A theory of data. *Psychol. Rev.*, 1960, **67,** 143–159.

Edwards, A. L. *Techniques of attitude scale construction.* New York: Appleton-Century-Crofts, 1957.

Guilford, J. P. *Psychometric methods.* New York: McGraw-Hill, 1954, chaps. 2, 10.

Gulliksen, H., and Messick, S. (Eds.) *Psychological scaling: Theory and applications.* New York: Wiley, 1960.

Torgerson, W. *Theory and methods of scaling.* New York: Wiley, 1958.

CHAPTER THREE

VALIDITY

After a model has been chosen for the construction of a measuring instrument and the instrument has been constructed, the next step is to find out whether or not the instrument is useful. This step is usually spoken of as determining the *validity* of an instrument. The term has some misleading connotations, but it is too well engrained in the litera-ture to permit an easy transition to terms that more properly denote the processes involved; consequently the term is used in this book, although efforts are made to sharply distinguish the different meanings which "validity" can have.

In a very general sense, a measuring instrument is valid if it does what it is intended to do. Proper performance of some instruments is rather easily verified, e.g., of the yardstick as a measure of length. It takes very little "research" with this instrument to find that resulting measurements (1) fit in perfectly with axiomatic concepts of the nature of length and (2) relate to many other variables. If all measures so perfectly met these standards, there would be little need to consider the validation of measuring instruments, but such is not the case. For example, whereas it might seem highly sensible to develop measures of emotions from physiological indices such as heart rate, muscle tonus, and palmar sweat, it has proved very difficult to find combinations of such indices to measure various emotions. So it is with many proposed measures in the physical, biological, and behavioral sciences: what seem to be good approaches to measurement on an intuitive basis fail to produce the desired empirical results.

Validation always requires empirical investigations, the nature of the evidence required depending on the type of validity. Validity is a matter of degree rather than an all-or-none property, and validation is an unending process. Whereas measures of length and of some other simple physical attributes may have proved their merits so well that no one seriously considers changing to other measures, most measures should be kept under constant surveillance to see if they are behaving as they should. New evidence may suggest modifications of an existing measure or the development of a new and better approach to measuring the attribute in question, e.g., the measurement of anxiety, intelligence, or the temperature of stars.

Strictly speaking one validates not a measuring instrument, but rather some use to which the instrument is put. For example, a test used to select college freshmen must be valid for that purpose, but it would not necesarily be valid for other purposes, such as measuring how well students have mastered the curriculum in high school. Whereas an achievement test in spelling might be valid for that purpose, it might be nearly worthless for other purposes, such as forecasting success in high school. Similarly, a valid measure of the response to stressful experimental treatments would not necessarily be a valid measure of neuroticism or anything else. Although a measure may be valid for many different purposes, e.g., as intelligence tests are, the validity with which each purpose is served must be supported by evidence.

Psychological measures serve three major purposes: (1) establishment of a functional relationship with a particular variable, (2) representation of a specified universe of content, and (3) measurement of psychological traits. Corresponding to these are three types of validity: (1) predictive validity, (2) content validity, and (3) construct validity. Examples of measures intended to serve those purposes are a test for selecting college freshmen, a test for measuring spelling ability in the fifth grade, and a measure of anxiety. Each of these three types of validity will be discussed in turn.

predictive validity

Predictive validity is at issue when the purpose is to use an instrument to estimate some important form of behavior, the latter being referred to as the *criterion*. The example given above was that of a test employed to select college freshmen. The test, whatever it is like, is useful in that situation only if it accurately estimates successful performance in college. The criterion in this case probably would be grade-point average obtained over four years of college. After the criterion is obtained, the validity of a prediction function is straightforwardly, and rather easily, determined. Primarily it consists of correlating scores on the predictor test with scores on the criterion variable. The size of the correlation is a direct indication of the amount of validity.

The term "prediction" will be used in a general (and ungrammatical) sense to refer to functional relations between an instrument and events occurring before, during, and after the instrument is applied. Thus a test administered to adults could be used to make "predictions" about events occurring in their childhood. A test intended to "predict"

basic principles

brain damage is, of course, intended not to forecast who will suffer brain damage at some time in the future, but rather to "predict" who does and who does not have brain damage at the time the test is administered. When a test is used to predict success in college, "prediction" properly means forecasting. Others have referred to predictive validity at those three points in time, respectively, as "post-diction," "concurrent validity," and "prediction." Using different terms, however, suggests that the logic and procedures of validation are different, which is not true. In each case a predictor measure is related to a criterion measure, and after the data are available, it does not matter when they were obtained. The nature of the problem dictates when the two sets of measurements are obtained. Thus to forecast success in college, it is necessary to administer the predictor instrument before students go to college; and to obtain the criterion of success in college, it is necessary to wait four years.

Predictive validity is determined by, and only by, the degree of correspondence between the two measures involved. If the correlation is high, no other standards are necessary. Thus if it were found that accuracy in horseshoe pitching correlated highly with success in college, horseshoe pitching would be a valid measure for predicting success in college. This is not meant to imply that sound theory and common sense are not useful in selecting predictor instruments for investigation, but after the investigations are done, the entire proof of the pudding is in the correlations.

Perhaps because of the simplicity of the ideas and the related methods of research, up to about 1950 it was frequently said that the validity of a measure is indicated by the correlation between the measure and its criterion. Actually, predictive validity is seldom the important issue in psychological science; concepts of validity which will be discussed later are of much more importance. Predictive validity is the major issue only in certain types of applied problems in psychology and education—e.g., in using tests to select office clerks, civil service workers, and officer candidates for the armed forces, and in making decisions about the hospitalization and treatment of mental patients.

In no other area is predictive validity as important as it is in using tests to help make decisions about schooling. In schools, predictive validity is at issue in measures of "readiness." Thus, for underage children, a test of readiness for the first grade is valid only to the extent that it predicts how well children will perform in the first grade. A test used to divide children into different ability levels is valid only to the extent that it predicts how well children will do in their different levels of instruction. A test used to select students for special programs of study in high school is valid only to the extent that it actually predicts performance in those programs. And so it is with all other tests used for the selection and placement of students—they are valid only to the extent that they serve prediction functions well.

Clear as the difference may seem, some people confuse predictor instruments with the criteria they are meant to predict. A story (a true one) will help to illustrate this confusion. A college graduate applied for entrance to a graduate training program to work toward a master's degree. He failed to score sufficiently high on an entrance examination (a predictor test) but was given special permission to enter on a trial basis. Once in training, he performed very well, doing better than most of his fellow students. Near completion of the student's training, the dean of the college insisted that the student would need to retake the entrance examination and make a satisfactory grade before his degree could be granted! Many other equally foolish examples could be given to show how predictor tests are confused with the criteria they are meant to predict.

Whereas it is easy to talk about correlating a predictor test with its criterion, in actuality obtaining a good criterion may be more difficult than obtaining a predictor test. In many cases either no criterion is available or the criteria that are available suffer from various faults, about which more will be said in Chapter Eight.

VALIDITY COEFFICIENTS Techniques for employing predictor tests and for validating such usages are part of the applied psychology of personnel selection. In personnel selection, there are numerous decision strategies and numerous statistical designs that relate to the employment of different types of predictor measures for different types of jobs with respect to different types of criterion variables. Although these matters are of considerable practical importance, for several reasons they need not be discussed in detail here. First, this book is intended for psychologists and future psychologists in general rather than only for future specialists in personnel selection. Second, as was mentioned previously, predictive validity is not nearly so important in the science of psychology as a whole as are other types of validity, ones to be discussed in the following sections. Third, even though some of the details of employing and validating predictor instruments are technically complex, the *logic* of validating prediction functions is relatively simple.

The validity of individual predictor instruments and combinations of predictor instruments is determined by correlational analysis and extensions of correlational analysis to multivariate analysis (methods of analysis to be discussed in later chapters). The simplest example of a validity coefficient is the correlation of an individual predictor test with an individual criterion, e.g., the correlation of a test of scholastic aptitude with average grades over four years of college training. In eval-

basic principles

uating the worth of predictor tests, it is a mistake to think in terms of perfect correlations in any case or even of high correlations in most cases.

In most prediction problems, it is reasonable to expect only modest correlations between a criterion and either an individual predictor test or a combination of predictor tests. People are far too complex to permit a highly accurate estimate of their performance from any practicable collection of test materials. Equally complex are the situations in which criterion data are obtained, e.g., the immense complexity of all the variables involved in determining the average grades of students over four years of college. Considering the immense complexities of the problem, it is remarkable that some predictor tests correlate as highly as they do with criterion variables. For example, scholastic aptitude tests are as predictive of grades in college four years hence as meterologists' predictions are of the weather in Chicago 10 days in advance.

The proper way to interpret a validity coefficient is in terms of the extent to which it indicates a *possible improvement in the average quality of persons* that would be obtained by employing the instrument in question. Tests that have only modest correlations with their criteria (e.g., correlations of .30 and .40) often are capable of markedly improving the *average* performance of personnel in different positions. Of course, many mistakes would be made in predicting the performance of individuals, but on the average, persons who score high on the test perform considerably better than persons who score low on the test. Such differences in mean performance frequently are highly important in applied settings. As a simple example, suppose that a test is being validated for the selection of vacuum cleaner salesmen, and it is found that the test correlates .30 with the dollar volume of sales each year by salesmen. On examination of the scatter plot of the relationship between the two variables, it is seen that the average sales of persons who score high on the test is 10 percent greater than the average sales of all persons combined. Then, by using the test to select future salesmen, the company increases gross sales by 10 percent, which might make the difference between going into bankruptcy and becoming a very profitable enterprise. In a similar way, tests that have only modest correlations with their criteria can frequently make highly important improvements in the average performance of groups in educational institutions, industry, government services, and other activities.

content validity

For some instruments, validity depends primarily on the adequacy with which a specified domain of content is sampled. A prime example would be a final examination for a course in introductory psychology. Obviously, the test could not be validated in terms of predictive validity, because the purpose of the test is not to predict something else but to *directly measure* performance in a unit of instruction. The test must stand by itself as an adequate measure of what it is supposed to measure. Validity cannot be determined by correlating the test with a criterion, because the test itself *is* the criterion of performance.

Even if one argued that course examinations should be validated in terms of correlations with other behaviors, what behaviors would serve as adequate criteria? A student might, by any standard, deserve an A in the course but never take another course in psychology or ever work in a position where knowledge from the course would be evidenced. Of course, one would expect the test to correlate with some other variables, and the size of such correlations would provide hints about the adequacy of the test. For example, one would expect to find a substantial correlation between scores on the final examination in introductory psychology and scores on the final examination in abnormal psychology (for those students who took both courses). If the correlation were zero, it would make us suspect that something were wrong with one or both of the examinations (or with one or both of the units of instruction). However, such correlations would offer only hints about the validity of the examinations, the final proof resting on the adequacy with which content had been sampled.

There are many other examples of measures that require content validity. Such is the case with all course examinations in all types of training programs and at all levels of training. All achievement tests require content validity, as would be the case, for example, with a comprehensive measure of progress in school up to the end of the fourth grade or a comprehensive measure of the extent to which men had performed well in a school for electronics technicians in the armed forces.

Rather than test the validity of measures such as those above after they are constructed, one should *ensure* validity by the plan and procedures of construction. To take a very simple example, an achievement test in spelling for fourth-grade students could obtain its content from a random sampling of words occurring in widely used readers. The plan is to randomly sample from a specified domain of content, and most potential users of the test should agree that this procedure ensures a reasonably representative collection of words. In addition, a sensible procedure would be required for transforming the words into a test. It might, for example, be decided to compose items by putting each correctly spelled word in with three misspellings and requiring the student to circle the correct one. Other decisions would need to be made about ordering the items in the test and about the oral or written instructions to students. These and other details are part of the plan for selecting content and for test construction. The validity of the measure is judged by the character of the plan and by the apparent skill with which the plan has been carried out. If it is agreed by most potential users of the test, or at least by persons in positions of responsibility, that the plan was sound and well carried out, the test has a high degree of content validity.

The simple example above illustrates the <u>two major standards for ensuring</u> content validity: (1) <u>a representative collection of items</u> and (2) <u>"sensible" methods of test construction</u>. Of course, in most instances these standards are not so easy to judge as was the case with the spelling test. <u>Often, it is logically impossible or unfeasible to actually sample content</u>. For example, how would one sample (in a strict sense of the word) items for an achievement test in geography? <u>Neither the sampling unit nor the domain is well specified</u>. One could sample sentences from textbooks and turn them into true-false items, but for obvious reasons such a test would not be adequate. Rather, what is done in such instances is to *formulate* a collection of items that broadly represents the unit of instruction. To ensure that the items actually represent the unit of instruction, it is necessary to have a detailed outline, or blueprint, of the kinds of questions and problems that will be included. (How such outlines are developed and used is explained in a number of introductory texts on educational and psychological measurement: Cronbach, 1960; Nunnally, 1964; Thorndike and Hagen, 1961.) In such cases, judging the quality of the outline is an important part of assessing content validity.

<u>The simple example of a random sampling of content is unrealistic in most situations for a second reason: the selection of content usually involves questions of values</u>. Thus, for the spelling test, one might decide that it is more important to measure performance on nouns, adjectives, and verbs than performance on other parts of speech; consequently one would restrict sampling to those types of words. In an achievement test for arithmetic, one might decide that it is more important to stress questions concerning quantitative concepts than those on numerical computations. And so it is with nearly all measures based on content validity: <u>values determine the relative stress on different types of content</u>. Of course, where values are important, there are differences in values among people; consequently there usually is some disagreement about the proper content coverage of particular tests. Also, since values sometimes change, it can be expected that a test which is viewed today as having high content validity may not be considered so high in that regard later. The values behind the construction of a measure should be made explicit, e.g., in test manuals, and it should be indicated how those values guided formulation of the test outline and the construction of items.

A second point at which content validity becomes somewhat complex is in ensuring that "sensible" methods of test construction are employed. This is not much of a problem with spelling tests, because it is relatively easy to construct items that most people will agree are satisfactory. It requires much more skill, however, to construct items in some other domains of content, e.g., geography, history, and salesmanship training; and there often is controversy about the employment of different types of items (using the word "item" to refer broadly to questions, problems, work samples, and other evidence of accomplishment).

Even though there often are problems with ensuring content validity, inevitably content validity rests mainly on appeals to reason regarding the adequacy with which important content has been sampled and on the adequacy with which the content has been cast in the form of test items. In addition there are various methods of analyzing data obtained from the test which will provide important circumstantial evidence. For example, at least a moderate level of internal consistency among the items within a test would be expected; i.e., the items should tend to measure something in common. (Methods for performing such analyses will be described in Chapter Eight.) This is not an infallible guide, however, because with some subject matters, it is reasonable to include materials that tap somewhat different abilities. For example, abilities for numerical computation are not entirely the same as those for grasping some of the essential ideas about quantification, but a good argument could be made for mixing these two types of content to measure overall progress in arithmetic.

Another type of circumstantial evidence for content validity is obtained by comparing performance on a test before and after a period of training. If the test is intended to measure progress in training, scores should increase from before to after; and the improvement in scores on individual items can be considered evidence for the validity of those items. There are, however, numerous flaws in this line of reasoning. An item can be obviously trivial yet show marked changes from the beginning to the end of the course—e.g., spelling of the teacher's name. Many students would not make the correct spelling the first day of class, but nearly all would be able to spell the teacher's name correctly by the last day of class. Conversely, on some very important items, there may be little change from before to after; but that may be because of inadequate texts, unskilled teachers, or lazy students.

Another type of evidence for content validity is obtained from correlating scores on different tests purporting to measure much the same thing, e.g., two tests by different commercial firms for the measurement of achievement in reading. It is comforting to find high correlations in such instances, but this does not guarantee content validity. Both tests may measure the same wrong things.

In spite of efforts on the part of some to settle every issue about psychological measurement by a flight into statistics, content validity is mainly settled in other ways. Although helpful hints are obtained from analyses of empirical findings, content validity mainly rests upon an appeal to the propriety of content and the way that it is presented.

construct validity

Whereas up to 1950 most textbooks on measurement spoke only of predictive validity and content validity, with many different names being used to refer to the two, actually those two types of validity are mainly important only in certain types of measurement problems in applied psychology. Predictive validity is important in selecting students for college, placing soldiers in special courses of training, making decisions about the treatment of mental patients, and placing people on jobs. Content validity is important for examining progress in elementary school, studying the effectiveness of different methods for training accountants, and making decisions about the promotion of civil service workers. Whereas these and other measurement problems are of vast practical importance, such applied problems are not close to the measurement problems that occur in the basic science of psychology.

Like all basic science, psychological science is concerned with establishing functional relations among important variables. (What is an "important" variable is determined either by intuition or by the content of psychological theories.) Of course, variables must be measured before they can be related to one another in experiments; and for statements of relationship to have any meaning, each measure must, in some sense, validly measure what it is purported to measure. Examples of important variables in psychology are reaction time, habit strength, intelligence, anxiety, drive level, and degree of frustration. How does one validate measures of such variables? (Later the word "validate" will be challenged as a proper name for what is required.) Take, for example, an experiment where a particular treatment is hypothesized to raise anxiety. Can the measure of anxiety be validated as a predictor of some specific variable? No, it cannot, because the purpose is to measure the amount of anxiety then and there, not to estimate scores on any other variable obtained in the past, present, or future. Also, the measure cannot be validated purely in terms of content validity. There is no obvious body of "content" (behaviors) corresponding to anxiety reactions, and if there were, how to measure such content would be far more of a puzzle than it is with performance in arithmetic.

As another illustration of why predictive validity and content validity do not suffice in most basic-science problems, consider a study investigating the effects of heredity and environment on intelligence. After an intelligence test is administered, correlations are obtained between spouses, between identical twins, between nonidentical twins, and between nontwin siblings. Analyses of the correlations are made so as to indicate the different contributions of heredity and environment to intelligence. The intelligence test cannot be validated by correlating it with a "criterion," because there is no better measure known. (If there were, why not use it in the study?) The test cannot be validated primarily in terms of content validity, because the "content" (relevant behavior) is somewhat in dispute, and even more in dispute is how to turn such content into workable measures. Thus whereas all may agree that "problem solving" is an important aspect of intelligence, this narrows the field very little. What types of problems? How should the problems be presented? How should the results be scored? Many more question marks could be expended in illustrating why it is not feasible to employ content validity as a primary standard for the usefulness of particular measures of psychological variables.

The degree to which it is necessary and difficult to validate measures of psychological variables is proportional to the degree to which the variable is concrete or abstract. A highly concrete variable would be reaction time, which would be measured, say, by the length of time taken to press a button on a given signal. How quickly subjects press the button *is* the variable of interest, and how to measure the variable is rather obvious. Specialists in studies of reaction time might quibble over microscopically fine differences in measurement techniques, but such slight differences in measurement methods would have scant effects on experimental results. In this case the operations of measurement are of direct interest, and there is no need to "validate" the measure; consequently the researcher can go about the business of finding interesting relations between that measure and other variables. There are, however, very few variables that are so obviously manifested in simple operations. In most instances the particular operations are meant to measure a variable which extends well beyond the operations in question. Consider the use of an activity wheel for investigations with rats. How rapidly the rat treads the wheel really is of little interest in itself, except to the extent that it represents a general level of activity that logically should be manifested in many ways, e.g., in the amount of movement around the floor of a box. Thus the intention is to measure a somewhat abstract variable of activity level, and consequently the validity of any particular measure is open to question. So it is with most measures: they represent efforts to measure relatively abstract variables, ones that are thought to be evidenced in a variety of forms of behavior and not perfectly so in any one of them.

To the extent that a variable is abstract rather than concrete, we speak of it as being a *construct*. Such a variable is literally a construct in that it is something that the scientist puts together from his own imagination, something that does not exist as an isolated, observable dimension of behavior. This construct represents a hypothesis (usually only half-formed) that a variety of behaviors will correlate with one another in studies of individual differences and/or will be similarly affected by experimental treatments.

It is important to realize that all theories in science mainly concern statements about constructs rather than about specific, observable variables. A prime example of confusion in this regard comes from the final oral examination for a Ph.D. candidate who had investigated the effects of different drugs on how rapidly mice would swim through a water maze filled with cold water. The dependent measure was time taken to traverse the maze. The candidate spoke of the dependent measure as representing "reaction to stress," the cold water supposedly being stressful to the mice. A member of the examining committee objected to speaking of the dependent measure as representing reaction to stress and took the student to task for not sticking to a description of the experimental results purely in terms of the observables, i.e., mice swimming in cold water. Both the student and the committee member were partly right and partly wrong. By speaking of the dependent measure as representing reaction to stress, the student assumed that the measure had a generality far beyond the actual observables. By suggesting that science is concerned only with the particular observables in an experiment, the committee member was painting a very faulty picture. No one really cares how rapidly mice swim in cold water. The particular measure is of interest only to the extent that it partly mirrors performance in a variety of situations that all concern "stress" or some other construct.

Scientists cannot do without constructs. Their theories are populated with them, and even in informal conversation scientists find it all but impossible to discuss their work without using words relating to constructs. It is important to keep in mind not only that proposed measures of constructs need to be validated for that purpose, but also that science is primarily concerned with developing measures of constructs and finding functional relations between measures of different constructs.

Constructs vary widely in the extent to which the domain of related observable variables is (1) large or small and (2) tightly or loosely defined. Regarding point 1, in some cases the domain of related variables

Is so small that any one of the few observable variables in the domain will suffice to measure the construct. This is true of reaction time, where, as mentioned previously, the alternative methods of measuring are so few and so closely related that any one of them can be spoken of as measuring reaction time without doing much injustice to the "construct." At a higher level of complexity, activity level in the rat logically should be manifested in at least a score of observables, and as it turns out, some of these do not correlate well with others. At the extreme of complexity are constructs like anxiety and intelligence, where the domains of related observables are vast indeed.

Considerations in point 1 above tend to correlate with considerations in point 2: the larger the domain of observables related to a construct, the more difficult it tends to be to define which variables do or do not belong in the domain. Thus it might be relatively easy to get agreement among psychologists about whether or not a particular observable should be related to activity level, e.g., a measure of muscle tonus. The boundaries of this domain are relatively well prescribed. In contrast, for many constructs the domain of related observables has "fuzzy edges," and the scientist is not sure of the full meanings of his own constructs. Typically, the scientist holds a firm belief about some of the more prominent observables related to the construct, but beyond that he can only guess how far the construct extends. In measuring the construct of intelligence, for example, all would agree that the construct should be evidenced to some extent in various types of problems involving reasoning abilities; but it is a matter of dispute as to what extent some measures of perceptual and memory abilities should be considered part of the construct. Such is the case with most constructs (e.g., anxiety and habit strength): the boundaries of the domain of related observables are not clear.

Because constructs concern domains of observables, logically a better measure of any construct would be obtained by combining the results from a number of measures of such observables than by taking any one of them individually. Since, however, the work is often tedious enough with one measure, let alone a handful, it sometimes is asking too much of the scientist to expect him to employ more than one measure in a particular investigation. Thus any particular measure can be thought of as having a degree of construct validity depending on the extent to which results obtained from using the measure would be much the same if some other measure, or hypothetically, all the measures, in the domain had been employed in the experiment. Similarly, the combined scores from a number of measures of observables in the domain can be thought of as having a degree of construct validity for the domain as a whole.

The logical status of constructs in psychology for constructs concerning individual differences is the same as that for constructs concerning the results of controlled experiments. Thus whereas the construct of intelligence is more frequently discussed with respect to studies of individual differences and the construct of habit strength is more frequently discussed with respect to controlled experiments, problems of construct validity are essentially the same for both. (Of course, in different studies a construct may be investigated as the dependent variable in a controlled experiment or in terms of correlations between sources of individual differences; but most measures are predominantly used in one or the other of the two types of studies.)

If the measurement of constructs is a vital part of scientific activity, how then are such measures developed and validated? There are three major aspects of the process: (1) specifying the domain of observables, (2) determining to what extent all, or some, of those observables correlate with each other or are affected alike by experimental treatments, and (3) determining whether or not one, some, or all measures of such variables *act* as though they measure the construct. Aspect 3 consists of determining whether or not a supposed measure of a construct correlates in expected ways with measures of other constructs or is affected in expected ways by particular experimental treatments. These steps are seldom, if ever, purposefully planned and undertaken by any investigator or group of investigators. Also, although it could be argued that the aspects should be undertaken in the order 1, 2, and then 3, this order is seldom, if ever, followed. More likely, a psychologist will develop a particular measure that is thought to partake of a construct, then he will leap directly to aspect 3 and perform a study relating the supposed measure of the construct to measures of other constructs, e.g., correlating a particular measure of anxiety with a particular measure of response to frustration. Typically, other investigators will develop other particular measures of the same construct, and skipping aspects 1 and 2, they will move directly to aspect 3 and try to find interesting relations between their measures and measures of other constructs. As the number of proposed measures of the same construct grow and suspicion grows that they might not all measure the same thing, one or more investigators seek to outline in writing the domain of observables related to the construct, which is aspect 1. All, or parts, of one or more such outlines of the domain are subjected to investigation to determine the extent to which variables in the domain tend to measure the same thing, which is aspect 2. The impact of theorizing with respect to aspect 1 and the research results from aspect 2 tend to influence which particular variables are studied in aspect 3.

Since most scientists work as individuals rather than being tied to some overall plan of attack on a problem, each scientist does much what he pleases, and consequently there is seldom a planned, concentrated effort to develop valid measures of constructs according to a step-by-step procedure. Instead of the domain of observables for any construct being tightly defined initially (aspect 1), more likely the nature of the domain will be *suggested* by numerous attempts to develop particular measures relating to the construct; and subsequently, some investigators will attempt to more explicitly outline the domain of content. Instead of a planned, frontal attack on the empirical investigations required in aspects 2 and 3, more likely evidence *accrues* from many studies of different proposed measures of the construct; and subsequently, the available evidence is accumulated and evaluated. Hopefully the end product of this complex process is a construct (1) that is well defined in terms of a variety of observables, (2) for which there are one or several variables that well represent the domain of observables, and (3) that eventually proves to relate strongly with other constructs of interest. Some of the methods required to reach those goals are described in the following sections.

DOMAIN OF OBSERVABLES   Whereas, on the face of it, one might think that the scientist should outline the domain of observables before assuming that any one observable relates to a construct, this is seldom done. More frequently, scientists investigate only one observable and assume that it is related to the construct, at least for the time being. For example, there have been many studies relating the Taylor manifest anxiety scale (Taylor, 1953) to supposed measures of other constructs. The test is intended to relate strongly to other variables in a domain of behaviors constituting anxiety. Many studies have been done in spite of the fact that the domain of the construct has not been well outlined, and it is probably true that if different investigators in this area attempted to outline the domain, there would be considerable disagreement among them.

Scientists should not be criticized for assuming that particular observables relate to a construct even though the domain of the construct is only vaguely understood. In his lifetime each scientist can perform only a relatively small number of studies (100 might be the average even for very busy scientists), and consequently he does not have time to do all that is required to specify the domain of a construct, develop measures of the construct, and relate those measures to other variables of interest. As the evidence accrues from the work of different scientists interested in a particular construct, however, it is fruitful to attempt a specification of the domain of related variables.

✔   No precise method can be stated for properly outlining the domain of variables for a construct. The outline essentially constitutes a theory regarding how variables will relate to one another; and though theories themselves should be objectively testable, the theorizing process is necessarily intuitive. <u>Outlining a construct consists essentially of stating</u> <u>what one means by the use of particular words</u>—words such as "anxiety," "habit strength," and "intelligence." In the early attempts to outline a domain, the "outline" usually consists of only a definition in which the word denoting the construct is related to words at a lower level of abstraction. An example is the early attempt by Binet and Simon (1905) to define "intelligence": "The tendency to take and maintain a definite direction; the capacity to make adaptations for the purpose of attaining a desired end; and the power of auto-criticism." Brave as such attempts are, when they define a construct with words that are far removed from specific observable variables, they do little to specify the domain in question. An example of a more clearly specified domain is that by Hull (1952) for the construct of "net reaction potential," where the specification is in terms of the observables of probability of response, latency of response, amplitude of response, and number of responses to extinction. Further specifications are made of the observables in each of the four classes of observables.

Whether or not a well-specified domain for a construct actually leads to adequate measurement of the construct is a matter for empirical investigation; but until there is a well-specified domain, there is no way to know exactly which studies should be done to test the adequacy with which a construct is measured. In other words, <u>the major importance of aspect 1 (outlining the domain) is that it tells you what to do in aspect 2 (investigating relations among different proposed measures of a construct).</u>

RELATIONS AMONG OBSERVABLES The way to test the adequacy of the outline of a domain relating to a construct is to determine <u>how well the measures of observables "go together" in empirical investigations</u>. In studies of individual differences, the first step is to obtain scores for a sample of individuals on some of the measures; next, each measure is correlated with all other measures. An analysis of the resulting correlations provides evidence about the extent to which all the measures tend to measure the same thing. (Essentially this is a problem in factor analysis, which will be discussed briefly later in this chapter and in detail in Chapters Nine and Ten.)

In investigations of construct validity in controlled experiments, the logic is much the same as that in studies of individual differences. One investigates the extent to which treatment conditions have similar effects on some of the measures of observables in the domain. A hypothetical example is given in Figure 3-1, which shows the effects of five levels of stress (the independent variable) on four supposed measures of the construct of fear. Measures A and B are monotonically related to levels of stress, which means that they are affected in much the

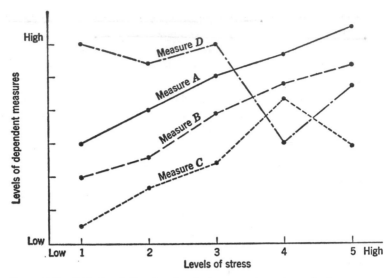

figure 3-1 *Effects of five levels of stress on four dependent measures.*

same way by the experimental treatments. Measure C is monotonically related to treatment levels up to level 4, but falls off sharply at level 5, and consequently measures something that is not entirely the same as that in A and B. Measure D is not related in any systematic manner to the treatment levels, and consequently it logically could not measure the same thing as measured by A, B, and C. To fully determine the extent to which these and other measures of fear "go together," it would be necessary to see how similarly they behaved with respect to other experimental treatments, e.g., different levels of electrical stimulation of "fear areas" in the brains of rats.

The test of how well different supposed measures of a construct "go together" is the extent to which they have similar curves of relationship with a variety of treatment variables. It does not matter what the form of the relationship is with a particular treatment variable as long as the supposed measures of the construct behave similarly. Thus, for two supposed measures of a construct, the relationship with one treatment variable could be monotonically increasing, the relationship with another curvilinear, and the relationship with another a flat line; but in all three instances the two measures of the construct would be affected much the same. If two measures were affected in exactly the same way by all possible experimental treatments, it would not matter which one were used in a particular experiment, and consequently one could speak of them as measuring the same thing. To the *degree* to which two measures are affected similarly by a variety of experimental treatments, they can be spoken of as measuring much the same thing. When

basic principles

a variety of measures behave similarly in this way over a variety of experimental treatments, it becomes meaningful to speak of them as measuring a construct. The measures that most consistently behave as the majority of measures do can be said to have the most construct validity.

Methods of investigating construct validity both in studies of individual differences and in controlled experiments involve correlations. Actual correlations are computed among measures of individual differences. A comparison of two curves is, in essence, a correlating of two curves, even though correlational methods might not be applied. Regardless of whether correlations are over individual differences or over levels of treatment effects, such correlations provide evidence about the structure of a domain of observables relating to a construct.

The results of investigations like those described above would lead to one of three conclusions. If all the proposed measures correlate highly with one another, it can be concluded that they all measure much the same thing. If the measures tend to split up into clusters such that the members of a cluster correlate highly with one another and correlate much less with the members of other clusters, it can be concluded that a number of *different* things are being measured. For example, in studying different supposed measures of anxiety, one might find that measures concerning bodily harm tend to go together and those concerning social embarrassment tend to go together. As a third possibility, if correlations among the measures all are near zero, they measure different things. Of course, the evidence is seldom so clear-cut as to enable one to unequivocally reach one of these three conclusions; rather, there usually is room for dispute as to which conclusion should be reached.

Evidence of the kind described above should affect subsequent efforts to specify the domain of observables for a construct and should affect theories relating the construct to other constructs. If all the measures supposedly related to a construct correlate highly, this should encourage investigators to keep working with the specified domain of observables and should encourage continued investigation of theories relating that construct to others. If the evidence is that more than one thing is being measured, the old construct should be abandoned for two or more new ones, and theories that assume only one construct should be modified to take account of the multiplicity of constructs. If none of the variables correlate substantially with the others, the scientist has an unhappy state of affairs. Of course, it is possible that one of the measures is highly related to the construct and the others are unrelated to the construct, but it is much more likely that none of them relate well to the construct. Either the investigator must postulate an entirely new domain of observables for a construct, as, for example, when questionnaire measures of anxiety are abandoned in favor of physiological measures, or he will have to abandon the construct altogether.

RELATIONS AMONG CONSTRUCTS In the previous section, means were discussed for studying construct validity in terms of the *internal consistency* with which different measures in a domain tend to supply the same information (tend to correlate highly with one another and be similarly affected by experimental treatments). To the extent that the elements of such a domain show this consistency, it can be said that *some* construct may be employed to account for the data, but it is by no means sure that it is legitimate to employ the construct name which motivated the research. In other words, consistency is a *necessary* but not *sufficient* condition for construct validity. A discussion of how one can, if ever, obtain sufficient evidence that a domain of observables relates to a construct requires an analysis of some of the deepest innards of scientific explanation.

First, we shall accept the assumption that it is possible to find immutable proof that a particular set of variables measures a particular construct, and we shall see what forms of evidence would be required. Later that assumption will be challenged, and different perspectives will be advocated for interpreting evidence regarding construct validity. If the assumption is accepted, sufficient evidence for construct validity is that the supposed measures of the construct (either a single measure of observables or a combination of such measures) *behave as expected*. If, for example, a particular measure is thought to relate to the construct of anxiety, common sense would suggest many findings that should be obtained with the measure. Higher scores (higher anxiety) should be found for (1) patients classified as anxiety neurotics than for unselected nonpatients, (2) subjects in an experiment who are kept threatened with a painful electric shock than for subjects not so threatened, and (3) graduate students waiting to undergo a final oral examination for the Ph.D. than for the same students after passing the examination. As another example, if a particular measure is thought to relate to the construct of intelligence, one would expect it to correlate at least moderately with grades in school, teachers' ratings of intelligence, and levels of professional attainment. So it is with all constructs: there are expected correlations with other variables and expected effects in controlled experiments.

If, according to the assumption above, it is possible to obtain immutable proof of the extent to which measures of observables measure a construct, the proof would come from determining the extent to which the measures "fit" in a network of expected relations. First would come the test of internal consistency of elements in the domain; then there would need to be many correlational studies and many controlled experiments. To the extent to which the measures met expectations in those regards, there would be proof of construct validity.

There is an obvious logical fallacy in claiming such evidence as "proof" of construct validity. To determine construct validity, a measure must fit a theory about the construct; but to use this as evidence, it is necessary to *assume* the theory is true. The circularity in this logic can be illustrated by the following four hypotheses:

1 Constructs A and B correlate positively.

2 X is a measure of construct A.

3 Y is a measure of construct B.

4 X and Y correlate positively.

To give meat to the bones of the example, assume that A is the construct of anxiety, B is the construct of stress, X is a questionnaire thought to measure anxiety, and Y is a parameter of experimental treatments that is thought to induce stress. Even though the four hypotheses are not independent, it should be obvious that one experiment cannot test them all simultaneously. All that can be tested directly by the experiment is hypothesis 4, that X correlates positively with Y. From this one finding, it would be necessary to *infer* the truth or falsity of the other hypotheses, but look at the many possibilities there are among the four hypotheses. Hypothesis 1 may be correct, but even if hypothesis 4 is correct, that would offer no direct proof for the truth of either or both hypotheses 2 and 3. Obviously X and Y could correlate positively, not because they relate to constructs A and B, respectively, but because they relate to still other constructs. As another possibility, hypothesis 2 could be correct, but if hypothesis 3 is incorrect, there would be no necessity for X to correlate with Y.

From the standpoint of inductive logic, it is apparent that the above paradigm for determining construct validity will not hold water. In the illustrative experiment, the experimenter hoped to obtain some evidence for hypothesis 2, that X is a measure of anxiety. All that can be validly tested by the experiment is whether or not hypothesis 4 is correct, whether or not X correlates with Y.

One who wanted to defend the above paradigm for testing construct validity could point out that the situation is not nearly as bleak as it has been painted. What is done in practice is to *assume* that two of the hypotheses 1 through 3 are correct, and by performing an empirical test of hypothesis 4, to allow a valid inference regarding the remaining hypothesis. Thus, for the example above, it would be assumed that hypothesis 1 is correct, that stress does relate to anxiety. Also, it would be assumed that hypothesis 3 is correct, that the threat of painful electric shock does induce stress. If these assumptions are correct, the actual correlation between X and Y permits a valid inference regarding the truth of hypothesis 2, that X is a measure of the construct of anxiety.

One could further argue that making such assumptions in the modified paradigm above is not really so dangerous. The danger can be lessened by restricting investigations of construct validity to those situations in which the truth of some of the hypotheses is very evident. The evidence of such truth could be based either on other experiments involving the variables, e.g., prior investigations of the construct validity of electric shock as an inducer of stress, or on strong appeals to common sense. Thus in performing studies of construct validity, one relates variables in situations where the assumptions are very safe. For example, nearly everyone will agree that increases in stress should be accompanied by increases in anxiety and that the threat of painful electric shock is a form of stress. Such assumptions are made even safer by correlating a supposed measure of one construct with the supposed measure of another where the domain of the latter is both well defined and highly restricted. Thus if a supposed measure of anxiety is correlated with a supposed measure of reaction time, it is rather safe to assume that the particular measure of reaction time validly represents the construct of reaction time.

In the limiting case, construct validity concerns a hypothesized relationship between a supposed measure of a construct and a particular, observable variable. Thus it would be hypothesized that tests of intelligence should correlate positively with grades in school, teachers' rating of intelligence, and level of professional accomplishment. Such "other" variables are constructs only in the sense that there are slight variations possible in the measurement of each of these, which, though, would probably have little effect on empirical correlations. In this way one can reduce the number of hypotheses in the above paradigm from four to three. The hypothesis "Y is related to B" becomes the assumption "Y is B." Then if the assumption is very safe that A relates to B, e.g., intelligence relates to progress in school, an empirical correlation of X with Y provides a safe basis of inference regarding the construct validity for the measurement of A with X. According to this point of view, studies of construct validity are safe when, and should be undertaken only when, (1) the domain of the "other" construct is well defined and (2) the assumption of a relationship between the two constructs is unarguable.

explication of constructs

The foregoing explanation of construct validation is the one currently accepted by many leading theorists, although perhaps the related procedures were specified in more detail than has been done by some authors. This is a workable set of standards, which provides a basis for the measurement of psychological constructs. If, however, the reader wants to go a step further in his thinking about the measurement of psychological constructs, there is a more defensible logic. Rather than referring to this logic as relating to construct validation, it would be more correct to refer to it as concerning _construct explication_, by which is meant the process of making an abstract word explicit in terms of observable variables.

The flaw in the paradigm described above is that it succinctly assumes that any construct has _objective reality_ beyond that of the particular observables used to measure the construct. Thus we speak of anxiety as though it were a real variable, one to be _discovered_ in the course of empirical studies. The evidence supplies support for arguments as to whether or not _it_ has been measured. One hears arguments such as, "This is not really a measure of anxiety." Inherent in these and other words used to discuss the measurement of constructs is the implicit assumption that constructs have objective reality. It is more defensible to make no claims for the objective reality of a construct name, e.g., "anxiety," and instead to think of the construct name as being a useful way to label a particular set of observable variables. Then the name is "valid" only to the extent that it accurately communicates to other scientists the kinds of observables that are being studied.

A more airtight set of standards for "construct validity" starts with the definition of a set of measures concerning observables. Thus set A would be said to consist of measures of particular observables X_1, X_2, X_3, etc., and set B would be said to consist of the particular observables Y_1, Y_2, Y_3, etc. (The X's could be thought of as different measures of anxiety and the Y's as different measures of learning.) Construct validation (later the term will be modified), then, consists of the following steps. Through a series of empirical studies, a network of probability statements is formed among the different measures in set A, and the same is done for B. There are many ways to do this, depending on the types of empirical studies undertaken and the types of probability statements thought to be most meaningful. The most straightforward example is where individual differences on the different measures within a set are correlated with one another. Thus it might be found that X_1 correlates .50 with X_2 and .45 with X_3, and that X_2 correlates .55 with X_3. Knowing these correlations, one could make probability statements concerning scores on the three measures. If, for example, it is known that a person has a score of 20 on measure X_1, the odds can be established as to whether or not that person has a score between 40 and 60 on X_2. Although it seldom is necessary to explicitly make such probability statements about correspondences between scores on different measures, correlations among the measures directly specify the extent to which such probability statements are possible.

After all possible correlations among the individual observables have been obtained, it then is possible to deduce correlations between different combinations of variables in the set (by methods that will be described in Chapter Five). Thus it would be possible to deduce the correlation between the sum of any three of the measures and the sum of any other three measures in the set. More importantly, it would be possible to deduce the correlation between any particular measure in the set and the sum of all measures that had been investigated in the set.

Gradually, in the course of many studies, more and more is learned about correlations among the measures of observables in a particular set. The total information in this regard can be spoken of as forming an *internal structure* for the elements of a set. The structure may indicate that all the variables tend to measure much the same thing, which would be support for retaining the set as it originally was defined; or the structure may be such as to indicate that two or more things are being measured by members of the set, e.g., two types of anxiety. If the latter is the case, it would be appropriate to break the original set A into two sets A_1 and A_2 corresponding to those variables that actually correlate well with one another. If all the correlations among members of the set are very low, it is illogical to continue speaking of the variables as constituting a set, and the investigator should turn his attention to other sets of variables. Regardless of which of these three conclusions is required by the evidence, eventually the evidence leads to a probability structure for the full set or for subdivisions of the set.

When the above has been accomplished, the internal consistency is known for the elements of a set A. Similarly, the internal consistency is determined for another set B. Taking the argument a step further, assume that a particular variable X_1 in A is correlated with a particular variable Y_1 in set B. Depending on the size of the correlation, it then would be possible to make many types of probability statements regarding unknown correlations between any other member of A and any other member of B. For example, if X_1 and X_2 are known to correlate highly and if Y_1 and Y_2 are known to correlate highly, finding a high correlation between X_1 and Y_1 permits a prediction of what the correlation would be between X_2 and Y_2. As another example, if the sum of all variables in A is known to correlate highly with the sum of all variables in B, it is possible to estimate the correlation between any particular variable from A and B or the correlation between any two combinations of variables from A and B. Thus there are *internal structures* for the variables in sets A and B separately and a *cross-structure* between variables in the two sets. If the internal structure of any set is satisfactory, it permits the scientist to explore cross-structures of that set with other sets. If such cross-structures are satisfactory, scientific progress is being made: either theories are being tested or interesting discoveries are being made.

Whereas, in the ultimate analysis, the "measurement" and "validation" of constructs can consist of nothing more than the determination of internal structures and cross-structures, that way of looking at it is disquieting to both the layman and the scientist. There is a need to put more meaning into the system. The scientist is not content to say only that members of set A relate to something else; he wants to say that anxiety, or a construct by another name, relates to something else. As was mentioned previously, words denoting constructs are essential to the scientist in thinking about problems, formulating theories, and communicating the results of experiments. This need for names pushes the scientist, and the layman even more, into assuming that corresponding to the name is some *real* variable which will be discovered some day. For example, some psychologists talk as though there is some real counterpart to the word "anxiety" that eventually will be found. The problem is not that of searching for a needle in the haystack, but that of searching for a needle that is not in the haystack.

The words that scientists use to denote constructs, e.g., "anxiety" and "intelligence," have no real counterparts in the world of observables; they are only heuristic devices for exploring observables. Whereas, for example, the scientist might find it more comfortable to speak of "anxiety" than set A, only set A objectively exists, empirical research concerns only set A, and in the final analysis only relations between members of set A and members of other sets can be unquestionably determined.

Although words relating to constructs are undeniably helpful to the scientist, they also can get him into real trouble. Such words are only symbols for collections of observables. Thus the word "fear" is a symbol for many possible forms of behavior. The difficulty is that the individual scientist is not sure of all the observables that should relate to such a word, and scientists disagree about the related observables. The denotations of a word can be no more exact than the extent to which (1) all possible related observables are specified and (2) all who use the word agree on the specification. Dictionary definitions of words concerning constructs help very little; they serve only to relate one unspecified term to other unspecified terms.

Considering the inexactness of denotations of words relating to constructs, it is not possible to *prove* that any collection of observables measures a construct. It would be much like the expedition starting out to catch a rare bird, the awrk. All scientists agree that the awrk has red wings, a curved bill, and only two toes, but everything else about the awrk is either unknown or a matter of dispute. How, then, would the expedition ever know for sure whether or not it had found an awrk? The analogy really is not farfetched; the same inconsistency is apparent in efforts to "find" measures of intelligence, anxiety, and other constructs. Looked at in this way, it logically is not possible to prove that any set of observables measures a construct.

Although, in a strict sense, "construct validity" is logically impossible, there are forms of proof that amount to much the same thing. The scientist starts with a word, e.g., "anxiety," and from that he hypothesizes a set of related observables. Proof can be obtained for the internal structure of those observables by methods described previously. If some combination of the members of this set of variables relates strongly to some combination of the members of another, this is proof that the first set has explanatory power. If it is useful to refer to these two steps as "construct validation," probably no harm is done, but it is important to understand what is being proved and how the related evidence is gathered.

Whereas it would be good if words denoting constructs were altered as evidence is obtained regarding sets of observables said to be related to the constructs, unfortunately this is not done as frequently as it should be. Ideally, one could envision a process whereby gradual refinements of a set of observables would be matched by gradual refinements of the words used to denote the set. Thus relatively inexact terms like "anxiety" and "intelligence" would be successively replaced by terms that were more denotatively exact for a set of observables, the set itself being continually refined in terms of an internal structure and a cross-structure with other sets of variables. It is doubtful, though, that any terms in common parlance will ever suffice to serve this purpose, and consequently only impartial designations such as "set A" can ever meet the full test of denotative explicitness.

Strictly speaking, scientists can never be sure that a construct has been measured or that a theory regarding that construct has been tested, even though it may be useful to speak as though such were the case. A construct is only a word, and although the word may suggest explorations of the internal structure of an interesting set of variables, there is no way to prove that any combination of those variables actually "measures" the word. Theories consist of collections of words (statements about natural events), and though such theories may suggest interesting investigations of cross-structures among sets of observables, the evidence obtained is not so much proof of the *truth* of the theories as it is proof of their *usefulness* as guides to empirical reality. Call it the "measurement" and "validation" of constructs if you like, but, at least as far as science takes us, there are only (1) words denoting constructs, (2) sets of variables specified for such constructs, (3) evidence concerning internal structures of such sets, (4) words concerning relations among constructs (theories), (5) which suggest cross-structures among different sets of observables, (6) evidence regarding such cross-structures, and (7) beyond that, nothing.

other issues concerning validity

OTHER NAMES   Other authors have called the three types of validity discussed in this chapter by different names. Predictive validity has been referred to as "empirical validity" and "statistical validity"; content validity has been referred to as "intrinsic validity," "circular validity," "relevance," and "representativeness"; and construct validity has been spoken of as "trait validity" and "factorial validity."

One frequently sees the term "face validity," which concerns the extent to which an instrument "looks like" it measures what it is intended to measure. For example, an achievement test for fourth-grade arithmetic would be said to have face validity if potential users of the test liked the types of items which were employed. Any instrument that is intended to have content validity should meet that standard, but the standard is far from complete. Face validity concerns judgments about an instrument *after* it is constructed. As was discussed previously, content validity more properly is ensured by the plan of content and the plan for constructing items. Thus face validity can be considered one aspect of content validity, which concerns an inspection of the final product to make sure that nothing went wrong in transforming plans into a completed instrument.

When an instrument is intended to perform a prediction function, validity depends entirely on how well the instrument correlates with what it is intended to predict (a criterion), and consequently face validity is irrelevant. There are many instances in which an instrument looks as though it should correlate well with a criterion although the correlation is close to zero. Also, there are many instruments that bear no obvious relationship to a criterion but actually correlate well with the criterion. With prediction functions, face validity is important only in formulating hypotheses about instruments that will correlate well with their criteria. Thus even though the correlations tell the full story, it is not wise to select predictors at random. Before research is done on a prediction problem, there must be some hope that a particular instrument will work. Such hope is fostered when the instrument looks as if it should predict the criterion. Also, tests usually are more predictive of a criterion if their item content is phrased in the language and the terms of the objects actually encountered in the particular type of performance. For example, if an arithmetic test is being constructed for the prediction of performance in the operation of particular types of machines, the test probably would be more predictive if problems were phrased in terms of numbers of nuts and bolts rather than numbers of apples and oranges. For these two reasons, face validity plays a part in decisions about types of tests to be used as predictors and in the construction of items for those tests.

In applied settings, face validity is to some extent related to public relations. For example, teachers would be reluctant to use an achievement test unless the items "looked good." Less logical is the reluctance of some administrators in applied settings, e.g., industry, to permit the use of predictor instruments which lack face validity. Conceivably, a good predictor of a particular criterion might consist of preferences among drawings of differently shaped and differently colored butterflies, but it would be difficult to convince administrators that the test actually could do a good job of selecting employees.

Although one could make a case for the involvement of face validity in the measurement of constructs, to do so probably would serve only to confuse the issues. It would be better to think directly in terms of the principles stated in the previous section.

PLACE OF FACTOR ANALYSIS   Methods of factor analysis and their use in the development of measures will be discussed in Chapters Nine and Ten and at other points in the book; but since factor analysis is intimately involved with questions of validity, it would be helpful to place some of the related issues in perspective. For those who are not already familiar with factor analysis, it should be noted that it essentially consists of methods for finding clusters of related variables. Each such cluster, or factor, is denoted by a group of variables whose members correlate more highly among themselves than they do with variables not included in the cluster. Each factor is thought of as a unitary attribute (a yardstick) which is measured to greater and lesser degrees by particular instruments, depending on the extent to which they correlate with the factor. Such correlations have been spoken of as representing the *factorial validity* of measures. It would be better to speak of such correlations as representing the *factorial composition* of measures, because the word "validity" is somewhat misleading.

The factorial composition of measures plays a part in all three types of validity discussed in this chapter. Factor analysis is important in the selection of instruments to be tried as predictors. Instead of constructing a new test for each applied problem as it arises, one selects a predictor instrument from a "storehouse" of available instruments. Factor analysis can serve to construct such a storehouse of measures with known factorial composition. It then is much easier to formulate hypotheses about the possible predictive power in particular instances of particular factors rather than to formulate hypotheses about the predictive power of instruments developed *ad hoc* for the problem. (In Chapter Eight it will be argued that in prediction problems developing measures *ad hoc* for applied problems as they arise is not only highly wasteful of energy, but also leads to some illogical methods of test construction.)

Factor analysis provides helpful circumstantial evidence regarding measures that are intended to have content validity. For example, a factor analysis of a battery of achievement tests might show that a test intended to measure mathematics correlates rather highly with a factor of verbal comprehension. This would suggest that the words and sentences used to phrase problems were sufficiently difficult to introduce an unwanted factor in the test, which would lead to revisions of the test for mathematics.

Factor analysis is at the heart of the measurement of psychological constructs. As was said previously, the explication of constructs mainly consists of determining (1) the internal statistical structure of a set of variables said to measure a construct and (2) the statistical cross-structures between the different measures of one construct and those of other constructs. Factor analysis is used directly to determine item 1, and procedures related to factor analysis are important in determining item 2. To take the simplest case, if all the elements of set A correlate highly with one another and all the elements of set B correlate highly with one another, the members of each set then have high correlations with a factor defined by that set. This would be evidence that the two sets, corresponding to two supposed constructs, meet the test of a "strong" internal structure. If, in addition, the two factors correlate substantially, this would provide evidence regarding the cross-structure of the two sets of measures.

Factor analysis plays important parts with respect to all three types of validity, but it plays somewhat different parts with each. Regarding predictive validity, factor analysis mainly is important in suggesting predictors that will work well in practice. With content validity, factor analysis mainly is important in suggesting ways to revise instruments for the better. With construct validity, factor analysis provides some of the tools that are most useful for determining internal structures and cross-structures for sets of variables.

SUGGESTED ADDITIONAL READINGS

Bechtoldt, H. P. Construct validity: A critique. *Amer. Psychologist,* 1959, **14,** 619–629.

Campbell, D. T. Recommendations for APA test standards regarding construct, trait, and discriminant validity. *Amer. Psychologist,* 1960, **15,** 546–553.

Cronbach, L. J., and Meehl, P. E. Construct validity in psychological tests. *Psychol. Bull.*, 1955, **52**, 281–302.

Lennon, R. T. Assumptions underlying the use of content validity. *Educ. psychol. Measmt*, 1956, **16**, 294–304.

Loevinger, Jane. Objective tests as instruments of psychological theory. *Psychol. Rep.*, 1957, **3**, 635–694.

PART 2

internal structure of measures

CHAPTER FOUR
VARIANCE AND COVARIANCE

A person who thoroughly understands some elementary concepts concerning the variance of measurements and covariance among different measures will have little difficulty in understanding the theory of measurement error, measurement of reliability, test construction, and multivariate analysis. Although most readers of this book already have been introduced to these topics, some reminders might prove helpful. Also, an effort will be made in this chapter to place issues regarding variance and covariance in tune with more complex issues to be discussed throughout the remainder of the book.

It might be said that scientific issues are posed only to the extent that objects or people vary with respect to particular attributes. For example, since the speed of light is a constant, there is little to investigate with respect to the speed of light. Once a constant is found in nature, it may prove useful in many equations specifying relations among attributes that do vary; but other than for its place in such equations, there is little to investigate about a constant per se. Thus if all stars had the same temperature, there would be nothing to investigate about the temperature of stars. If all people had the same intelligence, there would be nothing to investigate about intelligence. To stir interest of scientists, variation is as important in controlled experiments as it is in studies of individual differences. For example, if different groups are subjected to different levels of stress and the effects of such treatments are tested by a measure of anxiety, the results are of interest only to the extent that mean scores on the measure of anxiety are different for the differently treated groups. In studies of individual differences, variance of an attribute among people is of interest; in controlled experiments, variance among means for differently treated groups is of interest. Scientists look for attributes that vary considerably, develop measures of those attributes, and attempt to "explain" such sources of variation.

Variance is "explained" by studying covariance among measures of different attributes. The scientist hopes to find a relatively small number of basic variables that will explain the variation in many other variables. The variance of one variable is "explained" by another to the extent that the variables covary or correlate. Thus if performance in school correlates highly with measures of intelligence, social background, motivation, and others, the performance in school is "explained" by the other variables. To the extent that the rate of memorizing pairs of words in paired-associate learning correlates with familiarity with the words, familiarity serves to "explain" rate of memorization.

variance

Although there are many possible measures of variation, or dispersion, one has proved to be the most fruitful by far:

(4-1)
$$\sigma^2 = \frac{\Sigma x^2}{N}$$

where σ^2 = variance

x = deviation scores on a measure

N = number of measurements

Each x value is the deviation score for a particular person, obtained by subtracting the mean of a set of scores from each of the raw scores $(X - M_x)$. Since in most studies the grand mean of raw scores is of little interest, analyses of both studies of individual differences and controlled experiments can begin by converting all raw scores to deviation scores. The variance is the average squared deviation score. Squared deviations are worked with because they lend themselves very neatly to algebraic manipulations. A measure of variation cannot be developed from the deviations themselves, because by definition these sum to zero for any distribution. A possibility would be to develop measures of variation from the absolute deviations, disregarding signs, but such absolute deviations prove very awkward for mathematical developments.

Although the variance is easy to work with mathematically, the square root of the variance (the standard deviation) has useful descriptive properties. The standard deviation is expressed in the same units as the measure involved. Thus if a standard deviation of 5 is found on a 40-item test, it permits an easy interpretation of the amount of variability of the particular group of scores. It is somewhat more difficult to think in terms of variances. In the example above, the variance would be 25, which would be difficult to interpret with respect to scores on a 40-item test. The variance is more frequently used in mathematical developments, and the standard deviation is more frequently used in "making sense" out of the amount of variation. Since one is directly convertible to the other, which one is used in a particular instance is a matter of convenience.

In most methods of analysis, not only is the grand mean of raw scores unimportant, but the absolute sizes of deviations about the mean are unimportant. What are important are the *relative* sizes of deviations about the mean. The absolute sizes of deviations depend on artifacts of measurement. For example, a deviation of 2.5 about the mean might be a relatively large deviation if the test contained only 10 items, but it might be a relatively small deviation if the test contained 100 items. A good way to "relativize" deviation scores is to divide each by the standard deviation, which results in *standard scores*. Thus a particular individual who has a deviation score of 20 points above the mean, where the standard deviation of scores in the group is 10, has a standard score z of 2. Similarly, a person in that group with a deviation score of -10 would have a standard score of -1.

Standard scores are very easy to interpret—each specifies how many standard deviations an individual is above or below the mean. If a distribution of scores is approximately normal, standard scores can be easily interpreted in terms of the percentage of individuals above and below particular points on the score continuum. Since standard scores have such useful descriptive properties, it is important to think in terms of standard scores when discussing various methods of mathematical analysis. As will be discussed later, the correlation between any two measures would be exactly the same whether the analysis started with raw scores, deviation scores, or standard scores. Similarly, the results of a particular analysis of variance would be the same whether the analysis started with raw scores, deviation scores about the grand mean, or standard scores about the grand mean. The different ratios of variance would be the same regardless of which type of scoring were used. That is, the results of such analyses are invariant with respect to any linear transformation, such as

$$X' = bX + a$$

where X' = set of transformed scores
  b = any constant multiplier of X
  a = any constant added to bX

Of particular interest is the case in which the variance is computed for a variable that can have values of one and zero only—e.g., for a test item that is scorable only as pass or fail. In this example the variance can be expressed in terms of the proportion of persons who pass the item, p, and the proportion of persons who fail the item, q (which equals $1 - p$):

(4-2) $$\sigma^2 = pq$$

It is obvious from Eq. (4-2) that the variance of a dichotomous distribution is at a maximum when p and q are .5 and becomes less and less as p and q deviate from that point. Since $q = 1 - p$, the variance is entirely determined by the size of either of the two values. Thus two items have the same variance if 80 percent of the persons pass one item and only 20 percent of the persons pass the other item.

Some people find it odd to think of a dichotomous distribution as having "variance." Not only is it mathematically sound to speak of the variance of a dichotomous item, but also a moment's reflection will show that it makes intuitive sense. Variance is closely related to the concepts of uncertainty. Thus if a test has a large variance, there is more uncertainty as to the actual score of any person. Similarly, the nearer the p value is to .5, the more uncertainty there is about the scores of individuals. In that situation, if nothing were known about the individuals and it were required to make bets as to whether particular individuals passed or failed the item, the accuracy of such bets would be only 50 percent and thus no better than flipping a coin. In contrast, if 90 percent of the individuals pass an item, the variance is smaller, and there is much less uncertainty. By betting "pass" for each person in turn, 90 percent accuracy would be achieved.

TRANSFORMATIONS OF DISTRIBUTIONS   The formula for the variance [Eq. (4-1)] employs deviation scores (x). This is because the variance is computed about the mean score, the size of the mean being of no consequence. Thus the variance is left unchanged if any arbitrary constant is added to, or subtracted from, all the scores in a distribution. Whatever the mean of the original distribution, adding a constant to all scores increases the mean by the amount of the constant; but it has no effect on the standard deviation.

If all the scores in a distribution are multiplied by a constant, the variance is multiplied by the square of the constant, and the standard deviation is multiplied by the constant. For example, if all scores are multiplied by c,

(4-3)
$$
\begin{aligned}
\sigma_{cx}{}^2 &= \frac{\Sigma(cx)^2}{N} \\
&= \frac{\Sigma c^2 x^2}{N} \\
&= c^2 \left(\frac{\Sigma x^2}{N} \right) \\
&= c^2 \sigma_x{}^2
\end{aligned}
$$

Frequently it is useful to transform a distribution of scores to a distribution having a particular mean and standard deviation. For example, it might be found that the mean of obtained scores is 40 and the standard deviation is 5. To compare scores on the test with scores on another test or to place scores in an easily interpretable form, it might be desirable to transform the original distribution to one having a mean of 50 and a standard deviation of 10. The principles stated above permit the derivation of a formula for that purpose:

(4-4)
$$X_t = \frac{\sigma_t}{\sigma_o}(X_o - M_o) + M_t$$

where X_t = scores on transformed scale

X_o = scores on original scale

M_o, M_t = means of X_o and X_t, respectively

σ_o, σ_t = standard deviations of X_o and X_t, respectively

In the foregoing example, a score of 40 would be transformed to a score of 50, and a score of 25 to a score of 20. Because Eq. (4-4) provides a linear transformation, it does not change the shape of the score distribution.

correlation and covariance

Because correlational analysis is so intimately related to the development of measures and to the analysis of data obtained from research, a thorough understanding of some basic principles of correlational analysis is essential for the understanding of more advanced topics in this book. There are different indices of correlation, but they all have one thing in common: they describe the *degree* of relationship between two variables. Although it is fine to hope for the day when variables, or combinations of variables, will be found that correlate perfectly, such a day is a long way off for most scientific problems. Thus whereas the temperature of an enclosed gas may lawfully relate to the *average* molecular motion, that temperature relates only in a rough statistical sense to the activity of individual molecules. Whereas the density of different stars may correlate with their chemical compositions, such correlations are far from perfect. And whereas the number of mutations of genes would correlate with the amount of irradiation, the correlation would be far from perfect. So it is in most investigations of psychological variables—the most that the experimenter can hope for is a *trend* of correspondence between two variables, and experience has taught that in many cases the degree of correspondence between variables will not be high. For example, it is unreasonable to expect a very high relationship between predictor tests and success in college. Similarly, in controlled experiments, there usually is considerable dispersion on dependent measures for the different subjects in a treatment group, and distributions of different treatment groups usually overlap considerably. Correlational analysis is useful in specifying the form and degree of imperfect functional relationships.

internal structure of measures

The particular index of correlation used in a study depends on (1) assumptions about permissible operations with the measures involved (assumptions about scale properties) and (2) the "shape" of the relationship. Regarding point 1, it will be recalled from Chapter One that numbers may be used to represent ratio scales, interval scales, ordinal scales, categories, and as labels. Since psychologists seldom claim to have sensible ratio scales and correlational results with ratio scales are the same as those with interval scales, there is no problem regarding claims about ratio scales. Since numbers used as labels are not meant to imply quantities of attributes, such numbers can be excluded as possibilities for correlational analysis. The issues then concern assumptions regarding interval scales, ordinal scales, and categories. First will be described methods of correlational analyses that assume permissible operations relating to interval scales. Later will be described correlational methods appropriate to ordinal scales and categories.

Point 2 above (shape of relationship) mainly is important when one is dealing with interval scales. The only sense in which one can study the "shape" of the relationship between two ordinal measures is to investigate the relative monotonicity of the relationship. Thus if persons are ordered alike on the two measures, there is a monotonic relationship; but to the extent to which they are ordered differently on the two measures, there is departure from monotonicity. Correlational analysis will be discussed where there is a linear relationship between two interval scales, and subsequently nonlinear methods of correlational analysis will be mentioned.

product-moment correlation

This section deals with product-moment (PM) correlation of two relatively continuous distributions. Complete continuity of distributions is only a mathematical abstraction that never occurs in the actual measurement of attributes. For complete continuity, infinitely precise measurement would be required. More specifically, a distribution is continuous if no matter how close two points are on a scale, there is a point lying between the two. In actual measurement, all scales have discrete steps rather than infinitely fine gradations. Thus an instrument for measuring minute lengths would still be able to measure only to the nearest thousandth or millionth of an inch, and there would be a limit to which finer gradations would be possible. On a 40-item test where correct scores are counted 1 and incorrect scores 0, only 41 possible points are measurable (0 to 40). On a seven-point rating scale, measurement is made of only seven discrete levels.

Product-moment correlation is used to specify the degree of relationship between two variables expressed in the form of standard scores.

variance and covariance

The problem begins with standard scores, because in this type of analysis the means and standard deviations of raw scores are irrelevent. For illustration, the scores for nine persons on two tests, z_1 and z_2, are shown below.

PERSON	TEST z_1	TEST z_2	$z_1 \times z_2$
a	1.55	1.18	1.83
b	1.16	1.77	2.05
c	.77	.59	.45
d	.39	−1.18	−.46
e	.00	.59	.00
f	−.39	−.59	.23
g	−.77	−.59	.45
h	−1.16	−.59	.68
i	−1.55	−1.18	1.83

$$r = \frac{\Sigma z_1 z_2}{N}$$

$$= \frac{7.06}{9}$$

$$r = .78$$

A scatter diagram of the above pairs of scores is shown in Figure 4-1.

The problem in PM correlational analysis is to determine the straight line that best summarizes the trend of correspondence between two sets of standard scores. A straight line has only two parameters: the slope, which will be symbolized as r, and the point of intercept with the z_2 axis, which will be symbolized as a. The problem can be

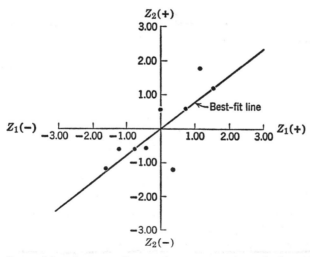

figure 4-1   *A scatter diagram for two sets of standard scores.*

internal structure of measures

phrased as that of obtaining a straight line that will "best estimate" scores on z_2 from scores on z_1 as follows:

(4-5) $\qquad z_2' = rz_1 + a$

where $z_2' =$ estimates of scores on z_2

The quality of the estimates would be gauged by some function of the differences between the estimated scores for z_2 and the actual scores on z_2:

$z_2 - z_2'$

This is the same as:

$z_2 - rz_1 - a$

Various ways could be used to obtain r and a, depending on what function of the foregoing differences was to be minimized. Thus one could try to derive r and a in such a way that the sum of absolute differences between z_2 and z_2' would be a minimum. Various other functions of the differences could be employed as a standard, each such function being referred to as a "loss function." The loss function that has proved most useful for this problem is that of *least squares:* r and a are determined so that the sum of squared differences between actual scores on z_2 and estimated scores z_2' is a minimum. Thus the problem is to minimize the following expression by the proper choice of r and a:

$\Sigma(z_2 - z_2')^2 = \Sigma(z_2 - rz_1 - a)^2$

Whether or not the foregoing expression has a unique minimum, and if it does, how to determine r and a are simple problems in calculus. Solving by the method of partial derivatives tells us three things. First, $a = 0$ for any comparison of sets of standard scores. Thus the line must go through the origin, as indicated in Figure 4-1. The problem then can be rephrased as finding an r that will minimize the expression

$\Sigma(z_2 - rz_1)^2$

Second, calculus tells us that r is unique in any problem, which means that there is only one value of r that minimizes the loss function. Third, calculus tells us that r is obtained as follows:

(4-6) $\qquad r = \dfrac{\Sigma z_1 z_2}{N}$

The proper value of r is obtained by multiplying pairs of standard scores on the two measures, summing these, and dividing the sum by the number of pairs (persons). These calculations were performed in the previous example of scores for persons on two tests. Once r is obtained,

variance and covariance

the line of best fit can be drawn, as was done in **Figure 4-1**. The best estimate of z_2 is obtained by multiplying each standard score on z_1 by r (which gives z_2'). Such estimates can be made from any particular score on z_1 either by using Eq. (4-6) or by reading off from the line of best fit to any point on z_2 corresponding to a point on z_1.

Because r is such a useful index, it is given a special name, the "PM correlation coefficient." It is used so much more frequently than any other index that, unless some other index of correlation is specified, the word "correlation" is usually assumed to stand for the PM correlation. The reason for calling it the "product-moment" coefficient is as follows. Deviations about a mean are spoken of as "moments" of a distribution. The deviates themselves are spoken of as the first moments of a distribution; squared deviates are second moments; cubed deviates are third moments; and so on. Since standard scores are deviates about a mean of zero, they are first moments of a distribution. Because the first step in obtaining r is to multiply corresponding standard scores on two measures, this can be spoken of as multiplying corresponding moments on two measures. Then r is the average product of first moments of two distributions—thus the name "product-moment correlation coefficient."

The usefulness of r extends far beyond that of determining the best-fit line. Because r cannot be greater than $+1.00$ or less than -1.00, its sign and size provide a very understandable indication of the direction and degree of relationship between two variables. As will be discussed more fully in subsequent sections, other advantages of the PM coefficient are that it (1) permits a partitioning of the variance of each of the two measures into meaningful components and (2) serves as a foundation for many complex methods of analysis, such as multiple correlation and factor analysis.

In discussing r, it makes no difference whether one phrases the problem as that of predicting z_2 from z_1 or vice versa. In either case the same numerical value would be found for r. This is not necessarily the case with some correlational methods applied to nonlinear relationships, which will be discussed later.

DIFFERENT FORMULAS   Although in a sense there is only one way to compute r, which is done by averaging the product of standard scores, the same numerical value can be obtained from many differently appearing formulas. These formulas vary in terms of ease of computation and the facility with which they permit more complex derivations. Regarding the former, Eq. (4-6) is almost never used in the actual computation of r, because it requires a tedious derivation of standard scores. Regarding the latter, it sometimes is easier to visualize the derivation of statistics based on r when one rather than another formula is used as a starting point. Some formulas for computing r are obtained from Eq. (4-6):

$$r = \frac{\Sigma z_1 z_2}{N}$$

Since any standard score equals a deviation score divided by the standard deviation of the distribution of deviation scores, the foregoing expression can be phrased in the following different ways:

$$r = \frac{\Sigma \left(\dfrac{x_1}{\sigma_1}\right) \left(\dfrac{x_2}{\sigma_2}\right)}{N}$$

(4-7)
$$= \frac{\Sigma x_1 x_2}{N \sigma_1 \sigma_2}$$

$$= \frac{\Sigma x_1 x_2}{\sqrt{\Sigma x_1{}^2} \sqrt{\Sigma x_2{}^2}}$$

Since any deviation score equals a raw score minus the mean of the raw scores in a distribution, Eq. (4-7) can be rephrased as follows:

$$r = \frac{\Sigma(X_1 \quad M_1)(X_2 - M_2)}{\sqrt{\Sigma(X_1 - M_1)^2} \sqrt{\Sigma(X_2 - M_2)^2}}$$

This can be transformed to the raw-score formula that appears most frequently in textbooks:

(4-8)
$$r = \frac{N\Sigma X_1 X_2 - \Sigma X_1 \Sigma X_2}{\sqrt{N\Sigma X_1{}^2 - (\Sigma X_1)^2} \sqrt{N\Sigma X_2{}^2 - (\Sigma X_2)^2}}$$

Many other formulas can be derived for actually computing r. The important point, however, is that r always specifies the degree of relationship between two sets of standard scores. Either standard scores are used directly for the computation of r or other formulas essentially convert raw scores or deviation scores to standard scores in the process of computation.

COVARIANCE The covariance σ_{12} is defined as the average cross product of two sets of deviation scores:

(4-9)
$$\sigma_{12} = \frac{\Sigma x_1 x_2}{N}$$

where x_1 = deviation scores on one measure
x_2 = corresponding deviation scores on another measure
N = number of pairs (persons)
σ_{12} = covariance

The covariance is a useful index of relationship, even though it does not lend itself to direct interpretation as easily as does r; for example, it is not restricted to the range from -1 to $+1$. In certain types of problems, however, the covariance is more important than r, which later will be shown to be the case, for example, in determining reliability. When, and only when, standard scores are placed in the formula, σ_{12} becomes r.

By dividing numerator and denominator of Eq. (4-7) by N, one obtains the following expression for the correlation coefficient:

$$(4\text{-}10) \qquad r_{12} = \frac{\sigma_{12}}{\sigma_1 \sigma_2}$$

The correlation between two measures can be thought of as the covariance of the two measures divided by the product of the standard deviations of the two measures. This way of phrasing r provides a very helpful starting point for understanding more complex forms of correlational analysis.

PARTITIONING OF VARIANCE As was mentioned previously, one of the reasons r is so useful is that it permits a partitioning of variance into meaningful components. Let us take the case where z_1 is being used to estimate z_2, but keep in mind that as long as both variables are in standard-score form it makes no difference which direction the predictions go. Before correlational analysis is undertaken, there are two variables, z_1 and z_2. After correlational analysis is completed, there are two additional variables. One is z_2', which is a set of estimates of z_2. The other is a set of error scores, obtained by subtracting the estimates of z_2 from the actual score on z_2, which will be symbolized as z_{2-1}. It is interesting to look at the means and variances of these four variables and the correlations among them.

It should be apparent that the means of all four variables above are zero. The means of z_1 and z_2 are zero by definition. Since z_2' is obtained by multiplying z_1 by a constant, r, the mean is left at zero. Since z_{2-1} is obtained by subtracting scores on z_2' from actual scores on z_2, the mean of z_{2-1} is zero.

By definition the variances of z_1 and z_2 are 1. Since $z_2' = rz_1$ and multiplying all the scores in a distribution by a constant multiplies the variance by the square of that constant, the variance of z_2' is r^2. The variance of z_{2-1} is obtained as follows:

internal structure of measures

$$\sigma_{2-1}{}^2 = \frac{\Sigma z_{2-1}{}^2}{N}$$

$$= \frac{1}{N} \Sigma (z_2 - z_2')^2$$

$$= \frac{1}{N} \Sigma (z_2 - rz_1)^2$$

(4-11)

$$= \frac{1}{N} \Sigma (z_2{}^2 - 2rz_1 z_2 + r^2 z_1{}^2)$$

$$= \frac{\Sigma z_2{}^2}{N} - 2r \frac{\Sigma z_1 z_2}{N} + r^2 \frac{\Sigma z_1{}^2}{N}$$

$$= 1 - 2r^2 + r^2$$

$$= 1 - r^2$$

Multiplying a variable by a constant does not change the correlation of that variable with any other variable. Consequently since $z_2' = rz_1$ and the correlation of z_1 and z_2 is r, the correlation of z_2' and z_2 likewise is r. The correlation of z_{2-1} with z_1 is obtained as follows:

$$r_{z_1 z_{2-1}} = \frac{\frac{1}{N} \Sigma z_1 z_{2-1}}{\sigma_{2-1}}$$

It will be sufficient to examine only the numerator of the expression to prove that z_1 and z_{2-1} correlate precisely zero:

$$\frac{1}{N} \Sigma z_1 z_{2-1} = \frac{1}{N} \Sigma z_1 (z_2 - rz_1)$$

$$= \frac{1}{N} (\Sigma z_1 z_2 - r \Sigma z_1{}^2)$$

$$= r - r$$

$$= 0$$

This also leads to the conclusion that predicted scores z_2' are independent of error scores z_{2-1}. (In this book uncorrelated variables will be referred to as "independent," which is not to be confused with the stricter definition of "independence" used in statistics.)

The correlation of z_2 with z_{2-1} is as follows:

$$r_{z_2 z_{2-1}} = \frac{\frac{1}{N} \Sigma z_2 z_{2-1}}{\sigma_{2-1}}$$

The denominator of the equation is the standard deviation of the errors of prediction. Previously the variance of the errors of prediction was shown to be $1 - r^2$; consequently the square root of that quantity is the denominator. The numerator can be expanded as follows:

$$\frac{1}{N}\Sigma z_2 z_{2-1} = \frac{1}{N}\Sigma z_2(z_2 - rz_1)$$

$$= \frac{1}{N}\Sigma(z_2{}^2 - rz_1 z_2)$$

$$= \frac{\Sigma z_2{}^2}{N} - r\frac{\Sigma z_1 z_2}{N}$$

$$= 1 - r^2$$

Placing numerator and denominator back in the original equation gives

(4-12)
$$r_{z_2 z_{2-1}} = \frac{1 - r^2}{\sqrt{1 - r^2}}$$

$$= \sqrt{1 - r^2}$$

The above relationships among means, variance, and correlations are summarized in Table 4-1. The reader should derive these simple principles on his own; then the results should be burnt into his brain. These simple principles are the foundation stones for more complex methods of multivariate analysis.

A number of important points should be understood from the foregoing discussion. Product-moment correlational analysis serves to summarize the relationship between two variables. The correlation coefficient r defines a line of best fit between one variable and another. For each score on one variable, there is a corresponding predicted score on the other variable. Unless the correlation is perfect, the variance of such predictions is less than that of the variable being predicted. Error scores are uncorrelated with predicted scores and uncorrelated with scores

table 4-1   *Means, variances, standard deviations, and correlations among scores involved in correlational analysis*

MEASURE	SCORE			
	Z_1	Z_2	Z_2'	Z_{2-1}
MEAN	.0	.0	.0	.0
σ^2	1.0	1.0	$r_{12}{}^2$	$1 - r_{12}{}^2$
σ	1.0	1.0	r_{12}	$\sqrt{1 - r_{12}{}^2}$
r with Z_1	1.0	r_{12}	1.0	.0
r with Z_2	r_{12}	1.0	r_{12}	$\sqrt{1 - r_{12}{}^2}$
r with Z_2'	1.0	r_{12}	1.0	.0

internal structure of measures

on the variable used as a basis of prediction. Correlational analysis then serves to partition the variance of a particular variable into two independent, or orthogonal, sources—one source which can be explained by another variable and a second source which cannot be explained by that other variable. In factor analysis, this logic is expanded to permit the partitioning of one variable into sources of variance that can, and cannot, be accounted for by *combinations* of other variables.

ERROR OF ESTIMATE   In addition to viewing PM correlation in terms of obtaining a best-fit straight line for the relationship between two sets of standard scores, it is also useful to think of correlation in terms of the errors of estimate. Previously the variance of the errors of estimate was symbolized as σ_{2-1}^2, which will now be abbreviated as σ_e^2. If both variables are expressed as standard scores

(4-13) $\sigma_e^2 = 1 - r^2$

and

(4-14) $\sigma_e = \sqrt{1 - r^2}$

The latter, being the standard deviation of the errors of estimate, is referred to as the *standard error of estimate*. If both variables are expressed as raw scores or deviation scores rather than as standard scores, Eqs. (4-13) and (4-14) would be modified as follows:

(4-15) $\sigma_e^2 = \sigma_y^2(1 - r^2)$

(4-16) $\sigma_e = \sigma_y \sqrt{1 - r^2}$

In Eqs. (4-15) and (4-16), σ_y^2 is the variance of the variable being estimated, the so-called dependent variable. The variance and standard deviation of errors of estimate depend only on the correlation between the two variables and the variance of the dependent variable. The standard-score formulas are special cases of Eqs. (4-15) and (4-16). Since for standard scores σ_y is 1.0, it "falls out" of the standard-score formulas.

Several points should be clear from an examination of the formulas regarding the variance and standard deviation of errors of estimate and from prior discussions of the nature of errors of estimate. First, there is an inverse relationship between the squared correlation and the variance of the errors of estimate. The more the points tend to scatter about the best-fit line, the less the correlation. Second, σ_e is useful in certain situations for setting confidence intervals for estimating scores on one variable from scores on another variable. Thus if it is known that an aptitude test correlates .50 with college grade-point averages, confidence intervals could be set for predictions of the dependent variable. It might be found, for example, that for students scoring 85

or higher on the aptitude test, the odds are less than 5 in 100 that a grade-point average of less than 1.0 (C average) would be obtained in college.

The third, and most important, point about the variance of errors of estimate is that it offers an approach to the development of many indices of relationship between variables. The formula for σ_e^2 can be rearranged as follows:

$$\sigma_e^2 = \sigma_y^2(1 - r^2)$$

(4-17)

$$r^2 = 1 - \frac{\sigma_e^2}{\sigma_y^2}$$

Thus the correlation is inversely related to the ratio of σ_e^2 to σ_y^2. When σ_e^2 is as large as σ_y^2, the correlation is zero; when σ_e^2 is very small relative to σ_y^2, the correlation is very high. This very important ratio will be spoken of as the *relative amount of error* (RE) in estimating any dependent variable. Also, it will be useful to talk about RE as a percentage. Thus if σ_e^2 is 5 and σ_y^2 is 10, it will be said that the RE is 50 percent. Whereas RE has been discussed with respect to a linear relationship between two variables, the concept extends to (1) any number of variables used to estimate a dependent variable and (2) any form of relationship, linear or otherwise. These extensions will be discussed in later sections.

other uses of PM correlation

In this section will be discussed three indices of relationship: phi, point-biserial, and rho. There apparently is some confusion in the minds of nonspecialists about these coefficients. It frequently is assumed that these coefficients are different from one another and that they are all different from the PM formula [Eq. (4-1)]. Both assumptions are incorrect. All three of these "other" coefficients are the same, and they are all the same as the "regular" PM coefficient. Such "other" coefficients are sometimes thought to be different because the computations "look" different, but this is entirely because of the type of data to which they are applied rather than a different mathematical rationale. Some shortcut formulas have been developed for cases where one or both of the variables are not continuous, e.g., for correlating two dichotomous variables. These are only special cases of the PM formula, and aside from the convenience of working with such shortcut formulas when computers are not available, the PM formula could be used to obtain exactly the same result that would be obtained from phi, point-biserial, or rho.

PHI   When both distributions are dichotomous, a shortcut version of the PM coefficient is available which is called "phi." Phi can be illustrated in the situation where two test items are being correlated:

ITEM 1

		fail	pass
	pass	17	30
ITEM 2			
	fail	33	20

The above diagram shows the scores for 100 students on two items. It indicates, for example, that 30 students pass both items and 33 fail both items. It is convenient to symbolize the four quadrants as follows:

ITEM 1

	b	a
ITEM 2		
	c	d

A shortcut version of the PM coefficient is obtained as follows:

$$(4\text{-}18) \qquad \text{phi} = \frac{ac - bd}{\sqrt{(a + b)(c + d)(b + c)(a + d)}}$$

There is a very useful relationship between phi and chi-square:

$$(4\text{-}19) \qquad \text{chi-square} = N(\text{phi})^2$$

Chi-square is obtained by squaring phi and multiplying by the number of persons involved in the correlation. A test of the null hypothesis for zero correlation can then be made by referring the obtained value to a table of chi-square with one degree of freedom.

As was mentioned previously, although the formula for phi looks different from the PM formula, the former is only a special case of the latter. When correlating two dichotomous distributions, exactly the same results as obtained from phi would be obtained by standardizing scores and placing these in the PM formula. If half the persons pass one item and passes are scored 1 and failures scored 0, all persons passing would have a standard score of $+1$ and all failing would have a standard score of -1. Such standard scores may look rather strange, but that does not disturb the mathematics of the problem.

Before the advent of high-speed computers, phi was frequently applied to artificially dichotomized variables. For example, in item analysis, dichotomous item scores can be correlated with artificially dichotomized total scores on the test. One way to dichotomize total scores is to make all scores below the median zero and all scores at or above the median 1. Phi could then be used to correlate each item with total test scores. Unless computational labor is a very important consideration, it is unwise to artificially dichtomize one or both of the variables being investigated. If both variables are continuous, it is best to apply the regular PM formula. If one variable is inherently dichotomous (e.g., pass-fail on test items) and one is continuous, it is best to apply point-biserial, which will be discussed in the next section. Information is always lost when a continuous variable is artificially dichotomized. As a shortcut version of the PM coefficient, phi is the preferred measure of relationship when variables are inherently dichotomous.

POINT–BISERIAL   When one dichotomous variable is to be correlated with a continuous variable, a shortcut version of the PM formula called "point-biserial" (r_{pb}) is available. The most frequent occasion for employing this formula is in correlating a dichotomous test item (e.g., pass-fail) with total scores on a test. The shortcut formula is as follows:

(4-20) $$r_{pb} = \frac{M_s - M_u}{\sigma} \sqrt{pq}$$

where M_s = mean score on continuous variable of "successful" group on dichotomous variable

M_u = mean score on continuous variable of "unsuccessful" group on dichotomous variable

σ = standard deviation on continuous variable for total group

p = proportion of persons falling in "successful" group on dichotomous variable

$q = 1 - p$

As was true of phi, r_{pb} was sometimes employed in former days where one of two continuous variables was artificially dichotomized. For example, rather than employ the regular PM formula to the continuous scores on two tests, scores on one of the two tests were dichotomized, the "cut" most frequently being done at the median. Then the shortcut formula was applied. This is very poor practice, however. The saving in computational time is not great, and fuller information would be obtained by correlating the two continuous variables. Point-biserial is the preferred measure of correlation when one variable is continuous and the other is inherently dichotomous, e.g., pass-fail or male-female. As was mentioned previously, the numerical result obtained by applying the regular PM formula is exactly the same as that which would be obtained from the shortcut version r_{pb}.

RHO   For correlating two sets of ranks, a shortcut version of the PM formula called "rho" is available. The formula could be used, for example, to correlate the rankings of two judges of the extent to which 20 patients had improved in the course of psychotherapy. The formula is as follows:

$$\text{(4-21)} \qquad \text{rho} = 1 - \frac{6\Sigma d^2}{N(N^2 - 1)}$$

where N = number of objects or persons ranked

d = algebraic difference in ranks for each object or person in two distributions of ranks

Although rho is sometimes spoken of as a "nonparametric" index of relationship, this certainly is not the case. Rho is only a shortcut version of the regular PM formula. Results obtained by applying rho are exactly the same as those obtained by applying the regular PM formula to two sets of ranks.

There are three possible reasons for employing rho. First, two continuous distributions can be converted to ranks and rho applied to save computational labor. This is a poor reason, though, because the saving in computational time is not great. In this instance, rho applied to the ranks would usually be very close to the regular PM formula applied to the continuous variables, particularly if both continuous variables are approximately normally distributed. A second reason for applying rho is to estimate what the PM correlation would be between two distributions which are markedly different in shape if the two were rescaled to have approximately the same shape. If, for example, one distribution is highly skewed to the left and the other is highly skewed to the right, the PM correlation will be less than it would be if both distributions had the same shape (for reasons that will be discussed in a later section). If both distributions were transformed to have the same shape, say, both were normalized, the correlation would increase somewhat. Before going to the labor of transforming the two distributions, it might be useful to estimate how much the variables would correlate after the transformation. This can be done with rho. By ranking scores on the two variables and applying rho, one will obtain a correlation that closely approximates the correlation that would be obtained from the two normalized variables. This is a legitimate reason for employing rho, but the circumstance arises infrequently.

The third, and best, reason for employing rho is to correlate two distributions that are inherently expressed as ranks. This would be the case for the example mentioned earlier where 20 patients were ranked with respect to improvement during the course of therapy. When measurement is in the form of rank order, rho provides a useful index of correlation. Because rho is a PM formula and PM formulas are often said to "require" interval scales, some would call this an "illegitimate" use of rho. It is hard to see much sense in such arguments. Since rho ranges between $+1$ and -1, it serves to describe the degree of relationship between two sets of ranks. Tests of statistical significance are available (McNemar, 1962) when both variables are inherently in the form of rank order. As a shortcut version of the regular PM formula, rho is the preferred measure of relationship when both variables are inherently in the form of ranks.

estimates of PM coefficients

Although they are not PM coefficients themselves, two coefficients have been used to estimate results that would, under special circumstances, be obtained from the PM formula. It will be recommended that these coefficients not be used in most cases, but they are spoken of so frequently in the literature relating to measurement theory that a brief discussion of them is required.

BISERIAL   When one variable is dichotomous and the other continuous, the biserial correlation r_{bis} can be used in place of the point-biserial correlation. The formula for r_{bis} is as follows:

(4-22) $$r_{bis} = \frac{M_s - M_u}{\sigma}\left(\frac{pq}{z}\right)$$

where M_s = mean score on continuous variable of "successful" group on dichotomous variable

M_u = mean score on continuous variable of "unsuccessful" group on continuous variable

σ = standard deviation on continuous variable for total group

p = proportion falling in "successful" group on dichotomous variable

$q = 1 - p$

z = ordinate of normal curve corresponding to p

Biserial can be used to estimate the PM correlation that would be obtained from two continuous distributions if the dichotomized variable were normally distributed. In the past, r_{bis} has been used to save computational time over that required for the PM coefficient. This could be done by "cutting" one distribution at the median and then computing r_{bis} rather than r. Another use of r_{bis} is to correlate scores on an inherently dichotomous variable with those on a continuous variable. For example, a preliminary form of a questionnaire might employ dichotomous items, e.g., agree-disagree. If the preliminary form is successful, it is planned to construct a form in which each item will be rated on an 11-point scale of agreement. The success of each item is in the extent to which it correlates with performance in a learning experiment. The biserial correlation of each dichotomous item with the criterion (success in the learning experiment) would be an estimate of the PM correlation that would be obtained by correlating the 11-point scale with the criterion.

TETRACHORIC CORRELATION   Taking the logic of biserial correlation a step further, the tetrachoric correlation coefficient r_t is used to estimate the PM correlation of two continuous variables from dichotomized versions of those variables. One use of r_t would be with two continuous variables that have been artificially dichotomized, such as two continuous variables each of which has been "cut" at the median. Another use of r_t is with two variables which are inherently dichotomous at the time of the analysis. The purpose here would be to estimate what the PM coefficient would be *if* the two variables were continuous, e.g., the correlation between two questionnaire items scored on 11-point scales rather than in terms of dichotomous responses.

Exact computing formulas for r_t are extremely complex, and even some of the approximate formulas are rather involved. Instead of employing the formulas, it is better to use the computing diagrams available for the purpose (discussed in McNemar, 1962).

USE OF r_{bis} AND r_t There are very strong reasons for *not* using r_{bis} and r_t in most of the ways that they have been used in the past. If continuous scores are available for both variables, any savings in computational labor over the regular PM coefficient is not worth the dangers involved. First, if one variable or both are inherently dichotomous, it usually is illogical to estimate what the PM coefficient would be if both variables were continuous. Unless subsequent steps are made to turn the dichotomous variables into continuous variables, such estimates only serve to fool one into thinking that his variables have explanatory power beyond that which they actually have. It is tempting to employ r_{bis} and r_t rather than phi and r_{pb}, because the former usually are larger. Unless the p values of both dichotomous variables are the same, phi will be less than r_t. Point-biserial is always less than r_{bis}, and if the p value of the dichotomous variable is considerably different from .50 in either direction, r_{bis} will be much larger than r_{pb}. Then to use r_{bis} is to paint a faulty picture of the actual size of correlations obtainable from existing data.

A second reason for not employing r_{bis} and r_t is that, even if it were sensible to make such estimates of the PM coefficient between two continuous variables, they frequently are very poor estimates. Both these coefficients very much depend on a strict assumption of the normality of the continuous variables, either of the variables that have been artificially dichotomized or of continuous variables that are to be generated later. When the assumption of normality is not met, the estimates can be off by more than 20 points of correlation. The author once had occasion to compare a biserial correlation between two continuous variables (one being dichotomized at the median for the analysis) with the regular PM coefficient applied to the continuous variables. The former was .71 and the latter was .52! The errors of estimate frequently found with these two coefficients show that they should generally not be employed.

If the foregoing are not reasons enough for generally avoiding use of r_{bis} and r_t, there is another important reason. Whereas it was said that one of the great virtues of PM correlation is that it opens the door to many powerful methods of analysis, this is not true for the two estimates of PM correlation. After one obtains r_{bis} and r_t, there is very little that can be done with them mathematically. It should be strongly underscored that these two estimates *cannot be used* in partial correlation, multiple correlation, factor analysis, or in any other form of multivariate analysis. There have been instances in the past of the use of r_t in factor analysis. Perhaps no harm was done, but there is no mathematical basis whatsoever for employing r_{bis} and r_t in multivariate analysis.

After this scathing denunciation of r_{bis} and r_t, it should be pointed out that there is one important, legitimate use for these coefficients. The use is in the development of mathematical models relating to measurement theory. It might be necessary, for example, in one mathematical model concerning test construction to assume that all the items have the same biserial correlation with total test scores or the same tetrachoric correlation with one another. This might permit the development of some useful principles which could be tested in empirical studies. There is nothing wrong with using r_{bis} and r_t in mathematical models, but they definitely should not be used to determine the correlation between sets of empirical data.

other measures of correlation

In addition to the measures of correlation discussed in the previous section, many other measures of the degree of relationship between two variables have been developed. None of these has achieved the prominence of the PM coefficient, because none fit as neatly into the mathematical developments required for multivariate analysis, e.g., factor analysis.

In this discussion of the value of different approaches to correlational analysis, it should become clear why it was stated in Chapter One that it is essential to employ methods of analysis appropriate to interval scales. It was shown that the PM coefficient is a function of the ratio of two variances, the variance of the errors of estimate divided

internal structure of measures

by the variance of the dependent measure [Eq. (4-17)]. The variance is a sensible index of dispersion only when the intervals of the scale are taken seriously. (A set of ranks has no variance.) To forsake the interval would be to forsake the variance, and to forsake the variance would be to forsake all the powerful methods of analysis that are needed.

What is lost when the assumption of an interval scale is forsaken is illustrated by the attempt to develop nonparametric correlation coefficients for ranked data. (Previously it was pointed out that rho is not a nonparametric index of relationship.) The only index that has achieved prominence is Kendall's tau (Kendall, 1948). Although tau is an index of the extent to which persons or objects are ordered alike on two variables, and the sampling distribution of the index is known, it has been used very little in research. The reason is that, like so many other non-PM measures, it is very difficult to extend tau to problems of multivariate analysis.

factors that influence the PM correlation

ASSUMPTIONS   It is frequently said that there are certain assumptions that must be met in employing the PM coefficient for two continuous distributions. First, it is said that there must be a linear relationship; that is, a straight line must do a good job of describing the trend, regardless of how much points may scatter above and below the line. If the trend of correspondence is highly irregular or there is a definite curve in the trend line, the assumption of linearity would not be met. (Methods of analysis for these situations will be mentioned later in the chapter.) Second, it is said that each of the variables must be normally distributed. Third, it is said that the relationship must be *homoscedastic* rather than heteroscedastic. In the former case, the spread about the best-fitting straight line is approximately the same at all levels of the two variables. In the latter case, the spread is much more at certain levels of the variables than at others. For the latter case, it might, for example, be found in correlating an aptitude test with college grades that the spread of grades about the best-fit line is considerably larger for persons who make high scores on the test than it is for persons who make low scores on the test.

There has been considerable controversy as to whether the above three characteristics should be considered "assumptions" in correlational analysis. Strictly speaking, they are only assumptions for employing *inferential statistics* relating to correlational analysis. When these three characteristics are present, the relationship is said to be *bivariate-normal*. The bivariate-normal distribution is an assumption in developing inferential statistics relating to PM correlations, e.g., "tests of significance" of the departure of a particular correlation from zero. To the extent to which any of the three assumptions are not met and consequently bivariate-normality is not precisely obtained, probability statements about the correlations might not be exactly correct. This, however, is not a great problem. Unless one of the assumptions were seriously violated, inferential statistics would not be highly erroneous. An example of a "serious" violation would be to correlate a normally distributed variable with scores from a J curve. Also, if there is some evidence of departure from the assumptions, a safe procedure is to use a higher level of "significance" than ordinarily would be required, e.g., to require that differences be significant at the .001 level rather than at the .01 level.

Other than for the assumptions required for the employment of inferential statistics, bivariate-normality is an assumption not so much for *using* the PM coefficient as for *interpreting* the results. Thus there is nothing to prevent the use of PM correlation even if one of the distributions is markedly different from the other in shape, if the relationship is far from linear and the spread of points is different at different places along the line. Unless these "assumptions" are seriously violated, no real problem in interpretation is involved. For example, if there is a moderate departure from linearity (say, the trend of correspondence tends to "flatten out" over the high end of the independent variable), no great damage is done in using the regular PM coefficient. It might be slightly more appropriate to employ a nonlinear measure (which will be discussed later), but the difference would not be large. Unless there is a marked curve in the relationship, the linear measure gives much the same results as does the curvilinear measure.

If the relationship were strongly heteroscedastic, the PM correlation would fail to reveal some important information. It would not reveal that the relationship was much stronger at certain levels of the variables than at others. This would be important in testing a theory or in using a test to select college freshmen. If the two variables have very differently shaped distributions, that is important, because it artificially forces a degree of nonlinearity and a degree of heteroscedasticity in the relationship.

RESTRICTION OF RANGE   Previously it was shown that the correlation is inversely related to the relative error (RE) σ_e^2/σ_y^2. It should be obvious that the correlation is a function of the variance of the dependent variable. Thus if a broader range of subjects is studied, the correlation will increase; if a narrower range of subjects is studied, the correlation will decrease. The change in variance must be a *real* change arising from differences in sampling methods. The correlation is not affected by *artificial* changes in the variance, as would be the case if all the scores on the dependent variable were multiplied by five. In that case σ_y and σ_e

would increase proportionally, and consequently the correlation would remain the same.

Whereas the effect of variance on correlation was illustrated with respect to the variance of the dependent variable, the effect is the same regardless of which of the two variances is altered. If a change in sampling doubles the variance of y, the effect on the correlation would be the same as if a change in sampling had doubled the variance of x. As mentioned previously, which variable in correlational analysis is called the dependent variable and which is called the independent variable is only a matter of convenience. The correlation is the same either way. Rather than obtain a standard error for estimating y from x, it would be just as sensible to obtain a standard error for estimating x from y. This could be done by substituting σ_x for σ_y in Eq. (4-16). Then it can be seen that the size of the correlation is inversely related to the standard error of estimating x from y divided by σ_x. The RE is the same either way.

The usual concern in correlational analysis is with sampling methods that _restrict_ the variances, and consequently the problem is referred to as that of _restriction in range_. Restriction in range may be either direct or indirect. A direct restriction occurs when sampling procedures are biased with respect to one of the two variables. Suppose, for example, that an aptitude test is being validated for the selection of college freshmen. The test is administered to all students applying for admission to a particular college. Only the top 50 percent of the students on the aptitude test are selected for admission. Later, scores on the aptitude test of those admitted to college are correlated with grade-point averages. In this case there has been a direct restriction of range on the aptitude test. The variance of scores on the test would have been much larger had _all_ the applicants been admitted to college. Since the test will be used with all applicants, the validity manifested in the restricted sample is spuriously low.

Indirect restriction of range occurs when the restriction is on a variable that correlates with one of the two variables under study. If the two variables correlate, direct restriction on one automatically results in an indirect restriction on the other. Thus in the example above, the direct restriction was on the aptitude test, but also there would have been an indirect restriction on grade-point averages. If all the applicants had been admitted, grade-point averages would have stretched out more on the lower end, and consequently the variance would have been larger.

Sometimes the restriction is because of a third variable. If, for example, all applicants were admitted to college and, regardless of grades, allowed to remain for four years of study, there would be no direct restriction of either variable. But suppose the situation were such that only those applicants who had B averages in high school were even considered for admission. Since grade averages in high school probably would correlate positively with the aptitude test and with grades in college, there would be an indirect restriction of range on the latter two variables. Then the correlation between test scores and grades in college would be lower than it would have been had the indirect restriction not occurred.

Although the problem has been posed as one of restriction in variance, it is no different when there has been an inflation of variance, either direct or indirect. In any study, what is important to consider is the *appropriate* variance for each variable. What is appropriate depends on the types of scientific statements that are made about data. If the results are to be discussed with respect to people in general, the appropriate variance is found by investigating an unbiased sample of the population in general. If the results are to be discussed with respect to boys between the ages of seven and ten, the appropriate variance is found in an unbiased sample of that group. If an aptitude test is to be used for the selection of college students only after certain preliminary hurdles are successfully passed, e.g., B average in high school, the appropriate variance is found for all applicants who have B averages in high school.

In any correlational study, if variances are known for the appropriate populations, these variances can be compared with the variances employed to compute a correlation. If the two sets of variances differ appreciably, estimates can be made of what the correlation would be if there were no restriction or elevation of range. Formulas for this purpose are discussed in Guilford (1965).

DISTRIBUTION FORM   Regardless of the shape of either distribution, normal or otherwise, if one is shaped differently than the other, the size of the correlation is restricted. The most obvious evidence of this principle is found in the fact that it is not possible to obtain a perfect correlation between two variables unless they have exactly the same distribution form (normal or otherwise). This is illustrated in Figure 4-2. The variable X is highly skewed toward the low end, and the variable Y is highly skewed toward the high end. The author tried to depict the highest correlation he could by pairing high scores on X with high scores on Y and vice versa for low scores. Why a perfect correlation is not possible is obvious when one tries to place the top eight people on X. For there to be a perfect correlation, all eight would have to lie at the highest point on Y. But since there are only two persons at the highest point on Y, it is necessary to place six of the eight persons at lower points on Y. Not only is the correlation less than 1.00, but also the relationship is curvilinear, which is the usual accompaniment of correlating differently shaped distributions.

internal structure of measures

The restriction of the correlation depends on (1) how high the correlation would be if the distributions had the same shape and (2) how different in shape the distributions are. Regarding point 1, whereas the effect was demonstrated with the attempt to obtain a perfect correlation, differences in shapes of distributions have an effect regardless of the size of the correlation. Suppose, for example, two variables have the same-shaped distributions and the correlation is found to be .50. Also assume that the relationship is linear. Then if the form of one distribution is artificially altered, the correlation tends to be less than .50. How much the correlation is lowered depends on the size of the correlation when the distributions are of the same shape. For a correla-

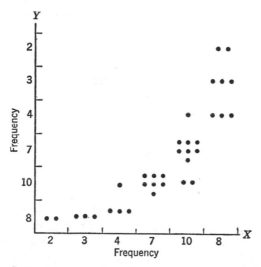

figure 4-2 *A scatter diagram for two differently shaped distributions of scores.*

tion of 1.00, a change in shape of one distribution might lower the correlation by 10 or 20 points. As the correlation between the same-shaped distributions becomes less and less, altering the shape of one distribution has less effect. Although no formulas are available for forecasting the amount of change, experience indicates that changes in the shape of one distribution seldom alter a correlation of .50 by more than five points. For correlations of .30 or lower, even drastic changes in the shape of one distribution (e.g., changing a normal distribution to one that is distinctly bimodal) tend to have very little effect. Thus the results of correlating two continuous variables in most studies in psychology would be about the same whether the distributions were shaped the same or somewhat differently. Correlations as high as .70 are rare, and the average of all correlations reported in the literature probably is less than .40.

Although differences in shapes of distributions tend to have slight effects in studies of *continuous* variables, the effect can be quite large when one or both of the variables is *dichotomous*. At first thought, it might seem odd to speak of a dichotomous distribution as having a "shape," but it is useful to think in that way. All distributions can be thought of as containing a standard area. One can think of pulling and squeezing the area under a normal distribution to form differently shaped distributions, all of which would cover the same area. For a dichotomous distribution, the total area available could be divided into two rectangles proportional to the percentage of persons in each half of the dichotomy. Then it is meaningful to talk about the similarity in shape of two dichotomous distributions or the similarity in shape of a dichotomous distribution to a continuous distribution.

table 4-2 *Correlation table for two items with different p values*

PERCENTAGE OF PERSONS
ITEM a

		fail (30)	pass (70)
PERCENTAGE OF PERSONS ITEM b	pass (50)	0	50
	fail (50)	30	20

The PM correlation between two dichotomous variables (phi) is restricted by the extent to which the percentage of persons in the "pass" group on one variable is different from the percentage of persons in the "pass" group on the other variable. An example should suffice to show why this is so. Suppose that on item a 70 percent pass and 30 percent fail and on item b 50 percent pass and 50 percent fail. In Table 4-2 an effort is made to achieve the highest correlation possible in that case. It is quite evident that a perfect correlation cannot be obtained: it would require that all who passed item a would have to pass item b, but this obviously is not possible. Because 70 percent passed a and only 50 percent passed b, 20 percent must be placed as failing b.

In correlating two dichotomous variables, a perfect positive correlation cannot be obtained unless the p values are the same for both variables. To the extent to which they are different, a ceiling is placed on the possible size of a positive correlation. The ceiling on negative correlations is proportional to the extent to which the p value on one item is different from the q value on the other item, and vice versa. Thus if 30 percent pass one item and 70 percent pass another item, it is possible to obtain a correlation of -1.00 but not one of $+1.00$. The reverse would be true if 70 percent had *failed* the second item.

Figure 4-3 illustrates the degree to which correlations are restricted by differences in p values for the two variables. The figure shows, for example, that if the p value of one item is .5 and the p value of the other item differs by as much as .3 (being either .2 or .8), the correlation cannot be greater than .50. It should be emphasized that the restriction on phi is because of the *difference* in p values for the two variables. A perfect correlation can be found when two variables both have p

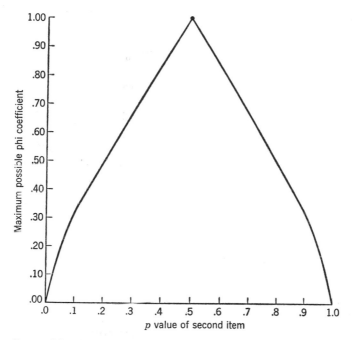

figure 4-3 *Maximum possible value of the phi coefficient between two test items when the p value of the first item is .5 and the p value of the second item varies from .0 to 1.0.*

values of .90 as well as it can for two variables that both have p values of .50.

Whereas it is possible to obtain a perfect correlation between two dichotomous variables (phi), it is not possible to obtain a perfect correlation between one dichotomous variable and one continuous variable r_{pb}. The reason is that, whereas the distribution shapes can be the same for two dichotomous variables, it is not possible for a dichotomous variable and a continuous variable to have the same shape. Why there cannot be a perfect relationship between a dichotomous variable and a continuous variable is illustrated in Figure 4-4. For the dichotomous variable, all the scores are on two points. To have a perfect correlation, it would be necessary for all the scores at those two points to fall exactly on two points on the other variable. But since the other variable is continuous, this is not possible. Consequently scores at either of the two points on the dichotomous variable must correspond to a range of points on the continuous variable.

The maximum size of r_{pb} between a dichotomous variable and a normally distributed variable is about .80, which occurs when the p value of the dichotomous variable is .50. The further the p value deviates from

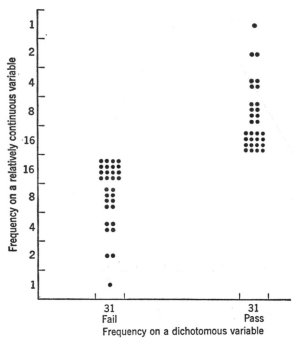

figure 4-4 *Scatter diagram of the maximum possible correlation between a dichotomous variable that has a p value of .5 and a variable that is relatively continuous.*

.50 in either direction, the lower the ceiling on r_{pb}. This is because the shape of a dichotomous distribution is most similar to that of a normal distribution when p is .50. When p departs from .50, the shape of the dichotomous distribution becomes less and less like that of the normally distributed variable. The ceiling on the correlation between a dichotomous variable and a normally distributed variable r_{pb} as a function of the p value of the dichotomous variable is shown in Figure 4-5. There it is seen, for example, that when p is as high as .90 or as low as .10, the maximum possible correlation is about .58.

internal structure of measures

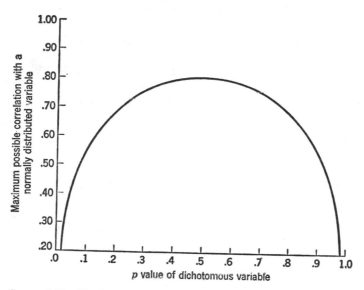

figure 4-5 *Maximum possible point-biserial correlation between a normally distributed variable and dichotomous variables ranging in p value from .0 to 1.0.*

a universal measure of relationship

Correlational analysis has been discussed so far in this chapter in terms of the best-fitting straight line, but it is entirely possible that relationships in particular studies will not be linear. Linear methods are used wherever possible, because they are easily extended to more complex forms of analysis, e.g., factor analysis. Even if there is some departure from linearity in particular comparisons, a best-fitting straight line often does a reasonably good job of describing the degree of relationship. In those instances where the relationship is markedly nonlinear, however, the PM correlation is inappropriate.

Previously it was shown that the PM coefficient is inversely related to the relative error (RE) about the best-fitting straight line, the variance about the line divided by the variance of the dependent measure. The same logic can be used to develop a universal measure of relationship, one that can be used regardless of the form of the relationship. The universal measure is called "eta." The first step in obtaining eta is to compute the variance about *any* curve of relationship. This is then divided by the variance of the dependent variable to obtain an RE. When this is subtracted from 1, the result is eta squared. The equation for eta is as follows:

(4-23) $(\text{eta})^2 = 1 - \text{RE}$

variance and covariance   **133**

How eta is used is illustrated in Figure 4-6, which shows a hypothetical relationship between scores on a measure of anxiety and scores on a learning task. Since the relationship is distinctly nonlinear, the PM coefficient would not do a good job of summarizing the trend. What one can do is compute the correlation about the best-fitting smooth curve. The sum of squared deviates about the curve is divided by the number of points (persons) to obtain the error variance. This is divided by the variance of learning scores to obtain an RE. The RE is subtracted from 1, and the square root of that quantity is eta.

Eta is said to be a "universal" measure of relationship because (1) it can be applied regardless of the form of the relationship, (2) either it can be applied to a predicted curve of relationship or the

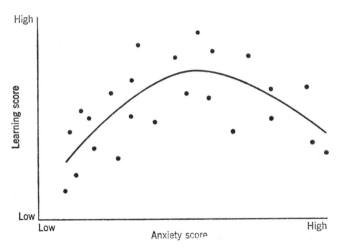

figure 4-6 *Hypothetical scatter diagram for learning scores and anxiety scores.*

best-fitting curve can be sought after the data are in hand, and (3) it applies equally well when independent variables are continuous measures and when they are only categorical in nature. It already has been demonstrated why point 1 holds: the RE is as meaningful about a complex curve as it is about a straight line. Regarding point 2, the form of a relationship might be predictable from a theory. Thus the form of the relationship between two variables might be predicted as parabolic or hyperbolic. Curves of these forms could be tried on the data, and eta would tell how well the curves explained scores on the dependent measure. (The mechanics of fitting curves and obtaining eta in different problems are presented in Lewis, 1960.) If no particular curve is predicted for the data, a variety of curves can be tried. The one with the largest eta provides the best fit (in the sense of least squares).

internal structure of measures

Regarding point 3 above, eta can be applied when the independent variable is a set of categories rather than a continuous variable. This is illustrated in Figure 4-7, which shows the effect of four different drugs on bar pressing (in a Skinner box) by rats. The independent variable consists of different drugs, and consequently it is arbitrary which drug is listed as A and which is listed as D. In this instance it is not meaningful to talk about the "form" of the relationship. There would be nothing wrong with reordering the drugs on the graph, which would drastically change the visible "form" of relationship. Eta can be applied in this case, however, in the same way that it is applied

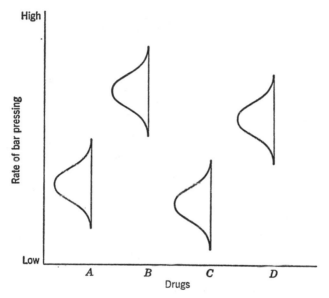

figure 4-7 *Distributions of effects of four drugs on rate of bar pressing.*

when both variables are continuous. The sum of squared departures from the mean score on the dependent measure for each drug can be calculated. These can be pooled and divided by the total number of rats, which provides a measure of error variance. This can be divided by the variance of all scores on the dependent measure to provide an RE, which can, in turn, be converted to eta.

Eta can be applied in any study where the *dependent* measure is continuous, or at least relatively so. The logic extends to all forms of analysis of variance. Customarily one thinks in terms of the F ratio, in which the variance estimate from any systematic source (e.g., different drugs) is divided by an appropriate error term (pooled "within" variance of scores on the dependent measure). Although the F ratio is useful in applying inferential statistics, eta indicates *how strong* the relationship is. Eta measures the *explanatory power* of an independent variable. The statistical significance of the F ratio depends on the number of subjects, but eta is independent of the number of subjects. If a large number of subjects is involved in the study, it is possible for the F ratio to be "highly significant," but when the F ratio is converted to eta it might be found that only a small portion of the variance of the dependent measure is explained by the independent measure. Whereas it is important to employ inferential statistics, it also is important to determine the strength of relationships, which can be done with eta. (When eta is employed with analysis of variance designs, "degrees of freedom" rather than numbers of subjects are used to compute sources of variance. In that case the measure is called "epsilon" rather than "eta," but the numerical values of the two measures usually are much the same. For the computation of epsilon in analysis of variance, see Peters and Van Voorhis, 1940.)

The PM coefficient can be thought of as a special case of eta. When both variables are continuous and the RE is computed with respect to the best-fitting straight line, eta reduces to the PM coefficient. What has been intended in this section is to show that the logic behind the PM coefficient is very general. The concept of relative error can be used to measure the degree of relationship regardless of whether or not (1) the investigation is of correlations among sets of individual differences or concerned with the effects of experimental treatments, (2) the relationship is linear or of some other form, (3) the form of the relationship is hypothesized before the study is undertaken or sought after the data are in hand, and (4) the independent variables are in the form of ratio scales, interval scales, ordinal scales, or only categories.

SUGGESTED ADDITIONAL READINGS

Guilford, J. P. *Fundamental statistics in psychology and education.* New York: McGraw-Hill, 1965, chaps. 5, 6, 14.

McNemar, Q. *Psychological statistics.* New York: Wiley, 1962, chaps. 8, 12.

internal structure of measures

CHAPTER FIVE

MULTIVARIATE CORRELATIONAL ANALYSIS

As was mentioned in the previous chapter, one of the benefits of working with PM correlation formulas is that they are easily extended to problems of multivariate analysis. Multivariate analysis is possible with nonlinear counterparts (eta) of the PM coefficient, but such methods are difficult to derive and very tedious to apply. Probably for some time to come most forms of multivariate analysis will be outgrowths of linear PM correlation. As was stated previously, even in cases where relations are not strictly linear, linear measures often do a satisfactory job of describing the trends. Also, if a variable typically has monotonic, but nonlinear, relations with other variables, it can be rescaled to achieve relations more nearly linear. As some have suggested, until the *data* in psychology are better than they are, it would be unwise to abandon linear methods of multivariate analysis for more cumbersome methods that take account of nonlinear relations.

Multivariate analysis will be treated more extensively in Chapters Nine to Eleven. In this chapter it will be necessary to discuss some of the foundations of multivariate analysis to make meaningful the material in Chapters Six to Eight. Also to be discussed in this chapter are the variance of linear combinations (sums) of variables, characteristics of score distributions, the correlation of sums, multiple correlation, and partial correlation.

variance of linear combinations

Usually distributions of scores being studied are obtained by summing other distributions of scores. In the simplest case, the total scores on a test are obtained by summing item scores. Then the total-score distribution is a linear combination, or sum, of the dichotomous distributions of item scores. As another example, an attitude scale might consist of 20 statements, half of them favorable toward the United Nations and half unfavorable. Each statement would be rated on a seven-step scale of agreement-disagreement. A total scale score could be obtained by adding all the ratings of positive statements and subtracting ratings of negative statements. The total score would then be a linear combination of the item scores. As another example, if standard scores on three tests are added (with or without weights) for assigning grades in introductory psychology, the total distribution is a linear combination of the three distributions of test scores.

There are some very important relations between the characteristics of score distributions and linear combinations of such distributions. Once these are thoroughly understood, more complex methods of multivariate analysis are easily developed. A simple linear combination (y) of three variables is as follows:

$$(5\text{-}1) \qquad y = x_1 + x_2 + x_3$$

Because the results from most multivariate analyses are the same regardless of whether one starts with raw scores or deviation scores, it will be more convenient to develop methods from equations employing deviation scores, like that above. In Eq. (5-1), each person's score on y is obtained by summing his score on the three x measures. It should be obvious that the mean of y is zero—y is in deviation-score form. A typical nonlinear measure would be one in which some of the x variables are multiplicatively combined, as follows:

$$y = x_1 + x_2 + x_3 + x_1 x_2 + x_1 x_3 + x_2 x_3$$

A very useful principle in studying linear combinations of variables is that many of the mathematical properties of linear combinations can be learned by substituting the linear combination in the equations that hold for individual distributions. Thus the variance of the previously given linear combination is obtained as follows:

$$(5\text{-}2) \qquad \begin{aligned} \sigma_y{}^2 &= \frac{\Sigma y^2}{N} \\ &= \frac{\Sigma (x_1 + x_2 + x_3)^2}{N} \\ &= \frac{1}{N} \Sigma (x_1{}^2 + x_2{}^2 + x_3{}^2 + 2x_1 x_2 + 2x_1 x_3 + 2x_2 x_3) \\ &= \sigma_1{}^2 + \sigma_2{}^2 + \sigma_3{}^2 + 2\sigma_{12} + 2\sigma_{13} + 2\sigma_{23} \end{aligned}$$

In the general case, the variance of any sum of variables $\sigma_\Sigma{}^2$ is obtained as follows:

$$(5\text{-}3) \qquad \sigma_\Sigma{}^2 = \Sigma \sigma_i{}^2 + 2\Sigma \sigma_{ij}, \qquad i \neq j$$

The variance of a sum of variables equals the sum of the variances of the variables plus twice the sum of all possible covariances among variables.

There is a very useful method for depicting the variance of a linear combination, one that will make it easier to understand more complex matters regarding multivariate analysis. One way to expand the terms in the variance of a linear combination is as follows. First, the terms in the linear combination are placed along the top and side of a rectangular table, as follows:

	x_1	x_2	x_3
x_1			
x_2			
x_3			

Corresponding elements are multiplied as follows:

	x_1	x_2	x_3
x_1	x_1^2	$x_1 x_2$	$x_1 x_3$
x_2	$x_1 x_2$	x_2^2	$x_2 x_3$
x_3	$x_1 x_3$	$x_2 x_3$	x_3^2

To obtain the elements in the variance of a linear combination of the three variables above [Eq. (5-3)], a summation sign is placed in front of each of the nine elements in the table above, and each resulting sum is divided by the number of persons in the study N. This results in the following table:

	x_1	x_2	x_3
x_1	σ_1^2	σ_{12}	σ_{13}
x_2	σ_{12}	σ_2^2	σ_{23}
x_3	σ_{13}	σ_{23}	σ_3^2

A look back at Eq. (5-2) will show that the above table contains all the elements in the variance of a sum of three variables. The sum of the elements in the table is then the variance of the sum of the variables (y). Any rectangular table of variables such as the one above is called a *matrix*. The matrix above is called a *covariance matrix*. Going down from left to right, the diagonal elements of the matrix are the covariances of the variables with themselves, which are the variances of the variables. Off of the diagonal are the covariances of the variables with one another. All possible covariances (three in this instance) are shown above the diagonal and again below the diagonal. What has been shown is that the variance of the linear combination of k variables is equal to the sum of all the elements in the covariance matrix for those k variables.

A covariance matrix will be symbolized as C. Later, subscripts will be used to distinguish different covariance matrices in particular problems. The symbol $\bar{C}$ will be used to symbolize "the sum of all the elements in the covariance matrix C." Then the variance of a sum of variables is $\bar{C}$.

VARIANCE OF A WEIGHTED SUM   Often weights are applied to each variable before they are summed, as follows:

$$y = b_1x_1 + b_2x_2 + b_3x_3$$

Such weights might be determined either on some a priori basis to give greater importance to some of the variables or a posteriori so as to maximize some characteristic of the variables. An example of the latter is in multiple regression, where weights are derived in such a way that the weighted sum will correlate as highly as possible with some variable not included in the sum. The variance of a weighted sum is obtained by an extension of the matrix approach for obtaining the variance of an unweighted sum. The only difference is that weights for the variables are shown with the variables on the top and side of the covariance matrix, as follows:

	b_1x_1	b_2x_2	b_3x_3
b_1x_1			
b_2x_2			
b_3x_3			

Corresponding elements are multiplied, summation signs are placed before each product, and each such sum is divided by N. Each element in the resulting matrix will be a covariance multiplied by the product of the two weights for the two variables. The resulting matrix is as follows:

	b_1x_1	b_2x_2	b_3x_3
b_1x_1	$b_1^2\sigma_1^2$	$b_1b_2\sigma_{12}$	$b_1b_3\sigma_{13}$
b_2x_2	$b_1b_2\sigma_{12}$	$b_2^2\sigma_2^2$	$b_2b_3\sigma_{23}$
b_3x_3	$b_1b_3\sigma_{13}$	$b_2b_3\sigma_{23}$	$b_3^2\sigma_3^2$

The variance of a weighted sum equals the sum of the elements in the weighted covariance matrix, as shown above. The variances of both weighted and unweighted sums will be said to equal $\bar{C}$. Where there is any likelihood of confusion in a particular instance, it will be stated whether or not weights are involved.

VARIANCE OF A SUM OF STANDARD SCORES   The simplest case is that in which the variables to be summed are each expressed as a standard score, as in the following linear combination:

$$y = z_1 + z_2 + z_3$$

In terms of the matrix arrangement for the calculation of the variance of a sum, it is easy to see what results. There are no weights, so no b terms appear in the matrix. The variance of any set of standard scores is 1; consequently 1s will appear in the diagonal spaces. Since the covariance of any two sets of standard scores is the PM correlation between them, r's will appear in the off-diagonal spaces. The result is a correlation matrix, illustrated as follows:

	z_1	z_2	z_3
z_1	1.00	r_{12}	r_{13}
z_2	r_{12}	1.00	r_{23}
z_3	r_{13}	r_{23}	1.00

Correlation matrices will be symbolized as R. The variance of the sum of k sets of standard scores equals the sum of all the elements in the correlation matrix of those sets of scores. That sum will be symbolized as $\bar{R}$. If variables expressed as standard scores are weighted before they are summed, products of the weights will appear in the correlation matrix in the same way as was shown for a covariance matrix.

VARIANCE OF SUMS OF DICHOTOMOUS DISTRIBUTIONS One of the most important cases for measurement theory is when the variance of a sum is obtained for k dichotomous variables, as when the total-score variance for k dichotomous items is studied. Where one response is scored 1 and the other zero, the matrix representation shows that the variance of total test scores for a three-item test would be as follows:

	x_1	x_2	x_3
x_1	$p_1 q_1$	σ_{12}	σ_{13}
x_2	σ_{12}	$p_2 q_2$	σ_{23}
x_3	σ_{13}	σ_{23}	$p_3 q_3$

The off-diagonal elements would be covariances. Since the variance of a dichotomous item scorable only as 1 and zero is pq, the diagonal is populated with pq values for the items. It will be remembered that the covariance between any two variables equals the PM correlation of the variables multiplied by the product of the standard deviations of the two variables. Consequently the covariance between any two items, say, between items 1 and 2, would be as follows:

(5-4) $\qquad \sigma_{12} = r_{12} \sqrt{(p_1 q_1)(p_2 q_2)}$

The correlation between the two items could be computed by the shortcut formula phi. Since pq grows smaller as p departs from .5 in either direction, the term under the radical will be relatively large when both p values are near .5 and relatively small when both p values are well removed from .5. These considerations will prove very important in discussing the variance of score distributions and in discussing test reliability.

The variance of the sum of k dichotomous items equals the sum of the elements in the covariance matrix for those items, which also will be symbolized as $\bar{C}$. (Only for the sum of the elements in a correlation matrix will the special symbol $\bar{R}$ be employed.) With dichotomous items, $\bar{C}$ equals the sum of pq values plus the sum of all off-diagonal covariances in the matrix.

characteristics of score distributions

The principles described in the previous section, plus some other principles that will be described in this section, will permit the development of numerous other useful principles concerning the mean, variance, and shape of distributions of test scores. The principles will be developed with respect to test scores obtained by summing scores on dichotomous items, but these principles also hold when items are scorable on more than two points.

THE MEAN   The mean of the scores on any test composed of dichotomous items can be developed as follows:

$$M_y = \frac{\Sigma y}{N}$$

where $y = x_1 + x_2 + \cdots + x_k$
The distribution of scores on the total test y is a linear combination of scores on the dichotomous items. The mean of y can be expressed in terms of the item scores as follows:

$$M_y = \frac{\Sigma(x_1 + x_2 + \cdots + x_k)}{N}$$
$$= \frac{\Sigma x_1}{N} + \frac{\Sigma x_2}{N} + \cdots + \frac{\Sigma x_k}{N}$$

Since the sum of the scores on any item is simply the number of persons who pass the item and since the number passing the item divided by the total number of persons N is p, the mean of y can be expressed as

(5-5)
$$M_y = p_1 + p_2 + \cdots + p_k$$
$$= \Sigma p_i$$

The mean equals the sum of the p values. This holds not only for pass-fail items, but also for any type of dichotomous item. It would be the case, for example, on an attitude scale containing dichotomous, agree-disagree items. Agreement with positive statements would be scored 1, and *disagreement* with *negative* statements would be scored 1. Other responses would be scored zero. The p value of each positive item would equal the number of persons agreeing divided by the number of persons in the study; the p value of each negative item would equal the number of persons disagreeing divided by the total number of persons. The mean score on the total scale would then equal the sum of the p values.

VARIANCES   Since the variance of a sum equals the sum of the variances plus twice the sum of the covariances, the variance of any set of test scores is dependent on these two factors. Where the sum of the covariances is zero, the variance of total scores will equal the sum of the item variances. If the items are scored only as 1 or zero (which will be assumed to be the case throughout this section), the variance of test scores will equal the sum of pq values. The sum of covariances will be zero if all correlations between items are zero or if there is a balance of negative and positive covariances among items.

An interesting case is that where the sum of covariances among items is zero and all items have the same p value. In this case the sum of pq would reduce to $k(pq)$, with k standing for the number of items. Thus on a 10-item test, if all items had a p value of .5, the variance of total scores would be 2.5; if all items had a p value of .2 (or .8), the variance of total scores would be 1.6.

In the special case where the sum of the covariance terms is zero and all items have the same p value, the variance of total test scores is the same as that of the *binomial distribution*. An example of the binomial distribution is presented in Figure 5-1, which shows the expected number of heads obtained when 10 pennies are tossed 1,024 times. The variance of that distribution is precisely $k(pq)$, where k is 10 and p is .5. This tie-in with the binomial distribution permits the development of some very useful principles concerning the properties of score distributions. In the coin toss example, each coin is analogous to a dichotomous test item. A head can be thought of as passing, receiving a score of 1, and a tail can be thought of as failing, receiving a score of zero. A toss of 10 coins is analogous to the performance of one person on a test, the number of heads being the person's score.

Several principles should be clear from the foregoing discussion. First, the variance of score distributions tends to be less as the p values of the items are removed from .5. This is so even if the *average* p value is .5 but the individual p values vary widely about that point.

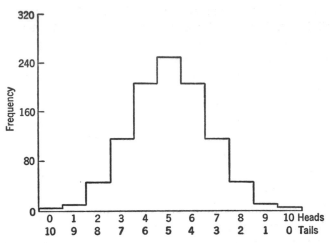

figure 5-1 *Graph of expected occurrences of heads and tails for 10 coins tossed 1,024 times.*

Second, the average size of correlations (and thus covariances) among items is directly related to the variance of total scores. High positive correlations among items make for a large variance among test scores, and vice versa for low correlations.

DISTRIBUTION SHAPE   The shape of the test-score distribution is determined by the p values, the covariances among items, and the number of items. As the number of items increases, the distribution becomes less and less jagged and more like a smooth curve. The binomial distribution in Figure 5-1 is a series of discrete steps rather than a smooth curve, and the same would be true of scores on a 10-item test. The binomial distribution approaches the smooth normal distribution as the number of coins is increased, and a similar smoothing of the curve comes as the number of test items is increased.

Strictly speaking, test scores are seldom normally distributed, even if the number of items is very large. Because of the positive correlations among items, a normal distribution would not be obtained. In a coin toss experiment the "items" are expected to be uncorrelated: the probability of one coin turning up heads would be independent of (uncorrelated with) what occurred for the other coins. But it certainly is not expected that the items on psychological measures will be uncorrelated. If they are, they have nothing in common; there is no central "theme," or factor, in their content. If items are uncorrelated, they all measure different things. Then it would not be sensible to give the total score a name or to assume that the total score measures any trait, or even to add scores on the items to obtain a total score.

Most measures of psychological attributes are obtained by adding scores over a collection of responses, of which test items are a special example. The principle applies equally well in studies of the learning rate in rats where the total error score is obtained by adding the number of errors at different points in a maze. Reflection will indicate that most measures are compounded of "items." Seldom is a trait measured by only one response.

A precisely normal distribution of test scores, or a binomial distribution, usually would represent *dead data*. Because the items must correlate positively with one another for the measurement method to make any sense, the variance of total scores usually would be larger than that obtained from a binomial distribution. The correlations also serve to flatten the distribution of test scores over that expected in a normal distribution, which is illustrated in Figure 5-2. When the average correla-

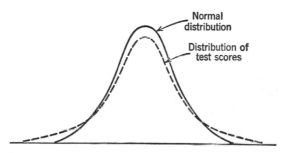

figure 5-2 *Comparison of a normal distribution with a distribution of test scores.*

tion among items is small, as is typically the case, the flattening will be slight. Average correlations as high as .40 would tend to produce a distribution that was markedly flatter than the normal distribution. Further increases in the size of correlations would tend to produce a bimodal distribution. In the limiting case where all correlations among items were 1.00, a person who passed one item would pass all items, and vice versa for a person who failed one item. In that case the total test scores would be distributed over only two points. (In the above cases the shapes of distributions would depend both on the correlations among items and on the p values, but the rules above are approximately correct for widely different sets of p values.)

Whether a distribution is symmetrical or skewed (lopsided) mainly depends on the average p value and the number of items. The influence of p values can be illustrated with a 10-item test in which all p values are .1 (only 10 percent of the subjects pass each item). Since the mean equals kp, in this case the mean is 1.0. Then there is practically no room for scores to occur below the mean but considerable room for scores to occur above it. A typical distribution for this case is shown in Figure 5-3. The nearer p values are to .5, the more symmetrical distributions tend to be. Whenever the average p value departs from .5, there is a tendency for the distribution to be skewed.

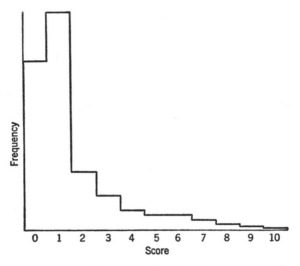

figure 5-3 *A skewed distribution of test scores where the p value of each item is .1.*

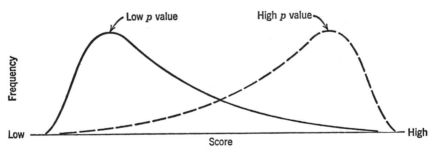

figure 5-4 *Skewed distributions of scores when the average p value is high and when the average p value is low.*

Average p values below .5 tend to produce distributions that are skewed toward the high end of the scale (said to be "skewed to the right") and the opposite occurs for average p values above .5. Typical distributions for these cases are shown in Figure 5-4.

    In cases where the p values of items have not been determined, one can simply look at the shape of a score distribution and tell if

internal structure of measures

the average p value is far removed from .5. Thus if the distribution of total scores is markedly skewed to the right, the average item must be rather difficult, and vice versa if the skew is to the left.

If a distribution is skewed with a particular number of items, a very important principle is that the skewness tends to *decrease* as the *number of items* is *increased*. This occurs regardless of the average p value of items. Previously it was shown that a very nonsymmetrical distribution would be obtained for a 10-item test whose items all had p values of .1. If the number of items were increased to 100, the distribution would tend to be more symmetrical. For 1,000 items the distribution would not be skewed in a way that could be seen. In the limiting case where a hypothetical infinity of items was involved, all distributions would be perfectly symmetrical regardless of the p values of the items. The reason this is so is that, even if the average p value is extreme in one direction or the other, with a large number of items there is still ample room for scores to spread out above and below the mean.

The analogy of the coin toss experiment with results from psychological measures provides other ways of visualizing how the symmetry of distributions is determined by p values and numbers of items. For this purpose, it will be useful to think of a coin toss experiment in which 10 biased coins are used. For each coin, the probability of a head is .2, and thus the probability of a tail is .8. The average number of heads for many tosses of the 10 coins would be 2.0. The distribution would be skewed to the right; i.e., the tail of the distribution would be stretched out over the higher numbers of heads. With only 10 coins on each toss, the skewness of the distribution would be marked. As the number of coins on each toss was increased above 10, the skewness would become less and less. In the hypothetical limiting case of an infinite number of such biased coins, the distribution would be precisely normal. It must be firmly kept in mind that the relative symmetry of the distribution is related to the number of test items or the number of coins. It is not systematically related to the number of *people* taking a test or the number of times the collection of coins is tossed.

covariance of linear combinations

In the previous section it was shown that by "looking inside" the variance of a linear combination, one can generate some useful principles regarding the characteristics of score distributions. In this section will be discussed some principles concerning the covariance between linear combinations of variables. The principles will be illustrated with two linear combinations, each having three variables, but the principles hold regardless of the number of variables in each combination. Following are two linear combinations.

$$y = x_1 + x_2 + x_3$$
$$w = x_4 + x_5 + x_6$$

The x's could be dichotomous items, items scorable on more than two points, or total scores on tests. In the previous section it was shown that the variance of y equals the sum of all the elements in the covariance matrix for the variables entering into the linear combination. This sum will be symbolized as $\bar{C}_y$. Similarly, the variance of w would equal $\bar{C}_w$. The covariance of the two linear combinations would be obtained as follows:

(5-6)

$$\sigma_{wy} = \frac{\Sigma wy}{N}$$

$$= \frac{1}{N}\Sigma(x_1 + x_2 + x_3)(x_4 + x_5 + x_6)$$

$$= \sigma_{14} + \sigma_{15} + \sigma_{16} + \sigma_{24} + \sigma_{25} + \sigma_{26} + \sigma_{34} + \sigma_{35} + \sigma_{36}$$

The covariance of y and w equals the sum of all covariances *between* members of the two linear combinations. Note that none of the variances is involved and none of the covariances of members *within* each of the two linear combinations is involved. Just as it was useful to display the variance of a linear combination in terms of a matrix of variance and covariance terms, it also is useful to display the covariance of two linear combinations in matrix form. This is done by placing the variables in one linear combination on the top of the matrix and the variables in the other linear combination on the side, as follows:

	x_4	x_5	x_6
x_1			
x_2			
x_3			

Corresponding terms are multiplied, summed over people, and divided by the number of people. The resulting matrix contains all covariances *between* the two sets of variables, as follows:

	x_4	x_5	x_6
x_1	σ_{14}	σ_{15}	σ_{16}
x_2	σ_{24}	σ_{25}	σ_{26}
x_3	σ_{34}	σ_{35}	σ_{36}

The sum of the elements in the above matrix is equal to the covariance of w and y. It will be useful to speak of such a matrix as

internal structure of measures

		y set			w set		
		x_1	x_2	x_3	x_4	x_5	x_6
y set	x_1	σ_1^2	σ_{12}	σ_{13}	σ_{14}	σ_{15}	σ_{16}
	x_2	σ_{12}	σ_2^2	σ_{23}	σ_{24}	σ_{25}	σ_{26}
	x_3	σ_{13}	σ_{23}	σ_3^2	σ_{34}	σ_{35}	σ_{36}
w set	x_4	σ_{14}	σ_{24}	σ_{34}	σ_4^2	σ_{45}	σ_{46}
	x_5	σ_{15}	σ_{25}	σ_{35}	σ_{45}	σ_5^2	σ_{56}
	x_6	σ_{16}	σ_{26}	σ_{36}	σ_{46}	σ_{56}	σ_6^2

a matrix of "between" covariances to distinguish it from the matrix
of "within" covariances involved in the variance of a linear combination.
A between matrix will be symbolized as C_{wy}, with different sets of double
subscripts used where necessary to indicate which linear combinations
are involved. The covariance of two linear combinations then is equal
to $\bar{C}_{wy}$.

If weights were applied to the terms in each linear combination
before they were summed, the weights would appear on the top and
side of the matrix and would be appropriately multiplied as follows:

	$b_4 x_4$	$b_5 x_5$	$b_6 x_6$
$b_1 x_1$	$b_1 b_4 \sigma_{14}$	$b_1 b_5 \sigma_{15}$	$b_1 b_6 \sigma_{16}$
$b_2 x_2$	$b_2 b_4 \sigma_{24}$	$b_2 b_5 \sigma_{25}$	$b_2 b_6 \sigma_{26}$
$b_3 x_3$	$b_3 b_4 \sigma_{34}$	$b_3 b_5 \sigma_{35}$	$b_3 b_6 \sigma_{36}$

In the study of the variance and covariance of linear combinations,
it is helpful to think in terms of the total matrix of covariances, which
is illustrated in Table 5-1 for two linear combinations with three variables
in each. Lines are drawn in the table to show elements respectively
concerning the variance of y, the variance of w, and the covariance
of y and w. These can be symbolized as follows:

	y	w
y	C_y	C_{wy}
w	C_{wy}	C_w

The variances of the two linear combinations, and the covariance between
them, can be obtained by summing the elements in the appropriate
sections of the matrix. If all variables were expressed as standard scores,

the appropriate sections of the correlation matrix would enter into these computations.

CORRELATION OF LINEAR COMBINATIONS The correlation of the two linear combinations w and y can be obtained as follows:

$$r_{wy} = \frac{\sigma_{wy}}{\sigma_w \sigma_y}$$

It should be obvious by this point that the correlation between two linear combinations of variables can be written in terms of the separate variables as follows:

(5-7) $$r_{wy} = \frac{\bar{C}_{wy}}{\sqrt{\bar{C}_w}\sqrt{\bar{C}_y}}$$

The numerator is the covariance of w and y expressed in terms of the elements of w and y. The denominator equals the product of the standard deviations of w and y expressed in terms of their respective elements. If all variables are standardized, the equation reduces to

(5-8) $$r_{wy} = \frac{\bar{R}_{wy}}{\sqrt{\bar{R}_w}\sqrt{\bar{R}_y}}$$

If variables were weighted, the elements of the covariance matrix or correlation matrix would be appropriately weighted.

Although the correlation of linear combinations has been illustrated in the situation where there is an equal number of variables in the two combinations, the formulas in this section are general to any case. Most important is the case where a linear combination of variables is correlated with a single variable, one that is not a linear combination of other variables. The elements relating to the correlation are schematized as follows:

	y	x_1	x_2	x_3	x_4
y	$\sigma_y{}^2$		C_{wy}		
$w \begin{cases} x_1 \\ x_2 \\ x_3 \\ x_4 \end{cases}$	C_{wy}		C_w		

In the above case, $\bar{C}_y$ reduces to $\sigma_y{}^2$, there being only one variable in the "linear combination." The sum of between covariances $\bar{C}_{wy}$ equals the sum of all the elements in the first row or first column of the matrix

internal structure of measures

excluding the diagonal term for y, $\sigma_y{}^2$. Then the correlation will be as follows:

(5-9) $\quad r_{wy} = \dfrac{\bar{C}_{wy}}{\sigma_y \sqrt{\bar{C}_w}}$

If all variables are expressed as standard scores, Eq. (5-9) reduces to

(5-10) $\quad r_{wy} = \dfrac{\bar{R}_{wy}}{\sqrt{\bar{R}_w}}$

In that case, since $\sigma_y = 1.0$, it will "fall out" of the denominator of Eq. (5-9).

The equations in this section hold equally well when the elements in linear combinations are dichotomous items. On the diagonals of the total covariance matrix would be pq values. The off-diagonal elements would consist of phi coefficients multiplied by the square root of the product of the two respective pq values. Equation (5-7) would give the correlation between total scores on two tests composed of dichotomous items. Equation (5-9) would, for example, give the correlation between one test item and the sum of scores on the remaining items of the test.

The principles developed so far in this chapter are the basis of linear, multivariate correlational analysis. Once they are thoroughly understood, it will be relatively easy to understand such extensions as multiple correlation, factor analysis, and discriminatory analysis.

partial correlation

The effort in science is to find a relatively small set of variables which will suffice to "explain" all other variables. A small set of variables "explains" a larger set if some combination of the smaller set correlates highly with each member of the larger set. For example, in the study of factors of human ability, it has been found that about six factors do a relatively good job of explaining most tests of human ability. When the six are combined in multiple-regression analysis, the combined scores correlate highly with most tests of human ability. To achieve such a small set of "explainer" variables is the essence of scientific parsimony.

Before a new variable is added to the set of "explainers," it should be demonstrated to actually add something to the existing "explainers." In this connection, the concept of "partialing" is very important. An example would be in the development of a new measure of anxiety.

After the test is developed, scores are correlated with speed of solving simple problems in arithmetic, and a positive correlation is found. This is taken as evidence that the measure of anxiety is a useful "explainer" of speed of solving simple problems. Later it is found that both measures correlate positively with scores on an intelligence test. Since IQ has proved to be an important "explainer," it must be determined if the new measure of anxiety *adds* something to the prediction of problem solving. For this purpose, scores on the intelligence test could be partialed from scores on the other two measures. If the partialed scores on the anxiety test still correlate with partialed scores on the measure of problem solving, the measure of anxiety actually adds something to what could be explained by the intelligence test alone; but if not, there is no evidence from the study to demonstrate that the anxiety test is an important new "explainer."

A partialed score is simply the error score when the PM correlation is used to estimate one variable from another. Using the example above, the partialed score for the anxiety test would be as follows:

(5-11) $$z_{1-3} = z_1 - r_{13}z_3$$

where $z_1 = $ standard scores on anxiety test

$z_3 = $ standard scores on intelligence test

$r_{13} = $ PM correlation between 1 and 3

$z_{1-3} = $ partialed score on anxiety test after variance explainable by intelligence test is removed

Similarly, the partialed score for the problem-solving test, holding intelligence constant, would be

$$z_{2-3} = z_2 - r_{23}z_3$$

where $z_2 = $ scores in problem solving

It will be remembered that partialed scores correlate precisely zero with the variable used for the estimation (z_3 in this case). Consequently any correlation between z_{1-3} and z_{2-3} is independent of scores on the intelligence test. Such a correlation is called a *partial correlation,* symbolized as $r_{12.3}$. The formula is developed as follows. The correlation between any two variables can be stated as

(5-12) $$r_{xy} = \frac{\sigma_{xy}}{\sigma_x \sigma_y}$$

For partial correlation the symbols are

(5-13) $$r_{12.3} = \frac{\sigma_{(1-3)(2-3)}}{\sigma_{1-3}\sigma_{2-3}}$$

The denominator is the product of the standard deviations of the two sets of partialed scores. Previously it was shown that the variance of any set of partialed scores is 1 minus the squared correlation between the two variables. Thus the equation can be transformed to

$$(5\text{-}14) \qquad r_{12.3} = \frac{\sigma_{(1-3)(2-3)}}{\sqrt{1 - r_{13}^2} \; \sqrt{1 - r_{23}^2}}$$

In the numerator, the covariance equals the sum of cross products of the two sets of partialed scores divided by N. The numerator can be expanded as follows:

$$\sigma_{(1-3)(2-3)} = \frac{1}{N} \Sigma(z_1 - r_{13}z_3)(z_2 - r_{23}z_3)$$

$$= \frac{1}{N} \Sigma(z_1 z_2 - r_{23}z_1 z_3 - r_{13}z_2 z_3 + r_{13}r_{23}z_3^2)$$

$$= r_{12} - r_{23}r_{13} - r_{13}r_{23} + r_{13}r_{23}$$

$$= r_{12} - r_{13}r_{23}$$

Reassembling numerator and denominator gives the following formula for the partial correlation:

$$(5\text{-}15) \qquad r_{12.3} = \frac{r_{12} - r_{13}r_{23}}{\sqrt{1 - r_{13}^2} \; \sqrt{1 - r_{23}^2}}$$

It will be important to remember that the numerator in Eq. (5-15) is the covariance of two sets of partialed scores and the denominator is the product of the standard deviations of two sets of partialed scores.

A number of points should be understood about partial correlation. First, partial correlation is the correlation expected between two variables when a third variable is held constant. Thus in the example above, if subjects who all had the *same* intelligence test score had been selected, the raw correlation between anxiety and problem solving would be expected to equal the partial correlation obtained when intelligence was allowed to vary. Unless there were homoscedastic relations between intelligence and the other two variables, however, the exact correlation between anxiety and problem solving for all subjects at the same level of intelligence would depend somewhat on *which* level of intelligence. For example, the partial-correlation coefficient might underestimate the raw correlation between anxiety and problem solving if all subjects had high intelligence and overestimate for subjects who were average in intelligence; but in practice, the partial correlation is usually a good estimate of the correlation found between two variables when a third variable is actually held constant.

The second important point is that the size of the partial correlation depends on the signs of the three correlations involved. If r_{12} is positive,

$r_{12.3}$ usually is *smaller* than r_{12} when r_{13} and r_{23} have the same sign, regardless of whether the sign is positive or negative. It usually is larger than r_{12} when the signs for the other two correlations are different. The reverse usually is true in both instances when r_{12} is negative. The word "usually" is an essential part of the foregoing three rules, because there are instances in which the rules are incorrect. This occurs, for example, in computing $r_{12.3}$ when $r_{12} = .30$, $r_{13} = .10$, and $r_{23} = .80$. In this instance $r_{12.3}$ is .37, which is larger than r_{12} rather than smaller as would be predicted from the first rule given above.

A third important point is that the amount of change frequently expected in partialing a third variable is an overestimate. For example, when anxiety and problem solving correlate .60 and each variable correlates .40 with intelligence, it might be thought that partialing intelligence will markedly reduce the correlation of .60. In fact, what occurs is as follows:

$$r_{12.3} = \frac{r_{12} - r_{13}r_{23}}{\sqrt{1 - r_{13}^2}\ \sqrt{1 - r_{23}^2}}$$

$$= \frac{.6 - (.4 \times .4)}{\sqrt{1 - .16}\ \sqrt{1 - .16}}$$

$$= \frac{.6 - .16}{.84}$$

$$= \frac{.44}{.84}$$

$$r_{12.3} = .52$$

The partial correlation is only eight points less than the raw correlation, which would not matter a great deal. Sometimes partial correlations differ markedly from raw correlations, but that tends to be the exception rather than the rule.

A fourth important point is that the variable which is partialed from the relationship between two other variables may itself be a linear combination of other variables. Thus if y is a linear combination of variables x_1 through x_5, there is nothing wrong with partialing y from variables x_6 and x_7. Saying it another way, there is nothing to prevent partialing the variance of a linear combination of variables from the correlation between two particular variables. This point will prove important in the discussion of factor analysis, which consists essentially of successively partialing linear combinations of variables from the correlations among the variables.

SEMIPARTIAL CORRELATION   In partial correlation, variable 3 is held constant in *both* variables 1 and 2. A possibility not previously mentioned is to hold variable 3 constant in one of the other two variables but not in both of them. In the previous example, scores on the Intelligence test could have been partialed from the anxiety test only, and not partialed from scores in problem solving. This could be justified on the grounds that intelligence is a "natural" part of problem solving and therefore the variance because of intelligence should be left in the latter variable. Then the task would be to determine the correlation of problem solving with the anxiety test after intelligence is partialed from anxiety scores but not from problem solving. This could be done with the *semipartial*-correlation coefficient, which is very similar to the partial correlation. If problem solving is variable 1, anxiety is variable 2, and intelligence is variable 3, the problem is to correlate z_1 with z_{2-3}. These scores can be placed in the regular PM formula, and after terms are expanded in a manner similar to that done previously in developing the formula for the partial correlation, the following formula is developed for the semipartial correlation $r_{1(2.3)}$:

$$(5\text{-}16) \qquad r_{1(2.3)} = \frac{r_{12} - r_{13}r_{23}}{\sqrt{1 - r_{23}^2}}$$

The only difference between Eq. (5-15) and Eq. (5-16) is that in the latter the denominator contains the standard deviation of partialed scores for variable 2 but not for variable 1. Since the standard deviations of partialed scores are almost always less than 1, the semipartial correlation is almost always less than the partial correlation. This is to be expected, since with semipartial correlation a systematic source of variance is removed from one variable but left in the other variable, which reduces the extent to which the variables can correlate either positively or negatively.

In most practical problems, it makes more sense to employ the partial correlation than to employ the semipartial correlation. Where semipartial correlation proves important is in the development of methods of multivariate analysis such as multiple correlation and factor analysis. Some of these uses will be shown later in this chapter in the section on multiple correlation. What is referred to here as the "semipartial correlation" is called the "part correlation" by some authors.

A GENERAL APPROACH TO PARTIALING   Whereas the partial-correlation coefficient has been developed above for only three variables, there is available a more general approach, which will not only facilitate computations but provide the basis for some other methods of multivariate analysis. Steps in the method are shown in Table 5-2. The more general approach starts with a matrix of correlations, the number of variables being irrelevant. Starting with such a matrix, it is possible to first partial the variance of variable 1 from the relations between the remaining variables, then partial variable 2, and so on, as far as one wants to go. The first step in partialing variable 1 is to take the correlations from the first row of the correlation matrix and place them at the top and side of an empty matrix. Appropriate correlations are then multiplied as indicated in Table 5-2. Element by element this matrix of products is then subtracted from the original matrix of correlations. This is spoken of as a matrix of residual coefficients; more specifically, in this case, the *first residual matrix*. A careful inspection of this matrix will show that (1) the diagonal elements are partial variances, where variable 1 is partialed from the other variables, and (2) the off-diagonal elements are partial covariances for that case. Thus to obtain the partial correlation between any two variables, variable 1 being partialed, all that is required is to divide the element in the residual matrix corresponding to the intersection of the two variables by the product of the square roots of the diagonal elements for the two variables. For example, when variable 1 is to be partialed from variables 2 and 3, the partial correlation for the latter two variables will be:

$$(5\text{-}17) \qquad r_{23.1} = \frac{r_{23} - r_{12}r_{13}}{\sqrt{1 - r_{12}^2}\,\sqrt{1 - r_{13}^2}}$$

Note that the numerator is the term appearing at the intersection of variables 2 and 3 in the first residual matrix, and the denominator consists of the product of square roots of the diagonal elements for 2 and 3. The whole residual matrix can be converted to a matrix of partial correlations, variable 1 being partialed, by dividing all the elements in each row of the residual matrix by the square root of the diagonal element in that row and then dividing each element in each column of the matrix by the square root of the diagonal element in that column. The result is illustrated in Table 5-2.

In the matrix of first-order partial correlations in Table 5-2, the column and row corresponding to variable 1 are filled with zeros. This is to be expected, because when variable 1 is partialed from variable 1, there are no scores left to correlate with other scores. Since the matrix of first-order partial correlations shows the correlations between variables when the variance because of variable 1 is removed, one can then proceed to partial another variable from the remaining ones. This can be done by employing the first-order partial correlations from Table 5-2 in the formula for the partial correlation. For example, if after variable 1 is partialed, it is desired to partial variable 2 from the correlation between variables 3 and 4, the formula would be as follows:

$$(5\text{-}18) \qquad r_{34.12} = \frac{r_{34.1} - r_{23.1}r_{24.1}}{\sqrt{1 - r_{23.1}^2}\,\sqrt{1 - r_{24.1}^2}}$$

CORRELATION MATRIX

	1	2	3	4
1	1.00	r_{12}	r_{13}	r_{14}
2	r_{12}	1.00	r_{23}	r_{24}
3	r_{13}	r_{23}	1.00	r_{34}
4	r_{14}	r_{24}	r_{34}	1.00

FIRST MATRIX OF PRODUCTS

		1	2	3	4
		1.00	r_{12}	r_{13}	r_{14}
		1.00	r_{12}	r_{13}	r_{14}
1	1.00	1.00	r_{12}	r_{13}	r_{14}
2	r_{12}	r_{12}	r_{12}^2	$r_{12}r_{13}$	$r_{12}r_{14}$
3	r_{13}	r_{13}	$r_{12}r_{13}$	r_{13}^2	$r_{13}r_{14}$
4	r_{14}	r_{14}	$r_{12}r_{14}$	$r_{13}r_{14}$	r_{14}^2

FIRST MATRIX OF RESIDUALS

	1	2	3	4
1	.00	.00	.00	.00
2	.00	$1.00 - r_{12}^2$	$r_{23} - r_{12}r_{13}$	$r_{24} - r_{12}r_{14}$
3	.00	$r_{23} - r_{12}r_{13}$	$1.00 - r_{13}^2$	$r_{34} - r_{13}r_{14}$
4	.00	$r_{24} - r_{12}r_{14}$	$r_{34} - r_{13}r_{14}$	$1.00 - r_{14}^2$

COMPUTATION OF PARTIAL CORRELATIONS

$$r_{23.1} = \frac{r_{23} - r_{12}r_{13}}{\sqrt{1 - r_{12}^2}\ \sqrt{1 - r_{13}^2}}$$

$$r_{24.1} = \frac{r_{24} - r_{12}r_{14}}{\sqrt{1 - r_{12}^2}\ \sqrt{1 - r_{14}^2}}$$

$$r_{34.1} = \frac{r_{34} - r_{13}r_{14}}{\sqrt{1 - r_{13}^2}\ \sqrt{1 - r_{14}^2}}$$

FIRST-ORDER PARTIAL CORRELATIONS

	1	2	3	4
1	.00	.00	.00	.00
2	.00	1.00	$r_{23.1}$	$r_{24.1}$
3	.00	$r_{23.1}$	1.00	$r_{24.1}$
4	.00	$r_{24.1}$	$r_{34.1}$	1.00

Note the similarity of Eqs. (5-18) and (5-17), the only difference being that in the former each coefficient is a partial correlation rather than a raw correlation. The raw correlations are called "zero-order coefficients"; when one variable is partialed, they are called "first-order partial correlations"; and so on for any order of partial correlation, depending on the number of variables appearing after the decimal point.

table 5-3 *A worked-out example of a general approach to the computation of partial correlations*

CORRELATION MATRIX

	1	2	3	4	5
1	1.00	.43	−.23	.45	.39
2	.43	1.00	−.34	.36	.09
3	−.23	−.34	1.00	−.23	.26
4	.45	.36	−.23	1.00	.32
5	.39	.09	.26	.32	1.00

FIRST PRODUCT MATRIX

		1	2	3	4	5
		1.00	.43	−.23	.45	.39
1	1.00	1.00	.43	−.23	.45	.39
2	.43	.43	.18	−.10	.19	.17
3	−.23	−.23	−.10	.05	−.10	−.09
4	.45	.45	.19	−.10	.20	.18
5	.39	.39	.17	−.09	.18	.15

FIRST RESIDUAL MATRIX

	1	2	3	4	5
1	0	0	0	0	0
2	0	.82	−.24	.17	−.08
3	0	−.24	.95	−.13	.35
4	0	.17	−.13	.80	.14
5	0	−.08	.35	.14	.85
square root of diagonal		.9055	.9747	.8944	.9220

The second-order partial correlations can be obtained in the same way that the first-order partial correlations were obtained. Partial correlations for variable 2 (variable 1 being previously partialed) are placed on the top and side of an empty table. Corresponding elements are multiplied to form a second matrix of cross products. This matrix of cross products is subtracted, element by element, from the table of first-order partial correlations. The square root of the diagonal element in each row is divided into each element in the row, and the same is done for each column. The result is a matrix of second-order partial correlations. By repeating this procedure, one can partial any number of variables from any other number of variables. Computational procedures for this method are illustrated in Table 5-3.

The procedure described above is very useful for "taking apart" relations among variables. The zero-order correlations show relationships

internal structure of measures

table 5-3 *A worked-out example of a general approach to the computation of partial correlations (Continued)*

FIRST-ORDER PARTIAL CORRELATIONS

	1	2	3	4	5
1	0	0	0	0	0
2	0	1.00	−.27	.21	−.10
3	0	−.27	1.00	−.15	.39
4	0	.21	−.15	1.00	.17
5	0	−.10	.39	.17	1.00

SECOND PRODUCT MATRIX

		1	2	3	4	5
		0	1.00	−.27	.21	−.10
1	0	0	0	0	0	0
2	1.00	0	1.00	−.27	.21	−.10
3	−.27	0	−.27	.07	−.06	.03
4	.21	0	.21	−.06	.04	−.02
5	−.10	0	−.10	.03	−.02	.01

SECOND RESIDUAL MATRIX

	1	2	3	4	5
1	0	0	0	0	0
2	0	0	0	0	0
3	0	0	.93	−.09	.36
4	0	0	−.09	.96	.19
5	0	0	.36	.19	.99
square root of diagonal			.9644	.9798	.9950

SECOND-ORDER PARTIAL CORRELATIONS

	1	2	3	4	5
1	0	0	0	0	0
2	0	0	0	0	0
3	0	0	1.00	−.10	.38
4	0	0	−.10	1.00	.20
5	0	0	.38	.20	1.00

among variables when none is held constant. First-order partial correlations show what remains when the influence of one variable is removed. One can remove any number of variables to see if there is any remaining correlation between two variables. For that purpose, the result is the same regardless of the order in which variables are partialed, e.g., $r_{12.345} = r_{12.543}$. Whereas previously it was shown that the first-order partial correlation frequently is not very different from the zero-order coefficient, the zero-order coefficient often is drastically altered when a number of variables are partialed.

multiple correlation

Previously it was stated that the problem in simple (zero-order) correlation is to find the line of best fit between two sets of standard scores. "Best fit" was defined in terms of the minimization of the sum of squared errors of estimation—the principle of least squares. The logic and method are easily extended to the problem of estimating a dependent variable from some combination of a number of independent variables. Let the dependent variable be designated z_y and the independent variable be designated $z_1, z_2, \ldots, z_k$. Let any combination of the independent variables which is used to estimate the dependent variable be designated z_y'. Although many different kinds of combinations of the independent variables could be used to estimate z_y, the kind used most frequently is a linear combination, as follows:

(5-19)
$$z_y' = \beta_1 z_1 + \beta_2 z_2 + \beta_3 z_3$$

where $z_y' = $ estimates of z_y

$z_1, z_2, z_3 = $ independent variables

$\beta_1, \beta_2, \beta_3 = $ weights for independent variables

The β's are called *beta weights,* and the problem is that of finding a set of beta weights such that

$$\Sigma(z_y - z_y')^2 = \text{a minimum}$$
$$\Sigma(z_y - \beta_1 z_1 - \beta_2 z_2 - \beta_3 z_3)^2 = \text{a minimum}$$

After the last expression is squared and summed, a solution for the beta weights can be sought through calculus. What is learned is that a unique set of beta weights is obtainable for any problem. The weights are found by the solution of a set of simultaneous equations. When only two independent variables are involved, the solution is very simple:

(5-20)
$$\beta_1 = \frac{r_{y1} - r_{y2}r_{12}}{1 - r_{12}^2}$$

$$\beta_2 = \frac{r_{y2} - r_{y1}r_{12}}{1 - r_{12}^2}$$

When more than two independent variables are involved, the computations are straightforward but complex. Computational routines for the general case are discussed in Guilford (1965) and in McNemar (1962).

Once the beta weights are computed, they are applied to the independent variables to obtain z_y', least-squares estimates of z_y. One could then correlate z_y' with z_y using the regular PM formula. This would be referred to as the *multiple correlation,* which would be symbolized as

internal structure of measures

$R_{y.12}$ for two independent variables and as $R_{y.1\cdots k}$ in the general case. Rather than actually compute z_y' and then calculate the correlation with z_y, one can obtain the multiple correlation directly from the zero-order correlations and beta weights as follows:

(5-21) $$R_{y.1\cdots k}^2 = \beta_1 r_{y1} + \beta_2 r_{y2} + \cdots + \beta_k r_{yk}$$

Since proof of Eq. (5-21) would take more space than could be justified in this book, the reader will have to take it on faith. (The proof is presented in McNemar, 1962.) If it is not necessary to obtain beta weights, the multiple correlation for two independent variables can be obtained as follows:

(5-22) $$R_{y.12}^2 = \frac{r_{y1}^2 + r_{y2}^2 - 2r_{y1}r_{y2}r_{12}}{1 - r_{12}^2}$$

A number of important principles should be understood about multiple correlation. First, R tends to be high when the independent variables have high correlations with the dependent variable. If all the independent variables correlate zero with the dependent variable, the multiple correlation must be zero also. If some of the independent variables have high correlations with the dependent variable, the multiple correlation will be high. Second, the multiple correlation cannot be less than the highest correlation of any one of the independent variables with the dependent variable. If, for example, one of the independent variables correlates .50 with the dependent variable, no matter what the other correlations are, R cannot be less than .50.

Third, R is larger when the independent variables have relatively *low* correlations among themselves. When correlations among independent variables are low, each *adds* something to the predictive power obtainable from the others. When correlations among independent variables are high, each is highly redundant of the others, and consequently they tend to add little predictive power to one another. When all correlations among independent variables are zero, the squared multiple correlation equals the sum of the squared correlations with the dependent variable. For example, if two independent variables correlated zero and each correlated .50 with the dependent variable, the squared multiple correlation would be .50 ($R = .71$). In that case, if the two independent variables correlated .50, R would be only .58. Further increases in the correlation between the independent variables would further reduce R. In the case of a perfect correlation between the two independent variables, R would be .50.

A fourth important principle is that the multiple correlation often produces results that would be hard to estimate when looking at the zero-order correlations. This is particularly so when there are numerous independent variables and a mixture of positive and negative correlations. An outstanding example is where a *suppressor variable* is present among the independent variables, as follows:

$$r_{y1} = .60$$

$$r_{y2} = .00$$

$$r_{12} = .50$$

$$\beta_1 = \frac{.6 - (.0 \times .5)}{1 - .5^2} = .8$$

$$\beta_2 = \frac{.0 - (.5 \times .6)}{1 - .5^2} = -.4$$

$$R^2 = (.8 \times .6) + (-.4 \times .0)$$

$$R = .69$$

Even though the second independent variable correlates zero with the dependent variable, when it is included in the multiple correlation with the first independent variable, the multiple correlation is substantially higher than the correlation between the first independent variable and the dependent variable. Even though variable 2 has a zero correlation with the dependent variable, the high correlation with variable 1 supplies important information. This correlation between the two independent variables necessarily concerns variance that is not related to the dependent variable. Consequently when this component of variance is subtracted from the first independent variable (note that the beta weight for variable 2 is negative), the predictive power of the first variable is increased. Actually, such suppressor variables are rarely found in practice, but when found, they serve to illustrate the distinct surprises that sometimes come from multiple correlation.

A fifth important principle is that in practice the multiple correlation usually does not increase dramatically as the number of independent variables is made larger and larger. For example, where 10 tests are being investigated for their ability to predict performance in college, a typical finding is that (1) one of the tests has a moderately high correlation with the criterion, (2) when that test is combined with another test that also has a high correlation with the criterion, the multiple correlation is considerably higher than any of the zero-order correlations, (3) adding a third test provides a small increment to the multiple correlation, and (4) beyond that, adding additional tests produces only small increases in the multiple correlation. There is no necessary reason why adding tests beyond three, four, or five does not continue to produce substantial increases in multiple correlation. It typically does not continue to increase because of the redundancy among the independent variables, as manifested in the correlations among them. After a point, the redundancy begins to catch up with the possible information that can be obtained from adding more and more independent variables to the prediction equation. Of course, there is always the hope and possibility of finding a new independent variable that will be less redundant of existing variables and will considerably increase the multiple correlation.

A sixth important principle is that the multiple correlation tends to be systematically biased "upward"; that is, it tends to be larger than the population parameter. The major reason for the bias in most studies is that there is a preselection of independent variables from a larger set. This would be the case, for example, if 10 tests were correlated with a criterion and then the 3 tests having the highest correlation with the criterion were placed in the multiple-correlation formula. Preselecting in this way would be "taking advantage of chance." Some of the variables preselected would have relatively high correlations with the criterion because of sampling error, and consequently their correlations would tend to be lower in another sample. Even more advantage is taken of chance when numerous combinations of variables are placed in the formula for multiple correlation. For example, if there are 10 independent variables, many different sets of 3 each could be placed in the formula, many different sets of 4 variables each could be tried, and so on for sets of different sizes. Then advantage is taken of chance not only in terms of the correlations with the criterion, but also in terms of the many different patterns of correlations among independent variables.

The extent to which it is possible to take advantage of chance depends inversely on the number of persons being studied and directly on the size of the total collection of variables from which a smaller set is to be selected. For example, if there are only 100 persons in the sample and a set of 3 variables is to be selected from a total group of 20, the multiple correlation will be so spuriously high as to be worthless. In contrast, if 1,000 persons are sampled and 3 variables are to be selected from a total of 6, the multiple correlation will be only slightly biased upward. Whereas in the former case the multiple correlation might be as much as 40 points higher than the population value, in the latter it might be only several points higher.

Even when there is no preselecting among independent variables, the multiple correlation is still biased upward. This would be the case, for example, when only three tests were being tried as predictors of a criterion and all three were placed in the formula for multiple correlation. There would be no possibility of taking advantage of chance through preselection, but advantage would be taken of chance in another way. Whenever a set of weights is chosen to minimize or maximize some function, there is an opportunity to take advantage of chance. This is the case with the beta weights in multiple correlation. They are selected in such a way as to wring the last ounce of predictive power out of a set of variables. In so doing they will capitalize on sampling error among correlations. The test that "happens" to have a high correlation because of sampling error will receive a large beta weight, and a test which "happens" to have a relatively small correlation will receive a small beta weight. Consequently the multiple correlation obtained in a relatively small sample of persons will tend to be smaller in a larger sample of persons. This tendency for the multiple correlation to decrease as the sample grows larger (even when no preselection occurs) is called *shrinkage*. The following formula can be used to estimate the shrinkage in going from a sample of any particular size to an infinitely large sample:

(5-23)
$$\hat{R}^2 = 1 - (1 - R^2)\left(\frac{N-1}{N-k}\right)$$

where $\hat{R}$ = unbiased estimate of population multiple correlation

R = multiple correlation found in sample of size N

k = number of independent variables

Equation (5-23) can be illustrated in the situation where a multiple correlation of .50 is found with 100 persons and 8 independent variables. The unbiased estimate of the population multiple correlation would be .44. From Eq. (5-23), one can see that the amount of bias is directly related to the number of independent variables divided by the number of persons sampled. When that ratio is a 100:1, the bias is insignificant. When it is 10:1, the bias is important. When the ratio is as high as 3:1, the multiple correlation in the sample is highly biased upward. When the number of independent variables is as large as the number of people, a perfect multiple correlation will always be found. In that case there would be complete opportunity to take advantage of chance. This result would hold even if the dependent variable consisted of social security numbers and the independent variables were drawn from tables of random numbers. When there are as many unknowns (here, beta weights) as persons in the study, the equations can be solved so as to obtain a perfect multiple correlation. Of course, the multiple correlation would not "hold up" when other samples were employed.

As is true of most other problems in psychological measurement, in dealing with multiple correlations nothing helps so much as to have a large sample of subjects. If there are only 2 or 3 independent variables and no preselection is made among them, 100 or more subjects will provide a multiple correlation with little bias. In that case, if the number of independent variables is as large as 9 or 10, it will be necessary to have from 300 to 400 subjects to prevent substantial bias. When there is no preselection among variables, the shrinkage formula can be used to obtain an unbiased estimate of the multiple correlation. But if, as usually happens, there is some preselection among variables, the shrinkage formula may not "shrink" as much as is needed. If there are as many as 10 variables from which the best several are to be selected, it will be wise to employ 500 or more persons in the study.

A GENERAL APPROACH TO MULTIPLE CORRELATION   Previously it was stated that if the independent variables correlate precisely zero with one another, the squared multiple correlation will be as follows:

(5-24) $R_{y.123}{}^2 = r_{y1}{}^2 + r_{y2}{}^2 + r_{y3}{}^2$

Of course, almost never will independent variables all correlate precisely zero with one another, and consequently methods are required to "untangle" the correlations among variables before the multiple correlation can be obtained. Equation (5-22) showed how the "untangling" is done when there are only two independent variables. Here will be presented a general approach to multiple correlation, which can be used with any number of variables and should provide some insights into methods for obtaining multiple correlations. The method is based on the semipartial correlation, which can be used to "untangle" correlations among independent variables. The method will be illustrated with three independent variables. Regardless of the size and sign of correlations among the variables, the multiple correlation can be obtained as follows:

(5-25) $R_{y.123}{}^2 = r_{y1}{}^2 + r_{y(2.1)}{}^2 + r_{y(3.12)}{}^2$

where r_{y1} = raw correlation between y and 1

$r_{y(2.1)}$ = semipartial correlation between y and 2, with 1 partialed from 2

$r_{y(3.12)}$ = semipartial correlation between y and 3, with both 1 and 2 partialed from 3

In using Eq. (5-25), it does not matter which independent variable is designated 1, 2, and so on. The formula works equally well for any ordering of the variables. The same multiple correlation would have been obtained if the first term on the right-hand side of the equation were $r_{y2}{}^2$ and the second term were $r_{y(1.2)}{}^2$.

The first step in computing R is to square any one of the correlations between the dependent variable and the independent variables. Next, take any one of the remaining independent variables and obtain the semipartial correlation between that variable and the dependent variable, holding constant the variable in the first term. This is squared and entered as the second term in the equation. Next, take any variable from the remaining independent variables and compute the semipartial correlation with y, holding constant the variables in the first two terms. This is squared and entered as the third term. This process can be

	1	2	3	4	y
1	1.0	r_{12}	r_{13}	r_{14}	r_{1y}
2	r_{12}	1.0	r_{23}	r_{24}	r_{2y}
3	r_{13}	r_{23}	1.0	r_{34}	r_{3y}
4	r_{14}	r_{24}	r_{34}	1.0	r_{4y}
y	r_{1y}	r_{2y}	r_{3y}	r_{4y}	1.0

ZERO-ORDER CORRELATIONS WITH VARIABLE 1

	1	2	3	4	5
F_1	1.0	r_{12}	r_{13}	r_{14}	r_{1y}

FIRST MATRIX OF CROSS PRODUCTS

	1.0	r_{12}	r_{13}	r_{14}	r_{1y}
1.0	1.0	r_{12}	r_{13}	r_{14}	r_{1y}
r_{12}	r_{12}	r_{12}^2	$r_{12}r_{13}$	$r_{12}r_{14}$	$r_{12}r_{1y}$
r_{13}	r_{13}	$r_{12}r_{13}$	r_{13}^2	$r_{13}r_{14}$	$r_{13}r_{1y}$
r_{14}	r_{14}	$r_{12}r_{14}$	$r_{13}r_{14}$	r_{14}^2	$r_{14}r_{1y}$
r_{1y}	r_{1y}	$r_{12}r_{1y}$	$r_{13}r_{1y}$	$r_{14}r_{1y}$	r_{1y}^2

carried on for any number of independent variables. Successive terms in the equation are successively higher orders of squared semipartial correlations. The first term is the square of a zero-order (raw) correlation, the second term is the square of a first-order semipartial correlation, the third term is the square of a second-order semipartial correlation, and so on.

It might not be obvious why semipartial correlations rather than partial correlations are used in the formula. The reason is that what is needed is to partial the independent variables from one another but not to partial their variances from the dependent variable. The partial-correlation coefficient answers a hypothetical question: What would the correlation be for two variables if one or more other variables were held constant? This would be the same as the result that, hypothetically, would be obtained if such "other variables" really were constants rather than variables, in which case all persons would have exactly the same score on each variable. In multiple correlation, one asks another hypothetical question: What would be the sum of squared correlations with y if the independent variables correlated zero with one another? In this instance, however, the question is hypothetical only with respect to the independent variables, not with respect to the dependent variable. In multiple correlation, one wants to leave the dependent variable *intact* and not partial any variance attributable to the independent variables. The problem is one of determining how much an *actual* variable y corre-

FIRST MATRIX OF RESIDUALS

	1	2	3	4	y
1	.0	.0	.0	.0	.0
2	.0	$1 - r_{12}^2$	$r_{23} - r_{12}r_{13}$	$r_{24} - r_{12}r_{14}$	$r_{2y} - r_{12}r_{1y}$
3	.0	$r_{23} - r_{12}r_{13}$	$1 - r_{13}^2$	$r_{34} - r_{13}r_{14}$	$r_{3y} - r_{13}r_{1y}$
4	.0	$r_{24} - r_{12}r_{14}$	$r_{34} - r_{13}r_{14}$	$1 - r_{14}^2$	$r_{4y} - r_{14}r_{1y}$
y	.0	$r_{2y} - r_{12}r_{1y}$	$r_{3y} - r_{13}r_{1y}$	$r_{4y} - r_{14}r_{1y}$	$1 - r_{1y}^2$

F_2

1 $\dfrac{0}{\sqrt{1 - r_{12}^2}} = 0$

2 $\dfrac{1 - r_{12}^2}{\sqrt{1 - r_{12}^2}} = \sqrt{1 - r_{12}^2} = r_{2(2.1)}$

3 $\dfrac{r_{23} - r_{12}r_{13}}{\sqrt{1 - r_{12}^2}} = r_{3(2.1)}$

4 $\dfrac{r_{24} - r_{12}r_{14}}{\sqrt{1 - r_{12}^2}} = r_{4(2.1)}$

y $\dfrac{r_{2y} - r_{12}r_{1y}}{\sqrt{1 - r_{12}^2}} = r_{y(2.1)}$

F

	F_1	F_2	F_3	F_4
1	1.0	.0	.0	.0
2	r_{12}	$r_{2(2.1)}$	.0	.0
3	r_{13}	$r_{3(2.1)}$	$r_{3(3.12)}$	.0
4	r_{14}	$r_{4(2.1)}$	$r_{4(3.12)}$	$r_{4(4.123)}$
y	r_{1y}	$r_{y(2.1)}$	$r_{y(3.12)}$	$r_{y(4.123)}$

lates with a linear combination of independent variables which have been *orthogonalized* (made to correlate zero with one another).

A COMPUTATIONAL APPROACH TO MULTIPLE CORRELATION   In this section will be presented a method for easily obtaining the semipartial correlations required for the multiple-correlation formula. The method will be explained in detail because it is a very useful approach to multiple correlation and it will prove very useful later in the discussion of factor analysis. Also, the method is easily programed for computers.

The method is similar to that for successive partialing discussed in a previous section. Steps in the method are shown in Table 5-4. The first step is the computation of a matrix of zero-order correlations, showing all correlations among independent variables and all correlations with the dependent variable y. Correlations for y are placed in the last row and last column of the matrix. The derivation of semipartial correlations will be done in the order of 1 through 4 for the independent variables. In looking back at Eq. (5-25) for the multiple correlation in terms of semipartial correlations, one will see that the first term is the square of one of the zero-order correlations with the dependent variable. Consequently the first term is "computed" merely by picking out r_{1y}, the correlation of the first variable with y.

The first row (or column) of the correlation matrix shows the correlations of variable 1 with the other variables. This is then set aside and labeled F_1. The next problem is to obtain first-order semipartial correlations with y, in which case variable 1 will be partialed from the independent variables but not from y. The first step in doing this is to place the elements of F_1 along the top and side of an empty table. Corresponding elements are then multiplied, which produces the *first matrix of cross products*. Elements in this matrix are subtracted from corresponding elements in the original matrix of correlations, and this results in the *first matrix of residuals*. The diagonal elements of that matrix are partial variances, variable 1 being held constant, and the off-diagonal terms are partial covariances. As was shown in a previous section, the first residual matrix can be converted to a matrix of first-order partial correlations by dividing each off-diagonal element by the product of the square roots of the two corresponding diagonal elements. This can be done because the partial correlation equals the partial covariance divided by the product of the square roots of the two partial variances.

Since the formula for semipartial correlation is only slightly different from that for partial correlation, it is easy to turn the first matrix of residuals into a matrix of first-order semipartial correlations. The only difference between the two formulas is that, in obtaining the semipartial correlation, one divides the partial covariance of any two variables by the square root of only one of the two variances. Since in the residual matrix the only interest is in the variable next to be used in obtaining semipartial coefficients, the major concern in the first residual matrix is with the elements in column 2. By dividing each element in that column by the square root of the diagonal element, one obtains first-order semipartial correlations, where variable 1 is partialed from variable 2 but not from the other variables. One can see how this works by looking at the formula for the semipartial correlation for variables 2 and 3, with variable 1 held constant only in 2:

(5-26) $$r_{3(2.1)} = \frac{r_{23} - r_{12}r_{13}}{\sqrt{1 - r_{12}^2}}$$

The above is precisely what one would obtain by dividing the element in the first residual matrix corresponding to variables 2 and 3 by the square

internal structure of measures

root of the diagonal element corresponding to variable 2. All the semi-partial correlations are listed as F_2. Naturally the semipartial correlation for variable 1 is zero, since when variable 1 is held constant in variable 1, there is nothing left to correlate with any other variable. The semipartial correlation for variable 2 is the square root of the variance of scores on 2 after 1 has been partialed. The most important correlation in F_2 is that of y with 2 when 1 is held constant in 2, which is $r_{y(2.1)}$. When squared, this serves as the second term in the formula for the multiple correlation [see Eq. (5-25)]. If one wanted the multiple correlation for variables 1 and 2 with y, $R_{y.12}^2$ could be obtained by squaring r_{y1} and adding that to the square of $r_{y(2.1)}$.

The above process of obtaining multiple correlations for different numbers of variables can be repeated as many times as necessary. These steps are not shown in Table 5-4, because they are only repetitions of the steps required to obtain F_2. If a third independent variable is to be added to the multiple correlation, the first step is to obtain a second matrix of cross products. The elements in F_2 are placed on the top and side of an empty table, and corresponding elements are multiplied. This matrix is then subtracted, element by element, from the first matrix of residuals. If variable 3 were next to be added to the prediction of y, each element in column 3 would be divided by the square root of the diagonal element for variable 3. This would produce semipartial correlations where variables 1 and 2 were held constant in variable 3, which would be F_3. The square of $r_{y(3.12)}$ could be added to r_{y1}^2 and $r_{y(2.1)}^2$ to obtain $R_{y.123}^2$.

The fourth variable could be added to the multiple correlation in the same way that variables 2 and 3 were added. A third matrix of cross products would be obtained by appropriately multiplying the elements of F_3. That matrix would be subtracted from the second matrix of residuals, which would give the third matrix of residuals. All the elements would be zero in columns and rows for variables 1, 2, and 3. The square root of the diagonal element for variable 4 would be divided into the element corresponding to 4 and y. This would give $r_{y(4.123)}$, which when squared could be added to the other terms in the multiple correlation.

The final results of the analysis are shown in the last part of Table 5-4 under the label F. The sum of the squares of the elements in the bottom row of F would be the squared multiple correlation with y. This procedure offers a very useful way of "picking apart" the relative contribution of variables to a multiple correlation.

SELECTION OF VARIABLES   So far in this section it has been assumed that the intention in a particular study is to find the multiple correlation of *all* independent variables with y, but this often is not the case. Frequently the researcher is seeking a relatively small number of variables that will do an adequate job of predicting a dependent variable. For example, in predicting success on a particular job (y), as many as 10 or more tests might be applied. If in practice it will not be possible to use more than, say, 3 or 4 of the tests, the problem is to find a small set of variables that has a higher multiple correlation with y than any other set with the same number of variables. The only foolproof way to solve that problem is to try the variables in all possible combinations two at a time, three at a time, and so on, but this would be prohibitively time-consuming and would provide many opportunities for taking advantage of chance.

The previous method for computing the terms required for multiple correlation can be adapted to the problem of selecting a smaller set of independent variables from a larger set. In this case imagine that the problem is that of picking the best set of 4 variables from a total collection of 10. First obtain a matrix of correlations for all 10 independent variables and for correlations with y. Next select the variable which has the highest correlation with y. This will be one of the variables used in the set of 4. Next compute the matrix of first residuals. (In doing this it is not necessary to place the variable which has the highest correlation with y on the first row and column of the correlation matrix or to place the second variable to be partialed on the second row and column of the first residual matrix. The operations can be carried out regardless of where variables are in the matrix of correlations and in the successive matrices of residual coefficients.) In the first residual matrix, divide each element in the row for y by the square root of the diagonal element in the column for the element. This would give all possible semipartial correlations with y. The variable with the highest coefficient would add the most to the first variable in the multiple-regression formula for predicting y.

After the second variable is found, the next step is to convert all the elements in the column for that variable into semipartial correlations, by the method shown in Table 5-4. These are then used to compute a second matrix of residual coefficients. Elements in the row for y are divided by the square roots of corresponding diagonal elements. The variable with the largest value is selected as the third variable for the set. A fourth variable is obtained by the same method.

A test can be applied to determine the "statistical significance" of the increment in multiple correlation supplied by each variable (McNemar, 1962, pp. 281–284). One would stop adding variables when the next variable to be added failed to have a "significant" semipartial correlation with y.

There is no guarantee that the method described above for obtaining a set of independent variables will always obtain the most predictive

internal structure of measures

set. This is because the method selects variables one at a time. It is possible that one could obtain a more predictive set of variables by trying all possible combinations of variables. For example, this might occur if the most predictive set does not contain the variable which has the highest zero-order correlation with the dependent variable, but the method described above always includes that variable as a member of the set. In practice, however, this method usually does pick the most predictive set of variables. In those instances where some other combination of variables is more predictive than the set chosen by the method, the difference usually is small. Also, since more advantage is taken of chance by trying variables in all possible combinations than by the method described above, the latter tends to shrink less when larger numbers of persons are studied.

SUGGESTED ADDITIONAL READINGS

Guilford, J. P. *Fundamental statistics in psychology and education.* New York: McGraw-Hill, 1965, chaps. 14, 16.

Hays, W. L. *Statistics for psychologists.* New York: Holt, 1963, chap. 15.

McNemar, Q. *Psychological statistics.* New York: Wiley, 1962, chap. 11.

CHAPTER SIX
THEORY OF MEASUREMENT ERROR

Some error is involved in any type of measurement, whether it is the measurement of the temperature of liquids, blood pressure, or intelligence. Measurement error can be in the form of either a systematic bias or random errors. The former would be the case if a chemist had only one thermometer, and although he read it with high fidelity, the thermometer always registered two degrees higher than it should. Random error would be at work if the thermometer were accurate but the chemist nearsightedly misread it while making different measurements. A systematic bias is not important in most psychological measures. It contributes only to the mean score of all subjects being studied, and as has been pointed out previously, the mean score of all subjects is not very important in studies of individual differences and in most psychological experiments. Random errors are important in all studies, because to the extent they are present, limits are placed on the degree of lawfulness that can be found in nature. Why this is so can be illustrated with the nearsighted chemist. Suppose that when no measurement error is present there is a smooth curve relating temperature to the ratio of one chemical to another in a compound. To the extent to which random errors of measurement occur, the smooth curve will not be found, and instead the curve will appear somewhat jagged. In all areas of science, random errors of measurement tend to jumble up any form of lawfulness that exists in nature.

Random errors of measurement are never completely eliminated; but to portray nature in its ultimate lawfulness, efforts are made to reduce such errors as much as possible. To the extent to which measurement error is slight, a measure is said to be *reliable*. Reliability concerns the extent to which measurements are *repeatable*—by the same individual using different measures of the same attribute or by different persons using the same measure of an attribute. Science is concerned with repeatable experiments; and for experiments to be repeatable, any particular object in any particular circumstance must have a set quantity of any particular attribute. When one investigator can find different measurements for the object in the particular circumstance or other investigators can find different measurements with the same or different instruments, experimental results are not exactly repeatable. Thus science is limited by the reliability of measuring instruments and/or the reliability with which scientists use them.

Of course, high reliability does not necessarily mean high validity. One could, for example, seek to measure intelligence by having children throw stones as far as they could. How far stones were tossed on one occasion might correlate highly with how far they were tossed on another occasion, and thus, being repeatable, the measure would be highly reliable; but obviously the tossing of stones would not constitute a *valid* measure of intelligence. The amount of measurement error places a limit on the amount of validity that an instrument can have, but even in the complete absence of measurement error, there is no guarantee of validity. Reliability is a *necessary* but not *sufficient* condition for validity.

It is interesting that the theory of measurement error has been developed largely in the context of psychology, and largely by psychologists. One might imagine that this is because psychological measures are plagued by measurement error, but this is only a partial explanation. Measures in other areas of science often are accompanied by as much, or more, random error as is the case in psychology. For example, the measurement of blood pressure in physiological studies is far less reliable than most psychological measures, and similar examples could be drawn from the physical and social sciences. The development of the theory of measurement error by psychologists can be attributed either to an accident of history or to the fact that, being self-conscious about problems of measurement, psychologists have developed the theory of measurement error along with other advances they have made in the methodology of measurement. Among his many other contributions to psychological measurement, Charles Spearman (1904) laid the foundation stones for the theory of measurement error.

For two reasons, it is easy to overstate the importance of the theory of measurement error in psychological measurement. First, as will be shown later, measurement error usually does not harm most investigations as much as might be thought. Second, there are numerous topics regarding psychological measurement that are more important than the theory of measurement error, as evidenced throughout this book. A large proportion of journal articles on psychological measurement and a major portion of some books on the topic have been devoted to measurement error. This is probably because the theory of measurement error is so neatly expressible in mathematical terms, in contrast to some other important issues, e.g., validity, where grounds for argument are not so straightforward. The theory of measurement error is *one* important topic in psychological measurement, and consequently this and the next chapter will be devoted to it.

The theory of measurement error which will be presented is surely one of the most workable mathematical models in psychology. The theory can be derived with few assumptions about the nature of data, and the same formulas can be derived from quite different sets of assumptions. The theory is very "robust," in the sense that it tends to hold well even when the assumptions of the model are markedly violated. Even very elegant, highly complicated mathematical models have failed to improve substantially on the principles which Spearman gave us.

The basic issues in the discussion of measurement error are illustrated in Figure 6-1. It is assumed that each person has a "true score," one that would be obtained if there were no errors of measurement. In the figure, person *A* has a relatively high true score and person *B* has a relatively low true score. Since there is some random error

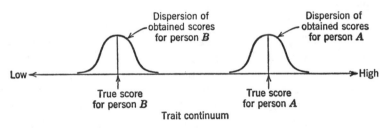

figure **6-1** *True scores and distributions of obtained scores for two persons.*

in the score obtained for a person on a particular occasion, obtained scores would differ from true scores on a random basis. If it were possible to give many alternative forms of a test, e.g., many different spelling tests constructed by the same procedures, the average score on the tests would closely approximate true scores. Scores obtained from the alternative forms would be distributed symmetrically above and below the true scores. Since such distributions of random errors are expected to be normally distributed, it is expected that distributions of obtained scores will be normally distributed about true scores.

The wider the spread of obtained scores about true scores, the more error there is in employing the type of instrument. The standard deviation of the distribution of errors for each person would be an index of the amount of error. If the standard deviation of errors were much the same for all persons, which usually is assumed to be the case, one standard deviation of errors could typify the amount of error to be expected. This typical standard deviation of errors is called the *standard error of measurement*, σ_{meas}. The size of σ_{meas} is a direct indica-

internal structure of measures

tion of the amount of error involved in using a particular type of instrument.

the domain-sampling model

The most useful model for the discussion of measurement error is that which considers any particular measure as being composed of *a random sample of items from a hypothetical domain of items*. An example would be a particular spelling test for fourth-grade students, which could be thought of as constituting a random sample of spelling words from all possible words appropriate for that age group. Another example would be the number of errors made by rats in a particular maze, in which case the errors made could be thought of as a random sample of the errors that would be made if there were an infinite number of turns in the maze and rats were capable of traversing an infinitely long maze. Many other examples could be given of how it is reasonable to think of a particular measure as representing a sample of items from a hypothetical domain of items.

Of course, at the outset it is obvious that the model is not true to life, because strictly speaking, items are almost never actually sampled randomly; rather, items are *composed* for particular measures. The model usually does, however, lead to accurate predictions in practice. First, it is stated that the purpose of any particular measurement is to estimate the measurement that would be obtained if *all* the items in the domain were employed, e.g., all the spelling words or an infinitely long maze. The score that any subject would obtain over the whole domain is spoken of as his *true score*. To the extent to which any sample of items correlated highly with true scores, the sample would be highly reliable.

The model can be developed without consideration of the number of items sampled for particular measures. Each sample could contain many items, or at the lower extreme, only one item. Also, the model can be developed without concern for the type of item employed or the factorial composition of items.

Basic to the model is the concept of an infinitely large correlation matrix showing all correlations among items in the domain. The average correlation in the matrix, $\bar{r}_{ij}$, would indicate the extent to which some common core existed in the items. The dispersion of correlations about the average would indicate the extent to which items varied in sharing the common core. If the assumption is made that all items have an equal amount of the common core, the average correlation in each column of the hypothetical matrix would be the same, which would be the same as the average correlation in the whole matrix. Keep in mind that the assumption is not necessarily that all correlations in the matrix are the same, but rather that the sum of correlations, or average, of each item with all the others is the same for all items. The latter is a much less restrictive assumption than the former.

If the above assumption holds, it is possible to directly compute (not just estimate) the correlation of any particular item with the sum of all items in the domain as follows. If all items are expressed as standard scores, the formula for the correlation of item 1 with the sum of scores on k items is

(6-1)
$$r_{1(1 \cdots k)} = \frac{\dfrac{1}{N} \Sigma z_1(z_1 + z_2 + z_3 + \cdots + z_k)}{\sqrt{\dfrac{\Sigma z_1^2}{N}} \sqrt{\dfrac{1}{N} \Sigma(z_1 + z_2 + z_3 + \cdots + z_k)^2}}$$

Equation (6-1) is simply the formula for the correlation of one variable with the sum of k variables. It is important to note that variable 1, being an item in the domain, is included in the sum of variables 1 through k. The numerator of the equation could be transformed as follows:

$$\frac{1}{N} \Sigma z_1(z_1 + z_2 + z_3 + \cdots + z_k)$$

$$= \frac{1}{N} \Sigma(z_1^2 + z_1 z_2 + z_1 z_3 + \cdots + z_1 z_k)$$

$$= \frac{1}{N} (\Sigma z_1^2 + \Sigma z_1 z_2 + \Sigma z_1 z_3 + \cdots + \Sigma z_1 z_k)$$

$$= 1 + r_{12} + r_{13} + \cdots + r_{1k}$$

$$= 1 + (k - 1)\bar{r}_{ij}$$

After the summation sign is "run through" terms (the third expression above), in parentheses is the product of sets of standard scores for variable 1 with all other variables. When these are divided by the number of people N, the fourth expression results. Each element in the sum is the correlation of variable 1 with one of the other variables. Since the first term is the correlation of variable 1 with itself, that term equals 1. If the assumption holds that the average correlation of each item with the others is the same, and thus the same as the average correlation in the matrix, the sum of the correlations of item 1 with the remaining $k - 1$ items (excluding item 1) would equal $(k - 1)\bar{r}_{ij}$.

In the denominator of Eq. (6-1), the term on the left is the standard deviation of standard scores on variable 1. Being 1, this "falls out" of the denominator. In the denominator, under the radical in the term on the right is the variance of the sum of k sets of standard scores.

Note that variable 1 is included in the sum. Previously it was shown that the variance of the sum of k sets of standard scores equals the sum of all the elements in the correlation matrix for those scores. There are k^2 elements in any symmetric matrix of correlations. Of these, k are diagonal elements and consequently $k^2 - k$ are off-diagonal elements. Since in a correlation matrix each diagonal element is 1, the sum of the diagonal elements equals k. Rather than sum the off-diagonal elements, one could obtain the same value by multiplying the average off-diagonal element by $k^2 - k$. With these considerations in mind, it should be understandable why the denominator of Eq. (6-1) can be phrased as follows:

$$\sqrt{k + (k^2 - k)\bar{r}_{ij}}$$

Reassembling numerator and denominator gives the following formula for the correlation of item 1 with the sum of the k items in the domain.

(6-2)
$$
\begin{aligned}
r_{1(1\cdots k)} &= \frac{1 + (k-1)\bar{r}_{ij}}{\sqrt{k + (k^2 - k)\bar{r}_{ij}}} \\
&= \frac{1 + k\bar{r}_{ij} - \bar{r}_{ij}}{\sqrt{k + k^2 r_{ij} - k\bar{r}_{ij}}}
\end{aligned}
$$

If, as the model assumes, the domain of items is Infinitely large, we can see what happens as k approaches Infinity. The first step is to divide each term in the numerator and denominator by k. Since the elements in the denominator are under the radical, this would require dividing each term by k^2. The result is as follows:

(6-3)
$$
r_{1(1\cdots k)} = \frac{\dfrac{1}{k} + \bar{r}_{ij} - \dfrac{\bar{r}_{ij}}{k}}{\sqrt{\dfrac{1}{k} + \bar{r}_{ij} - \dfrac{\bar{r}_{ij}}{k}}}
$$

$k \to \infty$

As k approaches infinity, any term divided by k approaches zero. Since there are only two terms in Eq. (6-3) that are not divided by k, the equation reduces to

(6-4)
$$
r_{1(1\cdots k)} = \frac{\bar{r}_{ij}}{\sqrt{\bar{r}_{ij}}} = \sqrt{\bar{r}_{ij}}
$$

$k \to \infty$

The correlation of item 1 with the sum of an infinite number of items in a domain would equal the square root of the average correlation among items in the domain. This holds only under the assumption that all items have the same average correlation with other items. Since in that case the average correlation of item 1 with the other items would equal $\bar{r}_{ij}$, Eq. (6-4) can be written as

(6-5) $\qquad r_{1(1\ldots k)} = \sqrt{\bar{r}_{1j}}$

$\qquad k \longrightarrow \infty$

where $\bar{r}_{1j}$ is the average correlation of item 1 with all other items in the domain. Since when k approaches infinity, the correlation of item 1 with the k items approaches the correlation of item 1 with *true scores*, it will be meaningful to use the following abbreviation of symbols:

(6-6) $\qquad r_{1(1\ldots k)} = r_{1t} = \sqrt{\bar{r}_{1j}}$

$\qquad k \longrightarrow \infty$

The correlation r_{1t} of variable 1 with true scores in the domain (the sum of all items in the domain) would equal the square root of the average correlation of item 1 with all other items.

The formulas derived so far are the foundations of the theory of measurement error, and if they are properly understood, it will prove easy to develop many principles from them.

MULTI-ITEM MEASURES   In the previous section, the basic formulas for measurement error were developed with respect to a hypothetical domain of *items,* but in nearly all measurement problems, measures are composed of a number of items. The model can be easily extended to take care of this. The infinitely large matrix of correlations among items can be thought of as divided into groups, each containing h items. The sum of scores on each group of items would constitute a test. If items were randomly sampled to compose the tests, correlations among different tests would tend to be the same. Such randomly sampled collections of items are said to constitute *randomly parallel* tests, since their means, standard deviations, and correlations with true scores differ only by chance. If it is assumed that the average correlation of each test with the sum of all other tests is the same for all tests, one can start back with Eq. (6-1) and insert standard scores for whole tests rather than for individual items. The successive steps are the same for proving that

(6-7) $\qquad\qquad r_{1t} = \sqrt{\bar{r}_{1j}}$

where 1 = scores on test 1

$\qquad t$ = true scores in domain

$\qquad \bar{r}_{1j}$ = average correlation of test 1 with all tests in domain

The same formula results whether one is considering individual items or whole tests and no matter how many items are in each of the whole tests. (It should be kept in mind that the average correlation among whole tests will be larger than the average correlation among items,

internal structure of measures

and consequently correlations with true scores will be higher for the whole tests.)

By convention, the average correlation of one test, or one item, with all tests or items in the domain is called the *reliability coefficient,* which will be symbolized as $\bar{r}_{11}$ for variable 1, $\bar{r}_{22}$ for variable 2, and so on. Then the square root of $\bar{r}_{11}$ equals the correlation of item 1 or test 1 with true scores in the domain.

ESTIMATE OF RELIABILITY If the assumption made previously regarding correlations among elements of a domain is correct, the correlation of any test with true scores is precisely equal to the square root of $\bar{r}_{11}$, which is not an estimate, but an actual determination. Of course, in practice one never knows $\bar{r}_{11}$ exactly, because it is not possible to generate an infinite number of tests. Consequently $\bar{r}_{11}$, and thus r_{1t}, can be only *estimated* in practice. An estimate of $\bar{r}_{11}$ will be symbolized as r_{11}, which is the conventional symbol for the reliability coefficient.

Obviously r_{11} is a better estimate of $\bar{r}_{11}$ when the former is obtained by averaging the correlations of test 1 with a large, rather than a small, number of tests from the domain. If the tests were obtained actually by randomly drawing items from the domain, the key assumption regarding correlations among tests would be approximately correct. The average correlation of test 1 with a number of other tests would then be an estimate of the average correlation of test 1 with all tests in the domain. For example, the average correlation between one spelling test and five other spelling tests with the same number of items would be an estimate of $\bar{r}_{11}$, and the square root of that would be an estimate of the correlation between test 1 and hypothetical true scores in spelling. What usually occurs in practice is that test 1 is correlated with only one other test (test 2) and the correlation is symbolized as r_{11}, which is taken as an estimate of $\bar{r}_{11}$. (It could be symbolized equally well as r_{22} and taken as an estimate of the squared correlation of test 2 with true scores in the particular domain.) When only one correlation is taken as an estimate of a hypothetical infinite number of correlations, however, it rightly should be questioned how efficient such estimates are, as will be considered in a later section.

THE IMPORTANCE OF THE RELIABILITY COEFFICIENT Care has been taken to show that it follows that r_{1t} is equal to the square root of $\bar{r}_{11}$ and to show how r_{1t} is estimated by the square root of r_{11} (the average of any number of correlations between test 1 and other tests from the domain, including the "average" of only one such correlation). Once a good estimate of $\bar{r}_{11}$, and thus a good estimate of r_{1t}, is obtained, many important principles can be developed about measurement error. In this section it will be assumed that a precise method of estimating $\bar{r}_{11}$ is being used in particular problems; in later sections the precision of such estimates in different circumstances will be discussed. Assuming, then, that $r_{11} = \bar{r}_{11}$, r_{1t} equals the square root of r_{11}.

The scores on a particular test are often spoken of as *fallible scores*, "fallible" because there is a degree of measurement error involved. In contrast, true scores are, in that sense, infallible. Although r_{1t} is the correlation between an existing variable and a hypothetical variable rather than between two existing variables, it can be used in mathematical derivations in the same way that any correlation can. One

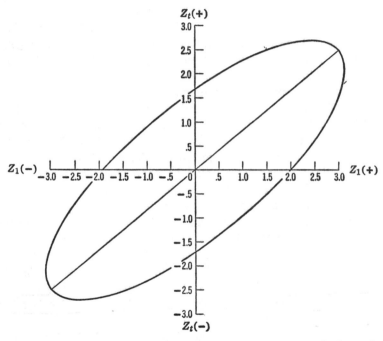

figure 6-2 *Regression line and scatter contour for hypothetical relationship between obtained scores and true scores.*

can visualize a scatter diagram showing the relationship between the fallible scores on any test and true scores. This is illustrated in Figure 6-2. Then, according to what has been learned about correlational analysis, the line of best fit for estimating true scores from fallible scores would be obtained as follows:

(6-8)
$$z_t' = r_{1t} z_1 = \sqrt{r_{11}}\, z_1$$

where z_t' = estimates of true standard scores

z_1 = standard scores on fallible measure

r_{1t} = correlation of fallible scores with true scores

r_{11} = reliability coefficient for variable 1

internal structure of measures

More about the estimation of true scores will be given in a later section. The important point here is that r_{1t} can be placed in the usual equations for correlational analysis. It is particularly important to realize that, since the square of any correlation equals the variance in one variable explainable by variance in another variable, r_{1t}^2 equals the percentage of true-score variance explainable by a fallible measure. Then it can also be said that r_{11} equals the same percentage of true-score variance in the fallible measure. This percentage takes on even more meaning when the fallible measure is expressed as deviation scores or raw scores rather than as standard scores. In the former two instances, the reliability coefficient could be expressed as follows:

(6-9)
$$r_{11} = \frac{\sigma_t^2}{\sigma_1^2}$$

where σ_1^2 = variance of variable 1

σ_t^2 = variance of variable 1 explainable by true scores

What Eq. (6-9) shows is that r_{11} equals the amount of true-score variance in a measure divided by the actual variance of the measure. This way of viewing the reliability coefficient opens the door to the development of many principles concerning measurement error, but before those principles are developed, another model will be described for deriving the same principles.

the model of parallel tests

The model discussed in the previous section concerned *randomly parallel* tests, which are assumed to differ somewhat from true scores in means, standard deviations, and correlations because of random errors in the sampling of items. It was stated that the best way to estimate the reliability is to correlate one test with a number of other tests from the same domain of content. Since in practice that is impractical, usually one test is correlated with only one other test to obtain an estimate of the reliability. But since, on the face of it, there may be much inaccuracy in letting one correlation stand for the average of many unknown correlations, it rightly could be questioned whether the correlation between only two tests can be considered a precise estimate of the reliability of either test.

If it is assumed that two tests actually are parallel, rather than just tending to be so on a sampling basis, the reliability coefficient and related measures can be directly derived without need for considering the precision of estimates. Two tests are parallel if (1) they have the same standard deviation, (2) they correlate the same with a set of true scores, and (3) the variance in each test which is not explainable by true scores is because of purely random error. (For some purposes, it also is useful to assume that the two tests have the same mean, but that assumption will not be necessary for developments here. Some of the other assumptions usually made about the characteristics of parallel tests will be shown to be derivable from the assumptions above.)

The scores on two parallel tests can be broken down as follows:

$$x_1 = t + e_1$$

$$x_2 = t + e_2$$

where x_1 = obtained deviation scores on test 1

$\qquad x_2$ = obtained deviation scores on test 2

$\qquad t$ = true score in domain

$\qquad e_1$ = errors on test 1

$\qquad e_2$ = errors on test 2

Since only the fallible scores on the two tests would actually be open to observation, the only way to learn about the true and error scores would be through the correlation of obtained scores on the two tests. Above it was assumed that the two tests correlate the same with true scores. If that correlation were known, it could then be used in a regression equation to estimate scores on the two fallible variables. From simple principles of correlation, much can be deduced about components of true and error variance.

In addition to principles incorporated in the above three basic assumptions for parallel tests, other principles can easily be deduced from the third assumption, that the portion of variance in each test not explainable by true scores is because of purely random error. First, by definition random errors tend to cancel one another, and consequently the mean of the errors on each test is expected to be zero. Second, since random errors do not correlate with one another, (1) errors on one test are expected to correlate zero with errors on the other test and (2) errors on either test are expected to correlate zero with true scores.

With this model, the following principles have been assumed or deduced:

$$\sigma_1 = \sigma_2$$

$$r_{1t} = r_{2t}$$

$$r_{te_1} = 0$$

$$r_{te_2} = 0$$

$$r_{e_1 e_2} = 0$$

$$M_{e_1} = 0$$

$$M_{e_2} = 0$$

internal structure of measures

Since error scores are uncorrelated with true scores, it follows that

(6-10) $\sigma_1^2 = \sigma_t^2 + \sigma_{e_1}^2$

and

(6-11) $\sigma_2^2 = \sigma_t^2 + \sigma_{e_2}^2$

Because variances of obtained scores are equal on the two tests and variances of true scores are equal, it follows that variances of error scores also are equal.

It is important to examine the correlation between the two parallel tests, as follows:

$$r_{12} = \frac{\frac{1}{N} \Sigma x_1 x_2}{\sigma_1 \sigma_2}$$

Since x_1 and x_2 can be expressed as the sum of true and error scores, and in the denominator the two standard deviations are equal, the correlation can be written as

$$r_{12} = \frac{\frac{1}{N} \Sigma (t + e_1)(t + e_2)}{\sigma_1^2}$$

$$= \frac{\frac{1}{N} (\Sigma t^2 + \Sigma t e_1 + \Sigma t e_2 + \Sigma e_1 e_2)}{\sigma_1^2}$$

$$= \frac{\sigma_t^2 + \sigma_{t e_1} + \sigma_{t e_2} + \sigma_{e_1 e_2}}{\sigma_1^2}$$

Because errors are uncorrelated with true scores and uncorrelated with each other, the three covariance terms in the numerator drop out, leaving

(6-12) $r_{12} = \dfrac{\sigma_t^2}{\sigma_1^2} = r_{11}$

The correlation between two parallel tests equals the true-score variance in either test divided by the variance of either test. The same ratio was derived from the domain-sampling model. Since the ratio is the same for both tests, it is symbolized as r_{11}, r_{22}, or r_{xx}, rather than as r_{12}.

A number of different methods could be used to prove that the correlation of test 1 with true scores equals the square root of the correlation between the two parallel forms. One method for showing this will prove useful later in discussing the assumptions of the model. It is implicit in the assumptions and derivations so far in this section that, when true scores are partialed from the two parallel tests, the residual scores on the two tests correlate zero. The error scores on the two tests would be the residuals after true scores were partialed, and these errors are uncorrelated. Thus the partial correlation would have to be zero, in which case the numerator of the partial correlation would have to be zero, as follows:

$$r_{11} - r_{1t}r_{2t} = 0$$

Since the model assumes that both tests correlate the same with true scores, the foregoing equation could be transformed to

$$r_{11} = r_{1t}^2 \quad \text{or} \quad r_{1t} = \sqrt{r_{11}}$$

With the correlation of obtained scores with true scores derived, it is possible to develop many principles concerning measurement error, but first it would be wise to look carefully at some relations between the two models that have been presented.

perspectives on the two models

It may seem paradoxical that two such different-appearing models reach the same conclusions about measurement error. Many other identical formulas can be derived from the two models. Actually, though, as can be seen on careful inspection, they are not different models—the parallel-test model is a special case of the more general domain-sampling model. If in the latter all sample tests have the same standard deviation and correlation with total scores in the domain (true scores), and when true scores are partialed from all sample tests, the partial correlations among sample tests are zero, the domain will be populated with parallel tests rather than randomly parallel tests. In this case the correlation between any two tests will be the same as the average of all correlations among tests, and the square root of that correlation will be the correlation of each test with true scores.

In making the three assumptions necessary for the parallel-test model, one primarily ignores the actual problem involved in estimating the correlation of obtained scores with true scores. The assumptions in that model are tantamount to assuming that the correlation between any two tests in a domain is a completely precise determination of the reliability coefficient, rather than only an estimate. The domain-sampling model frankly faces the fact that there is a problem regarding the precision of estimation.

The parallel-test model offers a conceptual dead end for the development of theories of measurement error. Since true scores are defined by only two tests, one naturally wonders, "True scores on what attribute?" It is easier to think in terms of a domain of possible items

internal structure of measures

and of any test being a sample, random or otherwise, of those items. If there are three supposedly parallel tests rather than two and the three correlations among them are different, what then is the reliability? Since the model explicitly assumes that all parallel tests have the same reliability, one is placed in a quandary. This is no problem for the domain-sampling model, where this possibility is admitted and an estimate of the reliability of any one test is the average of its correlations with the other two tests.

Although the parallel-test model involves three assumptions, only one of these assumptions, the equality of variances, can be empirically determined. That, however, is the least important of the assumptions. A more crucial assumption is that the two tests have the same correlation with true scores, and there is no way to determine if this assumption is correct. Equally crucial is the assumption that errors on the two tests are uncorrelated, which was shown to be tantamount to the assumption that, when true scores are partialed from scores on the two tests, the partial correlation is zero. There is no way to determine if that assumption is correct.

The parallel-test model has probably achieved its popularity because of its simplicity and because it ignores problems regarding the precision of reliability estimation. An important principle is that any formula obtained from the parallel-test model which *specifies* a characteristic of measurement error is matched by a formula from the domain-sampling model that *estimates* the same characteristic. For example, in the former model the correlation between two tests supposedly specifies the reliability, whereas in the latter model, the correlation is considered only an estimate. The same is found true for all formulas that have been derived from the parallel-test model: an identical formula, albeit an estimate rather than a specification, can be found in the domain-sampling model. However, the reverse of the principle does not hold. There are many principles and formulas relating to principles that can be derived from the domain-sampling model but cannot be matched by the parallel-test model. An example was mentioned previously of unequal correlations among three tests. Another example is that the domain-sampling model permits deductions about the precision of the estimate of reliability obtained with different numbers of items and with different distributions of correlations among them. The parallel-test model precludes even asking questions about such issues. The only way that the latter model can handle any question regarding relations among numerous tests is to postulate numerous parallel tests. Inevitably, thinking in this way encourages one to relax the assumptions regarding parallel tests, and what starts as a parallel-test model soon evolves into a domain-sampling model.

The author is strongly in favor of the domain-sampling model as a theoretical framework for discussing and investigating reliability. Actually, the basic idea of randomly sampling items from a domain leads to many different models for measurement error. The one developed previously was the simplest of all these, its only assumption being that the average correlation of each item with the others is the same for all items. The precision of estimates of reliability employing this assumption will be discussed in a later section.

FACTORIAL COMPOSITION It sometimes is said that both the models which have been described for considering measurement error assume that all items measure one factor only. Strictly speaking, this is not correct. Both models would hold if items were equally divided between two factors, e.g., if half the items in the domain concerned spelling and the other half concerned arithmetic. In the domain-sampling model, random samples from this two-factor domain would tend to correlate the same with one another. True scores would consist of combined ability in spelling and arithmetic. The square root of average correlations among sample tests would approximate the correlation of individual tests with true scores, which is the key deduction from the model. All other formulas for measurement error could be derived for this two-factor domain. The model would hold as well if instead of two kinds of items relating to two factors, all items were compounded in equal proportions of a number of factors. For example, if each item simultaneously measured anxiety, reaction time, and muscle coordination, all items would tend to correlate much the same with one another, and consequently the average correlation among 20 or more of them would serve well to represent the average correlation that would be obtained among much larger numbers of them.

The domain-sampling model would still hold, and the parallel-test model would hold approximately, even if half a dozen factors were randomly scattered among the items. In this case some of the items would be dominated by one factor only, some would share two or more factors, and some would share the variance of all factors involved. The reliability estimate would not be as precise as it would be if only one factor dominated the items, but predictions from the models would still hold.

The domain-sampling model concerns the extent to which one "anything" correlates with an infinite number of other "anythings." This correlation is estimated by taking the square root of the average correlation of one "anything" with a number of other "anythings" or the square root of the correlation with only one other "anything." All the mathematical properties of the models, particularly the domain-sampling model, hold regardless of the factorial composition of the items.

The factorial composition of items is important in two ways. First, to the extent that the items diversely measure a number of factors rather than only one factor, correlations among items are likely to be rather heterogeneous in size. As will be discussed more fully in the next section, the more homogeneous the correlations in the domain are, the more precise are estimates of correlations with true scores. Consequently even though the domain-sampling model leads to *unbiased* estimates of correlations with true scores when the domain is factorially complex, such estimates might be accompanied by a considerable amount of *content-sampling error*.

The second important consideration regarding factorial composition is that, in actual investigations, the *intention* is to investigate a domain of items that principally concerns one factor. No one is, or should be, interested in studying the internal consistency of a polyglot domain of test materials. As has been mentioned previously and will be stressed in future chapters, the purpose in the development of a new measure is to tap a unitary attribute. Even though the model holds when items concern more than one factor, the problem is more meaningful and estimates of reliability are more precise when items are dominated by only one factor.

precision of reliability estimates

At a number of places so far the question has arisen as to the precision of reliability estimates from the domain-sampling model. Such estimates are precise to the extent that different random samples of items correlate the same with true scores. If an item correlated exactly the same with all other items in the domain, the correlation with any other item would be a precise indication of reliability. If all items in the domain correlated exactly the same with one another, all items would have exactly the same correlation with true scores, which would equal the square root of the typical correlation. To the extent that correlations among items in the domain vary, there is some random error connected with the average correlation found in any particular sampling of items. For example, if item 1 had correlations with other items in the domain ranging from .10 to .30, the average correlation of item 1 with a number of other items randomly selected from the domain would provide a relatively precise estimate of the reliability of item 1. In contrast, if such correlations ranged between −.30 and .60, the average correlation of item 1 with the other items might give only a rough approximation of the reliability.

Related to the precision of estimates of reliability is a double problem of sampling—that concerned with the sampling of people and that concerned with the sampling of items. As was mentioned previously, it is all but impossible to consider both problems of sampling simultaneously. For this reason, it was said that measurement theory is a "large sample" theory, in which it is assumed that sufficient numbers of persons are studied so that this source of sampling error is a minor consideration. This is necessary not only to simplify measurement theory, but also because the precision required in measurement theory cannot tolerate large doses of sampling error because of a small number of subjects. Consequently, in this discussion it will be assumed that a minimum of 300 persons is employed in studies of measurement error, in which case the sampling error because of the sampling of people will be a minor consideration. In the theory of measurement error, the concern is with the *sampling of items*.

A domain of items is of interest only if the average correlation among items is positive. If the average correlation is zero or near zero, the items as a group have no common core, and it is not sensible to consider them as measuring a unitary attribute. Assuming that the average correlation is positive and sufficiently higher than zero to encourage further investigation, the next point of interest is the relative homogeneity of correlations. As was mentioned previously, it is hoped that the correlations will be relatively homogeneous. Whatever the case, there will be a distribution of correlations about the average value. An approximate statistical model will help to evaluate the influence of that distribution on the precision of estimates of reliability. The model assumes that correlations are normally distributed about the average value and statistically independent of one another, both of which assumptions are known to be at least slightly incorrect. If the average correlation is positive, a random distribution of correlations about that average tends to be skewed rather than strictly normal. Also, correlations in a matrix are not independent of one another. For example, the correlation of item 1 and item 2 is not independent of the correlation of item 2 and item 3. When, however, correlations are as low as they usually are among test items (typically ranging between .10 and .40), those assumptions are violated only slightly, and consequently the model probably will hold well in practice.

As will be explained more fully in a later section, regardless of the number of items sampled from a domain to obtain a test, the reliability of the test is directly related to the average correlation among those items. Longer tests have higher reliability coefficients than shorter tests, but in both cases the reliabilities of the tests are deducible from the average correlations among their items. This being so, the precision with which the reliability is estimated for any test is a direct function of the precision with which the average correlation of items in a test estimates the average correlation of all items in the domain. If such correlations are normally distributed in the domain, an approximate standard error for the estimation of $\bar{r}_{ij}$ is obtained as follows:

internal structure of measures

$$(6\text{-}13) \qquad \sigma_{\bar{r}_{ij}} = \frac{\sigma_{r_{ij}}}{\sqrt{\frac{1}{2}k(k-1)-1}}$$

where $\sigma_{\bar{r}_{ij}}$ = standard error of estimating $\bar{r}_{ij}$ in whole domain

$\sigma_{r_{ij}}$ = standard deviation of distribution of actual correlations within test

k = number of test items

Equation (6-13) is merely an adaptation of the customary formula for the standard error of the mean, in which case people would be sampled rather than test items. In that instance the standard error of average scores for people would equal the standard deviation of scores divided by the number of persons minus 1. In Eq. (6-13), each correlation is considered analogous to a score made by one person. The standard deviation of correlations within a test is taken as an estimate of the standard deviation of correlations in the whole domain. At first glance, the denominator of Eq. (6-13) may look complicated, but it is only the square root of the number of possible correlations among k items minus 1, the 1 being subtracted to obtain the proper "degrees of freedom." In a correlation matrix, there are k^2 terms. From this must be subtracted the k diagonal 1s. What remains must be divided by 2, because each correlation appears twice in the matrix. Proper manipulation shows that these steps end with the finding that the number of off-diagonal coefficients either above or below the diagonal is $\frac{1}{2}k(k-1)$. Thus when 1 is subtracted from this number, the proper degrees of freedom appear under the radical in the denominator.

What is immediately apparent from the formula is that the error of estimating $\bar{r}_{11}$ is directly related to the standard deviation of correlations among items. Also apparent from an inspection of the denominator is that the precision (the inverse of the standard error) of estimating $\bar{r}_{11}$ is directly related to the number of test items. Thus an important principle is deduced: Not only are longer tests more reliable (which will be proved later), but also their estimates of reliability are more precise than would be the case for shorter tests.

A typical situation is that in which the average correlation among items is .20 and the standard deviation of correlations is .10. Then the standard error for estimating $\bar{r}_{ij}$ from a 10-item test is obtained as follows:

$$\sigma_{\bar{r}_{ij}} = \frac{.10}{\sqrt{(5 \times 9) - 1}}$$

$$= \frac{.10}{\sqrt{44}}$$

$$= \frac{.10}{6.63}$$

$$\sigma_{\bar{r}_{ij}} = .016$$

theory of measurement error

In any sampling problem, the expectation is that 95 percent of sample means will lie in a band stretching from approximately two standard errors below the population mean to two standard errors above it. The analogous expectation here is that, for random samples of items, the average correlation among items will be distributed in a like manner. Using this logic, if the average correlation among items in a domain is .20 and the standard deviation of correlations is .10, the standard error for average correlations obtained from 10-item tests is only .016. Then the expectation is that 95 percent of the sample values lie between approximately .168 and .232. If in this instance there were 40 items on each test, the standard error would be only .0036!

What is illustrated in the above example is that, even when tests have as few as 10 items, reliability estimates are rather precise. When there are as many items as appear on most tests, the sampling error because of the selection of items is vanishingly small. The reason for this precision is that as the number of items is increased, the number of correlations among items increases at a rapid rate, the factor being that appearing in the denominator of Eq. (6-13). For example, there are 780 possible correlations among 40 items. One then obtains approximately the same precision for estimating the average correlation that would be obtained in sampling people if 780 subjects were used in the study. Thus, in most measurement problems, there is very little error in the estimation of reliability that could be attributed to random error in the selection of items. A very important point is that if two tests supposedly from the same domain correlate less with one another than would be predicted from the average correlation among items within each test, the difference usually is caused not by random errors in the selection of items, but by either sampling error because of the numbers of persons or systematic differences in the way items are obtained for the two tests. In other words, when this occurs in a large sample of persons, the indication is that the two tests are representative of somewhat different domains of content, a point which will be discussed more fully later.

It should be kept in mind that if, for example, the average correlation in a sample of 40 items is .20, the estimated correlation of total scores on the test with true scores will not be .20, but considerably higher than that (exactly how much will be discussed later). A confidence zone for the reliability of the whole test can be obtained by extrapolating the upper and lower bounds of the confidence zone for the average correlation among items on the test. This can be done with Eq. (6-18), which will be discussed later. First, the lower bound of the confidence zone for the average correlation among items is placed in the formula, which provides a lower bound of the confidence zone for the reliability r_{11} of the whole test. Next, the upper bound of the confidence zone

internal structure of measures

for the average correlation among items is placed in the formula, which provides an estimate of the upper bound of the confidence zone for the reliability of the whole test. Although confidence zones for whole tests are larger than confidence zones for individual items, if the test has as many as 40 items, the confidence zone usually is surprisingly small.

If the assumptions of the domain-sampling model hold and the numbers of persons and test items are relatively large, there is practically no error in estimating the correlation of a collection of items with true scores. Henceforth it will be assumed that those conditions hold, and consequently we shall speak of "determining" rather than "estimating" various statistics regarding measurement error.

It should be reiterated that the foregoing principles concerning the precision of reliability estimates are based on an approximate model which does some injustice to actuality by assuming that correlations among items in a domain are normally distributed and statistically independent of one another. As was mentioned previously, however, these assumptions hold reasonably well for the usual correlations among test items; consequently formulas based on those assumptions should provide useful information about the amount of error to be expected in estimating the reliability coefficient in particular investigations.

VARIANCES OF ITEMS   In this chapter the basic formulas for reliability were derived on the assumption that all items are expressed as standard scores, but in practice items are rarely standardized before they are summed to obtain test scores. One might wonder if such differences in variances that exist among items would disturb the principles that have been developed so far. For example, since dichotomous items will not all have the same p value and thus will not all have the same variance, this might introduce difficulties for the domain-sampling model. In fact, it does not. The model could have been developed from the covariances among items as well as it was from the correlations among items, and the same principles would have resulted. Also, it is clear that differences in p values of items usually have very little effect on the precision of reliability estimates, particularly if the number of items is 20 or more. This was made quite clear in a study by Cronbach and Azuma (1962), in which they randomly sampled artificial items having a range of p values. They found that such random variation in p values had very little effect on the reliability estimates.

deductions from the domain-sampling model

When the domain-sampling model is accepted as a useful foundation, it is possible to deduce many principles regarding measurement error.

These principles are useful both for the development of measurement theory and for handling problems of measurement error in research.

TEST LENGTH   As was mentioned previously, the reliability of scores obtained on a sample of items from a domain increases with the number of items sampled. Thus the individual item would be expected to have only a small correlation with true scores; a 10-item test might correlate .50 with true scores, and a 100-item test might correlate above .90 with true scores. The rate at which the reliability increases as a function of the number of items can be deduced in the following way. The matrix below depicts the correlations of items with true scores and with one another:

The first column and first row of the matrix would contain correlations of true scores with all variables. The first diagonal element would contain the correlation of true scores with themselves, which would be 1.0. Also, all the other diagonal elements would equal 1.0. The remaining portions of the matrix would contain all possible correlations of items with one another. From what was learned previously about the correlation of sums, one can develop the correlation of the k items with true scores in the following steps:

$$(6\text{-}14) \qquad r_{t(1 \cdots k)} = \frac{\Sigma r_{it}}{\sqrt{r_{tt}} \sqrt{k + 2\Sigma r_{ij}}}$$

Equation (6-14) is simply the correlation of the sum of k variables with one variable, t. The numerator can be expressed as k times the average correlation of items with true scores. In the denominator, the term on the left is 1.0; thus it drops out of the equation. The remaining term of the denominator is the square root of the sum of the elements in that part of the matrix showing correlations among the k items. There would, of course, be k diagonal elements. Instead of having two times the sum of correlations among items, one can place in the denominator two times the average correlation multiplied by the number of

internal structure of measures

correlations. With these considerations in mind, Eq. (6-14) can be transformed as follows:

(6-15) $$r_{t(1 \cdots k)} = \frac{k\bar{r}_{it}}{\sqrt{k + k^2\bar{r}_{ij} - k\bar{r}_{ij}}}$$

The formula is theoretically correct, but since the numerator contains the average hypothetical correlation of items with true scores, as it stands It is of no practical use. It is instructive to see what happens when both sides of the equation are squared ($r_{t(1 \cdots k)}^2$ will be symbolized as r_{kk}):

(6-16) $$r_{kk} = \frac{k^2\bar{r}_{it}^2}{k + k^2\bar{r}_{ij} - k\bar{r}_{ij}}$$

(6-17) $$r_{kk} = \frac{k\bar{r}_{it}^2}{1 + (k - 1)\bar{r}_{ij}}$$

Since the correlation of any item with true scores is estimated by the square root of the average correlation of that item with other items, in the numerator $k\bar{r}_{ij}$ can be substituted for $k\bar{r}_{it}^2$, resulting in

(6-18) $$r_{kk} = \frac{k\bar{r}_{ij}}{1 + (k - 1)\bar{r}_{ij}}$$

It is hard to overestimate the importance of Eq. (6-18) for the theory of measurement error. An example will serve to show what can be learned from applying the formula. If, in a 20-item test, the average correlation among items is .25, these values could be substituted in Eq. (6-18) as follows:

$$r_{kk} = \frac{20 \times .25}{1 + (19 \times .25)}$$

$$= \frac{5.00}{1 + 4.75}$$

$$= \frac{5.00}{5.75}$$

$$r_{kk} = .87$$

Previously it was shown that r_{kk} is the square of the correlation of scores on a collection of items with true scores. Consequently, in the above example, the correlation with true scores would equal the square root of .87, which is .93. Thus it can be seen how a highly reliable total test score can be obtained from items that correlate only .25 with one another on the average.

Although r_{kk} was introduced as a way of obtaining the correlation of a collection of items with true scores, it has considerable meaning in its own right. It is the expected correlation of one k-item test with other k-item tests drawn from the same domain. Thus r_{kk} is the *reliability coefficient* for a k-item test determined from the *intercorrelations of items* on the test. As will be discussed more fully in the next chapter, in many ways this is the most meaningful measure of reliability.

Equation (6-18) holds regardless of the size of units that are added. All one needs to know is the average correlation among the units. Thus the formula would hold if the k units being combined were pairs of items, groups wth 10 items in each, or groups with 1,000 items in each. If the assumptions of the domain-sampling model hold, one will come to approximately the same conclusion about the reliability of a test with a particular number of items regardless of the number of items in each unit which is combined to obtain the final test. For example, for a 40-item test, rather than estimate the reliability by placing the average correlation among items in Eq. (6-18), a different approach would be to randomly divide the 40 items into four groups of 10 each. The average correlation among the four groups of items would be inserted in Eq. (6-18), with k equaling 4 rather than 40. The estimated reliability of the 40-item test would be approximately the same by the two approaches.

One of the most frequent uses of Eq. (6-18) is with respect to the split-half measure of reliability, which will be discussed more fully in the next chapter. For this, the items of a test are divided in half, and the two half-tests are correlated. The question is then one of what would be the reliability of the whole test. When only two samples of items from the domain are being added, Eq. (6-18) reduces to

(6-19) $$r_{kk} = \frac{2r_{12}}{1 + r_{12}}$$

where r_{12} = correlation between two half-tests
r_{kk} = reliability of whole test

RELIABILITY OF AN ITEM SAMPLE   The logic developed in the previous section for determining the effect of test length on reliability can be extended to determine the reliability of any particular sample of items. It was shown that the reliability depends entirely on the average correlation among items and the number of items. These values could be substituted in Eq. (6-18) to obtain the reliability for any particular test. In practice, however, it is tedious to compute all correlations among items or other units being summed. There is a much easier way to obtain the same result. Looking back at Eq. (6-16), one can see that in the numerator $\bar{r}_{ij}$ could be used instead of $\bar{r}_{it}^2$. Equation (6-18) then would be

(6-20) $$r_{kk} = \frac{k^2 \bar{r}_{ij}}{k + k^2 \bar{r}_{ij} - k \bar{r}_{ij}}$$

The denominator equals the sum of all elements in the matrix of correlations for the k variables. Thus Eq. (6-20) could be rewritten as

(6-21) $\quad r_{kk} = \dfrac{k^2 \bar{r}_{ij}}{\bar{R}}$

The numerator equals the sum of all the elements in a square table of correlations where the average element is $\bar{r}_{ij}$. This is almost the same as the sum of elements in the matrix of correlations among items, except for two important differences. First, the former matrix would not have variances on the diagonal (unities, in this case, with standardized scores). Consequently the sum of variances (k) would have to be subtracted from R to give a first approximation of the numerator. It would be only an approximation, because the sum of elements with zeros in the diagonal would equal $(k^2 - k)\bar{r}_{ij}$ rather than $k^2\bar{r}_{ij}$. In other words, after the sum of variances is subtracted from R, the result would need to be inflated by the following ratio to obtain $k^2\bar{r}_{ij}$:

$$\frac{k^2}{k^2 - k} = \frac{k}{k - 1}$$

With these considerations in mind, it then is possible to write the formula for the reliability of a k-item test as

(6-22) $\quad r_{kk} = \dfrac{\left(\dfrac{k}{k-1}\right)(\bar{R} - \Sigma \sigma_i{}^2)}{\bar{R}}$

$$= \frac{k}{k-1}\left(\frac{\bar{R} - \Sigma \sigma_i{}^2}{\bar{R}}\right)$$

Since variables are expressed as standard scores, Eq. (6-22) would reduce to

(6-23) $\quad r_{kk} = \dfrac{k}{k-1}\left(\dfrac{\bar{R} - k}{\bar{R}}\right)$

Whereas up to this point it has proved convenient to work with standardized scores, in actual computations it is more convenient to work with the covariances among items rather than with their correlations. Also, as was mentioned previously, the assumption that all items have the same variance (same p value for dichotomous items) is a potential source of imprecision in the estimation of reliability. All the formulas and principles that have been developed could have been developed on the basis of the average covariance among items. In that case Eq. (6-22) would change to

(6-24) $\quad r_{kk} = \dfrac{k}{k-1}\left(\dfrac{\bar{C} - \Sigma \sigma_i{}^2}{\bar{C}}\right)$

It will be remembered that $\bar{C}$ is the sum of the elements in a covariance matrix, in this case the square matrix showing all variances of items and all covariances among them.

Equation (6-24) could actually be used to estimate the reliability of a k-item test. After the covariance matrix was obtained, the proper sums of elements could be placed in the formula. But what was learned previously about the variance of sums points to a much simpler approach. Since the variance of a sum of items σ_y^2 equals the sum of the elements in the covariance matrix for the items entering the sum, $\bar{C} = \sigma_y^2$. Thus Eq. (6-24) may be rewritten as

$$(6\text{-}25) \quad r_{kk} = \frac{k}{k-1}\left(\frac{\sigma_y^2 - \Sigma\sigma_i^2}{\sigma_y^2}\right)$$

It also can be written as

$$(6\text{-}26) \quad r_{kk} = \frac{k}{k-1}\left(1 - \frac{\Sigma\sigma_i^2}{\sigma_y^2}\right)$$

Equation (6-26) is one of the most important deductions from the theory of measurement error. In that form it is referred to as *coefficient alpha*. The same formula is derivable from the parallel-test model, and very similar formulas are derivable from other mathematical models for measurement error. Although it may look very different, coefficient alpha is identical to Eq. (6-18) for estimating the reliability of a k-item test when (1) the average covariance among items is employed in the latter rather than the average correlation among items and (2) the average of the item variances (pq values for dichotomous items) is substituted for 1 as the first item in the denominator of Eq. (6-18). All these considerations converge to justify the statement that coefficient alpha is a very important formula in the theory of reliability. It represents the expected correlation of one test with an alternative form containing the same number of items. The square root of coefficient alpha is the estimated correlation of a test with errorless true scores. It is so pregnant with meaning that it should routinely be applied to all new tests.

When, as is usually the case, an investigation is being made of the reliability of a test composed of dichotomous items, coefficient alpha takes on the following special form:

$$(6\text{-}27) \quad r_{kk} = \frac{k}{k-1}\left(1 - \frac{\Sigma pq}{\sigma_y^2}\right)$$

The first step in determining the reliability of a test composed of dichotomous items is to find the p value for each item, which is then multiplied by $1 - p$. These products are then summed. The second step is to com-

internal structure of measures

pute the variance of scores on the total test, which is then divided into the sum of pq values. After this is subtracted from 1, the result is multiplied by the ratio of the number of test items to the number of test items minus 1. This version of coefficient alpha is referred to as "Kuder-Richardson Formula 20" (KR-20). It is easy to compute, and there is no excuse for not computing it for any new measure.

Another way of looking at coefficient alpha will serve to further indicate its importance. It will be remembered that the reliability coefficient of any test is the estimated average correlation of that test with all possible tests with the same number of items which are obtainable from sampling a domain. Thus coefficient alpha is the expected correlation of one test with another test of the same length when the two tests purport to measure the same thing. Coefficient alpha can also be derived as the expected correlation between an actual test and a *hypothetical* alternative form, one that may never be constructed. If the actual test is called x and the hypothetical test is called y, then the total covariance matrix for all items on the two tests can be schematized as follows:

	x	y
x	C_x	C_{xy}
y	C_{xy}	C_y

From the domain-sampling model, it is expected that the average diagonal term in C_x is the same as that in C_y and the average off-diagonal elements in the two matrices are the same. Also, it is expected that the average element throughout C_{xy} equals the average off-diagonal element in C_x. Thus coefficient alpha can be derived from the correlation of sums as follows:

$$r_{xy} = \frac{\bar{C}_{xy}}{\sqrt{\bar{C}_x}\,\sqrt{\bar{C}_y}}$$

According to the model, $\bar{C}_x$ approximately equals $\bar{C}_y$, so the equation can be rewritten as

$$r_{xy} = \frac{\bar{C}_{xy}}{\bar{C}_x}$$

According to the model, the average coefficient in C_{xy} (and thus the sum of coefficients) is derivable from C_x. First, it would be necessary to subtract from C_x the variances of items lying on the diagonal. Then it would be necessary to inflate the result by the factor developed previously, that is, $k/(k-1)$. This then brings one right back to coefficient alpha. It is at the heart of the theory of measurement error.

VARIANCE OF TRUE AND ERROR SCORES   Previously it was shown that the reliability coefficient can be expressed as follows:

$$r_{11} = \frac{\sigma_t^2}{\sigma_x^2}$$

The reliability coefficient equals the ratio of true-score variance to the actual variance of the measure. Then it is apparent that

(6-28) $\sigma_t^2 = r_{11}\sigma_x^2$

and that

$$\sigma_t = \sqrt{r_{11}}\,\sigma_x$$

Unless x is perfectly reliable, the variance of true scores will be less than the variance of obtained scores by a factor of r_{11}. Since error scores are uncorrelated with true scores, it follows that

(6-29) $\sigma_x^2 = \sigma_t^2 + \sigma_e^2$

These facts might lead one to the erroneous conclusion that, generally speaking, reliable tests tend to have smaller standard deviations than unreliable tests have. Just the reverse is true. A look back at coefficient alpha [Eq. (6-26)] will show why this is so. The larger the average covariance among items, the more reliable is the test. When the sum of covariance terms is zero, the reliability is zero. It will be remembered that the variance of a sum equals the sum of variances *plus* the sum of all covariances in the covariance matrix. The variance of a totally unreliable test equals the sum of variances only. Consequently the more reliable the test, the larger is the variance of test scores. If, for example, two 20-item tests have the same average pq value, the one with the larger variance is more reliable.

✔ It is true that the error variance adds to *whatever reliable variance is present,* but it also is true that the reliable variance adds to whatever error variance is present. Since, in a completely unreliable measure, the variance of scores equals the sum of the variance of items, this places a limit on the size of the measurement error that can be present. As the test becomes reliable, the covariance terms become positive, and as the covariance terms are made larger, the variance of test scores becomes larger. Whereas there is a severe limit on the size of the variance of errors, there is a much less severe limit on the sum of covariance terms. For example, in the typical 30-item test with moderately high reliability, the covariances among items contribute at least three times as much to the variance of test scores as do the item variances. Thus it is seen that reliable tests tend to have large variances of total scores relative to that found on unreliable tests of the same length.

ESTIMATION OF TRUE SCORES   Since the square root of r_{11} (r_{1t}) is the estimated correlation of obtained scores with true scores, it can be used to estimate true scores from obtained scores. It will be remembered that when variables are expressed as deviation scores, the regression equation for estimating one from the other is as follows:

$$y' = \frac{\sigma_y}{\sigma_x} r_{xy} x$$

The problem to be considered is the estimation of true scores t from obtained scores x. Previously it was shown that the standard deviation of true scores equals $\sqrt{r_{xx}}\, \sigma_x$ (r_{xx} being the reliability of x). Then estimates of true scores can be obtained as follows:

(6-30)

$$t' = \frac{\sigma_t}{\sigma_x}(r_{xt})x$$

$$= \frac{\sqrt{r_{xx}}\,\sigma_x}{\sigma_x}(r_{xt})x$$

$$= \sqrt{r_{xx}}\,(r_{xt})x$$

Since r_{xt} equals the square root of r_{xx},

(6-31)

$$t' = \sqrt{r_{xx}}\,\sqrt{r_{xx}}\,x$$

$$= r_{xx}x$$

Estimates of true scores are computed by multiplying obtained scores by the reliability coefficient.

Although Eq. (6-31) is the best least-squares estimate of true scores from *linear* regression, it was not assumed in the domain-sampling model that tests in the domain necessarily have linear regressions with true scores. There are models for measurement error that lead to the conclusion that the regression of true scores on obtained scores frequently is nonlinear (but always monotonic); such models are discussed by Lord (1959). The assumption of linear regression of true scores on obtained scores is not crucial for most of the principles derivable from the domain-sampling model, e.g., the effect of test length on reliability, but it is crucial for the development of any relatively simple methods for the estimation of true scores. (Some of the models that permit nonlinear regression of true scores on obtained scores are so complex as to be understood and appreciated only by the ultra specialist in the study of measurement error.) Consequently in this section it will be assumed that the regressions are linear.

As is true in any correlational analysis, obtained scores must be *regressed* to obtain a best least-squares estimate of true scores. Hidden in this fact is an important principle: *Obtained scores are biased estimates of true scores.* Scores above the mean are biased upward, and scores below the mean are biased downward. The further scores are in either direction from the mean of obtained scores, the more, in an absolute sense, scores are biased. As a group, people with high obtained scores have a preponderance of positive errors of measurement, and the opposite is true for people who have low obtained scores. In one sense this fact makes little difference. Estimated true scores correlate perfectly with obtained scores; they both have means of zero, and the shapes of distributions are identical. For these reasons, in most investigations there is nothing to be gained by estimating true scores, which is a point that will be considered more fully in the next chapter. The only practical importance of estimating true scores is in setting confidence zones for the effects of measurement error on obtained scores, which will be discussed in the next section.

The fact that obtained scores are biased raises an important theoretical point. If one actually had true scores, these could be used in the usual regression equation for estimating obtained scores. To simplify the problem, imagine that both true scores and obtained scores were standardized, in which case the regression equation would be given as

(6-32)
$$z_x' = r_{xt}z_t$$

where z_x' = estimates of obtained standard scores for x

z_t = true scores

r_{xt} = correlation of true and obtained scores

Subtracting values of z_x' from the actual values of z_x would provide the errors of estimation, which are the errors because of unreliability. It will be remembered that such errors of estimation correlate zero with the variable used to make the estimates (true scores), which is another way of stating the assumption that error scores are uncorrelated with true scores. But it also should be remembered that errors of estimate do correlate with the variable being estimated, in this case with obtained scores. The amount would be as follows:

(6-33)
$$r_{xe} = \sqrt{1 - r_{xt}^2}$$
$$= \sqrt{1 - r_{xx}}$$

Thus it would be found, for example, that if x had a reliability of .64, obtained scores would correlate .60 with error scores. The correlation would be positive, because high obtained scores are biased upward and low obtained scores are biased downward. In spite of the obvious conclusion that errors must correlate positively with obtained scores,

It is surprising how often this point is either overlooked or misunderstood.

STANDARD ERROR OF MEASUREMENT The standard error of estimating obtained scores from true scores is computed as it is in all correlational problems. In the general case, the standard error of estimating one variable in deviation-score form (x) from another variable in deviation-score form (y) is

$$\sigma_{\text{est}} = \sigma_x \sqrt{1 - r_{xy}^2}$$

If x is a set of obtained scores and y is a set of true scores, the formula is

(6-34)

$$\sigma_{\text{est}} = \sigma_x \sqrt{1 - r_{xt}^2}$$
$$= \sigma_x \sqrt{1 - r_{xx}} = \sigma_{\text{meas}}$$

The standard error of estimating obtained scores from true scores is called the *standard error of measurement* and is given the special symbol σ_{meas}.

The standard error of measurement is the expected standard deviation of scores for any person taking a large number of randomly parallel tests. One can use it to set confidence zones for obtained scores, but in so doing one must understand that such confidence zones *are not symmetrical about the obtained score.* Thus, although it usually is done in practice, it is incorrect to set the 95 percent confidence zone as equaling two standard errors of measurement below and two above the obtained score. The confidence zone is symmetrical about the estimated true score t', as will be discussed more fully in the next chapter.

The use of σ_{meas} implicitly assumes that the distribution of errors has the same shape and size for people at different points on the continuum of true scores. These assumptions are not made by the domain-sampling model, and they are not needed for the most important deductions from the model. They are required, however, if one is to set confidence zones for estimated true scores, but there are reasons to believe that both assumptions are somewhat incorrect in most empirical problems. One can see why this is so by looking at another mathematical model for measurement error, a model that is not as generally useful as the domain-sampling model, but is particularly relevant to determining the shape and width of the distributions of errors at different points on the continuum of true scores. The model is based on the assumption that errors have a *binomial* distribution about true scores. The model can be illustrated in the special case where all items in a domain would have p values of .5 if they were administered to a large group of people. Then a person with an average true score would have a probability of .5 of correctly answering any item selected at random from the domain. His expected score on any random sample of items would be half the number of items, but this would vary from sample to sample in terms of the binomial distribution. Since errors are random, for any person the scores obtained on one sample of items would be statistically independent of scores obtained on other samples, and consequently a binomial distribution of obtained scores would be found for each person. As was mentioned previously, the shape of the binomial distribution and its standard deviation depend on p values and the number of test items. For this hypothetical person, one would expect to find a symmetrical distribution, approaching the normal distribution as the number of items in different tests were made larger and larger.

With this model, it is interesting to see what deductions would be made about a person who had a very high true score. He would have a high probability of correctly answering items drawn at random from the domain. Consequently the distribution of scores on different

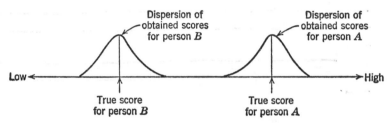

figure 6-3 *True scores and skewed distributions of obtained scores for two persons.*

samples of items would not be symmetrical, but would tend to be skewed to the left, toward the lower end of the continuum of obtained scores. Also, his standard deviation of obtained scores would be *less* than that for a person with an average true score. For a person with a very low true score, the distribution of obtained scores would be skewed to the right, and he also would have a smaller standard deviation of such scores than would a person with an average true score. The amount of skewness for persons at either extreme of the true-score continuum would be inversely related to the number of test items. With no more than 20 items, the skewness might be quite marked; with as many as 100 items, the skewness might be unnoticeable.

Since the binomial model is a very sensible model for determining the shape and distribution of obtained scores, it forces one to reconsider the simple model depicted in Figure 6-1. The situation illustrated in Figure 6-3 is more realistic than that of depicting the standard error of measurement as the same at all points on the continuum of true scores and the distribution of such errors as normal. In Figure 6-3, it is indicated that as true scores depart from the average, distributions

.of obtained scores tend to have smaller standard deviations and tend to be skewed toward the opposite end of the continuum. Even if this is the more realistic picture, it does not change the great practical advantages of using the standard error of measurement as an overall index of the amount of error. The latter holds true on the average, and this is sufficient for most uses of such tools in research.

ATTENUATION   At the start of this chapter it was said that measurement error is "bad," because it tends to obscure—or, as it is called, "attenuate"—any lawfulness in nature. This means that it makes correlations less than they would be if measurement error were not present. From the theory of measurement error, it is possible to estimate how much effect measurement error has on particular correlations, or conversely, how much correlations between true scores would be higher than those between fallible scores. The proper formulas could be developed in a number of ways. A simple approach is as follows. Any two tests from two different domains would be expected to have uncorrelated errors, and errors on either test would be uncorrelated with true scores on either test. Then the correlation between fallible scores on the two tests can be "taken apart" as follows:

$$r_{12} = \frac{\sigma_{12}}{\sigma_1 \sigma_2}$$

$$= \frac{\frac{1}{N} \Sigma (t_1 + e_1)(t_2 + e_2)}{\sigma_1 \sigma_2}$$

$$= \frac{\frac{1}{N} \Sigma (t_1 t_2 + t_1 e_2 + t_2 e_1 + e_1 e_2)}{\sigma_1 \sigma_2}$$

$$= \frac{\frac{1}{N} (\Sigma t_1 t_2 + \Sigma t_1 e_2 + \Sigma t_2 e_1 + \Sigma e_1 e_2)}{\sigma_1 \sigma_2}$$

All but the first term in the numerator are zero, so the formula can be written as

(6-35) $r_{12} = \dfrac{\sigma_{t_1 t_2}}{\sigma_1 \sigma_2}$

This transformation of the numerator shows that *the covariance of obtained scores is equal to the covariance of true scores*. If there were no error present, the covariance term in the numerator would remain the same, but the standard deviations in the denominator would shrink by the amount derived previously. Thus if there were no error present, the correlation $\hat{r}_{12}$ between the two sets of scores would be as follows:

$$\hat{r}_{12} = \frac{\sigma_{12}}{(\sqrt{r_{11}}\,\sigma_1)(\sqrt{r_{22}}\,\sigma_2)}$$

(6-36)

$$= \frac{\dfrac{\sigma_{12}}{\sigma_1 \sigma_2}}{\sqrt{r_{11}}\,\sqrt{r_{22}}}$$

$$= \frac{r_{12}}{\sqrt{r_{11}}\,\sqrt{r_{22}}}$$

Equation (6-36) is spoken of as the "correction" for attenuation, but it is really an estimate rather than a correction—an estimate of how much the correlation would be if two variables were made perfectly reliable. In other words, Eq. (6-36) estimates the limiting value of the correlation between samples of items from two domains when the number of items from each domain is made larger and larger.

Equation (6-36) also applies to samples of items drawn from the *same* domain, but in this case the result is trivial. The correlation between two such tests would be expected to equal the product of terms in the denominator, and consequently $\hat{r}_{12}$ would equal 1.0.

One important principle derivable from Eq. (6-36) concerns the maximum correlation that any set of fallible scores can have with any other set of scores. If $\hat{r}_{12}$ were 1.0, r_{12} would be limited only by the reliabilities of the two tests:

(6-37)

$$1.00 = \frac{r_{12}}{\sqrt{r_{11}}\,\sqrt{r_{22}}}$$

$$r_{12} = \sqrt{r_{11}}\,\sqrt{r_{22}}$$

Thus it can be seen that it is possible for one test to have a correlation with another test which is higher than its own reliability coefficient. In the limiting case, if the second test were perfectly reliable, the first test could correlate with the second test as high as the square root of its reliability coefficient. Since the square root of the reliability is the correlation of a test with true scores, this naturally places a limit on the extent to which a sample of items from one domain can correlate with a sample of items from another. Had any other conclusion been reached, the utility of the domain-sampling model would have been seriously questioned. In the next chapter various uses of formulas concerning attenuation will be discussed and illustrated.

alternative models

Major emphasis in this chapter has been placed on the domain-sampling model because (1) it is easy for most persons to understand; (2) it permits simple derivations of important principles; and (3) deductions from the model have a high degree of internal consistency. Regarding this last point, it was seen in numerous places that there are several different approaches to deriving the same formulas, and formulas serving quite different purposes were shown to be derivable from one another.

Other models are available to "compete" with the domain-sampling model. One of these is the parallel-test model, which some authors prefer. It was shown that this model is only a special case of the domain-sampling model and any advantages it supposedly has are illusory. Another model which was illustrated is the binomial model, which is useful for discussing the distribution of errors of measurement and can be used for that purpose as an adjunct to the domain-sampling model. Other models assume only that errors of measurement are random, without assuming a particular shape for the distribution of errors and without assuming that items are sampled from a domain. From this assumption alone it is possible to derive equations specifying the distribution of true scores underlying a number of alternative forms of a test. These and other models for measurement error are discussed by Lord (1959). It should be emphasized, however, that these other models do not present a serious challenge for the domain-sampling model. Some of the models are very complex, and to actually use them in research places a strain on the best of high speed computers. Estimates obtained from these models seldom differ materially from estimates obtained from the domain-sampling model. Also, deductions from the domain-sampling model tend to hold well in actual research. These are reasons why it was said that the domain-sampling model is surprisingly "robust."

SUGGESTED ADDITIONAL READINGS

Cronbach, L. J. Coefficient alpha and the internal structure of tests. *Psychometrika,* 1951, **16**, 297–334.

Guilford, J. P. *Psychometric methods.* New York: McGraw-Hill, 1954, chaps. 13, 14.

Guilford, J. P. *Fundamental statistics in psychology and education.* New York: McGraw-Hill, 1965, chap. 17.

Gulliksen, H. *Theory of mental tests.* New York: Wiley, 1950, chaps. 1–8.

CHAPTER SEVEN
ASSESSMENT OF RELIABILITY

Whereas the previous chapter presented the theory of reliability, this chapter will discuss principles for applying the theory in empirical research. Also, some additional formulas will be developed for problems that frequently occur in the investigation of the effects of measurement error on research results. Previously it was said that measurements are reliable to the extent that they are repeatable and that any random influence which tends to make measurements different from occasion to occasion is a source of measurement error. The domain-sampling model was offered as a way of investigating such random sources of error. Each test is considered as a random sample of items from a domain, and measurement error is present only to the extent that samples are limited in size. Thus if the average correlation among items is positive, a very long test is always a highly reliable test, the degree of reliability being estimated by Eq. (6-18). This line of argument assumes that all measurement error is because of content sampling. But is content sampling the only factor that prevents measurements from being exactly the same on two occasions? First we shall look at some of the factors that reduce the repeatability of measurements, and then we shall see if these can be adequately handled by the domain-sampling model.

sources of error

In practice there are many factors that prevent measurements from being exactly repeatable, the number and kind of factors depending on the nature of the test and how the test is used. Some of the principal sources of measurement error are described in the following sections.

VARIATION WITHIN A TEST It is important to make a distinction between errors of measurement that cause variation in performance from item to item within a test and errors that are manifested only in variation

In performance on different forms of a test given at different times. Errors of the former kind can easily be handled by the domain-sampling model, but a modification of the model is necessary to handle errors of the second kind.

The major source of error within a test is because of the sampling of items. According to the domain-sampling model, each person has a particular probability of correctly answering each item, depending on his true score and the difficulty of the item for people in general. In the simplest case, if a person has an average true score and all the items have p values of .5 for people in general, that person has a probability of .5 of correctly answering any item chosen at random from the domain. He would be expected to correctly answer half the items on any test drawn from the domain, but that expectation would be accompanied by some error. The more items in each test, the less would be the error. The same logic can be extended to items that have no "correct" responses, e.g., to items concerning agreement and disagreement with statements. Each person can be thought of as having a set probability of agreeing with each statement, which in turn would lead to an expected number of agreements with a sample of items. Depending on the number of items in each sample, there would be some variability in scores from test to test.

The error because of the sampling of items is entirely predictable from the average correlation. Consequently coefficient alpha would be the correct measure of reliability for any type of item, and the special version of that formula, KR-20, would be used with dichotomous items.

On multiple-choice tests, guessing is a source of measurement error. If, for example, an individual does not really know the answer to two questions, he might pass one and fail the other purely because of guessing. (Effects of guessing will be discussed more fully in Chapter Fifteen.) Guessing causes some variation in performance from item to item, which tends to lower the test reliability. Guessing is easily handled by the domain-sampling model. The domain can be thought of as consisting of multiple-choice items. The typical correlation among such items would allow an estimate of the reliability of any sample of items. Guessing would serve to lower the typical correlation, but once that typical correlation were estimated from the correlations within a test, it could be used to estimate reliability.

In addition to guessing, many other factors produce variation in scores from item to item within a test. Halfway through a test, a person might get a headache, and this would tend to lower his scores on the remaining items. A person might intend to mark alternative a for a particular item, but purely as a clerical error, mark alternative b instead. Another person might inadvertently skip an item which he could have answered correctly. Halfway through a test, a person might realize that he misinterpreted the test instructions regarding how to respond to items, and not having time to go back to earlier items, he would do better on the remaining items than on the earlier items. Even if a person actually knew the answer to a question, he might give the wrong answer because he accidentally misread "is not an example of" as "is an example of." There are many other factors that produce errors within tests.

To some extent errors of scoring can be assessed within a test. On objective tests, errors of scoring are purely mechanical, but since they tend to lower correlations among items, they are within the scope of the domain-sampling model. On some tests the scoring is largely subjective, as in essay examinations or in most projective tests. The element of chance in the scores given on such tests provides a source of measurement error. Measurement error is caused by fluctuations in standards by the individual grader and by differences in standards of different graders. For the individual grader, such errors are manifested within a test if each item is graded *independently* of other items. For example, on an essay examination the instructor might grade all responses to question 1, then grade all responses to question 2, and so on. If such scores are independent, the average correlation among the items can be used to obtain an accurate estimate of reliability. Although it infrequently occurs, if half the items are scored by one person and the other half are independently scored by another person, the average correlation among items will provide an estimate of the reliability.

All the errors that occur *within* a test can be easily encompassed by the domain-sampling model. The assumptions of the model can be extended to the case where situational influences are randomly "assigned" to the items. Thus not only would each person be administered a random sample of items from the domain, but also each item would be accompanied by a random set of situational factors. Then whether or not a person passes any item drawn at random from the domain is a function partly of the happenstance of which item is selected and partly of the happenstance of the situational factors that accompany the item. All such sources of error will tend to lower the average correlation among items within the test, but the average correlation is all that is needed to estimate the reliability.

VARIATION BETWEEN TESTS If alternative forms of a test are administered two weeks apart, almost never will the two sets of scores correlate perfectly. The domain-sampling model provides a prediction of the correlation, and as was shown in the previous section, the prediction takes account not only of the sampling of content, but also of many sources of errors within each testing session. There are, however, three major sources of error intervening between administrations of different tests that are not precisely estimated from the average correlation of items within each test. The first is because of systematic differences in content of the two tests. The model envisions an actual sampling of items from a hypothetical domain, but of course, in practice items are composed rather than drawn from a hat. For example, two spelling tests independently composed by two persons might emphasize different kinds of words. Then the correlation between the two tests might be less than would be predicted from the average correlation among the items within each test. Similarly, alternative forms of a measure of attitudes toward the United Nations might be systematically different in content, and consequently the correlation between the two forms would be less than that predicted by the domain-sampling model.

A second factor causing variation in scores on some tests from one occasion to another is because of subjectivity of scoring. For example, on an essay examination or a projective test, the same examiner might give somewhat different scores to the same persons; and even larger differences would be expected between the scores given by two examiners. Previously it was said that some of the error because of the subjectivity of scoring by one person could be estimated from the correlation among items within one test if items are scored independently, but this might tap only part of the error. The scorer might change his standards somewhat from one occasion to another. For example, between the two testings, the projective tester might come to regard a particular type of response as more pathological than he previously had regarded it. Previously it was said that if different parts of a test are independently scored by different examiners, the average correlation among all items would be indicative of the error entailed in using different examiners; but since two examiners rarely collaborate in that way, there is an unassessed amount of error because of the examiner who "happens" to score responses for a particular person. Then the average correlation among items on a test scored by one person would tend to overestimate the correlation between alternative forms scored by different persons.

Another source of variation in test performance from one occasion to another is because of the fact that people actually change with regard to the attribute being measured. A person might feel much better on one occasion than on another, might study in the domain of content, or might change his attitude toward the United Nations. It is reasonable to think there is some fluctuation in abilities from day to day, depending on a host of physiological and environmental factors. Even more to be expected are variations in moods, self-esteem, and attitudes toward people and issues. Such changes in people would tend to make correlations between alternative forms less than what would be predicted from the average correlations among items on each test.

Systematic differences in content of tests and variations in people from one occasion to another cannot be adequately handled by a model which is based on the random sampling of items. For adequately handling these factors, the model must be extended to consider the random sampling of *whole tests*, in which case the tests are thought of as being randomly sampled for particular occasions and correlations among tests are permitted to be somewhat lower than would be predicted from the correlations among items within tests. In that case the average correlation among a number of alternative forms administered on different occasions, or the correlation between only two such forms, would be a better estimate of reliability than that provided by coefficient alpha or KR-20.

estimation of reliability

Because measurement error is an important issue in the use of any measurement method, investigations of reliability should be made when new measures are developed. Following are some recommendations regarding how such investigations should be undertaken.

INTERNAL CONSISTENCY   Estimates of reliability based on the average correlation among items within a test are said to concern the "internal consistency." This is partly a misnomer, because the size of the reliability coefficient is based on both the average correlation among items (the internal consistency) and the number of items. Coefficient alpha is the basic formula for determining the reliability based on internal consistency. It, or the special version applicable to dichotomous items (KR-20), should be applied to all new measurement methods. Even if other estimates of reliability should be made for particular instruments, coefficient alpha should be obtained first.

Coefficient alpha sets an upper limit to the reliability of tests constructed in terms of the domain-sampling model. If it proves to be very low, either the test is too short or the items have very little in common. In that case there is no need to make other estimates of reliability (e.g., correlation of alternative forms), because they will prove to be even lower. If, for example, coefficient alpha is only .30 for a 40-item test, the experimenter should reconsider his measurement problem.

Even though potentially there are important sources of measurement error that are not considered by coefficient alpha, it is surprising what little difference these sources of measurement error usually make.

This is particularly so if the test instructions are easily understood and there is little subjectivity of scoring. If coefficient alpha for a particular test is compared with the correlation between alternative forms and at least 300 persons are studied, the two coefficients typically are very close. If, say, the former is .85, it might be found that the latter is .80, but it is rare to find the latter as low as .60. There are exceptions, which will be discussed in the next section, but reliability estimated from internal consistency is usually very close to the reliability estimated from correlations between alternative forms.

Coefficient alpha provides a good estimate of reliability in most situations, since *the major source of measurement error is because of the sampling of content*. Also, previously it was shown that reliability estimates based on internal consistency actually consider sources of error that are based not, strictly speaking, on the sampling of items per se, but on the "sampling" of situational factors accompanying the items.

ALTERNATIVE FORMS   In addition to computing coefficient alpha, with most measures it also is informative to correlate alternative forms. Usually the forms would be administered about two weeks apart. This would provide time for variations in ability and attitude to occur. If the correlation between alternative forms is markedly lower than coefficient alpha, say, by as much as 20 points, it indicates that considerable measurement error is present because of some combination of the three sources of error mentioned previously: systematic differences in content, subjectivity of scoring, or large variations in people over short periods of time. Investigations can be made to determine which of these factors is causing the reduction in reliability.

To investigate variation in scores over short periods of time (two weeks), the correlation obtained on one group of subjects with a two-week interval between testings can be compared with the correlation between forms when they both are administered on the same day. If the correlation between forms administered on the same day is much higher than that between forms administered two weeks apart, it indicates that the trait being measured tends to fluctuate somewhat over short periods of time. In one sense this is not measurement error, since such changes need not be random. For example, a measure of moods would be expected to change somewhat from one occasion to another, because we all have ups and downs in that regard. Usually, however, the effort is to measure some relatively enduring characteristic, one that at least stays relatively stable over a period of two weeks. Consequently, for most purposes, such variations in traits over short periods of time *act* like measurement error in that they tend to attenuate correlations with other variables.

If the correlation between alternative forms administered two weeks apart is low and the correlation between those administered on the same day is equally low, the indication is not that people are changing over time, but that the two forms have largely different types of content. If the average correlation among the items on one form is higher than that among items on the other form, one form is more reliable than the other. This would suggest that something went wrong in the construction of one of the forms. The decision might be to construct a new form and then correlate that with the existing reliable form.

If the average correlation within the two test forms is substantial, but the average cross-correlation between items in the two forms is low, it indicates that the two forms reliably measure somewhat different traits. For example, if the average correlation within each of the two sets of items were .20 and the average correlation between items in the two sets were .10, it would indicate systematic differences in content. This should lead the investigator to think more carefully about the intended domain of content. An inspection of the content might make it evident why the forms differ, which could lead either to emphasizing in the future the type of content in one of the forms or to seeking a type of item that bridges the gap between the two types of content.

It is somewhat more difficult to determine the measurement error because of subjectivity of scoring. Let it be assumed that differences in content of the two forms and variations over short periods of time have been ruled out as major sources of unreliability by the methods described above. Then a separate set of comparisons would be needed for each scorer. Each would score responses to alternative forms given (1) two weeks apart to one group of subjects and (2) on the same day to another group of subjects. If correlations between scorers are high for both groups, it indicates that there is little unreliability from any source, including that because of subjectivity of scoring. If the correlation for the two-week interval is substantially less than the correlation for tests taken on the same day, it indicates that scoring is reliable but the trait varies over short periods of time. If both correlations are low in a number of studies made of different scorers, it is difficult to tell whether the measurement error is because of subjectivity of scoring or some other factor. Since in essence the scorer is "a part of the item," there is no easy way to pick apart the contribution of scoring to the measurement error. There would be many hints as to the possible unreliability of scoring, such as (1) good reason to believe that the trait actually exists, e.g., intelligence, (2) the existence of reliable objective tests of the trait, and (3) considerable variability in the reliability of raters. If the measurement problem is important and it is felt necessary to continue employing subjective methods of scoring, the rules for scoring should be improved. If this results in an increased reliability,

internal structure of measures

it is indicated that unreliability of scoring contributed to the earlier amount of measurement error.

If raters do tend to agree with themselves when scoring the same subjects on alternative forms, another question which arises is whether or not there is measurement error because of differences in scoring by different scorers. This can be easily determined by correlating scorings of alternative forms by different scorers. It is sometimes found that scorers develop their own idiosyncratic methods of scoring, and although each scorer is consistent in employing his method, the scorers do not agree with one another. This works like other sources of measurement error to attenuate relations found between variables in research.

The need to investigate alternative forms of a measure depends very much on the type of measure. Where the domain of content is easily specified, where there is little subjectivity of scoring, and where people tend to vary little over short periods of time, coefficient alpha will provide an excellent estimate of reliability. This is the case, for example, for most tests of aptitude and achievement. It is necessary to investigate alternative forms if the trait is suspected to vary considerably over relatively short periods of time, as would be true for measures of moods and some measures of attitudes. In some cases the experimenter is challenged to compose alternative forms to satisfy others that there is a definable domain of content. This occurs with some projective techniques, such as the Rorschach, where there is some question as to whether or not it is possible to construct an alternative form. If an alternative form cannot be constructed, it is not possible to define the domain of content, and there is no way to accurately communicate what is being measured; furthermore, it is doubtful that anything of importance is being measured.

OTHER ESTIMATES OF RELIABILITY   Coefficient alpha and correlations between alternative forms (under the various conditions mentioned previously) are the basic estimates of reliability. There are other ways of estimating reliability which, though not recommended for most measurement problems, are frequently encountered in research reports. Instead of employing coefficient alpha or KR-20, one may estimate reliability from various subdivisions of a test. The most popular method is the *split-half* approach, in which items within a test are divided in half and scores on the two half-tests are correlated. Usually the items are halved by placing the even-numbered items in one group and the odd-numbered items in the other group. There are many other ways to make the division, e.g., randomly dividing items into two groups or separately scoring the first and second halves of the items. After the correlation is obtained, it must be corrected by Eq. (6-19) to obtain the reliability coefficient.

The difficulty with the split-half method is that the correlation between halves will vary somewhat depending on how the items are divided, which raises some questions regarding what *the* reliability is. Actually, it is best to think of the corrected correlation between any two halves of a test as being an estimate of coefficient alpha. Then it is much more sensible to employ coefficient alpha than any split-half method. The only reason for employing a split-half method occurs when the items are scored not dichotomously, but on three or more points. In that case it is not possible to use the KR-20 version of the coefficient alpha. With KR-20, it is very easy to obtain the p values for items and thus the variances of items; but if the number of items is large and computer services are not available, it might prove excessively time-consuming to compute variances for multipoint items (which would be required by coefficient alpha). It is much easier to separately score odd and even items, correlate the two sets of scores, and make the necessary correction [Eq. (6-9)].

There are many other ways to obtain reliability estimates from subdivisions of items. For example, the items can be randomly divided into four equal parts. The average correlation among the four sets of scores can be placed in Eq. (6-18) to obtain an estimate of the reliability of the whole test. There would, however, be nothing to gain by such methods of estimating reliability. The results would serve only to estimate coefficient alpha. If items are scored dichotomously, there is no excuse for not computing KR-20. If items are scored on more than two points, it is wise to compute coefficient alpha. When saving computational time is an important consideration, the corrected correlation betwen odd and even items will provide a good approximation of coefficient alpha.

One appropriate use of the split-half method is in measuring variability of traits over short periods of time when alternative forms are not available. For example, the odd items can be given as one test on the first occasion, and the even items can be given as an alternative form on the second occasion. The corrected correlation between the two sets of scores will indicate the relative stability of the trait over that period of time. The result will be an accurate estimate of the correlation to be found between alternative forms if (1) the items are not markedly affected by fatigue, (2) there are enough items in each half-test to provide a precise estimate of reliability (at least 20), and (3) the actual alternative forms do not differ systematically in content. It is better to actually construct alternative forms and correlate them, but if that is not feasible, the split-half measure over time can be employed instead.

In place of using the alternative-form method for determining reliability, the *retest method* can be used, in which the same test is given to the same people after a period of time. Except for certain special instances, there are serious defects in employing the retest method.

internal structure of measures

The major defect is that experience in the first testing will influence responses in the second testing. To the extent that responses to the first testing are remembered, they will tend to be repeated on the retest. Also, the individual will tend to repeat his work habits and make much the same guesses on items where he is unsure. This works to make the correlation between testings higher than it would be for alternative forms.

Another difficulty with the retest method is that it does not fit very well into the domain-sampling model. In the model, the reliability of any test is strictly a function of the average correlation among items. As was mentioned previously, estimates derived from that model, e.g., KR-20, tend to be approximately the same as correlations actually obtained between alternative forms. The reason the retest method does not fit the model is that the retest correlation is only partly dependent on the correlation among items within a test. Thinking back about principles concerning the correlation of sums will show why that is the case. Even if the items within each testing correlated zero on the average with one another, it still would be possible to obtain a positive correlation between scores in the two testings. The numerator of the correlation of sums is the sum of all the cross-covariances (correlations, if scores are standardized) between the two sets of items being summed. Even if all the cross-correlations between different items were zero, each item might correlate well with itself on the two testings. Such correlations would be expected to be much higher than those usually found between different items, and they could produce a substantial correlation between retests.

If coefficient alpha is low for a test, a relatively high correlation between retests should not be taken as an indication of high "reliability." As has been mentioned in a number of places, a test should "hang together" in the sense that the items should correlate with one another. Otherwise it makes little sense to add scores over items and speak of the total scores as measuring any attribute. The major information supplied by the retest method is "negative": if the retest correlation is low, the alternative form correlation will be even lower. If a test does not even correlate with itself when administered on two occasions, it is hopeless to seek other evidence of reliability and hopeless to employ the test in research.

It is recommended that the retest method generally not be used to estimate reliability, but there are some exceptions. In some types of measures, the retest probably would not be markedly affected by the first testing. This would tend to be the case, for example, if an individual were required to rate the pleasantness of 200 designs. The sheer number of ratings would make remembering the ratings of individual designs very difficult, and consequently the retest would be largely independent of the earlier testing. Also, scores would be more nearly independent if there were a long time between testings, say, six months or more.

LONG-RANGE STABILITY   Previously it was said that alternative forms should be administered about two weeks apart to permit short-range fluctuations in abilities and personality characteristics to be manifested. Another issue concerns the stability of scores over relatively long periods of time—upward of six months. If, for example, alternative forms given six months apart correlate less than those given two weeks apart, in a sense the difference is not because of "error," but because of systematic changes in people. As was mentioned previously, what is considered error and what is considered systematic change depends on the way measurement tools are used. If a measure is intended to represent the *relatively enduring* status of a trait in people, it would need to remain relatively stable over the period in which scores were employed for that purpose. A good example is the IQ, which is considered by most people to be a relatively enduring characteristic of the individual, something that might change gradually over a period of years, but not markedly in a period of only one year. If an earlier measurement is used at a later time either to make practical decisions about people or to make decisions about the outcomes of research, then to the extent that the trait being measured has not remained stable, measurement error will reduce the validity of the decisions. As a practical example, if scores on intelligence tests given in the second year of high school are used to make decisions about college entrance for students two years later, the effectiveness of such decisions will be limited by (among other things) the extent to which the trait of intelligence has remained stable during that time. If the correlation between alternative forms of the test over that period of time were very low, some bad mistakes would be made in advising students about college. If, for example, on the earlier testing the student had an IQ of 130 and no later testing were made, it would be tempting to strongly encourage the student to enter college. But suppose that an alternative form of the test were administered near the end of high school and the student's IQ were only 95; with this new evidence in hand, it would be a bad mistake to strongly recommend college training.

As an example of how long-range instability can attenuate research results, suppose that an experiment is being conducted to measure the effect of anxiety on difficult learning tasks. Also, suppose that the test of anxiety is administered six months prior to the learning tasks. If the retest correlation or correlation with an alternative form over the six-month period were low, the possible results from using the first test would be highly attenuated. Of course, instead of relying on measures administered much earlier, it is far better to make measurements shortly before practical decisions are to be made about people or shortly before they are used in experiments.

Aside from questions of measurement error, long-range stability is an important research issue in its own right, as, for example, in studies of the growth and decline of human abilities. Some have accused measurement specialists of assuming that psychological traits remain largely stable throughout life and, thus, that very little can be done to improve people. Such a philosophy is not at all necessary for the theory of measurement error. The theory would hold as well if people changed markedly in their characteristics from day to day; but if that occurred, it would make chaos out of efforts to make practical decisions about people and to find general principles of human behavior. People do change, but fortunately, in most traits they change slowly enough to allow valid uses of psychological measures in daily life and in research investigations.

uses of the reliability coefficient

In the previous section it was shown that it is meaningful to think of a test as having a number of different coefficients of reliability, depending on the major sources of measurement error that are considered. In practice, however, it is useful to speak of a reliability coefficient for a test which summarizes the amount of measurement error expected from using the instrument. In most cases this should be the correlation between alternative forms administered about two weeks apart. If there is an element of subjectivity in the scoring, the alternative forms should be independently scored by different persons. If, for example, five persons score the first form and five other persons score the second, the average correlation between the two sets of scores (25 correlations in this instance) would provide a good reliability coefficient. If alternative forms are not available, the corrected correlation between split-halves given two weeks apart can be used as the reliability coefficient. When alternative forms are not available and testing subjects more than once is not feasible, coefficient alpha can be used as the reliability coefficient.

The major use of the reliability coefficient is in communicating the extent to which the results obtained from a measurement method are repeatable. The reliability coefficient is one index of the effectiveness of an instrument, reliability being a necessary but not sufficient condition for any type of validity. In addition there are other uses that can be made of the reliability coefficient; the major uses are discussed in the following sections.

CORRECTIONS FOR ATTENUATION   One of the most important uses of the reliability coefficient is in estimating the extent to which obtained correlations between variables are attenuated by measurement error. Previously it was shown that the correction for attenuation is as follows:

$$\bar{r}_{12} = \frac{r_{12}}{\sqrt{r_{11}r_{22}}}$$

In this case, $\bar{r}_{12}$ is the expected correlation if both variables are perfectly reliable. If the correction is to be made for only one of the two variables, the reliability coefficient for only that variable will appear under the radical in the denominator.

There is some controversy about when the correction for attenuation should be applied. One could argue that the correction for attenuation provides a way of fooling one's self into believing that a "better" correlation has been found than that actually evidenced in the available data. Another justifiable criticism of many uses of the correction for attenuation is that the so-called correction sometimes provides a very poor estimate of the correlation actually obtained between variables when they are made highly reliable. This can occur if a poor measure of reliability is made, in terms of principles discussed previously, and if the reliability coefficient is based on a relatively small number of cases (less than 300). That poor estimates are often obtained is illustrated by the fact that corrected correlations sometimes are greater than 1.00!

If, however, good estimates of reliability are available, there are some appropriate uses of the correction for attenuation. The most important use is in basic research, where the corrected correlation between two variables is an estimate of how much two traits correlate. In an investigation of the correlation between anxiety and intelligence, for example, the real question is that of how much the two traits go together. If the two measures have only modest reliability, the actual correlation will suggest that the two traits go together less than they really do.

Another important use of the correction for attenuation is in applied settings where a test is used to forecast a criterion. If, as often happens, the criterion is not highly reliable, correcting for unreliability of the criterion will estimate the real validity of the test. Here, however, it would be wrong to make the double correction for attenuation, since the issue is how well a test actually works rather than how well it would work if it were perfectly reliable. In prediction problems, the reliability of the predictor instrument places a limit on its ability to forecast a criterion, and the correction for attenuation cannot make a test more predictive than it actually is. The only use for this double correction would be in estimating the limit of predictive validity of the test as both test and criterion are made more and more reliable.

Since perfect reliability is only a handy fiction, results from applying the foregoing formula for the correction for attenuation are always hypothetical. It is more important to estimate the increase in the correlation

internal structure of measures

between two variables when the reliability is increased by any particular amount. A formula for doing this is as follows:

(7-1)
$$\bar{r}_{12} = \frac{r_{12} \sqrt{r_{11}'r_{22}'}}{\sqrt{r_{11}r_{22}}}$$

where $\bar{r}_{12}$ = estimated correlation between two variables if reliabilities are changed

r_{11}' = changed reliability for variable 1

r_{22}' = changed reliability for variable 2

The use of Eq. (7-1) can be illustrated in the situation where two tests correlate .30 and each test has a reliability of $^\bullet$.60. If the reliability of each test were increased to .90, the expected correlation between the more reliable tests would be obtained as follows:

$$\bar{r}_{12} = \frac{.3 \sqrt{.9 \times .9}}{\sqrt{.6 \times .6}}$$

$$\bar{r}_{12} = .45$$

For the sake of computations, a handier version of Eq. (7-1) is as follows:

(7-2)
$$\bar{r}_{12} = r_{12} \sqrt{\frac{r_{11}'r_{22}'}{r_{11}r_{22}}}$$

The formula also can be used to estimate what the correlation would be if both reliabilities were _lowered_. This is useful when it is necessary to employ shortened versions of longer tests. If the reliabilites are known for both the longer tests and the shortened versions and the correlation is known between the longer tests, the reliabilities of the shortened tests can be placed in Eq. (7-2) as r_{11}' and r_{22}', and the reliabilities of the longer tests as r_{11} and r_{22}. Equation (7-2) applies equally well when the reliability of one test is increased and the reliability of the other is decreased. If the reliability of only one of the two variables is to be changed, Eq. (7-2) becomes

(7-3)
$$\bar{r}_{12} = r_{12} \sqrt{\frac{r_{11}'}{r_{11}}}$$

This version of the formula is useful in estimating how much the correlation of the predictor test with a criterion will change if the reliability of the test is either increased or decreased by particular amounts.

What should be evident from inspecting the formulas concerning corrections for attenuation is that such corrected correlations seldom are dramatically different from the actual correlations. Thus, in the example above, a dramatic increase in the reliability of each test from .60 to .90 resulted in an increase in correlation from .30 to only .45. Such a difference is important, but it is much less than intuitively might be thought to occur. As another example, if the correction were made for only one variable and the reliability were increased from .60 to .80, a correlation of .30 would be expected to rise only to .35. The author once heard a colleague suggest that some low correlations found in a study probably would have been much higher if test reliabilities had been higher. The average correlation was about .15, and the average reliability was about .60. Even if the average reliability of the tests were increased to .90, the average correlation would be less than .25. The colleague had in mind an increase in average correlation to .40 or .50, which could not possibly occur.

CONFIDENCE ZONES   Another use of the reliability coefficient is in establishing confidence zones for obtained scores. Previously it was shown that for any variable x the standard error of measurement is

$$\sigma_{\text{meas}} = \sigma_x \sqrt{1 - r_{xx}}$$

The standard error of measurement is the estimated standard deviation of obtained scores if any individual is given a large number of tests from a domain. It then is useful in establishing confidence zones for scores to be expected on many alternative forms of a test. It was pointed out, however, that it is incorrect to establish such confidence zones symmetrically about the score that a person makes on a particular test. If, for example, an individual has an IQ of 130 on a particular test and the σ_{meas} is 5, it is incorrect to say that the 95 percent confidence zone for that person extends from 120 to 140 ($130 - 2\sigma_{\text{meas}}$ to $130 + 2\sigma_{\text{meas}}$). Even though the practice in most applied work with tests has been to center confidence zones about obtained scores, this is incorrect, because obtained scores tend to be biased, high scores tending to be biased upward and low scores downward.

   Before establishing confidence zones, one must obtain estimates of unbiased scores. Unbiased scores are the average scores people would obtain if they were administered all possible tests from a domain, holding constant the number of items randomly drawn for each. These are true scores, which are estimated as follows:

(7-4) $t' = r_{xx}x$

In the previous example, the individual with an IQ of 130 would have a deviation score x of 30. If the reliability were .90, his estimated true score t' would be 27 in deviation-score units. Adding back the mean IQ of 100 would give an estimated true score of 127 in units of IQ. Then the correct procedure would be to set the 95 percent confidence zone as extending from two standard errors of measurement below 127 to two standard errors above 127. With a σ_{meas} of 5, the zone then would extend from 117 to 137. If a person were administered a large number of alternative forms of the test, 95 percent of the obtained scores would be expected to fall in that zone, and the expected average of the obtained scores would be 127 (not 130).

In most applied work with tests, there is little reason for estimating true scores except for the establishment of confidence zones. Since estimated true scores correlate perfectly with obtained scores and making practical interpretations of estimated true scores is difficult, in most applied work it is better to interpret the individual's obtained score. The estimated true score would be used only to obtain the center for a confidence zone. Thus, in the example above, the individual would be said to have an IQ of 130, with the 95 percent confidence zone extending from 117 to 137. On that same test, a person with an IQ of 70 would have a 95 percent confidence zone extending from 63 to 83. Actually, such asymmetrical confidence zones have a real practical advantage: they continually remind people that scores obtained on any test tend to be biased outward on both sides of the mean.

In contrast to applied work with tests, there seldom is need in basic research to estimate true scores or establish confidence zones. In basic research the major concerns are with how much the measurement error lowers correlations and how much it increases the error components in statistical treatments. It is sometimes necessary in basic research to consider the effect of measurement error on the mean of a group of obtained scores. This would be the case, for example, if extreme groups on a measure were subjected to an experimental treatment and then either a retest were made or an alternative form were applied. The gain or loss scores for individuals, and the average gain and loss scores for the two groups, would be partly determined by regression effects from measurement error. In essence what one must do is estimate average true scores for the two groups on both tests and then see if the average change is different for the two groups. Except for this special problem, however, in basic research there is little to be gained by estimating true scores or establishing confidence zones.

EFFECT OF DISPERSION ON RELIABILITY   It should be realized that, since the reliability coefficient is a correlation coefficient, the size of the reliability coefficient is directly related to the standard deviation of obtained scores for any sample of subjects. Previously it was shown that the reliability coefficient could be expressed as follows:

$$(7\text{-}5) \qquad r_{xx} = 1 - \frac{\sigma_{\text{meas}}^2}{\sigma_x^2}$$

The variance of the errors of measurement is expected to be at least approximately independent of the standard deviation of obtained scores.

In other words the standard error of measurement is considered to be a fixed characteristic of any measurement tool regardless of the sample of subjects under investigation. Then it is apparent that the reliability coefficient will be larger for samples of subjects that vary more with respect to the trait being investigated. An example would be in studying the reliability of scores on a test used to select college freshmen. If the correlation between alternative forms is used as the measure of reliability and the correlation is computed only for persons who actually were accepted for college, the correlation will be less than it would have been if persons who were not permitted to enter college had been included in the study.

A look back at Eq. (7-5) will indicate how estimates can be made of how much the reliability would change if the variance of obtained scores were either larger or smaller. If, for one sample, the variance of errors were 2.0 and the variance of obtained scores were 8.0, the reliability would be .75. If a new sample had a variance of 10.0, the variance of errors would be expected to remain at 2.0, and consequently the reliability would be .80. Thus after the standard error of measurement is found for one sample, it is easy to estimate what the reliability would be in another sample with either a larger or smaller standard deviation of scores.

Even though it is important to keep in mind that the reliability varies with the disperison of scores, this does not alter the direct meaning of the reliability coefficient in any particular sample of people. The reliability coefficient is the ratio of true-score variance to obtained-score variance. If that ratio is small, measurement error will attenuate correlations with other variables and will make it difficult to find significant effects with statistical treatments. If the total group of subjects in a study has a standard deviation of scores which is not much larger than the standard error of measurement, it is hopeless to investigate the variable. Approximately this condition has occurred in some studies. For example, in some studies of creativity, investigations have been made of only those children who had IQs of at least 120. With the children pre-selected in this way, the standard deviation of IQs in the group being studied would not be much larger than the standard error of measurement for the measure of intelligence. Then if IQs for the preselected groups are correlated with scores on tests of creativity, the correlations obviously will be very low.

making measures reliable

Of course, doing everything feasible to prevent measurement error from occurring is far better than assessing the effects of measurement error after it has occurred. Measurement error is reduced by writing items clearly, making test instructions easily understood, and adhering closely to the prescribed conditions for administering an instrument. Measurement error because of subjectivity of scoring can be reduced by making the rules for scoring as explicit as possible and by training scorers to do their jobs. On the better individual tests of intelligence, even though the scorer is a potential source of measurement error on some items, rules for scoring are so explicit and scorers usually are so well trained that very little measurement error is present. Of course, the ideal always is to completely remove subjectivity in scoring, but for practical reasons, that sometimes is difficult to do. For example, in studies of discrimination learning, experimenters have been interested in "observing responses" in the rat—the tendency for the rat at the choice point in a T maze to look back and forth a number of times before making a choice. Conceivably, the number of such observing responses could be objectively recorded with a complex set of instruments, but if different scorers agree reasonably well on the numbers of observing responses made by different rats, the presence of some subjectivity in the scoring may be preferable to the expense and awkwardness of employing objective instruments. Still, though, the ultimate ideal in science is to have measures that are unaffected by errors of human judgment.

TEST LENGTH The primary way to make tests more reliable is to make them longer. If the reliability is known for a test with any particular number of items, the following formula can be used to estimate how much the reliability would increase if the number of items were increased by any factor k:

(7-6) $$r_{kk} = \frac{kr_{11}}{1 + (k - 1)r_{11}}$$

If, for example, the reliability of a 20-item test is .70 and 40 items from the same domain are added to the test (making the final test three times as long as the original), the estimated reliability of the 60-item test will be

$$r_{kk} = \frac{3(.7)}{1 + (3 - 1).7} = .88$$

The only assumption in employing Eq. (7-6) in this case would be that the average correlation among the 20 items in the shorter test be the same as the average correlation among the 60 items in the augmented test. The assumption would be violated if old items and new items differed systematically in content (if they were from somewhat different domains) or if they differed in reliability (if the average correlation in

assessment of reliability

one set were higher than that in the other set). In spite of these sources of imprecision, it is surprising how accurately the effects of test length on reliability are usually estimated by Eq. (7-6). This is particularly so if the shorter test contains at least 20 items. (As will be remembered, the precision of the reliability estimate is directly related to the number of test items.)

Equation (7-6) also can be used to estimate the effects on reliability of shortening a test. In this case k equals the number of items in the shorter test divided by the number of items in the longer test, r_{kk} is the estimated reliability of the shortened test, and r_{11} is the reliability of the longer test. In the previous example, one could work backward from the reliability of .88 for the 60-item test and estimate the reliability of a 20-item test. Then, by placing .88 as r_{11} in Eq. (7-6) and making $k = \frac{1}{3}$, one recovers the original reliability of .70 for the 20-item test. For either lengthening or shortening a test, the precision of the estimate obtained from Eq. (7-6) depends mainly on the number of items in the *shorter* test. To take an extreme case, one would not expect a very precise estimate if the known reliability of a 5-item test were used to estimate the reliability of a 40-item test, or vice versa.

Since Eq. (7-6) shows the test reliability to be a direct function of the number of test items only, one might wonder how it can give accurate estimates where there are other sources of measurement error in tests, e.g., variation in scores over short periods of time. As was argued previously, many such sources of error are considered by the domain-sampling model. Coefficient alpha is sensitive not only to the sampling of items but also to sources of measurement error that are present within the testing session. The alternative-form measure of reliability can be made sensitive to all sources of error, including subjectivity of scoring and variations in abilities and personality characteristics over short periods of time. If coefficient alpha is placed in Eq. (7-6), the estimated coefficient alpha for a longer or shorter test takes into account the sampling of items and numerous sources of error in the testing situation. If the correlation between alternative forms is placed in Eq. (7-6), the estimate takes account of variations over short periods of time and any factors that have been systematically varied for the two testings, e.g., using different scorers for the two tests. A good estimate would then be obtained of the alternative-form reliability for a longer or shorter test over the same period of time and with the same factors systematically varied. For these reasons, Eq. (7-6) is not blind to sources of error other than those because of the sampling of items per se. Coefficient alpha placed in Eq. (7-6) usually gives a good estimate of the coefficient alpha that will be obtained from a lengthened or shortened test. If the alternative-form reliability is placed in Eq. (7-6), it usually will give a good estimate of the alternative-form reliability for a longer or shorter test. Since coefficient alpha usually is a good estimate of the alternative-form reliability, when the former is placed in Eq. (7-6), it usually will give a good estimate of the correlation to be expected between alternative forms with any particular number of items.

An inspection of Eq. (7-6) shows that if the average correlation among items in a domain is positive, no matter how small, then as the number of items in a test is made larger and larger, the reliability necessarily approaches 1.00. If the average correlation is positive, the correlation between any two sample of items (r_{11}) is expected to be positive. If numerator and denominator of Eq. (7-6) are divided by k, and k is allowed to approach infinity, r_{kk} approaches 1.00. At first glance this might seem to be an easy way to obtain highly reliable tests, but often in practice Eq. (7-6) estimates that to reach even a moderately high reliability a huge number of items would be required. A conversion of Eq. (7-6) can be used to estimate the number of items required to obtain a particular reliability:

(7-7)
$$k = \frac{r_{kk}(1 - r_{11})}{r_{11}(1 - r_{kk})}$$

where r_{kk} = desired reliability
r_{11} = reliability of existing test
k = number of times test would have to be lengthened to obtain reliability of r_{kk}

In the situation where a 20-item test has a reliability of .50, the estimated lengthening required to obtain a reliability of .80 is found as follows:

$$k = \frac{.8(1 - .5)}{.5(1 - .8)} = \frac{.4}{.1} = 4$$

Thus the estimate is that to reach a reliability of .80 an 80-item test would be required. In many cases it would be feasible to use a test of that length, but let us see what happens when a 40-item test has a reliability of only .20 and a reliability of .80 is desired:

$$k = \frac{.8(1 - .2)}{.2(1 - .8)} = \frac{.64}{.04} = 16$$

It is estimated that 640 items would be required to reach a reliability of .80. Unless the items were of a kind that could be administered very quickly, a test of that length would be impractical in most applied work and in most experiments. Thus one can see that if the average correlation among items in a domain is very low (e.g., only .05), the correlations between samples of items will not be large, and to obtain high correlations would require a prohibitively large number of items in each sample.

STANDARDS OF RELIABILITY   What a satisfactory level of reliability is depends on how a measure is being used. In the early stages of research on predictor tests or hypothesized measures of a construct, one saves time and energy by working with instruments that have only modest reliability, for which purpose reliabilities of .60 or .50 will suffice. If significant correlations are found, corrections for attenuation will estimate how much the correlations will increase when reliabilities of measures are increased. If those corrected values look promising, it will be worth the time and effort to increase items and reduce measurement error in other ways.

For basic research, it can be argued that increasing reliabilities beyond .80 is often wasteful. At that level correlations are attenuated very little by measurement error. To obtain a higher reliability, say, of .90, strenuous efforts at standardization in addition to increasing the number of items might be required. Thus the more reliable test might be excessively time-consuming to administer and score.

In contrast to the standards in basic research, in many applied settings a reliability of .80 is not nearly high enough. In basic research, the concern is with the size of correlations and with the differences in means for different experimental treatments, for which purposes a reliability of .80 for the different measures involved is adequate. In many applied problems, a great deal hinges on the exact score made by a person on a test. If, for example, in a particular school system children with IQs below 70 are placed in special classes, it makes a great deal of difference whether the child has an IQ of 69 or 70 on a particular test. If a college is able to admit only one-third of the students who apply, whether or not a student is in the upper third may depend on only a few score points on an aptitude test. In such instances it is frightening to think that any measurement error is permitted. Even with a reliability of .90, the standard error of measurement is almost one-third as large as the standard deviation of test scores. In those applied settings where important decisions are made with respect to specific test scores, a reliability of .90 is the minimum that should be tolerated, and a reliability of .95 should be considered the desirable standard.

reliability of linear combinations

So far this discussion of reliability has been concerned with the reliability of particular traits (e.g., spelling ability), as manifested in the average correlation among items. Another issue is that of the reliability of linear combinations of measures of different traits. An example of such a linear combination would be the total score on an achievement test battery for elementary school children, which would be the sum of scores obtained on separate parts of the test for spelling, arithmetic, word usage, and others. This simple linear combination can be depicted as

$$y = x_1 + x_2 + x_3$$

Then the question is that of estimating the reliability of y from a knowledge of the reliabilities of the x variables and the covariances among them.

At first thought it might seem that the reliability of y could be estimated by coefficient alpha. For this, the sum of the variances of the x variables would be divided by the variance of y, the quotient would be subtracted from 1, and the result would be increased by the factor concerning the number of "things" being summed [see Eq. (6-26)]. This could be done, but the result would be quite erroneous unless the x variables were all measures of the same trait, e.g., alternative forms of a test of spelling ability. The reliability of samples of items from the *same* domain depends entirely on the average correlation among the samples, but this does not hold for samples of items from *different* domains. Suppose that, in the example concerning three subtests of an achievement test, each test had a respectable reliability, but the three all correlated zero with one another. In that case coefficient alpha would lead to the conclusion that the sum of the three tests had a reliability of zero, but that would be absurd.

The actual reliability of a linear combination would be determined by correlating alternative forms of the linear combination. Thus if there were alternative forms of the test battery, each with tests of spelling, arithmetic, etc., the alternative forms could be administered approximately two weeks apart. The correlation between total scores on the two occasions would be a good measure of reliability for the linear combination.

In cases where alternative forms are not available or administering them is not feasible, an estimate of the alternative-form reliability can be derived as follows. Previously it was shown that the reliability of any variable equals the true-score variance in that variable divided by the variance of that variable. Thus the reliability of the linear combination would be

(7-8)
$$r_{yy} = \frac{\sigma_{t_y}^2}{\sigma_y^2}$$

where $\sigma_{t_y}^2$ = variance of true scores for linear combination
σ_y^2 = variance of obtained scores for linear combination

assessment of reliability

In the previous example of a simple sum of three variables, the denominator would be the variance of that sum, which equals $\bar{C}_y$, the sum of all elements in the covariance matrix for the three variables. The numerator could be expressed as follows:

$$\sigma_{t_y}{}^2 = \frac{1}{N} \Sigma(t_1 + t_2 + t_3)^2$$

By definition the variance of true scores on y equals the variance of the sum of true scores (t_1, t_2, and t_3) of the x variables. Previously it was shown how the variance of a linear combination could be obtained by placing the variables in the sum on the sides of a square table, multiplying corresponding elements, and dividing each product by the number of persons being studied (N). This would result in a covariance matrix of true scores for the three variables. Each off-diagonal element would be the covariance between two sets of true scores. In Chapter Six it was shown that the covariance of true scores for any two variables is identical to the covariance of obtained scores for those two variables. Thus the off-diagonal elements in the covariance matrix for true scores would be identical to the off-diagonal elements in the covariance matrix for obtained scores. The only difference between the two matrices would be in the diagonal elements. Each diagonal element in the covariance matrix of obtained scores would be a variance of obtained scores. Each diagonal element in the covariance matrix of true scores would equal the sum of squares of true scores for that variable divided by N, which would equal the variance of true scores for that variable. Since the reliability of any variable in the linear combination equals the true-score variance divided by the variance of obtained scores, the true-score variance equals the obtained-score variance multiplied by the reliability. Thus the covariance matrix of true scores for the sum of three variables would be as follows:

	t_1	t_2	t_3
t_1	$r_{11}\sigma_1{}^2$	σ_{12}	σ_{13}
t_2	σ_{12}	$r_{22}\sigma_2{}^2$	σ_{23}
t_3	σ_{13}	σ_{23}	$r_{33}\sigma_3{}^2$

Since the covariance matrix of true scores in the numerator of the equation differs from the covariance matrix in the denominator only in terms of diagonal elements, the former can be expressed in terms of the latter, as follows. To obtain the sum of the elements in the matrix of true scores, first subtract the sum of variances (the sum of diagonal elements) from the covariance matrix for obtained scores; then add to the remainder the sum of products of reliability coefficients and variances (the sum of diagonal elements in the covariance matrix for true scores). The reliability of the sum of variables will then be as follows:

(7-9) $\quad r_{yy} = \dfrac{{}^{t}\bar{C}_y - \Sigma\sigma_i^2 + \Sigma r_{ii}\sigma_i^2}{\bar{C}_y}$

(7-10) $\quad r_{yy} = 1 - \dfrac{\Sigma\sigma_i^2 - \Sigma r_{ii}\sigma_i^2}{\bar{C}_y}$

Since $\bar{C}_y$ is identical to $\sigma_y{}^2$, Eq. (7-10) can be rewritten as

(7-11) $\quad r_{yy} = 1 - \dfrac{\Sigma\sigma_i^2 - \Sigma r_{ii}\sigma_i^2}{\sigma_y{}^2}$

With this version of the formula, one would need to compute only the variance of the linear combination (y) and the standard deviation of each variable in the linear combination and to have foreknowledge of the reliability of each variable. A concrete example would be in the case where (1) the variances of three variables are 1, 2, and 3, respectively, (2) the reliabilities are .60, .70, and .80, respectively, and (3) the variance of the sum of the three variables is 12. The reliability of the sum would be obtained as follows:

$$r_{yy} = 1 - \frac{(1 + 2 + 3) - (.6 + 1.4 + 2.4)}{12}$$

$$= 1 - \frac{6 - 4.4}{12}$$

$$r_{yy} = .87$$

If, as is usually the case, variables were placed in the form of standard scores before they were summed, the covariance of the sum of obtained scores would equal the sum of the elements in the correlation matrix for the variables which were summed. The diagonal elements in the matrix would be 1s, and the off-diagonal elements would be correlations between variables in the sum. The covariance matrix for true scores would have off-diagonal elements the same as those in the correlation matrix for obtained scores, but the diagonal elements would be reliability coefficients rather than 1s. Then Eq. (7-11) could be transformed for the case of k variables expressed in standard scores as follows:

(7-12) $\quad r_{yy} = \dfrac{\bar{R}_y - k + \Sigma r_{ii}}{\bar{R}_y}$

(7-13) $\quad r_{yy} = 1 - \dfrac{k - \Sigma r_{ii}}{\bar{R}_y}$

(7-14) $\quad r_{yy} = 1 - \dfrac{k - \Sigma r_{ii}}{\sigma_y{}^2}$

assessment of reliability

The standard-score version of the formula for the reliability of a sum can be illustrated in the case where three variables being summed each have reliabilities of .60 and each pair correlates .50. Then $k = 3$, and the sum of reliabilities equals 1.8. The variance of y would equal $k + (6 \times .50)$ (there being six off-diagonal elements in the correlation matrix). The result would be as follows:

$$r_{yy} = 1 - \frac{3 - 1.8}{6} = .8$$

Going back to Eq. (7-14), one can see that in the special case where only two sets of standard scores are summed, the following special formula can be used:

(7-15) $$r_{yy} = 1 - \frac{2 - r_{11} - r_{22}}{\sigma_y{}^2}$$

Where each of the two variables being summed has a reliability of .60 and the correlation between the two is .50, the computations are as follows:

$$r_{yy} = 1 - \frac{2 - 1.2}{3} = .73$$

The variance of y equals the sum of the elements in the correlation matrix for only two variables, which equals 2.0 plus two times the correlation between them. This makes the denominator of the fraction on the right equal 3.0.

NEGATIVE ELEMENTS Up to this point it has been assumed that the problem is that of estimating the reliability of positive sums of variables, but the logic applies equally well when some of the variables are subtracted rather than added, as would be the case in the following linear combination:

$$y = x_1 + x_2 - x_3$$

The previously derived formulas for a linear combination apply equally well when some of the variables in the linear combination have negative signs. If the three variables were in standard-score form, Eq. (7-14) could be applied. In the second term on the right-hand side of the equation, the numerator would not be affected by the minus sign for variable 3 in the example above. There would still be k variables (three), and the reliabilities of the three variables would not be affected. What would be affected is the denominator of that ratio, the variance of the linear combination. If variable x_3 correlated positively with the other two variables, placing a minus sign before that variable in the linear combination would reverse the signs of the correlations of variable 3 with the other two variables. This would make the variance of y less than it would have been if variable 3 had been added rather than subtracted. But if variable 3 had a negative correlation with the other two variables, the minus sign in the linear combination would serve to make the variance of the linear combination more than it would have been if the variable had been added. Since the larger the variance of the linear combination, the more the reliability, the pattern of positive and negative signs in the linear combination has a direct effect on the reliability of the combination.

WEIGHTED SUMS   The method for estimating the reliability of a sum can be extended to the case of weighted sums. A weighted sum of variables expressed as standard scores would be as follows:

$$y = b_1 z_1 + b_2 z_2 + b_3 z_3$$

The variance of y would equal the sum of all elements in the weighted correlation matrix. The diagonal elements would consist of squared weights, and each off-diagonal element would consist of the correlation between two variables multiplied by the products of the weights for the two variables. The sum of elements in this matrix would be divided into the sum of elements in the matrix corresponding to the variance of the sum of true scores. The off-diagonal elements would be the same in the two matrices, but in the latter the diagonal elements would consist of squared weights multiplied by reliability coefficients. Then Eq. (7-14) could be modified to obtain the following formula for the reliability of a weighted sum of variables expressed as standard scores:

(7-16)
$$r_{yy} = 1 - \frac{\Sigma b_i^2 - \Sigma b_i^2 r_{ii}}{\sigma_y^2}$$

where b_i = weight for variable z_i
r_{ii} = reliability of variable z_i

To apply Eq. (7-16), one would first obtain the variance of the sum of weighted standard scores, which would be the denominator of the expression on the far right of the equation. For the numerator, the sum of squared weights would be obtained. The square of each weight would be multiplied by the corresponding reliability, these would be summed, and the sum would be subtracted from the sum of squared weights. Then it would be only a simple problem in arithmetic to obtain the reliability of the linear combination.

When variables are expressed as deviation scores rather than as standard scores, Eq. (7-16) can be modified as follows to obtain the reliability of the weighted sum:

(7-17)
$$r_{yy} = 1 - \frac{\Sigma b_i^2 \sigma_i^2 - \Sigma b_i^2 \sigma_i^2 r_{ii}}{\sigma_y^2}$$

assessment of reliability

231

Equations (7-16) and (7-17) can be applied equally well in the case where some of the weighted variables have minus signs in the linear combination.

PRINCIPLES CONCERNING THE RELIABILITY OF LINEAR COMBINATIONS
Because linear combinations of variables are encountered so frequently in practice, it is important to look at some principles that govern their reliability. The multiple-regression equation is a weighted linear combination of variables, weighted so as to correlate as highly as possible with a criterion variable. Later it will be seen that, in factor analysis, factors consist of linear combinations of variables, and most other methods of multivariate analysis deal with linear combinations of variables. Consequently the reliability of a linear combination of variables is an omnipresent issue in psychological measurement.

Although previously it was said that the reliability of a sum cannot be estimated by coefficient alpha [Eq. (6-26)], a reinspection of the basic formula for the reliability of a linear combination [Eq. (7-11)] will show that the two formulas look very similar. In the former there is a multiplier in which the number of test items is divided by the number of test items minus 1, but otherwise the two equations look much alike. The difference is that, in the formula for the reliability of a linear combination, the sum of reliabilities multiplied by variances is subtracted in the numerator of the ratio from the sum of variances. Thus the reliabilities of the variables tend to increase the reliability of a linear combination over that which would be predicted from coefficient alpha.

When the correlations among items are all zero, coefficient alpha is necessarily zero. A look at the standard-score version of the reliability of a sum of variables [Eq. (7-12)] will show what happens when the correlations between variables are all zero. In that case $\bar{R} = k$, the number of variables. Then Eq. (7-12) can be reduced to the following:

$$(7\text{-}18) \qquad r_{yy} = \frac{\Sigma r_{ii}}{k}$$

Equation (7-18) leads to the important deduction that when the variables in a sum of standard scores correlate zero, the reliability of the sum is the average reliability of the variables. Thus if three variables expressed as standard scores had reliabilities of .60, .70, and .80, and correlations among the three variables were all zero, the reliability of the sum would equal .70. This would hold even if some of the variables had negative signs in the sum. Obviously Eq. (7-18) also applies when the *average* correlation is zero (excluding the diagonal elements in the matrix).

Another look at Eq. (7-14) will show what happens when the average correlation is not zero. It is possible for the average correlation to be negative, which obviously would be the case when two variables correlated positively and one were given a negative sign in the combination. Then there would be only one correlation, which would have to be negative. There is, however, a severe limit to the possible average negative correlation obtainable among the variables of a linear combination. One can readily see what the limit would be. Since the sum of all elements in a correlation matrix (including the diagonal elements) is the variance of the sum of variables expressed as standard scores and since a variance cannot be negative, a negative sum of off-diagonal correlations cannot be greater than the sum of diagonal values, which equals k. By expressing the denominator of the ratio in Eq. (7-14) as k plus the sum of off-diagonal correlations, one can see that the reliability approaches zero as the sum of off-diagonal correlations approaches minus the sum of reliabilities.

If, as is usually the case, the average correlation is positive, the higher the average correlation, the higher the reliability of the linear combination. To understand this rule, one must make a very careful distinction between correlations among variables *before* they are placed in linear combinations and *after* they are placed in linear combinations. The reason this distinction is so important is that the correlation between two variables before they are placed in a linear combination is reversed in sign if they are given *different* signs in the linear combination. In the simplest case, if two variables have a positive correlation and a linear combination is formed by subtracting one from the other, in the linear combination (in the correlation matrix corresponding to the variance of the combination) the correlation will be negative. So far all the discussion of the reliability of linear combinations has concerned correlations *after* linear combinations are formed. To prevent confusion in that regard, all formulas were developed so that sums or averages of correlations did not explicitly appear. Instead, the correlations among variables in the linear combination were "hidden" in the variance of the linear combination. Of course, when actually computing the variance of a linear combination, one would add or subtract variables depending on their signs in the combination. When that is done, the correct value is obtained for the variance of y. The remaining terms in the computing formulas are reliabilities for variables expressed as standard scores and both reliabilities and variances for sets of deviation scores. Since these are always positive, regardless of the signs variables are given, there is no way to become confused about the proper use of the formulas.

There is, however, considerable value in looking at correlations among variables *before* they are placed in linear combinations. This will show how much reliability is expected from a particular linear combination. Here is an extreme case. If two variables correlated .60 and each had a reliability of .60, then if one variable were subtracted from the other [Eq. (7-15)], the reliability of the linear combination would be zero. Obviously such a linear combination would be worthless. Less extreme cases occur frequently in practice. In the case where the reliabilities were each .80 and the correlation between the two variables was .60, the reliability of the difference between the two variables would be only .50. In both cases the same reliability would have resulted if before variables were combined, the correlations were negative, and both variables were given a positive sign in the combination.

Since the reliability of a sum increases with the size of the average correlation among variables, any set of signs in a linear combination that maximizes the positive sum of correlations will maximize the reliability. The problem is illustrated in the following correlation matrix for six variables:

	1	2	3	4	5	6
1	1.0	+	+	−	−	−
2	+	1.0	+	−	−	−
3	+	+	1.0	−	−	−
4	−	−	−	1.0	+	+
5	−	−	−	+	1.0	+
6	−	−	−	+	+	1.0

The matrix is meant to illustrate correlations among variables *before* they are placed in a linear combination. Variables 1, 2, and 3 form a set whose members all correlate positively, and the same is true for variables 4, 5, and 6. All correlations between members of the two sets are negative. If a linear combination were formed in which all six variables had positive signs, the sum of the elements in the above matrix would be the variance of the linear combination. The size of the reliability of the linear combination is positively related to the size of the variance of the linear combination, and thus it is positively related to the sum of correlations among variables. If, in the example above, all variables were given positive signs, there would be more negative correlations than positive correlations, and consequently the sum of correlations might be either near zero or even negative. In this example, one could obtain the maximum reliability for any possible linear combination by giving negative signs to all three variables in *either* (but not both) set. If one chose to give negative signs to variables 4, 5, and 6, all correlations among the three would remain positive and would not change in size. They would remain positive because all three variables would still have the *same* sign. The important difference would be that the signs of all correlations between the two sets of variables would change from negative to positive. Then all correlations in the matrix would be positive, the variance of the linear combination would be at a maximum, and the reliability of the linear combination would be at a maximum.

The problem is seldom as neat as in the example discussed above; however, an inspection of correlations among variables *before* they are placed in a linear combination will often indicate that a planned linear combination of variables would not be very reliable and that a different linear combination would be much more reliable. Of course, maximization of reliability is seldom the most important goal either in basic research or in applied work. For example, in the former, if a hypothesis concerns how much *better* people do on the sum of three measures than they do on the sum of three other measures, in the linear combination there is no choice but to give positive signs to the first three variables and negative signs to the other three variables. An inspection of correlations among the variables might, however, show that such a linear combination would have a very low reliability, in which case the study would be doomed before it started.

SUGGESTED ADDITIONAL READINGS

Guilford, J. P. *Psychometric methods.* New York: McGraw-Hill, 1954, chap. 14.

Gulliksen, H. *Theory of mental tests.* New York: Wiley, 1950, chaps. 10, 15, 16.

Thorndike, R. L. Reliability. In F. F. Lindquist (Ed.), *Educational measurement.* Washington: American Council on Education, 1951. Pp. 560–620.

CHAPTER EIGHT
TEST CONSTRUCTION

Until recent years there was considerable disagreement about proper methods of test construction. Much of the disagreement apparently arose from a failure to state fundamental principles of scaling, validity, and reliability. Without agreement on these principles, different measurement specialists advocated different approaches to test construction. The situation was much like that of three motorists who sit and argue about the best roads to travel when either they do not know where they want to go or they plan to go to different places. Now there apparently is more agreement on basic objectives. If the principles discussed in previous chapters are largely correct, it is rather easy to develop satisfactory principles of test construction.

In Chapter Two, the *linear model* was accepted as the most appropriate for the development of most measures of psychological attributes. The model stipulates that test scores are to be obtained by summing scores over items. The items can be either weighted or unweighted, and either they can all have positive signs in the combination or some can have negative signs. All these possibilities are subsumed under the concept of a linear combination of test items. Although there are competing models for special problems of measurement, there is no general competitor to the linear model. Probably 95 percent of all psychological measures are based on the linear model, and this probably will continue to be the case. For these reasons, it will be assumed that the linear model should be used as a guide in nearly all test construction. Some possible uses of other models were mentioned in Chapter Two and will be discussed again in later chapters.

Whereas it will be convenient to speak of "test construction," the principles in this chapter apply to all forms of psychological measurement, e.g., to physiological measures of anxiety, to measures of activity in the rat, and to measures of learning rate in paired-associate learning. The principles apply to any measure that is obtained from a linear combination of individual responses, items on mental tests constituting

internal structure of measures

only a special case. The principles apply to measures of ability, personality, and attitudes; and they apply both to dichotomous items and to items scorable on more than two points.

Previously it was said that, depending on the way tests are used, one of three standards of validity apply—predictive validity, content validity, or construct validity. As will be discussed more fully later in the chapter, the methods of test construction used for measures intended to have predictive validity and for those intended to have construct validity should be the same. Somewhat different methods of test construction are required, however, for instruments that depend primarily on content validity. First, brief mention will be made of principles concerning the construction of measures intended to have content validity, and then the remainder of the chapter will be devoted to principles concerning the construction of measures intended to serve the other two functions.

construction of achievement tests

As was mentioned in Chapter Three, the achievement test is the most obvious example of a measure that requires content validity. The term "achievement test" will be used in a general sense to refer to (1) examinations In individual courses of instruction in schools of all kinds and at all levels, (2) standardized measures of achievement used routinely by all the instructors in a particular unit of instruction, and (3) commercially distributed tests of achievement used throughout the country. Such measures of achievement are very frequently employed at all levels of education up through graduate school and professional training, in civil service examinations, and in special training programs in military establishments and in industry.

In terms of sheer numbers of tests administered, achievement tests outrank all other tests by far. For three reasons, however, only brief mention will be made here of procedures for the construction of achievement tests. First, the basic principles for constructing achievement tests are rather simple and can be stated quickly. Second, although there are hundreds of special techniques for constructing achievement tests of particular kinds for particular purposes, e.g., achievement tests for grammatical skills and mechanical drawing, these special techniques are of interest mainly to professional educators and specialists in measurement. Since this book is aimed at future psychologists in general rather than any special group, a lengthy discussion of such special techniques would be out of place. Third, there are comprehensive books devoted either wholly or in large part to the construction of achievement tests. These are listed in the Suggested Additional Readings at the end of this chapter (see readings by Gerberich, Nunnally, and Wood).

THE TEST PLAN   As was mentioned in Chapter Three, ensuring the content validity of an achievement test by an explicit plan for constructing the test is more appropriate than determining the content validity after the test is constructed. If representative persons who are to use the test agree in advance on the appropriateness of the plan, arriving at an acceptable instrument is mainly a matter of technical skill and applied research.

The major part of the test plan is an outline of content for the instrument which is to be constructed. Since content validity depends on a rational appeal to an adequate coverage of important content, an explicit outline of content provides a basis for discussing content validity. For example, an outline of content for a comprehensive achievement test for the fourth grade would need to indicate whether or not a section on "study skills" was to be included. If such a section was to be included, it would also be necessary to list the aspects of study skills that would be covered, e.g., use of the dictionary and locating topics in reference books.

In addition to the outline of content, the plan should describe the types of items to be employed, state the approximate number of items to be employed in each section and each subsection of the test, and give examples of the types of items to be used. The plan also should state how long the test will take to administer, how it will be administered, how it will be scored, and the types of norms that will be obtained.

When the plan is completed, it is reviewed by numerous persons, including teachers, subject-matter experts, administrative officials (in public schools, industry, the military, and other organizations), and specialists in educational and psychological measurement. Many suggestions might be made for changes, and the revised plan would be resubmitted to reviewers. Hopefully, the eventual plan is one that receives general approval from reviewers.

Of course, such an elaborate plan would be undertaken only for achievement tests that were to be used quite widely, such as for commercially distributed tests of overall achievement for elementary school and achievement tests used in large training programs in military establishments. At the other extreme, an instructor probably would not develop an elaborate plan for constructing a course examination (an achievement test) which was to be used only with his students. But even in this case it is wise for the instructor to make an outline of the intended coverage. This will provide a basis for judging the adequacy of coverage,

internal structure of measures

and a discussion of the outline with fellow instructors will help ensure content validity.

TEST ITEMS   Of course, a test can be no better than the items of which it is composed. A good plan represents an *intention* to construct a good test, but unless items are skillfully written, the plan never materializes. Although there are some rules for writing good items (see Nunnally, 1964, chap. 6), writing test items is an art that few people seem to master. Most frequently, items are marred by two shortcomings. First, they are ambiguous, because they fail to adequately "aim" students toward the type of response required. A classic example is, "What happened to art during the fifteenth century?" The question is so vague that the student could take many different directions on an essay examination and could legitimately select several different alternatives on a multiple-choice item. A second major fault is that items often concern trivial aspects of the subject matter. To write items that are unambiguous and to write them as quickly as possible, it is tempting to populate tests with items concerning dates, names, and simple facts. Most instructors will agree that the memory for simple details is not the important thing to be measured; what is important is to measure various aspects of "reasoning with" the subject matter. But regardless of the type of item employed, it takes considerable skill to write items that adequately measure a true understanding of principles.

There is a choice as to which type of item will be employed, including short-answer essay questions, longer essay questions, and numerous types of objective items. Among objective items, the multiple-choice item is considered the best for most purposes. For three reasons, commercially distributed achievement tests rely almost solely on multiple-choice items. First, they are very easy to administer and score. Second, expert item writers who are highly skilled at composing such items are available. Third, when multiple-choice items are skillfully composed, they can accurately measure almost anything. Time and again it has been shown that a test composed of good multiple-choice items correlates with an essay test of the same topic almost as highly as the reliability of the latter will permit. Since the multiple-choice test typically is much more reliable than the essay test, the conclusion is inescapable that the objective test is more valid. This relationship tends to hold even with material where intuitively it would not seem possible, e.g., in comparison of a multiple-choice test for the pronunciation of a foreign language with scores given on oral exercises.

Although in some instances it logically would be very difficult to employ multiple-choice items to measure achievement (e.g., English composition), most of the major achievement tests have no essay questions.

In practice, though, this is not always a major disadvantage. When essay questions are used in achievement tests, they usually correlate so highly with other sections of the test that they can be omitted. Thus, for example, when essay questions are tried as measures of English composition, they tend to add little new variance to what can be explained by multiple-choice tests of vocabulary, reading comprehension, and grammar. This is partly because of a much higher reliability for the objective sections of the test and partly because of a high degree of overlap between abilities required in the objective items and ability in English composition. There is a very important principle here: Rather than employ a factor-pure measure of an attribute which is not highly reliable (an essay test for English composition), it is sometimes a more valid approach to employ a highly reliable measure of a second attribute which correlates highly with the first.

In addition to higher reliability and ease of scoring, another advantage of multiple-choice items is that they usually sample the topic much more broadly than would be possible on essay examinations. For example, a 50-minute classroom examination could easily employ 50 multiple-choice items without excessively "speeding" students, but it would be difficult to employ more than 5 one-page essay questions in the same amount of time. How well students performed on the essay questions would depend to some extent on their "luck" regarding which questions were asked, but such luck (measurement error because of the sampling of content) would tend to average out over 50 multiple-choice items. Since there is measurement error because of the sampling of content and an equally large amount of measurement error because of the subjectivity of scoring, the multiple-choice examination is usually much more reliable than the essay examination. A typical finding would be an alternative-form reliability between .60 and .70 for the essay examination and a reliability between .80 and .90 for the multiple-choice examination.

Although the skillful item writer can measure almost anything with multiple-choice items, this is not true for many instructors, particularly those not familiar with principles of measurement and without considerable practice in constructing objective tests. In classes with a large number of students (50 or more), there usually is no choice but to employ an objective examination. To do a careful job of grading that many essay examinations would be a monstrous chore. When there are no more than 15 students in a class, it actually saves time to construct and score an essay examination rather than a multiple-choice examination. Even if the multiple-choice examination is very easy to score, a good one is time-consuming to construct. When there are as many as 30 students, the practical advantage is on the side of the multiple-choice examination. When the class contains between 15 and 30 students, there is no strong practical advantage for either type of test, and consequently the decision between them should be made on other grounds. If instructors feel more comfortable in constructing one type of test rather than the other, they should probably follow their own intuitions in that regard.

The labors of constructing a multiple-choice test are greatly diminished if the instructor has a pool of items that has been accumulated from previous classes. Once such a pool of items is developed, usually most of the items for a new test can be drawn from that pool, with some new items being written to take into account changing emphases in the unit of instruction. When such a pool of items is available, constructing and scoring a multiple-choice test nearly always takes less time than constructing and scoring an essay test for the same subject matter.

If essay questions are used, it generally is best to employ short-answer questions which can be answered in no more than half a page. Short-answer questions have a number of advantages over long-answer questions. Since more questions can be included, the short-answer examination makes it possible to provide a broader coverage of the content. In short-answer questions, it is easier to "aim" the student toward the intended types of responses. There then will be fewer instances in which a student writes brilliantly on something different from what the instructor intended. Also, short-answer questions are much easier for the instructor to grade. Not only do students get lost while responding to long answer questions, but instructors get lost in trying to grade them. With short-answer questions, it is much easier for the instructor to formulate a concrete basis for grading and to keep the standards in mind while looking at responses.

After test items are constructed, they should be critically reviewed. Of course, for a classroom examination, the instructor probably would do his own reviewing, but for important achievement tests, a careful review is done by a number of persons. First, the items would be reviewed by experts in test construction. They would consider each item for its appropriateness, apparent difficulty, and clarity. The items that survived that review would then be reviewed by teachers and other potential users of the test.

ITEM ANALYSIS   Although content validity mainly rests on rational rather than empirical grounds, results from applying an instrument do provide some important types of information. Large-scale investigations are undertaken for important achievement tests. In contrast, the individual instructor may not seek such information at all or may obtain it only incidentally. The first step in obtaining such information is to administer a large collection of items to a large sample of persons who are representative of the individuals with whom the final test will be employed. To have ample room to discard items that work poorly, there should be at least twice as many items as will appear on the final test. All items should be administered to at least 300 persons, preferably to 1,000 or more. Because there are so many opportunities for taking advantage of chance in item analysis, unless there are at least five times as many persons as items, the results may be highly misleading. For this reason, few instructors obtain enough data for their test items to warrant an item analysis.

If computational resources are available for the purpose, the most important type of item analysis of achievement tests is done by correlating each item with the total test score. If the test has different parts for different topics (e.g., reading and science), each item should be correlated with the subscore for its section rather than with scores on the test as a whole. The proper coefficient is point-biserial, which, as was said previously, is the PM formula applied to the relationship between a dichotomous item and a multipoint distribution of scores.

Any item that correlates near zero with test scores should be carefully inspected. In an achievement test, it is possible for an item to correlate near zero with total scores and still be a valid item, but that rarely is the case. It is more likely that the item is excessively difficult or easy, is ambiguous, or actually has little to do with the topic. Unless there are strong grounds for deciding otherwise, such items generally should be discarded. Among the remaining items, the items that correlate higher with total scores generally are the better items. They probably are less ambiguous; they cannot be very extreme in difficulty in either direction; and they will tend to make the final test highly reliable.

The next step in item analysis depends on the number of items that have relatively high correlations with total scores. For example, where 100 multiple-choice items are being investigated for a subtest of a large achievement test, correlations with subtest scores are expected to range from zero to about .40. In tests of ability, such correlations are seldom negative, and when they are, it usually is because of sampling error. Correlations above .20 are usually considered good. (An artifact in such correlations will be discussed later.) If there are more than enough items at that level, one can proceed to the next step. If there are barely enough items at that level for the eventual test, there is no choice but to employ those items, and consequently there is no room for further pruning of items. If the number of items at that level is far less than required for the eventual test, the only recourse is to start over with a larger collection of items.

When there are plenty of items that correlate well with total scores, the next step is to investigate the reliability for successive collections of the items. First, the items would be ranked in accordance with their

internal structure of measures

correlations with total scores. Successive sets would be selected, and coefficient alpha, or KR-20, would be computed for each set. Since usually at least 30 items are required to have a high reliability, coefficient alpha would be applied to the 30 items having the highest correlations with total scores. If the reliability were as high as desired, one would stop adding items. If not, one would add the 5 or 10 items next in terms of correlations with total scores, and coefficient alpha would be computed for the collection of items. One would keep adding sets of items 5 or 10 at a time until the reliability was as high as desired.

After a set of items which has a high reliability has been obtained, the next step is to plot the frequency distribution for total scores on the items. If the distribution is "satisfactory," the selection of items is complete. For commercially distributed achievement tests, it usually is helpful to have a symmetrical, approximately normal distribution of scores. The distribution of scores can be compared with that expected from a normal distribution with the same mean and standard deviation. If the distribution of scores is highly skewed in either direction, corrective measures can be taken. If the distribution is skewed toward the higher end, this means that the test is too difficult. If there are some relatively easy items which correlate satisfactorily with total scores and which were not included in the final collection of items, these can be used to replace some of the more difficult items in the final collection. This will tend to make the distribution of total scores more closely resemble the normal distribution. If the distribution is skewed toward the lower end, some more difficult items can be used to replace some of the easier items. Some cut-and-try methods in this regard will make the distribution symmetrical.

For reasons which will be made clearer in later sections of this chapter, in the item analysis of achievement tests it is best to lay major stress on the correlations of items with total scores rather than on the difficulties (p values) of items. After items have passed reviews by measurement experts and other persons, the steps in item analysis are almost identical to those in the item analysis of predictor tests and measures of constructs; consequently a more complete discussion of methods of item analysis will be reserved for a later section of the chapter.

Again it should be emphasized that item analysis of achievement tests is secondary to content validity. Contrary to what is done with predictor tests and measures of constructs, with achievement tests considerable pains are taken to ensure that all items have content validity *before* they are submitted to item analysis. Thus all items submitted for analysis are assumed to be good, and the analysis only provides additional information. But more important than the information obtained from item analysis is the initial decision to use a particular item in a tryout form of the test. Also, regardless of what is found in item analysis, the final decision to include or reject an item is based primarily on human judgment. For example, in each section of most achievement tests, the first several items are very easy. These are included to prevent some students from becoming discouraged and to give all students some practice with the particular type of item. Because nearly everyone correctly answers these items, purely on the basis of an item analysis these items might appear worthless.

NORMS In standardizing achievement tests, one of the most important steps is the establishment of norms. In the broadest sense of the word, "norms" are any scores that provide a frame of reference for interpreting the scores of particular persons. With achievement tests for measuring progress in elementary school, usually the set of norms would be based on scores made by a representative cross section of students across the country. In addition it is useful to have local norms, such as norms based on samples of students in a particular locality and in a particular school. Then the score of a particular student can be compared with scores of students across the country, students in the same locality, and students in the same school.

In the construction of important achievement tests, the construction of norms is almost as much work as the construction of tests. (For some of the particulars, see Lindquist, 1951, and Nunnally, 1964.) Great care must be taken to ensure that the sample of students is representative of the country as a whole, and for this purpose, thousands of students must be tested. Then statistical analyses must be undertaken to obtain the final norms. Also, it usually is necessary to obtain separate norms for different parts of the test.

Norms usually are expressed both in the form of transformed standard scores and as percentiles. For the former, a widely used method is to convert raw scores to a distribution having a mean of 500 and a standard deviation of 100. Essentially, a percentile indicates the percentage of persons in the normative sample that is *below* a particular score. Thus if 80 percent of the students score less than 122, a person with a score of 122 is at the 80th percentile. Such percentiles would be completely interpretable, however, only if no two students made the same score. Consequently, in practice, percentiles are computed by dividing the total number of students tested into the number of students below a particular score plus half the students who make that score.

A strong case can be made that percentiles are easier to interpret than are transformed standard scores. The only way to accurately interpret transformed standard scores is to do some mental arithmetic to figure how many standard deviations a person is above or below the mean and how many persons would be above and below that point.

internal structure of measures

Obviously, then, working with percentiles directly is easier than going through such mental gyrations.

Good norms, although crucial for important tests of achievement, are not highly important for predictor tests and measures of constructs. For the former, one could effectively employ a predictor test in a particular setting even if he had no idea how people in general would score on the instrument. For measures of constructs, the major effort is to obtain reliable variance for the groups being investigated regardless of any information that might be supplied by norms. With predictor tests and measures of constructs, norms mainly are useful in indicating whether research results might have been somewhat different with different types of people, e.g., effects on correlations because of restriction in range of scores.

the criterion-oriented approach to test construction

There are two *incorrect* ways to construct tests: one is to select items according to their correlations with a criterion and the other is to select items according to their difficulty. Even if both methods are thought to be incorrect, they have been advocated and used so much in the past that it will be necessary to explain them in some detail. In this section will be discussed the criterion-oriented approach. By "criteria" are meant scores relating to some type of performance in daily life, such as school grades, amount of sales by insurance agents, and ratings of the skill of airplane pilots.

The criterion-oriented approach evolved from the following faulty line of reasoning. First, you ask yourself, "Why construct a test?" Then you answer, "To predict a criterion." If that were so, what would be the best items for the test? Obviously, items that individually correlate well with the criterion. The more each item correlates with the criterion, the more the total test score will correlate with the criterion. According to this line of reasoning, the obvious thing to do is (1) compose a large group of items, (2) administer them to a large sample of individuals in the situation where the test will be used, (3) correlate each item with the criterion, e.g., grades in some course of training, and (4) fashion a test out of those items that correlate most highly with the criterion.

Following this line of reasoning further, there is a way to improve on the foregoing method for the selection of test items. Assuming that one has found a large number of items that correlate well with the criterion, one can further select items in terms of their correlations with one another. Should the items in the final test correlate highly with one another? According to the criterion-oriented approach, the answer is "No." This conclusion follows from the logic of multiple correlation. It will be remembered that, if a number of variables each correlate positively with a criterion, the multiple correlation is higher when the predictors correlate as little as possible with one another. The maximum multiple correlation would be obtained when the predictors had zero correlations with one another. The same logic would hold for a linear combination of items. When items have low correlations with one another and each correlates positively with the criterion, each item adds information to that provided by the other items; and when scores are summed over items, a relatively high correlation with the criterion will be found.

It will be remembered that the average correlation of an item with the other items on a test is highly related to the correlation of that item with total scores on the test. Then, according to this logic, one

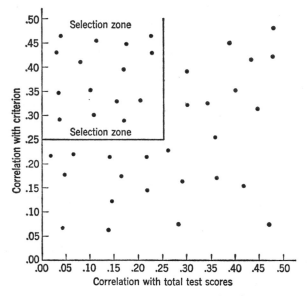

figure 8-1 *Scatter diagram of item correlations with a criterion and with total test scores.*

would select items that correlated highly with the criterion and had low correlations with total test scores. After these two sets of correlations are obtained, they can be plotted as in Figure 8-1. One then selects items from the indicated region of the figure. If there are enough items in that region, they are used to form the final test.

WHAT IS WRONG WITH THE CRITERION-ORIENTED APPROACH   By this point it must be apparent that something is badly wrong with the criterion-oriented approach. By this method one would select a polyglot group of items with low internal consistency. Coefficient alpha would be low, and consequently there would be no strong common core (factor) in the items. Since the items would tend to measure different things, there would be no rational basis for the construction of an alternative form. The problem could be approached empirically by selecting another set of items that correlated well with the criterion and for which the internal consistency was low, but according to principles concerning the correlation of sums, the "alternative forms" would not correlate highly.

The major error in the criterion-oriented approach is in the original premise that the purpose of constructing a test is to predict a *particular* criterion. This is seldom the guiding principle in constructing a test. It obviously is not the reason for constructing measures that require content validity and construct validity. In either case, if one had a criterion (whatever that would be), there would be no need to construct tests. As has been argued previously, with measures that require content validity there logically is no empirical criterion. Although construct validity partly depends on correlations among different proposed measures of a construct, no one of them can be considered *the* criterion. Since most measures used in basic research require construct validity, the criterion-oriented approach clearly does not apply. Since in applied work there are many more uses of achievement tests (measures that require content validity) than of predictor tests, the logic obviously does not hold in most applied work.

The only sphere in which the criterion-oriented approach is not obviously inappropriate is in applied work with predictor tests. It will be shown, however, that the logic does not apply there either. It is almost always poor strategy to *construct* a test to measure a particular criterion; it is better to *select* tests of known factorial composition as potential predictors of a criterion. Instead of forming hypotheses about types of *items* that might be predictive of a criterion, it is better to form hypotheses about types of *whole tests* that might be predictive of a criterion.

Other than for measures that require content validity, the purpose of constructing tests should be to investigate factors of human ability and personality. Each test should follow from a hypothesis about relations between a particular type of item and other types of items. Each test should be homogeneous in content, and consequently the items on each test should correlate substantially with one another. Correlations among different tests should be studied by factor analysis. The resulting factors constitute a standard set of "yardsticks" regarding abilities and personality traits. Gradually, as evidence accrues from factor analysis, the major dimensions of human attributes are determined. In the long run this will result in a catalog of measures for the important dimensions. Then, when one wants to measure a particular factor, the proper measure, or combination of measures, can be taken from a drawer or off a shelf. This logic applies both to measures of psychological constructs and to predictors of particular criteria. The "shelves and drawers" already contain measures of many important factors, and one can select among them for the prediction of particular criteria.

There is no intention to imply here that it is wrong to construct new tests with respect to applied problems of prediction, but when they are so constructed, they should not be constructed according to the criterion-oriented approach. Each such test should be homogeneous in content. Of course, one would want to find the correlation of scores with the criterion, and if that were reasonably high, one would want to learn the factor composition of the measure by correlating it with measures of existing factors. Gradually, in this way, tests constructed for prediction problems add to what is known about factors in general.

How, though, can one adequately predict criteria from homogeneous tests? As some will argue, the criterion usually is factorially complex and consequently can be predicted best by a factorially complex predictor test. Instead of building the factorial complexity into a particular test, it is far better to meet the factorial complexity by combining tests in a battery by multiple regression, in which case tests would be selected to measure the different factors that are thought to be important. If items are selected by the criterion-oriented approach, one really does not know *what* factors are being measured. Also, the importance of each factor in the test would be determined by the number of items that happened to be present for the factor, and thus would not be rationally related to the importance of the factor in the criterion. The ideal way to combine factors is by multiple regression, and this can be done only by having relatively homogeneous tests relating to each factor. With the criterion-oriented approach, one knows neither what factors are involved in the omnibus test nor what weights are being given to different factors. The fallacy is in assuming that the criterion is to be predicted with *one* test, which to be effective must be heterogeneous in content. It is far better to predict a criterion with a battery of tests, each of which is homogeneous in content.

Even if one accepted the logic of the criterion-oriented approach, it would work poorly in practice. It is very difficult to find items that correlate well with a criterion and have low correlations with one another. Usually the two types of correlations tend to go together, and consequently very few items that met the standards would be found. When the method appears to work, it usually is because only a small sample of subjects is being used, and consequently there is considerable room to take advantage of chance. Subsequent studies would show that the test was not nearly as predictive of the criterion as was suggested by the item analysis. Usually one has a choice of using items that have (1) low correlations *both* with one another and with the criterion or (2) relatively high correlations with one another and with the criterion.

Obviously, then, the homogeneous test would predict the criterion as well or better than the heterogeneous test.

Even if one selects items purely in terms of correlations with a criterion and ignores correlations among items, the criterion-oriented approach is not good. Such a test usually would be factorially complex and would run into the difficulties mentioned previously. Also, such a test would contribute very little to one's understanding of either the applied situation or basic issues concerning human attributes. For the former, since one would not fully understand what factors were involved in the test, no information would be supplied about the factors that make for success in a school or on a job. If the factors that lead to success are known, opportunities are provided for training students or employees. For example, if it is known that reading speed is important for success on a particular job, employees can be trained in that respect. If, in a school situation, it is found that successful performance correlates more with memory factors than with other factors, this might suggest changes in the curriculum.

If an omnibus test were constructed for each prediction problem as it arose, we would never come to understand human attributes. Rather than have the "drawers and shelves" filled with measures of a limited number of factors, we would have warehouses filled with thousands of unclassifiable measures.

Even if one ignored the weight of argument given so far against the criterion-oriented approach, he would find that the method works poorly in practice. Obviously, it is very wasteful of time and money to construct tests for each new prediction problem. It is much easier to investigate existing measures with known factor compositions. An omnibus test constructed for a particular criterion often is predictive only of that criterion. For example, in an industrial situation, a psychologist involved in the selection of employees for 20 different jobs might need to construct 20 different criterion-oriented tests. In the same situation, a battery of 3 to 7 tests (with different weights for different jobs) might be predictive of all jobs, and usually the battery would be more predictive of success on any particular job than would the test constructed specifically for that purpose.

The criterion-oriented test that is predictive of a job in one setting often is not very predictive of an apparently similar job in another setting. Thus a test that successfully selects insurance salesmen might be very poor at selecting magazine salesmen. Also, for any particular job in any particular setting, criteria have a way of changing over time. What people do in particular jobs and the abilities and personality attributes required for successful performance frequently evolve with changes in the organization and developments in technology. Thus the criterion-oriented test that works well now might not work well in five years. One could meet these problems with a battery of tests of known factor composition by investigating different weights required for different jobs and for the same job at different points in time. Also, the evidence might indicate that one or more tests would need to be replaced by more predictive tests.

Because of the obvious bad features of the criterion-oriented approach, it is surprising to find some authors of recent books on psychological measurement flirting with that approach. Related methods of item analysis clearly are not applicable to measures that require content validity or construct validity. Conceivably they would be appropriate for particular problems in prediction, but it is hoped that sufficient arguments have been made against the use of the criterion-oriented approach there also. In prediction problems, a far better approach is to form a battery of tests from homogeneous measures of known factor composition. How to construct such homogeneous measures will be discussed in a later section.

Before concluding this section it should be made clear that the foregoing criticisms are leveled at methods of test construction based on the correlations of items with *criteria of success in daily life*, such as grades in college, amounts of sales by insurance salesmen, and ratings of effectiveness of airplane pilots. Criticisms in this section are not leveled at *all* attempts to construct tests wholly or in part by the investigation of correlations of items with some variable external to the items. An example in point is that of selecting items in terms of their correlations with a known factor of human ability or personality. This is a very useful adjunct to the methods for constructing homogeneous tests which will be discussed in a later section.

constructing tests in terms of item difficulties

For constructing measures of constructs and measures to be used as predictors, a second *incorrect* approach concerns the selection of items in terms of their difficulties. Although the difficulty levels of items do provide important information, this information is secondary to information obtained from correlations among the items. (How to use the latter type of information will be discussed in the next section.)

It will be remembered that the difficulty of any dichotomous item (p value) is the fraction of persons tested who receive a score of 1 rather than a score of zero. On tests of ability, a score of 1 means that the individual passes the item; on nonability tests (e.g., a measure of suggestibility), a score of 1 is indicative of a high rather than a low score on the attribute. On a spelling test, a p value of .9 would mean that 90 percent of the persons tested passed the item—correctly

internal structure of measures

spelled the spoken word or marked the correct alternative on a printed test.

In test construction, p values are important for two interrelated reasons. First, they influence the characteristics of score distributions. The p values directly determine the mean score, the mean being the sum of the p values. The mean is only of incidental importance, however, in the construction of tests. More important, the p values influence the shape and dispersion of test scores. (These are also influenced by the number of items and the correlations among items.) If the average p value is far removed from .5 in either direction, the distribution will tend to be skewed (particularly when the number of items is small, e.g., less than 20), and the standard deviation will tend to be small. Consequently, since it usually is desired to have an approximately symmetrical distribution and to disperse people as much as possible, an argument can be made for having an average p value of .5. In addition, even if the average p value is .5, the standard deviation of test scores is larger when all the p values are near .5 rather than scattered widely above and below that point. Then, to disperse people as much as possible (to discriminate among them), one could argue that it is desirable for all test items to have p values close to .5. A test composed of items of that kind is referred to as a *peaked test*.

The other reason why p values are important is that they relate to the reliability. According to coefficient alpha and KR-20, the higher items correlate with one another, the higher the reliability. From Chapter Four it will be remembered that the restriction on the size of the phi coefficient does *not* depend on the p value of either item; rather, it depends on the *difference* in p values of the two items. Thus a correlation of 1.00 can be obtained between two items with p values of .9 as well as it can between two items with p values of .5. An important point not mentioned previously, however, is that a particular difference in p values has a very different effect on the ceiling of the phi coefficient when it is a difference between items having p values near .5 rather than a difference between items having p values far removed from .5 in either direction. For example, a difference in p value of .4 to .5 would place very little restriction on the phi coefficient, but a difference in p value from .89 to .99 would greatly restrict the maximum size of the phi coefficient. It is for this reason that items with an average p value that is extreme in either direction tend to have relatively low correlations with one another on the average. For the same reason, coefficient alpha and KR-20 tend to be lower for tests composed of items with extreme average p values than for tests with average p values near the middle of the range. Since coefficient alpha and KR-20 usually are good estimates of the alternative-form reliability, a similar lowering of the reliability is expected when correlating alternative forms of a test if the forms are composed of items whose average p values are extreme in either direction.

Both from the standpoint of the desirable properties of score distributions and from the standpoint of test reliability, one arrives at the conclusion that a peaked test is best. Although no one would take this argument to the extreme of insisting that all items be at the .5 level, it could be argued that the items should be selected in the range from .4 to .6. This is what one would do if he were to construct a test solely in terms of difficulty levels.

WHAT IS WRONG WITH THIS APPROACH   The faults in selecting items in terms of p values are not nearly so blatant as those in selecting items in terms of the criterion-oriented approach. Also, the point is not that selecting items in terms of p values is incorrect, but rather that there is a much better way to select them. Purely by selecting items so as to obtain a peaked test, one might end up with a very good instrument. If after the items were selected, they proved to have a high reliability, it might be subsequently found that the new measure related importantly with other supposed measures of a construct and/or proved effective in predicting particular criteria. If these things happened, after the fact it could not be argued that the method of test construction failed to work well in that instance. The important point, however, is that, a priori, there are reasons why such pleasant results might not be obtained.

For reasons which were discussed previously, "good" items are ones that correlate well with one another. Since the correlations of items with total scores on a test are directly related to their sums of correlations with one another, it thus can be said that "good" items are ones that correlate highly with total test scores. This doctrine will be explained more fully in the next section, but first it will be useful to see what implications this doctrine has for the selection of items in terms of p values.

The p values only place *upper limits* on correlations of items with total scores. A p value near .5 does not *guarantee* a high correlation with total scores. In a particular analysis, it is possible to find that all the items with p values near .5 have correlations near zero with total scores and that items with p values well removed from .5 have respectable correlations with total scores. Actually, in addition to the possible advantages of having p values near .5, there are reasons for being suspicious of such items. Clearly, one would not consider it good to have true-false items with p values of .5, because that would suggest that the items were so difficult that everyone guessed. A test composed of such items would have a reliability near zero. There is even more reason to be suspicious of items on some nonability tests that have

internal structure of measures

p values near .5. For example, on a personality inventory composed of agree-disagree items, any item that is highly ambiguous will tend to have a p value near .5. Since subjects are unable to understand the item, they mentally "flip coins" in giving an answer. In a sense, on personality inventories it is comforting to find that an item has a p value somewhat removed from .5 (e.g., .7), because that at least suggests that the majority of people were able to understand the item well enough to reject or accept it.

An item on a peaked test *may* be a good item, the crucial standard being whether or not it actually correlates well with total scores on the test. It is equally possible, however, that the item might not have a high correlation with total scores. This could be either because the item is very unreliable or because it reliably measures something different from the majority of items in the test. Since the crucial consideration is how much the item actually correlates with total scores, why not select items mainly in terms of those correlations? That is what will be advocated in the next section. Before that method is discussed, however, some additional comments should be made about selecting items in terms of p values.

Even if one were to admit that p values are all-important in constructing tests, the logic of so doing is clear only for *free-response* items that are *scored dichotomously*. An example of such an item would be if students were provided a space to answer the question, "When did Columbus discover America?" For two reasons such items are rare. First, most tests employ multiple-choice items rather than free-response items of any kind. Second, even in those tests that employ free-response items, the items usually are scored on a multipoint basis rather than dichotomously. The former would be the case, for example, in scoring each question in an essay examination on a six-point scale.

When multipoint items are employed, there no longer is a "p value." On dichotomous items the p value is the mean, and it is directly related to the variance (pq). On multipoint items the mean and variance tend to be related, but they are far from perfectly correlated. For example, on seven-point scales used in measures of attitudes, the nearer the mean is to the middle of the scale, the larger the variance tends to be. In that case, however, should one select items in terms of the mean score or in terms of the variance? One could argue that both should be considered, but there are no obvious principles concerning how these two kinds of information should be combined. It is far better to construct tests concerning multipoint items by methods to be described in the next section.

Considering dichotomously scored multiple-choice items, the selection of items in terms of p values is greatly complicated by the effect of *guessing*. (The effects of guessing will be discussed in detail in Chapter

Fifteen.) The p value is determined by both the intrinsic difficulty of the item and the effect of guessing. Guessing tends to make p values higher, the amount of "elevation" being inversely related to the number of alternative responses for each item. Where there are only two alternative responses (a true-false test), it obviously would be inappropriate to peak a test at .5. Less obviously, it also would be inappropriate when there are four or five alternative responses, as typically found on multiple-choice tests.

One might think that the ideal difficulty for test items could be obtained with a proper correction for the expected effects of guessing, but this would solve only part of the problem. Guessing not only tends to raise p values, but also introduces measurement error. Since the less guessing there is, the less measurement error there is, easy items tend to have less measurement error than more difficult items. Consequently the most discriminating item would tend to be somewhere between a corrected p value of .5 and 1.0. There is, however, no certainty as to what the exact value should be. All one can do is generate a model to predict the ideal level and then test how well the model works in practice. Employing one such model, Lord (1952b) deduced that the most discriminating two-choice item would have an *uncorrected* p value of .85, a three-choice item .77, a four-choice item .74, and a five-choice item .69. There has not, however, been enough research to determine whether those deductions, or deductions from other models, hold in the general case.

Even if mountains of research were done to find the "ideal" p values for multiple-choice tests with different numbers of alternatives, the previously described shortcomings of selecting items purely in terms of p values still would be present. At best the p values can only indicate the types of items that are not highly restricted in their possible correlations with total scores. It is far more sensible to construct tests primarily in terms of the actual correlations of items with total scores.

construction of homogeneous tests

Much of what has been said so far in this book argues for the construction of homogeneous tests. Only some of the most important arguments will be reiterated. The first page of Chapter One emphasized that measurement always concerns an *attribute*. An attribute is some isolatable characteristic of organisms, some dimension of structure or function along which organisms can be ordered. Items within a measure are useful only to the extent that they share a common core—the attribute which is to be measured. The linear model was accepted as providing a reasonable approach to the construction of most measures in psychology, particularly for the construction of measures concerning individual differences among subjects. Most frequently, the model leads to a simple summation of item scores to obtain total scores. In summing scores, it is assumed that each item adds something to the others, and unless the items shared an attribute, it would not be meaningful to sum scores over items.

The major theory of reliability is based on the domain-sampling model, which assumes that each test is a random sample of items from a domain. Although the model holds when the domain contains items from different factors, it makes more sense, and estimates from it are more precise, when items from the domain share only one major factor. Eventually it will be possible to understand the cardinal dimensions of human attributes only when relatively complete factor structures are known for different types of abilities and personality characteristics. The best measures of each factor will be those that correlate highly with one factor and have low correlations with other factors.

Implicit in the considerations above is the premise that tests should be as homogeneous in content as possible. The homogeneity of content in a test is manifested in the average correlation among items and in the pattern of those correlations. If the average correlation among items is very low (and thus the average correlation of items with total scores is low), the items as a group are not homogeneous. This may be because all the correlations are low or because a number of different factors are present in the items. In the latter case there would be a number of item clusters, each cluster being relatively homogeneous, but the clusters would have either correlations near zero with one another or negative correlations. The ideal is to obtain a collection of items which has a high average correlation with total scores and is dominated by one factor only.

FACTOR ANALYSIS OF ITEMS   Considering the last statement above regarding the ideal statistical properties of a good test, it might be thought that the ideal approach to test construction would be through factor analysis. It will be argued, however, that *constructing* tests on the basis of factor analysis is not as wise as investigating the factorial composition of tests after they are constructed. This is a controversial point of view, and it is recognized that those who advocate the construction of tests through factor analysis have some good points on their side.

One important reason for not beginning test construction with factor analysis is that such analyses are seldom highly successful. As will be made evident in Chapter Nine, the results from factor analysis usually are clearest when the correlations among whole tests or individual items vary considerably. For example, if some of the correlations among tests are zero and other correlations are as high as .70, this suggests that the tests tend to divide up into clearly defined clusters, or factors.

If two tests relate strongly to a factor, they are expected to correlate substantially and to have low correlations with tests that relate strongly to other factors. Then it becomes apparent that for a group of variables (either whole tests or test items) to clearly define a number of factors, there must be a wide range of correlations in the matrix. This very seldom occurs in matrices of correlations among items. On most tests the average correlation among items is less than .20, and the variance of correlations among items is small. A typical finding would be that two-thirds of the correlations were between .10 and .30. To the extent the variance of correlations is larger than that, it typically indicates that there is considerable sampling error because of a relatively small number of subjects being investigated. Because of the small variance in correlations among items, it usually is not possible to clearly document a number of factors by the analysis of such correlations. This is particularly so when the items are scored dichotomously. With multipoint items (e.g., rating scales), the correlations among items usually are higher than they are with dichotomous items, and correspondingly, the variance in correlations among items is greater with multipoint items. Consequently factor analyses of multipoint items have a higher probability of success.

Another reason for not beginning the construction of tests with factor analysis is that such analysis of test items is extremely laborious. Imagine that one is constructing tests of "dominance" and it is thought that there are a number of different factors concerning different forms of dominance. Many items supposedly concerning different aspects of dominance are collected from the literature or constructed for the particular study. Each item requires agree-disagree responses. It is very difficult for the investigator to tell which items should go with different forms of dominance, so he tries to settle the issue with factor analysis. Not only is there a low probability of getting neat factors from this approach; but also the analysis, if properly done, will be extremely tedious. Some rules of thumb will indicate why this is the case. Since about 30 dichotomous items are usually required for respectable reliability, constructing three tests relative to three factors of dominance will require 90 items. Since many of the items either will be very unreliable or will not relate to any of the three factors, a good guess is that it will take a total collection of at least 180 items to obtain the three tests. To prevent taking advantage of chance, a minimum standard (not an ideal) in a factor analysis is that there be at least ten times as many subjects as variables. This means that at least 1,800 subjects are required before a factor analysis can be undertaken. Even with the best of high-speed computers, the actual factor analysis will be expensive. After the analysis is completed, many more hours will be required to study the results, try out different combinations of items for different tests, and investigate reliabilities of the tests and relations among them. Properly done, from start to finish it may take over three years to complete the job, and it will be an expensive operation.

Factor analyses of items seldom are undertaken with the thoroughness described above. Typically, considerably fewer than 100 items are included in the study. Consequently, even if the analysis suggests that there are a number of prominent factors present, there are not enough items to measure the factors. Then another analysis must be done with some of the items from the first collection and with new items that are thought to be related to the factors found in the first analysis. One may need to repeat this process a number of times in order to understand the factor structure and obtain reliable measures of each factor.

Frequently factor analyses of items are undertaken with many fewer subjects than the minimum recommended (10 subjects per item). There are some horrible examples in the literature where the number of subjects was approximately the same as the number of items. Unless the number of subjects is at least ten times as large as the number of items, factor analysis can take great advantage of chance. Then what appear to be factors are only artifacts because of sampling error. For example, if each of 100 subjects flipped coins to decide whether to agree or disagree with 100 questions, a factor analysis probably would indicate a number of apparently strong factors. This is because factor analysis essentially provides a method of searching for clusters of variables that correlate with one another and correlate less with members of other clusters. When the number of subjects is not much larger than the number of items, such clusters of correlations will occur purely by chance. Of course, such "factors" do not hold up in subsequent studies.

For the reasons mentioned above, most efforts to construct tests through factor analysis have not met with notable success. The literature is filled with unclear results from factoring items, disputes about how many and what kinds of factors are present in a particular collection of items, and supposed measures of factors that have very low reliability. This is not to deny that the *logic* of test construction is closely related to factor analysis—it definitely is. The question concerns when factor analysis should be applied. It is argued that factor analysis should usually not be applied to items before tests are constructed, but should be applied to whole tests *after* they are constructed. Although ideally it would be good to know the factor composition of items before they are placed in a test, for the reasons discussed above this is not easy to learn. A wiser strategy is to construct the most homogeneous test possible. Then, in later factor analyses of whole tests, it is possible to learn how successful one has been in developing a relatively pure measure of an important factor. Also, by methods which will be discussed later, at that point it is possible to purify a test of items that prevent it from being a relatively pure measure of a factor.

In addition to the statistical considerations discussed above, there is another important reason for not initiating test construction with a factor analysis of items. This approach tends to encourage an unhealthy form of "shotgun empiricism," which, however, is not a necessary accompaniment of the approach. Although none will admit it, some still work as though factor analyses, and other methods of analysis, automatically grind out the "true nature of things" even if there is no theory at all regarding the construction of items and regardless of the character of the items themselves. One can almost hear such persons saying to themselves, "What I need is a large collection of items to factor-analyze so that I can find the nature of human attributes." The reader surely has heard the evils of "shotgun empiricism" on numerous other occasions. Progress in science must be guided by theories rather than by a random effort to relate things to one another. Theories serve to greatly reduce the amount of trial-and-error effort, and it is the people who explore theories who tend to stand at the vanguard of each field of science. Some measurement specialists have been rightly criticized for being far more concerned with methods of analysis than with theories regarding the attributes which are intended to be measured. This criticism applies with great force when a polyglot collection of items is factor-analyzed in the hope of obtaining important measures of human attributes.

THE HYPOTHESIS   A new measure should spring from a hypothesis regarding the existence and nature of an attribute. In some cases a formal hypothesis is deduced from a theory regarding a construct. An example would be deducing hypotheses from theories concerning the construct of anxiety. If, as many people assume, anxiety is a form of "generalized drive," many hypotheses follow regarding the attributes of people who are high in the trait (construct) of anxiety. It would be expected that people who are high in anxiety would be characterized by a relatively low ability to solve familiar problems in novel ways, e.g., to write the alphabet from z to a or to solve simple arithmetic problems by a novel approach. Based on this hypothesis, one could construct a pool of items. Although in many cases there are no formal hypotheses regarding the existence of attributes, at least the investigator should have an informal hypothesis that can be communicated to others. For example, it might be hypothesized that reliable individual differences exist in the tendency to have common rather than uncommon associations. Although the hypothesis would not be deduced from a formal theory, such individual differences, if they exist, might be important for cognitive and affective processes. The hypothesis suggests a number of types of items that might be used to measure the attribute in question. In one type of item, the subject would be given a stimulus word and two possible response words. One of the response words would be a highly common associate of the stimulus word and the other would be a less common associate of the stimulus word. On each item, the subject would be required to mark the most appropriate associate. Whether the hypothesis follows from a theory or is only a "good idea," it guides the construction of items. Subsequent investigations of the items provide a test of the hypothesis.

CONSTRUCTION OF ITEMS   One cannot know for sure how many items should be constructed for a new measure until *after* they are constructed and submitted to item analysis. If the standard is to obtain a test with a coefficient alpha of .80, item analysis might show that the desired reliability can be obtained with as few as 20 items or that as many as 80 items are required. There are some rules of thumb that can be used to determine the number of items to be constructed. Usually between 20 and 30 dichotomous items are required to obtain an internal-consistency reliability of .80. Also, usually fewer multipoint items than dichotomous items are required to obtain a particular reliability. For example, it is not unusual to find a coefficient alpha of .80 for 15 agree-disagree attitude statements rated on a seven-point scale. How many more items should be constructed than the minimum required depends on what is known from previous studies about the type of item. If it were known that items of a particular type tended to have high internal consistency (e.g., items on vocabulary tests), at most no more than twice as many items would be constructed as has been found in previous studies to be required for a reliable test. In that case, to obtain a reliability of .80, 30 items probably would suffice for the final test. To provide room for the item analysis to eliminate unsatisfactory items, 60 items would be constructed initially. If very little is known about the homogeneity of items of a particular kind, it is wise to err on the conservative side and construct more items than would be the case in the previous example. For example, with the previously mentioned measure of the tendency to give common word associations, if it were desired to obtain a test with a reliability of .80, it would be wise to construct 100 items.

A somewhat different strategy in deciding how many items to construct starts by purposefully constructing a smaller number of items than is thought to be adequate, e.g., constructing only 30 items when it is suspected that 30 items will be required to obtain a coefficient alpha of .80. These items are then applied to a relatively small sample of subjects (say, 100), and the results are submitted to item analysis. If either the total collection of items (30) or the most homogeneous subset (say, of 15 items) has a coefficient alpha of at least .50, this indicates that it is worth the effort to construct more items, gather responses from a much larger group of subjects, and perform a more complete item analysis. The eventual labor is greater for constructing the test in stages rather than in one large step, but if the results from the first stage of the former method are very discouraging, the project can be abandoned without further loss of time and effort.

SAMPLE OF SUBJECTS   After items are constructed and before they are sub-
mitted to item analysis, they must, of course, be administered to a sample of people. So that the required types of analyses may be performed, all the items should be administered to all the people. Of course, the sample of people used in this phase of test construction should be reasonably representative of the types of people that will be studied with the eventual test. To take a very bad example, if a test is intended to be used primarily with children from eight to ten years of age, it should not be constructed on the basis of data obtained from college students. Except for such extremes, however, the subjects used in test construction need not be exactly representative of those with whom the final test will be used. Also, often a test is used with many different types of subjects (e.g., some attitude scales), and in such cases it is very difficult to ensure that the group of subjects used in test construction is highly representative of all the different groups with which the test eventually will be used.

   As is true of all methods of analysis, it is not possible to say in advance exactly how many subjects should be used to obtain data for item analysis. A good rule of thumb, however, is that there should be at least ten times as many subjects as items. (This rule was mentioned previously for factor analysis. It also is a reasonable standard for all forms of multivariate analysis, such as multiple correlation.) In some cases this rule is impractical if there are more than about 70 items. For example, if there are 100 items, it might not be possible to obtain 1,000 subjects. In any case, though, 5 subjects per item should be considered the minimum that can be tolerated.

   In gathering data for item analysis, one should administer items under conditions that closely resemble those under which the eventual test will be used. If subjects in the tryout sample are given all the time that they want to complete the items and one intends to place a severe time limit on the eventual test, an item analysis probably will provide very misleading information. If items for a personality inventory are being administered in an atmosphere that encourages frankness and the eventual test is to be administered in an atmosphere where subjects will be reluctant to say bad things about themselves, the item analysis will tell a faulty story.

ITEM–TOTAL CORRELATIONS   The remainder of this section will consider methods of item analysis when most of the correlations among items (say, at least 90 percent) are positive. This is almost always the case in measures concerning abilities, i.e., where there is a "correct" response for each item. Some of the correlations may be very close to zero, but if the sample size is large, very few are negative. A later section will consider methods of item analysis when some of the items tend to correlate negatively with the others, as occurs on many personality inventories.

When items predominately correlate positively with one another, those with the highest average correlations are the best items. Since the average correlations of items with one another are highly related to the correlations of items with total scores, the items that correlate most highly with total scores are the best items. Compared to items with relatively low correlations with total scores, those that have higher correlations with total scores have more variance relating to the common factor among the items, and they add more to the test reliability.

The first step in item analysis, then, is to correlate each item with total scores. Thus if there are 60 items, scores are summed over items, and 60 correlations are obtained. If multipoint items are employed, the regular PM coefficient is the correct measure. If dichotomous items are employed, the correct measure is point-biserial, which, it will be remembered, is only a differently appearing version of the PM formula. The obtained coefficients are then ranked from highest to lowest. If numerous correlations are relatively high (with respect to standards that will be discussed shortly), one is "in business," and a few simple steps can be taken to obtain a final test that has (1) a desired level of reliability and (2) a desired distribution form, this usually being a symmetrical distribution.

There are numerous measures of item-total relationship other than point-biserial. An argument can be made for employing the item-total covariance rather than the correlation, because the former takes account of the p values of items as well as the correlation with total scores. The covariance tends to give added weight to items that have p values near .5. Correlational methods other than point-biserial have been employed for item analysis. Biserial can be used; and if the continuous total scores are divided at the mean or median, either phi or tetrachoric can be applied.

In addition to the different measures of correlation that can be used in item analysis, numerous other measures of item-total relationship are available. One of the most popular measures is obtained as follows. First, the top and bottom 25 percents of persons in total test scores are found. Second, for each item, the percentages of persons in top and bottom groups that pass the item are determined. Third, the percentage in the bottom group is subtracted from the percentage in the top group. Items that have a large difference in this regard tend to discriminate persons with high total test scores from persons with low total test scores.

Although many different measures of item-total relationship can be employed in item analysis, there is a wealth of data to demonstrate that they all provide much the same information. In a typical study, four different measures of item-total relationship are applied to the same items, and then items are ranked on the different measures. Typically it is found that correlations between the different sets of ranks are .90 or higher, demonstrating that essentially the same set of items would have been selected by any of the methods.

It is recommended that the PM correlation be used in item analysis, which with dichotomous items is point-biserial. Not only does the PM correlation give very much the same information any other measure of item-total relationship would provide, but to the extent that item selection would be slightly different by different measures, the PM correlation is logically better than the other measures.

When the PM correlation is used for item analysis, account must be taken of an artifact in such correlations. In correlating an item with total test scores, one must remember that the item is a part of the total test. This makes the correlation of an item with total scores higher than it would be if the item were correlated with scores on all other items. In the extreme case, if there were no more than five items, even if all correlations among items were zero, each item would correlate positively with total scores; but if each item were correlated with the sum of scores on the other four items, the correlations would be zero. This spurious source of item-total correlation can be removed with the following formula:

(8-1)

$$r_{1(y-1)} = \frac{r_{y1}\sigma_y - \sigma_1}{\sqrt{\sigma_1^2 + \sigma_y^2 - 2\sigma_1\sigma_y r_{y1}}}$$

where r_{y1} = correlation of item 1 with total scores y

σ_y = standard deviation of total scores

σ_1 = standard deviation of item 1

$r_{1(y-1)}$ = correlation of item 1 with sum of scores on all items exclusive of item 1

Although the artifact can be large when the number of items is small, with the numbers of items that are involved in most analyses,

internal structure of measures

the artifact is quite small. The effect can be illustrated in the case of 80 items where (1) the item-total correlation is .24, (2) the p value of the item is .5, and (3) the variance of total scores is 191. In this case the corrected correlation would be .22, which is only slightly lower than the item-total correlation.

Equation (8-1) is of potential importance mainly in establishing the level of statistical significance in an item analysis. Logically, one should stop adding items to a test when the item-total correlations are well below accepted standards of statistical significance, say, below the .05 level of statistical significance. The significance level should be determined *after* correlations are corrected by Eq. (8-1). In practice, however, it usually is not necessary to bother with the slight artifact that is present. Frequently there are as many as 80 items in the analysis, and thus, as was illustrated above, the bias is slight. If 625 persons were used for the analysis, the standard error of the correlation would be approximately the reciprocal of 25. Then corrected correlations of .08 would be significant beyond the .05 level, which means that uncorrected correlations around .09 or .10 would be significant at that level. Where one has at least 80 items for the analysis, there usually are more items with uncorrected item-total correlations above .10 than are required for the eventual test. Consequently, in most item analysis, one can work directly with the item-total correlations without applying Eq. (8-1). If, however, the number of items is considerably less than 80 and the number of subjects is relatively small, Eq. (8-1) should be employed.

Although it is useful to compute the standard error of the correlation coefficient and let it serve as a guide to the minimum level of item-total correlation that will be used in the selection of items, there usually is no need to be highly concerned about the statistical significance of item-total correlations. Worries in this regard are greatly lessened by dealing with a large sample of persons, e.g., a very minimum of five persons per item. More important, if all or nearly all the item-total correlations are positive, as is usually the case, the only sensible hypothesis is that *all* the items actually would correlate positively with total test scores in the population of persons being sampled. When over 90 percent of the item-total correlations are positive, as is usually the case, one is being conservative to reject items whose correlations with total scores do not reach the .05 level of statistical significance.

STEP-BY-STEP PROCEDURES   If there are numerous uncorrected item-total correlations above .20, the remaining steps in item analysis are simple. Since about 30 dichotomous items usually are required to reach a reliability of .80, KR-20 would be computed for the 30 items having the highest correlations with total scores. If the reliability is as high as desired, the item analysis is complete. If it is not, one increases the number of items, adding those items that have the next highest correlations with total scores. How many items are added depends on their correlations with total scores and on the reliability of the first set of 30 items. When the correlations with total scores are very low (e.g., .05), little can be gained by adding more items. When there are numerous additional items with correlations above .10, how many of them are added depends on how much the reliability needs to be increased. If the reliability of the original group of items is .65 and a reliability of .80 is desired, a good strategy is to add 10 items. Then KR-20 is computed for the 40 items. If the desired reliability is obtained, the item analysis is complete; if not, more items are added. If, for example, the 40-item test had a reliability of .75 rather than .80, a good strategy would be to add the next 5 items in terms of their correlations with total scores. If this did not achieve the desired reliability, one could add several more items. If at any point the reliability fails to increase or decreases, there is no use in trying out larger numbers of items.

When one wants to undertake the labors involved, a highly systematic approach to test construction is to compute KR-20 for cumulative sets of items, starting with the 5 items having the highest correlations with total scores and adding items in sets of 5. Then one can plot a curve showing the size of KR-20 for tests of different lengths. A typical curve is shown in Figure 8-2. Also shown is the expected increase in reliability from lengthening a 5-item test when the 5 items have a reliability of .40. As can be seen, the empirically obtained reliabilities are lower than the results predicted from Eq. (7-6). This is to be expected, because Eq. (7-6) assumes that the items which are added at each step have the same correlations with total scores as did the original 5 items. By the method of item analysis recommended here, the first 5 items would correlate highest with total scores, and later items would correlate less with total scores. Consequently the curve of obtained reliabilities is lower than that predicted from Eq. (7-6). Employing this approach, one would select the number of items that reached a desired level of reliability. Because this method of selecting items takes some advantage of chance, it would be well to continue adding items until KR-20 is comfortably above the reliability needed for the final test. For example, if a reliability of .80 were needed in the final test, it would be wise to select enough items to achieve a KR-20 of .85 or higher. If there were no set standard for the size of the reliability, one would quit adding items when the curve began to level off, as it does in Figure 8-2 for more than 50 items.

The more complete procedure illustrated in Figure 8-2 is not necessary in most item analyses. A quicker approach with dichotomous items

internal structure of measures

is to compute KR-20 for the 30 items having the highest correlations with total scores. If the desired reliability is not obtained, adding a few more items usually will suffice. If the analysis is of multipoint items, it is wise to compute coefficient alpha for the 15 items having the highest correlations with total scores, and if the reliability is not high enough, to add items 5 at a time until the desired reliability is obtained.

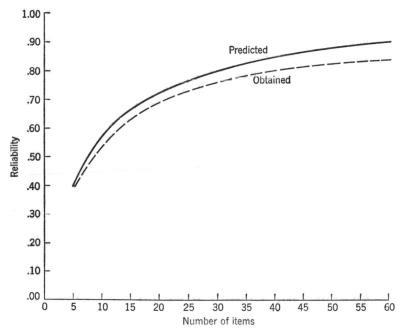

figure 8-2 *The predicted and obtained reliabilities of tests varying in length from 5 to 60 items when the reliability of the first 5 items is .40.*

What should one do if this approach to test construction fails? It will probably fail if the reliability of the first 30 dichotomous items is no more than .40. Since by this point one has already used the "cream" of the items, there may not be enough good items left to reach a reliability of .80. There are three reasons why the method may fail to produce a homogeneous test. The first possibility is that the items are from a domain where correlations among items are uniformly low. In that case the reliability would grow slowly as the number of items was increased, but the curve would not flatten out altogether. One could then achieve a reliable test, but it would take a very large number of items.

The second possibility is that the collection of items is factorially complex, in which case clusters of items will tend to have relatively high correlations with one another but very low correlations with members of other clusters. It usually would be very difficult to distinguish this circumstance from the first circumstance discussed. In both cases correlations with total scores would be low; KR-20 would tend to rise as more items were added, but the curve would go up very slowly.

The third possibility is that some of the items have relatively high correlations with one another but the other items have correlations near zero with all items. In that case one would have some good items to form the nucleus of a test, but the reliability could not be increased by adding items. This condition could be detected by a sudden drop-off in the size of item-total correlations as one inspected the correlations ranked from highest to lowest. This would be evidenced, for example, if the thirty-fifth item in the list had a correlation with total scores of .17 and the thirty-sixth item had a correlation of only .06.

How can one recognize which of the three circumstances prevail, and what should be done after the circumstance is recognized? As was mentioned above, it is relatively easy to distinguish the third circumstance from the other two by the marked falloff in item-total correlations at some point in the list of items. If that occurs, one should study the good items and try to determine the nature of their content. Then one should try to construct more items of the same kind, administer them along with the original good items to a new group of subjects, and submit all items to the type of analysis which has been described.

If the average item-total correlation is low, it is very difficult to tell whether this is because of the first or second circumstance. If it is caused by factorial complexity (the second circumstance), it cannot be because of the presence of only two or three strong factors. If that were the case, correlations with total scores would not be very low. Indeed, the major criticism that can be made of selecting items in terms of correlations with total scores is that the method apparently works as well as when several groups of items relate strongly to different factors as it does when all items relate only moderately to the same factor. From previous discussions of the correlation of sums, one can well see why this would be the case. Where there are 60 items, half of which relate strongly to one factor and the other half to another factor, typically the items belonging to each factor have average correlations with one another of around .20 and with items belonging to the other factor of less than .10. In this case, regardless of the presence of two factors, all items have respectable correlations with total scores. The method of item analysis which has been discussed will select items from both factors. Thus if there are several prominent factors in the items, the problem is not so much that the item analysis will fail, but rather that it will work deceivingly well.

internal structure of measures

There is another reason why the item analysis probably would not fail because of the presence of several strong factors in the items. The investigator probably would have guessed the presence of the factors and would have constructed different tests to measure the different factors. Consequently it is unlikely that he would construct an item pool containing items relating to several strong factors.

If the reliability of the first 30 dichotomous items is not above .50 and the difficulty cannot be traced to the third circumstance (marked falloff in item-total correlations at some point in the list of items), it can be argued that factor analysis should be applied. For reasons which were discussed previously, this would be very laborious, and the results probably would not be very clear. Since if there were only several strong factors among the items the need for a factor analysis would not be apparent, the most the investigator could hope to find would be numerous rather weak factors among the items. There then would not be enough items to construct a reliable test for any of the factors found. If the average item-total correlation were low and the variance of correlations were small, the better part of valor in this circumstance might be to abandon the type of item being employed. The investigator would conclude that the attribute either did not exist or needed to be measured by a different type of item. If he were doggedly determined to continue investigating the particular type of item, his only choices would be (1) not to factor-analyze, but to construct a very long test in the hope that later it will be found to primarily measure one factor or (2) to factor-analyze the collection of items in the hope of eventually learning how to measure one, or some, of the small factors involved.

SUCCESSIVE APPROXIMATIONS A possibility not mentioned in the previous section is that the selection of items in terms of item-total correlations can be improved by successively correlating items with subpools of the items. This can be illustrated where an analysis is being made of 100 items and only 50 of them have nonzero average correlations with the others. In this case, if it were known in advance that there were only 50 items from which to select the final group of items, the other 50 items would be removed from the analysis. If all items were correlated with total scores on the 100 items, the 50 bad items would tend to "water down" the correlations of the 50 good items with total scores. If one has the time and patience and the problem is sufficiently important, a refinement of the basic approach can be made as follows. In the first go-around, all items are correlated with total scores on all items. All items are removed that have item-total correlations which are either statistically insignificant or below some minimum value, e.g., .10. For example, say that 40 items are removed from a total collection of 100. Total scores are then obtained on the remaining 60 items, and each of the 60 items is correlated with those total scores. Then KR-20 is computed for the items that stand highest in those correlations, and if the desired level of reliability is not reached, successive sets of items are added.

One could go through the above steps a number of times, each step leading to a more and more homogeneous group of items. However, it is seldom necessary to work with anything other than the original correlations of items with total scores. Usually the rank order of item-total correlations in successive sets of items refined in that way is much the same as it is for the initial item-total correlations. Where such successive refinements are sometimes required is with pools of items where many of the correlations among items are negative, as is sometimes the case with items on personality inventories. This problem will be discussed in a later section.

THE DISTRIBUTION FORM One of the supposed advantages of selecting items in terms of p values is that it permits control of the distribution form for total test scores. How can the same control be exercised when one selects items in terms of item-total correlations rather than p values? There is a way to control the distribution form *after* good items have been selected in terms of item correlations. The method will be illustrated in the situation where the first 30 items in terms of item-total correlations produce the desired level of reliability but there still are more items that correlate reasonably well with total scores—say, 20 more such items. The first step would be to plot a frequency distribution for total scores on the first 30 items. If the distribution was symmetrical, the item analysis would be complete. If not, it would be necessary to study the p values of both the 30 items and the remaining 20 good items.

If the distribution is skewed toward the higher end of the continuum, it means that the test is too difficult. To make the distribution more symmetrical, some of the items in the 30-item test having low p values should be replaced by items from the remaining 20 that have p values above .5. If 5 items having p values between .2 and .3 are replaced by 5 items having p values between .5 and .7, this will tend to make the distribution symmetrical. The distribution of the new group of 30 items is then plotted, and if it is symmetrical, the item analysis is complete. If the distribution still is slightly nonsymmetrical, replacement of a few more items will solve the problem. In replacing items in this way, one must recheck the reliability at each step to make sure it is not falling below the desired standard. If it does fall slightly, then at each step in the replacement of items, several more items should be added than are removed. Thus, for example, to achieve both the desired reliability and the desired distribution form, one might end up with a 38-item test rather than a 30-item test.

Actually, though, it is quite unlikely that the distribution of scores will be markedly nonsymmetrical if items are selected purely in terms of correlations with total scores. This method tends to select items in the middle range of p values rather than those at the extremes. Since the restriction on the size of point-biserial is rather severe for items with p values below .2 or above .8, it is unlikely that items with such extreme p values will be high enough in the rank order of item-total correlations to be included in a test. Since the least restriction in point-biserial is for items having p values at .5, items with p values near .5 have a greater likelihood of having high correlations with total scores, and consequently such items tend to stand high in the rank order of item-total correlations. (It is important to remember, however, that picking items in terms of item-total correlations favors only those items with p values near .5 that actually correlate well with total scores.) Because choosing items in terms of item-total correlations tends to select items that are "average" in p value, this method of item analysis almost always produces a symmetrical distribution of scores, and consequently no further refinements are necessary. Also, one seldom seeks anything other than a symmetrical distribution.

Another reason why it is not important in most problems to be highly concerned about the p values of the items which are selected is that the exact shape of the distribution of total scores is seldom a very important issue. This is particularly so in measures of constructs to be used in basic research. For example, with a new measure of introversion, the major concerns are that the reliability be sufficiently high and the distribution be approximately symmetrical. Whether it is slightly skewed in either direction will make very little difference in research. The most the skewness could do is have a very slight effect on the size of correlations with variables which are symmetrically distributed.

special problems in test construction

In the remainder of the book it will be assumed that the best way to construct most tests is in terms of item-total correlations, as described in the previous section. This section will consider some special problems that arise in employing that method.

BIPOLAR DOMAINS OF ITEMS   The discussion in the previous section assumed that most correlations among items are positive, which usually is the case for any test concerning abilities, but is not necessarily the case for measures of personality, attitudes, interests, and others. For example, if an attitude scale regarding the United Nations were being constructed, one approach would be to start by writing 60 statements, half of which were thought to be favorable toward the United Nations and half thought to be unfavorable. Each item would require dichotomous, agree-disagree responses. If all agreements were scored 1 and all disagreements scored zero, the negative statements would tend to correlate negatively with the positive statements. Then the average correlation of each item with the others would be close to zero, and thus all the items would have item-total correlations close to zero. Obviously, then, it would not be possible to select items in terms of item-total correlations, and the analyses would provide no hints as to what should be done to improve the situation.

If items are selected purely in terms of item-total correlations, the success of this method depends on the investigator's ability to devise a scoring key initially that will make the majority of correlations among items positive. In most cases this is easily done. In the previous example of constructing a measure of attitudes toward the United Nations, the investigator would score agreements with the positive statements as 1 and *disagreements* with the *negative* statements as 1. Then most of the correlations among items would be likely to be positive, and there would be no difficulty in selecting items in terms of item-total correlations. Of course, the investigator might misjudge some of the items, and consequently some items would have negative correlations with total scores. For selecting items in terms of item-total correlations, however, it is not necessary that all the correlations among items be positive, but only most of them. The method usually will work if a scoring key is devised such that 70 percent of the correlations among items are positive. In this case the majority of item-total correlations are positive, and some probably are sufficiently high to encourage further item analysis.

After the first attempt to devise a scoring key that will make most correlations among items positive, the next step is to rank the items in terms of item-total correlations. If at least 70 percent of the correlations are positive and numerous correlations are above .15, one can proceed to the next step, which is to reverse the scoring for all items having statistically significant negative item-total correlations. Thus if an item that correlated —.15 with total scores had previously been scored 1 for "agree," in the new scoring key it would be scored 1 for "disagree," and vice versa for an item with that same negative correlation which previously had been scored 1 for "disagree." The scoring would not be changed for all items having positive correlations with total scores or nonsignificant negative correlations. Next, a new set of total scores would be obtained with the new scoring key, and each item would be correlated with the new total scores. This time the number of positive item-total correlations would probably increase markedly, and the average size of the correlations would increase. If there still are numerous items having negative item-total correlations, the process can be repeated.

In most bipolar item domains, it is not necessary to go through the iterative procedure described above. Usually the investigator can intuit a scoring scheme that will make most correlations among items positive. This usually is easy to do with attitude scales, interest inventories, and most personality inventories. It might be necessary to go through one rekeying of the items, but seldom would it be necessary to repeat the process a number of times. But, as was said previously, even if the scoring key produces only 70 percent positive item-total correlations among items, the iterative approach will usually produce the needed positive item-total correlations. After these correlations are obtained, rather than make only one rank order in terms of item-total correlations, it is better to make a different order for items scored "agree" (or "yes") than for items scored "disagree" (or "no"). Then one would select an equal number of items from each list to form the first trial test. For example, one would select the top 15 items from both lists and form a 30-item test. If KR-20 is not as high as desired, additional items would be added from both lists. A balanced scoring key of this kind tends to eliminate response styles such as the tendency to agree regardless of the item content. (Response styles will be discussed in Chapter Fifteen.)

DISCRIMINATION AT A POINT   Although it rarely occurs in practice, a potential problem in test construction is to devise a test that will most effectively discriminate persons from one another at a particular point in the distribution of persons, e.g., a test that will most effectively discriminate the lower 30 percent of persons from the upper 70 percent. The problem might occur in a training program in the Armed Forces where only the top 70 percent of the persons at one stage of training are allowed to enter the next stage of training. Another situation in which discrimination at a point would be important is in the selection of students for scholarships. If only 10 percent of the students can be given scholarships, it is important to reliably distinguish the top 10 percent from the bottom 90 percent.

It has been suggested that the most effective way to discriminate at a point is by controlling the p values of items (Lord, 1952a and b). Models used for this purpose lead to the conclusion that one would *not* choose items with p values as extreme as the "cut" desired in the distribution of persons. Thus, to discriminate the upper 70 percent, one would not choose items with p values near .7; instead, one would select items closer to .5. Interesting as such developments are, they are beside the point.

The most discriminating item for any division of a distribution is the one that correlates highest with that division. Thus, to discriminate at a point, one would select items as follows. First, one would construct a very long test in terms of item-total correlations, by methods which were described in previous sections. In this case it would be wise to have at least twice as many items in the first test as are thought to be needed for the eventual test. In terms of total scores, subjects would be split into the divisions required, e.g., bottom 30 percent and top 70 percent. Persons in the top group would receive a score of 1, and those in the bottom group would receive a score of zero. A phi coefficient would be computed between each dichotomous item and each dichotomous score on the total test. Items would be ranked from highest to lowest in this regard. The items with the highest phi coefficients would be the most discriminating items at the particular point.

One would obtain the final test by selecting enough items high in the rank order of phi coefficient to obtain the desired level of reliability. Subsequently, of course, one would employ continuous scores on the total test rather than dichotomous scores. One can improve this method of test construction by going through an iterative process as follows. After the first selection of items in terms of phi coefficients and the formation of a test, subjects would again be split into the desired proportions on this new test. Phi coefficients would again be computed between dichotomous items and dichotomized total scores. Items near the top of the list in terms of those correlations would be used to form a new test, and the procedure could, if required, be repeated again. Such an iterative approach would, however, seldom be necessary. Usually, the items that were high in the first listing of phi coefficients would be high in subsequent listings of phi coefficients.

Even though it is true that, individually, the items that have the highest coefficients with any split in terms of total scores are the most discriminating items, there is no guarantee that the sum of scores on such items will be more discriminating than the sum of scores on some other set of items. The most discriminating *set* of k items will be that set which has the highest multiple correlation with dichotomized total scores. It would, however, be impractical to undertake the analyses that would be involved or to use the differential weights for items required by multiple regression. Also, that approach would take great advantage of chance even if large numbers of subjects were used. The method described above usually will provide better discrimination at a point than any other method that is feasible.

The method described above for discriminating at a point will tend

internal structure of measures

to select items that have p values in the general region of the point. Thus, in using the method to discriminate the upper 70 percent of people and employing free-response items, one would select more items with p values near .7 than at points far removed from .7. The crucial consideration, though, is the phi coefficient between dichotomous scores on the item and dichotomized total scores. In some instances one finds that items with p values near the upper proportion being discriminated have low phi coefficients, and similarly, one frequently finds that items with p values 20 points or more removed from the split have relatively high phi coefficients. What this method does, essentially, is concentrate the test reliability near a particular point in the score continuum, more about which will be said in the next section.

An obvious reason why it usually is not wise to construct a test so as to maximally discriminate at a particular point is that such a test will be useful either for only one purpose or for only a narrow range of purposes. In different situations, different points of discrimination are important. The test which has been constructed specifically to discriminate the top 80 percent of the persons in one situation obviously will do a poor job in another situation of discriminating the top 20 percent. Also, the score that would correspond to a particular percentage in one situation might correspond to a very different percentage in another situation. For example, if 70 percent of the persons in one situation had a raw score of 65 or higher, in another situation it might be found that only 30 percent of the persons had a score of 65 or higher. In most cases, one wants to construct a *general-purpose test*, one that is discriminating at all levels of the attribute and hence can be used for many different purposes in many different situations. One can do this by selecting items in terms of item-total correlations as described previously rather than in terms of phi coefficients between items and total scores dichotomized at a point. Also, possibly one would want to employ the refinement described in the next section to ensure approximately equal reliability at different points in the continuum of scores on the eventual test.

AN EQUIDISCRIMINATING TEST   As was mentioned previously, when items are selected so as to most effectively discriminate at a particular point in the distribution, this tends to concentrate the test reliability at that point. In previous chapters, we were concerned with the *overall* reliability of a test, which is the consistency with which people at all levels of the attribute are differentiated from one another on alternative measures. Thus the overall reliability (coefficient alpha or the correlation between alternative forms) can be thought of as an "average" of the reliabilities at different levels of the attribute. Instead of examining the overall reliability, one could make investigations of reliability at different levels of the attribute, e.g., for people who score between the 20th and 40th percentiles on a particular form of a test. If a test were constructed to maximally discriminate at the 30th percentile by methods described previously, this would provide good reliability (discrimination) in the range from the 20th to the 40th percentile, but would, for example, provide poorer discrimination in the range from the 60th to 80th percentiles. On an alternative form constructed by the same standards, the rank order of persons in the lower range would tend to change less than would the rank order of persons in the higher range. There is a way to partially ensure equal discrimination at different levels of the attribute, this leading to an *equidiscriminating test*.

An equidiscriminating test would be useful in any situation where (1) important practical decisions are made about people with regard to their particular test scores and (2) the population of persons under study is highly diverse with respect to the type of item being employed. This would be the case for vocabulary items being employed as part of a battery for the measurement of scholastic aptitude. Assume that the vocabulary test is to be used with children in grades four through eight. One list of words will be used with all grades, but different norms will be constructed for each grade. Thus it is important that scores on the test discriminate among children in each grade and not just among the average children in different grades.

In the example above, if it were not important to discriminate among the children within grades, a test could be constructed purely in terms of item-total correlations as described previously. First, a large number of items would be constructed. Considering the diversity of the sample of people, the items would need to vary widely in difficulty. All items would be administered to samples of students in grades four through eight. In the item analysis all students would be pooled, and each item would be correlated with total scores. The additional steps in item analysis would be those described previously.

If the test were constructed without considering the diversity of the students involved in the analysis, it probably would be more discriminating among children in the middle grades, probably being most discriminating among the children in the sixth grade. This is because the p values of more items will be ones that permit relatively higher item-total correlations for children in the sixth grade considered separately than for children in either the fourth grade or eighth grade considered separately. For a sufficient range of difficulty, many items would be so difficult for fourth graders as to provide practically no discrimination among members of that group. For eighth graders, many of the items would be so easy as to provide no discrimination among the members of that group. For sixth graders, the average item would be "just right," and consequently the test would discriminate well among the members of that group. Of course, the test probably would discriminate well between average children in the different grades, but that is not the important consideration. The primary purpose of the test is to discriminate *within* grades, not *between* grades.

There are a number of approaches to constructing an equidiscriminating test; the procedure which is recommended is as follows. By its nature, an equidiscriminating test is usually a long test, because it must discriminate well at different levels of the attribute. For example, the vocabulary test required in the illustrative problem above probably would require at least 80 items. Since more room will be required to pick and choose among the items than is required when items are selected purely in terms of item-total correlations, it is necessary to start with a larger ratio of initial-to-final items in constructing an equidiscriminating test. Also, it is wise to construct items that vary greatly in difficulty. If prior information is available about the approximate difficulty of words for the different grades, one can use equal numbers of items that are thought to be of average difficulty for the different grades. If a personality test were being constructed for adults rather than a vocabulary test for children, the investigator would simply have to intuit a pool of items diverse in p values.

After all items were administered to the samples involved, the total sample would be split at a particular percentile level, and phi coefficients would be computed between all items and dichotomized total scores. A good way to start would be to divide the total distribution of persons at the 20th percentile, giving everyone above that point a score of 1 and everyone below a score of zero. Each item would be correlated with that dichotomy. Items would then be ranked in terms of their phi coefficients. Next, the original total-score distribution would be divided at the 40th percentile, persons above that point receiving a score of 1 and persons below a score of zero. Phi coefficients would then be computed for all items with this second set of dichotomized total scores. This would provide a rank ordering of phi coefficients for the 40–60 split. Subsequently, splits would be made at the 60th percentiles and at the 80th percentiles, which would lead to two more rank orderings of phi coefficients.

After the four lists of item-dichotomy correlations were obtained, the next step would be to select an approximately equal number of items at each dichotomy to obtain the same average phi coefficient at each level. For example, by this approach one might end up with 20 items at each of the four percentile levels, the average phi coefficients at the respective levels being .19, .21, .23, and .18. Of course, cut-and-try methods would be required to obtain such a result. The average correlations of items at one level (e.g., the 60–40 split) are likely to be higher, in general, than the correlations with respect to another split. Also, an item that correlates well with one split is likely to correlate well with another split, and some of the items are likely to have very low correlations with all splits. One can, however, by a considerable amount of shifting items from dichotomy to dichotomy, achieve approximately the desired properties.

There usually would be little worry about the equidiscriminating test having a high overall reliability. One would not construct such a test unless he already knew that the overall reliability of the type of item was reasonably high. Also, the number of items required for an equidiscriminating test would tend to ensure a high overall reliability. Of course, an investigation would be made of the overall reliability after the test had been constructed through the steps described above.

Numerous refinements of the basic approach described above are possible for the construction of an equidiscriminating test. Dichotomies could be formed at 8 or 10 levels rather than the 4 mentioned in the illustrative problem above; however, that probably would do little to improve the final test. After items were selected on the first go-around, one could iteratively improve the results at each stage by forming new distributions of total scores and recomputing phi coefficients with dichotomized scores on the new distributions. Also, new items could be constructed and then correlated with dichotomized scores at different levels of the existing test. A final refinement could be made with respect to adjusting the average phi coefficient at each level. Previously it was said that one should strive for an equal number of items at each level and for equal average phi coefficients in item groups for their respective splits. This, however, is only an approximate solution to the ideal, whicn is to obtain a final collection of items where the average phi coefficient over the *total* collection of items is the same at the different splits. Thus if there are 80 items in the final test and 20 items are selected to represent each level, the ideal is for the 80 phi coefficients with each level to be approximately the same, on the average, as the 80 phi coefficients with other levels. Usually one approximates this ideal by attending to the average correlations of the 20 items selected specifically for each level. Since the correlations of all 80 items at each level would have been obtained for the analysis, the approximation to the ideal can be determined. If there are appreciable differences in the average correlations of the 80 items at the different levels, additional items (if there are any good items left at this point) can be added so as to increase the average correlation at particular levels.

The person who enjoys Rube Goldberg methods of statistical analysis can easily think of additional refinements of the methods that have been described for the construction of an equidiscriminating test. It is doubtful, though, that the elaborate procedures discussed so far will find frequent use, and even less likely that more elaborate methods will be regarded as anything other than museum pieces. Obviously, analyses such as those described are out of the question where high-speed computers are not available, and even with such computers, the analyses are time-consuming and expensive. One should consider these labors only in the situation described previously—where the population is very diverse with respect to the type of item being studied and important decisions will be made about people on the basis of the eventual test.

The problem of obtaining an equidiscriminating test was illustrated with a scholastic aptitude test for children in grades four through eight. That example was used because it fits the requirements of practical importance for the children concerned and it neatly illustrates the problem of trying to obtain a good test when the population differs greatly with respect to the type of item being investigated. In that situation, however, there would be two competing approaches. If it were feasible to construct separate tests for the different grades, this would be better than constructing an equidiscriminating test to cover students in all five grades. Another approach would be to construct an equidiscriminating test on the basis of point-biserial correlations between each item and the continuous scores of students within each grade. In most test-construction problems, however, there are no "grades" that serve to stratify the population with respect to the attribute in question. For example, in the construction of a measure of intelligence to be used with adults, there are no "grades" that serve to indicate different levels of the attribute. Consequently, in the general case, determining "grades" in terms of the obtained distribution of total scores is better than searching for natural groupings of people with respect to the attribute in question. This is why it was recommended that, in the general case, equidiscriminating tests be constructed by successively forming dichotomies of total scores at various levels.

In basic research, it seldom is worth the trouble to strive for an equidiscriminating test. The major requirement in basic research is to have high *overall* reliability of a size that will support significant mean differences among treatment groups or high correlations among different sources of individual differences. In tests that are used widely across the country and are used to make important practical decisions about people, at least an approximation of an equidiscriminating test should be obtained.

WEIGHTING OF ITEMS   The methods of item analysis discussed in this chapter assume that all items are to be weighted equally in the eventual test, and no mention has been made of the possibility of obtaining differential weights for items. Rather than simply adding the number of correct responses on a test of ability, one could count correct responses on some items 3, correct responses on some other items 2, and correct responses on the remaining items 1. This possibility has not been discussed because it is almost always a waste of time to seek differential weights for items.

A number of different standards could be used for obtaining differential weights for items. If items were being selected in terms of their correlations with an external criterion, they could be weighted by a method that would tend to maximize the correlation of total test scores with the criterion. An approximate method for doing this would be to weight the score on each item by the item-criterion correlation. Since it was strongly recommended that tests not be constructed in terms of item-criterion correlations, it also is strongly recommended that items not be weighted by any function of the item-criterion correlations. Also, as was said before, in most test-construction problems there is no criterion, and consequently there is no possibility of using that method.

A more sensible approach is to obtain differential weights for items by a method that will tend to maximize the reliability of total test scores. Such a method would fit well with the procedures described previously for selecting items in terms of item-total correlations. An approximate method for obtaining such differential weights is to weight each item by its item-total correlation. To take an overly simplified example, if 10 items all had item-total correlations of .15 and 10 more items had item-total correlations of .3, a higher reliability for the 20 items would be obtained if the former items were weighted 1 and the latter were weighted 2 than if all items were weighted 1.

The crucial question in seeking differential weights for items is that of how much difference it makes to use differential weights. It would make a difference if the weighted and unweighted scores on whole tests did not correlate highly and if the reliability of the weighted test was considerably higher than the reliability of the unweighted test. However, there is overwhelming evidence that the use of differential weights seldom makes an important difference. Regardless of how differential weights are determined, typically it is found that on tests containing at least 20 items, the weighted test correlates in the high nineties with the unweighted test. Also, the slight increase in reliability obtained by weighting items can be matched in nearly all instances by adding several items to the unweighted test. Since it is much easier to add several items to a test than to go through the labors of determining and using differential weights for items, seeking differential weights is almost never worth the trouble.

Differential weights tend to make a difference when (1) the number of items is relatively small (less than 20) and (2) item-total correlations vary markedly. Seldom do both these conditions occur with dichotomous items, since most such tests contain more than 20 items and the item-total correlations are concentrated in a narrow zone. Some measures composed of multipoint items do have considerably less than 20 items, and the item-total correlations vary more than they typically do on tests composed of dichotomous items. This would be the case in a measure of attitudes which contained 10 seven-point rating scales. In this case an increase in reliability of from 5 to 10 points might be achieved by the differential weighting of items. Even there, however, the same increase in reliability probably could be obtained by adding two or three new items.

For the reasons discussed above, in nearly all cases it is recommended that total scores be obtained by an unweighted summation of item scores. If the reliability is not as high as desired, by far the best approach is to increase the number of items.

REMOVAL OF AN UNWANTED FACTOR   Sometimes it is known in advance that items which are being analyzed to measure one attribute will tend to correlate with an unwanted attribute. This is the case, for example, in tests constructed to measure different factors of human ability, where experience has shown that many types of items concerning human ability tend to correlate with the factor of verbal comprehension. Since no matter what factor is being measured, the items will require some understanding of words and sentences, obtaining relatively independent measures of factors other than verbal comprehension is rather difficult.

Another example is in the construction of a measure of anxiety where previous studies have indicated that the type of item being used is likely to produce a test which will correlate substantially with measures of intelligence. This will make it somewhat difficult to perform studies on anxiety, since any results obtained will be confounded with intelligence.

An extension can be made of the method of selecting items in terms of item-total correlations to lessen the effect of an unwanted factor. One would need a larger collection of items initially than is usually required in selecting items in terms of item-total correlations. For example, if the best guess is that a 30-item test will be required to achieve the desired level of reliability, it will be well to start with over 100 items. Each item is then correlated with total scores and with scores on the unwanted factor. To facilitate the selection of items, a scatter diagram should be made of correlations of items with both variables. The desired items are those that have relatively high correlations with total scores and relatively low correlations with the unwanted factor. Although there will tend to be few items in this category, those that correlate highly with total scores and negatively with the unwanted factor are particularly helpful in purifying the test being constructed.

After a set of items is selected from the scatter diagram, the next steps are to compute KR-20 for the collection of items and correlate the total scores on those items with scores on the unwanted factor. If the former is high and the latter is low, the item analysis is complete. If that is not the case, new items need to be added, and some compromise might have to be reached between the two considerations. If the overlap between measures of the two attributes is a particularly bothersome problem in research, it will be wise to have the reliability of the new test somewhat lower than desired to prevent the new test from correlating substantially with the unwanted factor.

TAKING ADVANTAGE OF CHANCE   All forms of item analysis tend to capitalize on sampling errors to make the results appear better than they will in subsequent studies. One tends to take advantage of chance in any situation where something is optimized from the data at hand. This occurs in multiple correlation, in selecting items in terms of item-total correlations, in selecting items for an equidiscriminating test, in seeking differential weights for items, and in purifying a test of an unwanted factor. Since the opportunities to take advantage of chance are related positively to the number of variables and negatively to the number of persons, it was recommended that a bare minimum in item analysis is to have 5 persons for each item, and that a safer number is 10 persons per item.

When there are at least 10 persons per item, the methods of item analysis will take very little advantage of chance. A collection of items found to have a reliability of .84 might in subsequent studies prove to have a reliability of .80, but the drop in reliability is seldom more than a few points. If the exact level of reliability is a crucial issue when items are being selected, a safe procedure is to strive for a reliability at least five points above the crucial level.

The considerable amount of "playing around" with data sometimes required in constructing tests from bipolar domains of items provides more of an opportunity to take advantage of chance than is provided when items are selected in terms of the initial item-total correlations. For this reason, when dealing with such domains of items, one should strive to obtain even more than 10 persons per item if that is feasible.

To investigate the extent to which item analyses (and other forms of analysis that strive to optimize some function of the data) take advantage of chance, it has been recommended that a "holdout" group of subjects be employed. For example, if only 600 subjects are available for testing, one approach would be to base the item analysis on half of the subjects. Then KR-20 (or whatever else was being optimized) would be computed for the first group and for the holdout group. That

internal structure of measures

certainly would provide evidence about the extent to which the analysis had capitalized on sampling errors, but it would be as imprudent an approach as it would be to permit fire prevention to fall to a dangerously low level in order to invest heavily in fire-fighting equipment. If the number of subjects is limited, as it usually is, the far wiser strategy is to use every last subject in the item analysis. This way one tends to ensure in advance that the reliability (or any other function being optimized) will not fall off markedly in subsequent studies.

speed tests

So far in this chapter it has been assumed that test construction concerns *power tests*, i.e., tests on which subjects are given about as much time as they want. With some types of tests, however, subjects are not given as much time as they want; instead, a highly restrictive time limit is imposed. Issues regarding speed and power tests will be discussed in detail in Chapter Fifteen, but here it is necessary to discuss some of the special principles that apply to the construction of speed tests.

In their purest form, speed tests consist of items of *trivial difficulty*. That is, the difficulties would be trivial if subjects were given as much time as they wanted in making responses. By "trivial difficulty" is meant a p value of .95 or higher when items are administered under power conditions. One type of item that fulfills this requirement is the simple problem in addition or subtraction. If problems of this type were employed in testing normal adults, all persons would answer almost all the problems correctly if they were given as much time as they wanted. The only way, then, to obtain a reliable dispersion of scores is to employ a highly restrictive time limit, in which, for example, the average person has time to answer only about half the questions. Another example of items of trivial difficulty is letter groups used in measures of perceptual speed. Each item consists of two pairs of letter groupings, each group containing about eight letters of the alphabet mixed with numbers and punctuation marks. In each pair of letter groups, either the groups are identical or one letter in one group is different from the corresponding letter in the other group. The subject is asked to indicate whether each pair of letter groupings is identical or not. Obviously, if subjects were given all the time they wanted, all the items would be of trivial difficulty. The only way, then, to obtain a reliable distribution of scores is to employ highly restrictive time limits, e.g., to allow only 10 minutes for responding to 100 items.

The rules that apply to the construction of power tests do *not* apply to the construction of speed tests. Rather, a special set of principles apply to the construction of speed tests. These principles will be outlined in this section and further amplified in Chapter Fifteen.

INTERNAL STRUCTURE OF SPEED TESTS   Previously in this chapter it was shown that the construction of power tests depends very much on the sizes and patterns of correlations among items. Also, in Chapters Six and Seven it was shown that the theory of reliability relates directly to the size and patterns of correlations among items. Here it will be shown that with speed tests the size and patterns of correlations among items are artifacts of time limits and of the ordering of items within a test. Consequently test construction cannot be based on the correlations of items with one another, and the reliability of speed tests cannot be based on internal consistency.

In a speed test, the average correlation among items is directly related to the amount of time allotted for taking the test. If subjects are given all the time they want, the p values of all items will be either 1.0 or close to that, and consequently the correlations among items will be either zero or close to zero. At the other extreme, if subjects are given practically no time for taking the test, the p values will all be zero or close to zero, and consequently the correlations among items will be near zero on the average. Between these two extremes of time limits, the average p values of items range from zero to 1.0. One could, for example, experiment with time limits to obtain an average p value near .5, in which case the average correlation among items might be substantial.

In addition to the average correlation among items being related to the time limit, the patterns of correlations among items are determined by the time limit. Let us look at the case where a time limit is employed such that (1) the average p value of items is near the middle of the possible range and (2), by methods to be discussed later, the distribution of total scores is found to be highly reliable. Suppose that one employed the methods discussed previously for constructing a power test. Essentially this consists of selecting those items that correlate highly with total scores, but on speed tests this depends directly on the ordering of items within the test. Items near the beginning of the test probably would have such high p values that they would tend to correlate very little with the other items, and consequently they would correlate very little with total scores. Items near the end of the test would have such low p values that they also would correlate very little with the other items and with total scores. In contrast, items near the middle of the test would tend to have substantial correlations with one another and with total test scores. Since, in a speed test, the ordering of items is arbitrary, the correlations of items with total scores are arbitrary, and it makes no sense to select items on the basis of item-total correlations. The construction of speed tests, then, must be based on principles other than those that apply to construction of power tests. These principles will be discussed throughout the remainder of this section.

THE ITEM POOL   As is true in the construction of all tests, the first step in the construction of a speed test is to develop an item pool. Usually this is rather easily done, because the items on speed tests usually are so simple that it is easy to compose them by the dozens. Whereas previously it was possible to give some rules of thumb regarding the numbers of items required for the item pool for a power test, this is very difficult to do with speed tests. This is because the reliability of speed tests is not as highly related to the number of items as is the case with power tests. For example, a speed test with 50 arithmetic items might be more reliable than a speed test containing 200 pairs of letter groupings. The reliability of different types of speed tests tends to be intimately related not to the number of items, but to the *testing time* required to obtain the most reliable distribution of scores. Thus if the ideal testing times for two different types of speed tests are both 15 minutes, the tests will tend to have roughly the same reliability regardless of the number of items in each. When one constructs the item pool, the number of items should depend on intuitive judgments about how rapidly the items can be answered by the average person. If later it is found that the original item pool was too small, it usually is easy to construct new items.

TIME LIMITS   Constructing a speed test consists almost entirely of finding the *time limit* that will produce the *most reliable distribution of total scores.* The amount of experimentation required to find the ideal time limit depends on previous experience with employing time limits with the particular type of item. Say, for example, that the items consist of simple problems in subtraction and addition and the test is to be used with unselected adults. Previous experience indicates that the average adult can correctly solve such problems at the rate of two per minute. The purpose of test construction is to develop a highly reliable test of numerical computation. The experimenter thinks that a test of about 80 such items will produce a highly reliable distribution of scores. He then constructs 80 such items and performs experiments to determine the ideal time limit. Previous experience suggests that the ideal time limit would be somewhere near 40 minutes, but it is safest to perform experiments to make sure. Consequently, the experimenter administers the items with five different time limits to five different groups, the groups consisting of random selections from a larger sample of subjects. The experimenter elects to try time limits of 30, 35, 40, 45, and 50 minutes, respectively.

In the experiment above, the ideal time limit is the one that produces the most reliable distribution of scores, the reliability being determined by methods to be discussed later. Rather than perform studies of reliability at this stage, however, one can use a simpler approach which will usually produce much the same results. In a speed test the reliabilities produced by different time limits are highly related to the standard deviations of scores produced by those time limits. Consequently one selects the time limit that produces the largest standard deviation of scores. Hypothetical results from the experiment discussed above are shown in Figure 8-3. As is typically the case, the standard

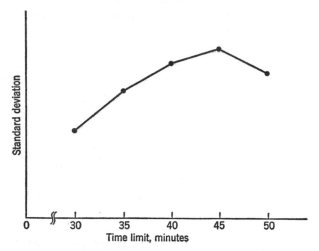

figure 8-3 *Standard deviation of scores on a speed test as a function of different time limits.*

deviation (and thus the reliability) is highest at some point in between the extreme time limits being investigated and tapers off on either side of that point. In this case, however, the ideal time limit is 45 minutes rather than the 40 minutes originally guessed by the experimenter.

MEASUREMENT OF RELIABILITY It is not correct to measure the reliability of a speed test in terms of internal consistency, as is the case with coefficient alpha and KR-20. The most appropriate measure of reliability is made by correlating alternative forms. Thus, in the previous example, rather than construct only one 80-item test of numerical computation, one would construct two 80-item tests. The correlation between scores on the two tests would be the best estimate of the reliability. A time-sav-

internal structure of measures

ing approximation to the alternative-form reliability can be obtained by correlating separately timed halves of only one test, which will save the labors of constructing an alternative form. In that case, even-numbered items on the test would constitute one form, and odd-numbered items the other form. The first half of the items would be administered with a time limit equal to half that employed with the test as a whole. Immediately after time is called, the second half of the items would be administered with a time limit equal to half that employed with the whole test. The correlation between the separately timed halves would then be corrected by Eq. (6-19) to provide an estimate of the alternative-form reliability of the whole test. The estimate usually is rather precise if (1) the trait does not change markedly over the time used for applying alternative forms and (2) performance within a testing session is not markedly influenced by fatigue.

Why the reliability of speed tests cannot be determined from formulas relating to internal consistency is not as simple as it may seem on first thought. This does not necessarily follow from the fact that the average correlation among items is an artifact of the time limit. It was said that the reliability is closely related to the size of the standard deviation of total scores, and the standard deviation of total scores is highly related to the average correlation among items within the test. (If the p values of items did not change somewhat with different time limits, there would be perfect relations between the standard deviation, the reliability, and the average correlation among items.) There is a subtle reason why formulas concerning internal consistency (e.g., KR-20) cannot be legitimately employed with speed tests. Such formulas are predictive of the alternative-form reliability only if it can be assumed that the average correlation (or covariance) among items *within* a test is the same as the average correlation (or covariance) *between* items on alternative forms. On speed tests the average correlation between items on alternative forms tends to be *smaller* than the average correlation between items within each test. For this reason, reliability estimates concerning internal consistency tend to *overestimate* the alternative-form reliability of speed tests.

FACTOR COMPOSITION   As was mentioned previously, the patterns of correlations among items in a speed test are determined almost entirely by the time limit and the ordering of items within the test. Items near the middle of the test tend to correlate more highly with other items than do items near either end of the test. Consequently, in a factor analysis, items near the middle of the test would tend to have the highest loadings on a general factor, purely because of the way items are ordered on the test. In addition, items tend to correlate more highly with items near their ordinal position on the test than they do with items further removed in the ordering. For example, the fourteenth item would probably correlate more highly with the thirteenth and fifteenth items than it would with the tenth and twentieth items. Consequently items tend to break up into different factors because of the proximity of items to one another in the test. The factor structure of speed tests is interesting from the standpoint of psychometric theory, but it tells one nothing about factors of ability, personality, and sentiment. The proper way to learn about the factors measured by speed tests is to factor-analyze whole tests *after* they have been constructed by methods discussed previously in this section.

SUGGESTED ADDITIONAL READINGS

Davis, F. B. Item analysis in relation to educational and psychological testing. *Psychol. Bull.*, 1952, **49,** 97–121.

Gerberich, J. R. *Specimen objective test items: A guide to achievement test construction.* New York: Longmans, 1956.

Gulliksen, H. *Theory of mental tests.* New York: Wiley, 1950, chaps. 9, 18, 19, 20, 21.

Nunnally, J. C. *Educational measurement and evaluation.* New York: McGraw-Hill, 1964, chaps. 5, 7.

Wood, Dorothy A. *Test construction: Development and interpretation of achievement tests.* Columbus, Ohio: Merrill, 1960.

multivariate analysis

CHAPTER NINE

FUNDAMENTALS OF FACTOR ANALYSIS

Up to this point the book has been concerned mainly with the measurement of *particular attributes,* which have been defined in a circular sense in terms of whatever a group of items tend to measure in common. Thus a multiple-choice vocabulary test is a measure of that particular attribute of word knowledge. Theories of scaling, reliability, and test construction assume that the items within a measure all tend to measure the same thing; i.e., they are dominated by one factor. A possibility that has not been discussed so far is that the factor inherent in a collection of items might be peculiar, or specific, to that collection of items. In psychological research, however, one is seldom interested in measuring *specific factors;* rather, one wants to measure a *common factor* that extends to a variety of types of items. It is found, for example, that vocabulary tests correlate with numerous other types of tests concerning the understanding of written material. Thus scores on vocabulary tests are dominated not by a specific factor, but rather by a common factor of verbal comprehension.

In some cases it is found that the factor which "holds together" a collection of items is mainly specific to those items. For example, numerous attempts have been made to develop measures of *acquiescence,* the tendency to agree rather than disagree in situations in general (Rorer, 1965). One type of test for that purpose requires the subject either to agree or disagree with highly ambiguous statements. Such collections of items tend to be internally consistent, and thus each collection of items tends to measure some factor. Unfortunately, however, the tests have very low correlations with one another. There is a factor in each test, but mainly it is a factor which is specific to that test. Apparently there is no broad common factor concerning acquiescence, and thus the construct loses its appeal.

In Chapter Three it was said that most theories concern constructs rather than particular variables, examples of such constructs being habit strength, intelligence, anxiety, activation, and self-esteem. Particular measures, and research with particular measures, are important mainly to the extent that they eventually help explicate a construct and show relations with measures of other constructs. To take a simple example, assume that one wants to learn the correlation between acquiescence and a conventional test of intelligence. Since the various supposed measures of acquiescence correlate very little with one another, they could have very different correlations with intelligence. The result from correlating any one measure with intelligence would have almost no generality to other supposed measures of the same construct.

In a sense, in applied work with tests, one also is interested in measuring constructs rather than particular attributes. There is, for example, a well-documented factor of *perceptual speed* which tends to be present in any task requiring the rapid recognition of similarities and differences in visual patterns. Tests relating to this factor are useful in programs of personnel selection, e.g., for the selection of filing clerks. Different types of items intended to measure this factor all correlate substantially with one another, and consequently research results with one of those measures tend to be general to the other measures.

Factor analysis is important mainly because it is useful in the explication of constructs. The first step in the explication of constructs is to develop measures of particular attributes which are thought to be related to the construct. Such particular measures are developed by the procedures described in previous chapters. The second step is to correlate scores on the different measures. The correlations are analyzed to determine whether (1) all measures are dominated by specific factors, (2) all measures are dominated by one common factor, or (3) the measures tend to break up into a number of common factors. If the analysis indicates, for example, that item 2 is the case, the third step in the explication of a construct is to perform experiments relating that construct to other constructs. "Factor analysis" is a broad term referring to numerous methods of analysis to be used in the second step described above. It is a crucial aspect of construct validation.

Factor analysis can be used either to test hypotheses about the existence of constructs, or if no credible hypotheses are at issue, to search for constructs in a group of interesting variables. Because there are numerous types of factor analysis and numerous auxiliary methods of analysis, it is difficult to adequately cover the topic even in sizable books. The computational routines require considerable space to present and illustrate. All these methods, however, are based on a few simple principles of linear algebra, and the proper employment of the methods is based on a few principles concerning psychological research. The remainder of the chapter will consider these principles. Details of mathematical developments and computational routines are found in the Suggested Additional Readings. The most up-to-date and complete sources are Harman (1960) and Horst (1965).

table 9-1 *Data matrix*

	MEASURES					
	a	b	c	· · ·		k
1	a_1	b_1	c_1	· · ·		k_1
2	a_2	b_2	c_2	· · ·		k_2
3	a_3	b_3	c_3	· · ·		k_3
4	a_4	b_4	c_4	· · ·		k_4
PERSONS ·	·	·	·	· · · ·		
·	·	·	·	· · · ·		
·	·	·	·	· · · ·		
N	a_N	b_N	c_N	· · ·		k_N

Properly considered, factor analysis is only a prelude to more extensive investigations of constructs. Factor analysis is useful only to the extent that it aids in the development of principles of human behavior, and the best methods of analysis are those that aid most in the search. Because of the opportunities for developing elegant, highly complex methods related to factor analysis, there has been a tendency to overdo the mathematical requirements of factor analysis and underdo the requirements of factor analysis for empirical research. This is a bad case of "the tail wagging the dog." In judging the usefulness of a particular method of analysis, the experimenter should ask himself, "How much will this help in my program of research?" Looking at it in this way, one will see that many of the mathematical issues in the literature on factor analysis concern inconsequential problems for empirical research and that some of the most important problems for empirical research frequently are subverted by Rube Goldberg mathematical developments. This book will argue that some of the simpler approaches are not only more practical, but also more commensurate with the strategies of empirical research.

mathematical basis

Factor analysis concerns a rectangular matrix (table) of data such as that illustrated in Table 9-1. A data matrix (or "score matrix," as it frequently is named) will be symbolized as S. The matrix contains the scores of N persons on k measures. Thus a_1 is the score of person 1 on measure a, a_2 is the score of person 2 on measure a, and k_N is the score of person N on measure k. It is assumed that scores on each measure are standardized. Then the sum of scores in any column of the table is zero, and the variance of scores in any column is 1.0.

The term "measures" is used in a very general sense to refer to any set of attributes that can be quantified. The measures might be printed tests, scores in different types of learning tasks, physiological variables, or items of personal history. The term "persons" is used in an even more general sense to refer to any class of objects on which measurements are made. The problem is the same whether the measurements are made on people, insects, vegetables, countries, rocks, or rivers. The only essential is that there be a score for each object on each measure. In practice, the data matrix is much taller than it is wide, because to keep from taking advantage of chance in the factor analysis, it is necessary to have many more persons than measures.

FACTORS *Any linear combination of the variables in a data matrix is said to be a factor of that matrix.* That is all there is to it. Any linear combination (A) would be as follows:

(9-1) $A = w_a a + w_b b + w_c c + \cdots + w_k k$

If, for example, the weight for variable a (w_a) is .8, the score for each person on measure a is multiplied by .8. The weights can be either all the same or different. Some can be positive and some can be negative. Different methods for deriving factors are defined in terms of the *ways that weights are used for obtaining linear combinations.* Any consistent method, whether it makes sense or nonsense, for determining such weights is the basis for a particular type of factor analysis. For example, as will be made clearer in a later section, the *centroid method* requires that all weights be either $+1$ or -1.

It must be kept in mind that any factor is a real (observable) set of scores, i.e., each person has a score on the factor. Thus one obtains the score for person 1 on factor A by combining that person's scores on measures a through k. The same weights are used for all persons, but since people will tend to have different scores on the various measures, they also will tend to have different scores on the factor. It is useful to express factor scores in standard form. This is done either in the course of the analysis itself or after the weights are applied.

Although conceivably factor analysis could employ nonlinear combinations of variables, nearly all existing methods are based on linear combinations. A nonlinear combination would be involved if, for example, one of the terms in the combination were $w_{ab}ab$, which would be the weighted product of variables a and b. When the basic data of psychology merit such complex methods of analysis, nonlinear methods of factor analysis may be employed more frequently. For the time being, the linear methods would seem to be sufficient.

FACTOR CORRELATIONS After a factor is obtained, scores on the factor can be correlated (PM formula) with scores on each of the individual variables in the data matrix. Since the factor is a column of numbers, that column of numbers can be directly correlated with any column of numbers in the data matrix. Such correlations usually are spoken of as *factor loadings;* "factor loadings" will always refer to factor-variable correlations in this book. Depending on the nature of the variables and the method of factor analysis employed, some of the correlations might be high and others low, and some might be positive and others negative. It is important to make a very clear distinction between factor scores and factor loadings. The former are the actual scores of people obtained from a linear combination of variables; the latter are the correlations of the variables with factor scores.

SUCCESSIVE FACTORING   In most problems, it is important to go beyond one factor and see what, if any, other factors are involved in the data matrix. The number of factors to be obtained is suggested by the first set of factor loadings. If these are very high, it suggests that only one factor is needed. If they are near zero, it suggests that there are no common factors. If they are moderately high (e.g., around .50), it suggests that more factors may be needed.

Basic to obtaining factors after the first one is the concept of partialing, as it has been examined in detail in previous chapters. The way to obtain a second factor (B) is as follows. Partial factor A from each of the variables. For partialing factor A from variable a, the loading of a on $A(r_{aA})$ is multiplied by each standard score on A. This is subtracted from each score on a. When A is partialed from b, r_{bA} is used to perform the operation. It would then require k different formulas to transform the original variables to partialed variables. The partialed matrix of data will be symbolized as S_1 to indicate that one factor has been removed. All variables in S_1 are converted to standard scores to facilitate subsequent analyses.

By definition A correlates precisely zero with each variable in S_1. What is not immediately apparent is that it necessarily follows that A will correlate precisely zero with any linear combination of the variables in S_1. Then no matter what linear combination of the variables in S_1 is used to obtain a second factor (B), r_{AB} must be precisely zero. This fact provides the basis for obtaining a set of uncorrelated (orthogonal) factors.

Factor B can be obtained by any linear combination of the variables (partialed variables) in S_1. (This is not to imply that some types of linear combinations are not better than others, a matter which will be discussed in detail later in the chapter.) For convenience, B would be placed in standard form. How then would one obtain loadings on factor B? Here it is easy to make a mistake by assuming that the loadings would be obtained by correlating the partialed variables in S_1 with B. What is done instead is to correlate the original variables (in S) with

table 9-2 *Matrix of factor loadings*

| | FACTORS | | | |
	A	B	C	h^2
a	.60	−.06	.02	.36
b	.81	.12	−.03	.67
c	.77	.03	.08	.60
d	.01	.65	−.04	.42
e	.03	.80	.07	.65
VARIABLES f	.12	.67	−.05	.47
g	.19	−.02	.68	.50
h	.08	−.10	.53	.30
i	.26	−.13	.47	.31
sum of squared loadings	1.76	1.56	.98	
V_i	.19	.17	.11	$V(\Sigma V_i) = .47$

B. This is done because the effort is to "take apart" the original variables in terms of a number of uncorrelated linear combinations or factors. The matrix S_1 is important only as a way of obtaining B.

After obtaining factors A and B, one can then go on to obtain additional factors by the same iterative approach. With second-order partial correlations, A and B could be simultaneously partialed from S. An easier way to arrive at the same result is to partial B from S_1. This results in S_2, and any linear combination of the twice-partialed variables in S_2 would produce another factor; that factor necessarily would be uncorrelated with the first two factors. Mathematically, the only general limit on the number of factors obtained in that way is the number of variables. If, for example, there are 20 measures, all scores in S_{20} will be zero.

THE MATRIX OF FACTOR LOADINGS   A matrix of factor loadings is shown in Table 9-2. Variables a, b, and c tend to have substantial loadings only on factor A; d, e, and f have substantial loadings only on factor B; and g, h, and i have substantial loadings only on factor C. There are some principles concerning the properties of matrices of factor loadings which form the basis for interpreting results. The square of any factor loading tells the proportion of variance explained in a particular variable by a factor. The correlation of a variable with a factor has the same interpretation that any correlation coefficient does. Thus since variable a has a loading of .60 on factor A, it can be said that factor A explains 36 percent of the variance of a. The sum of squares in any column of the factor matrix indicates the total amount of variance explained by that factor for the variables as a group. More important, the average squared loadings (V_i) in a column is the proportion (without the decimal, a percentage) of variance of the variables as a group explained by that factor. Thus factor A explains 19 percent of the total variance in the original data matrix S. The sum of average squared loadings for the several factors (V) indicates the percentage of variance explained by the factors, which provides an indication of the extent to which a set of factors does a good job of explaining the original variables. It also is an indication of the extent to which the variables tend to have common factors among them rather than only specific factors.

The sum of squared loadings in any row of factor loadings (h^2) tells the proportion (or percentage) of variance of the variable which is explained by the factors. The more a variable tends to share common factors with the other variables, the larger will be h^2. In this context it would be useful to think of how one would estimate one of the original variables from the factors. If as many factors are extracted as there are variables, any variable can be perfectly "estimated" from those factors. But usually the number of factors is small relative to the number of variables, and thus it is not probable that a perfect estimate can be obtained. In terms of the principle of least squares, the best estimate of any variable would be obtained from the multiple regression of the factors on that variable. Thus one would obtain an estimation of variable a from three factors as follows:

(9-2)
$$a' = \beta_a A + \beta_b B + \beta_c C$$

where a' = least squares estimate of a from multiple regression
A, B, C = standard scores on three factors
$\beta_a, \beta_b, \beta_c$ = multiple-regression weights

The above approach to estimating any variable from a set of factors leads to some useful deductions. It will be remembered from Chapter Five that, when the predictor variables are uncorrelated, the squared multiple correlation equals the sum of squared predictor-criterion correlations. Since in this discussion the factors are assumed to be uncorrelated, the sum of squared loadings in any row of the matrix of factor loadings is the squared multiple correlation of the factors with the particular variable. Consequently the column in Table 9-2 labeled h^2 shows the squared multiple correlations of the three factors with the nine variables. This is why h^2 can be interpreted as a percentage of variance explained.

Another deduction from Eq. (9-2) is that the factor loadings in any row are the beta weights (β_i) required for multiple regression:

(9-3)
$$a' = r_{aA}A + r_{aB}B + r_{aC}C$$

Equation (9-3) holds in any instance where (1) all variables are in the form of standard scores and (2) all predictor variables (factors, here) are uncorrelated. This holds regardless of how the linear combinations (factors) are determined. One might choose a method of obtaining linear combinations that would lead to a very poor estimate of the original variables; but regardless of how good or poor the estimate, the multiple-regression weights would equal the factor loadings. Also, the reader should not confuse the present issue concerning the estimation of variables from factors with the issue of going the other way around—estimating factor scores from variables. The latter issue will be discussed in Chapter Ten.

Another important principle follows from the discussion above. If all the variables are reproduced perfectly by the factors, the correlation between any two variables equals the sum of products of the loadings of the variables on the factors:

(9-4) $$r_{ab} = r_{aA}r_{bA} + r_{aB}r_{bB} + \cdots + r_{aK}r_{bK}$$

This principle can be derived from the discussion in Chapter Five regarding the correlation of sums. If any variable can be reproduced perfectly from a set of factors, that variable can be expressed as a linear combination of those factors. The correlation between any two such variables can be expressed in terms of the correlation of sums, in the usual way. As will be remembered, the correlation of sums equals the sum of elements in the cross-covariance matrix divided by the square root of the product of the sums of elements in both covariance matrices. If the factors are uncorrelated, all the terms in each covariance matrix vanish except those on the diagonal. The diagonal terms are the squares of the loadings of the variables on the factors. Since the sum of these is 1.0 in each of the two covariance matrices whenever the variables are perfectly reproduced, the denominator of the formula for the correlation of sums "falls out." The correlation then equals the sum of elements in the cross-covariance matrix. Since factors are uncorrelated, only terms involving the same factor are different from zero, for example, $r_{aA}r_{bA}$. Thus the correlation between any two variables equals the sum of cross products of their factor loadings.

Of course, seldom will the number of factors actually used in a study exactly reproduce the original variables. It would be a waste of time if one had to employ as many factors as there are variables, and when that is not done, the factors being used very seldom account for as much as 80 per cent of the total variance. Even when only part of the variance is explained by the factors, however, the cross products of factor loadings provide a partial explanation of the correlations between variables. Thus if only three factors are used, a partial explanation of the correlation between variables a and b is as follows:

(9-5) $$r_{ab}' = r_{aA}r_{bA} + r_{aB}r_{bB} + r_{aC}r_{bC}$$

fundamentals of factor analysis

That is why it is said that factors serve to *explain correlations* among variables or explain the common variance among variables. For any set of factors, one can attempt to reconstitute the original correlation matrix by forming all possible pairs of cross-product terms, as was illustrated above for variables a and b. This can be subtracted, element by corresponding element, from the matrix of correlations among the original variables. These are then *residual coefficients*. If they are small (by standards that will be discussed later), the set of factors does a good job of explaining the common variance; but if they are large, it indicates that prominent factors are still to be obtained from the data.

THE CORRELATION MATRIX   It frequently is said that one "factors a correlation matrix." In previous sections it was stated that it is more appropriate to think of factoring the data matrix. For two reasons, however, correlations among the variables play important parts in factor analysis. Preparatory to any factor analysis, the first step is to compute the full matrix of correlations among variables. The first important part played by the correlation matrix is in determining the signs and sizes of coefficients in the linear combinations that produce factors. For example, if all the correlations are positive, which tends to indicate that all the variables have something in common, it might be decided to give all variables positive weights in the first linear combination. If, on the other hand, some of the variables tend to correlate negatively with the others, it might be decided to give negative weights to those. If, instead of assigning weights on some a priori basis, one derives weights mathematically in a way that optimizes some property of the data, the correlation matrix indicates how that optimization is to be done. Thus the correlation matrix is very useful in determining the signs and sizes of coefficients in linear combinations. Without the information provided by the correlation matrix, it would be very difficult to form useful linear combinations.

A second importance of the correlation matrix is that it greatly facilitates the correlation of variables with factors. Since each factor is a linear combination of the variables, the correlation of any variable with a factor can be obtained from the correlation of sums by the usual formulas (Chapter Five). A simple example will illustrate how this is done; in a later section the methods will be discussed in detail. In this example, imagine that there are only five variables; say that they are supposed measures of anxiety. A hypothetical correlation matrix for the variables is shown in Table 9-3.

In Table 9-3, all the variables correlate positively with one another, but some tend to have higher correlations than others. Since the variables all correlate positively, a decision is made to give all the variables

table 9-3 *Correlation matrix for five measures of anxiety*

	1	2	3	4	5	A
1	1.00	.43	.18	.08	.48	.60
2	.43	1.00	.51	.49	.63	.84
3	.18	.51	1.00	.27	.55	.69
4	.08	.49	.27	1.00	.44	.63
5	.48	.63	.55	.44	1.00	.91

positive weights in the first linear combination. Also, it is decided to give them all equal weights. Since the weights are all equal, it is easier to give all variables a weight of 1 than to employ any other weight. In other words, one obtains the first linear combination (factor) by simply adding scores on the five variables. One would obtain the factor score for person 1 by simply adding that person's scores on the five tests, and so on for the other persons. For convenience, factors scores would then be standardized. Finally, each of the variables would be correlated with the factor to obtain factor loadings.

If the correlation matrix is available, there is an easier way to obtain factor loadings. Since in the example above the factor is a simple sum of the variables, the correlation of variables with the factor can be obtained from the correlation of sums. When all variables are in the form of standard scores, it was shown in Chapter Five that the correlation of one variable with the sum of other variables is as follows:

(9-6)
$$r_{1y} = \frac{\Sigma r_{1i}}{\sqrt{\bar{R}}}$$

where y = linear combination

$\quad 1$ = variable being correlated with y

$\quad \Sigma r_{1i}$ = sum of correlations between variable 1 and each variable in y

$\quad \bar{R}$ = sum of all elements in correlation matrix for y variables

To put it in words, the numerator equals the sum of correlations between variable 1 and each of the variables in the linear combination. Under the radical in the denominator is the sum of all elements in the matrix of correlations among the y variables. This includes the diagonal 1s.

The formula for the correlation of sums was developed in Chapter Five for the situation where one variable is correlated with the sum of a number of *other* variables, but the formula applies equally well when the variable itself is a member of the linear combination. Thus the formula can be applied in the situation above where, for example, variable 1 in Table 9-3 is to be correlated with the sum of all variables in the matrix. In this case variable 1 is to be correlated with the sum of variables 1 through 5. In the numerator of Eq. (9-6), there are five correlations. One of these is the correlation of variable 1 with itself, which by definition is 1.0. The other four correlations are between variable 1 and the other four variables. The sum (T) of all elements in the correlation matrix is 13.12. The square root of T is 3.6221, which is the denominator of Eq. (9-6). The correlation of variable 1 with the sum of variables 1 through 5 would then be obtained as follows:

Sum of variable 1's correlations $= 2.17$

$$\frac{2.17}{3.6221} = .60$$

In the same way, the loadings of all five variables on the factor would be computed. These are shown in column A of Table 9-3.

In the example above, a very simple linear combination was used to illustrate how factor loadings can be computed from the correlation matrix rather than from the data matrix itself. The logic applies, however, to *any* type of linear combination. All such possibilities are covered by formulas for the correlation of individual variables with the weighted combination of a set of variables (see Chapter Five). For example, in the method of principal axes (to be described later), the first factor is determined so as to maximize the "variance explained"—maximize the sum of squared loadings on the first factor. To do this requires a set of weights determined by a particular method of analysis. The weights could be applied to the data matrix; then the factor loadings could be obtained by correlating each variable with the weighted combination of variables. It is easier to use the same weights in the correlation of weighted sums, which can be done directly on the correlation matrix.

To obtain a succession of uncorrelated (orthogonal) factors, a method was previously described for partialing each factor in turn from the original matrix of data. One can accomplish the same, and much more easily, by partialing the factor loadings from the correlation matrix. For example, previously it was shown how a second factor could be obtained as a linear combination of the partialed matrix of data, the influence of the first factor having been removed. Factor loadings on the second factor were obtained by correlating each of the original variables with a linear combination of the partialed variables. The same can be obtained from the correlation matrix as follows. First, by formulas for the correlation of sums, loadings on the first factor are determined. These correlations are partialed from the original correlations by the usual methods of partial correlation. This can be illustrated for variables 1 and 2. Each variable has a loading on (correlation with) factor A. It is an easy matter to partial factor A from the correlation between variables 1 and 2. All that is needed are three correlations: r_{12}, r_{1A}, and r_{2A}. In the same way, correlations with factor A can be partialed from all correlations in the original matrix. Loadings on the second

multivariate analysis

factor can then be determined from the matrix of partial correlations rather than from the matrix of partialed scores. It is the same either way, but working from the matrix of correlations is much more convenient than working from the data matrix.

The original correlation matrix supplies all the information required for determining factor loadings on any kind, and any number, of factors. This fact should not, however, be allowed to obscure the basic nature of factors. Even if loadings of variables on factors can be computed from the correlation matrix, the factors themselves are linear combinations of the actual variables. Also, after factor loadings are obtained, to obtain scores of people on factors one must return to the data matrix and apply methods that will be described in Chapter Ten.

GEOMETRIC INTERPRETATIONS   There are some very useful analogies between factor analysis and geometry. The correlation between any two variables can be pictured as the angle between two vectors (straight lines). Specifically, the correlation is pictured as the cosine of the angle between two vectors. Both vectors have the same origin, and both are of length 1.0 (unit length). Each vector can be thought of as a "correlation yardstick" with the numbers .00, .01, .02, . . . , .99, 1.00 along it. One obtains the correlation between any two variables by extending a perpendicular line from either one of the vectors to the tip of the other. This is illustrated in Figure 9-1 for the correlations of variables b and c with variable a. Variable b correlates .70 with variable a, and variable c correlates .30 with a. One would find the same correlations by lowering perpendiculars

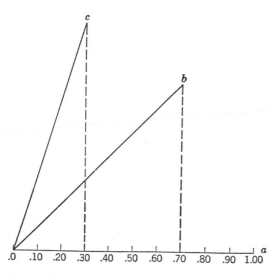

figure 9-1   *Geometrical representation of the correlations among three variables.*

from b to a and from c to a. Also, the cosine of the angle between b and c specifies their correlation, this being .91. Two vectors at right angles have a cosine of .00 and a correlation of .00; two vectors that lie atop one another have a cosine of 1.00 and a correlation of 1.00. For two vectors having a 45° angle of separation, the cosine and correlation are .71. In between these points are represented all possible sizes of correlations.

Negative correlations are represented by angles greater than 90°, as is illustrated in Figure 9-2 for a negative correlation of .50. Each vector can be thought of as extending in both directions from the origin, as is illustrated by the dashed line extending past the origin at the end of variable a. Usually only one end of the vector is shown in illustrations, but it is understood that vectors go to length 1.00 on both sides

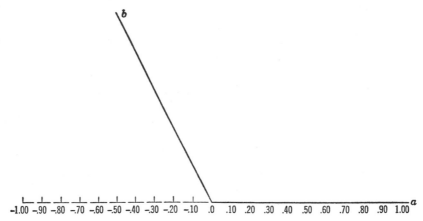

figure 9-2 *Geometrical representation of a negative correlation between two variables.*

of the origin. This permits the depiction of all possible correlations, positive and negative, by the cosines of angles. Angles between 90 and 180° have negative cosines. For example, an angle of 180° has a cosine of −1.00, and an angle of 135° (45° beyond a right angle) has a cosine of −.71.

Any matrix of correlations can be thought of as a matrix showing all possible cosines among a set of vectors, each vector representing one of the variables. Thus the correlation matrix in Table 9-4 can be thought of as a matrix of cosines. The geometric configuration for the variables is shown in Figure 9-3. Such configurations have an arbitrary frame of reference. That is, as long as the cosines among angles are left the same, the whole configuration can be rotated about the origin without changing the problem. Whereas, in Figure 9-1, variable a is shown as coming out horizontally to the right of the origin, one could

table 9-4 *Correlation matrix for four variables*

	a	b	c	d
a	1.00	.73	−.04	−.67
b	.73	1.00	.66	.05
c	−.04	.66	1.00	.78
d	−.67	.05	.78	1.00

represent the same set of cosines among vectors equally well by having variable *c* come out horizontally to the right of the origin. In that case all variables would be rotated to the right through equal angles. Then, for example, the vector for variable *b* would slope downward to the right of the origin. All that is important is that the configuration correctly show the cosines of angles corresponding to the correlations among variables.

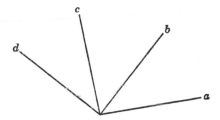

figure 9-3 *Geometrical representation of the correlations in Table 9-4.*

The matrix of correlations in Table 9-4 is an idealization of what is found in practice. It is unusual in that all the cosines (correlations) can be represented in two dimensions (a two-space). Usually the correlations cannot be represented even in three dimensions. Then it is necessary to think of the correlations as being represented in a *hyperspace,* a space of more than three dimensions. Of course, there is no physical representation of spaces of more than three dimensions, but this does not hinder the use of geometric conceptions.

Factors often are spoken of as dimensions, and factoring is spoken of as dimensionalizing a space of variables. Imagine, for example, that the vectors for 20 variables all lie in a three-dimensional space. Factor analysis can be thought of as inserting a framework of three new vectors (factors) to explain the correlations (cosines) among the variables. If all 20 vectors lie in a three-space, the variables are "redundant" of one another. They all can be "explained" by three factors. Following are some useful principles regarding relations between factoring and hyperspace geometry.

If a set of variables is represented in an *r*-dimensional space, any linear combination of the variables is also represented in that r-dimensional space. This would apply in the example above where 20 variables are represented in a three-dimensional space. *Any* linear combination of those variables would also be a vector in that space. This applies no matter what the coefficients are for the linear combination, e.g., some of the coefficients can be zero and some can be negative. In other words, a factor (a linear combination of variables) is another vector in the same space as that of the variables themselves. Thus factoring can be thought of as putting new variables in a space of variables. The important point is that the vector representing any factor cannot "get out of" the space formed by the variables themselves.

If any set of variables lies in an r-dimensional space, any r number of nondependent linear combinations of those variables is said to constitute a *basis* for the space. The term "nondependent" means that none of the linear combinations can be expressed as a linear combination of the other linear combinations, e.g., none of five factors can be totally explained from the others by multiple regression. The principle is easier to visualize when all factors are uncorrelated with one another, in which case the vectors for the factors all are at right angles to one another. If the vectors representing variables lie, say, in three dimensions, any three uncorrelated (orthogonal) factors will explain all the correlations among the variables.

The loading of a variable with a factor is represented by the cosine of the angle between the vector for the variable and the vector for the factor. If the variables lie in an r-dimensional space, any r orthogonal factors will explain the vectors for all variables. In that case the sum of the squared loadings in each row of the matrix of factor loadings will equal 1.00, and the sum of cross products of loadings in any two rows of that matrix will equal the correlation between the two variables. Thus a row of factor loadings can be thought of as a row of cosines between a variable and a number of factors.

Usually the number of factors employed will not explain correlations perfectly. In other words, the space of variables has more dimensions than factors. In that case the factors are said to form a *semibasis* for the space of variables. Suppose, for example, that the variables cannot be represented in less than 10 dimensions, but only five factors are used. Some of the variables might lie almost entirely in the space of factors, and others might lie mainly outside that space. The sum of squared loadings for any variable is a direct measure of the extent to which that variable lies in the space defined by the factors. Then h^2 is the squared length of a vector explainable by a space of factors. If, for example, h^2 for a variable on five factors is .64, .8 of the length (h) of that variable is explained by the factors, and .2 of the length cannot be explained by those factors.

multivariate analysis

The number of dimensions required to represent a matrix of correlations is said to be the *rank* of that matrix. Consequently factor analysis is often said to involve finding the rank of a matrix of correlations.

As useful as these geometric interpretations are, it is possible to carry them too far. First, there is nothing necessarily geometric about factoring. It can all be developed and used without ever talking about cosines of angles, dimensions, and the like. Geometric interpretation is a useful isomorphism which sometimes helps one to think about problems of factoring, but it should be invoked only when it is useful. Second, the talk about "rank" and "the basis for a space" can easily mislead one into assuming that these are frequently obtained. In nearly all problems, the rank is as large as the number of variables. This is mainly because each variable tends to have its own specific factor in addition to that part of its variance which can be explained by common factors. Even in the ideal situation where variables could be entirely explained by a relatively small number of common factors, e.g., 20 variables and five factors, the sampling error of correlations would usually prevent a perfect "fit." Also, in most problems, no one is interested in completely explaining the correlations among variables. Usually one is interested in the prominent factors, the ones that have at least moderate-sized loadings. Typically, the factors with very small loadings (e.g., none higher than .30) are not interpreted.

In terms of hyperspace geometry, it is most useful to think of factoring as establishing a semibasis for a space of variables. Then, from a statistical point of view, a good factoring method is one that constitutes a semibasis which explains as much as possible of the variance (h^2) of the variables. From the standpoint of empirical research, a good semibasis is one that (1) is easily interpreted and/or (2) relates most clearly to psychological theories.

TYPES OF FACTORS   Whereas previously we have spoken only of common and specific factors, a more detailed breakdown is usually employed. Some people like to speak of two types of common factors—general factors and group factors. A *general factor* is a factor on which all variables in the particular study have substantial loadings, e.g., .40 or higher. A *group factor* is a factor on which only some of the variables have substantial loadings, e.g., only 5 of 20 variables have substantial loadings on a particular factor. There is nothing necessary about the distinction between general and group factors, but it provides a useful way of discussing the relative generality of a common factor over variables in a study. Actually, rather than a sharp distinction, in most studies it is a matter of degree.

In addition to the specific factor in each variable, there also is an error factor. The error factor concerns the amount of unreliability (measurement error) in each variable. Rather than being a factor in the usual sense of the word, the error is the leftover, nonexplainable variance. By definition specific factors are uncorrelated with one another, error factors are uncorrelated with one another, and both are uncorrelated with common factors. Thus the total variance of any variable a can be sectioned into the following uncorrelated components:

(9-7) $\sigma_a{}^2 =$ variance explainable by common factors
$+$ variance because of specific factor
$+$ variance because of errors of measurement

Since in most analyses it is difficult to separate specific variance from error variance, they are usually lumped together and called the *unique variance* (u^2). Because it is customary to express variables in the form of standard scores, the variance of a can be expressed as follows:

(9-8) $\sigma_a{}^2 = h^2 + u^2$

It is apparent, then, that the unique variance equals the sum of squared loadings on common factors subtracted from 1.0 (which is $1 - h^2$).

It frequently is said that factor analysis serves to partition variables into sources of common and unique variance. One determines the common variance by forming linear combinations of the variables, and the unique variance is the part not explainable by the common factors. As was mentioned previously, though, this is only approximately done in most studies. There still is common variance left in most studies after the investigator stops factoring. Consequently, in most studies, the portion of variance left over is partly because of unique variance and partly because of nonanalyzed common variance. Also, for reasons which will be made clear later, there is no foolproof way to distinguish common variance from unique variance. This is because in forming linear combinations, the unique variance of each variable usually becomes part of the factors, which tends to confound the two sources of variance. Lacking exact methods for partitioning variance into these components, it is best to think of Eqs. (9-7) and (9-8) as idealizations of what actually is done in factor analysis. It is, however, useful to think of the variance of any variable as being partitionable into three uncorrelated components—common variance, specific variance, and error variance (the latter two summing to equal the unique variance).

DIRECT AND STEPWISE SOLUTIONS   Factor analysis can be used either to test hypotheses about constructs, or if appealing hypotheses do not exist, to search for common factors. In the former case one employs *direct* solutions. For example, if the hypothesis were that six measures of introversion are dominated by only one common factor, one would obtain a direct solution to test that hypothesis, e.g., by correlating each test with the simple sum of the six tests. As another example, it might be hypothesized that six tests concerning introversion evolve into two common factors, with three of the tests belonging to one factor and the other three belonging to another factor. One could then obtain a direct solution to test this hypothesis, e.g., by making the first linear combination (factor) a simple sum of the first three variables and the second factor a simple sum of the second three variables. One might hypothesize as many as half a dozen or more factors and then form linear combinations accordingly. The essence of any direct solution is that (1) it is performed so as to test hypotheses about the existence of factors and (2) the nature of linear combinations is stated in advance of obtaining the correlation matrix.

Although for obvious reasons it is better to begin an analysis with hypotheses, this has not been the case in most factor analyses to date. The investigator either is unwilling to formulate hypotheses, does not trust the hypotheses he has, or has so many variables to analyze that the end result is difficult to estimate. In these cases one starts with a large collection of "interesting" measures (e.g., 20 tests concerning different aspects of memory) and leaves it to the statistical methods to say what factors are present. Many attempts have been made in this way to explore "interesting" domains of variables, e.g., motor skills, perceptual abilities, interests, and personality characteristics.

When one is searching for factors rather than testing hypotheses about them, it is useful to perform the analysis stepwise. The first step is to *condense* the variables into a relatively small number of common factors. In this case the standard of statistical parsimony is given paramount consideration. It does not matter in the first step how interpretable the factors are; the only concern is with the extent to which they serve to condense the data. The degree to which condensation is obtained is reflected in the average percentage of variance explained (average h^2) by a number of factors. If a method of condensation is used in which each factor takes out more variance than the succeeding one, the rate at which variance is extracted indicates the degree of condensation. Imagine that in the analysis of 20 tests, the first five factors explain 50 percent of the variance and the succeeding five factors explain another 10 percent of the variance. This means that the first five factors do a good job of condensing the correlations among the 20 variables. Another way of looking at it is that, after the first five factors are partialed from the correlation matrix, the partial correlations among variables are near zero, and thus there is little common variance left to analyze. In other words, five factors provide a good semibasis for the space of variables.

After one has used one of the methods for condensing a space of variables, the next step usually is to *rotate* factors. This is done because it usually is very difficult to interpret the original factors. They are good from a statistical point of view, but when the loadings of variables on factors are inspected, it is hard to find clear-cut patterns of loadings, a point which will be illustrated in a later section. A rotated factor is simply a linear combination of the original factors. Thus a rotated factor is simply a linear combination of other linear combinations. If one has five factors which condense the variables reasonably well, one can rotate those factors by making five linear combinations of the original factors. Means are available for ensuring that the rotated factors are orthogonal if that is desired. The important point is that any set of rotated factors explains exactly the same variance as the original factors. Variables will have different patterns of loadings on the rotated factors than they have on the original factors, but the h^2 for each variable will remain exactly the same (assuming that the rotated factors are uncorrelated). The rotated factors explain the same amount of variance as the original factors, but they "slice it up" in a way that is more interpretable. The distinction between direct and stepwise solutions and the concept of rotation are mentioned briefly here to prepare the reader for extensive discussions of these matters in the remainder of the chapter.

the centroid method of condensation

The *centroid* method surely has been used more frequently than any other method in the first step of a stepwise analysis. Whereas here it is referred to as a method of condensation, generally it is referred to simply as the centroid method of factoring. Actually it is not quite as efficient at condensing variables as is a method to be discussed in a later section—the method of principal axes. The effectiveness of the centroid method, however, usually is rather close to that of principal axes. Also, the centroid method is far simpler to compute and understand. If one understands the centroid method, he will have a good grasp of the mechanics involved in all methods concerned with condensation.

THE GEOMETRICAL CONFIGURATION   A geometrical interpretation of the centroid method starts with the space of variables shown in Figures 9-3 and 9-4. In Figure 9-4 only the end points of vectors are shown for four measures. This is an idealized example, because all the vectors go to unit length in a two-space, which means that two factors can perfectly explain all variables. If more than two factors were required, the vectors would not go to unit length in the figure, because part of the length would be evidenced in other dimensions.

As was mentioned previously, a factor can be thought of as a new vector which is obtained from a linear combination of the variables. The first centroid factor produces a vector which is the average of the vectors for the variables. That is, it is the mean, or centroid, of the other variables, and thus the vectors for the variables balance in all directions about the centroid. In Figure 9-4, the first centroid factor (A) is inserted. As can be seen, it is precisely in the middle of the vectors for the variables, only the end points of these vectors being

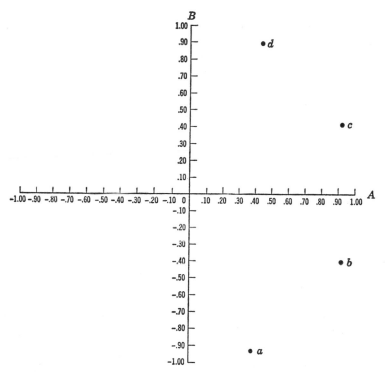

figure 9-4   *Plot of centroid factor loadings.*

shown. Just as the vectors for the variables can be thought of as extending in both directions from the origin, this is also true of factor vectors.

The correlation (loading) of each variable with the first centroid can be read from the factor axis, as noted previously. The factor axis is sectioned in tenths to show how this is done.

The second centroid factor is made orthogonal (uncorrelated or at a right angle) with the first. Since the variable can be represented perfectly in a two-space, there is only one place for the second centroid to go. It is shown in Figure 9-4 as vector B. Loadings on B can also be read directly. Loadings on the two centroid factors are shown in Table 9-5. In each case h^2 is 1.00, and the loadings are exceptionally

table 9-5 *Centroid loadings for factors shown in Figure 9-4*

		FACTOR	
		A	*B*
VARIABLE	*a*	.38	−.93
	b	.92	−.40
	c	.91	.42
	d	.44	.90

table 9-6 *Correlation matrix for six variables and computation of loadings on first centroid factor*

	1	2	3	4	5	6
1	1.00	.55	.43	.32	.28	.36
2	.55	1.00	.50	.25	.31	.32
3	.43	.50	1.00	.39	.25	.33
4	.32	.25	.39	1.00	.43	.49
5	.28	.31	.25	.43	1.00	.44
6	.36	.32	.33	.49	.44	1.00
column sums	2.94	2.93	2.90	2.88	2.71	2.94

$$T = 17.30 \qquad \sqrt{T} = 4.1593 \qquad M = .2404$$

A	.71	.70	.70	.69	.65	.71

high, which would be the case only in an idealized example like the one here.

THE CORRELATION MATRIX   Like other forms of factor analysis, a centroid analysis starts with the computation of a matrix of correlations. A matrix for six variables is shown in Table 9-6. The PM formula should always be employed, which results in point-biserial and phi for special cases where one or both variables are dichotomous. Non-PM estimates of PM coefficients such as biserial and tetrachoric cannot legitimately be used in factor analysis. This is because the correlation of a variable with a linear combination of variables requires the use of PM coefficients in the correlation of sums. This cannot legitimately be done with biserial or tetrachoric. Numerous analyses have been undertaken with these formulas, and perhaps the results have been approximately correct. There is, however, no mathematical basis for employing such coefficients in factor analysis.

The correlation matrix in Table 9-6 has been arranged to indicate that the six variables tend to break up into two clusters, one formed by variables 1, 2, and 3 and the other formed by the remaining three variables. A person who is experienced with factor analysis could see at a glance that the common variance among the variables can be condensed to a high degree by two factors. For the factor analysis, *unities* are placed in the diagonal spaces of the matrix. (So-called *communality estimates* are frequently placed in the diagonal spaces, a matter which will be discussed in the next chapter.)

THE FIRST CENTROID FACTOR   As was mentioned previously, factoring methods are defined in terms of the way they form linear combinations of variables. The centroid method is defined by linear combinations in which all weights are either $+1.0$ or -1.0. In other words, the variables are simply summed, with the possibility that some of them might be given negative weights (subtracted rather than added).

To simplify the discussion, let it be assumed that the sum of correlations in each column (and thus each row), disregarding the diagonal unities, is positive. This would mean that, disregarding the diagonal elements, each variable has a larger sum of positive correlations than of negative correlations. This usually holds for the original correlation matrix. When this condition holds, the matrix is said to be of *positive manifold*. For the following discussion, it is not necessary that all correlations be positive, but only that the sum of nondiagonal entries in each column be positive. What to do if the sum of one or more columns is negative will be discussed later.

If the correlation matrix is of positive manifold, the centroid method requires that the weights for all variables be $+1.0$. In other words, the variables are not weighted; they are simply summed. After the sum of variables is standardized, it is a unit-length vector at the centroid of the other vectors, as was illustrated in Figure 9-4. It is then the mean vector, the one that balances the others in all directions.

In Table 9-6 are shown the steps required to obtain factor loadings on a first centroid factor. The correlation of each variable with the sum of all six variables (the first centroid factor) is determined as follows. First, the sum of coefficients in each column of the matrix is computed. This includes every element from the top to the bottom of each column, *including* the diagonal unity. The sum of the column sums (T) is obtained, which, of course, is the sum of all elements in the correlation matrix including diagonal elements. To compute each centroid loading, the sum of elements in each column is the numerator in the correlation of sums, and the square root of T is the denominator. It is easier to multiply the former by the reciprocal of the latter (M). Thus when each column sum is multiplied by M, a loading on the first centroid

table 9-7 *First matrix of factor cross. products* (Q_1)

	.71	.70	.70	.69	.65	.71
.71	.50	.50	.50	.49	.46	.50
.70	.50	.49	.49	.49	.46	.50
.70	.50	.49	.49	.48	.45	.49
.69	.49	.49	.48	.48	.45	.49
.65	.46	.46	.45	.45	.42	.46
.71	.50	.50	.49	.49	.46	.50

factor is obtained. The full set of loadings on the first centroid is shown in row A.

MATRIX OF RESIDUAL COEFFICIENT   After the first factor is obtained, by the centroid method or by any other method, and as a prelude to seeking a second factor, one must obtain a matrix of residual coefficients. The residual coefficient corresponding to any element in the original correlation matrix is obtained as follows. First, the loadings for the two variables on the first centroid factor are multiplied. For variables 1 and 2, this product is .50. This is done for all possible pairs of variables. One simplifies the computations by placing the loadings at the proper points on the top and side of an empty matrix and then multiplying corresponding pairs of elements. This is shown in Table 9-7. In each diagonal space is the square of the particular factor loading. The resulting matrix is labeled Q_1, to stand for the first matrix of factor cross products. Then Q_1 is subtracted element by element from the original matrix of correlations (R), resulting in the first matrix of residual coefficients (R_1), shown in Table 9-8.

It is important to understand the nature of the elements in the residual matrix. They are sometimes mistakenly spoken of as "residual correlations." Each diagonal element is a partial variance, the variance remaining after the influence of the first factor is partialed. Each off-diagonal element is a partial covariance, the covariance between two variables after the influence of the first factor is removed. One can see why this is so by looking at the partial correlation between variables 1 and 2 when factor A is held constant:

(9-9) $$r_{12-A} = \frac{r_{12} - r_{1A}r_{2A}}{\sqrt{1 - r_{1A}^2}\sqrt{1 - r_{2A}^2}}$$

In the partial correlation formula, the numerator is the partial covariance for the two variables being partialed, and the denominator is the product of the square roots of the partial variances for the two variables. The

table 9-8 *First matrix of residual coefficients* (R_1)

	1	2	3	4	5	6
1	.50	.05	−.07	−.17	−.18	−.14
2	.05	.51	.01	−.24	−.15	−.18
3	−.07	.01	.51	−.09	−.20	−.16
4	−.17	−.24	−.09	.52	−.02	.00
5	−.18	−.15	−.20	−.02	.58	−.02
6	−.14	−.18	−.16	.00	−.02	.50

numerator is exactly what is found in R_1 corresponding to the entry for variables 1 and 2. In the denominator, the square of the term on the left (the partial variance for variable 1) is exactly what is found in the diagonal element for variable 1 in R_1. Likewise, the partial variance for 2 is found in the diagonal space for that variable in the residual matrix.

Since in R_1 the diagonal terms are partial variances and the off-diagonal terms are partial covariances, it is easy to convert the entire table to a matrix of partial correlations. One can accomplish this by dividing the elements in each row by the square root of the diagonal element for that row and then dividing the elements in each column by the square root of the diagonal element for that column. To obtain a second factor (by the centroid method or by any other method), it is not necessary to convert residual coefficients to partial correlations. The computations can be more easily performed on the partial variances and partial covariances. It will be remembered that formulas for the correlation of sums apply as easily to covariance matrices as they do to correlation matrices.

REFLECTION   One obtains a second factor by applying formulas for the correlation of sums to R_1. In R_1, however, it is not a good strategy to make the second factor the sum of partialed scores. This is because this matrix has an even balance of negative and positive coefficients. Consequently the sum of elements in each column of R_1 differs from zero only by rounding errors. Since the first centroid is the mean vector, when its influence is partialed the residual coefficients in the whole table sum to zero. Obviously, then, it is not possible to compute factor loadings for the second factor by the same method of weighting used for the first factor.

What is done to remedy this situation is to *reflect* some of the variables in R_1. All this means is that some of the variables are given negative signs in the sum. For any variable which is so reflected, the signs of all coefficients in that column and row of the residual matrix are changed. Thus, rather than actually changing the signs of scores in the matrix of partialed scores (making positive standard scores negative and negative standard scores positive), one can obtain the same final result by changing the signs of rows and columns of R_1. There is nothing "wrong" with performing such reflections; it is simply a step required in correlating each of the variables with a particular linear combination of the partialed variables. All that is required is that, after the loadings are obtained from the reflected variables, the variables which were reflected be given negative signs for their loadings.

The aim of reflecting variables is to obtain a reflected matrix (symbolized as R_1') which will have the highest possible sum of coefficients (T). This is because the sum of factor loadings increases with T. Since, in any method of condensation, the object is to make each factor account for as much variance as possible, one should reflect in a way that makes T as large as possible. The ideal is when reflections can be made so that all coefficients in R_1' are positive, in which case it is obvious that T is a maximum. Frequently it is not possible to make all coefficients positive, so some cut-and-try methods are necessary for finding the largest sum of coefficients. Detailed methods for doing this are described by Thurstone (1947).

When only a few variables are involved in the analysis (which is rarely the case these days), the best method of reflection can be determined by inspection. In Table 9-8, it can be seen that the two groups of variables have all negative coefficients between them. Then one can make most of the coefficients in the table positive by giving negative signs to variables 4, 5, and 6. (The same could have been accomplished by giving negative signs to variables 1, 2, and 3.) The resulting matrix of reflected residuals (R_1') is shown in Table 9-9.

Loadings on the second centroid factor are obtained from R_1' (not from R_1). The same procedures are employed as were employed with the original matrix of correlations. First, one finds the sum of coefficients in each column, including the diagonal term. One then finds the sum of the column sums (T), the square root of that, and the reciprocal of that, which is M. Each column sum is multiplied by M. Then the proper signs must be given to these values before they become loadings. All variables which were reflected receive minus signs, and all nonreflected variables receive positive signs. When the proper sign changes are made, the second centroid factor (B) is obtained.

Although one can easily get lost in the mechanics of reflection to obtain linear combinations and the subsequent rereflections to obtain the proper signs for loadings, actually it is only a computational routine for doing something very simple. Since after the influence of the first

table 9-9 *Reflected residual matrix* (R_1') *and extraction of second centroid factor*

	1	2	3	4*	5*	6*
1	.50	.05	−.07	.17	.18	.14
2	.05	.51	.01	.24	.15	.18
3	−.07	.01	.51	.09	.20	.16
4*	.17	.24	.09	.52	−.02	.00
5*	.18	.15	.20	−.02	.58	−.02
6*	.14	.18	.16	.00	−.02	.50
column sums	.97	1.14	.91	1.00	1.07	.96

$$T = 6.05 \quad \sqrt{T} = 2.46 \quad M = .406$$

B	.40	.46	.37	−.41	−.43	−.39

* These variables were reflected.

centroid factor is removed from the variables there is a balance of negative and positive correlations among the partialed variables, the partialed variables do not add up to anything. Each variable would correlate zero with the simple sum of partialed variables. To obtain a linear combination that correlates highly with each of the variables, one must give some of the partialed variables negative signs. The ideal system of signs makes all correlations among partialed variables positive, or if that is not obtainable, makes the sum of correlations as large as possible. Instead of determining signs for reflection from the matrix of partialed scores, it is much easier to see how this should be done from an inspection of the matrix of residual coefficients.

Once the sign changes are made, the correlation of each variable with the second centroid factor can be determined directly from the correlation of weighted sums, in which some weights will be +1.0 and others will be −1.0. A computational shortcut is to change the signs of coefficients in the appropriate rows and columns of R_1 producing R_1', compute the loadings from the latter matrix, and then reverse signs for variables that were reflected.

In obtaining loadings on the first centroid factor, it was assumed that positive manifold exists. If that is not the case, reflections must be made before the first centroid factor is obtained. One does this by exactly the same procedures described above for the more usual case where reflection is required only after the first factor is extracted.

ADDITIONAL FACTORS   There is little more to explain about the centroid method of factoring. Methods of condensing variables are repetitive procedures.

fundamentals of factor analysis

table 9-10 *Second residual matrix* (R_2)

	1	2	3	4	5	6
1	.34	−.13	−.21	−.01	−.01	.02
2	−.13	.29	−.16	−.05	.05	.00
3	−.21	−.16	.37	.06	−.04	−.02
4	−.01	−.05	.06	.36	−.20	−.16
5	−.01	.05	−.04	−.20	.39	−.19
6	.02	.00	−.02	−.16	−.19	.35

Once one knows how to obtain loadings and residual matrices and make reflections, he simply repeats the same process over and over for subsequent factors. After the second centroid factor is obtained, cross products of loadings are computed, forming matrix Q_2. This is then subtracted from R_1 (the unreflected residual matrix), not from R_1' (the reflected first residual matrix). This produces R_2, which for the six-variable problem is shown in Table 9-10.

To obtain a third factor, one would operate on R_2 in the same way that he did on R_1. First, some of the variables would have to be reflected to maximize the sum of loadings, which would produce R_2'. Loadings would be computed from R_2' as they were from R_1'. Again it would be necessary to give negative signs to the loadings of variables which were reflected, which would result in factor C.

Two factors are sufficient to explain most of the common variance in our illustrative problem (note how small most of the coefficients are in R_2), but if the problem warrants it, the methods which have been described can be applied repeatedly until any number of factors (up to the number of variables) is obtained.

CHARACTERISTICS OF THE CENTROID METHOD   The ideal standard for any method of condensation is that it extract as much variance as possible with each factor. This is done by the method of principal axes, and it is approximated by the centroid method. In the centroid method, if reflection at each stage is done so as to maximize T, the centroid method has definable statistical characteristics. In that instance the sum of absolute loadings (disregarding signs) for each factor is a maximum. If one looks back at the way unreflected loadings were obtained from the reflected residual matrix, he can easily see that the sum of such loadings necessarily equals the square root of T. Thus, before loadings are reflected, their sum increases with T. After loadings are reflected, the sum of absolute loadings also increases with T.

It will be remembered that the variance explained by any factor equals the sum of *squared* loadings in a column of the matrix of factor loadings. Thus a method which maximizes that sum (which the method of principal axes does) extracts more variance than any other method. Instead of maximizing the sum of squared loadings, the centroid method tends to maximize the sum of loadings, disregarding signs. It is said that the centroid method "tends" to do this, because in practice this will be the case only if reflections are made so as to maximize T. An example will serve to illustrate why this does not always occur. Suppose that one is reflecting elements in the first residual matrix and sufficient reflections have been made to produce positive sums for each column of the matrix. One could then go on to obtain loadings on a second factor. It is possible, however, that a better system of sign changes could have been employed, which would have made T larger and thus would have produced a larger sum of absolute loadings. When computer routines are employed which guarantee that T is maximized before each factor is extracted, the centroid method is strictly defined: It is the method which extracts the largest sum of absolute loadings for each factor in turn.

The centroid method, it should be pointed out, is a "good" method. It is a very simple method to understand, and consequently one does not have to be an expert to grasp the mathematical essentials of the method. Also, compared to some other methods, it requires relatively simple computations. For this reason, before the advent of large-capacity, high-speed computers, the centroid method was by far the most favored method of condensation. Now it is being edged out by the method of principal axes. From the standpoint of the degree of condensation, however, the advantage of the principal-axes method is not great.

other methods of condensation

In stepwise analyses, only two methods other than the centroid method are widely used today. These are the method of *principal axes* and the *square-root* method. The former is used very generally as the first step in a stepwise analysis. The latter is used for only a number of special problems.

PRINCIPAL AXES   The method of principal axes also is variously called the method of *principal components* and the *principal-factor solution*. The first principal axis is defined as that linear combination of variables which explains the most variance. That is, weights for the first factor are selected so that the average squared factor loading (V_1) is a maximum. Then the first residual matrix is obtained by methods discussed with respect to the centroid method of factoring. A linear combination is then formed of the partialed variables so that the average squared loading on the second factor (V_2) is as large as possible. This procedure is repeated until the desired number of factors is extracted.

To obtain weights that will maximize the variance extracted by each factor in turn, one must seek a solution through calculus. Obtaining a solution for principal axes requires some rather complex mathematical developments which would be beyond the scope of this book. (See Harman, 1960, for a discussion of the mathematical developments required for principal axes.) Also, even though there is a theoretical solution, the direct solution would be too laborious for general use. What is usually done instead is to obtain a solution iteratively. First, one selects a trial set of loadings for the first principal axis. For example, loadings on the first centroid factor would provide a good approximation of the first principal axis. To the extent that the trial values are different from the actual loadings on the first principal axis, certain known properties of the principal-axes solution will not be realized. The discrepancies is this regard suggest how to modify the first set of trial values so as to obtain a second set of trial values. These are then tested to see how closely they fit the mathematical requirements. This suggests how a third set of trial values is to be selected. The steps are repeated until the amount of change from one set of trial values to the next is very small. The final set of trial values then will differ from the first principal axis only by negligible amounts. All the principal axes are obtained by similar procedures.

As was mentioned previously, the method of principal axes is the ideal method of condensing variables during the first step of a two-step analysis (the second step involving the rotation of factors). Logically, the best method of condensing variables is the one that explains the most variance for any set number of factors, and the method of principal axes does that. In Table 9-6 was shown a correlation matrix for six variables, which was used to illustrate the workings of the centroid method. In Table 9-11 are shown two factors extracted from that table by the centroid method and the method of principal axes. One can see that the two sets of loadings are very similar. The first factor is almost identical, and the largest difference on the second factor is only .05 (for variable 3). In this example, the total variance explained is the same in both analyses (65 percent). The more usual finding, however, is that the method of principal axes explains slightly more variance on the first two factors than does the centroid method, and the relative advantage of the method of principal axes increases as additional factors are extracted.

Another advantage of the method of principal axes is that it ties in very well with numerous other forms of analysis. For example, inferential statistics regarding factors obtained from principal axes are much

table 9-11 *A comparison of factors obtained by the centroid method with factors obtained by the method of principal axes*

	CENTROID FACTORS				PRINCIPAL AXES		
	A	*B*	h^2		*A*	*B*	h^2
1	.71	.40	.66		.71	.39	.66
2	.70	.46	.70		.71	.48	.73
3	.70	.37	.63		.70	.32	.59
4	.69	−.41	.64		.69	−.42	.65
5	.65	−.43	.61		.64	−.45	.61
6	.71	−.39	.66		.71	−.38	.65
V	.48	.17	(total = .65)	*V*	.48	.17	(total = .65)

easier to develop than are inferential statistics regarding factors obtained from any other method (see Anderson, 1958). Whereas previously it was shown that the centroid method is statistically defined only in the case where T is maximized, the method of principal axes is statistically defined in all cases. Putting it another way, although it is possible for two centroid analyses of the same correlation matrix to produce somewhat different loadings because somewhat different systems of reflection are employed on residual matrices, there is only one possible principal-axes solution for any correlation matrix.

Even with iterative solutions available, a monstrous amount of calculation is required to obtain principal axes. To perform such an analysis for only eight variables on a desk calculator would require a great deal of time. Consequently, until recent years, the principal-axes method was mainly an unattainable ideal. Now, with the proliferation of high-speed computers, it is feasible to perform such analyses of correlation matrices containing more than 50 variables. Harman (1960) outlines the procedures for programing solutions for principal axes. In the years ahead, the method of principal axes will probably supplant the centroid method as the preferred approach to condensing a matrix of correlations. (The passing of the centroid method should be accompanied by a small show of sadness. Whereas almost anyone can understand the mathematics of the centroid method, few nonspecialists will fully understand the mathematics of principal axes. Consequently investigators will in many cases have to work with methods whose mathematical innards are something of a mystery. Also, since in many cases the centroid method has been computed "by hand," this has given investigators an intimate "feel" for the meaning of loadings, residual coefficients, reflections, and other constituent parts of factor analysis. The method of principal axes necessarily must be done on computers, so many investigators will see only the end products of their analyses, and there is a danger that they will lose the all-important "feel" for how factor analysis works.)

THE SQUARE-ROOT METHOD   The square-root method is also known as the *diagonal* method of factoring and the *sweep-out* method. In the square-root method, the rule for establishing linear combinations is that one of the variables receives a weight of 1 and all the other variables receive a weight of zero. Thus the first factor equals one of the variables, and loadings on the first factor equal correlations of that variable with all other variables. The variable selected to form the first factor would have a loading of 1.0 on the factor. These loadings are then used to obtain a matrix of residuals (R_1) in the usual way. It will be remembered that the diagonal elements of that matrix are partial variances, and the off-diagonal elements are partial covariances. The variable used to form the first factor necessarily will have a column and row filled with zeros.

From the first residual matrix, a second variable is selected to form the second factor. One obtains the correlations of the original variables with any one of the partialed variables by dividing all the elements in a column of R_1 by the square root of the selected variable's diagonal element in R_1. This transforms the partial covariances in the column into semipartial correlations. How this works was described in Chapter Five. Semipartial correlations are wanted rather than partial correlations, because the object in factor analysis is to correlate the *original variables* with a succession of uncorrelated linear combinations of those variables. The semipartial correlations are loadings on the second factor.

On the second factor, the variable used to form the first factor will necessarily have zero loadings, and it will have zero loadings on any subsequent factors. Since the loading for the variable used to form the second factor equals the diagonal element divided by the square root of the diagonal element, the loading equals the square root of that element.

A third factor can be obtained by the same method used to obtain the second factor. The second residual matrix is obtained in the usual manner. The elements will all be zero in the columns and rows for the variables used to obtain the first two factors. A third variable is used to form the third factor. All elements in the column are divided by the square root of the diagonal element. This produces loadings on the third factor. Loadings on the third factor for variables used to form the first two factors will necessarily be zero.

Each of the variables used in turn to form a factor is called a *pivot*. A relatively efficient method of condensation is obtained by the

table 9-12 *Two factors extracted by the square-root method*

	A	B	h²
1	.55	.19	.34
2*	1.00	.00	1.00
3	.50	.27	.32
4†	.25	.97	1.00
5	.31	.36	.23
6	.32	.42	.28
V	.30	.23	(total = .53)

* First pivot variable.
† Second pivot variable.

judicious choice of pivots. One rule is to select as the first pivot the variable which has the highest sum of correlations (disregarding signs) in the correlation matrix. The second pivot is selected as that variable with the largest sum of absolute coefficients in the first residual matrix, and so on for the selection of subsequent pivots. A better procedure is to base the selection of pivots on the sum of squared coefficients in each column of the correlation matrix and the residual matrices. After the first pivot is determined in this way, in choosing the pivot for each of the subsequent residual matrices, it is best to divide the sum of squared coefficients in each column by the diagonal element in each column. Some simple algebraic manipulations will show that the resulting quantities equal the sum of squared loadings that would be obtained if different variables were used as the pivot. In other words, the variable that has the largest quantity can be used to explain more variance than would be explained by making any other variable the pivot. This rule is then applied to all subsequent residual matrices.

When the rule stated above is employed for selecting pivots, the square-root method does a reasonably good job of condensation. That is, the elements in residual matrices tend to become small as the influence of successive factors is removed. With the above rule employed, Table 9-12 shows two square-root factors for the six-variable problem in Table 9-6. The total percentage of variance explained (V) and that explained by each factor can be compared with that for the centroid method and the method of principal axes (Table 9-11).

Actually, the square-root method is hardly ever used these days as the first step in a two-step analysis (the second step being rotation). It is appealing as a method of condensation, because the computations are so simple. One can see that it requires much less work than the centroid method. Loadings are far simpler to obtain, and there is no need to reflect signs of correlations in residual matrices. The computations are made even simpler if one is willing to use a less exact procedure than the one described above for selecting pivots. If, by inspecting the correlation matrix, one can decide on all pivots without waiting to examine each residual matrix, all the computations can be performed on the columns of the correlation matrix corresponding to those variables. For example, suppose it is decided to pivot successively on variables 8, 11, and 2. One would first form a rectangular table containing only the columns for those three variables from the correlation matrix. All three factors could then be extracted directly from this abbreviated table. This would permit a very rapid determination of factor loadings. Using a desk calculator, one could derive three factors in an afternoon from a matrix with 100 variables. To extract three centroid factors from the same matrix with only desk calculators would be prohibitively time-consuming.

The major fault of the square-root method in a stepwise analysis is that it leans too heavily on the variance of the pivot variables. The purpose of factor analysis is to examine the common variance. Although there is no sure method for distinguishing common variance from unique variance, the centroid method and the method of principal axes tend to do this. When either of these methods is used, after a number of factors has been removed, coefficients in the residual matrix tend to be uniformly low. At the same stage of analysis by the square-root method, all residuals corresponding to pivot variables are zero, but there are likely to be patches of relatively high coefficients among some of the other variables. Compared to the centroid method and the method of principal axes, the square-root method does a better job of explaining the common variance among a small number of variables (the pivot variables), but it does a poorer job of explaining the common variance among the remaining variables.

Because the square-root method capitalizes so heavily on the variance of the pivot variables, it makes the interpretation of factors, qua common factors, somewhat difficult. The first pivot variable *is* the first factor. The loading of the second pivot variable on the second factor usually is much higher than the loading of any other variable, and so it is with subsequent factors. Since pivot variables load so heavily on their respective factors, the interpretation of each factor must be heavily influenced by the pivot variable. The interpretation of common factors is facilitated by having a number of variables with uniformly high loadings on each factor.

Now that high-speed computers are widely available, there is little need to employ the square-root method as the first step in a stepwise analysis. Either the centroid method or the method of principal axes should be used instead. The square-root method remains very useful, however, for numerous auxiliary problems relating to multivariate analysis. In Chapter Six it was shown how the mechanics of square-root factoring can be used to obtain partial correlations and multiple correlations. The square-root method is also very useful for performing some of the steps required in the rotation of factors, e.g., for orthogonalizing a set of correlated factors (Harman, 1960; Thurstone, 1947).

rotation of factors

The second step in a stepwise analysis is to rotate factors. Although some factorists try to interpret factors obtained in the first step (e.g., factors obtained from the centroid method), by far the majority of factorists prefer to rotate factors. This is done to obtain a more interpretable pattern of factor loadings and to facilitate estimations of the scores of people on the factors.

THE GEOMETRIC ANALOGY   It is in the rotation of factors that the analogy between factoring and hyperspace geometry proves most useful. In Figure 9-4 were shown the placements of two centroid vectors in a two-space of four variables. There is nothing to prevent one from rotating those two factor vectors. If one wants to maintain uncorrelated (orthogonal) factors, the rotation must be done so as to keep the rotated factor vectors at right angles to each other. Rotation can be illustrated by imagining that the factor vectors are movable like the hands on a clock. One of the factor vectors then could be moved to any position desired. The other would be moved to a position where it formed a right angle with the rotated first factor vector.

The geometry of rotation is illustrated in Figure 9-5, which is a graphic plot of loadings on two centroid factors for the six-variable problem shown in Table 9-6. A and B are the centroid factor vectors, and A_1 and B_1 are the rotated vectors. Loadings for the six variables can now be read off of the rotated factors in the same way that they were from the unrotated factors. Loadings on the rotated factors are shown in Table 9-13. If rotated factors are orthogonal, two important properties of the unrotated matrix of factor loadings carry over to the rotated matrix of factor loadings. First, the sum of squared loadings in any row (h^2) remains the same. That is, the rotated factors explain the same amount of variance as did the unrotated factors. Second, the sum of products of loadings in any two rows of the rotated factor matrix is the same as that in the unrotated matrix. Thus the same common variance is explained in both the rotated and unrotated matrices. In other words, from a statistical point of view, the rotated factors are "just as good" as the unrotated factors. Thus if rotated factors are more easily interpreted than unrotated factors, the investiga-

table 9-13 *Orthogonal rotation of centroid factors*

	A_1	B_1	h^2
1	.23	.78	.66
2	.18	.82	.70
3	.25	.75	.62
4	.78	.18	.64
5	.77	.14	.61
6	.78	.21	.65
V	.33	.32	(total = .65)

tor has every right to rotate. The first step in a stepwise analysis (e.g., use of the centroid method) can then be thought of as determining the starting points for rotation. The first step serves its purpose in condensing the common variance, and the second step (rotation) serves its purpose in "slicing up" that common variance in a manner that is more easily interpreted.

MECHANICS OF ROTATION   One way to rotate is illustrated in Figure 9-5. First, one plots loadings on factors with the use of graph paper. The rotated loadings can be read directly from the rotated factors. One way to do this is to develop a transparent grid that can be placed over the graph. The zero point on the grid is placed over the zero point on the graph. The abscissa of the grid is placed along the vector for A_1, which makes the ordinate of the grid fall along the vector of B_1. Loadings on A_1 and B_1 are read from the grid in the same way that they were read from the graph for unrotated factors A and B. What rotation does is to construct a new coordinate system.

Although it is seldom done these days in large analyses, one can perform all rotations by the graphical method described above. This method requires that only two factors be rotated at a time. Thus one might start off by rotating A and B to A_1 and B_1. Then A_1 would be rotated with factor C, which would lead to A_2 and C_1. B_1 and C_1 could then be rotated to obtain B_2 and C_2, and so on. If there are numerous factors, there are even more numerous possibilities for rotating factors two at a time.

One can rotate factors two at a time and still maintain the essential properties of the original matrix of loadings. If orthogonal rotations are made in each binary comparison, no matter what pairs are formed for rotation and no matter how many such rotations are done, h^2 for each variable will remain the same. Also, the sum of cross products in any two rows of factor loadings will remain the same, and all factors will remain orthogonal.

If more than three or four factors are submitted to rotation, the graphical method of rotation may take considerable time. This is because there are so many possible comparisons of the factors two at a time. Suppose, for example, that in the first round of rotations, five factors are compared two at a time in all possible pairs. This would require 10 graphical comparisons, rotations, and the computation of rotated loadings. Usually the full matrix of rotated factors would not produce

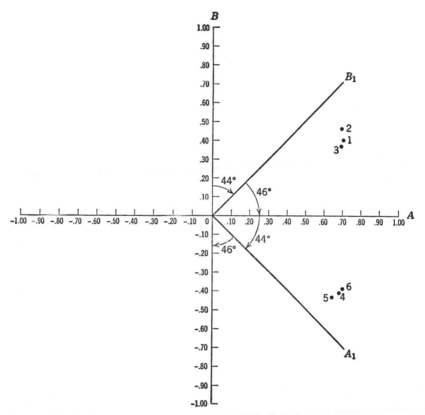

figure 9-5 *Orthogonal rotation of centroid factors.*

the desired pattern of loadings (according to standards which will be discussed later). It would then be necessary to start in again and rerotate the once-rotated factors. From 10 to 20 such rounds of rotation might be required to reach the desired solution, which would be very time-consuming. For this reason, numerous efforts have been made to develop *analytic methods of rotation,* ones that "do the job for you" on computers. These will be discussed later.

MATHEMATICS OF ROTATION   It will be recalled that a factor is a linear combination of variables. A rotated factor is simply a linear combination of a set of factors. In other words, a rotated factor is a linear combination of a set of linear combinations. For example, the rotation of factor A in Figure 9-5 can be done with the following linear equation:

(9-10) $$r_{iA_1} = a_1 r_{iA} + b_1 r_{iB}$$

where r_{iA_1} = rotated loadings on A_1
r_{iA} = unrotated loadings on A
r_{iB} = unrotated loadings on B
a_1, b_1 = weights for rotation

In the rotation shown in Figure 9-5, a_1 is .72, and b_1 is $-.69$. The weights are the cosines of the angles of rotation of A_1 with A and B, respectively. Rather than rotate visually with the use of a grid as was discussed previously, one can use the graph of factor loadings to obtain the proper weights and then perform the rotations on a desk calculator. This is not necessarily faster than using a grid, but it is somewhat more accurate.

Rather than form a rotated factor as the linear combination of only two factors as is illustrated in Eq. (9-10), one can form a factor as a linear combination of a larger number of factors. Thus a set of rotated factor loadings (A_1) could be obtained from a linear combination of four factors as follows:

(9-11) $$r_{iA_1} = a_1 r_{iA} + b_1 r_{iB} + c_1 r_{iC} + d_1 r_{iD}$$

When a rotated factor is formed as a linear combination of more than two factors, it is difficult to obtain the weights from graphical comparisons. This is because one is rotating simultaneously in more than two dimensions, and consequently the weights cannot be determined by the movement of factor vectors on the flat surface of a piece of graph paper.

Equations (9-10) and (9-11) illustrate an important principle concerning rotation. If the original factors are orthogonal (which has been assumed in all discussions so far), the sum of squared weights for rotation must equal 1.0. This is true both for the rotation in Eq. (9-10) and for that in Eq. (9-11). This is necessary for the rotated factor to remain at unit length.

Another important principle about rotation can be illustrated by the linear combination that would produce B_1 in Figure 9-5. In general terms the formula would be as follows:

(9-12) $$r_{iB_1} = a_2 r_{iA} + b_2 r_{iB}$$

The weights for obtaining loadings on B_1 are a_2 and b_2. For the rotation in Figure 9-5, a_2 is .69, and b_2 is .72. Note that the sum of the squares of these two coefficients equals 1.0, as it must. The principle to be illustrated is this: If the original factors are orthogonal and the rotated factors are orthogonal, the sum of products of the two sets of factor weights must equal zero. Thus in this instance $a_1a_2 + b_1b_2$ does, and must, equal zero. This is true regardless of how many terms there are in the linear combination used to obtain rotated factors. Thus if factors A_1 and B_1 are orthogonal rotations of factors A, B, C, and D, it necessarily follows that

(9-13) $a_1a_2 + b_1b_2 + c_1c_2 + d_1d_2 = 0$

If that condition does not hold, A_1 and B_2 are not orthogonal, i.e., the correlation between the two factors is different from zero. If all rotated factors are orthogonal, the sum of cross products of weights for rotation for any pair of rotated factors equals zero.

OBLIQUE ROTATIONS   Up to this point it has been assumed that, in rotation, the original factors are orthogonal and the rotated factors also are orthogonal. There is, however, no mathematical necessity for maintaining right angles among rotated factors. Nonorthogonal (correlated) factors are referred to as *oblique*, because the angles among them differ from 90°. It is tempting to employ oblique factors to place rotated factor vectors through clusters of variables, which tends to maximize the loadings on a factor for the members of a cluster. An oblique rotation for the data from Figure 9-5 is shown in Figure 9-6, and the corresponding loadings on oblique factors are shown in Table 9-14. The cosine of the angle between A_1 and B_1 is .48, which is the correlation between the two factors. One can determine loadings on oblique factors by raising a perpendicular line from the rotated factor vector to the tip of the vector for a variable. This also can be done with a transparent grid in a manner similar to that described previously for orthogonal rotations. First, one obtains loadings on A_1 by placing the abscissa of the grid along A_1. Then, to obtain loadings on B_1, it is necessary to rotate the grid to a point where the ordinate of the grid lies on B_1. Loadings on B_1 can then be read from the ordinate of the grid.

Rather than compute loadings on obliquely rotated factors with a grid, one can form linear combinations of the unrotated factors. Contrary to what is true of orthogonal rotations, however, the sum of squared weights for rotation would be greater or less than 1.0, depending on the angle between the rotated factors. Also, the sum of cross products of weights for rotation of two rotated factors would not equal zero.

Oblique rotations change some of the essential characteristics of the original matrix of factor loadings. The sum of squared loadings in any row would equal h^2 only by chance, and the sum of average squared loadings in the columns of the matrix would equal V only by chance. Also, the sum of cross products in any two rows of the matrix of rotated loadings would be unlikely to equal the same quantity computed from the unrotated loadings.

There are numerous other "statistical losses" in employing oblique rather than orthogonal rotations. For example, in an orthogonal rotation, the sum of squared loadings in any row of the matrix of factor loadings

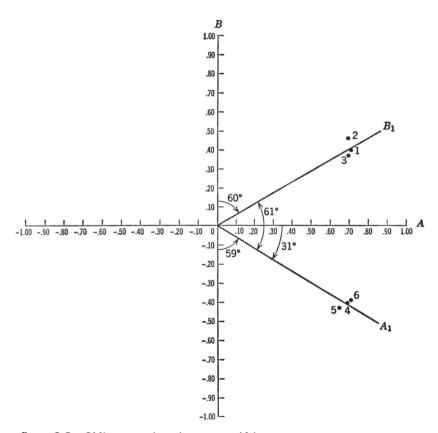

figure 9-6   *Oblique rotation of two centroid factors.*

equals the squared multiple correlation of the factors with the particular variable; in oblique rotations, this would not be the case. Also, in numerous auxiliary methods of analysis that cannot be discussed here, working with orthogonal factors is far simpler than working with oblique factors.

The supposed advantages of oblique rotations are mainly conceptual rather than mathematical. As was mentioned previously, when one looks at plots of factor loadings, it is intuitively appealing to place factor

table 9-14 *Loadings on obliquely rotated factors*

	A_1	B_1
1	.40	.81
2	.36	.84
3	.41	.79
4	.80	.39
5	.78	.35
6	.81	.42

vectors through dominant clusters of variables, which usually leads to oblique rotations. Also, it is easy to think of many variables that are conceptually independent but are correlated in real life. For example, it is meaningful to discuss heights and weights of people as separate dimensions of size, but the two are correlated. From this and other examples, it can be argued that it is meaningful to work with correlated factors in factor analysis.

Because there are good things to say about both orthogonal rotations and oblique rotations and because both are mathematically legitimate, which is used boils down to a matter of taste. In the early years of factor analysis, most rotations were orthogonal. Then, from about 1935 until recent years, there was a swing toward the use of oblique rotations, but now one gets the impression that orthogonal rotations are predominating. Also, since most rotations are performed today by analytic methods on high-speed computers, the type of rotation is determined by the particular analytic method. The method which is apparently used most frequently (the varimax method) results in orthogonal rotations.

The author has a mild preference for orthogonal rotations, because (1) they are so much simpler mathematically than oblique rotations and (2) there have been numerous demonstrations that the two approaches lead to essentially the same conclusions about the number and kinds of factors inherent in a particular matrix of correlations. This preference is "mild," because as will be discussed more fully later, in the act of estimating the scores of people on orthogonal factors, one frequently does the equivalent of additional rotations. After estimates of factor scores are obtained, it usually is found that the estimates are correlated even if the factors themselves are orthogonal. For this reason, the author can understand why some persons prefer the use of oblique rotations to place factor axes through dominant clusters of variables. There are some systems of oblique rotation, however, which definitely are not recommended. These will be discussed in the next section.

CRITERIA FOR ROTATION   What is a *good* set of rotations? As was mentioned previously, the unrotated factors are as good in a statistical sense as any rotation of them. The major reason for rotating factors is to obtain a more interpretable solution. The ideal case of an easily interpreted solution is illustrated in Table 9-15, where an X stands for a substantial positive loading. There are at least three "pure" variables for each factor. Factor A can be interpreted in terms of whatever variable 1, 2, and 3 have in common. Since the variables that define one factor have zero loadings on the other two factors, this aids the interpretation of factors. In addition to simplifying the interpretation of factors, an ideal rotation like that in Table 9-15 would make it very easy to estimate scores of people on factors. One could estimate scores on factor A by simply summing (and then standardizing) scores on variables 1, 2, and 3. Similarly, one could obtain factor scores for the other two factors by averaging scores on the related clusters of variables.

If it were reasonable to expect factor results like that in Table 9-15, it would be easy to get almost everyone to agree on the criterion for rotation: *Rotation should be performed so that each variable loads on one and only one factor.* The rule need not require that there be the same number of pure variables for all factors; the only requirement is that there be some pure variables for each factor. Attempts to approximate this ideal led to Thurstone's (1947) concept of *simple structure.* The concept is embodied in a set of rules regarding the form of the rotated matrix of factor loadings, e.g., each row of the factor matrix should have at least one zero.

Although most factorists today talk about "rotating to simple structure," no one can say for sure what constitutes simple structure. The rules given by Thurstone and others are not nearly sufficient. The condition is definable in the ideal case, as in Table 9-15, but when one departs from the ideal case, no one can completely specify the best approximation of simple structure. It is like trying to specify the essential physical ingredients that combine to form a beautiful woman. In both cases, by looking at the product, one can form an impression of how well the criterion is met, but the processes of judgment are illusive.

Rather than talk about simple structure, perhaps it would be better to talk about *simpler structures.* Thus a rotated factor matrix is usually simpler to interpret than the unrotated matrix, and some rotations are simpler to interpret than others. Generally what one seeks is a rotation where there are *some relatively pure variables for each factor.* The orthogonal rotation in Table 9-13 meets this standard. Variables 1 through

table **9-15** *Ideal set of rotated factor loadings*

		FACTOR		
		A	B	C
	1	X	0	0
	2	X	0	0
	3	X	0	0
	4	0	X	0
VARIABLE	5	0	X	0
	6	0	X	0
	7	0	0	X
	8	0	0	X
	9	0	0	X

3 have much higher loadings on B_1 than on A_1, and vice versa for variables 4 through 6. Such simpler rotations can be sought either with graphic comparisons of factors two at a time or with one of the analytic methods used on computers.

Efforts can be made to find a simpler structure either with orthogonal factors or with oblique factors. The example in Table 9-13 shows how this can be done with orthogonal rotations. In searching for methods to define simple structure, Thurstone (1947) and his colleagues developed a special system of oblique rotation, one that is *not* recommended by the author of this book. The usual difficulty in approaching the ideal of simple structure is that the clusters of variables (when the variables tend to cluster) are not at right angles. Typically, if factors are rotated into clusters, the factors will correlate positively. This is particularly likely to occur in studies of human abilities, because all abilities tend to correlate positively with one another. Thus if one rotates in this way rather than using orthogonal rotations, the rotated factors will look less "simple." One can see this by comparing the orthogonal solution in Table 9-13 with the oblique solution in Table 9-14.

Instead of placing oblique vectors through clusters of variables, the method employed by Thurstone essentially backs each oblique vector off 90° from one of the clusters. This method of oblique rotation is illustrated in Figure 9-7 for the six-variable problem used in the preceding figures. When factor vectors are backed off from a cluster, the members of that cluster are made to have near-zero loadings on the factor. Thus, in Figure 9-7, variables 4, 5, and 6 are made to have near-zero loadings on B_1, and variables 1, 2, and 3 are made to have near-zero loadings on A_1. The resulting oblique rotation is shown in Table 9-16.

fundamentals of factor analysis

Factor vectors placed like those in Figure 9-7 were referred to by Thurstone as *reference vectors*. In addition he spoke of *primary factors*, which were at right angles to the reference axes. The loadings on reference axes are shown in Table 9-16, and the loadings on primary factors were shown previously in Table 9-14. Where there are only two factors to be rotated, a primary factor would go through a cluster (if there

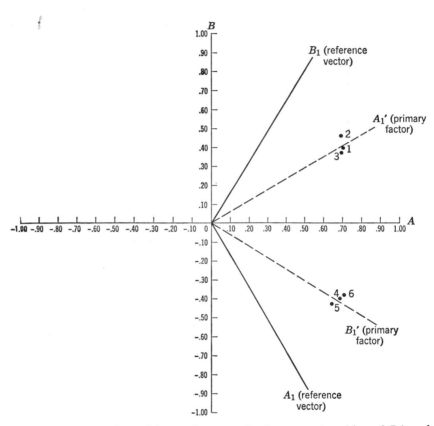

figure 9-7 *Rotations of factors in terms of reference vectors (A_1 and B_1) and primary factors (A_1' and B_1').*

are only two clusters, as in Figure 9-7), and the reference axes would be backed off at 90° from the primary factor.

For a number of good reasons, this method of seeking a simpler structure is not recommended. The use of two systems of factor vectors has led to considerable confusion in the literature. For example, authors frequently label tables as "correlations with primary factors" when they actually are depicting correlations with reference vectors. Further con-

multivariate analysis

table 9-16 *Loadings on oblique reference vectors depicted in Figure 9-7*

	A_1	B_1
1	.01	.71
2	−.05	.76
3	.02	.69
4	.70	.02
5	.70	−.02
6	.69	.04

fusion arises in the use of the word "loading," which is used sometimes to refer to the correlation of a variable with a factor and sometimes to refer to the weight applied to factor scores for estimating observed scores (the two are different in the oblique case).

Another criticism of the Thurstone approach to oblique rotation is that it can, and often does, fool the investigator into thinking his data are simpler than they actually are. In most problems, even an approximation to simple structure by this method forces negative correlations among the factor axes (the reference vectors). Whereas thinking in terms of positively correlated factors is difficult enough, it is even more difficult to think in terms of negatively correlated factors. Thus the simple-appearing table of loadings comes at the expense of confusion in interpreting the overall results. Such confusion can be illustrated with the following example. This method of rotation can be used to show that an arithmetic test has a substantial loading on factor A and a zero loading on factor B, and vice versa for a vocabulary test. But since the two variables would be positively correlated, the only way that one could obtain the rotation would be by making the factors correlate negatively. If one does not look at the negative correlation between the two factors, he might be misled into thinking that the two variables are independent. There are, in the literature, many examples of confusions resulting from efforts to interpret oblique rotations made in this way.

It is recommended that only one system of rotated factors be employed, the rotated factors being referred to simply as factors. Their geometric counterparts can be referred to as factor vectors or factor axes. If it is decided to rotate these factors obliquely rather than orthogonally, it is recommended that the oblique factors not be backed off 90° from clusters. Rather, it is recommended that factors be placed through clusters. This seldom will lead to a simple-appearing matrix of factor loadings, but it will clearly represent the actual relations among variables.

ANALYTIC METHODS OF ROTATION   Since the advent of methods of factor rotation, there have been numerous attempts to formulate analytic criteria. An analytic criterion is one that is stated in terms of a precise mathematical rule, or set of rules, rather than only in terms of a verbal description. Most attempts to specify such analytic methods have been based on the rules stated by Thurstone for attaining simple structure. Because of the immense amount of computations required to apply analytic criteria in rotations, it has been only during the last dozen years that practicable methods have evolved. (An excellent summary of the technical details of these methods is given by Harman, 1960. More recent developments regarding analytic methods of rotation are discussed by Horst, 1965.)

So far only the orthogonal methods of analytic rotation have been employed sufficiently to know how well they work in practice. The first such attempt led to the *quartimax* method. It is based on one of the salient requirements of simple structure—that the variance of loadings in each row of the factor matrix should be as large as possible. When a variable has substantial loadings on a number of factors, it is not a pure measure of any of them, and the variance of loadings is then relatively small. If the factors can be rotated so that a variable loads mainly on one factor, that variable is a relatively pure measure of that factor, and the variance of loadings is relatively large. Thus, by maximizing the sum of variances in different rows of the factor matrix, one approaches one of the goals of simple structure. Since, however, the actual variance in any row would be affected by both the sizes of loadings and their signs, the criterion is applied to the squared loadings rather than to the loadings themselves. A number of different investigators independently arrived at this criterion. The particular method used to maximize the sum of variances of rows in the factor matrix is called "quartimax" (Neuhaus and Wrigley, 1954).

The quartimax method, although still used in some studies, has not proved very successful in producing simpler structures. The difficulty is that it tends to produce a general factor in the rotations. One can see why this would be so, because the criterion would be perfectly satisfied if all variables had a loading on only one factor.

Kaiser (1958) approached the problem in a somewhat different way. Rather than maximize the sum of variances of rows in the factor matrix, his *varimax* method maximizes the sum of variances of squared loadings in the columns of the factor matrix. In each column of the matrix, this tends to produce some high loadings and some loadings near zero, which is one aspect of simple structure. The varimax method is also applied to the squared loadings rather than to the loadings themselves. The varimax method has proved very successful as an analytic approach to obtaining an orthogonal rotation of factors. Even in those cases where the results do not meet the investigator's concept of a simple structure, the solution usually is close enough to greatly reduce the labor of finding a satisfactory rotation.

methods for testing hypotheses

The methods of factor analysis discussed so far concern stepwise solutions. These methods are dominated by statistical criteria concerning the formation of linear combinations in the first step of the analysis and the rotation of factors in the second step of the analysis. The methods are used primarily to *discover* factors rather than to test theories regarding the existence of factors. Because these methods are sometimes used in the absence of explicit theory, some investigators feel that factor analysis, in all its forms, is an unhealthy type of "shotgun empiricism." In this section it will be shown that some forms of factor analysis are very useful for testing theories regarding the existence of factors.

As is true of all methods for testing hypotheses, methods of factor analysis used for that purpose hypothesize the existence of particular patterns of relationship in the data. In factor analysis, the patterns of relationship concern properties of the correlation matrix. For example, if one hypothesizes that a single general factor accounts for the correlations among a set of variables, this is the same as hypothesizing that the correlation matrix will possess certain mathematical properties. By testing to see if the mathematical properties are present, one makes a test of the tenability of the hypothesis. If instead of hypothesizing one factor, it is hypothesized that particular collections of variables will evolve into a number of common factors, this also can be tested by an analysis of particular characteristics of the correlation matrix.

Although, in the best scientific tradition, the hypotheses should be available before data are collected, in testing hypotheses with factor analysis, the hypotheses frequently are formulated only after an inspection of the correlation matrix. This can be thought of as halfway between pure efforts at discovery and pure efforts at the testing of hypotheses.

In all methods of factor analysis used for the testing of hypotheses, one goes directly to the desired solution, and rotations are not required. If the hypotheses are supported poorly by the obtained factors, one might start over and employ one of the stepwise methods. In other words, if the theory does not lead to a good explanation of the matrix of correlations, an effort can be made to discover factors by the stepwise approaches.

First will be discussed two methods which mainly are of historical interest—Spearman's general-factor solution and the bifactor solution. Then we shall discuss the method which is used most frequently today for testing hypotheses, the multiple-group method.

SPEARMAN'S GENERAL-FACTOR SOLUTION Charles Spearman (1904) was the originator of factor analysis, and more recent theorists have been strongly influenced by his ideas. Although he modified his ideas later (Spearman, 1927), his early theory was that all mental abilities are underlain by one general factor G. The general factor was thought of as a type of mental yardstick of intelligence, and only one yardstick was thought necessary to explain the common ground among all forms of individual differences in abilities. Thus tests as diverse as tests of arithmetic, spelling, and the judgment of illusions were thought to share in G. In addition, it was theorized that each source of individual differences (test) possessed a unique factor. Since by definition the unique factors in different tests are uncorrelated, all correlations among tests could be accounted for by one general factor. The theory is sometimes called Spearman's *two-factor theory*, because it hypothesized that each test could be explained by a general factor and a unique factor.

Spearman developed a test for his general factor according to the following lines of reasoning. If correlations among tests can be accounted for by one common factor (G), this means that the correlations among the tests can be accounted for by the correlations of the tests with (loadings on) G. If the loadings of tests on G were known, these could be used to predict the correlation between any two tests. To use a concrete example, say that there are five tests numbered 1 through 5. Their correlations would be r_{12}, r_{13}, etc., and the loadings of these on G would be r_{1G}, r_{2G}, etc. According to the logic of PM correlational analysis, if one variable can explain the correlation between two other variables, the partial correlation between the latter two variables (partialing the first variable) is zero. Consequently if G explained the common variance among the five variables, the partial correlations among those five variables (holding G constant) would all be zero. In that case it would necessarily follow that the correlation between any two variables would equal the product of their loadings on G. Why this is so can be seen from the following formula for partialing G from the correlation between variables 1 and 2:

$$(9\text{-}14) \qquad r_{12.G} = \frac{r_{12} - r_{1G}r_{2G}}{\sqrt{1 - r_{1G}{}^2}\,\sqrt{1 - r_{2G}{}^2}}$$

The only way for the expression on the right to be zero is for the numerator to be zero, and the only way for the numerator to be zero is for the correlation between the two tests to equal the product of their loadings on G. Thus the correlations in any matrix explainable

	TEST				
	1	*2*	*3*	*4*	*5*
1		ab	ac	ad	ae
2	ab		bc	bd	be
TEST 3	ac	bc		cd	ce
4	ad	bd	cd		de
5	ae	be	ce	de	

by a general factor would be the products of loadings on the general factor.

To simplify the following discussion, let the loadings of the five tests on G be symbolized as a, b, c, d, and e, rather than as r_{1G}, r_{2G}, etc. Then if the correlations can be explained by a general factor, $r_{12} = ab$, $r_{13} = ac$, $r_{23} = bc$, etc. The full matrix of correlations would equal the products of loadings on G, as shown in Table 9-17. (For the time being, it will be assumed that there is no concern with the diagonal elements, and consequently they are left blank in Table 9-17. Later, when the concept of *communality* is discussed, we shall consider questions regarding the diagonal elements.)

Matrices that can be explained by a general factor have some interesting characteristics. One characteristic of Table 9-17 is that, exclusive of diagonal elements, the elements in each column are proportional to those in other columns. For example, taking elements from columns 1 and 2 gives the following:

$$(9\text{-}15) \qquad \frac{r_{13}}{r_{23}} = \frac{r_{14}}{r_{24}} = \frac{r_{15}}{r_{25}}$$

One can prove this by substituting for the correlations their counterparts in terms of products of loadings on G:

$$\frac{r_{13}}{r_{23}} = \frac{ac}{bc} = \frac{a}{b}$$

$$(9\text{-}16) \qquad \frac{r_{14}}{r_{24}} = \frac{ad}{bd} = \frac{a}{b}$$

$$\frac{r_{15}}{r_{25}} = \frac{ae}{be} = \frac{a}{b}$$

Thus the elements in any two columns (ignoring those pairs of elements where either is a diagonal element) are proportional to the loadings of the two variables on G. Obviously this holds for any two rows of the matrix as well as for any two columns.

The test for a general factor in terms of this model essentially is a test for the proportionality of columns in the matrix of correlations. This is done in the following manner. Let a *tetrad* be defined as any four correlations (excluding diagonal elements) where two correlations are from one column and the other two are from corresponding rows of another column. The following three tetrads (t_1, t_2, t_3) are obtainable for the columns of coefficients for variables 1 and 2:

$$t_1 \begin{bmatrix} r_{13} & r_{23} \\ r_{14} & r_{24} \end{bmatrix}$$

$$t_2 \begin{bmatrix} r_{13} & r_{23} \\ r_{15} & r_{25} \end{bmatrix}$$

$$t_3 \begin{bmatrix} r_{14} & r_{24} \\ r_{15} & r_{25} \end{bmatrix}$$

A *tetrad difference* equals the correlation in the upper left of the tetrad multiplied by the correlation in the lower right, from which is subtracted the product of the two remaining elements. Thus the tetrad difference d_1 for t_1 above equals

(9-17) $\qquad d_1 = r_{13}r_{24} - r_{14}r_{23}$

If a matrix of correlations is explainable by a general factor, all tetrad differences will be zero. This follows from the criterion of proportionality of columns, which can be illustrated for t_1 above. Since the rows of the matrix are proportional, it follows that

$$\frac{r_{13}}{r_{14}} = \frac{r_{23}}{r_{24}}$$

(9-18)
$$\frac{r_{13}}{r_{14}} - \frac{r_{23}}{r_{24}} = 0$$

$$r_{13}r_{24} - r_{14}r_{23} = 0 = d_1$$

In the early attempts to test for the presence of a general factor, Spearman and his colleagues investigated distributions of tetrad differences. Although the model requires that all tetrad differences be precisely zero, this is not expected to happen in any particular study. Even if G were capable of accounting for the correlations, sampling error would prevent correlations from fitting the requirements exactly. As can be seen, there are numerous tetrads in a matrix of correlations. After these are computed, a frequency distribution can be erected. If the differences were because of sampling error only, one would expect to find a mean of zero and a relatively small variance about zero. Spearman and Holzinger (1924) developed some formulas concerning the sampling error related to such distributions, which permitted a statistical test for the sufficiency of a general factor.

Rather than test for the presence of a general factor by the investigation of distribution of tetrad differences, there is an easier approach. First, estimates are made of the loadings of the variables on G. Second, products of the loadings are obtained and compared with the correlations. If differences between the two (as shown in a matrix of residual coefficients) are very small, a general factor is accepted as sufficient. If some of the residuals are large, the hypothesis of a general factor must be rejected in favor of hypotheses concerning more than one common factor.

In the ideal case where columns of the correlation matrix are exactly proportional, the loading of any variable on G can be directly computed from equations formed among the correlations. One equation for determining the squared loading a^2 of variable 1 on G is as follows:

(9-19)
$$\frac{r_{12}r_{13}}{r_{23}} = \frac{(ab)(ac)}{bc} = \frac{a^2bc}{bc} = a^2 = r_{1G}{}^2$$

The same result can be obtained from different equations:

(9-20)
$$\frac{r_{14}r_{15}}{r_{45}} = \frac{(ad)(ae)}{de} = \frac{a^2de}{de} = a^2 = r_{1G}{}^2$$

In a matrix of five variables, there are six equations for computing the loading on G for any one of the variables. If the proportionality requirements were met exactly, all the equations would give the same result. Since this is not likely to occur, the different equations provide somewhat different estimates of loadings on G. One can combine all equations to obtain an overall estimate of the loading. In our illustrative problem, one does this by adding the numerators of all six equations and adding the denominators of all six equations:

(9-21)
$$a^2 = \frac{r_{12}r_{13} + r_{12}r_{14} + r_{12}r_{15} + r_{13}r_{14} + r_{13}r_{15} + r_{14}r_{15}}{r_{23} + r_{24} + r_{25} + r_{34} + r_{35} + r_{45}}$$

The denominator contains the sum of all correlations exclusive of those of variable 1 with the other variables. The numerator contains the sum of paired products of correlations of variable 1 with the other variables. When the proportionality criterion is not met exactly, as it almost never will be, Eq. (9-21) provides an estimate of the loading of variable 1 on G. Similar expressions could be generated for determining the loadings of the other variables.

table 9-18 *Computational procedures for determining loadings on a general factor*

CORRELATIONS

	1	2	3	4	5
1		.48	.40	.40	.30
2	.48		.40	.40	.25
3	.40	.40		.34	.28
4	.40	.40	.34		.20
5	.30	.25	.28	.20	
column sums (L)	1.58	1.53	1.42	1.34	1.03
sums of squares (Q)	.6404	.6129	.5140	.4756	.2709
$M = 3.45$					
r_{iG}^2	.50	.45	.37	.31	.16
r_{iG}	.71	.67	.61	.56	.40

RESIDUAL COEFFICIENTS

	1	2	3	4	5
1		.00	−.03	.00	.02
2	.00		−.01	.02	−.02
3	−.03	−.01		.00	.04
4	.00	.02	−.00		−.02
5	.02	−.02	.04	−.02	

SOURCE: Adapted from Harman, 1960.

Rather than go through the arithmetical operations required to estimate loadings by the method illustrated in Eq. (9-21), one can use the available computational routines. The same results are obtainable from the following formula:

(9-22)
$$r_{iG}^2 = \frac{L^2 - Q}{2\sqrt{(M - L)}}$$

where r_{iG}^2 = squared loading of any variable on G
$\quad\quad L$ = sum of correlations in column i excluding diagonal element
$\quad\quad Q$ = sum of squared correlations in column i
$\quad\quad M$ = sum of all correlations below diagonal of matrix
The computations are illustrated in Table 9-18.

After the estimated loadings on G are obtained, a matrix of cross products of the loadings would be obtained in the usual way. The matrix of cross products would be subtracted from the matrix of correlations, which would produce a matrix of residual coefficients. An examination of the size and patterning of residual coefficients would lead to either the acceptance or rejection of the general-factor hypothesis.

multivariate analysis

table 9-19 *An idealized bifactor solution for nine tests*

| | | GENERAL FACTOR | GROUP FACTORS | | |
		A	B	C	D
	1	X	X	0	0
	2	X	X	0	0
	3	X	X	0	0
	4	X	0	X	0
TESTS	5	X	0	X	0
	6	X	0	X	0
	7	X	0	0	X
	8	X	0	0	X
	9	X	0	0	X

Spearman's general-factor solution has been out of style for over 30 years. Since matrices of correlations obtained from diverse mental tests do not fit the mathematical requirements very well, there began a search for the number and kinds of factors that do exist among tests of ability. The methods of discovery discussed previously (the stepwise solutions) are better for that purpose. Now that more consideration is being given to factor analysis as a method for testing theories about constructs, the general-factor solution may again become useful. If, for example, one did considerable research on anxiety and developed eight plausible methods of measuring attributes related to the construct, it would be interesting to test for the presence of a general factor. Of course, no one should expect a perfect fit in this or any other example, but if the fit is reasonably good, it provides a partial test for the hypothesis of a general factor.

BIFACTOR METHOD Holzinger (1941) developed a bifactor solution which is a direct extension of Spearman's general-factor solution. In the bifactor solution, it is hypothesized that the common variance among variables can be explained by two types of common factors, a general factor and group factors. (It will be remembered that a group factor is simply a common factor shared by only some of the variables.) The method does not state in advance how many group factors are required in addition to the general factor; instead, the number of factors is determined by the correlations.

An idealized bifactor solution for nine tests is shown in Table 9-19, in which an X denotes a substantial positive loading. Note that each test has a positive loading on the general factor and a positive loading on one group factor.

Essentially, there are three steps in a bifactor solution. First, the variables are divided into groups on the basis of their correlations. Variables which correlate highly are placed in one group. Variables which have low correlations with members of the first group but relatively high correlations among themselves are made members of a second group, and so on for the determination of other groups. The second step is to compute the loadings of all variables on the general factor. One does this by essentially the same approach as was shown previously for the general-factor solution. Then the matrix of residual coefficients is obtained. The third step is to compute factor loadings within each of the designated groups. The general-factor solution illustrated in Table 9-18 is obtained separately for each group. Thus one obtains a general-factor solution for all variables combined, and then one obtains group factors for the small matrices of residual coefficients for particular groups.

Although the bifactor solution is conceptually simple, in practice the computations can be quite tedious, and numerous aspects of the computations are not well specified. The major difficulty lies in the original assignment of variables to groups. It is difficult to say how many groups should be posited and which variables belong to which groups. Rather complex cut-and-try methods are used to perform the groupings (Harman, 1960), and the results are by no means unique. One investigator might reach the conclusion that there are four groups of variables in a particular matrix, and another investigator might decide that there are only three groups. Also, the investigators might reach different decisions about the placement of particular variables in one or another of the groups.

After the groups are specified, the arithmetic of obtaining loadings on the general factor is somewhat complex. In this step, one does not compute loadings in exactly the same way as in the general-factor solution illustrated in Table 9-18. In that solution, loadings take account of all correlations of one variable with the others. In the bifactor solution, loadings are obtained in a slightly different way. If the loadings take account of all correlations among variables, this will confound the general factor with the group factors. To circumvent this difficulty, the general-factor loadings for the members of one group are obtained only from their correlations with the members of other groups. Thus if variable 1 is a member of group 1 and there are three groups, the loading of variable 1 on the general factor would be determined from the correlations of variable 1 with the members of groups 2 and 3, but not from the correlations of variable 1 with the other members of group 1. One can see how this can be done by looking back at Eq. (9-21). In that example assume that variables 1 and 2 form one group and variables 3, 4, and 5 form a second group. One can obtain an estimate of the general-factor loading for variable 1 by ignoring all terms containing variable 2, which results in the following formula:

(9-23) $$a^2 = \frac{r_{13}r_{14} + r_{13}r_{15} + r_{14}r_{15}}{r_{34} + r_{35} + r_{45}}$$

In this way, one can estimate loadings on the general factor without considering the correlations among the variables in a cluster. When the necessary operations are performed for large matrices containing numerous groups, however, the computations are tedious.

In addition to the tedious computations, there are three major problems with the bifactor method. First, as was mentioned previously, there is considerable indeterminacy in the establishment of groups of variables. Second, the final factor solutions are misleadingly neat. If variables tend to correlate positively, they all will have positive loadings on the general factor. On the group factors, the members of a group will have positive loadings if their residual coefficients (after G is removed) are positive. What is misleading is the suggestion that the group factors are uncorrelated with one another, which seldom is the case. In the same vein, since only the members of a group are shown as having loadings on their group factor, it is suggested that other variables are unrelated to the factor. Once a group is defined, there is no way to compute the loadings on the group factor for a variable which was not included in the group. If, however, an additional variable were made a member of the group and the general-factor formula were applied, the loading would tell to what extent the variable has something in common with the other variables. This can be illustrated by the hypothetical results in Table 9-19. Variable 5 has no loading on the group factor found for variables 1 through 3. One could redo the analysis and include variable 5 in the first group rather than in the second group. Would variable 5 then have a zero loading on the first group factor? It is quite unlikely that the loading would be zero, but this is what is suggested by an examination of bifactor solutions.

The third major problem with the bifactor method as it has frequently been used is that it is only partly a method for testing hypotheses about factors. This is because groups are determined by their correlations rather than in terms of a theory about the variables. Usually the investigator has a semitheory about how the variables will fall into groups, but in the end the grouping is done in terms of the correlations. Another reason why the bifactor method is only partly concerned with testing hypotheses is that no statement is made in advance of the analysis as to how many group factors are expected. All that is stated is that the common variance of any variable can be partitioned into a general factor and a group factor. A method which is more purely concerned with testing hypotheses requires that the number of factors be stated in advance and the relative sizes of loadings on those factors be predicted.

The bifactor method could be used more directly for testing hypotheses. To do this would require that the investigator formulate the groupings of variables before data are collected. Then the bifactor solution would be applied to the a priori groupings, and the pattern of factor loadings would indicate the effectiveness of the groups in explaining the common variance. This can, however, be done much better and more easily by the multiple-group method.

MULTIPLE-GROUP METHOD   The multiple-group method offers the best overall approach to testing hypotheses about the existence of factors. In the limiting case, it can be used to test for the presence of a general factor, much as is done with the general-factor solution. At the other extreme, it can test for the presence of any number of hypothesized factors.

The multiple-group method will be illustrated with the six-variable problem used to illustrate methods of condensation. For the example, suppose that the problem concerns hypotheses about two factors of anxiety. One factor is hypothesized to concern bodily harm, and the other is hypothesized to concern anxiety in social situations. Tests 1 through 3 are hypothesized to concern the first factor, and tests 4 through 6 are hypothesized to concern the second factor. It also is hypothesized that, in an oblique solution, there will be a moderate correlation between the two factors.

The mathematics of the multiple-group method are very simple. They are obtained directly from formulas for the correlation of sums, much about which has already been said in this book. The multiple-group method might better be called the "group-centroid method," because it is only a variation of the centroid method which was discussed previously. Although one can place a centroid among *all* the variables, it is equally easy to place a centroid among only some of them. In the example above, the first centroid factor is placed among variables 1, 2, and 3 only. (It could equally well be placed among the other three variables only.) Then the correlations of *all* variables with this centroid are obtained, which are the loadings on the first factor. Next, a second centroid is placed among variables 4, 5, and 6 only. The correlations of all six variables with the second centroid will be the loadings on the second factor.

Going back to the basic concept of factor analysis as concerning the linear combination of variables in a matrix of data, a group centroid equals the sum of scores over a specified set of variables. One obtains loadings on the factor by correlating all the variables (including ones not included in the sum) with the factor scores. It is easier to perform these calculations on the matrix of correlations than on the data matrix, which can be done with formulas for the correlation of sums. It will be remembered that the general formula for the correlation of sums of standard scores is as follows:

(9-24) $$r_{xy} = \frac{\bar{R}_{xy}}{\sqrt{\bar{R}_x}\,\sqrt{\bar{R}_y}}$$

The numerator is the sum of all elements in the cross-correlation matrix for the two sums x and y. Under each radical in the denominator is the sum of elements in the correlation matrix for the variables in a sum. If either x or y is not a sum of other variables but an individual variable instead, one term of the denominator equals 1.0, and the numerator equals the sum of correlations between the individual variable and the members of the sum of variables. Various uses of Eq. (9-24) constitute the major computational steps in the multiple-group method.

A worked-out example of the multiple-group method is shown in Table 9-20. The first factor consists of the sum of variables 1, 2, and 3. The loading of any variable on this group-centroid factor is obtained from Eq. (9-24), as follows. Since a loading will equal the correlation of an individual variable with the sum of variables 1 through 3, only one term appears in the denominator. The square of the denominator equals the sum of all the elements in the submatrix of correlations for variables 1 through 3. This part is blocked off in Table 9-20. The sum T_1 includes the correlations above and below the diagonal of the submatrix for the three variables, and it also includes the three diagonal unities. The square root of this sum is the denominator in the equation for computing each loading, but again, it is easier to multiply by m, the reciprocal of the square root of T_1. The numerator of the equation equals the sum of correlations of each variable with variables 1 through 3. Each variable has three correlations with these three variables. Since variables 1 through 3 are members of the group which defines the factor, one of their three correlations is 1.0. Thus the sum of correlations for variable 1 equals $1.0 + r_{12} + r_{13}$. For any variable not included in the group defining the centroid, there are three empirical correlations, and the diagonal entry would not enter the computations. Thus for variable 4, the numerator equals $r_{14} + r_{24} + r_{34}$. In this way, loadings of the six variables on the first group-centroid factor are obtained.

How loadings are obtained on the second group factor depends on whether one decides to use oblique factors or orthogonal factors. The former case will be considered first. In this case loadings on the second centroid factor can be obtained directly from the original matrix of correlations as illustrated in Table 9-20. In Eq. (9-24), the denominator is the square root of the sum T_2 of all elements in the submatrix of correlations for variables 4, 5, and 6. This submatrix is

CORRELATION MATRIX

	1	2	3	4	5	6
1	1.00	.55	.43	.32	.28	.36
2	.55	1.00	.50	.25	.31	.32
3	.43	.50	1.00	.39	.25	.33
4	.32	.25	.39	1.00	.43	.49
5	.28	.31	.25	.43	1.00	.43
6	.36	.32	.33	.49	.43	1.00

T_1 (sum 1, 2, 3) = 5.96 $\sqrt{T_1}$ = 2.4413 m_1 = .4096

T_2 (sum 3, 4, 5) = 5.70 $\sqrt{T_2}$ = 2.3875 m_2 = .4188

VARIABLE	SUMS OF CORRELATIONS WITH GROUPS		FACTOR LOADINGS	
	first group	second group	A	B
1	1.98	.96	.81	.40
2	2.05	.88	.84	.37
3	1.93	.97	.79	.41
4	.96	1.92	.39	.80
5	.84	1.86	.34	.78
6	1.01	1.92	.41	.80

blocked off in Table 9-20. The numerator of the equation for each variable equals the sum of correlations of that variable with variables 4, 5, and 6. In this instance the numerator for each of the variables in that group contains two empirical correlations and a diagonal unity. For variables 1, 2, and 3, the numerator will equal the sum of three empirical correlations with the other three variables. Thus the numerator for variable 1 equals $r_{14} + r_{15} + r_{16}$. In this way all loadings on the second group factor are obtained.

After the two factors are obtained, it is easy to compute the correlation between them from Eq. (9-25). The matrix of correlations can be sectioned as follows:

R_A	R_{AB}
R_{AB}	R_B

According to formulas for the correlation of sums, the correlation between the two factors A and B is obtained as follows:

(9-25)
$$r_{AB} = \frac{\bar{R}_{AB}}{\sqrt{\bar{R}_A}\,\sqrt{\bar{R}_B}}$$

$$r_{AB} = .48$$

Since the two terms in the denominator have been obtained for previous computations, all that is needed is to compute the sum of elements in the cross-correlation matrix R_{AB} and use this as the numerator.

It will be noted that the loadings on the two oblique group-centroid factors in Table 9-20 are similar to the loadings shown in Table 9-14 for an oblique rotation of two centroid factors, except that what was designated factor A there is designated factor B here, and vice versa. In both cases, the final factors go through clusters of variables. There is, however, a very important difference in how the two sets of results are obtained. In rotating the centroid solution, it is necessary to search for factors. In the group-centroid solution, the factors are hypothesized in advance of the analysis, and a direct solution for the factors is made. In general, there is no assurance that the two approaches will lead to the same results.

Note that the factor matrix in Table 9-20 does not look very "simple." The variables that define factor A have appreciable loadings on factor B, and vice versa. This typically occurs when oblique rotations are to the dominant clusters.

If orthogonal factors are desired when hypotheses are tested with the multiple-group method, the procedures are slightly different from those discussed for the oblique case. Factor A would be obtained from the correlation matrix as was shown in Table 9-20, but factor B would not be obtained from the correlation matrix. A matrix of residuals would be obtained in which the influence of factor A is removed. This would be done in the usual way. Products of loadings would be obtained for factor A, and these would be subtracted from the correlation matrix. Then the computations for B would be performed on the residual matrix. The same procedures would be applied that were illustrated in Table 9-20.

Although one can obtain loadings on orthogonal group-centroid factors by operating on successive residual matrices as described above, there is an easier way to perform the computations. First, oblique factors are obtained from the correlation matrix. Then a mathematical transformation is made which orthogonalizes the oblique axes. (The computations are discussed in Harman, 1960, and in Thurstone, 1947.) Although this approach is computationally much simpler than the one described above, it would be difficult to discuss without assuming some knowledge of matrix algebra on the part of the reader.

The multiple-group method can be used to test for any number of hypothesized factors. If a group of variables is hypothesized to be explainable by only one common factor (a general factor), the first "group" centroid will go among all the variables. In other words, the first factor will be the first factor obtained from applying the regular centroid method of condensation, discussed previously.

The multiple-group method can be easily applied to more than two groups of variables. Oblique factors can be determined directly from the correlation matrix. One does this by sectioning off the variables that constitute the different groups. From these sections, one obtains the proper quantities for formulas concerning the correlation of sums. After all factors are extracted from the correlation matrix, they can be mutually orthogonalized by the transformations mentioned above. These loadings can be used to obtain a final matrix of residuals. If, for example, four factors have been obtained, one can compute the fourth residual matrix without going through the steps of computing the earlier residual matrices (Harman, 1960; Thurstone, 1947).

When the multiple-group method is employed, it is not necessary for all variables to be assigned to one of the groups. In some analyses, there are firm hypotheses about the factorial composition of some of the variables, but other variables are included in the analyses purely in the hope that interesting relations will be discovered. In the analysis in Table 9-20, six additional variables could have been included but assigned to neither of the two groups. It should be obvious how their loadings would be computed via the correlation of sums. The loadings for the original six variables would not change, but loadings would be obtained for the six additional variables.

In previous years the multiple-group method frequently was used as a method of condensation in a stepwise analysis rather than as a method for testing hypotheses. When clusters are judiciously chosen in terms of the correlations, a number of group-centroid factors will explain considerable common variance. Then some or all of the factors obtained in this way can be rotated. The multiple-group method is not as efficient in condensing common variance as either the full centroid method or the method of principal axes. Since the availability of computers makes it practicable to employ the latter two methods in stepwise analyses, there no longer is need to employ the multiple-group method for this purpose. This fact has probably led to the unfortunate conclusion by some persons that the multiple-group method is "not as good" as the full centroid method or the method of principal axes. It is not as good for condensing common variance in a stepwise analysis, but it is far better for testing hypotheses.

In using the multiple-group method, it is appropriate to ask whether or not it is possible to find *disconfirming* results regarding the existence of factors. There are a number of ways for this to happen. First, a variable assigned to a group might not correlate highly with the centroid for that group, which would mean that the variable does not strongly share a common factor with the other variables. This is not as likely to happen when the groups contain only a small number of variables, because each variable is then prominently represented in the centroid.

In actual research, however, there frequently are half a dozen or more variables assigned to each group, and thus it is possible to obtain rather low correlations of variables in a group with the centroid for that group. [Also, if there is a small number of variables in a cluster, the spurious inflation of loadings for those variables can be corrected by Eq. (8-1).]

A second type of disconfirming information is obtained when variables assigned to one cluster correlate substantially with the centroid for another cluster. For example, it might be found that a test intended to measure anxiety regarding bodily harm actually correlates more with the centroid for tests intended to measure anxiety in social situations than with the centroid for tests of the former kind.

A third type of discomfirming information is obtained from an inspection of the final residual matrix after all the hypothesized factors have been extracted. The average, absolute value of those residuals should be low. If that quantity is large in proportion to the average absolute correlation in the original matrix, it means that the hypothesized factors do a poor job of explaining the common variance.

SUGGESTED ADDITIONAL READINGS

Fruchter, B. *Introduction to factor analysis*. Princeton, N.J.: Van Nostrand, 1954.

Harman, H. H. *Modern factor analysis*. Chicago: Univer. Chicago Press, 1960.

Horst, P. *Factor analysis of data matrices*. New York: Holt, 1965.

Thurstone, L. L. *Multiple-factor analysis*. Chicago: Univer. Chicago Press, 1947.

CHAPTER TEN
SPECIAL ISSUES IN FACTOR ANALYSIS

Although the fundamentals of factor analysis were covered in the previous chapter, there still are numerous special issues which need to be discussed. These include the estimation of factor scores, comparisons of factors in different analyses, and statistical decisions in factor analysis. One of the major issues which has not been discussed up to this point concerns the "communality problem," which is discussed in the following section.

the communality problem

In the previous chapter it was assumed that unities are placed in the diagonal spaces of correlation matrices before factor analysis is undertaken. Spearman's general-factor solution and Holzinger's bifactor solution did not require consideration of the diagonal elements, but the other methods of factor analysis were illustrated with correlation matrices containing unities in the diagonal spaces. This was done for two reasons. First, the actual correlation of any variable with itself is 1.0, and consequently the diagonal elements of any real correlation matrix are unities. Second, if a factor loading is defined as the correlation of a standardized variable with a standardized linear combination of a set of variables, then to compute that loading from the correlation of sums, the formulas require that unities be placed in the diagonals of the correlation matrix. If anything other than unities are placed in the diagonal spaces, one is not correlating an *actual variable with* a *linear combination of actual variables.*

Although the author prefers to think of factor analysis as concerning the linear combination of actual variables, there are others who view the matter quite differently. It was mentioned previously that factor analysis attempts to distinguish common variance from unique variance. When unities are placed in diagonal spaces of the correlation matrix, this goal is only approximately accomplished. The two sources of variance become somewhat mixed, because the variables themselves, including their uniqueness, determine the factors. Some would speak of this type of analysis as *component analysis* (because the factors are actual linear combinations, or components, of the variables) and distinguish this from some loftier approach which alone deserves the name of factor analysis.

Perhaps it would be best to speak of the approach developed in the previous chapter as concerning *actual factors,* since the factors are actual combinations of the variables and loadings are actual correlations with those factors. The other approach is concerned with *hypothetical factors*—hypothetical because they can only be estimated from the actual variables. The second approach is to seek mathematical solutions that specify factors entirely in terms of the common variance among variables. Such approaches involve *communalities,* numbers in the diagonal spaces of the correlation matrix which generally are less than 1.0.

The search for hypothetical common factors is appealing for a number of reasons. (Later it will be argued, however, that there presently is no firm basis for performing such analyses and also that there are some logical fallacies underlying the concepts involved.) That approach is appealing because if there were some way to cleanly disentangle common variance and unique variance, it would accomplish one of the major purposes of factor analysis. The approach is appealing also because it would help explain the influence of hypothetical factors on correlation matrices. One can see why this is so by returning to the general-factor solution.

A general factor G is thought of as a hypothetical factor. It accounts for the correlations among variables, but it is not completely defined by the actual variables. In other words, even if the proportionality criterion is met, the multiple correlation of the variables with G could be much less than 1.0. This is different from what happens in solving for actual factors (as distinguished above from hypothetical factors). For example, if unities are placed in the diagonal spaces of the correlation matrix, centroid factors, or any rotations of them, are completely defined by the actual variables in the data matrix. Then the multiple correlation of all variables with each factor is precisely 1.0.

If a hypothetical general factor accounts for all the correlations in a matrix, the products of loadings on G equal the correlations. When that notion was introduced earlier, no mention was made of the diagonal spaces of the correlation matrix. In the matrix of products of G loadings, in each diagonal space would be the squared loading for the variable. Thus the diagonal terms would be a^2, b^2, etc., as illustrated in Table 10-1. These terms would equal 1.0 only if each variable correlated perfectly with G, in which case all the correlations would be 1.0. The diagonal elements in the matrix of cross products are called *communali-*

table 10-1 *Corelation matrix computed from loadings of four variables on a general factor*

	1	2	3	4
1	a^2	ab	ac	ad
2	ab	b^2	bc	bd
3	ac	bc	c^2	cd
4	ad	bd	cd	d^2

ties. Each communality equals the variance explained (h^2) by the hypothetical factor G.

If a matrix of correlations like that in Table 10-1 meets the requirements for a general factor and unities are placed in the diagonal spaces of that matrix, no existing method of condensation will arrive at only one factor. If, for example, the centroid method is applied, there probably will be as many factors as there are variables. There will be a general factor, and the remaining factors will tend to explain rather small percentages of variance; but all elements in the first residual matrix certainly will not be zero. There is, however, a way to accomplish this feat if the squared loadings on G are placed in the diagonal spaces, which is illustrated in Table 10-1.

The foregoing result can be accomplished by applying the usual method of centroid condensation to the matrix in Table 10-1, in which communalities are inserted in the diagonal spaces. The sum of coefficients in the first column equals $a(a + b + c + d)$. The sum of coefficients in any column equals the loading of the particular variable times the sum of loadings for all variables. Then the sum of columns sums (T) equals the squared sum of all loadings, which shows that the square root of T equals the sum of loadings. By the usual method of centroid analysis, one finds the loading of any variable by dividing the column sum for that variable by the square root of T. Then the centroid loadings would be a, b, c, and d—the hypothetical loadings on G. The products of these loadings would equal the coefficients in Table 10-1, including the communality values. All elements in the first residual matrix would be precisely zero. Such a beautiful result as this appeals to the imagination and makes one wonder if all factor analysis could not be founded on the search for hypothetical factors. Before the difficulties in this line of reasoning are discussed, the issue of communalities in the general case will be examined.

It was Thurstone who most fully explored the derivation of hypothetical common factors through the use of communality estimates. He discussed the issues in terms of the *rank* of the space of variables, which was mentioned in the previous chapter. The rank equals the number of factors required to reduce residual coefficients to zero (to explain all correlations among variables). He saw that Spearman's general factor was a special case of rank 1 and that regardless of the number of hypothetical factors required to account for observed correlations, the problem could be posed as finding the rank of a matrix of correlation. In this way one could try to learn the number of hypothetical factors and loadings on those factors which would account for the correlations. Although there is no direct way to obtain both these types of information simultaneously, there are some methods of estimation.

When the rank of the matrix actually is less than the number of variables (hopefully much less), if one could somehow guess the correct communalities, one of the methods of condensation, such as the centroid method, could be used to obtain the proper loadings. If, for example, the "true" rank is 4, all coefficients in the fourth residual matrix will be zero, and the sum of squared loadings for any variable (h^2) will equal the communality for that variable. This then turns into a "bootstrap" operation, in which, by some means, the communality must be known before the analysis is undertaken. If one can ascertain the correct values for the communalities and place these in the correlation matrix, any method of condensation applied to that matrix will reveal the "true" rank and will determine loadings on the factors. Many models have been developed for determining hypothetical factors, and many particular methods have been proposed for estimating communalities (see the discussion in Harman, 1960, and in Horst, 1965).

The method of estimating communalities proposed by Thurstone, which is the one still used most frequently, is an iterative approach. First, by some means, estimates are made of communalities and placed in the diagonal spaces. One of the methods of condensation is applied, typically principal axes or the centroid method, to the point where the matrix of residual coefficients contains only very small values. The number of factors required to do that is considered the rank of the matrix. To obtain proper loadings, the following steps are then required. First, h^2 for each variable is computed and compared with the estimated communality used in the analysis. Unless the differences are very small (e.g., an average absolute difference over all variables of only .02), the analysis must be performed again. This time, instead of the original estimates of the communalities, the h^2 found for each variable in the first analysis is used. These new communality estimates are placed in the diagonal spaces of the correlational matrix, and the same number of factors is extracted as was obtained in the first analysis. The new set of h^2 values is then compared to the ones used in the second round of factoring. If the differences are not small, the obtained communalities in the second analysis are used as estimated communalities for a third analysis. One can keep going in this way until differences between estimated communalities and derived communalities are very small. The loadings obtained in the final analysis are taken as the correct loadings.

Regarding the original estimates used in the iterative approach described above, almost any numbers between zero and 1.0 taken at random will do. Wrigley (1957) has shown that widely different initial estimates all tend to converge. Many proposals have been made for choosing the initial trial values (Guttman, 1958; Harman, 1960; Thurstone, 1947). One that has been followed frequently is to employ the highest absolute value of correlation in each column as the trial value.

In spite of the intuitive appeal of hypothetical factors and their resolution through the use of communality estimates, 60 years of searching for an acceptable model have brought only confusion and doubt. The illustrations used to demonstrate the potential usefulness of hypothetical factors (such as that in Table 10-1 for the general-factor case) start by *defining* loadings on factors so that they will exactly explain the correlations in a matrix. One can do this easily for more than one factor by composing hypothetical matrices of factor loadings. The only requirement is that the sum of squares on any row not be greater than 1.0 and the sum of cross products of any two rows not be greater than 1.0 or less than −1.0. Then, by cross-multiplying the elements in any two rows, one obtains a hypothetical correlation. In this way a full matrix of correlations can be obtained. After h^2 is placed in each diagonal space of the matrix, factor analysis can be applied so as to recover the original loadings. For this purpose, the obtained loadings have to be rotated so as to be the same as the hypothetical loadings used to obtain the correlation matrix. Thus, given any set of hypothetical factors, a unique correlation matrix is obtainable. From this fact, it is tempting to argue that the reverse is true—that, given any empirical matrix of correlations, one can deduce unique loadings on a unique number of hypothetical factors. This is about as convincing as the argument that, since one can scramble an egg, he also can unscramble it. In the remainder of this section the major models that have been proposed for the derivation of hypothetical factors will be discussed.

The major difficulty in finding an acceptable solution for hypothetical factors (and thus for communalities to obtain those factors) is that many persons have not been specific in defining "common variance" and "unique variance." Different efforts to define these concepts have led to different models for investigating hypothetical factors. Thurstone's model concerning minimum rank most closely approximates what most people mean by hypothetical factors relating to common variance. For the model to work in practice, however, there must be a reasonable, unique way of partitioning the variance of each variable into portions attributable to common and unique factors. This means that the model must lead to a unique h^2 for each variable, one that does not violate other mathematical requirements of correlational analysis and factor analysis. There is no acceptable, unique solution available. The iterative approach discussed previously is not unique, because at one stage of the analysis, an assumption must be made about the rank (about the number of hypothetical factors). Then one can iteratively find a set of communalities that will fit that rank, but there is no assurance that the rank is correct. No solution is known in the case where both the number of factors and communality estimates are allowed to vary simultaneously. Also, even if one accepts particular ways of estimating the rank, the iterative approaches have their problems. Different initial estimates of communalities result in convergence to somewhat different iterative solutions for communalities and factor loadings. Also, the iterative approach sometimes leads to the conclusion that the communalities for some variables are greater than 1.0, which certainly casts suspicion on all attempts to obtain communalities through iterative approaches.

In addition to the iterative approach, another approach to estimating communalities is with multiple correlation. The squared multiple correlation (SMC) for estimating each variable from the remaining variables is obtained. Thus for variable 1 in a group of 20 variables, this would be the SMC for variables 2 through 20 with variable 1. Guttman (1956) has proved that the SMC is a *lower bound* for the communality. If the rank of a matrix is less than the number of variables, h^2 for any variable will be at least as large as the SMC for that variable. There are two major difficulties with the use of SMCs as estimates of communalities. First, they obviously determine one type of common variance, the variance that a particular variable has in common with the other variables in a matrix. However, this is not the intuitive concept of common variance that many people have in mind. To many people, common variance concerns how much a particular variable has in common with a set of hypothetical factors, not just how much it has in common with the variables in a particular study. A second problem with the use of SMCs is that they do not reproduce the expected results in artificial problems where stated sets of factor loadings are used to generate tables of correlations. In those cases SMCs seldom reproduce the initial loadings used to obtain the artificial matrices, and thus SMCs do not entirely match the intuitive concept of common factors. If, however, one steadfastly refuses to place unities in the diagonal spaces of the correlation matrix, the use of SMCs is the most sensible approach currently available. The SMCs have the advantages of being (1) unique, (2) directly obtainable on computers, and (3) definitive of at least one type of common variance.

A third approach to the estimation of hypothetical factors is with Guttman's (1953) *image analysis*. Essentially this is undertaken as follows. For each variable in the data matrix, one substitutes an estimate of that variable from the remaining variables. The estimation is done with multiple regression. The estimated variables are then intercorrelated and factor-analyzed by one of the methods of condensation, the diagonal spaces of the correlation matrix being filled with SMCs. (A more direct approach is to make some mathematical transformations of the original correlation matrix, which is less laborious than having to transform the data matrix as described above. The required transformations are discussed by Guttman, 1953.) Although this is an interesting approach which may eventually find acceptance, it suffers from the same two difficulties as does the use of SMCs in the original matrix of correlations: it does not entirely fit the intuitive concept of common variance, and it does not generally reproduce the factors used to generate artificial matrices of correlations.

A fourth approach to deriving hypothetical factors is with the *maximum-likelihood* approach to factor analysis (Harman, 1960), about which more will be said in a later section of this chapter. Essentially what the method does is to obtain factors so as to provide the best estimate (in terms of the principle of maximum likelihood) of a hypothetical population correlation matrix from the actual correlation matrix at hand. A statistical test is available for judging the significance of residual matrices. The communality of each variable is defined as the sum of squared loadings over the statistically significant factors. The major problem with this approach is that the communality of each variable tends to increase as the number of persons tested is made larger and larger. This does not fit the usual concept of common-factor variance, which is thought to be independent of the number of persons tested.

There are numerous other possible models for deriving hypothetical factors, but none of these has led to acceptable solutions. The problem is that no one knows for sure how to define common-factor variance separately from the variance of unique factors. All estimates of communality tend to increase (e.g., SMCs) as the number of variables in the study is increased. If, by common-factor variance, one has in mind the SMC that a variable would have with an infinitely large random sample of variables, then if there were any sampling error at all, the SMC would approach unity (because of the tendency for the multiple correlation to take advantage of chance). If there were no sampling error, the SMC would equal the reliability of the variable in question.

This is because in an infinite sampling of variables, one would obtain alternative forms of all measures.

There simply is no way to cleanly define common-factor variance when the common factors are not completely specified by the variables at hand. Fortunately, however, the diagonal cells of the correlation matrix usually make little difference in the number and kinds of factors obtained. There have been numerous demonstrations that the results obtained with unities in the diagonal spaces tend to closely match the results obtained with different types of communality estimates (e.g., Tyler and Michael, 1958). Thus even though the use of unities in the correlation matrix tends to confound common variance and unique variance, the confounding usually is slight. This is particularly so when the number of variables is relatively large (say, 20 or more), as it is in most analyses. In this case one can take numbers from zero to 1.0 at random, place them in the diagonal spaces, and still not greatly affect the loadings obtained on the several most prominent factors.

Unless, and until, someone develops a cleaner definition of common-factor variance, it is strongly recommended that factors be thought of as actual linear combinations of variables, in which case unities are placed in the diagonal spaces of the correlation matrix. This approach has its feet on the ground both theoretically and mathematically.

statistical decisions

Factor analysis in psychology has, as the name implies, been considered mainly as a mathematical method of analysis rather than as a statistical tool, in the stricter meaning of the term. This is the way that the author thinks it should remain. There are, however, points in factor analysis where decisions must be made regarding the statistical confidence to be placed in results. Chief among these is the question of when to stop factoring. The answer is different in terms of whether the analysis is to test hypotheses concerning the existence of factors or to explore a set of variables for factors.

Regardless of which of the two types of analyses is being performed, one should make questions of sampling error trivial by employing a large sample of persons. Since there are so many opportunities to take advantage of chance in factor analysis, particularly when employing one of the methods of condensation prior to rotation, a good rule is to have at least ten times as many subjects as variables. Then there will be little sampling error, and as experience has shown (Harman, 1960; Sokal, 1959), there probably will be more "significant" factors than the investigator will care to interpret.

With methods for testing hypotheses, the chief method being with the use of group centroids, as many factors should be extracted as were hypothesized initially. The question then concerns whether or not the average loading on each factor is significantly high to lend confidence that the factor exists beyond the confines of the particular group of subjects. A highly conservative rule of thumb will usually suffice for that purpose. First, one computes the average correlation among the variables hypothesized to form a particular factor. If some of the variables were hypothesized to have negative loadings, signs of their correlations would be reversed in the proper columns and rows of the correlation matrix. The average value would be over all nondiagonal elements. This average value would then be compared with the usual standard error of a correlation coefficient. An example will help illustrate this rule of thumb. It is hypothesized that six variables form a factor. All correlations among the variables are positive, and the average correlation is .30. There are 300 subjects, and consequently the standard error for a correlation coefficient (not for the average correlation among variables) is approximately the reciprocal of the square root of 300. Then a correlation as low as .15 would be significant beyond the .01 level. Thus one could have a great deal of confidence in a factor based on an average correlation of .30. If the factor does not possess a high degree of confidence by this very conservative standard, either the number of persons is too small to provide meaningful results or the variables are related so weakly that substantial factor loadings probably cannot be obtained.

Statistical tests have been developed for the number of factors obtained in employing the method of principal axes in stepwise solutions. These methods are summarized by Burt (1952), Harman (1960), and Maxwell (1959). After each principal axis is extracted, a test of statistical significance is applied to the residual matrix. If the residuals are significantly different from zero, an additional factor is extracted, and the test is applied to the resulting matrix of residual coefficients. In a stepwise solution, another approach is with the method of maximum likelihood mentioned previously (which is described in detail by Harman, 1960). The fault with this method, though, is that it strains even the best of high-speed computers, and to date there are only a few examples of its use.

In spite of the mathematical elegance of statistical methods used to determine the number of factors for principal axes and for the maximum-likelihood method, such methods are of little use in empirical research. They are far too liberal in determining the number of factors. This is made quite clear by the examples given by Sokal (1959) and by Harman (1960). For example, in one problem where it makes psychological sense to obtain only three factors, the method of maximum likelihood says that there are five "significant" factors (Harman, 1960, pp. 378–379). To use these methods of determining the number of factors would in some cases lead psychologists to work with factors where the highest loading is less than .20. In that case no variable would have as much as 4 percent of its variance attributable to the factor. In such instances how would one ever interpret the factor properly or know how to investigate the factor in subsequent studies?

The purpose in factor analysis should *not* be to find all the factors that are statistically significant. If the number of subjects is large, the number of statistically significant factors tends to approach the number of variables. This is particularly so if unities are placed in the diagonal spaces of the correlation matrix preparatory to employing one of the methods of condensation. The purpose in factor analysis should be to test for, or discover, factors that can be reasonably well defined by the actual variables. This relates to the problem of estimating factor scores, which will be discussed in a later section.

A conservative rule of thumb for accepting a factor as "real" is as follows. No attempt is made to make decisions about the significance of unrotated loadings, e.g., as obtained from the centroid method or the method of principal axes. If ample computer services are available, a useful rule is to rotate one-third as many factors as there are variables. Thus if there are 30 variables, one would derive 10 factors by the method of principal axes and then rotate those by, say, the varimax method. It is suggested that one-third as many factors as variables be employed because seldom would more factors either have substantial loadings or be of scientific interest.

After factors are rotated, the next step is to note the number of variables that have loadings of .30 or higher. It is doubtful that loadings of any smaller size should be taken seriously, because they represent less than 10 percent of the variance. Imagine in a particular study that on factor 5 there are six variables with loadings of .30 or higher. Since these variables must be used to interpret the factor, it is proper to ask how well the factor is defined by these variables. This is determined by the multiple correlation of the six variables with the factor, about which more will be said in a later section. After that multiple correlation is computed, a conservative rule of thumb for accepting the factor as "real" is obtained as follows. First, to partially take account of the extent to which advantage is taken of chance, the obtained multiple correlation should be "shrunk" with the use of Eq. (5-23). In Eq. (5-23), rather than use the number of variables employed to compute the multiple correlation, one should use the total number of variables in the study. Then the shrunken multiple correlation is compared with the standard error for a multiple correlation. So that one can have any real confidence in the factor, the shrunken multiple correlation should be considerably larger than the multiple correlation which would be significant at the .01 level. Thus if a multiple correlation of .30 would be significant at the .01 level, one would hope to have a shrunken multiple correlation of at least .50.

The results of any factor analysis should be "more significant" than would be required by any exact statistical test. If the variables used to interpret a factor do not have a multiple correlation with the factor of at least .50, the estimates of factor scores will be highly inexact. Since there are very few instances in which an investigator would attempt to interpret a factor which failed to meet that criterion, the question is one of how much confidence can be placed in a multiple correlation of .50. If there are at least ten times as many people as variables, such a multiple correlation will be highly significant in most instances.

Worrying about exact tests of statistical significance or employing the conservative rules of thumb discussed above, however, is of far less importance than considering the "reality" of factors as a problem of replication. No factor analysis should be an end in itself. If the results are interesting, some of the same variables will be included in other investigations. Then it will be found to what extent the variables used to define a factor actually "hang together" and measure something different from variables used to define other factors. This can be illustrated in the problem where two factors are thought sufficient to explain most of the common variance among 20 supposed measures of anxiety. Suppose it is found that three variables have a high multiple correlation with one factor and three other variables have a high multiple correlation with the second factor. Scores on these variables are then used to estimate the two factors, and these estimates of factor scores are used as dependent measures in controlled experiments. In addition to examining the treatment effects, the experimenter should also intercorrelate the six measures used to define the two factors. If correlations among the three variables used to define a factor are substantial and correlations between the variables belonging to the two factors are much smaller, this is direct evidence that the factors are "real."

estimation of factor scores

If factors are linear combinations of actual variables, factor scores for people can be perfectly "estimated." This is the case, for example, when unities are placed in the diagonal spaces of the correlation matrix and factor analysis is undertaken with the centroid method, the method of principal axes, the square-root method, or the multiple-group method. With information provided by the matrix of factor loadings, equations can be established for determining factor scores from the data matrix. (The nature of these equations is discussed in Harman, 1960, and in Thurstone, 1947.) Essentially these equations concern a multiple-regression analysis in which the factor is the variable to be predicted and all the variables are the predictors. Each loading is a correlation with the factor, and correlations among the predictor variables are obtained from the original matrix of correlations. A different prediction equation would be required for each factor. When unities are placed in the diagonal spaces of the correlation matrix preparatory to the analysis, the multiple correlations of variables with the factors are all precisely 1.0. So in this instance one uses multiple regression in the trivial case where all multiple correlations are known in advance to be 1.0.

With any of the methods concerned with hypothetical factors, scores of people on the factors can only be estimated, not directly measured. This is true in Spearman's general-factor solution, the bifactor solution, and any method of condensation where values other than unities are placed in the diagonal spaces. The preferred procedure in these cases is to estimate factor scores with multiple-regression analysis, in the same way it is done when factors are actual linear combinations of variables. This can be done either with all the variables in the analysis or with a subset of the variables. In either case, however, the multiple correlation will almost always be less than 1.0, and in most cases it will be considerably less.

The estimation of factor scores is a crucial step in the continuing explication of constructs. For example, suppose it is found that two factors do a good job of accounting for the correlations among 20 supposed measures of anxiety. The next step would be to use the two factors in controlled experiments and in investigations concerning correlations among sources of individual differences. Unless there are continuing investigations of this kind, a factor analysis does little to advance our science. A very important point, however, is that in such continuing investigations of the factors, it is quite unlikely that all 20 tests will be employed. The hope in factor analysis is to reduce a larger collection of variables to a smaller set of "potent explainers." In the example above, it might be found that three tests relate strongly to one factor of anxiety and another three tests relate strongly to the second factor of anxiety. These tests can then be used to estimate factor scores in subsequent studies. In this instance, however, factor scores could only be estimated, and not perfectly so. This is true regardless of whether unities were placed in diagonal spaces of the correlation matrix. If unities were employed, even if each factor has a perfect multiple correlation with *all* the variables, a perfect multiple correlation with only some of them is not likely.

For the above reasons, in nearly all empirical studies it is better to think of *estimating* factor scores rather than of measuring them directly. Of course, if unities are employed, one can directly measure factor scores for the particular people who participated in the factor analysis, but this is the trivial case. If a factor is of any importance, it will be used in many investigations, and employing all the tests used to define the factor initially is not feasible.

That factor scores usually must be estimated by multiple regression is a fact which provides some perspectives on other issues in factor analysis. Frequently only one variable is used to estimate factor scores in subsequent investigations, e.g., only one test is used to measure a factor of anxiety in a controlled experiment on the effects of anxiety on the rate of solving particular types of problems. For two interrelated reasons, this usually is bad practice. First, a variable seldom loads so heavily on a factor that it provides precise estimates of factor scores. In this instance the "multiple correlation" with the factor is simply the loading of the variable on the factor. Then, even if the variable has a loading as high as .70, only about 50 percent of the variance of the factor can be accounted for by the variable. Second, estimates of factor scores in this instance would be heavily weighted by the unique variance of the particular variable. Almost always, at least two variables are needed to estimate a factor. The multiple correlation between the two variables is likely to be considerably higher than the loading of either, and combining the two variables in multiple regression averages out some of the unique variance in each variable.

At the other extreme, in continuing studies of a factor, it seldom is feasible to use more than three or four variables to estimate factor scores. This has two important implications. The first is that one should look carefully at the multiple correlation of the variables with the factor. Regardless of how "statistically significant" the factor may be in other ways, if that multiple correlation is not high, the factor is not ready for continuing investigations. If the multiple correlation is less than .70, one is in trouble. In that instance the error variance in estimating the factor would be approximately the same as the valid variance. As a very minimum, one should be quite suspicious of factor estimates obtained with a multiple correlation of less than .50, because in that case less than 25 percent of the variance of factor scores can be predicted from the variables. Then one could not trust the variables as actually representing the factor, and it would be of doubtful value to perform further studies supposedly concerning the factor. For these reasons, decisions about the acceptance or rejection of a factor as "real" should be based on the size of the multiple correlation with the factor for those variables which will be used to estimate the factor in subsequent studies. Thus mere statistical significance of a factor is not nearly as important as having a factor that can be estimated well from a relatively small subset of the variables. When the latter standard is employed, factors frequently are rejected that would appear "highly significant" by the former standard (assuming that there are at least 10 subjects per variable). Of course, even if a factor fails to meet the requirement of having a high multiple correlation, it might be investigated with new variables in a new factor analysis. But the factor should be "released" to other scientists only when good estimates of factor scores are possible.

A second implication of the fact that only a relatively small subset of variables can be used in continuing investigations of a factor concerns the rotation of factors in stepwise analyses. As was mentioned previously, the estimation of factors usually results in an additional rotation, one beyond that performed in the rotational process per se. If, for example, three variables are used to define a factor, in essence one is placing a factor axis among those variables. If the factor is estimated by a simple sum of scores on three variables, it is rotated to the centroid of those three variables. Then even if factors are kept orthogonal in the rotations, the estimates of factor scores are likely to be correlated.

factor-analytic designs

The problem of factor analysis was posed with respect to a data matrix, which was illustrated in Table 9-1. The columns of the table were different variables, and rows of the table showed the scores of persons on those variables. The problem was posed in terms of the correlations between column variables. This type of analysis is referred to as R technique, which is to be distinguished from numerous other possibilities for factor-analytic designs. These possibilities have been discussed in detail by Cattell (1952). A variant of R technique is to have the *same* person on each row of the data matrix, showing changes in scores at different points in time and/or under different circumstances. An example would be in the study of physiological processes in one person from day to day. Measurements on the same variables are made each day for a period of several months. These measures are intercorrelated and factor-analyzed. A factor would concern a group of physiological variables that tend to go up and down together from day to day. This variant of R technique is called P technique, the P standing for observations at different points in time. It is similar to R technique in that it concerns the factor analysis of correlations among variables. P technique also can be employed when each row of the data matrix shows the average scores of a group of subjects on different occasions. This might be useful in the study of longitudinal trends in physiological processes or personality characteristics for people in general.

In contrast to R technique and P technique, there are designs concerning correlations among the rows of the data matrix rather than among the columns. These methods are frequently referred to as "transposed" or "inverted" analyses. The parent name for these different possibilities is Q technique. A detailed discussion of Q technique is given by Stephenson (1953).

A study performed by Fiedler (1950) will serve to illustrate Q technique. (A more detailed description of Q technique will be given in Chapter Fourteen.) The study was of 60 psychotherapists who represented three different approaches to treatment. Each therapist rated his agreement with a list of statements concerning different ways of conducting therapy sessions. The columns of the data matrix related to the statements, and the rows showed the ratings of each therapist. Scores were standardized *over statements* for each therapist separately, not over therapists for each statement as would be the case in R technique. Correlations were computed between therapists, showing the relative amount of agreement between therapists. Factor analyses were then performed to describe the different schools of thought.

A variant of Q technique, which some call O technique, is to have the same person on all rows of the data matrix, showing different scores on the same variables for the same individual on different occasions. This is the same type of data matrix employed in P technique. With O technique, however, one correlates rows of the data matrix with one another rather than doing this for columns. An example of this variant of Q technique is a study by the author (Nunnally, 1955), in which an individual was required to make ratings of her self-concept from 16 different points of view, e.g., "the way you really are," and "the way your parents view you." These were intercorrelated, resulting in a 16×16 matrix of correlations. A factor analysis found "three selves," and changes in these were investigated over the course of psychotherapy.

In both R technique and Q technique, one must be careful how scores are standardized before correlations are computed. In the typical R-technique study, common sense indicates how this should be done. Scores should be standardized over people separately for each variable. Essentially the same should be done in P technique, in which case scores are standardized over occasions for one person (or group of persons) on each variable separately.

In the Q-technique family of designs, more thought is required to determine the proper approach to standardization. An example would be where the columns represented different tests of ability and rows showed the scores of different subjects. It would be misleading to standardize over tests for each person and then intercorrelate persons. Since the tests probably would have different means over persons, the correlations between persons would be strongly influenced by these mean differences. In that case the proper approach would be to first standardize over persons on each variable and then restandardize over variables for each person. This would remove spurious effects because of differences in means and standard deviations of variables. In some types of studies, this can be accomplished by the method of collecting data. This cannot be done with tests of ability, but it can be done with ratings concerning preferences and agreement. One does this by forcing all subjects to have the same mean rating and the same standard deviation of ratings. The method for doing this is called the Q *sort*, which will be discussed in detail in Chapter Fourteen.

There are some obvious differences between R technique and Q technique. In the former, the variables have factor loadings, and the persons have factor scores, and vice versa in Q technique. Another obvious difference between the two approaches concerns the number of persons and variables required for meaningful analyses. In R technique, the number of persons should be much larger than the number of variables, and vice versa in Q technique. Whereas in the former, it is meaningful to apply inferential statistics to correlations, this poses some problems in the latter. In Q technique, the sample size consists of the number of variables, and to employ that as N in the usual formulas (e.g., significance of difference from zero correlation) forces one to consider random samples of variables in a specifiable domain, which, to say the least, is a matter that is not well thought out at the present time.

There have been numerous attempts to show that nothing can be obtained from Q-technique designs that could not be obtained from R-technique designs. For several reasons, this is not correct. In certain hypothetical cases there are some equations that will permit a transformation of the results obtainable in Q technique to results obtainable in R technique, and vice versa (Burt, 1941). The circumstances in which that can be done, however, are not likely to prevail in actual studies. Second, even if there were precise mathematical relations in all cases, the rotational choice in one method of analysis probably would not lead to the most desirable solution in the other method of analysis. Third, and most important, the different approaches have very different implications for psychological theory. If a person has theories concerning factors among variables, he should use R technique. If he has theories concerning factors among persons, he should employ Q technique. Even if it were true that transforming one type of analysis to the other usually would be possible, this would be beside the point. To think otherwise would be analogous to thinking that because the same machine could be used to measure heart rate and brain waves, it would make no difference which were measured.

The difference between the two basic approaches to factor analysis is in terms of the ease with which they can be fitted into psychological theories. The constructs in most theories concern clusters of related variables (e.g., anxiety, intelligence), and R technique is the proper approach. In contrast, Q technique concerns clusters of persons, and each factor is a hypothetical "person." The hypothetical person is defined in terms of "his" complete set of responses to the variables involved. Factors must be thought of as idealized "types" of persons, and the loadings of actual people specify to what extent they are mixtures of the various types. Such constructs simply are more difficult for most psychologists to "think with" than are the constructs of concern in R technique. For this reason, the R-technique family of possible analyses is used much more frequently than the Q-technique family of analyses. There are, however, some types of studies where Q technique is sensible and where interesting results have been obtained in studies to date (some of these are mentioned in Chapter Fourteen). Q technique also is closely related to profile analysis, which will be discussed in the next chapter.

cluster analysis

The purpose of cluster analysis is very similar to that of factor analysis. As the name implies, cluster analysis consists of methods of classifying variables into groups, or clusters. A cluster consists of variables that correlate highly with one another and have comparatively low correlations with variables in other clusters. This is essentially what a factor is in factor analysis. Instead of formal methods of factor analysis, however, there are some ways of searching for clusters in the correlation matrix. An approximate approach is as follows. First, if some variables have a negative sum of correlations in the correlation matrix, one reflects variables so as to obtain a maximum sum of positive correlations for the matrix as a whole. Next, the highest correlation in the matrix is found. The two variables involved form the nucleus of the first cluster. Then one looks for variables that have high correlations with both of the first two variables and includes them in the cluster.

One obtains the nucleus for the second cluster by finding two variables that correlate highly but have low correlations with members of the first cluster. Variables that correlate highly with the two variables serving as the nucleus of the second cluster are included in the cluster. Then one proceeds in this way to search for a third cluster, and so on.

If clusters were quite clear, as is seldom the case, it would be better to use cluster analysis than to go the long way round through formal procedures of factor analysis. For a number of reasons, however, this frequently is not the best strategy. When the number of variables is small, one frequently can see the patterns of relationship easily simply by inspecting the correlation matrix, which was the case for the six-variable problem in Table 9-6. When there are many variables in the study (e.g., more than 20), it is easy to get lost in the maze of correlations and become entirely confused about which variables should be placed in clusters. For problems containing large numbers of variables, numerous cut-and-try methods have been proposed for locating clusters. McQuitty (1961) has developed a number of rather elaborate computational routines for that purpose, and his article provides references to some of the major approaches to cluster analysis. There are two major problems with these methods. First, they are mathematically "messy." Numerous, semiarbitrary decisions must be made about the number of clusters and the composition of clusters. Second, these methods require as much computational time as a formal factor analysis would.

If one likes to think of all factor analysis as being forms of cluster analysis (a point of view which has considerable merit), the multiple-group approach to factor analysis is recommended. If clusters are hypothesized in advance, the multiple-group method can test for how well the clusters actually hang together. If clusters are not defined a priori with regard to hypotheses about constructs, one can search for clusters with the multiple-group method. A first group centroid can be placed among those variables that have the highest correlations with one another. The residual matrix is obtained, and a second factor is placed among those variables that have high residual coefficients with one another, and so on for additional factors.

Whether one uses the cut-and-try methods of cluster analysis or formal methods of factor analysis, in the end all factors can be thought of as clusters. As was mentioned previously regarding the estimation of factor scores, almost always no more than three or four variables are used to measure a factor in studies subsequent to the factor analysis. Then, for all intents and purposes, those several variables define the factor, and in practice, a factor is a linear combination of the scores on a cluster of variables.

ad-lib factoring

In obtaining successive factors from a particular matrix of correlations, it is not necessary to employ only one method of factoring. It is entirely legitimate, for example, to extract the first factor by the method of principal axes, the second factor by the centroid method, the third factor by the square-root method, and the fourth factor by still another method. Factor analysis can be applied to the successive matrices of residual coefficients without regard to the methods of factoring used to obtain the factors. When there are hypotheses to guide the analysis, an ad-lib approach to factoring offers a flexible method for "taking apart" the common variance among variables. An example of how this is done comes from a study by Nunnally and Hodges (1965) in which the variables were measures of individual differences in word association. Each variable concerned the tendency to give a particular type of associate. Prior to the analysis, three scales had been studied extensively, and these were included as variables in the factor analysis. The other variables in the analysis were new scales intended to measure five new factors. The first step in the analysis was to employ the square-root method. The three old scales were used successively as pivots. This tested for the relative independence of the old scales and removed the variance of the old scales from the variance of the new scales. The group-centroid method was then applied to the residual matrix. Five group centroids were placed among the five hypothesized groups of variables. The complete-centroid method was then applied to the resulting residual matrix, in an effort to discover factors that had not been hypothesized originally. Rotations were made of the complete-centroid factors by the varimax method, but the three factors derived by the square-root method and the five factors obtained by the group-centroid method were not included in the rotations. A flexible approach to factor analysis of this kind allows one to directly test the explanatory power of hypotheses regarding the nature of psychological constructs. It is easy to let good ideas about a domain of variables get lost in the brutish mechanics of a ready-made, rigid approach to factoring.

higher-order factors

If correlated factors are obtained, it is possible to factor the correlations so as to obtain higher-order factors. The original factors are called "first-order factors." Say, for example, that 10 first-order factors are obtained and the correlations among those factors are known. Then the 10×10 matrix of correlations among factors can be submitted to any desired method of factor analysis, and the obtained factors can be rotated. In this example, say that 4 factors are obtained. These would be called "second-order factors." The correlations among the second-order factors also could be analyzed to obtain third-order factors. A first-order factor is a linear combination of the variables; a second-order factor is a linear combination of the first-order factors; and so on for higher-order factors. Since there is a direct link between the original variables and higher-order factors, there are methods for computing the loadings of all variables on higher-order factors (Harman, 1960).

For two reasons, the author has somewhat ambivalent feelings about the usefulness of higher-order factors. First, they tend to confuse nonspecialists. The average psychologist has difficulty in understanding first-order factors, and this difficulty is increased with higher-order fac-

multivariate analysis

tors. This is not such a problem if loadings are interpreted only with respect to the highest order of factors investigated—e.g., if the loadings of all variables are shown and discussed only for the second-order factors. If, however, the average psychologist must interpret loadings on first- and second-order factors, he is likely to make some misinterpretations. Also, if factor analysis is partly founded on the principle of parsimony, it is reasonable to question the parsimony of having different orders of factors. For the sake of parsimony, the fewer the factors, the better; but the use of higher-order factors adds more and more factors. In this way one could end up with more factors than variables.

A second reason for the author's ambivalent feelings about the use of higher-order factors is that, in some cases, approximately the same information can be obtained in a simpler way. This is particularly the case with second-order factors. Loadings on a second-order general factor mainly reflect the tendency of variables to correlate positively or negatively with the other variables. Much the same information is obtained from the loadings of variables on a first-order factor obtained by either the centroid method or the method of principal axes. There is nothing wrong with interpreting such loadings on a general factor even if that factor subsequently is rotated in conjunction with other factors. As a final observation about the employment of higher-order factors, if first-order factors are kept orthogonal, there is, of course, no possibility of obtaining higher-order factors.

comparisons of factors in different analyses

An important problem in research is to determine the similarity of factors in different analyses. For example, in the literature, one frequently finds discussions of whether two factors from two different analyses actually are the same. In deriving methods for settling such issues, it is important to remember that factors are linear combinations of the variables. These are to be distinguished from factor loadings, which are the correlations of variables with the factors. It is a mistake to argue about the comparability of factors in terms of the patterns of loadings in two analyses. One proposal, for example, has been to correlate the loadings on factors in different analyses to measure their comparability. Various other indices have been proposed for comparing two matrices of factor loadings (Pinneau and Newhouse, 1964). These, however, all miss the point, because the loadings are not the factors. It is easy to rig an example where the loadings on two orthogonal factors in the *same* analysis correlate highly. One can do this by drawing two orthogonal axes and then putting in points for variables so that a high correlation is obtained.

The proper method of comparing factors in different analyses is to compare *factor scores* in the different analyses. This can be done straightforwardly only if the same persons are involved in the different analyses. If such is the case, it does not matter whether all the variables are the same in the different analyses, only some of the variables are the same, or all the variables are different. The first step is to obtain factor scores on all factors. For this, it is better to use all the variables in the analysis to obtain factor scores than to estimate them from subsets of the variables. The next step is to correlate the factor scores in the different analyses. The comparability of factors is judged by the sizes of the correlations. If only some of the persons participate in two studies, one can obtain an approximate notion of the comparability of factors by correlating factor scores for those persons.

If different persons are involved in the different analyses, it is arguable what method should be used to compare factors. If in that case the variables also are different in the different analyses, there is no conceivable way of comparing factors. If the variables are the same, one method of comparing factors is as follows. To obtain factor scores in one analysis, a set of weights must be applied to the variables. The set of weights required in one analysis can be applied to the scores of the different people in a different analysis. In each analysis, this would then provide two sets of factor scores—the weights for one obtained from the analysis of a different group of subjects. The correlations between these two sets of factor scores could be used to judge the comparability of factors in the analysis of the same variables in different groups of subjects. If only some of the same variables are involved in the two analyses, an approximate test of comparability can be made as follows. Factor scores are estimated from only those variables that appear in both analyses, if that is possible, and correlations of the type described above are computed between the sets of factor scores.

how to fool yourself with factor analysis

It would be appropriate at this point to mention some cautions regarding the use of factor analysis. One way to fool yourself with factor analysis is to ignore the correlations that are used to define a factor. In some cases the variables used to define a factor have correlations near zero with one another. This can happen because of the successive partialing that goes on in the derivation of factors. An example will indicate how this occurs. Suppose that two variables each have loadings of .50 on one of two factors; on the second factor, one variable has a loading of .50 and the other has a loading of − .50. If one were not careful, he might use the two variables to define the first factor, but the pattern of loadings on the two factors would stem from a correlation of zero between the two variables. Mathematically there is nothing wrong with this eventuality, but it might lead to some misinterpretations. It is mathematically possible for variables that have very low correlations to have substantial loadings on a factor, but if those variables are used to define a factor in studies subsequent to the factor analysis, people will tend to expect substantial correlations among the variables.

A second way to fool yourself with factor analysis relates to the first way. It is easy to overinterpret the meaning of small factor loadings, e.g., those below .40. It must be remembered that in some methods of factor analysis, such as the centroid method, factor vectors are placed so as to make loadings on successive factors as large as possible. Even if the average correlation in the matrix (disregarding signs) is rather low, the factor loadings may look substantial. This is particularly the case when unities are placed in the diagonal spaces of the correlation matrix. As an extreme example, suppose that there are only four variables and all correlations are precisely zero. In this case, think what the first centroid factor loadings will be. Each column sum is 1.0. The sum of elements in the matrix is 4.0. Each variable will then have a loading of .50 on the first factor. When unities are placed in the diagonal spaces and the number of variables is small, one should be cautious in interpreting small loadings. As was advised previously, the safe procedure is to inspect the original matrix of correlations to ensure that variables used to define a factor actually have substantial correlations.

A third way to fool yourself with factor analysis is to misinterpret the meaning of orthogonal factors. Although the factors themselves are uncorrelated, this does not mean that estimated factor scores are uncorrelated. If unities are placed in the diagonal spaces and all variables in the study are used to obtain (not estimate) factor scores, the factor scores will be uncorrelated; but this is seldom the way factor scores are obtained. Usually, they are only estimated, not obtained directly. This is true in all cases where anything other than unity is placed in each diagonal space of the correlation matrix prior to factoring. Even if unities are placed in the diagonal spaces, usually, for practical purposes, factors are estimated by no more than four variables. In these cases the estimated factor scores are likely to correlate substantially even if the factors themselves are orthogonal. Consequently, one should be careful in using the word "orthogonal" to discuss a particular set of factors.

A fourth way to fool yourself with factor analysis is to employ variables that are experimentally dependent, which can occur in a number of ways. One way this occurs is in employing variables that have overlapping items. This most frequently happens in personality inventories, where it is common practice to derive a number of different scales from the same items. An outstanding example is in the Minnesota Multiphasic Personality Inventory (MMPI), where numerous scales are based on the same items. The overlapping items force correlations among the scales, which produce "factors." A study by Shure and Miles (1965) showed that when overlapping items are removed from the scales, the factor structure of the MMPI is quite different from what was thought. Another way to obtain experimental dependence is by including in the analysis various combinations of the separate variables. This would be the case, for example, if one variable equaled the difference between two other variables. The difference scores necessarily would correlate with the two variables used to obtain the differences, which would tend to confuse the results of a factor analysis. Generally it is best to avoid any form of experimental dependence among variables employed in factor analysis. The intention is to investigate "natural" correlations among variables, not the correlations that are forced through experimental dependence.

A fifth way to fool yourself with factor analysis concerns the selection of subjects. If subjects are relatively heterogeneous with respect to age, sex, and education, factors sometimes are produced by differences in those regards. Whether or not one should permit samples of persons to be heterogeneous with respect to such variables depends on the population over which the results of factor analysis are to be generalized. For example, if the factors are to be interpreted with respect to individual differences in children *within* particular age levels, the sample of children investigated in the factor analysis should be relatively homogeneous with respect to age. On the other hand, if one is interested in factors relating to developmental trends in children, the sample of children should vary over the age range under consideration.

Regarding the sex of subjects, one of the truisms in psychology is that males and females tend to differ with respect to almost everything. If both sexes are included in an analysis, it is wise to standardize scores separately for the two before correlations are computed. If that is not done, sex should be included as another variable in the analysis. Either group can be given a score of 1, and the other group can be given a score of zero. The correlation of sex with the other variables can be observed. The influence of sex can then be removed by the square-root method, and factor analysis can be done on the matrix of residual coefficients. Unless one is specifically interested in factors relating to age and education, it is wise to employ groups that are rather homogeneous in those regards. Otherwise, one often finds large general factors that disappear when more homogeneous groups are studied. Rather than seek homogeneous groups, another approach is to include age and years of education as additional variables in the analysis and to remove their influence by the square-root method.

an outlook on factor analysis

More important than an understanding of the technical details of factor analysis is a proper outlook on the methods. Factor analysis is neither a royal road to truth, as some apparently feel, nor necessarily an adjunct to shotgun empiricism, as others claim. Since it usually is necessary to combine scores on a number of variables to obtain valid measures of constructs, some method is required for determining the legitimacy of particular methods of combining variables. Important in determining this legitimacy are the patterns of correlations among variables. Factor analysis is nothing more than a set of mathematical aids to the examination of patterns of correlations, and for that purpose, it is indispensable.

SUGGESTED ADDITIONAL READINGS

Cattell, R. B. The three basic factor-analytic research designs—their interrelations and derivatives. *Psychol. Bull.*, 1952, **49**, 499–520.

Harman, H. H. *Modern factor analysis.* Chicago: Univer. Chicago Press, 1960.

Horst, P. *Factor analysis of data matrices.* New York: Holt, 1965.

Maxwell, A. E. Statistical methods in factor analysis. *Psychol. Bull.*, 1959, **56**, 228–235.

CHAPTER ELEVEN

PROFILE ANALYSIS, DISCRIMINATORY ANALYSIS, AND MULTIDIMENSIONAL SCALING

Although factor analysis is used more frequently than any other form of multivariate analysis, it is only one of a number of types of multivariate analysis that are useful in psychological measurement. The three classes of multivariate analysis to be discussed in this chapter do not, by any means, exhaust the multivariate methods that are available, but they are the ones that are employed most frequently in addition to factor analysis. Like factor analysis, profile analysis and discriminatory analysis are concerned with the scaling of people. Multidimensional scaling is primarily concerned with the scaling of stimuli rather than the scaling of people. It is employed when data fail to "fit" the models for unidimensional scaling of stimuli discussed in Chapter Two. First will be discussed profile analysis and discriminatory analysis, and then the final section of the chapter will be devoted to multidimensional scaling.

Like factor analysis, profile analysis and discriminatory analysis are concerned with a rectangular data matrix, with variables appearing on the columns of the matrix and persons appearing on the rows. The major purpose of factor analysis is to examine relations between the columns to test for, or discover, clusters of variables. Each such cluster consists of variables that tend to measure the same thing and to measure something different from what is measured by other clusters. Instead of being concerned with relations among the columns (variables), profile analysis and discriminatory analysis are concerned with relations among the rows (persons). Just as factor analysis is mainly concerned with clusters of variables, profile analysis and discriminatory analysis are mainly concerned with clusters, or groups, of persons.

problems in profile analysis

"Profile analysis" is a generic term for *all* methods concerning groupings of persons. One class of problems in profile analysis is that in which the groups are known in advance of the analysis and the purpose is to distinguish the groups from one another on the basis of scores in the data matrix. For example, the problem would start with groups of normals, neurotics, and psychotics, and the purpose of the analysis would be to distinguish these three groups in terms of scores on a dozen tests. This class of problem concerns discriminatory analysis, which is concerned with a priori groupings of people and is one class of analysis in the more general family of profile analyses.

The other major class of problems in profile analysis occurs when groupings of people are not stated in advance of the analysis, in which case the purpose of the analysis is to "cluster" persons in terms of their profiles of scores. Thus discriminatory analysis is concerned with testing hypotheses about the extent to which a priori groups "hang together" in the data matrix, and the clustering of profiles is concerned with discovering groups of persons that "hang together." In the remainder of this section will be discussed some general features of score profiles, and following this will be separate sections on the clustering of profiles and discriminatory analysis.

CHARACTERISTICS OF SCORE PROFILES   The term "profile" apparently comes from the practice, in applied work with tests, of plotting scores on a battery of tests in terms of a graph or profile. Examples of profiles for two persons on six variables are shown in Figure 11-1. The variables can be thought of as six tests of ability, six measures of physiological responses to stress, or six measures of different traits relating to mental illness. For convenience, the variables are expressed as standard scores (standardized separately over all persons in the study), but this relates to an issue which will need to be discussed later.

There are three major types of information in the profile of scores for any person: level, dispersion, and shape. The *level* is defined by the mean score of the person over the variables in the profile. In Figure 11-1, for person a, one would obtain this by adding scores on the six variables and dividing that by 6, and one would do the same for person b. It can be seen that the level for a is higher than that for b. Without the application of other forms of analysis, the level is directly interpretable only if all variables are "pointed" in the same direction and only if they concern the same domain of behavior. This would be the case if all variables concerned different tests of reasoning and the profile were plotted so as to show high scores on the right and low scores on the left. The level is not directly interpretable if the variables are from very different domains of behavior, as would be the case if they consisted of two personality tests concerning mental illness, two reasoning tests, and measures of height and weight. Although it is conceivable that such a polyglot collection of variables would relate to the same construct, it is doubtful that a sensible interpretation could be made of the mean score (level) on those measures. Even if the variables all relate to the same domain of behavior, the level is difficult to interpret if variables are "pointed" in different directions. This would be the case with six tests concerning aspects of mental illness if on half the tests a high score indicated "sickness" and on the other tests a high score indicated adjustment.

As the word implies, the *dispersion* relates to how widely scores in a profile diverge from the average (level). Some speak of this as

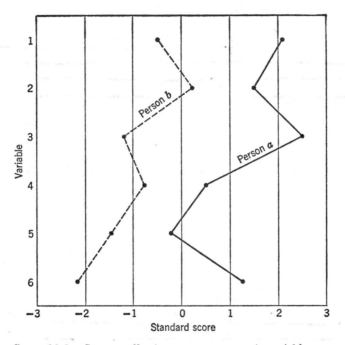

figure 11-1   *Score profiles for two persons on six variables.*

the *scatter* rather than as the dispersion. A measure of the dispersion is the standard deviation of scores for each person. In Figure 11-1, one would determine this for person a by subtracting his level from his scores on each of the six variables, squaring these six deviates, and obtaining the square root of their average. The same would be done to obtain the dispersion for person b.

Whereas under the conditions stated previously it is possible to make a direct interpretation of level, this is difficult to do for the profile dispersion. It is difficult because the profile dispersions for people in general depend upon the correlations among variables in the profile. If high positive correlations exist among the variables, people in general will tend to have small dispersions. If the correlations among variables are low, the dispersions will tend to be relatively large. If some of the correlations are positive and others are negative, the dispersions will be even larger. The most sensible way to interpret the dispersion of scores for a particular person is to compare it with the dispersions of scores for other persons. For example, if person a has a much larger dispersion than person b on six physiological measures, it can rightly be concluded that person a is much more variable than person b. Also, although it is seldom done, the interpretation of profile dispersions is facilitated by obtaining a distribution of dispersions over people. The distribution could then be converted to percentiles, which could be used as a basis for interpreting the profile dispersions for particular persons.

The last remaining information in the profile, the *shape,* concerns the "ups and downs" in the profile. Even though two persons have the same level and dispersion, the high and low points for the two might be quite different. The shape is defined by the rank order of scores for each person. Thus in Figure 11-1, person a is highest in variable 3, next in variable 1, and so on to his lowest score, which is on variable 5. As can be seen, the order (the shape) is quite different for person b. In studies of human abilities, the shape indicates the particular talents of the person. In a controlled experiment, the shape indicates the dependent variables which are most sensitive to the effects of the experimental treatments on a particular person.

It should be obvious that level, shape, and dispersion are not entirely independent in samples of persons. If the level is either very high or very low, the dispersion must be relatively low. Thus one would expect to find at least a moderate curvilinear correlation over people between level and dispersion. Although shape is not related to level, in a sense it is related to the dispersion. If the dispersion is small, the ordering of variables for a person (the shape) may represent only tiny differences in performance. Also, if this is the case, the observed differences may be because of measurement error. (This point was discussed in Chapter Seven in terms of the reliability of linear combinations of variables.) Consequently, unless the dispersion is relatively large, it may be hazardous to interpret the shape of a particular profile.

It should be obvious that the physical appearance of a particular profile depends on the way variables are listed. Since it is arbitrary which variable is listed in which position, the physical appearance of the profile can be arbitrarily changed without affecting level, dispersion, or shape.

clustering of profiles

In spite of the considerable controversy in recent years over proper methods for clustering profiles, there are some straightforward methods for handling the problem. The problem starts with the measurement of N persons on k variables. The variables can be anything, but to place the problem in focus, imagine that each variable concerns a physiological response to stress. (Readers with different turns of mind can imagine that the variables are MMPI scales or tests of abilities.) The experimenter is curious regarding possible individual differences in patterns of responses, so he plots profiles for some of the subjects. He sees not only marked differences in levels, but also what appear to be marked differences in shapes. He would like to perform some type of analysis to determine whether or not people fall into different clusters regarding their measurements. This is the problem of clustering profiles.

MEASURES OF PROFILE SIMILARITY   Before it is possible to develop methods for clustering profiles, one must define measures of profile similarity. In the clustering of variables with factor analysis, the measure of relationship is the PM correlation coefficient. In some instances the PM coefficient has also been used to measure the similarity of profiles. This is what is done in Q technique, as it was described in the previous chapter. In our illustrative problem, the physiological measurements for each person would be standardized. The level would be subtracted from scores on each of the variables, and each deviation score would then be divided by the profile dispersion for that person. In the same way, the profiles for all persons would be standardized. (Keep in mind that this is very different from standardizing scores over persons on each variable. The probability is near zero that the two approaches to standardization would produce the same scores.) The PM correlation between two standardized profiles would be computed in the usual way, and the correlation would constitute one measure of the degree of relationship between two profiles.

If, however, it is important to consider profile level and profile dispersion, the PM correlation is not a proper measure of the degree of similarity of two profiles. The mechanics of computing the PM formula equate all profiles for level and dispersion. The level of all profiles is zero, and the standard deviation of all profiles is 1.0. Thus it is apparent that the PM coefficient is sensitive only to similarities in shape and not to similarities in level and dispersion. Two examples will indicate how this could produce misleading results. If a moron and a genius had exactly the same shapes of profiles on tests of abilities, the PM coefficient would be 1.00, but this would hide the fact that they differed markedly in level. If two persons had the same shape on profile variables and had the same level, the PM correlation would be 1.00, but this could hide the fact that they differed greatly in dispersion.

There are two primary standards in choosing any measure of relationship: first, it should include all the information important in making comparisons, and second, it should lend itself to powerful methods of mathematical analysis. The first is largely a matter of taste and judgment, but once the measure is selected, it may place severe limits on the methods of analysis that can legitimately be employed. _If it is thought wise to cluster profiles with consideration of level, dispersions, and shape, obviously the measure of relationship should consider all three types of information. (Later it will be argued that in some instances it is better to use measures of relationship that ignore one or more of the three sources of information._) Numerous measures have been proposed for this purpose (Cronbach and Gleser, 1953; Helmstadter, 1957; Muldoon and Ray, 1958).

An example will serve to illustrate one possible measure that considers level, dispersion, and shape. One obtains this measure by summing the absolute differences in scores for any two profiles. This would be zero for two identical profiles and would tend to grow larger as profiles differed in level, dispersion, or shape. Although this measure makes sense as a descriptive index, it suffers from the same fault as do most of the other proposed measures of profile similarity: it does not lend itself to powerful methods of analysis. (For the reasons why it does not, see Nunnally, 1962.)

THE DISTANCE MEASURE   The most appealing measure of profile similarity is the distance measure D which was proposed by Osgood and Suci (1952) and by Cronbach and Gleser (1953). _D is simply the generalized Pythagorean theorem_ for the distance between two points in Euclidean space. In the case of two persons and two variables, this is the length of the hypotenuse of a right triangle, as illustrated in Figure 11-2. The distance between the points for persons a and b is obtained as follows:

(11-1) $D_{ab}^2 = (X_{a1} - X_{b1})^2 + (X_{a2} - X_{b2})^2$

The square root of the above expression is the distance between points a and b. For any number of variables (k), the squared distance is as follows:

(11-2)
$$D_{ab}^2 = (X_{a1} - X_{b1})^2 + (X_{a2} - X_{b2})^2 + \cdots + (X_{ak} - X_{bk})^2$$
$$= \Sigma(X_{aj} - X_{bj})^2$$

The distance D between the two points corresponding to the profiles for two persons equals the square root of the sum of squared differences on the profile variables.

All the scores for one person on k variables serve to define one point in a k-space of variables, each variable being plotted as orthogonal to the others. The point for the person then summarizes all the information in the profile. Although there is no physical representation for such

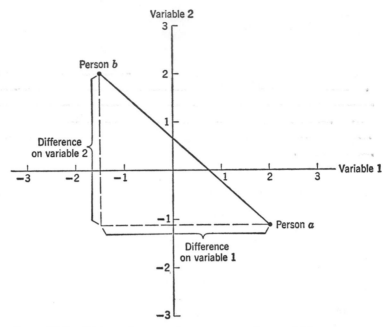

figure 11-2 *Distance between two persons on two variables.*

points when more than three variables (dimensions) are involved, the logic of measuring distance with D still holds.

D is intuitively appealing, because it considers profile level, dispersion, and shape. Also, it does lend itself to powerful methods of analysis. For these reasons, the author recommends, as others have, that problems of profile analysis be discussed in terms of the D measure. For reasons which will be discussed later, however, in deriving methods for the clustering of profiles, it is better to use a function of D rather than D itself.

Returning to the illustrative problem concerning profiles of physiological variables, the experimenter could use the D measure to search for clusters of people. First, he would compute D between all possible pairs of persons, forming an $N \times N$ symmetric matrix of distances. Persons with small D's have similar profiles, and persons with relatively large D's have dissimilar profiles. Numerous methods of cluster analysis have been employed for determining the numbers of clusters and the membership of each cluster. (For some proposed solutions, see Osgood, Suci, and Tannenbaum, 1957; Sawrey, Keller, and Conger, 1960.)

raw-score factor analysis

Most of the methods of cluster analysis that have been proposed for the analysis of matrices of distance measures suffer from the same

table 11-1 *Matrix of D's for points shown in Figure 11-3*

PERSON

	a	b	c	d	e	f
a	.0	1.0	1.4	7.8	7.1	6.4
b	1.0	.0	1.0	7.2	6.4	5.8
c	1.4	1.0	.0	6.4	5.7	5.0
PERSON d	7.8	7.2	6.4	.0	1.0	1.4
e	7.1	6.4	5.7	1.0	.0	1.0
f	6.4	5.8	5.0	1.4	1.0	.0

faults as do all such cut-and-try methods: they lack any general algebra, they are indeterminate, and they are computationally messy. Powerful methods for this purpose are available, which will be discussed in this section. The answer is to factor-analyze the raw-score cross products of pairs of profiles.

To set the issues in focus, imagine that a problem concerns the profiles of six persons on 10 physiological variables (or on 15 measures

figure 11-3 *Interpoint distances for six persons.*

of abilities). The distances D between all pairs of persons are obtained, and these are shown in Table 11-1 and plotted in Figure 11-3. In this hypothetical example, the distances were formed so that they could be exactly portrayed in a two-space, which would almost never be the case in actual research.

In looking at Figure 11-3 and Table 11-1, one can see that there are two clusters, defined, respectively, by persons a, b, and c, and by persons d, e, and f. If, in actual research, there were so few cases involved and such definite clusters were present, no refined method of analysis would be needed; but this is almost never the case. A method of analysis will be described which can recover those clusters and can be used equally well with any number of persons and regardless of the relative "visibility" of clusters.

It apparently is not widely known that matrices of D's such as that in Table 11-1 can be factored. The method was derived by G. J. Suci (Osgood, Suci, and Tannenbaum, 1957). Suci and this author cooperatively explored his method of factoring D and found it to be a special case of raw-score factor analysis. This is where a major misconception arises: some persons are evidently unaware that raw-score cross products can be factored in the same way that correlation coefficients are factored. The failure to realize that factor analysis is not restricted to correlation coefficients is either directly evident or implied in many papers concerning methods of clustering profiles.

AN EXAMPLE OF RAW-SCORE FACTOR ANALYSIS   Because of the unfamiliarity of factoring raw-score cross products, a worked-out example will be given. The first step is to obtain the sum of raw cross products over the profile variables. An example is as follows for the profiles of persons a and b on four variables:

	PERSON a	PERSON b	CROSS PRODUCTS
VARIABLE 1	1.5	1.0	1.5
VARIABLE 2	.5	2.0	1.0
VARIABLE 3	−2.0	−1.0	2.0
VARIABLE 4	1.2	−.5	−.6
SUM			3.9

The sum of cross products for persons a and b is 3.9. In the same way, the sum of cross products is obtained for all pairs of persons, resulting in a symmetric matrix of terms. It is said that these are sums of *raw* cross products because the mathematical procedures to be described place no limits on the scoring units employed for each variable. Later will be discussed the question of employing a common system of units for all variables, e.g., expressing all variables as standard scores as was done in Figure 11-1.

A hypothetical matrix of cross products for physiological variables is shown in Table 11-2. The matrix was constructed so as to be compatible with the D's shown in Table 11-1 and the plot of those distances shown in Figure 11-3. Actually, the matrix of cross products was constructed by working backward from the distances in Figure 11-3, but one could obtain them equally well by actually summing cross products on 10 physiological variables (or 15 tests of abilities). Each diagonal space contains the sum of cross products of a person with himself, which is simply the sum of squared scores over the profile variables.

(This is analogous to placing unities in the diagonal spaces of a correlation matrix preparatory to factoring correlation coefficients.) It will be noted that large sums of cross products in Table 11-2 correspond to small D's in Table 11-1, and vice versa. One could perform various types of cluster analysis on the matrix of cross products as well as on the matrix of distances, but there are much better ways to go at it.

How should one analyze the sums of cross products to obtain clusters? The answer is to factor-analyze, and *all* the methods used with correlation coefficients can be applied: square root, multiple group, centroid, principal axes, or whatever. In doing this, one applies the customary formulas in the customary ways. Let us see what a centroid analysis provides.

For the first centroid factor, one sums the elements in each column, finds the square root of the sum of the column sums, and divides this into each of the column sums. These are loadings on the first centroid factor in the raw-score space. One uses the first factor loadings to obtain a first set of residuals, reflects, extracts a second set of factor loadings, and continues in this manner until residuals are small (relative to the sizes of the original sums of cross products) or until enough factors have been obtained to satisfy one's curiosity.

By choosing a set of points in a two-space, one needs only two factors to explain the cross products, and consequently the second residuals differ from zero only by rounding errors in the computations. Also, as would necessarily be the case, the sums of squares of loadings in rows of the factor matrix are identical to the original diagonal elements in the matrix of cross products.

After raw-score factors are obtained, there is nothing to prevent rotating them in the same way that one rotates factors obtained from correlation matrices. (Also, there is nothing to prevent employing analytic methods of rotation such as those discussed in Chapter Nine.) In Table 11-2, an orthogonal transformation of centroid factors A and B is made to obtain rotated factors A_1 and B_1. The clusters shown in Figure 11-3 and Table 11-1 are clearly evidenced in the rotated factor loadings, and the factor loadings tell how strongly each person relates to each factor. In Figure 11-4, the rotated factor loadings are plotted, and it can be seen that the obtained set of interpoint distances is identical to that shown in Figure 11-3.

HOW RAW-SCORE FACTOR ANALYSIS WORKS   Variables in profiles (e.g., physiological measures or tests of abilities) can be considered as mutually orthogonal axes in Euclidean space. Each profile can be plotted as a point in the space, and D measures the distance of such points from one another. Raw-score factor analysis provides a basis (or semibasis) for the profile space; i.e., the factors provide a geometrical frame

table 11-2 *Raw-score cross products and factor solution for points shown in Figure 11-3*

CROSS PRODUCTS

		person				
	a	*b*	*c*	*d*	*e*	*f*
a	36	30	30	6	6	12
b	30	25	25	5	5	10
c	30	25	26	11	10	15
person *d*	6	5	11	37	31	32
e	6	5	10	31	26	27
f	12	10	15	32	27	29
column sums	120	100	117	122	105	125
first factor	4.58	3.81	4.46	4.65	4.00	4.77

FIRST RESIDUALS

	a	*b*	*c*	*d*	*e*	*f*
a	15.02	12.55	9.57	−15.30	−12.32	−9.85
b	12.55	10.48	8.01	−12.72	−10.24	−8.17
c	9.57	8.01	6.11	−9.74	−7.84	−6.27
person *d*	−15.30	−12.72	−9.74	15.38	12.40	9.82
e	−12.32	−10.24	−7.84	12.40	10.00	7.92
f	−9.85	−8.17	−6.27	9.82	7.92	6.25
column sums						
after reflection	74.61	62.17	47.54	75.36	60.72	48.28
second factor	−3.89	−3.24	−2.48	3.92	3.16	2.51

SECOND RESIDUALS

	a	*b*	*c*	*d*	*e*	*f*
a	−.11	−.05	−.08	−.05	−.03	−.09
b	−.05	−.02	−.03	−.02	.00	−.05
c	−.08	−.03	−.04	−.02	.00	−.05
person *d*	−.05	−.02	−.02	−.07	.01	−.02
e	−.03	.00	.00	.01	.01	−.01
f	−.09	−.05	−.05	−.02	−.01	−.05

of reference where no frame of reference existed originally. Because any sufficient basis preserves distances between points, the factor loadings preserve the original D's. In the example shown in Table 11-2, this can be tested by obtaining D's from the rotated factor loadings. This shows, for example, that the D between persons a and b is almost exactly 1.0, which is what was given in Table 11-1. Similarly, all the D's can be calculated from the matrix of centroid loadings or from the matrix of rotated loadings. If factoring is not complete, the factor matrix will serve to explain the bulk of the distances. Thus any informa-

CENTROID FACTORS

	A	B	h^2
a	4.58	−3.89	36
b	3.81	−3.24	25
c	4.46	−2.48	26
person d	4.65	3.92	37
e	4.00	3.16	26
f	4.77	2.51	29

TRANSFORMATION MATRIX

	A_1	B_1
A	.763	.647
B	−.647	.763

ROTATED FACTORS

	A_1	B_1
a	6.01	.00
b	5.00	−.01
c	5.01	1.00
person d	1.01	6.00
e	1.01	5.00
f	2.02	5.00

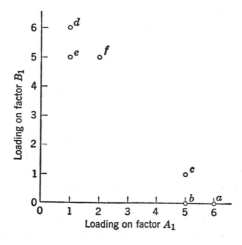

figure 11-4 *Loadings on rotated factors.*

tion regarding clusters that could be obtained from a matrix of D's also can be obtained from a matrix of cross products, and whereas it is difficult to directly factor matrices of D's, this is very easy with matrices of cross products. Consequently, although it is useful to think of profiles as represented by points in Euclidean space, it is better to analyze those points with the sums of cross products than with D.

Since it has been shown that working with sums of cross products is more useful than working with D, it is instructive to examine the relationship between the two measures:

(11-3)
$$D_{ab}{}^2 = \Sigma(X_{aj} - X_{bj})^2$$
$$= \Sigma(X_{aj}{}^2 + X_{bj}{}^2 - 2X_{aj}X_{bj})$$
$$= \Sigma X_{aj}{}^2 + \Sigma X_{bj}{}^2 - 2\Sigma X_{aj}X_{bj}$$
$$\Sigma X_{aj}X_{bj} = \frac{\Sigma X_{aj}{}^2 + \Sigma X_{bj}{}^2 - D_{ab}{}^2}{2}$$

If both profiles are standardized over the k profile variables and both sides of Eq. (11-3) are divided by k, the following is obtained:

(11-4) $$r_{ab} = 1 - \frac{D_{ab}{}^2}{2K}$$

Thus it can be seen that when the two profiles are in the form of standard scores (standardized over profile variables, not over people), the PM correlation between the two profiles is a monotonically decreasing function of D^2, and thus of D. [Incidentally, Eq. (11-4) offers another approach to obtaining the PM correlation in any case. Instead of computing products of standard scores in the customary approach, one would compute the sum of squared differences between standard scores and enter that in Eq. (11-4).]

TRANSFORMATIONS OF VARIABLES   Much of the controversy about the clustering of profiles has concerned what transformations, if any, should be made of the raw data prior to the analysis. There are two kinds of transformations that can be made: transformations of distributions of individual differences on the separate variables and transformations of intraindividual profile scores. The former will be discussed in this section, and the latter will be discussed in the next section.

One reason why it is important to consider possible transformations of the variables prior to the search for clusters is that the variables may have very different standard deviations (over people). For example, a number of physiological variables are likely to be expressed in very different units. Then, purely as an artifact, the standard deviation of one variable might be 1.2, and that of another, 522.8. Less extreme differences might be expected on different tests of abilities or different scales of adjustment. If such differences are allowed to remain, some variables will more strongly influence the clustering of profiles than will others. If the variables differ markedly in standard deviations, it usually is wise to equate variables in that regard prior to the analysis of cross products. One way to do this is to convert all variables to standard scores.

Another possible type of transformation of variables must be considered because of the correlations among variables (over people). Since in most problems concerning the clustering of profiles all variables concern either the same construct or related constructs, one expects to find positive correlations among the variables. This is what one would expect in studying profiles of scores on 10 physiological variables or on 15 tests of abilities. If correlations among such variables are near zero, one could rightly ask why it makes sense to lump them all together in the search for clusters.

Some have argued that if the variables are correlated, it makes no sense to employ D or to perform analyses of cross products. This is because D treats variables as orthogonal, and the analysis of cross products deals with an orthogonal space of variables. For two reasons, the author disagrees with this point of view. First, if this point of view is correct, many types of analyses customarily employed in psychology make little sense. For example, even if there is a positive correlation between two variables, we customarily *depict* them as orthogonal in making scatter diagrams. Another example relates to Eq. (11-4), which shows that the correlation coefficient can be expressed as a monotonically decreasing function of D. When the correlation is between two variables rather than between two profiles, D is the distance between two variables (not two persons) in a space of persons. In that instance, each person can be represented by an axis which is orthogonal to that for all other persons. The correlation between any two variables can be obtained either as a function of D, or more customarily, as the average product of standard scores. Would anyone seriously question the customary use of correlational analysis simply because it can be depicted in a space of orthogonal persons? Of course, since profiles will tend to correlate with one another, people will not be orthogonal in that sense, but does that prevent the use of the correlation coefficient? It is doubtful that anyone would answer "yes," but for some reason, there are people who think it is not correct to use D or the sum of cross products unless the variables are orthogonal.

The second, and most important, reason for disagreeing with the point of view that variables must be uncorrelated is that a distinction should be made between the mathematical necessities of profile analysis and the interpretability of results. There is no mathematical necessity for restricting the use of D and of cross-products analysis to those situations where variables are uncorrelated. For the mathematical analyses, an orthogonal space is *constructed,* and there is no need to make the angles among vectors proportional to their natural correlations. The real issue concerns the interpretability of analyses.

Regarding the interpretability of analyses, there are two major standards. First, the results must be meaningful in the light of psychological theories and the common sense of scientific activity. Second, and most important, the interpretability depends on how well a particular clustering of profiles eventually fits in a network of lawful relations. Thus there is no simple rule of thumb regarding what transformations, if any, of variables should be made with respect to the correlations among them. If an investigator can make sense of profile clusters regardless of the correlations among variables, he has every right to use the methods of analysis discussed in previous sections. In the long run it may turn out that the investigator made a mistake, as would be evidenced in finding only "messy" relations with other variables; but at least temporarily, the scientist has to follow his intuitions in searching for natural laws.

If correlations among the variables are such that they suggest a number of prominent factors, the investigator might want to factor-analyze variables before searching for clusters of profiles. For example, it might be found that there are three factors underlying 10 physiological measures or that there are five factors underlying 15 tests of abilities. In either case the data matrix could be reduced to a matrix of factor scores. Then profile analysis could be performed on the matrix of factor scores rather than on the data matrix. In that case profiles could be plotted for the factor scores, and cross-products analysis could be used to search for clusters in the space of factor scores.

TRANSFORMATIONS OF PROFILES   Regardless of what transformations, if any, are made of distributions of individual differences on separate variables, it is also necessary to consider possible transformations of intraindividual distributions of profile scores. If it is meaningful to consider level, dispersion, and shape in clustering profiles, these should be permitted to vary when cross products are analyzed. If, however, one or more of these aspects is considered irrelevant, then it, or they, should be equated before the analysis is undertaken.

If level is considered unimportant in a particular analysis, the means of all profiles should be equated, preferably to zero. Then cross products would be formed among profiles expressed as deviation scores (deviates about the level for each person). It facilitates working with such sums of cross products to divide them by the number of variables.

multivariate analysis

In that case relations among profiles would be expressed as *covariances*. These can be factored by cross-products analysis in the same way as shown previously for the analysis of cross products of raw scores. This is called "covariance analysis," but it is only a special case of cross-products analysis.

If both level and dispersion are considered irrelevant in a particular problem, these should be equated in all profiles before cross-products analysis is applied. One best does this by reducing each profile to standard scores (standardized over each profile, regardless of whether or not scores have previously been standardized over variables). Then if the sums of cross products are divided by the number of variables, correlation coefficients are obtained, and no one needs to be told that these can be factor-analyzed. In that case one is performing a Q-technique analysis, as it was described in the previous chapter.

Regardless of whether the analysis concerns the raw matrix of data or whether transformations are made over variables or over profiles, cross-products analysis can be applied. It is a powerful method for clustering profiles.

IMPLICATIONS FOR RESEARCH Even if there are powerful mathematical methods for clustering profiles, this does not necessarily imply that it is wise to perform such investigations. The problems with clustering profiles are the same as those discussed previously with regard to Q technique. Factors represent hypothetical "types" of persons, and loadings specify the similarity of the profile for each person with the profiles for the various factors. There is nothing "illegitimate" about these concepts, and anyone who wants to base research on them has every right to do so. Most psychologists, however, apparently feel less comfortable with these concepts than with those attendant on the factoring of variables. In the short run, which approach is used must be left as a matter of scientific taste; in the long run, which proves to be more fruitful will be judged by the accumulated research results.

One of the difficulties in interpreting factors among profiles is that such factors involve the semiundefinable concept of *similarity*. D is a measure of the similarity of two profiles, and a loading in cross-products analysis is a measure of the similarity of the profile for a person with the profile representing a factor. Similarity is a meaningful concept only when the question is answered, "Similarity with respect to what?" This is why it was previously said that the collection of variables for clustering profiles should be representative of some definable domain of attributes, e.g., the major physiological variables thought to be affected by stress or numerous tests concerning different types of reasoning. If the variables represent very different domains of content or it is very difficult to describe the domain, the results from factoring profiles are not likely to be highly interpretable.

discriminatory analysis

Discriminatory analysis is employed when groups of persons are defined a priori, and the purpose of the analysis is to distinguish the groups from one another on the basis of their score profiles. Examples of groups are different types of mental patients, different vocational groups, and college seniors majoring in different fields. From a mathematical point of view, there is no limit to the types of variables that can be employed. Questions regarding the interpretability of results with different types of variables will be discussed later.

There are three related problems in discriminatory analysis: (1) determining whether or not differences in score profiles for two or more groups are statistically significant, (2) maximizing the discrimination among groups by combining the variables in some manner, and (3) establishing rules for the placement of new individuals into one of the groups. The first of these is the least important of the three for most research in psychology; however, appropriate statistical tests are available. Hotelling's T test can be employed for testing the statistical significance of the differences between the average profiles of two groups (Anderson, 1958; Hotelling, 1931). It could be used, for example, in testing the significance of differences in profiles of physiological variables for males and females. If the null hypothesis is rejected in this case, it is inferred that the total profiles for the sexes are different. Analogous tests are available for testing the significance of differences among more than two profiles, these being by-products of the discriminant function, which will be discussed later.

For two reasons, it was said that statistical tests like those described above are not highly important in most research problems. First, the results of such tests frequently are difficult to interpret. It is possible for two groups to have nonsignificant differences on all the variables but for the overall difference between profiles to be significant. Such tests combine all the information from the different variables in one overall test of significance. Unless there are significant differences on some of the variables, preferably on a majority of them, it is difficult to interpret the significance of difference in overall profiles. At best such tests provide rather meager information about significance of differences. Second, and more important, merely finding that the average profiles for two or more groups are significantly different does not solve the major problems, which are problems 2 and 3 as stated above.

The major problem in discriminatory analysis is problem 2, that of maximizing the discrimination among groups. A discussion of issues related to that problem will occupy most of this section. Later in the section, the problem of the placement of new individuals (problem 3) will be discussed.

GEOMETRIC INTERPRETATION OF DISCRIMINATORY ANALYSIS The geometric interpretations given previously for profile analysis will help one understand some of the issues in discriminatory analysis. If there are N persons and k variables, the profile for any person can be represented by a point in a k-dimensional space. Each axis of the space consists of one of the variables, and the variables are depicted as orthogonal to one another. In discriminatory analysis, it is useful to think of the

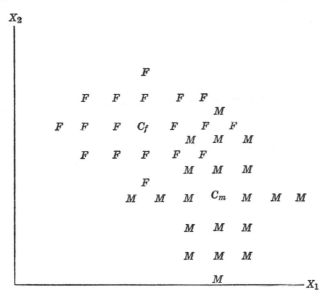

figure 11-5 *Scores of males M and females F on two measures of physiological reaction to stress.*

region of that space occupied by a particular group. If discriminatory analysis is to provide useful information, it is necessary for the members of each group not to be scattered randomly over the space, but it is necessary for the members of the different groups to occupy somewhat different parts of the space of variables. To the extent that individuals in each group are tightly clustered in a particular region of the k space, and to the extent that there is little overlap between the regions occupied by different groups, discriminatory analysis can provide useful information.

A simplified example of a space for two groups on two variables is shown in Figure 11-5. The groups are males and females, and X_1 and X_2 are raw scores on two physiological indices of reaction to stress.

The profile point for each male is represented by an M, and likewise the point for each female is represented by an F. It can be seen that the two groups tend to occupy different regions of the space. Males tend to be high on X_1 and low on X_2, and vice versa for females; however, there is a moderate amount of overlap between the two groups on both variables.

In Figure 11-5, C_m and C_f represent the centroids for males and females, respectively. A centroid is simply the point representing the average profile of a group. The average score for the group is obtained for each variable, and the resulting means are plotted as though they were scores for an individual. The centroid is the point about which the points for individuals in a group balance in all directions. It is

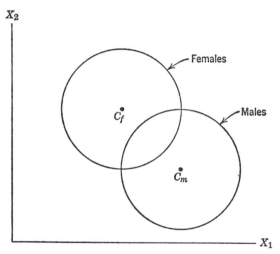

figure 11-6 *Areas of scatter for males and females on two measures of physiological reaction to stress.*

analogous to a centroid vector as it was discussed with regard to centroid factor analysis. If groups are well discriminated, centroids are far apart, and the members of each group hover near their centroid.

Instead of depicting a point for each person in each group, it is more convenient to depict only regions of scatter for the groups. This is done in Figure 11-6 for the profile points depicted in Figure 11-5. The amount of overlap between the contours of scatter indicates the extent to which the two groups are not discriminated by the two variables.

LINEAR DISCRIMINANT FUNCTION What would be helpful in the problem depicted in Figures 11-5 and 11-6 would be some means of combining the information from the two variables so as to discriminate the members of the two groups as well as possible. Potentially this could be done

multivariate analysis

with a number of types of functions of the variables, but a simple linear function has been used most often. Such a function is referred to as a *linear discriminant function:*

$$Y = a_1X_1 + a_2X_2$$

where Y = scores on discriminant function
X_1, X_2 = raw scores on variables
a_1, a_2 = weights for variables
Weights a_1 and a_2 are applied to raw scores on variables X_1 and X_2. The same set of weights is applied to the scores of each person in each group. This results in a new score for each person, Y, which

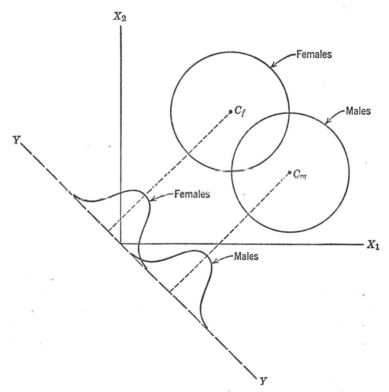

figure 11-7 *Projection of scores onto a discriminant function Y.*

combines the information from X_1 and X_2 regarding discrimination of the groups.

Before we discuss how the weights are obtained for the discriminant function, the example in Figure 11-6 illustrates how such a linear function can serve to discriminate two groups. After the weights are applied, a new line can be drawn in the space Y, and the scores of all persons can be projected on that line. This is done in Figure 11-7. Whereas

profile and discriminatory analyses and multidimensional scaling

there is considerable overlap between the two groups on each of the variables X_1 and X_2, there is less overlap on Y. The scores for persons on Y can be "taken out" of the space for the variables and depicted separately as a frequency distribution, which is shown in Figure 11-8. There it can be seen that the means for the two groups are far apart and there is little overlap between the two distributions. Then Y serves to condense the discriminatory information in the two variables.

As is true in all situations where optimum weights are sought, the method for obtaining the weights depends on a rule for optimization. For example, it will be recalled that the weights in multiple regression

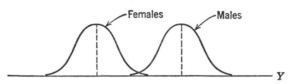

figure 11-8 *Distributions of scores on a discriminant function.*

are obtained according to the principle of least squares: the sum of squared errors of prediction is minimized. In the linear discriminant function, the weights are obtained so as to maximize the following ratio:

$$\frac{\text{Variance between means on } Y}{\text{Variance within groups on } Y}$$

After any set of weights is employed, the discriminant function Y is obtained, and each person has a score on Y. Then one can find the quantities required for the numerator and denominator of the above ratio. This is done as it usually is in analysis of variance. For the numerator, the sum of squared deviates of group means about the grand mean would be divided by the number of groups minus 1. For the denominator, the sum of squared deviates for individuals within a group would be determined with respect to the mean score for that group. These would be summed over groups, and the result would be divided by the total number of subjects in all groups minus the number of groups. This is similar to what is done when one calculates the ratio of the "between" to "within" variance in a one-classification analysis of variance. Thus it is seen that the rule of optimization with the linear discriminant function is to obtain weights so as to maximize the F ratio of between-means variances to within-groups variances. This rule was proposed by Fisher (1936) and has been the basis of most work in discriminatory analysis since that time.

After a rule for optimization is proposed, one then resorts to calculus to see if a mathematical solution is obtainable. It turns out that there is a solution, which results in a set of computational procedures for deriving the weights for linear discriminant functions. With only two groups and any number of variables, this proves to be very simple. In this case a solution is obtainable through a special use of multiple-regression analysis. The variable to be predicted consists of "group scores." The members of one of the two groups receive a score of 1, and the members of the other group receive a score of zero. It does not matter which group is given which score. Also, since correlational analysis is concerned only with standard scores, any other two numbers would do as well. The variables are then used in multiple regression to estimate the group scores. For this, the customary formulas are applied in the customary ways. If the variables are relatively continuous, correlations among them would be computed by the regular PM formula. The correlation of each variable with the group scores would be a point-biserial coefficient. The regression weights obtained in this case would serve as the weights for obtaining the discriminant function Y. The more general method to be discussed next can also be used when there are only two groups, but in that case the same result can be obtained much more simply by the method discussed above.

MULTIPLE LINEAR DISCRIMINANT FUNCTION In most research problems, there are more than two groups. Then it is possible, and usually desirable, to derive more than one linear discriminant function, and for this, one employs the *multiple discriminant function.* The first discriminant function derived is that linear combination of the variables which maximizes the ratio of the between-means variance to the within-groups variance. Next, a second discriminant function is derived which serves as the second-best explainer of variance. In any problem, it is possible to obtain as many discriminant functions as variables or one less than the number of groups, whichever is less. Usually there are more variables than groups, in which case the possible number of discriminant functions equals the number of groups minus 1. This leads to a family of linear discriminant functions, as follows:

$$Y_1 = a_1X_1 + a_2X_2 + \cdots + a_kX_k$$
$$Y_2 = b_1X_1 + b_2X_2 + \cdots + b_kX_k$$
$$Y_3 = c_1X_1 + c_2X_2 + \cdots + c_kX_k$$
$$\vdots \qquad\qquad \vdots$$
$$Y_h = h_1X_1 + h_2X_2 + \cdots + h_kX_k$$

After the weights are obtained, each person receives a score on each discriminant function. The discriminant functions are computed so that the scores on all functions are uncorrelated with one another (orthogonal). For example, the correlation between Y_1 and Y_2, above, over all persons in all groups combined would be zero. (This, however, does not necessarily hold for the correlation between two sets of discriminant scores *within* a particular group.) A sufficient condition for any two discriminant functions to be orthogonal is for the sum of cross products of their weights to equal zero. Thus, in the system of equations above, the following would hold for the weights on Y_1 and Y_2:

$$a_1b_1 + a_2b_2 + \cdots + a_kb_k = 0$$

To attempt a discussion of the mathematical procedures required for the multiple discriminant function would be far out of keeping with the level of mathematical sophistication presumed for the average reader of this book. Because the multiple discriminant function is employed rather infrequently, the literature on the subject which would be understandable by nonspecialists is scarce. The multiple discriminant function was introduced to American researchers by Phillip Rulon (1951) and his colleagues. Details of the computing procedures and a large-scale, worked-out example are given by Tiedman, Bryan, and Rulon (1952). An extensive mathematical treatment of the multiple discriminant function and related methods of analysis is given by Anderson (1958). Maxwell (1961) lucidly discusses the computational procedures and illustrates the use of discriminatory analysis with dichotomous variables. Another example of the use of the method on a major problem is given by Thorndike and Hagen (1959).

The major computational step in deriving multiple discriminant functions is to perform a principal-axes factor analysis; however, the analysis is not made of the correlations among variables as would be the case in the usual form of factor analysis. What is analyzed instead is a special table consisting of sums of squared deviates within groups. (That is not a highly enlightening description of the table which is analyzed, but it is the most that can be said without wandering off into rather deep mathematical water.) The first set of principal-axes loadings obtained from this table is the set of weights required to form the first discriminant function Y_1. For each variable, the proper weight is its loading on the factor. The second principal-axes factor supplies the weights for the second discriminant function, and so on. Analogous to methods for obtaining factor scores for people in factor analysis, scores on the discriminant functions are obtained for all persons. The method of analysis ensures that these sets of scores will be mutually uncorrelated over all persons in all groups.

Just as in factor analysis the average squared loading on a factor indicates the percentage of variance explained by that factor, in multiple-discriminant analysis the average squared weight on a factor indicates the percentage of total variance of all scores explainable by that discriminant. Also, as is true of factor analysis, the percentage of variance explained by each discriminant derived in turn tends to fall off rapidly after the first one. Thus the first discriminant tends to do a much better job of discriminating the groups than does any subsequent discriminant, and typically, very little variance is explained by discriminants beyond the second or third.

EXAMPLES OF MULTIPLE DISCRIMINANTS   A large-scale example of the use of the multiple discriminant function is from a study by Tiedeman, Bryan, and Rulon (1952). The groups were eight technical specialties in the

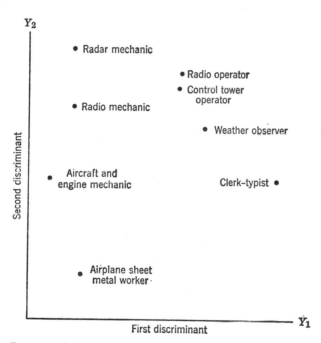

figure 11-9 *Centroids of occupational groups on two discriminant functions. (Adapted from Tiedeman, Bryan, and Rulon, 1952.)*

Air Force. The persons in each group had received satisfactory scores on achievement tests in their specialities. The number of persons in a group varied from 99 to 2,084. The variables consisted of 17 tests, mainly concerning intellectual functions such as word knowledge and knowledge of mechanical principles. After the first two discriminant functions were obtained, subsequent discriminants explained very little variance.

After discriminant functions are obtained, all persons can be depicted in the discriminant space rather than in the space of variables. One does this by plotting scores on the discriminants, as is done in Figure 11-9. In the figure are shown only the centroids for the groups.

If the scores were shown for each person, one would see that there is considerable overlap among groups, and in this problem there was more overlap than separation of the groups. The authors interpreted the first discriminant as a mechanical dimension, since the groups clearly are lined up in that way. Low scores on Y_1 correspond to specialties with high mechanical achievement, and vice versa for high scores on Y_1. Less definitely, the second discriminant was interpreted an an intellectual dimension, because specialties high on it tend to require more intellectual aptitude than those that are low.

Another example of multiple discriminants comes from a study by Maxwell (1961) of differences in symptoms of schizophrenics, manic

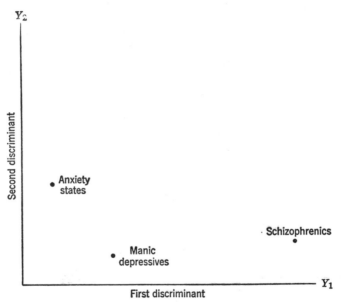

figure 11-10 *Centroids for three types of mental patients on two discriminant functions. (Adapted from Maxwell, 1961.)*

depressives, and patients characterized by severe anxiety. Centroids for the three groups on the first two discriminant functions are shown in Figure 11-10. The first discriminant was characterized by a high level of thought disruption and a low level of anxiety, the schizophrenics being high in this regard and the other two groups being low. The major symptom contributing to the second discriminant was "freedom from delusions of guilt," this dimension serving to differentiate the anxiety states from the manic depressives.

PLACEMENT   Placement concerns the assignment of new individuals to a group when their membership is unknown. With respect to the examples

multivariate analysis

above, this would be the case for a new member of the Air Force who is to be assigned to a technical specialty, or with respect to the second example, a new patient who has not yet been classified. To undertake such placement, one must compare the profile of scores for a person with the profiles of scores for persons who are known to belong to a group. Herein lies the difficulty of the placement problem, because first one must know the group membership of at least some persons to make valid decisions about the group membership of other persons. Also, if the average profiles of the groups are not different, placement is hopeless. In that case, flipping coins would do as well.

Placement can be performed either in the space of variables or in the discriminant space. (For the pro's and con's of these approaches, see Lohnes, 1961.) Some approximate approaches in the space of variables will indicate the nature of the problem. Let it be assumed that, prior to the placement problem, profiles of scores are obtained for persons who are known to belong to three different groups. Subsequently, score profiles are obtained for new persons, and decisions must be made about the placement (assignment or classification) of the new individuals. One approach would be to obtain D between the profile for each person and the average profile for each group, and then each individual would be assigned to the group for which D is smallest. A major problem with this approach is that it does not consider the variance of particular variables within groups or between groups. An individual may have a score on a particular variable which is close to the average for a particular group, but the group could vary widely on that variable. Then D would be unduly influenced (made small) by a variable which is not very important in discriminating the groups. An improvement would be to divide the squared difference between the score for a person and the average score for a group by the variance of scores within the group. The sum of such weighted squares could serve as a basis for placement. The major problem with this approach is that it does not take account of the correlations among variables. If two variables correlate highly, the discriminatory information in them is highly redundant, in the same sense that this is so in multiple-regression analysis. Thus an individual might have a large D with a particular group because he differs from the group only on three highly correlated measures but is very similar to the group on the remaining measures.

There is an approach to placement which circumvents the problems discussed above. First, let it be assumed that the multiple discriminant function has been applied. Then, in our illustrative problem, the scores of all persons in the three groups are known for the discriminants, and the centroid for each group is computed. It is necessary to assume that scores on each discriminant are normally distributed within each group. Then it is possible to compute contours of equal density about the centroid for each group. Since these contours are about the centroid for a group, they are referred to as *centours*. (How to obtain such centours is discussed by Lohnes, 1961.) It is easiest to visualize such centours in the two-space of only two discriminants, but the logic applies as well with any number of discriminants. In a two-space, the scatter of a group about its centroid can be pictured by a series of ellipses, as in Figure 11-11. As was mentioned previously, even though discriminant functions correlate zero with one another over all persons in all groups, this does not necessarily hold within any particular group. If the correlation is high (which is very rarely the case), the centours

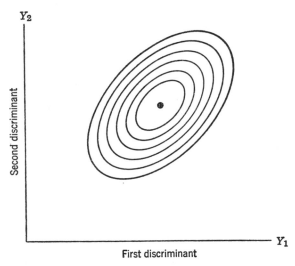

figure 11-11 *Centour ellipses around the centroid for one group on two discriminant functions.*

will be highly elliptical; if the correlation is zero, the centours will be circles. Regardless of which is the case, the centours indicate the percentages of persons "further in" and "further out" about the centroid.

In the use of centours, placement is performed by the assignment of the individual to the group where his centour score is highest. The centour score for an individual estimates the percentage of persons in a group that are further from the centroid. For example, if an individual has a centour score of 75 percent, this means that 75 percent of the members of the group are further from the centroid (irrespective of direction) than the centour on which the profile point for the subject lies. If an individual had centour scores of 75, 25, and 10 percent, respectively, for three groups, he would be assigned to the first group. Such centour scores do not usually add up to 100 percent. Depending

multivariate analysis

on the discrimination among groups, one person could have a high centour score on a number of groups, and another person could have a very low centour score on all groups.

The extent to which centour scores are successful in placing people is directly related to the variability of such scores for each person. If such scores are much the same for a person, placement is performed about as well by flipping coins for him. If that is the case for most subjects in a study, placement had better be based on variables other than those employed in the study.

EVALUATION OF DISCRIMINATORY ANALYSIS   In spite of the differences in the purposes of factor analysis and discriminatory analysis, mathematically they are closely related. The multiple discriminant function is based on a linear combination of variables, so in that sense, a linear discriminant function is a factor. Also, as was mentioned previously, linear discriminant functions are obtained by an application of principal-axes factoring to a special matrix concerning indices of discrimination among and within groups. Linear discriminant functions, then, are special types of factors, ones that serve to discriminate among a priori groups of subjects. It would be the sheerest of accidents if scores on any such discriminant function corresponded perfectly to scores on any factor obtained from analyzing correlations among variables. The fact that both the clustering of profiles and discriminatory analysis are based on special uses of factor analysis indicates how general are the concepts and procedures of factor analysis. Other uses of factor analysis in dealing with problems of multivariate analyses will be seen later, in the section on multidimensional scaling.

The wisdom of applying discriminatory analysis depends on the problem. Potentially, discriminatory analysis is most useful in applied psychology, where, for example, it might be used in assigning persons to jobs, students to courses of training, and patients to diagnostic groups. There are, however, some logical difficulties in employing discriminatory analysis for that purpose. One logical difficulty is in deciding how to designate the members of groups prior to performing discriminatory analysis. For example, in discriminating different professional groups on the basis of score profiles, should the group of engineers include all engineers, only highly successful engineers, or some modal group with regard to success? As another logical problem, in employing discriminatory analysis in applied psychology, it usually is assumed that all persons will be assigned to one of the groups, which is a poor strategy. In addition to these and other logical difficulties in employing discriminatory analysis in applied psychology, it simply has not worked very well in studies to date. The amount of overlap between groups in the discriminant space tends to overshadow the separation between groups. It is wishful thinking to hope that all engineers will differ markedly from all physicians, or that all schizophrenics will differ markedly from all neurotics, on any collection of variables.

Discriminatory analysis is more useful in *understanding* the major differences between groups than it is for placing individuals in groups. Thus, in the examples given in Figures 11-9 and 11-10, the nature of the discriminants does help one to understand the differences in central tendency of the groups, but the amount of overlap is so large that placement of new individuals would not be highly effective.

In basic research in psychology, there are a number of potential uses of discriminatory analysis. One use would be in analyzing the effects of different experimental treatments when there are multiple dependent measures. This would be the case, for example, if the different treatments consisted of different types of stress and the dependent measures consisted of different physiological variables. Each treatment would define an a priori group, and there would be as many groups as treatments. The multiple discriminant function could then be applied to scores on the physiological variables. This might provide a useful way of summarizing the most important differences among the treatment groups. In most investigations, however, the interest is in the individual variables rather than in a linear combination of them. The investigator usually is not so much interested in maximizing differences between groups in a statistical sense, as the discriminant function does, as he is in examining differences in means on the separate variables.

Another potential use of discriminatory analysis in basic research is with respect to independent variables rather than with respect to dependent variables, as described above. In that case, placement procedures are used to assign people to groups before the experiment, and either all subjects are given the same treatment or subjects within groups are randomly assigned to different treatments. An example would be the case in which, prior to the experiment, the discriminant function is applied to scores of neurotics, normals, and hospitalized psychotics on a dozen physiological variables. Placement procedures are then used to obtain groups of college students that differ in terms of their similarity to the three groups. The three groups of college students obtained in this way would then participate in an experiment. In that case the dependent variables could be anything of interest, e.g., learning rates in three tasks.

The problems with using discriminatory analysis in the way described above are the same as those in all post factum designs. The independent variable is the group classification, but that variable is likely to be confounded with numerous other variables. For example, psychotics are likely to differ from other groups on physiological variables for reasons that have nothing to do with psychosis per se, e.g.,

multivariate analysis

because of hospital diet. Then one would be selecting college students partly on the basis of dietary habits rather than on psychotic tendency.

pattern analysis

What is spoken of in this chapter as profile analysis is called "pattern analysis" by some persons. Here it will prove useful to make a distinction between the two in terms of the types of scores employed in each. The term "profile analysis" will be used for those situations in which variables are relatively continuous—e.g., when all variables consist of total scores on tests or when they consist of ratings obtained from seven-step scales. The term "pattern analysis" will be used for those situations in which the variables are dichotomous rather than relatively continuous. Most typically, pattern analysis is employed with the dichotomous items within a test. Another possibility would be to dichotomize scores on continuous variables (e.g., dichotomize scores at the median), but that would be throwing away much valuable information.

As has been mentioned at numerous points in this book, most measurement theory is based on the linear model. In this model, measures of attributes are obtained by a linear combination, usually a simple sum, of scores on individual items. It is possible, at least theoretically, to obtain more information from a collection of items than from the linear model. For example, even though two persons obtain the same total score on a test, it is unlikely that they have the same scores on all items. On a personality inventory concerning adjustment, two persons could obtain the same adjustment score but have different "patterns" of responses to the items. A pattern is simply any complete set of responses to a collection of items. A pattern would be the actual responses of a particular individual, the most popular responses in a group of persons, or even a hypothetical set of responses. It has been suggested that an analysis of such patterns might offer improvements over measures obtained from the linear model.

CLUSTERING OF PATTERNS Numerous cut-and-try techniques have been proposed for the clustering of persons in terms of patterns of responses. The proper approach, however, is to employ cross-products analysis, similar to the way that it is employed with relatively continuous measures. The first step in such an analysis is to compute an index of response agreements over items for each pair of individuals. If two individuals give the same response to an item, regardless of what that response is, that is counted as an agreement. In tests of ability, one type of response would consist of passing the item, and the other type of response would consist of failing the item. In nonability tests, one type of response would consist of agreeing with a statement, and the other would consist of disagreeing with the statement. An index of agreement in responses over dichotomous items is the mean cross product of scores when one of two dichotomous responses is scored 1 and the other is scored -1. Thus if two persons either pass or fail an item, the cross product is 1; but if one person passes the item and the other fails the item, the cross product is -1. Similarly for nonability tests, if two persons give the same response to an item, the cross product is 1; but if they give different responses, the cross product is -1. Sums of such cross products over items are then divided by the number of items. These can be factor-analyzed by all the methods employed with other types of sums of cross products.

In spite of the ease with which cross-products analysis can be applied to the problem of clustering profiles, the author knows of no instance in which this has been done. The theoretical possibilities are interesting. The loadings of each person on each factor could be considered as a score, each such score indicating how strongly each person related to each pattern (factor). Rather than having only one score on the collection of items, as would result from applying the linear model, each person would have a score on each factor. Such scores could be employed in subsequent investigations, either as variables in basic research or as predictor variables in applied problems.

DISCRIMINATORY ANALYSIS OF PATTERNS Analogous to methods of discriminatory analysis applied to sets of relatively continuous scores (profiles), there are methods of discriminatory analysis that can be applied to sets of dichotomous scores (patterns). For example, the multiple discriminant function can be applied. Discriminatory analysis with score patterns is discussed by Maxwell (1961). An illustrative problem would be that of discriminating different types of mental patients on the basis of patterns of symptoms, in which each symptom would be scored 1 when present and zero when absent.

EVALUATION OF PATTERN ANALYSIS In spite of the interesting possibilities for clustering persons in terms of patterns and for applying discriminatory analysis to patterns, pattern analysis has produced very little in the way of important research findings. Pattern analysis suffers from a crippling flaw: it takes individual items too seriously. As has been noted previously, the individual item usually is heavily loaded with uniqueness, part of which is pure measurement error and the rest reliable variance specific to the item. It will be remembered that items within a test usually have low correlations with one another, correlations above .30 being the exception. In other words, most of the variance in each item is trivial, and pattern analysis seeks to find important information in that trivia. It has not worked. Studies in which pattern analysis has been employed either failed to obtain clear results, or when they apparently did, the results did not hold up in subsequent samples. Regarding the latter point, pattern analysis is the "ideal" method for taking advantage of chance. This is because (1) there is a large component of measurement error in each item, (2) such studies usually employ a relatively large number of items, which gives more room for taking advantage of chance, and (3) the methods of analysis, such as the multiple discriminant function, are ones that capitalize on chance variance. There is still hope for the future, but so far pattern analysis has not added substantially to the linear model in the scoring of responses to collections of items.

multidimensional scaling

Although multidimensional scaling is based on the same mathematical models as are factor analysis and discriminatory analysis, it is used for a different purpose. As the term will be used in this book, "multidimensional scaling" usually is concerned with the scaling of stimuli rather than with the scaling of people. Multidimensional scaling is an extension of the methods of unidimensional scaling of stimuli which were discussed in Chapter Two. The subject would have been discussed there, but to understand multidimensional scaling, one must first understand the mathematical methods that have been discussed so far in this book.

From Chapter Two it will be remembered that methods of unidimensional scaling are applied only in those cases where there is good reason to believe that one dimension is sufficient. This would be the case, for example, in developing an interval scale for judgments of weight or an interval scale for preferential responses of women regarding the handsomeness of men. In unidimensional scaling, the experimenter tries to control extraneous differences among the stimuli to prevent them from influencing judgments or preferences. For example, in a study of lifted weights, the experimenter would ensure that the weights are all the same shape and color. In a study of preferential responses regarding the handsomeness of men, the experimenter would ensure that the photographs of men were either all in color or all in black and white and that they were of men in similar attire and in similar poses. More important than these efforts to control extraneous differences among stimuli is the control obtained from instructions to subjects. In unidimensional scaling, the investigator knows in advance of the study the dimension on which responses are to be made. Each subject is carefully instructed to make judgments or preferences with regard to the dimension of interest, and he is warned about letting other variables influence his responses.

In multidimensional scaling, subjects are not instructed to make responses with respect to a particular dimension; rather, they are asked to respond only in terms of similarities and differences among the stimuli, e.g., judging whether stimulus a is more similar to stimulus b or to stimulus c. Multidimensional scaling is used in two related types of studies. In one type of study, the investigator does not know what dimensions people typically use in responding to a class of stimuli, and the purpose of such investigations is to learn the dimensions. This would be the case in studying responses of college students to 20 well-known members of the United States Senate. Similarity judgments about the senators might be explainable by only one dimension of good-bad, or other dimensions might be evidenced in the judgments, such as liberal-conservative, North-South regional affiliation, and so on. The purpose of the study would be to learn something about the dimensions that people employ in judging senators.

In the second type of study in which multidimensional scaling is employed, the investigator is rather sure what the major dimensions of preference or judgment are, but he is not sure how people use those dimensions. An example would be in obtaining similarity judgments regarding colored chips. All chips would be of the same hue, but they would be systematically varied in terms of brightness and saturation. An analysis of the responses might indicate that subjects actually employ only one dimension rather than two; e.g., both saturation and brightness are combined into one overall dimension of "vividness." Equally possible would be to find that more than two dimensions are required to represent the responses. A third possibility would be that subjects employ only two dimensions in making responses but one is much more influential than the other.

THE GEOMETRIC MODEL   To illustrate geometrical models for multidimensional scaling, let it be assumed that (1) subjects have made similarity judgments regarding pairs of stimuli in a set and (2) these have been analyzed so as to obtain distances between all stimuli. How points 1 and 2 are accomplished are crucial issues in multidimensional scaling, but before they are discussed, it would be informative to see how that data may be represented and analyzed. To take a simplified example, think of the similarity judgments as being obtained from the ratings of pairs of stimuli on a seven-step scale of similarity-dissimilarity. Distances could then be represented by the mean rating over subjects for each pair of stimuli. Suppose that such distances have been obtained among senators.

In Figure 11-12 are shown hypothetical results for distances among six senators, the senators being labeled a, b, c, etc. It is a simplified example, because (1) most studies would employ considerably more than six stimuli (senators in this case) and (2) probably more than two dimensions would be required to portray the distances exactly. In Figure 11-12, stimuli are portrayed in terms of a Euclidean distance model, i.e., in terms of the geometry of real physical space. Theoretically there are other possible representations of distances among stimuli, but none of these has achieved the popularity of the Euclidean distance model. This is because it makes sense intuitively and leads to powerful methods of analysis.

In Figure 11-12, lines could have been drawn between all pairs of stimuli to represent distances, but to simplify the illustration, that was not done. After distances among stimuli have been obtained, how are these to be dimensionalized? If the points fit as neatly in a two-space as those shown in Figure 11-12, there would be no problem. One could simply pencil in two dimensions with a ruler, as is done in Figure 11-13.

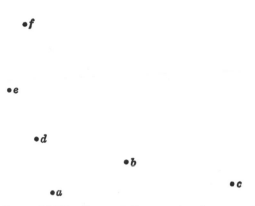

figure 11-12 *Space of distances for the mean similarity ratings of six senators.*

In that case the number of dimensions must be neither more nor less than two; but the exact placement is a matter of choice, as it is in the rotation of factors in factor analysis. One could employ an arbitrary scale for each dimension, e.g., ¼ inch equals a score of 1, ½ inch equals a score of 2, ¾ inch equals a score of 3, and so on. Then interpretations could be made of the dimensions in terms of the scores of senators, and the dimensions could be investigated in subsequent studies. Since, however, stimuli can seldom be represented in a two-space, as in Figures 11-12 and 11-13, it is necessary to develop methods of analysis that can handle all cases.

In the discussion of methods for clustering profiles, it was shown that distances could be analyzed by cross-products analysis. Let us see how essentially the same type of analysis can be used in multidimensional scaling. Previously it was shown that the dimensions obtained from the factor analysis of cross products explain distances among points (persons in profile analysis, stimuli in multidimensional scaling).

It was also shown that the sum of cross products of factor loadings for any two persons equals the sum of cross products on the variables, assuming that the factors constitute a sufficient basis for the space. In multidimensional scaling, one does not know what the dimensions (factors) are, but it is useful to think of the distances among stimuli as being explainable by the sums of cross products on those dimensions. For example, assume that people employ four dimensions for judging similarity among stimuli. If scores for the stimuli on those dimensions were known, a matrix of sums of cross products of those scores could be obtained. That could be factor-analyzed as any matrix of such sums of cross products can, and scores for stimuli on the underlying four dimensions could be recovered. The square root of the sum of squared

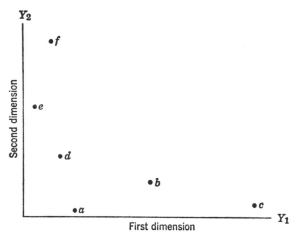

figure 11-13   *Two dimensions for the distances among senators.*

differences in loadings on those dimensions for any two stimuli would equal the distance found from similarity judgments.

Of course, if one knew the scores of stimuli on underlying dimensions, no analysis would be required; but let us see how the logic applies when that information is not available. Looking at measures of distance among stimuli, one can imagine that those are produced by differences on one or more underlying dimensions. If the distances can somehow be converted to sums of cross products on the underlying dimensions, a factor analysis of those will reveal the dimensions and determine the score of each stimulus on each dimension. In the clustering of persons in terms of score profiles, the sums of cross products are readily obtainable, but this is not the case in multidimensional scaling. In the latter case, distances are estimated by some method (methods will be discussed later), but there are no underlying variables on which sums of cross products can be obtained directly. Such sums of cross

multivariate analysis

products are then hypothetical, and only by employing some type of mathematical model can one estimate them.

Some simple principles of geometry will indicate how sums of cross products are estimated from measures of distance. Previously was shown [Eq. (11-3)] the following relationship between D for two points a and b and the sum of cross products $\Sigma X_{aj}X_{bj}$ for those two points:

$$\Sigma X_{aj}X_{bj} = \frac{\Sigma X_{aj}{}^2 + \Sigma X_{bj}{}^2 - D_{ab}{}^2}{2}$$

If D is known, which is assumed to be the case in this discussion, all that is required to obtain the sum of cross products is to find the

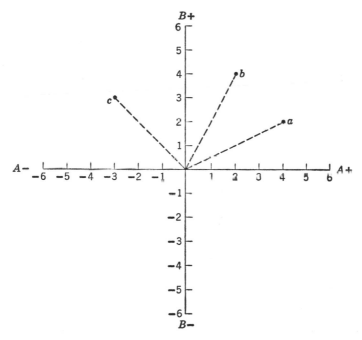

figure 11-14 *Vector lengths for three points in a two-dimensional space.*

sum of squared scores for each point on the dimensions. The sum of squared scores for any point has an important geometric interpretation: it is the squared length of a vector extending from the origin of the space to the point. This principle is illustrated in Figure 11-14, which shows three points in a two-space. Point a has a score of 4 on dimension A and a score of 2 on dimension B. The squared distance of a from the origin of the space (the intersections of A and B) is $4^2 + 2^2 = 20$. The distance (indicated by a dashed line) of a from the origin then equals the square root of 20, or approximately 4.47. Point *b* represents scores of 2 and 4 on *A* and *B*, respectively, so it also has a squared distance from the origin of 20. Point *c* represents scores of −3 and 3 on *A* and *B*, respectively, and thus the squared distance from the origin is 18.

After distances among stimuli are obtained, the major problem in multidimensional scaling is to establish an origin for the space. Once the origin is established, the squared distance of each point from the origin can be found, and this supplies the information necessary to compute sums of cross products. The set of distances provides no hint about an origin, as is evidenced by the lack of an origin in the space of distances portrayed in Figure 11-12. There are a number of ways to put an origin in a space of distances. One way to do this is to make one of the points the origin. Then all the other points could be represented by vectors extending from the point designated as the origin. In Figure 11-15, this is done for the points shown previously in Figure

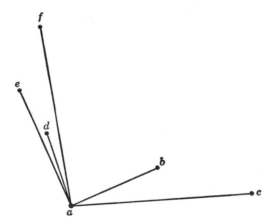

figure 11-15 *Space of distances among senators with an origin at the point for senator a.*

11-12. Point *a* is made the origin, and all other points are represented by vectors extending from *a*. The distances among points are unchanged, but now the points are shown as extending from an origin.

It would not be satisfactory to define the origin as the point of a particular stimulus, because (1) there is some error in establishing the point and (2) even if that were not the case, the results of subsequent analyses would depend very much on the point which was chosen. A solution which tends to circumvent these problems is to place the origin at the centroid of the space of points. In a two-space of points, this could be easily done by (1) putting any pair of orthogonal coordinates in the space and (2) computing the average scores of all points on the coordinates. It will be remembered that the centroid of points (for persons or stimuli) is represented by the average score of those points on any orthogonal basis for the space. In Figure 11-16 are shown the points from Figure 11-12 represented by vectors extending from the centroid of the space.

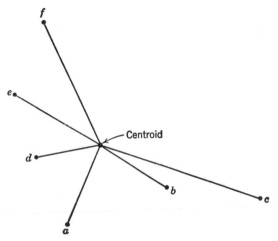

figure 11-16 *Space of points for six senators with an origin at the centroid.*

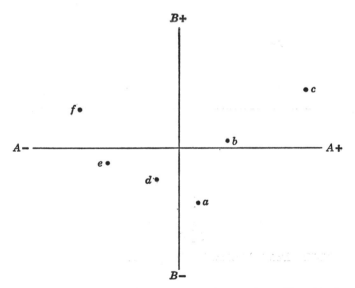

figure 11-17 *Loadings of six senators on two centroid factors.*

When all points cannot be exactly represented in a two-space, as they almost never will, there are straightforward ways of calculating the distance of each point from the centroid of the space. (These methods are discussed by Torgerson, 1958, chap. 11.) After these distances

profile and discriminatory analyses and multidimensional scaling   **409**

table 11-3 *Loadings of six senators on two rotated factors*

		FACTOR	
		A_1	B_1
	a	.02	−.31
	b	.26	−.05
SENATOR	c	.74	.07
	d	−.16	−.13
	e	−.37	.03
	f	−.42	.35

are obtained, the matrix of distances among stimuli can be converted to a matrix of sums of cross products. These can then be factored by *any* method of factor analysis. Also, there is nothing to prevent rotation of factors to positions that are more interpretable.

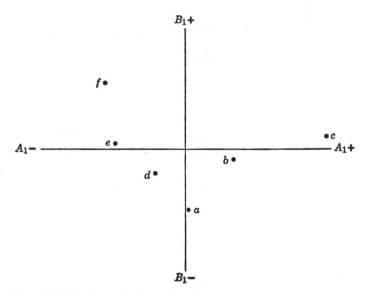

figure 11-18 *Rotated factors for six senators.*

In Figure 11-17 are shown the results of a centroid factor analysis of the vectors shown in Figure 11-16 (centroid factors are not to be confused with the centroid point of a space of points). These are rotated in Figure 11-18, and loadings for stimuli on the rotated factors are snown in Table 11-3. (The units in which loadings are expressed are the same as those used to express the distances of points from one another and from the centroid of the space.) Considering the patterns of loadings for the senators, it might be suggested that factor A_1 concerns liberalism versus conservatism and factor B_1 concerns attitudes regarding foreign affairs.

ESTIMATION OF DISTANCES   In the previous section it was assumed that distances among stimuli are known, in which case it is an easy task to (1) convert those to sums of cross products and (2) factor-analyze the sums of cross products. The major controversy in multidimensional scaling, however, concerns how those distances are obtained initially. Before particular methods for estimating those distances are discussed, it would be worthwhile to examine the requirements for the obtained distances.

In multidimensional scaling, the distances must be established on a ratio scale of measurement, that is, it must be possible to say, for example, that the distance between points a and b is twice the distance between points b and c. Also, since a ratio scale must have a rational origin, it must be possible for the distance between two stimuli to be zero. In Chapter One it was said that a ratio scale is invariant only over transformations of the type aX. Any ratio scale X can be multiplied or divided by an arbitrary constant a, and the resulting scale X' will also be a ratio scale. Then the distances used for multidimensional scaling must be determined only up to a criterion of proportionality. Thus if one method of estimating the distances produces distances of 1, 2, and 3 between three pairs of stimuli and another method produces distances twice as large (2, 4, and 6), the spatial configurations will look alike for both. The second configuration will cover more space than the first, but both will fit in the same number of dimensions, relative distances will be the same, and angles between vectors relating points will remain the same. Thus, up to a criterion of proportionality, the actual sizes of units used to express distances are arbitrary.

Even if a ratio scale of distances (or anything else) is invariant under transformations of the form aX, it is *not* invariant under transformations of the form $aX + b$, where b is different from zero in either the positive or negative direction. Thus one cannot add an arbitrary constant to a set of distances and maintain the same configuration of points. Then, for example, adding an arbitrary constant might change the shape of the triangle connecting three points or might change the number of dimensions required to represent half a dozen points. Another possibility is that the space would become non-Euclidean; i.e., the points could not be represented in any physical space or any extension of the properties thereof to hyperspaces. More about this matter will be discussed in a later section, but a simple example here will indicate the possibility of obtaining a non-Euclidean set of distances. Suppose that the distances between three stimuli are known on a ratio scale as follows:

$a - b = 2$

$b - c = 4$

$a - c = 6$

The points representing the above distances lie in one dimension, i.e., along a straight line. The distance from a to c equals the sum of the other two distances. If 1 is subtracted from each of the above distances, the new distances are 1, 3, and 5, respectively. This is an impossible set of distances, at least in Euclidean space. The distances will not plot on a straight line, because to do so, the largest distance (that between a and c) would have to be no larger than the sum of the other two distances. Also, those distances will not fit in any higher space. In a two-space, for example, the points would need to form a triangle; but since it is not possible for one side of a triangle to be larger than the sum of the other two sides, it is not possible to depict the points in Euclidean space.

The lesson to be learned from the discussion above is that, before one can dimensionalize distances among stimuli, those distances must be obtained on a ratio scale of distances. Then either some method of ratio estimation must be employed in gathering data from subjects, or if methods are employed that lead to an interval scale, some rationale must be developed for transforming the interval scale of distances to a ratio scale of distances. Regardless of which of these two approaches is used, the distances are only estimated, and there must be an examination of the extent to which the distances actually are Euclidean. Although there are a number of ways one can do this, the easiest way is by examining the results of a principal-axes factor analysis of the space of distances, after the distances have been transformed to sums of cross products in the manner discussed previously. If the space is non-Euclidean, results of the analysis will violate some rules regarding possible outcomes. (These circumstances are discussed by Torgerson, 1958. For the mathematically sophisticated reader, if the space is non-Euclidean, at least one latent root of the matrix of sums of cross products will be negative. No latent root can be negative if the space is Euclidean.) Thus if the method of principal axes is used to dimensionalize the space of stimuli, there is a built-in check on the legitimacy of analyzing the space as though it were Euclidean.

RATIO ESTIMATES OF DISTANCES   A careful distinction must be made between obtaining ratio estimates of distances, as they will be discussed here,

multivariate analysis

and obtaining ratio estimates of scale values, as they were discussed in Chapter Two. In the latter, for example, the subject would be required to estimate the ratio of brightness of one light to another. In the ratio estimation of distances, the analogous task would be to judge the ratio of *differences* in brightness of lights a and b to that of b and c. In multidimensional scaling, the scaling tasks concern judgments about the relative size of differences among the stimuli rather than about the amount of an attribute possessed by the stimuli.

A simple form of ratio estimation applied to obtain a ratio scale of distances among stimuli would be as follows. Subjects rate the similarity of all possible pairs of the stimuli, e.g., colored chips or senators. Ratings are performed on a percentage scale, with 100 being designated as "identical" and zero designated as "no similarity." Since the problem is to obtain estimates of distances among the stimuli, not estimates of nearness, the absolute difference between each mean rating and 100 would be computed. Thus if the average rating for one pair of stimuli were 80, the estimated distance between stimuli would be 20. After those calculations are made for all pairs of stimuli, the results are considered as forming a ratio scale of distances. Since ratio scales of distance are invariant up to a criterion of proportionality, expressing distances as percentages is as good as expressing them in any other form.

Another approach to obtaining ratio estimates of differences is as follows. The subject is presented with three stimuli and asked to state which two are most different. Next the subject is asked to state which two are least different (or more similar). In this instance suppose that the subject picks stimuli a and c on the first instruction and b nd c on the second instruction. This tells us that distances among stimuli are ordered from highest to lowest as follows: a-c, a-b, b-c. Next the subject would be required to estimate the ratios of those differences, and there are a number of ways in which this could be done. One approach would be as follows. Since the subject judges the distance between b and c to be the smallest, a judgment could be made about the ratio of the other two distances to that distance. The subject would be asked to pick any number, including fractional numbers, to indicate how much more different a is from b than b is from c. Next the subject would be asked to employ the same method in estimating how much more different a is from c than b is from c. The average ratios obtained in this way from a group of subjects could then be used to form a ratio scale of distances among stimuli.

After distances are obtained by either of the methods described above, they can be submitted to factor analysis. Distances could be determined from the centroid of the space, and then distances among stimuli could be transformed to sums of cross products. If these are factored by the method of principal axes, a check could be made on the Euclidean properties of the space.

Some investigators are reluctant to employ methods of ratio estimation to obtain distances among stimuli because they feel that such methods require too much of subjects. Instead they feel that it would be better to require much simpler responses from subjects and then estimate a ratio scale of distance with mathematical models.

INTERVAL ESTIMATES OF DISTANCES   Instead of employing methods of ratio estimation with differences among stimuli, one could employ methods of interval estimation. For example, the experimenter shows the subject two pairs of stimuli, one pair consisting of stimuli a and b and the other pair consisting of stimuli c and d. The subject is asked to pick a pair of stimuli from a set so that the distance between them is midway between the distances of a-b and c-d. Such methods of interval estimation of distances, however, would confuse the experimenter, and the subject would be even more perplexed. Even if this were an understandable task for subjects, it would lead only to an interval scale for the distances. Since methods of ratio estimation are more understandable to subjects and are intended to produce ratio scales for distances, those methods are preferable to methods of interval estimation. (This is so in multidimensional scaling, but it is not necessarily so in unidimensional scaling as it was described in Chapter Two.) The alternative is to start with methods of ordinal estimation, which is discussed in the following section.

ORDINAL ESTIMATES OF DISTANCES   Most of the work on multidimensional scaling so far has been based on ordinal estimates of distances. The method of *triads* is frequently used for this purpose. The subject is shown three stimuli from a larger set. First, he is asked to indicate which two of the three stimuli are most similar; next, he is asked to indicate which two are most different. This produces a rank ordering of the three differences possible among three stimuli. Judgments can then be made of the ordering of distances in all possible triads in a set.

Another method of ordinal estimation employed with distances among stimuli is the method of *multidimensional rank order*. An example would be as follows. The subject is given stimulus a and asked to rank the remaining stimuli in a set in terms of their similarity to a. Next, the subject is given stimulus b and asked to rank all other stimuli in terms of their similarity to b. As many rank orderings are made as there are stimuli.

Either of the above methods of ordinal estimation can be used to generate an interval scale of distances. The basic data obtained from subjects are the proportions of times that one stimulus is judged more similar to a second stimulus than to a third stimulus. For stimuli a, b, and c, this would be symbolized $_aP_{bc}$, which indicates the proportion of subjects that say a is more similar to b than to c. Since such proportions provide only ordinal information about distances, some type of mathematical model must be employed to convert the proportions to intervals. This is most frequently done with models relating to Thurstone's law of comparative judgment, which was discussed in Chapter Two. There are, however, two very important differences between the way those scaling methods are applied in unidimensional scaling and in multidimensional scaling. In the former, the methods are applied to proportions of persons who say that one stimulus is greater than another with respect to a stated attribute; in multidimensional scaling, the methods are applied to the proportions of people who say, in effect, that the distance between two stimuli is greater than that between two other stimuli. In the former case, the methods result in an interval scale of the stimuli with respect to an attribute; in the latter case, the result is an interval scale of *distances* among stimuli, with the attribute(s) involved in the distances not being known at that stage of the analysis. An illustrative interval scale of distances among three pairs of stimuli is as follows:

Smaller distances $\longleftarrow$ |$_{ab}$ |$_{bc}$ _____ |$_{cd}$ $\longrightarrow$ Larger distances

The interval of distance between pairs ab and bc is much smaller than that between pairs bc and cd. Since it is an interval scale rather than a ratio scale, no zero point is shown, and the ends of the line are anchored only by "smaller" and "larger." One can, however, take seriously the ratios of the three intervals depicted. For example, one can see that the interval bc-cd is several times larger than the interval ab-bc. The purpose of applying Thurstone's law of comparative judgment would be to obtain an interval scaling of all possible distances among stimuli in a set. Then, by methods to be discussed later, the interval scale would be transformed to a ratio scale, and the resulting distances would be factor-analyzed by the methods discussed previously.

Concerning an interval scale obtained as described above, it should be mentioned that the proportions $_iP_{jk}$ are redundant of one another in providing information about intervals among distances. For example, the proportions $_aP_{bc}$ and $_aP_{bd}$ both provide information about the size of the distance a-b on an interval scale of distances. To take advantage of these redundant sources of information, a method is available for obtaining an interval scale which produces the best fit, in the sense of least squares, to all the proportions. This method is discussed in detail by Torgerson (1958, chap. 11).

THE ADDITIVE CONSTANT   If the methods discussed in the previous section are employed to obtain an interval scale of distances, there still is the problem of converting to a ratio scale of distances. As was mentioned previously, to factor-analyze the distances among stimuli, one must measure distances on a ratio scale. After an interval scale is obtained for the distances, one can convert it to a ratio scale by adding or subtracting the proper quantity. This can be illustrated where one knows in advance the distances among stimuli on a ratio scale. Suppose that the distances a-b, b-c, and c-d were known to be 6, 5, and 2, respectively. If one were to subtract 2 from each of the distances, they would be 4, 3, and zero, respectively. The converted distances would be on an interval scale of measurement but not on a ratio scale. Obviously, one could add 2 to all the converted distances and reachieve the ratio scale of distances. Thus in this case the proper additive constant would be 2.

Of course, with an interval scaling of distances, there is no direct way to determine the additive constant that will produce a ratio scale. Rather, one must make some assumptions about the nature of the additive constant and then derive the constant on the basis of those assumptions. Most frequently, it is assumed that the additive constant should be selected so that (1) it results in Euclidean distances and (2) the dimensionality of the space of distances is as small as possible. (Methods for doing this are discussed by Torgerson, 1958.)

The above objectives are achieved iteratively. In doing this, it is important for one to know that he can always make the space of distances Euclidean by making the additive constant large enough. As the additive constant is made larger and larger, the dimensionality of the space approaches the number of stimuli minus 1. When that limit is reached, any set of distances must necessarily fit the requirements of Euclidean space. Then it would not be possible to find illogical relations among distances like those illustrated previously. Also, nothing would "go wrong" in applying principal-axes factoring methods to the distances, as it would if the space of points were non-Euclidean. In principle, then, the problem of finding the correct additive constant boils down to finding the smallest number that will preserve the Euclidean properties of the space.

The most popular method for finding the additive constant is as follows. The problem is easier to handle if the smallest distance on the interval scale of distances is set equal to zero, which is permissible with any interval scale. Then the additive constant must be either zero or a positive number. It could not be negative, because that would result in at least one negative distance among stimuli, which would be an outstanding example of a non-Euclidean set of distances. Theoretically, then, one could try all possible numbers from, say, .01 to 1,000. The smallest number that preserved the Euclidean properties of the space would be the additive constant. This would be an immense amount of labor, and consequently some shortcuts are required.

The additive constant usually is estimated in the following steps. First, a trial value is chosen, the average of all distances among stimuli on the interval scale being a good choice for this. Second, all distances on the interval scale are converted to distances on an approximate ratio scale. Third, the distance of each point is determined from the centroid of the points by methods discussed previously. Fourth, distances are converted to sums of cross products by methods which also were discussed previously. Fifth, the matrix of cross products is factored by the method of principal axes, and the results provide a check on the Euclidean properties of the space. Sixth, if the space is non-Euclidean, as usually will be the case, a larger additive constant must be selected, and the analysis must be redone from the beginning. This iterative approach is employed until the space is approximately Euclidean. Since there is some error in the data, an exact fit to Euclidean requirements is not expected; consequently the iteration is stopped when the fit is close. If in the fifth step above the space is Euclidean, a smaller additive constant is employed, and the resulting matrix of cross products is analyzed by the principal-axes method of factoring. Successive iterations in this way will lead to the smallest additive constant that approximately meets the requirements of a Euclidean space. The results on one iteration suggest how much larger or smaller the next trial value should be. (The particulars of these steps are discussed by Torgerson, 1958, and by Messick, 1956.) In studies to date, only several iterations have been required to achieve a good fit.

When the proper additive constant is determined, simultaneously a multidimensional scaling is achieved for the stimuli. The number of factors in the last iteration is taken as the dimensionality of the space, and the loadings of stimuli on those factors indicate the amount of each attribute (dimension) possessed by each stimulus.

Although logically the problem of finding an additive constant should be restricted to methods of scaling that lead to interval scales of distances, that is not necessarily the case. Previously, methods were described for estimating ratio scales of distances from ratio estimates of distances among stimuli. In the process of factor analyzing such differences, however, it might be found that the space is non-Euclidean, which would indicate that the supposed ratio scale of distances is not correct. Then it would be necessary to seek an additive constant to make the space Euclidean, and this would be done in exactly the same way as described above for interval scales of distances.

SCALING WITH AN UNKNOWN DISTANCE FUNCTION   All the methods for multidimensional scaling discussed so far in this chapter start with some type of model for determining distances among stimuli. A recent development has been the exploration of methods of multidimensional scaling that have no formal procedures for determining distances prior to the analysis (Kruskal, 1964; Shepard, 1962). These methods can, for example, be applied directly to the rank ordering of distances obtained from the method of multidimensional rank order. The method can be applied to any measure of similarity or difference, regardless of whether or not such measures can reasonably be assumed to represent distances in Euclidean space. For example, the methods can be applied to the proportion of times that one letter of the alphabet is confused with another in telegraph messages. In other words, these methods do not take seriously the actual distances which are analyzed; instead, they establish distances according to mathematical and statistical criteria.

Scaling with an unknown distance function consists essentially of (1) starting with rank-order information about distances and (2) stretching and compressing those approximate distances so as to meet certain mathematical requirements. There are three mathematical requirements, the first of these being that only monotonic transformations of the initial estimates of distances are permitted. If the approximate distances are known at least on a rank-order scale, it is not proper to make a nonmonotonic transformation of them. Second, however many transformations of those approximate distances are made, the final set of distances must meet the requirements of a Euclidean space. Third, transformations should be made so as to fit the distances as well as possible in as few dimensions as possible. These methods lead to factors which span the space, and the loadings of stimuli on the factors are obtained.

The mathematical basis for performing the above steps is very complex, and the computations are inconceivable without the best high-speed computers. In one sense, these methods are "frightening," because they replace rational models for obtaining distances with the brute force of mathematical methods. On the other hand, results from applying methods of multidimensional scaling with unknown distance functions impress one with how "robust" spatial relations among stimuli are. Results from applying these methods have been very similar to results from applying the more customary methods discussed in previous sections. Also, even more impressive, these methods have successfully reproduced known distances among stimuli. In one example, Kruskal (1964) used these methods to recover the actual distances among physical stimuli. The analysis started with a set of dots on a piece of graph paper, where it is known that (1) the distances are the real distances in a Euclidean two-space and (2) the axes of the graph can serve as two factors for describing the space. First, these actual distances were distorted by a monotonic transformation, and then random numbers were added to the resulting values. These were only roughly approximate to the actual distances. The approximate distances were submitted to the methods of analysis outlined above. The obtained configuration of points was amazingly similar to the actual configuration of points. Other demonstrations are quite convincing regarding the ability of these methods to produce results closely similar to those produced by other methods of multidimensional scaling. Because these methods are very difficult for nonspecialists to understand and because they require such immensely complex computations, it is questionable how widely they will be employed.

AN EXAMPLE OF MULTIDIMENSIONAL SCALING   An excellent example of multidimensional scaling was presented by Torgerson (1958). The problem concerned judgments about the similarity of colored chips. There were nine chips, all the same red hue but varying in terms of saturation and brightness. The physical characteristics (not necessarily the psychological characteristics) of the nine chips with respect to saturation and brightness are shown in Figure 11-19. The problem was to determine the dimensions that subjects employ in making similarity judgments about the colored chips.

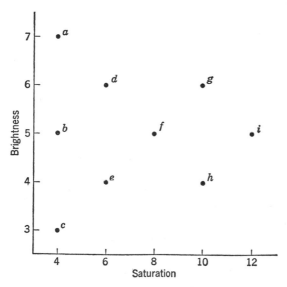

figure 11-19   *Saturation and brightness of nine colored chips. (Adapted from Torgerson, 1958, by permission of the author and publisher.)*

table 11-4 *Distances among nine colored chips*

	a	b	c	d	e	f	g	h	i
a		2.98	5.83	1.23	4.69	3.83	3.48	5.62	5.16
b	2.98		2.88	1.67	1.85	2.82	4.30	3.88	4.85
c	5.83	2.88		4.38	2.30	4.09	6.22	4.02	5.48
d	1.23	1.67	4.38		3.13	2.70	2.59	4.65	4.40
e	4.69	1.85	2.30	3.13		2.37	4.67	2.42	4.17
f	3.83	2.82	4.09	2.70	2.37		2.28	1.95	2.58
g	3.48	4.30	6.22	2.59	4.67	2.28		4.30	2.93
h	5.62	3.88	4.02	4.65	2.42	1.95	4.30		2.93
i	5.16	4.85	5.48	4.40	4.17	2.58	2.93	2.93	

SOURCE: Adapted from Torgerson (1958) by permission of the author and publisher.

table 11-5 *Sums of cross products among nine colored chips*

	a	b	c	d	e	f	g	h	i
a	10.35	2.41	−5.70	6.09	−3.99	−1.62	3.11	−7.12	−3.55
b	2.41	3.36	3.65	1.95	1.80	−1.76	−3.57	−2.35	−5.50
c	−5.70	3.65	12.24	−1.80	5.31	−1.70	−9.23	1.54	−4.31
d	6.09	1.95	−1.80	3.34	−1.40	−1.43	2.31	−5.64	−3.42
e	−3.99	1.80	5.31	−1.40	3.66	−.44	−5.08	2.40	−2.28
f	−1.62	−1.76	−1.70	−1.43	−.44	1.08	1.93	2.14	1.80
g	3.11	−3.57	−9.23	2.31	−5.08	1.93	7.99	−1.75	4.29
h	−7.12	−2.35	1.54	−5.64	2.40	2.14	−1.75	7.00	3.79
i	−3.55	−5.50	−4.31	−3.42	−2.28	1.80	4.29	3.79	9.17

SOURCE: Adapted from Torgerson (1958) by permission of the author and publisher.

The method of triads was employed with 38 subjects. The responses were then converted to the form $_iP_{jk}$, showing the proportion of times that stimulus i was judged more similar to stimulus j than to stimulus k. Those proportions were then scaled by a method (Torgerson, 1958) which provides a least-squares fit to interval scales based on Thurstone's law of comparative judgment. An additive constant was then sought to convert the interval scale of distances to a ratio scale of distances, the latter being shown in Table 11-4. Next, the distance of each stimulus from the centroid of the space of distances was determined, and these distances were used to transform distances to sums of cross products by the method discussed previously. The sums of cross products shown in Table 11-5 were factor-analyzed, for which purpose Torgerson employed the centroid method rather than the method of principal axes.

multivariate analysis

table 11-6 *A factor analysis of the sums of cross products among nine colored chips*

	CENTROID FACTORS		ROTATED FACTORS	
	A	B	A_1	B_1
a	−3.12	.18	2.71	−1.55
b	−.59	1.78	−.27	−1.85
c	1.86	2.84	−2.92	−1.69
d	−1.94	.49	1.52	−1.31
e	1.23	1.30	−1.68	−.62
f	.41	−.90	.04	.99
g	−1.40	−2.44	2.34	1.56
h	2.39	−.77	−1.80	1.76
i	1.16	−2.45	.06	2.71

SOURCE: Adapted from Torgerson (1958) by permission of the author and publisher.

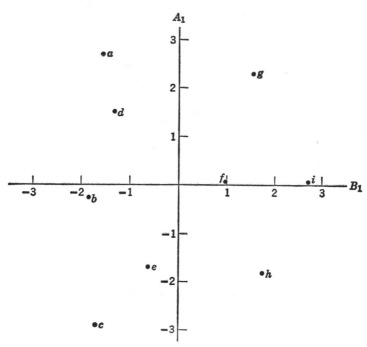

figure 11-20 *Plot of rotated factor loadings for nine colored chips. (Adapted from Torgerson, 1958, by permission of the author and publisher.)*

The first two centroid factors, and rotations of them, are shown in Table 11-6, and a plot of the rotated factors is given in Figure 11-20. Except for the placement of the origin at the centroid of the space, the configuration of points in Figure 11-20 is rather similar to the physical configuration of points (Figure 11-19) with which the problem began. Of course, in multidimensional scaling, one should not expect an exact correspondence between physical dimensions of stimuli and psychological dimensions of stimuli. In the case where stimuli can be described by physical dimensions, the problem is to determine the similarities and differences between the two types of spaces.

EVALUATION OF MULTIDIMENSIONAL SCALING Multidimensional scaling is still rather new. The number of examples in the literature is small, and there are many disputable issues regarding proper approaches. The potential advantage of multidimensional scaling is that it allows the investigator to go beyond the assumptions and procedures of unidimensional scaling and seek the number and kinds of dimensions involved in the actual responses of persons to stimuli of particular kinds.

As this author sees it, there are two major problems in multidimensional scaling. First, one can rightly question the assumptions in the different models for multidimensional scaling, either the purely mathematical assumptions involved in models for scaling with an unknown distance function or the psychological assumptions in models such as those relating to Thurstone's law of comparative judgment. The second major problem concerns the tasks required of subjects. In unidimensional scaling, the tasks usually are intuitively clear to investigators, and subjects apparently have no difficulty in understanding them, e.g., instructions to rate the handsomeness of men on a seven-step scale or to indicate which of two weights is heavier. In contrast, in multidimensional scaling, the tasks are not so intuitively clear to investigators, and it has been this author's experience that subjects are sometimes a bit confused by them. All the tasks set for subjects concern the concepts of similarity and difference, which are a bit elusive when the stimuli vary with respect to a number of possible dimensions. For example, one could, if he thought it appropriate, consider the ages of senators in making similarity judgments about them. Also, similarity judgments are *judgments,* and to request the same types of responses in situations relating to preferences would probably be confusing to subjects and might lead to wide individual differences in results. For example, if subjects were required to rate the similarity of different national groups, e.g., Russians, French, English, etc., responses would partly concern attitudes (a form of preference), and individual differences in such attitudes might strongly influence the results.

In addition to the somewhat elusive meaning of ''similarity'' in multidimensional scaling, some methods for gathering data require the subject to make complex judgments about the relative similarity of pairs of stimuli, as in obtaining similarity judgments by methods of ratio estimation, discussed previously in this chapter. Because of the complexities of the tasks required of subjects in some forms of multidimensional scaling, one wonders if the subject can do what is requested and whether or not the results make any sense.

As is true of all models in science, mathematical or otherwise, the proof of the pudding is in how well the results of employing a model eventually lead to parsimonious laws of nature. Most of the studies in multidimensional scaling to date have mainly been "demonstrations"—of particular approaches, of computational methods, and of the types of results to be obtained. The most encouraging evidence for the usefulness of presently available methods of multidimensional scaling comes from the third type of demonstration above. In those instances where stimuli could be described by physical dimensions (e.g., colored chips or geometrical forms), the dimensions obtained from multidimensional scaling have been surprisingly close to the actual physical dimensions. In those instances where the stimuli could not be described in terms of physical dimensions (e.g., senators), the results of multidimensional scaling have made good sense.

What is needed now is to go beyond the stage of demonstrations and determine to what extent the dimensions obtained from multidimensional scaling are predictive of results in controlled experiments. If such dimensions actually are psychological dimensions, they should, for example, be predictive of amounts of facilitation and inhibition in various types of learning and predictive of gradients of generalization in studies of classical conditioning.

SUGGESTED ADDITIONAL READINGS

Cronbach, L. J., and Gleser, Goldine C. Assessing similarity between profiles. *Psychol. Bull.,* 1953, **50,** 456–473.

Maxwell, A. E. Canonical variate analysis when the variables are dichotomous. *Educ. psychol. Measmt,* 1961, **21,** 259–272.

Tiedeman, D. V., Bryan, J. G., and Rulon, P. J. An application of the multiple discriminant function to data from the airman classification battery. *Res. Bull.* No. 52-37. San Antonio, Tex.: Lackland Air Force Base, 1952.

Torgerson, W. *Theory and methods of scaling.* New York: Wiley, 1958, chap. 11.

PART 4

the content areas

CHAPTER TWELVE

MEASUREMENT OF ABILITIES

Before we discuss human abilities, a definition is in order: *Abilities concern individual differences in how well people perform different tasks when they try*. The definition says that abilities concern "individual differences," but perhaps it would be better to say that psychologists mainly are interested in individual differences in abilities rather than in relatively constant characteristics of people. For example, it certainly requires abilities, and important ones, to lift objects from a table, but since individual differences in this regard are not very important, there would be little there to interest psychologists. In the definition, the words "how well" signify that abilities concern performance with respect to specified criteria of success. Examples are correct answers to factual questions, correct solutions of mathematical problems, accuracy of reproducing a geometrical figure from memory, and speed of response in a study of reaction time. Before a particular type of ability can be studied, the "how well" of performance must be objectively defined. The definition speaks of performance when people "try," which indicates that abilities can be measured only in those situations where all subjects are motivated to do their best.

Because this book is mainly concerned with measurement theory and methodology rather than with surveying empirical findings, this chapter will be mainly concerned with theory and methodology also. To satisfy that concern, however, it will be necessary to summarize some trends in studies of human abilities. Descriptions of particular measurement techniques and detailed accounts of research on human abilities can be found in the Suggested Additional Readings at the end of the chapter.

There is no end to the ways in which people differ from one another in abilities, but only some of these have proved worthy of attention. Most thoroughly investigated have been the so-called "intellectual" abilities, which are distinguished from the "special" abilities. There is no way to clearly make the distinction, but the *intellectual abilities* are usually thought of as those forms of ability that are important for scholarly accomplishment and scientific work. In contrast, the *special abilities* are those that are thought to be important for mechanical skills, artistic pursuits, and physical adroitness. Although the evidence to be summarized in this chapter will primarily concern the intellectual abilities, the theories and methods which will be discussed are general to all forms of ability.

historical perspective

It is rather surprising that systematic studies of human abilities were not undertaken until the second half of the last century. This cannot be explained in any large measure by physical problems of instrumentation, because even today most measures of human ability are paper-and-pencil instruments, and writing equipment has been available for thousands of years. One might think that this slow development was because of the absence of correlational methods (and their extensions to multivariate analysis), but this does not seem to have been the case. Correlational methods are very simple in comparison to systems of mathematics that were developed before the birth of Christ, and if they had seen a purpose in it, the ancient Greeks might have worked with correlational methods similar to those that we use today. Once an interest in studies of individual differences developed, and thus a need for correlational methods was seen, they were developed very quickly.

The slowness with which measures of human ability were developed seems to have paralleled the slowness with which man came to consider himself as a proper object of investigation. The earliest scientific concern of man was with the lower animals around him, natural phenomena on earth, and the heavenly bodies. This is evidenced in the fact that an accurate method was available for measuring the circumference of the earth 2,000 years before the first systematic measures of human ability were developed. The attitudes that led to those imbalances in scientific approach may have been the result of religious compunctions about investigating people, or they may have resulted from people taking one another so much for granted that they saw nothing to study in human beings; but whatever the causes, systematic studies of human abilities were late in coming, and they still have a long way to go.

DARWIN   The work of Charles Darwin had an immense influence on all studies of living organisms, including studies in psychology. If there is a "survival of the fittest" among plants and lower animals, there may also be a "survival of the fittest" among people. If it is meaningful to think of plants and lower animals as adjusting to, or coping with, the environment, it may be meaningful to think of much of human activity as

measurement of abilities

serving the same purpose. If individual differences among fishes in a species relate to differences in survival rate, individual differences in humans may be similarly important. If differences in survival rate result in slow changes in species of fish over many generations, individual differences in humans may slowly lead to changes in the average characteristics of the species as a whole. If physical characteristics of fish tend to be passed on from generation to generation, some individual differences in people may be influenced by heredity.

GALTON   Particularly important in the history of studies of individual differences was the influence that Darwin had on Francis Galton. Through this influence, Galton became interested in the heritability of human traits. He became convinced that most human traits are inherited, not only such physical characteristics as height and eye color, but also abilities and personality characteristics. Galton founded the *eugenics* movement, the avowed purpose of which is the betterment of the human race through selective mating. (The movement is still active today in England.) Being a scientist, he saw that before a program of eugenics was possible it would be necessary to understand the principles whereby traits are passed from father to son, and before that could be done, it would be necessary to measure human traits.

Galton coined the term "mental test" and made efforts to measure many human attributes. He recognized the need for standardization in testing—that all subjects should be presented the same problems under uniform conditions and instructions. Galton's tests bore little resemblance to the ones which are used most widely today. He and his immediate followers in England made much of the philosopher Locke's dictum that all knowledge comes through the senses. Their reasoning was that the person with the most acute "senses" would be the most gifted and knowledgeable. Most of Galton's tests were measures of simple sensory discrimination: the ability to discriminate tones from one another, the acuteness of vision, the ability to differentiate colors, and many other sensory functions.

Galton began the first large-scale testing program at his Anthropometric Laboratory in the South Kensington Museum in 1884. Each visitor was charged three pence for having his measurements taken on a variety of physical and sensory tests, including height, weight, breathing power, strength of pull, hearing, sight, and color sense. To analyze the obtained data, Galton made use of statistical methods, and with these he determined averages and measures of dispersion. His particular need was for a measure of association, or correlation, to determine the amount of resemblance between the characteristics of fathers and their sons. For this purpose, he made the first steps in the development of correlational analysis.

Galton's work came at a very important time, because during the last quarter of the nineteenth century, the newly founded field of psychology was concerned almost exclusively with the mental makeup of the typical person, and there was very little interest in individual differences. Galton's work made it obvious that the new field of psychology could not ignore individual differences. The study of individual differences has been an important activity in psychology since that time, particularly so in the United States.

PEARSON   Galton supported a younger colleague, Karl Pearson, in the development of statistical methods for the study of individual differences. Pearson was the genius in mathematical statistics that Galton was in studies of individual differences. He derived the PM correlation coefficient, multiple correlation, and partial correlation, and laid the groundwork for factor analysis and other methods of multivariate analysis. Once Galton pointed to a need for mathematical methods to deal with the measurement of human abilities, it did not take Pearson long to develop them.

BINET   Along with his many other interests in psychology, during the last quarter of the nineteenth century, Alfred Binet became interested in individual differences in human ability. This interest may have been fostered by his work with hypnotism, in which there had been much speculation about individual differences in hypnotizability. Also, his interest probably was fostered by the developing field of psychiatry in France at the time, with which he had been associated. Psychiatry and clinical psychology are, by their nature, concerned with individual differences, and it is only to be expected that persons in those fields would foster studies of human abilities and personality attributes.

Binet's early work on human abilities resembled the work of Galton in that he worked mainly with simple variables of sensory discrimination and physical attributes. He even studied palmistry as a possible source of measures of abilities. Binet's work on abilities took a practical turn in the opening years of the twentieth century, when he was commissioned by the French government to study mental deficiency in French schools. The French government had become alarmed by the number of children who were apparently unable to perform normal schoolwork, and some means was needed for distinguishing those children who could profit from remedial instruction from those that lacked the capacity to advance in school. Faced with this practical problem, Binet did what most other psychologists would have done in the circumstances: he turned from investigating the "elements" of human ability to investigating the use of a global measure of overall intellectual ability, or intelligence.

Binet, working in collaboration with Théodore Simon, completed his first test in 1905. It consisted of a list of 30 problems concerning the child's ability to understand and reason with the objects in the cultural environment. The problems ranged in difficulty from those that could be solved by very young children to those that would be difficult for the average adult. Five of the problems were as follows:

1 Touch head, nose, ear, cap, key, and string.

2 Judge which of two lines is longer.

3 Repeat immediately three digits read by the examiner.

4 Define house, horse, fork, and mamma.

5 Repeat sentence of 15 words after a single hearing.

The list of problems was tried on about 50 children, and provisional norms were established. The test obviously was only a rough beginning to the measurement of intelligence, but it constituted a very important first step. A revision of the test was made in 1908, in which items were arranged in terms of age levels, with a group of items representing average intelligence for each age. The highest age level at which a child could perform adequately was called his *mental age*. Later, William Stern suggested that this be divided by chronological age for each child, which (when multiplied by 100) is the IQ as it has come to be known.

It is hard to overstate Binet's influence on later investigations of human abilities. The measurement of intelligence was then, and still is, of immense practical importance. The thought that intelligence could be measured, even if only approximately, stirred many investigators to develop measures of intelligence and to use such measures in research. The scene soon shifted to America, where there were numerous translations and modifications of the Binet tests. The important point, however, is that all subsequent work on the measurement of intelligence has been modeled after Binet's work, to the extent that many of the items on modern tests of intelligence are very similar to ones that Binet used.

The strong influence that Binet's tests had on subsequent efforts to measure intelligence was, in one sense, very good, but in another sense it might have worked a harm. Binet's tests concerned the end products of intelligence—the mastery of language, reasoning, and the assimilation of facts. This is where one naturally would look for evidence of differences in overall intellectual ability. By weaving a measuring instrument from the global end products of intellectual functioning, one has a high probability of obtaining a valid measure. The type of test developed by Binet obviously has a rather high level of construct validity for the construct of intelligence. The influence of his tests in this regard was very good, because it rapidly led to the development of measures of intelligence with real practical importance.

The sense in which the influence of Binet may have worked a harm on subsequent studies of human abilities is in the fact that subsequent studies along the same lines as the work of Binet have not taught us much about the *nature* of human intellect. It is one thing to be able to measure an attribute and quite another to understand it. In turning away from the elements of intellect to work with global end products, Binet certainly was on the right course for the development of valid measures of intelligence. If one is interested only in measurement, rather than in understanding, one should always turn to global end products rather than try to pick apart an attribute in terms of simple functions. For example, if one wanted to measure the quality of different wines, the safest approach would be to have judgments made by professional wine tasters. Such judgments probably would be valid in the sense that they would be predictive of what wines people would like and what they would purchase, but they would tell us nothing about how grapes should be grown or how wine should be made.

Of course, if Binet's work had a somewhat stifling influence on subsequent studies of human intellect, this was not at all Binet's fault. His earlier work showed that he was aware of the need to pick apart the nature of human intellect in terms of simple functions, but given the practical job of developing measures of intelligence in a rather short period of time, he naturally turned to the use of global measures of end products.

APPLIED PSYCHOLOGY   The work of Binet had a strong influence on applied psychology, particularly in the United States. Tests of the type developed by Binet have been exceedingly useful in schools, psychological clinics, the armed forces, and in industry. There is hardly anyone today who has not taken an intelligence test of some kind, and the lives of many people have been strongly influenced by decisions based in large part on the results of such tests, e.g., a child being placed in a special school for retardates and a man being allowed to undertake officer training in the armed forces.

Because tests of the Binet type have worked so well in applied settings, in turn applied psychology has had a very strong influence on concepts of human abilities and on the research into human abilities. This has particularly been the case during the two great wars of this century, in which many psychologists were called to develop large-scale testing programs for many purposes in the selection of men, the measurement of progress in programs of training, and the assignment of men to sundry duties.

It would be silly to suggest that it is wrong for measures of human ability to have practical importance or that applied concerns should not influence the directions of research on human abilities. This applied influence has, however, probably had some adverse effects on the study of human abilities. There has been too much concern with predictive validity, whereas, as was mentioned previously, the major concern in most basic research in psychology is with the explication of constructs. For example, in the use of multiple regression to predict a criterion, the applied psychologist usually loses interest in those measures that fail to add to predictive validity, but such measures might be of great importance in basic research on the nature of human abilities. Also, partly because of the applied influence, there has been too little theory about human abilities and too much "shotgun empiricism." Even worse, studies of human abilities have in large measure been divorced from experimental psychology, where we probably should go to seek interesting new measures of differences in abilities and to investigate the importance of different factors of intellect. Of course, the applied psychologists cannot wait while the basic researcher wanders snail-paced through the crannies of natural phenomena, but on the other hand, the basic researcher should not be limited by the scope of present practical concerns or dominated by the concepts and procedures relating to applied efforts.

One of the important influences of applied psychology on the study of human abilities has been in terms of money. Much of the research support for studies of human abilities has come from government agencies, industry, and commercial distributors of tests. Apparently there still is not a lot of grant funds from government agencies and philanthropic organizations being given for basic research on human abilities, and this being so, it is only natural for researchers in this area to seek funds for research from applied enterprises. In consequence, research on human abilities, particularly in this country, has been strongly influenced by the needs and outlooks of applied psychology. For the sake of applied psychology, that is good, but for the sake of promoting the science of psychology, one would hope to see more basic research on human abilities and a closer tie with psychological theories and with experimental psychology.

THE BRITISH FACTORISTS After having followed the threads of the Binet influence up through modern applied psychology, it would be appropriate to return to Galton's followers in England. There was a remarkable parallel during the first several years of this century between the work of Binet in France and the work of Charles Spearman in England. (The work of Spearman is summarized in his book *The Abilities of Man,* 1927.) Like Binet, Spearman was concerned with the nature of human abilities, but his was a much more scholarly approach based on psychological theories concerning the nature of abilities and buttressed by mathematical models for studying human abilities. Implicit in Binet's efforts to measure intelligence was the assumption that either there is only one factor of intelligence or intelligence is dominated by one factor. Spearman asserted the presence of a general factor as a hypothesis to be tested. He developed the mathematical criteria for the presence of a general factor in a matrix of correlations among tests (discussed in Chapter Nine) and gathered data to test the hypothesis of a general factor.

In his early work, Spearman concluded that individual differences in all tests of ability can be accounted for by two factors: a general factor G and a specific factor for each test. Later Spearman had to recognize that G was not sufficient to explain the correlations among all tests of ability. He could see that it was necessary to deal with "correlated specific factors" (which is rather paradoxical terminology) or with "group factors." Whatever one wanted to call them, it became obvious that more factors than one would be required to explain correlations among tests of ability. Now that we have "splintered" human abilities into numerous factors, we have come to realize that much, but not all, of the common variance among tests of abilities can be explained by one general factor.

Although, in a sense, the theories and findings of Spearman tended to support the type of test developed by Binet, Spearman proposed a more refined method for measuring G. First, it would be necessary to determine which tasks actually measure G rather than being dominated by specific factors; second, to measure G would require a proper weighing of each intellectual task. Spearman was alarmed by Binet's practice of assembling a hodgepodge of problems without first testing for the presence of a general factor or without properly weighing the problems in terms of their loadings on the general factor. Since, however, Spearman was concerned more with basic research on human abilities than with the development of practical measures, he developed no tests with the wide appeal of the Binet measures of intelligence.

Spearman's work continues to be important for two major reasons. First, while developing mathematical models for studying G, he laid the foundation for factor analysis. He could see that, in the end, questions regarding the generality of intelligence rested on the nature of correlations among tests of ability. Once he showed how such correlations could be studied with respect to a general factor, it encouraged others to extend the logic to methods for investigating any number of factors among tests.

The second major importance of Spearman's work is that, in contrast to the tradition of applied work that followed from Binet's tests, it established a scholarly tradition in the investigation of human abilities. Spearman was concerned much more with *understanding* human abilities than with just measuring them (which perhaps is why few practical instruments developed from his research). Spearman had many interesting theories about G, about its biological basis, the influence of culture, the interaction of G with manifestations of abilities in daily life, and the relations of G to speed, fatigue, and other variables.

From 1930 until recent years, there was a tendency, particularly in this country, to dismiss Spearman as having been "wrong" and to forget the achievements of the man and the potency of his ideas. The statistical evidence is that he really was not entirely wrong about the importance, if not omnipotence, of a general factor. Also, Spearman's theories about human abilities still are stimulating, and they should provide a lesson to some of those modern factorists who are less concerned with a real psychology of human abilities than with obtaining more and more factors.

Spearman's influence still is strong among British psychologists. They no longer cling to Spearman's G as the sole factor of intellect, but they recognize the presence of a general factor in addition to a number of group factors. Perhaps because of Spearman's influence, they are reluctant to accept all the factors found by American psychologists as being important dimensions of intellect. Also, in Spearman's tradition, British psychologists have tried to make sense of the structure of human abilities by proposing "factor hierarchies," a matter which will be discussed later in this chapter. Although picking names tends to slight the numerous unmentioned British psychologists that have made major contributions to the study of human abilities, the names that stand out are Godfrey Thomson, Cyril Burt, and Phillip Vernon.

pioneering research by the Thurstones

Just as Binet's ideas about the testing of intelligence were rapidly imported to the United States, Spearman's ideas were also; but psychologists in this country were concerned not so much with Spearman's theories of human abilities as with his methods of factor analysis. During the 1920s and 1930s, American psychologists pushed mathematical methods of factor analysis far ahead of those developed by Spearman. Prominent in this work were T. L. Kelley and K. J. Holzinger. Subsequently, L. L. Thurstone did so much to develop mathematical methods of factor analysis and to explore human abilities with them that it is fair to say that he is the "father" of the American school of factorists.

The American school of factorists has, at least until recent years, been typified by a rough-and-ready bedrock empiricism. There has not been nearly enough theory, but there has been a great deal of technical elegance in the measurement of human abilities and in the mathematical analysis of correlations among them. Later it will be shown how this technical elegance has produced factors to the point of confusion, but before that stage in the history of the study of human abilities is discussed, let us see what the scene was like in the early 1940s when psychologists were learning about Thurstone's investigations of the "primary mental abilities."

Thurstone was an engineer before he was a psychologist, and as an engineer he worked for a time with Thomas Edison. Perhaps genius is infectious, because Thurstone became an Edison in the field of psychology. Although he is best known for studies of human abilities, particularly for his contributions to factor analysis, his inventive mind ranged over studies of learning, perception, personality, and other topics. For many years his Psychometric Laboratory at the University of Chicago was the world center for studies of human abilities, and many of the persons who are today prominent in psychometric work studied there with him. Thurstone made not only outstanding contributions to the theory and methodology of individual differences, but also the first large-scale onslaughts on the empirical problems.

Up until about 1930, the major argument in studies of human ability concerned whether or not Spearman was correct about the omnipresence of G. Thurstone, as he often stated it, turned the question around and asked *how many* and *what kinds* of factors are needed to account for the observed correlations among tests of ability. To answer these questions, Thurstone made major improvements in existing methods of factor analysis and gathered data on a scale that was unheard of in that day.

Before Thurstone's studies of human ability, most studies had been done on from 6 to 20 tests, and frequently the number of subjects was too small to obtain stable results. In one major analysis, Thurstone employed 60 tests, most of which had to be developed for the purpose. Only those who have participated in such studies can appreciate the labor that is involved in constructing instruments, administering them to subjects, and analyzing the data. Inherent in such studies is the great difficulty of administering all tests to all subjects. If a subject takes 59 tests but, for some reason, is unavailable to take the 60th test, none of his scores can be used in a factor analysis. When Thurstone performed his major studies of human abilities, only the most rudimentary of computational equipment was available. Consequently it was an immense and highly time-consuming job to compute all possible correlations among tests, employ methods of condensation (the centroid method being used most frequently for that purpose), and rotate the factors.

An understanding of what was known about factors of human abilities circa 1940 can be gained from reading the article to follow by Thelma Gwinn Thurstone, her husband's collaborator in many studies of human abilities. The article beautifully understates the magnitude

of the research and the importance of the findings for subsequent studies **of** human abilities.

PRIMARY MENTAL ABILITIES OF CHILDREN[1]

For many years psychologists have been accustomed to the problems of special abilities and disabilities. These are, in fact, the principal concern of the school psychologists who deal with children who cannot read, have a blind spot for numbers, or do one thing remarkably well and other things poorly. It seems strange with all this experience in differential psychology that we have clung so long to the practice of summarizing a child's mental endowment by a single index, such as the mental age, the intelligence quotient, the percentile rank in general intelligence, and other single average measures. An average index of mental endowment should be useful for many educational purposes, but it should not be regarded as more than the average of several tests. Two children with the same mental age can be entirely different persons, as is well known. There is nothing wrong about using a mental age or an intelligence quotient if it is understood as an average of several tests. The error that is frequently made is interpreting it as measuring some basic functional unity when it is known to be nothing more than a composite of many functional unities.

The researches on the primary mental abilities which have been in progress for several years have had as their first purposes the identification and definition of the independent factors of mind. As the nature of the abilities became more clearly indicated by successive studies, a second purpose of a more practical nature has been involved in some of the studies. This purpose has been to prepare a set of tests of psychological significance and practicable adaptability to the school testing and guidance program. The series of studies will be summarized in this paper, the battery of tests soon to be available will be described, and some of the problems now being investigated will be discussed briefly.

previous studies

The first study in this series involved the use of 56 psychological examinations that were given to a group of about 250 college students. That study revealed a number of primary abilities, some of which were clearly defined by the configuration of test vectors while others were indicated by the configuration but less clearly defined. All of these factors have been studied in subsequent test batteries in which each primary factor has been represented by new tests specially designed to feature the primary factors in the purest possible form. The object has been to construct tests in which there is a heavy saturation of a primary factor and in which other factors

[1] Reprinted from Thelma G. Thurstone, Primary mental abilities of children, *Educ. psychol. Measmt*, 1941, **1**, 105–116, by permission of the author and publisher.

are minimized. This is the purification of tests by reducing their complexity.

These latter studies of the separate abilities were in each case made in the Chicago high schools. . . . In each series of tests, one factor was represented by a large number of tests, but all factors were well represented. In all of these studies the same primary abilities were identified as had been found in the experiment with college students. These studies led to the publication by the American Council on Education of an experimental battery of tests for the primary mental abilities, adaptable for use with students of high school or college age.

The identification of the same primary mental abilities among high school students as we had previously found among college students encouraged us to look for differentiation among the abilities of younger children. In the Chicago Public Schools, group mental tests are made of all 1B, 4B, and 8B children in the elementary schools and of 10B students in the high schools. The demand for a series of tests to be used in the guidance program for high school entrants and the advisability of not making too broad a leap in age led us to select an eighth-grade population for the next study.

the eighth-grade experiment

In view of the purpose of investigating whether or not primary mental abilities could be isolated for children at the fourteen year age level, the construction of the tests consisted essentially in the adaptation for the younger children of tests previously used with high school students. In some of the tests little or no alteration was necessary, while for other tests it was considered advisable to revise vocabulary and other aspects of the tests to suit the younger age level. A number of new tests were added to those selected from previous experimental batteries. Sixty tests constituted the final battery.

When the tests had been designed and printed, they were given in a trial form to children in grades 7A and 8A in several schools. Groups of from 50 to 100 children in these two grades were used for the purpose of standardizing procedures and especially, for setting time limits. . . .

Eleven hundred and fifty-four children participated in this study. The complete battery of 60 tests was given in 11 one-hour sessions to the children in the 8B grades in each of the 15 schools. The children enjoyed the tests and, with very few exceptions, the sustained interest and effort were quite evident. One thing which a psychologist might fear in such a long series of tests would be fluctuating motivation on the part of the students. Although the adjustment teachers administered the tests, every session was observed by a member of our staff, and we were highly gratified by the sustained interest and effort of the pupils.

In addition to the 60 tests we used three more variables: chronological age, mental age, and sex. The latter test data were available in school records. They were determined by the Kuhlmann-Anderson tests which had been given previously to the same children. Therefore, the battery to be analyzed factorially contained 63 variables.

The total population in this study consisted of 1,154 eighth-grade children. When all the records had been assembled, it was found that 710 of these subjects had complete records for all of the 63 variables. We decided to base our correlations on this population of complete records rather than to use the large population with varying numbers of cases for the correlation coefficients. For convenience of handling with the tabulating-machine methods, the raw scores were transmuted into single digit scores from which the Pearson product-moment correlation coefficients were computed. With 63 variables there were 1,935 Pearson correlation coefficients.

This table of intercorrelations was factored to 10 factors by the centroid method on the tabulating machines by means of punched cards. Successive rotations made by the method of extended vectors yielded an oblique factorial matrix which is a simple structure.

Inspection of the rotated factorial matrix showed seven of the factors previously indicated: Memory, Induction, Verbal Comprehension, Word Fluency, Number, Space, Perceptual Speed, and three less easily identifiable factors. One of these is another Verbal factor; one is involved in ability to solve pencil mazes; and one is present in the three dot-counting tests which were used.

We have computed the intercorrelations between the 10 primary factors. Our main interest centers on the seven primary factors that can be given interpretation and, especially, on the first six of these factors for which the interpretation is rather more definite. Among the high correlations we note that the Number is correlated with the two Verbal factors. The Word Fluency factor has high correlation with the Verbal Comprehension factor and with Induction. The Rote Memory factor seems to be independent of the other factors. These correlations are higher than the correlations between primary factors for adults.

Because of the psychological interest in the correlations of the primary mental abilities, we have made a separate analysis of the correlations for those factors which seem to have reasonably certain interpretation. If these six primary mental abilities are correlated because of some general intellective factor, then the rank of the correlation matrix should be one. Upon examination, this actually proves to be the case. A single factor accounts for most of the correlations between the primary factors.

The single factor loadings show that the inductive factor has the highest loading and the Rote Memory factor the lowest loading on the common general factor in the primary abilities. This general factor is what we have called a second-order general factor. It makes its apperance not as a separate factor, but as a factor inherent in the primaries and their correla·· tions. If further studies of the primary mental abilities of children should reveal this general factor, it may sustain Spearman's contention that there exists a general intellective factor. Instead of depending on the averages or centroids of arbitrary test batteries for its determination, the present method should enable us to identify it uniquely.

We have not been able to find in these data a general factor that is distinct from the primary factors, but the second-order general factor should be of as much psychological interest as the more frequently postulated, independent general factor of Spearman. It would be our judgment that the second-order general factor found here is probably the general factor which Spearman has so long defended, but we cannot say whether he would accept the present findings as sustaining his contentions about the general factor. We have not found any occasion to debate the existence of a general intellective factor. The factorial methods we have been using are adequate for finding such a factor, either as a factor independent of the primaries or as a factor operating through correlated primaries. We have reported on primary mental abilities in adults, which seem to show only low positive correlations except for the two verbal factors. In the present study we have found higher correlations among the primary factors for eighth-grade children. It is now an interesting question to determine whether the correlations among primary abilities of still younger children will reveal, perhaps even more strongly, a second-order general factor.

Interpretation of factors

The analysis of this battery of 60 tests revealed essentially the same set of primary factors which had been found in previous factorial studies. Six of the factors seemed to have sufficient stability for the several age levels that have been investigated to justify an extension of the tests for these factors into practical test work in the schools. In making this extension we have been obliged to consider carefully the difference between research on the nature of the primary factors and the construction of tests for practical use. Several of the primary factors are not yet sufficiently clear as regards psychological interpretation to justify an attempt to appraise them generally among school children. The primary factors that do seem to be clear enough for such purposes are the following: Verbal Comprehension V, Word Fluency W, Number N, Space S, Rote Memory M, and Induction or Reasoning R. The factors which in several studies are not yet sufficiently clear for general application are the Perceptual factor P and the Deductive factor D.

The Verbal factor V is found in tests involving verbal comprehension, for example, tests of vocabulary, opposites and synonyms, completion tests, and various reading comprehension tests.

The Word Fluency factor W is involved whenever the subject is asked to think of isolated words at a rapid rate. It is for this reason that we have called the factor a Word Fluency factor. It can be expected in such tests as anagrams, rhyming, and producing words with a given initial letter, prefix, or suffix.

The Space factor S is involved in any task in which the subject manipulates an object imaginally in two or three dimensions. The ability is involved in many mechanical tasks and in the understanding of mechanical drawings. Such material cannot be used conveniently in testing situations, so we have used a large number of tasks which are psychologically similar, such as Flags, Cards, and Figures.

The Number factor N is involved in the ability to do numerical calculations rapidly and accurately. It is not dependent upon the reasoning factors in problem-solving, but seems to be restricted to the simpler processes, such as addition and multiplication.

A Memory factor M has been clearly present in all tests batteries. The tests for memory which are now being used depend upon the ability to memorize quickly. It is quite possible that the Memory factor will be broken down into more specific factors.

The Reasoning factor R is involved in tasks that require the subject to discover a rule or principle covering the material of the test. The Letter Series and Letter Grouping tests are good examples of the task. In all these experimental studies two separate Reasoning factors have been indicated. They are perhaps Induction and Deduction, but we have not succeeded in constructing pure tests of either factor. The tests which we are now using are more heavily saturated with the Inductive factor, but for the present we are simply calling the ability R, Reasoning.

In presenting for general use a differential psychological examination which appraises the mental endowment of children, it should not be assumed that there is anything final about six primary factors. No one knows how many primary mental abilities there may be. It is hoped that future factorial studies will reveal many other important primary abilities so that the mental profiles of students may eventually be adequate for appraising educational and vocational potentialities. In such a program the present studies are only a starting point in substituting for the description of mental endowment by a single intelligence index the description of mental endowment by a profile of fundamental traits.

the final test battery

In adapting the tests for practical use in the schools for the appraisal of six primary mental abilities, we must recognize that the new test program has for its object the production of a profile for each child, as distinguished from the description of a child's mental endowment in terms of a single intelligence index. For many educational purposes it is still of value to appraise a child's mental endowment roughly by a single measure, but the composite nature of such single indices must be recognized.

The factorial matrix of the battery of 60 tests was inspected to find the three best tests for each of seven primary factors. In making the selection of tests for each primary factor we considered not only the factorial saturations of the tests, which are, of course, the most important consideration, but also the availability of parallel forms which may be needed in case the tests should come into general use. Ease of administration and ease in understanding of the instructions are also important considerations.

The three tests for each primary factor were printed in a separate booklet and the material was so arranged that the three tests for any factor could be given easily within a 40-minute school period. The main purpose of the larger test battery was to determine whether or not the primary factors could be found for eighth-grade children, but the purpose of the present shorter battery was to produce a practical, useful test battery and to check its factorial composition. The selected tests were edited and revised so that they could be used for either hand-scoring or machine-scoring. The Word Fluency tests constitute an exception in that none of the tests now known to be saturated with this factor seems to be suitable for machine-scoring.

In order to check the factorial analysis at the present age level, we arranged to give the selected list of 21 tests to a second population of eighth-grade children. The resulting data were factored independently of the larger battery of tests. There were 437 subjects in this population who took all of the 21 tests. This population was used for a new factor analysis. The results of this analysis clearly confirmed the previous study. The simple structure in the present battery is sharp, with only one primary factor conspicuously present in each test, so that the structure could be determined by inspection for clusters.

A battery of 17 tests has been assembled into a series of test booklets for use in the Chicago schools. An experimental edition of 25,000 copies has been printed, and the plan for securing norms on these tests includes their administration to 1,000 children at each half-year grade level from grade 5B through the senior year in high school. These records have been obtained during the school year 1940 to 1941. The use of such a wide age range in standardizing the test is at first thought, perhaps, rather strange. The effort was made in order to secure age norms throughout the entire range of abilities found among eighth-grade children since the tests are to become a part of the testing procedure for all 8B children in the Chicago schools. Separate age norms will be derived for each of the six primary abilities. If a single index of a student's mental ability is desired, it is recommended that the average of his six ability scores be used. . . .

further problems

One of our principal research interests at the present time is to determine whether primary abilities can be identified in children of kindergarten or first-grade age. A series of about 50 tests is well under way, and some of them are now being tried with young children. If we succeed in isolating primary abilities among these young children, our next step will be to prepare a practical battery of tests for that age. A subsequent problem will be to make experimental studies of paper-and-pencil tests for appraising the primary abilities of children in the intermediate grades, approximately at the fourth-grade level. We are fairly confident that such tests can be prepared for use in the intermediate grades.

It is a long way in the future, but it is interesting to speculate on the possibility of using the tests of the primary mental abilities as the tool with which to study fundamental psychological problems of mental growth and mental inheritance. Absolute scaling of the tests at the different age levels will make possible studies on the rates of development of the separate abilities at various age levels. Modifiability of the abilities will be another problem to which we shall later turn attention.

present outlooks on studies of human abilities

Since the monumental work by the Thurstones, factor-analytic studies of human abilities have pushed far ahead. In the early 1940s, many psychologists were developing tests for the armed forces. Tests were developed for so many special types of aptitudes and with respect to so many types of training programs that excellent opportunities were provided to extend what was known about factors of human ability. Up through 1950, it could be reported that there were over 40 well-established factors of ability. (These are described in detail by French, 1951.) This was a far cry from the conception of human abilities originally held by Spearman, and it suggested that the Binet type of test was based on very false assumptions about the generality of intellect.

The number of factors of intellect has continued to grow since the survey by French, and now one could argue that there are between 50 and 100 factors, depending on how cautiously one interpreted the evidence. Whereas the purpose of employing factor analysis was to provide an understanding of the nature of human abilities, the results of factor-analytic studies served only to confuse us. Spearman hoped to show that only one factor of intellect was important, and one gathers that the Thurstones hoped to show that no more than about 10 would be required to cover the important ground of human intellect. Probably no one wanted to find over 50 factors, because having found so many, what is one to do with them? Is human intellect really splintered into so many separate dimensions?

In the search for factors, it gradually became apparent that one can artifactually force factors to occur in a number of ways. One way to do this is to compose several tests that are highly similar in terms

the content areas

of operations and materials. An example is as follows. On the first test, the subject is presented with a page of randomized alphabetical letters and told to circle as many a's as he can in 60 seconds. On the next test, the subject is presented with another page of randomized letters and told to circle b's; then on the third test, he is told to circle c's. The three tests will correlate well with one another, and the correlations among them cannot be accounted for by factors relating to other types of tests. Then, from a purely mathematical point of view, it must be admitted that the three tests define a factor; but is a factor that is so narrowly defined likely to be of any importance?

Another way to artifactually force factors is to include in the analysis subjects who are heterogeneous in numerous ways and to intercorrelate variables that relate to that heterogeneity. For example, French reports an age factor, with the largest loading on chronological age and smaller loadings on tests that change with age. He reports a sex factor which relates to differences in central tendency between men and women on tests of ability. Of course, it is important to learn of relations between such vital statistics and human abilities, but should one consider these as factors? One could prevent such factors from occurring either by selecting more homogeneous groups of subjects or by partialing age, sex, and other vital statistics from the correlations among tests before applying factor analysis.

There are numerous other ways to artifactually force factors to occur. One of these is to score the same items in a number of different ways, in which case there nearly always will be high correlations among the different scoring keys.

judging the importance of factors of ability

Aside from the point that many of the supposed factors that have been found would be better classed as *artifactors* (to coin a word), it is becoming increasingly clear that, to prevent utter chaos in the accumulation of factors, some consideration must be given to the *importance* of factors. Since it now is quite obvious that "laboratory" tests can be constructed so as to produce an endless array of factors, some means must be devised for separating the wheat from the chaff. How to determine the importance of factors will be the major issue for discussion in the remainder of this chapter.

MATHEMATICAL IMPORTANCE OF FACTORS   One way in which a factor can be important is in its relations to mathematical models for human abilities. For example, to the extent that a general factor is found in tests of human ability, that factor is important because it goes a long way in explaining correlations among all tests of ability. The mathematical importance of a factor depends, however, on the nature of the mathematical model. Thus a general factor would be important in a model that concerns a general factor and group factors, but it would not be important, or would be a downright nuisance, in other models. A later section will consider one of the models that has been proposed for explaining human abilities.

CONTENT GENERALITY OF FACTORS   A second way in which a factor can be judged important is with respect to the range of test materials involved. Previously it was described how an "artifactor" could be produced by the development of three almost identical tests (the circling of alphabetical letters). Although there are no concrete standards by which one can gauge the relative breadth of content covered by factors, some of the factors appearing in the literature appear to relate to very narrow domains of content. For example, French reports a factor of *length estimation*, for which some of the tests with highest loadings concern (1) estimating length with a meter stick, (2) estimating length with a meter stick after practice, (3) selecting the shorter of straight lines radiating from a point, and (4) selecting the shortest crooked line. This may prove to be an important factor, but from the narrowness of its content, one would suspect that it is not. There would be more intuitive support for the factor if it extended to judgments of area and volume and it related to both regular and irregular figures.

At the other extreme of content generality is the *verbal comprehension factor* which relates to almost any type of test that directly or indirectly concerns the understanding of words and connected discourse. That factor relates to so many types of intellectual tasks that there sometimes is a problem in reducing its effects in tests that are intended to measure other factors, e.g., because of the wording of written or oral instructions and because of the verbal material in test items.

There is no way to specify the ideal level of generality for a factor. At the upper extreme of generality, one could argue that a factor is not sufficiently analytic; i.e., it tends to hide subdimensions of abilities in a particular area. This has often been said about the factor of verbal comprehension, and consequently efforts have been made to break this factor down into several correlated factors. As was mentioned previously, the ideal generality of a factor depends in part on the mathematical model which is used to guide research on human abilities. At the lower extreme of content generality, however, it is doubtful that some of the highly specialized factors that have been reported will ever prove to be of general importance. Such is the case with the factor of *length estimation*. That factor might be important only for predicting success on a job concerned purely with the estimation of the length of things, and if there is such a job, it probably is so unimportant in the total enterprise that success in it would not be worth the labors of employing psychological tests. Also, aside from the possible use of tests as predictor instruments, it is doubtful that such a narrowly defined factor would prove to be important in the other ways discussed in this chapter. One gets the impression that this is true of many of the factors which have been reported: they are so narrowly defined in item content that, unless they can be shown to be somewhat more general in that regard, they have little likelihood of becoming important.

In a sense, one can argue that a factor is important partly to the extent that it produces some surprises. If, for example, one tells a colleague that he has found a factor of length estimation among half a dozen tests all obviously related to the same thing, he is likely to be met with a yawn. (Of course, in some instances the yawn is undeserved, because what frequently appear to be "obviously" similar tasks fail to correlate well with one another.) At the other extreme of surprise value are some of the perceptual and spatial factors, where moderate-sized loadings are found for some tests that do not obviously concern either perception or spatial relations. An example is the *gestalt flexibility factor* (French, 1951), which primarily concerns the ability to detect simple geometrical configurations within complex configurations. The surprise value of the factor comes in the fact that a *motor* test (two-hand coordination) has a high loading. Anyone who is interested in the nature of human abilities would not yawn on learning that. Such surprises stimulate us to think about the more basic factors of ability that underlie test materials that surperficially are so different.

IMPORTANCE IN PREDICTION One obvious way in which a factor can be important is in the prediction of significant criterion variables, such as success in pilot training, grades in college, and improvement in psychotherapy. As was mentioned previously, in a sense it is unfortunate that so much of the effort to understand human abilities has hinged on applied concerns. To some extent this has caused us to ignore factors that may be very important for understanding the nature of human abilities but have little predictive validity for the criteria most frequently investigated. Also, it has led us to deal with factors that probably should be ignored in basic research. For example, French (1951) reports a factor of pilot interest which concerned biographical data and items of information about aviation. That factor was useful in predicting success in pilot training during World War II, but since it was so specifically oriented toward one occupation, it is hard to see how it would be important otherwise. (Also, because airplanes have changed so rapidly and the duties of pilots have changed also, the factor probably no longer is very useful for predicting success in pilot training.)

In spite of the many potential uses for factors of ability in predicting performance in real-life situations, most of the uses have been with respect to either (1) success in school at all levels or (2) success in specific occupations. The most outstanding success has been with respect to the former, where it has been found that success in many different types of school settings is reasonably well predicted by factors of verbal comprehension, reasoning, numerical computation, and some of the perceptual and spatial factors; but beyond those, other factors tend to have little predictive validity. The validity of factors of human ability for predicting success in particular occupations depends considerably on the occupation. Much more success has been had with high-level occupations (e.g., engineers) than with low-level occupations (e.g., truck drivers).

Although it is doubtful that studies of predictive validity alone will do all that one requires to gain an understanding of the importance of different factors of human ability, there are ways in which such studies could help. It would, for example, be informative to learn more about how factors of ability relate to particular topics in college and to subparts of those topics. Instructive in this regard would be to learn more about how factors of verbal ability relate to the mastery of foreign languages, not only to overall grades in learning languages, but also to the rate of mastering various aspects of the language, e.g., grammar as opposed to vocabulary.

ECOLOGICAL IMPORTANCE OF FACTORS   Eventually, what will be needed for an understanding of the importance of factors in daily life is a correlation of those factors with individual differences manifested in real-life situations. Presently we do not know to what extent our factors of human ability extend beyond the "laboratory" to the things that people do every day. Are those factors of any importance for making change on a bus, recalling phone numbers, or giving a talk to the PTA? Of course, it is not possible to measure performance in a multitude of real-life situations, but at least it would be possible to conduct informal surveys of what people do in daily life. Persons who are familiar with the known factors of human ability could literally follow people around and watch the things that they do, and any task that possibly concerned one of the known factors could be noted. Also it would be useful to list important tasks that apparently do not relate to any known factors of ability. Gradually, in this way, a classification scheme could be developed for areas in real life that need to be explained by factors of ability, and studies could be made of the correlations between "laboratory" tests and daily behavior. It may sound rather far out now to talk of such developments, but issues relating to human abilities are sufficiently important to merit the efforts. In this process, we certainly will find much "chaff" among presently known factors of human abilities, but the remaining "wheat" will stimulate further basic investigations.

IMPORTANCE FOR PSYCHOLOGICAL CONSTRUCTS   More than anything else, factors need to prove their importance for controlled experiments in general psychology. There has always been a great deal of talk about the need to consider measures of individual differences in controlled experiments, but not much has been done about it. One can see numerous parallels between factors of human ability and processes that are investigated in controlled experiments. For example, one would expect to find individual differences in some of the perceptual factors to correlate with individual differences in various aspects of tachistoscopic recognition experiments. As another example, one would expect to find relations between verbal factors, memory factors, and various aspects of studies on verbal learning and verbal behavior. Interesting hypotheses can be generated about relations between various factors of ability and the functions mediated by different parts of the brain.

A suggestion by Ferguson (1954) is illustrative of the many possible links between factors of human ability and basic processes in controlled experiments. He suggested that transfer of training in experiments on learning is governed by factors of human ability. It is well known that practice in one type of learning situation may facilitate learning in new situations, but there has been no way of predicting the amounts and kinds of transfer that would occur. Ferguson's suggestion is that if a person is given training with respect to one type of problem relating to a particular factor of ability, there will be positive transfer to other types of problems relating to the same factor. For example, if an individual is given training with respect to one task concerning a particular factor of reasoning, that might transfer somewhat to different-appearing tasks concerning the same factor. This suggestion offers the possibility of investigating many links between the results of controlled experiments and factors of ability.

Guilford (1961) has pointed out numerous relations between factors of human ability and the processes that are investigated in controlled experiments—concept formation, learning, reinforcement, memory, and others. Fleishman and Hempel (1954) pioneered a type of study which serves to relate factors of ability to controlled experiments: they investigated correlations between factors of ability and progress in different trials of a learning task. They found that the importance of different factors differed with the stage of learning. In learning a psychomotor task, a factor of spatial relations was important in the early trials, but in later trials, it correlated much less with performance. On the early trials, factors concerning speed of movement had relatively small correlations with performance, but by the end of training, they were the most important factors. There are many other possibilities for investigating relations between factors of ability and learning processes.

Guilford's concept of the structure of intellect

In threading our way through the history of studies of human abilities, we are brought up to recent times by considering the work of J. P. Guilford and his colleagues. Guilford has collected mountains of data with respect to factors of intellect, and he has made notable contributions to methods of analysis; but more important, he has done more than anyone else to develop a systematic point of view about the nature of factors of intellect. His work epitomizes the good things that (in this author's opinion) should be done to mesh studies of human abilities with experimental psychology. Just as it was useful to quote Thelma Gwinn Thurstone in detail to show the best thinking about human abilities circa 1940, it now will be useful to quote Guilford in detail to show the best of modern thinking about human abilities.

THREE FACES OF INTELLECT[2]

My subject is in the area of human intelligence, in connection with which the names of Terman and Stanford have become known the world over. The Stanford Revision of the Binet Intelligence scale has been the standard against which all other instruments for the measurement of intelligence have been compared. The term IQ or intelligence quotient has become a household word in this country. . . .

It is my purpose to speak about the analysis of this thing called human intelligence into its components. I do not believe that either Binet or Terman, if they were still with us, would object to the idea of a searching and detailed study of intelligence, aimed toward a better understanding of its nature. Preceding the development of his intelligence scale, Binet had done much research on different kinds of thinking activities and apparently recognized that intelligence has a number of aspects. It is to the lasting credit of both Binet and Terman that they introduced such a great variety of tasks into their intelligence scales. . . .

Our knowledge of the components of human intelligence has come about mostly within the last 25 years. The major sources of this information in this country have been L. L. Thurstone and his associates, the wartime research of psychologists in the United States Air Forces, and more recently the Aptitudes Project at the University of Southern California, now in its tenth year of research on cognitive and thinking abilities. The results

[2] J. P. Guilford, Three faces of intellect, *Amer. Psychologist*, 1959, **14,** 469–479. Reprinted with minor changes by permission of the author and the American Psychological Association.

from the Aptitudes Project that have gained perhaps the most attention have pertained to creative-thinking abilities. These are mostly novel findings. But to me, the most significant outcome has been the development of a unified theory of human intellect, which organizes the known, unique or primary intellectual abilities into a single system called the "structure of intellect." It is to this system that I shall devote the major part of my remarks, with very brief mentions of some of the implications for the psychology of thinking and problem solving, for vocational testing, and for education.

The discovery of the components of intelligence has been by means of the experimental application of the method of factor analysis. It is not necessary for you to know anything about the theory or method of factor analysis in order to follow the discussion of the components. . . . I will say that each intellectual component or factor is a unique ability that is needed to do well in a certain class of tasks or tests. As a general principle we find that certain individuals do well in the tests of a certain class, but they may do poorly in the tests of another class. We conclude that a factor has certain properties from the features that the tests of a class have in common. I shall give you very soon a number of examples of tests, each representing a factor.

the structure of intellect

Although each factor is sufficiently distinct to be detected by factor analysis, in very recent years it has become apparent that the factors themselves can be classified because they resemble one another in certain ways. One basis of classification is according to the basic kind of process or operation performed. This kind of classification gives us five major groups of intellectual abilities: factors of cognition, memory, convergent thinking, divergent thinking, and evaluation.

Cognition means discovery or rediscovery or recognition. Memory means retention of what is cognized. Two kinds of productive-thinking operations generate new information from known information and remembered information. In divergent-thinking operations we think in different directions, sometimes searching, sometimes seeking variety. In convergent thinking the information leads to one right answer or to a recognized best or conventional answer. In evaluation we reach decisions as to goodness, correctness, suitability, or adequacy of what we know, what we remember, and what we produce in productive thinking.

A second way of classifying the intellectual factors is according to the kind of material or content involved. The factors known thus far involve three kinds of material or content: the content may be figural, symbolic, or semantic. Figural content is concrete material such as is perceived through the senses. It does not represent anything except itself. Visual material has properties such as size, form, color, location, or texture. Things we hear or feel provide other examples of figural material. Symbolic content is composed of letters, digits, and other conventional signs, usually organized in general systems, such as the alphabet or the number system. Semantic content is in the form of verbal meanings or ideas, for which no examples are necessary.

When a certain operation is applied to a certain kind of content, as many as six general kinds of products may be involved. There is enough evidence available to suggest that, regardless of the combinations of operations and content, the same six kinds of products may be found associated.

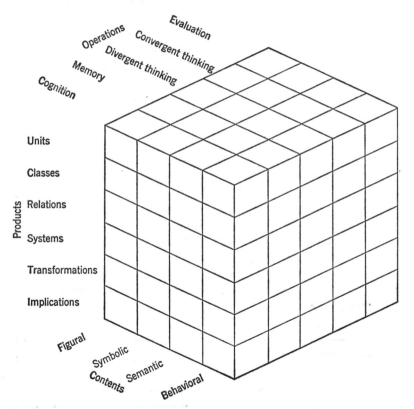

figure 12-1 *A cubical model representing the structure of intellect.*

The six kinds of products are: units, classes, relations, systems, transformations, and implications. So far as we have determined from factor analysis, these are the only fundamental kinds of products that we can know. As such, they may serve as basic classes into which one might fit all kinds of information psychologically.

The three kinds of classifications of the factors of intellect can be represented by means of a single solid model, shown in Figure 12-1. In this model, which we call the "structure of intellect," each dimension represents one of the modes of variation of the factors. Along one dimension are found the various kinds of operations, along a second one are the various kinds of products, and along the third are various kinds of content. Along the dimension of content a fourth category has been added, its kind of content being designated as "behavioral." This category has been added on a purely theoretical basis to represent the general area sometimes called "social intelligence." More will be said about this section of the model later.

In order to provide a better basis for understanding the model and a better basis for accepting it as a picture of human intellect, I shall do some exploring of it with you systematically, giving some examples of tests. Each cell in the model calls for a certain kind of ability that can be described in terms of operation, content, and product, for each cell is at the intersection of a unique combination of kinds of operation, content, and product. A test for that ability would have the same three properties. In our exploration of the model, we shall take one vertical layer at a time, beginning with the front face. The first layer provides us with a matrix of 18 cells (if we ignore the behavioral column for which there are as yet no known factors), each of which should contain a cognitive ability.

the cognitive abilities

We know at present the unique abilities that fit logically into 15 of the 18 cells for cognitive abilities. Each row presents a triad of similar abilities, having a single kind of product in common. The factors of the first row are concerned with the knowing of units. A good test of the ability to cognize figural units is the Street Gestalt Completion Test. In this test, the recognition of familiar pictured objects in silhouette form is made difficult for testing purposes by blocking out parts of those objects. There is another factor that is known to involve the perception of auditory figures—in the form of melodies, rhythms, and speech sounds—and still another factor involving kinesthetic forms. The presence of three factors in one cell (they are conceivably distinct abilities, although this has not been tested) suggests that more generally, in the figural column, at least, we should expect to find more than one ability. A fourth dimension pertaining to variations in sense modality may thus apply in connection with figural content. The model could be extended in this manner if the facts call for such an extension.

The ability to cognize symbolic units is measured by tests like the following:

Put vowels in the following blanks to make real words:

P_____W_____R

M_____RV_____L

C_____RT_____N

Rearrange the letters to make real words:

R A C I H

T V O E S

K L C C O

The first of these two tests is called <u>Disemvoweled Words</u>, and the second <u>Scrambled Words</u>.

The ability to <u>cognize semantic units</u> is the well-known factor of verbal comprehension, which is best measured by means of a vocabulary test, with items such as:

GRAVITY means _____

CIRCUS means _____

VIRTUE means _____

From the comparison of these two factors it is obvious that recognizing familiar words as letter structures and knowing what words mean depend upon quite different abilities.

For testing the abilities to know <u>classes</u> of units, we may present the following kinds of items, one with symbolic content and one with semantic content:

Which letter group does not belong?

XECM   PVAA   QXIN   VTRO

Which object does not belong?

clam   tree   oven   rose

A figural test is constructed in a completely parallel form, presenting in each item four figures, three of which have a property in common and the fourth lacking that property.

<u>The three abilities to see relationships</u> are also readily measured by a common kind of test, differing only in terms of content. The well-known analogies test is applicable, two items in symbolic and semantic form being:

JIRE   :   KIRE   : :   FORA   :   KORE   KORA   LIRE   GORA   GIRE

poetry   :   prose   : :   dance   :   music   walk   sing   talk   jump

Such tests usually involve more than the ability to cognize relations, but we are not concerned with this problem at this point.

The three factors for <u>cognizing systems</u> do not at present appear in tests so closely resembling one another as in the case of the examples just given. There is nevertheless an underlying common core of logical similarity. Ordinary space tests, such as Thurstone's Flags, Figures, and Cards or Part V (Spatial Orientation) of the Guilford-Zimmerman Aptitude Survey (GZAS), serve in the figural column. The system involved is an order or arrangement of objects in space. A system that uses symbolic elements is illustrated by the Letter Triangle Test, a sample item of which is:

```
   d   ‾‾‾‾
 b   e   ‾‾‾‾
a   c   f   ?‾‾
```

Which letter belongs at the place of the question mark?

The ability to understand a semantic system has been known for some time as the factor called general reasoning. One of its most faithful indicators is a test composed of arithmetic-reasoning items. That the phase of understanding only is important for measuring this ability is shown by the fact that such a test works even if the examinee is not asked to give a complete solution; he need only show that he structures the problem properly. For example, an item from the test Necessary Arithmetical Operations simply asks what operations are needed to solve the problem:

A city lot 48 feet wide and 149 feet deep costs $79,432. What is the cost per square foot?

A add and multiply
B multiply and divide
C subtract and divide
D add and subtract
E divide and add

Placing the factor of general reasoning in this cell of the structure of intellect gives us some new conceptions of its nature. It should be a broad ability to grasp all kinds of systems that are conceived in terms of verbal concepts, not restricted to the understanding of problems of an arithmetical type.

Transformations are changes of various kinds, including modifications in arrangement, organization, or meaning. In the figural column for the transformations row, we find the factor known as visualization. Common measuring instruments for this factor are the surface-development tests, and an example of a different kind is Part VI (Spatial Visualization) of the GZAS. A test of the ability to make transformations of meaning, for the factor in the semantic column, is called Similarities. The examinee is asked to state several ways in which two objects, such as an apple and an orange, are alike. Only by shifting the meanings of both is the examinee able to give many responses to such an item.

In the set of abilities having to do with the cognition of implications, we find that the individual goes beyond the information given, but not to the extent of what might be called drawing conclusions. We may say that he extrapolates. From the given information he expects or foresees certain consequences, for example. The two factors found in this row of the cognition matrix were first called "foresight" factors. Foresight in connection with figural material can be tested by means of paper-and-pencil mazes. Foresight in connection with ideas, those pertaining to events, for example, is indicated by a test such as Pertinent Questions:

In planning to open a new hamburger stand in a certain community, what four questions should be considered in deciding upon its location?

The more questions the examinee asks in response to a list of such problems, the more he evidently foresees contingencies.

the memory abilities

The area of memory abilities has been explored less than some of the other areas of operation, and only seven of the potential cells of the memory matrix have known factors in them. These cells are restricted to three rows: for units, relations, and systems. The first cell in the memory matrix is now occupied by two factors, parallel to two in the corresponding cognition matrix: visual memory and auditory memory. Memory for series of letters or numbers, as in memory span tests, conforms to the conception of memory for symbolic units. Memory for the ideas in a paragraph conforms to the conception of memory for semantic units.

The formation of associations between units, such as visual forms, syllables, and meaningful words, as in the method of paired associates, would seem to represent three abilities to remember relationships involving three kinds of content. We know of two such abilities, for the symbolic and semantic columns. The memory for known systems is represented by two abilities very recently discovered. Remembering the arrangement of objects in space is the nature of an ability in the figural column, and remembering a sequence of events is the nature of a corresponding ability in the semantic column. The differentiation between these two abilities implies that a person may be able to say where he saw an object on a page, but he might not be able to say on which of several pages he saw it after leafing through several pages that included the right one. Considering the blank rows in the memory matrix, we should expect to find abilities also to remember classes, transformations, and implications, as well as units, relations, and systems.

the divergent-thinking abilities

The unique feature of divergent production is that a variety of responses is produced. The product is not completely determined by the given information. This is not to say that divergent thinking does not come into play in the total process of reaching a unique conclusion, for it comes into play whenever there is trial-and-error thinking.

The well-known ability of word fluency is tested by asking the examinee to list words satisfying a specified letter requirement, such as words beginning with the letter "s" or words ending in "-tion." This ability is now regarded as a facility in divergent production of symbolic units. The parallel semantic ability has been known as ideational fluency. A typical test item calls for listing objects that are round and edible. Winston Churchill must have possessed this ability to a high degree. Clement Attlee is reported to have said about him recently that, no matter what problem came up, Churchill always seemed to have about ten ideas. The trouble was, Attlee continued, he did not know which was the good one. The last comment implies some weakness in one or more of the evaluative abilities.

The divergent production of class ideas is believed to be the unique feature of a factor called "spontaneous flexibility." A typical test instructs the examinee to list all the uses he can think of for a common brick, and he is given eight minutes. If his responses are: build a house, build a barn, build a garage, build a school, build a church, build a chimney, build a walk, and build a barbecue, he would earn a fairly high score for ideational fluency but a very low score for spontaneous flexibility, because all these uses fall into the same class. If another person said: make a door stop, make a paper weight, throw it at a dog, make a bookcase, drown a cat, drive a nail, make a red powder, and use for baseball bases, he would also receive a high score for flexibility. He has gone frequently from one class to another.

A current study of unknown but predicted divergent-production abilities includes testing whether there are also figural and symbolic abilities to produce multiple classes. An experimental figural test presents a number of figures that can be classified in groups of three in various ways, each figure being usable in more than one class. An experimental symbolic test presents a few numbers that are also to be classified in multiple ways.

A unique ability involving relations is called "associational fluency." It calls for the production of a variety of things related in a specified way to a given thing. For example, the examinee is asked to list words meaning about the same as "good" or to list words meaning about the opposite of "hard." In these instances the response produced is to complete a relationship, and semantic content is involved. Some of our present experimental tests call for the production of varieties of relations, as such, and involve figural and symbolic content also. For example, given four small digits, in how many ways can they be related in order to produce a sum of eight?

One factor pertaining to the production of systems is known as expressional fluency. The rapid formation of phrases or sentences is the essence of certain tests of this factor. For example, given the initial letters:

W_____ c_____ e_____ n_____

with different sentences to be produced, the examinee might write "We can eat nuts" or "Whence came Eve Newton?" In interpreting the factor, we regard the sentence as a symbolic system. By analogy, a figural system would be some kind of organization of lines and other elements, and a semantic system would be in the form of a verbally stated problem or perhaps something as complex as a theory.

In the row of the divergent-production matrix devoted to transformations, we find some very interesting factors. The one called "adaptive flexibility" is now recognized as belonging in the figural column. A faithful test of it has been Match Problems. This is based upon the common game that uses squares, the sides of which are formed by match sticks. The examinee is told to take away a given number of matches to leave a stated number of squares with nothing left over. Nothing is said about the sizes of the squares to be left. If the examinee imposes upon himself the restriction that the squares that he leaves must be of the same size, he will fail in his attempts to do items like that in Figure 12-2. Other

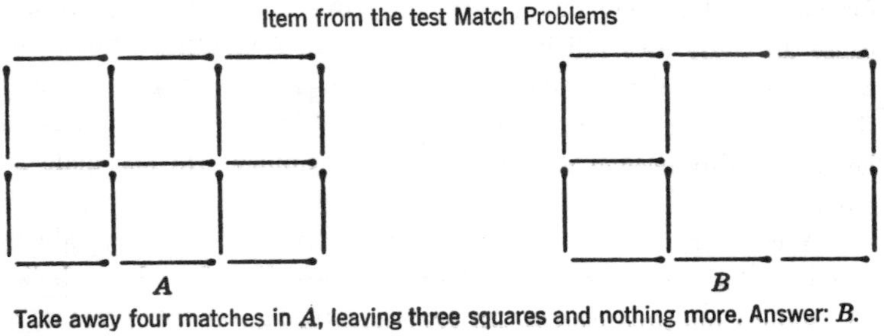

Item from the test Match Problems

A   *B*

Take away four matches in *A*, leaving three squares and nothing more. Answer: *B*.

figure 12-2 *A sample item from the test Match Problems. The problem in this item is to take away four matches and leave three squares. The solution is given.*

odd kinds of solutions are introduced in other items, such as overlapping squares and squares within squares, and so on. In another variation of Match Problems the examinee is told to produce two or more solutions for each problem.

A factor that has been called "originality" is now recognized as adaptive flexibility with semantic material, where there must be a shifting of meanings. The examinee must produce the shifts or changes in meaning and so came up with novel, unusual, clever, or farfetched ideas. The Plot Titles Test presents a short story, the examinee being told to list as many appropriate titles as he can to head the story. One story is about a missionary who has been captured by cannibals in Africa. He is in the pot and about to be boiled when a princess of the tribe obtains a promise for his release if he will become her mate. He refuses and is boiled to death.

In scoring the test, we separate the responses into two categories, clever and nonclever. Examples of nonclever responses are: African Death, Defeat of a Princess, Eaten by Savages, The Princess, The African Missionary, In Darkest Africa, and Boiled by Savages. These titles are appropriate but commonplace. The number of such responses serves as a score for

       the content areas

ideational fluency. Examples of clever responses are: Pot's Plot, Potluck Dinner, Stewed Parson, Goil or Boil, A Mate Worse Than Death, He Left a Dish for a Pot, Chaste in Haste, and A Hot Price for Freedom. The number of clever responses given by an examinee is his score for originality, or the divergent production of semantic transformations.

Another test of originality presents a very novel task so that any acceptable response is unusual for the individual. In the Symbol Production Test the examinee is to produce a simple symbol to stand for a noun or a verb in each short sentence, in other words to invent something like pictographic symbols. Still another test of originality asks for writing the "punch lines" for cartoons, a task that almost automatically challenges the examinee to be clever. Thus, quite a variety of tests offer approaches to the measurement of originality, including one or two others that I have not mentioned.

Abilities to produce a variety of implications are assessed by tests calling for elaboration of given information. A figural test of this type provides the examinee with a line or two, to which he is to add other lines to produce an object. The more lines he adds, the greater his score. A semantic test gives the examinee the outlines of a plan to which he is to respond by stating all the details he can think of to make the plan work. A new test we are trying out in the symbolic area presents two simple equations such as $B - C = D$ and $Z = A + D$. The examinee is to make as many other equations as he can from this information.

the convergent-production abilities

Of the 18 convergent-production abilities expected in the three content columns, 12 are now recognized. In the first row, pertaining to units, we have an ability to name figural properties (forms or colors) and an ability to name abstractions (classes, relations, and so on). It may be that the ability in common to the speed of naming forms and the speed of naming colors is not appropriately placed in the convergent-thinking matrix. One might expect that the thing to be produced in a test of the convergent production of figural units would be in the form of figures rather than words. A better test of such an ability might somehow specify the need for one particular object, the examinee to furnish the object.

A test for the convergent production of classes (Word Grouping) presents a list of 12 words that are to be classified in four, and only four, meaningful groups, no word to appear in more than one group. A parallel test (Figure Concepts Test) presents 20 pictured real objects that are to be grouped in meaningful classes of two or more each.

Convergent production having to do with relationships is represented by three known factors, all involving the "education of correlates," as Spearman called it. The given information includes one unit and a stated relation, the examinee to supply the other unit. Analogies tests that call for completion rather than a choice between alternative answers emphasize this kind of ability. With symbolic content such an item might read:

pots stop   bard drab   rats _?_

A semantic item that measures education of correlates is:

The absence of sound is _____

Incidentally, the latter item is from a vocabulary-completion test, and its relation to the factor of ability to produce correlates indicates how, by change of form, a vocabulary test may indicate an ability other than that for which vocabulary tests are usually intended, namely, the factor of verbal comprehension.

Only one factor for convergent production of systems is known, and it is in the semantic column. It is measured by a class of tests that may

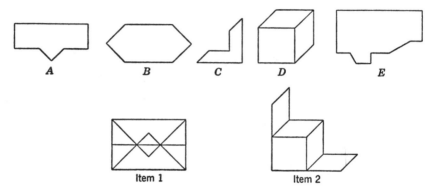

figure 12-3 *Sample items from a test Hidden Figures, based upon the Gottschaldt figures. Which of the simple figures is concealed within each of the more complex figures?*

be called ordering tests. The examinee may be presented with a number of events that ordinarily have a best or most logical order, the events being presented in scrambled order. The presentation may be pictorial, as in the Picture Arrangement Test, or verbal. The pictures may be taken from a cartoon strip. The verbally presented events may be in the form of the various steps needed to plant a new lawn. There are undoubtedly other kinds of systems than temporal order that could be utilized for testing abilities in this row of the convergent-production matrix.

In the way of producing transformations of a unique variety, we have three recognized factors, known as redefinition abilities. In each case, redefinition involves the changing of functions or uses of parts of one unit and giving them new functions or uses in some new unit. For testing the ability of figural redefinition, a task based upon the Gottschaldt figures is suitable. Figure 12-3 shows the kind of item for such a test. In recognizing the simpler figure within the structure of a more complex figure, certain lines must take on new roles.

In terms of symbolic material, the following sample items will illustrate how groups of letters in given words must be readapted to use in other words. In the test Camouflaged Words, each sentence contains the name of a sport or game:

I did not know that he was ailing.

To beat the Hun, tin goes a long way.

For the factor of semantic redefinition, the Gestalt Transformation Test may be used. A sample item reads:

From which object could you most likely make a needle?

A   a cabbage

B   a splice

C   a steak

D   a paper box

E   a fish

The convergent production of implications means the drawing of fully determined conclusions from given information. The well-known factor of numerical facility belongs in the symbolic column. For the parallel ability in the figural column, we have a test known as Form Reasoning, in which rigorously defined operations with figures are used. For the parallel ability in the semantic column, the factor sometimes called "deduction" probably qualifies. Items of the following type are sometimes used.

Charles is younger than Robert

Charles is older than Frank

Who is older: Robert or Frank?

evaluative abilities

The evaluative area has had the least investigation of all the operational categories. In fact, only one systematic analytical study has been devoted to this area. Only eight evaluative abilities are recognized as fitting into the evaluation matrix. But at least five rows have one or more factors each, and also three of the usual columns or content categories. In each case, evaluation involves reaching decisions as to the accuracy, goodness, suitability, or workability of information. In each row, for the particular kind of product of that row, some kind of criterion or standard of judgment is involved.

In the first row, for the evaluation of units, the important decision to be made pertains to the identity of a unit. Is this unit identical with that one? In the figural column we find the factor long known as "perceptual speed." Tests of this factor invariably call for decisions of identity, for example, Part IV (Perceptual Speed) of the GZAS or Thurstone's Identical Forms. I think it has been generally wrongly thought that the ability involved is that of cognition of visual forms. But we have seen that another factor is a more suitable candidate for this definition and for being in the very first cell of the cognitive matrix. It is parallel to this evaluative ability but does not require the judgment of identity as one of its properties.

In the symbolic column is an ability to judge identity of symbolic units, in the form of series of letters or numbers or of names of individuals.

Are members of the following pairs identical or not?

825170493_____825176493

dkeltvmpa_____dkeltvmpa

C. S. Meyerson_____C. E. Meyerson

Such items are common in tests of clerical aptitude.

There should be a parallel ability to decide whether two ideas are identical or different. Is the idea expressed in this sentence the same as the idea expressed in that one? Do these two proverbs express essentially the same idea? Such tests exist and will be used to test the hypothesis that such an ability can be demonstrated.

No evaluative abilities pertaining to classes have as yet been recognized. The abilities having to do with evaluation where relations are concerned must meet the criterion of logical consistency. Syllogistic-type tests involving letter symbols indicate a different ability than the same type of test involving verbal statements. In the figural column we might expect that tests incorporating geometric reasoning or proof would indicate a parallel ability to sense the soundness of conclusions regarding figural relationships.

The evaluation of systems seems to be concerned with the internal consistency of those systems, so far as we can tell from the knowledge of one such factor. The factor has been called "experimental evaluation," and its representative test presents items like that in Figure 12-4 asking "What is wrong with this picture?" The things wrong are often internal inconsistencies.

A semantic ability for evaluating transformations is thought to be that known for some time as "judgment." In typical judgment tests, the examinee is asked to tell which of five solutions to a practical problem is most adequate or wise. The solutions frequently involve improvisations, in other words, adaptations of familiar objects to unusual uses. In this way the items present redefinitions to be evaluated.

A factor known first as "sensitivity to problems" has become recognized as an evaluative ability having to do with implications. One test of the factor, the Apparatus Test, asks for two needed improvements with respect to each of several common devices, such as the telephone or the toaster. The Social Institutions Test, a measure of the same factor, asks what things are wrong with each of several institutions, such as tipping or national elections. We may say that defects or deficiencies are implications of an evaluative kind. Another interpretation would be that seeing defects and

figure 12-4 *A sample item from the test Unusual Details. What two things are wrong with this picture?*

deficiencies are evaluations of implications to the effect that the various aspects of something are all right.

some implications of the structure of intellect

for psychological theory

Although factor analysis as generally employed is best designed to investigate ways in which individuals differ from one another, in other words, to discover traits, the results also tell us much about how individuals are alike. Consequently, information regarding the factors and their interrelationships gives us understanding of functioning individuals. The five kinds of intellectual abilities in terms of operations may be said to represent five ways of functioning. The kinds of intellectual abilities distinguished according to varieties of test content and the kinds of abilities distinguished according to varieties of products suggest a classification of basic forms of information or knowledge. The kind of organism suggested by this way of looking at intellect is that of an agency for dealing with information of various kinds in various ways. The concepts provided by the distinctions among the intellectual abilities and by their classifications may be very useful in our future investigations of learning, memory, problem solving, invention, and decision making, by whatever method we choose to approach those problems.

for vocational testing

With about 50 intellectual factors already known, we may say that there are at least 50 ways of being intelligent. It has been facetiously suggested that there seem to be a great many more ways of being stupid, unfortunately. The structure of intellect is a theoretical model that predicts as many as 120 distinct abilities, if every cell of the model contains a factor. Already we know that two cells contain two or more factors each, and there probably are actually other cells of this type. Since the model was first conceived, 12 factors predicted by it have found places in it. There is consequently hope of filling many of the other vacancies, and we may eventually end up with more than 120 abilities.

The major implication for the assessment of intelligence is that to know an individual's intellectual resources thoroughly we shall need a surprisingly large number of scores. It is expected that many of the factors are intercorrelated, so there is some possibility that by appropriate sampling we shall be able to cover the important abilities with a more limited number of tests. At any rate, a multiple-score approach to the assessment of intelligence is definitely indicated in connection with future vocational operations.

Considering the kinds of abilities classified as to content, we may speak roughly of four kinds of intelligence. The abilities involving the use of figural information may be regarded as "concrete" intelligence. The people who depend most upon these abilities deal with concrete things and their properties. Among these people are mechanics, operators of machines, engineers (in some aspects of their work), artists, and musicians.

In the abilities pertaining to symbolic and semantic content, we have two kinds of "abstract" intelligence. Symbolic abilities should be important in learning to recognize words, to spell, and to operate with numbers. Language and mathematics should depend very much upon them, except that in mathematics some aspects, such as geometry, have strong figural involvement. Semantic intelligence is important for understanding things in terms of verbal concepts and hence is important in all courses where the learning of facts and ideas is essential.

In the hypothesized behavioral column of the structure of intellect, which may be roughly described as "social" intelligence, we have some of the most interesting possibilities. Understanding the behavior of others and of ourselves is largely nonverbal in character. The theory suggests as many as 30 abilities in this area, some having to do with understanding, some with productive thinking about behavior, and some with the evaluation of behavior. The theory also suggests that information regarding behavior is also in the form of the six kinds of products that apply elsewhere in the structure of intellect, including units, relations, systems, and so on.

The abilities in the area of social intelligence, whatever they prove to be, will possess considerable importance in connection with all those individuals who deal most with other people: teachers, law officials, social workers, therapists, politicians, statesmen, and leaders of other kinds.

for education

The implications for education are numerous, and I have time just to mention a very few. The most fundamental implication is that we might well undergo transformations with respect to our conception of the learner and of the process of learning. Under the prevailing conception, the learner is a kind of stimulus-response device, much on the order of a vending machine. You put in a coin, and something comes out. The machine learns what reaction to put out when a certain coin is put in. If, instead, we think of the learner as an agent for dealing with information, where information is defined very broadly, we have something more analogous to an electronic computor. We feed a computor information; it stores that information; it uses that information for generating new information, either by way of divergent or convergent thinking; and it evaluates its own results. Advantages that a human learner has over a computor include the step of seeking and discovering new information from sources outside itself and the step of programing itself. Perhaps even these steps will be added to computors, if this has not already been done in some cases.

At any rate, this conception of the learner leads us to the idea that learning is discovery of information, not merely the formation of associations, particularly associations in the form of stimulus-response connections. I am aware of the fact that my proposal is rank heresy. But if we are to make significant progress in our understanding of human learning and particularly our understanding of the so-called higher mental processes of thinking, problem solving, and creative thinking, some drastic modifications are due in our theory.

The idea that education is a matter of training the mind or of training the intellect has been rather unpopular, wherever the prevailing psychological doctrines have been followed. In theory, at least, the emphasis has been upon the learning of rather specific habits or skills. If we take our cue from factor theory, however, we recognize that most learning probably has both specific and general aspects or components. The general aspects may be along the lines of the factors of intellect. This is not to say that the individual's status in each factor is entirely determined by learning. We do not know to what extent each factor is determined by heredity and to what extent by learning. The best position for educators to take is that possibly every intellectual factor can be developed in individuals at least to some extent by learning.

If education has the general objective of developing the intellects of students, it can be suggested that each intellectual factor provides a particular goal at which to aim. Defined by a certain combination of content, operation, and product, each goal ability then calls for certain kinds of practice in order to achieve improvement in it. This implies choice of curriculum and the choice or invention of teaching methods that will most likely accomplish the desired results.

Considering the very great variety of abilities revealed by the factorial exploration of intellect, we are in a better position to ask whether any general intellectual skills are now being neglected in education and whether appropriate balances are being observed. It is often observed these days that we have fallen down in the way of producing resourceful, creative graduates. How true this is, in comparison with other times, I do not know. Perhaps the deficit is noticed because the demands for inventiveness are so much greater at this time. At any rate, realization that the more conspicuously creative abilities appear to be concentrated in the divergent-thinking category, and also to some extent in the transformation category, we now ask whether we have been giving these skills appropriate exercise. It is probable that we need a better balance of training in the divergent-thinking area as compared with training in convergent thinking and in critical thinking or evaluation.

The structure of intellect as I have presented it to you may or may not stand the test of time. Even if the general form persists, there are likely to be some modifications. Possibly some different kind of model will be invented. Be that as it may, the fact of a multiplicity of intellectual abilities seems well established.

There are many individuals who long for the good old days of simplicity, when we got along with one unanalyzed intelligence. Simplicity certainly has its appeal. But human nature is exceedingly complex, and we may as well face the fact. The rapidly moving events of the world in which we live have forced upon us the need for knowing human intelligence thoroughly. Humanity's peaceful pursuit of happiness depends upon our control of nature and of our own behavior; and this, in turn, depends upon understanding ourselves, including our intellectual resources.

hierarchical models

Although Guilford's classification scheme goes a long way in establishing a theoretical base for the nature of intellect, it would lead to an appallingly large number of separate factors. The classification scheme alone leads only to finding more and more factors, and it has nothing to say about possible relations among the factors. As Guilford recognizes, what is needed in addition to the classification scheme is a mathematical model for simplifying relations among the many factors following from the scheme. For this purpose, numerous persons have proposed the use of hierarchical models, which posit increasing levels of generality of factors. A hypothetical example of factors that would fit such a model was given by Humphreys (1962, p. 476):

> I shall assume that there are four discriminable levels of specificity of tests of mechanical information. These are as follows: (*a*) information about specific tools, e.g., the cross-cut saw or the socket wrench; (*b*) information about groups of tools having a common function, e.g., saws or wrenches; (*c*) information about areas of mechanical interest, e.g., carpentry or automotive; (*d*) general mechanical information, sampling from several areas such as carpentry, automotive, metal work, and plumbing.

A graphic representation of the above hierarchy is shown in Figure 12-5. At the top is general mechanical information, immediately below

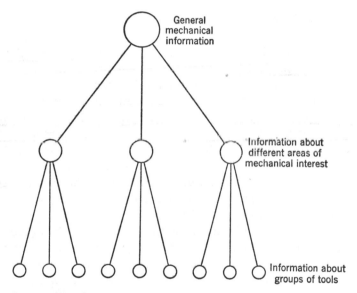

figure 12-5   *Factor hierarchy for mechanical information.*

are broad group factors relating to particular areas of mechanical interest, and below that are narrow group factors relating to information about different groups of tools. Further down could have been shown specific factors relating to information about particular tools within each group of tools.

A test of the adequacy of the above hierarchy for mechanical information could be obtained as follows. First, one would construct tests at level *b* above, concerning information about tools having a common function, e.g., saws or wrenches. (Little information probably would be supplied by starting at level *a*, concerning particular tools.) Scores on the tests would be intercorrelated and factor-analyzed to test for the

table 12-1 *Matrix of factor loadings corresponding to the factor hierarchy shown in Figure 12-5*

	GENERAL FACTOR	GROUP-CENTROID FACTORS		
	A	B	C	D
1	x	x		
2	x	x		
3	x	x		
4	x		x	
TESTS 5	x		x	
6	x		x	
7	x			x
8	x			x
9	x			x

adequacy of the hierarchy shown in Figure 12-5. One could make a test for the general factor by obtaining the first principal-axes factor or the first complete-centroid factor. The influence of the general factor would be removed from the correlation matrix in the usual way. Next, one could obtain group-centroid factors corresponding to the three hypothesized broad group factors relating to areas of mechanical interest. If the nine tests formed the hypothesized hierarchy, the matrix of factor loadings would appear like that in Table 12-1 (each x representing a substantial positive loading). Not shown in the table are the specific factors (reliable unique variance) for the tests corresponding to the nine hypothesized narrow group factors.

Another example of a hierarchy was given by Guilford (1959), concerning possible relations among different types of factors in his scheme of factors. The hierarchy is shown in Figure 12-6. Only the hierarchy for productive thinking is shown in detail. At the top is overall intellectual ability (like Spearman's G), below which is "thinking" as opposed to "memory." Below "thinking" is "productive thinking," and below that are two types of productive thinking. To make the hierarchy for productive thinking complete, one would need to put in additional lines going down to different types of convergent and divergent thinking.

✓ As one can see from Figure 12-6, to propose a complete hierarchical structure for human intellect would result in a very complex system, and to find tests to fit the system would be extremely difficult. Also, one can always find tests that will not fit the system, e.g., a test that has substantial loadings on more than one group factor at a particular level.

There are several principles that should be heeded in the search for hierarchical arrangements of factors. First, in the long run it probably will be more fruitful to start from near the bottom and work upward rather than from the top and work downward. For example, rather than start off at the top with "intellect" and look for hierarchical arrangements of factors below it, it probably would be better to start with, say, "productive thinking," and seek a hierarchy below that. One of the problems in so many studies of human abilities is that they bite off far more than they can chew. Consequently factors are poorly defined, and so many factors are found in each analysis that it is hard to make sense of the results. It would be better to make careful investigations

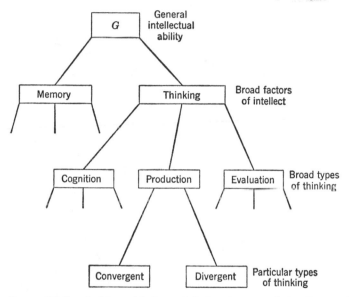

figure 12-6 *A hierarchical model for factors of intellect.* (*Adapted from Guilford, 1959.*)

of restricted aspects of intellectual functioning, such as productive thinking. If hierarchies can be found at a lower level, gradually these can be welded into larger hierarchies at higher levels.

A second principle in searching for hierarchies of factors is that such work has little chance of success without credible theories of human abilities. The importance of theory is evidenced in the hypotheses about hierarchical relations among factors that follow from Guilford's theories about the structure of intellect. It is inconceivable that one would find neat hierarchical structures in miscellaneous collections of tests covering a hodgepodge of abilities.

A third principle in searching for hierarchies is that we should abandon the needless assumption that *all* tests in a factor analysis must fit the hierarchy. As was mentioned previously, it would always be easy to produce a test that did not fit a hierarchy (or any other mathematical model concerning relations among factors of human ability). What is important is to find tests that *do* form a hierarchy regardless of how many other tests in an analysis do not conform to the hierarchy. If the tests that do fit the hierarchy explain most of the common variance among all tests in the analysis, the hierarchy offers a sufficient scheme of explanation. One can then throw away the tests that do not fit the hierarchy and continue to expand the hierarchy upward and downward in new investigations. The purpose of such studies should be to *impose lawfulness on nature*, not to hope vainly that it will be discovered in anything that anyone wants to call a test.

It may be too much to hope that hierarchies of factors can be found which will meet the mathematical requirements. To find such hierarchies will require a great deal of work, and more careful thought and investigation than have characterized many previous efforts. If such hierarchies can be found, they will go a long way toward making human abilities understandable. If they cannot be found, or some other mathematical model cannot be shown to fit, it will have to be admitted that there are many separate factors of intellect with no logical order among them. Then the only recourse will be to examine the importance of each separate factor with respect to criteria discussed previously. That not only would take a long, long time, but it would be a rather uninteresting pursuit.

SUGGESTED ADDITIONAL READINGS

Cronbach, L. J. *Essentials of psychological testing.* (Revised.) New York: Harper & Row, 1960, chaps. 7, 9.

Guilford, J. P. *Personality.* New York: McGraw-Hill, 1959, chap. 10.

Guilford, J. P. Factorial angles to psychology. *Psychol. Rev.,* 1961, **68,** 1–20.

Nunnally, J. C. *Tests and measurements: Assessment and prediction.* New York: McGraw-Hill, 1959, chap. 9.

Spearman, C. *The abilities of man.* New York: Macmillan, 1927.

CHAPTER THIRTEEN

MEASUREMENT OF PERSONALITY TRAITS

definitions of personality traits

Before we can meaningfully discuss the measurement of personality traits, we must define "personality." Since, however, different persons have different meanings for the word, the most we can do is indicate some types of human traits that most persons agree relate to personality. To some nonpsychologists, the word "personality" connotes social effectiveness and charm, which, of course, would be considered by psychologists as only one corner of the total domain of personality characteristics.

Some psychologists have given overly comprehensive and elegantly vague definitions of "personality" such as "the total functioning individual interacting with his environment." Such definitions would include all traits of human ability, which we have chosen to discuss separately from personality. One could make a good argument for including attitudes and interests in a definition of personality, but at least for the sake of understanding problems of measuring human traits, those will be discussed separately in the next chapter.

The overall study of personality concerns two broad issues: (1) what people are like at any point in time and (2) how they got that way. Personality measurement is mainly concerned with issue 1, the purpose of measurement being to describe individuals in terms of traits relating to dominance, extraversion, and others. Issue 2 relates to heredity and past experience. To explain how an individual developed a particular set of traits, one must resort either to genetic mechanisms or to learning theory. Of course, at the present time we know very little about possible genetic mechanisms relating to human traits; although we think that we know considerably more about the types of social learning that influence particular traits, there still is much speculation there.

Specialists in the study of personality can, and sometimes do, argue that a discussion of personality measurement is not a total discussion of personality. There is much merit in this argument. Although this chapter will be concerned only with personality measurement, it is freely recognized that this is only the first of the two issues discussed above. Also, we might have better measures of personality if all the persons who specialize in personality measurement had closer contacts with studies and theories concerning personality development.

As is true in the measurement of human abilities, the measurement of personality traits is mainly concerned with individual differences. We shall speak of personality measurement as concerning the following three broad classes of traits:

1 *Social traits:* The characteristic behavior of individuals with respect to other people. Typical social traits are honesty, gregariousness, shyness, dominance, and humor. Social traits are often said to constitute the surface layer of personality, the way that an individual appears in society.

2 *Motives:* Individual differences in "needs" or "drives," particularly the "nonbiological" drives such as the needs for affiliation, aggression, and achievement. Motives are often spoken of as constituting personality "dynamics."

3 *Adjustment versus maladjustment:* The relative freedom from emotional distress and/or socially disruptive behavior. Maladjustment relates to the so-called neuroses and psychoses, and adjustment relates to the opposite of these.

One could make further subdivisions of the above categories of personality traits, such as to divide social traits into character and temperament, but the three categories should suffice for the discussion in this chapter. Of course, these three kinds of traits are not independent. A person's motives certainly influence his social behavior, but there is no one-to-one correspondence. For example, even though it may be meaningful to speak of a person as having hostile motives, he may not act very hostilely, except in subtle ways that only the expert would recognize. Social traits can be observed directly, and it is for this reason that most of the standardized measures of personality concern social traits. Motives, or dynamics, cannot be observed directly, but must be inferred from overt responses, e.g., as is done with projective techniques such as the Rorschach.

Adjustment and maladjustment are related to the other two categories of traits. Whenever an individual is very extreme in social traits or motives, he usually is said to be maladjusted, as would be the case of extreme shyness for the former or suicidal motives for the latter. There are, however, some traits relating to adjustment that are not easily thought of as being either motives or social traits, such as hallucinations, imaginary illness, and bizarre associations. Definitions of adjustment and maladjustment necessarily concern values—what the individual values and what is valued by the society as a whole. If the individual is distressed by his own feelings and behavior and/or his behavior is highly distressful to others, we say that he is maladjusted.

PERSONALITY TRAITS   The title of this chapter speaks of the measurement of personality *traits*, the word "trait" being a synonym for "attribute" or "characteristic" as those terms have been used in previous chapters. A trait is simply a measurable dimension of behavior, either one that is measurable only dichotomously or one that is measurable in finer gradations. Traits vary in generality from specific habits, such as smoking rather than not smoking, to very general dimensions of behavior, such as extraversion rather than introversion. To have parsimonious descriptions of personality, it is necessary to find general traits, ones more general than specific habits.

idiographic and nomothetic theories

For some years now there has been a controversy as to whether or not general traits of personality exist. The controversy has been between those who espouse a *nomothetic* and those who expouse an *idiographic* point of view, the former referring to "general laws" applicable to all people, and the latter referring to a personalized approach. Essentially, the idiographic point of view is that each person is a law unto himself. In terms of factor-analytic approaches, this means that either there are no general factors among personality characteristics or those which do exist fail to capture the "essence" of the individual. The idiographic approach is the one used by novelists who explore in detail the inner workings and behavioral characteristics of one person. This is in contrast to the nomothetic approach, which strives to represent the important personality characteristics of all people in terms of profiles of measurable traits.

The idiographists have an important point: To find general traits (factors) of personality, it is necessary to find correlations among specific traits (habits); but everyday experience suggests that such correlations frequently are either very low or absent altogether. For example, it makes sense to deal with a general trait of dominance only if there are positive correlations among tendencies to be dominant in specific situations; but there are so many examples of persons who are dominant with their wives but not dominant at work, dominant with men but not with women, dominant in intellectual matters but not in practical matters, and so on.

For the nometheticist to be successful, he must hypothesize a general trait of personality and find it evidenced in the correlations

measurement of personality traits   471 among more specific traits, or if he has no hypotheses, he must find such clusters of correlated traits in his factor-analytic explorations. If the nometheticist does not find important factors by these approaches (important in terms of criteria discussed in the previous chapter), he has failed. Enough failures of this kind would eventually lead to the admission that the idiographist is correct: personality traits are "scattered" among people in such a way that the only approach to understanding the individual is by tracing out the life threads of how he came to be the way he is. Then it would have to be admitted that there are no general traits of dominance, extraversion, or others; instead, each individual would need to be considered a unique configuration of specific traits (habits).

The idiographists may be entirely correct, but if they are, it is a sad day for psychology. Idiography is an antiscience point of view: it discourages the search for general laws and instead encourages the description of particular phenomena (people). This would be like the astronomer who gave up on finding any general laws relating to heavenly bodies and instead devoted the rest of his life to describing the particular features of the planet Neptune.

Efforts to measure personality traits are based on the hypothesis that the idiographists are not entirely correct, that there are some general traits of human personality. The nomothetic point of view should be tested to the limit; otherwise, to accept an idiographic point of view in advance is to postulate that only chaos prevails in the description of human personalities. The remainder of this chapter will be concerned with efforts to find general traits of personality.

APPROACHES TO THE MEASUREMENT OF PERSONALITY   In contrast to the measurement of human abilities, there are a number of different basic approaches to the measurement of personality traits. Most measures of human ability, particularly those of the "intellectual" functions, are printed tests. In each such test, the subject understands that he is required to solve some type of problem, broadly speaking. In most tests of human ability, it is obvious how responses should be scored. With measures of personality, these matters are not nearly so clear. Personality traits are not highly concerned with "how well" a person can perform; rather, they are mainly concerned with the typical behavior of people in daily life, e.g., the typical amount of gregariousness or hostility. How such typical behavior is to be measured, if it can be, is a matter of dispute, and consequently various schools of thought have come forward. Also, the logic of measurement depends on the kind of personality trait which is being studied. Thus the logic of measurement required for the measurement of social traits might be different from that required for the measurement of motives.

The major approaches to the measurement of personality traits are with (1) self-inventories, (2) observational methods, (3) projective techniques, (4) physiological variables, and (5) perceptual variables. In the remainder of the chapter each of these approaches will be discussed in turn.

CURRENT STATUS OF PERSONALITY MEASUREMENT Before going into particular approaches to the measurement of personality characteristics, we should establish a proper emotional tone by stating in advance that the measurement of personality characteristics is still in an embryonic stage. Most of the so-called measures of personality traits either have no validity (predictive or construct validity) or have a small amount of valid variance in comparison to the nonvalid variance (the error variance and the reliable variance which is unrelated to the trait being measured). In those few instances where substantial validity has been demonstrated, there still are intolerable amounts of nonvalid variance.

In speculating why efforts to measure personality attributes to date have not been highly successful, one must realize that this is not because the problem has been neglected. Galton was interested in the measurement of personality traits and made some attempts to develop valid instruments, and the same was true of Binet, Spearman, Thurstone, and the other "greats" in psychometric theory. On the present scene are numerous distinguished psychologists who have devoted themselves in large measure to the study of personality traits. At the present time, it is safe to say that much more effort is being expended to develop measures of personality traits than to develop measures of human ability. In spite of all this effort and in spite of the talent that has been associated with some of it, the search has met with only very modest success.

The rapid success of early efforts to measure human abilities may have beguiled psychologists into thinking it would be easy to measure personality traits. Also, since printed tests of human abilities proved successful, this probably encouraged the idea that printed tests of personality would be equally successful.

Part of the difficulty in measuring personality traits is that, as the idiographists claim, there may be few important general traits of personality, if any. If, as the idiographists claim, specific traits (or habits) combine idiosyncratically in people, there is no hope of measuring general traits of personality. One cannot measure a trait that does not exist, no matter what approach is followed. Let us hope, however, that the idiographists are not entirely correct and that, when we find the correct approaches, some important general traits of personality will be measurable.

The present state of personality measurement is in strong contrast to the need for such measures. Psychological theories are populated with personality traits such as anxiety, self-esteem, ego strength, dogmatism, empathy, rigidity—none of which can be measured very well at the present time. In addition there are many needs for measures of personality traits in applied settings—in psychological clinics, schools, psychiatric practice, industry, the armed forces, and others. In spite of these obvious needs, there are very few instances in which supposed measures of personality traits have proved to be *consistently* valid. This point is emphasized by the fact that, whereas vocabulary tests are consistently valid for selecting college freshmen for many different colleges, no personality test (as far as the author knows) has shown itself to be consistently valid for the same purpose. Worse than the lack of validity of most personality measures in applied settings is the fact that the use of such measures has tended to make a mockery of psychology in the public eye.

self-inventory measures

By far the most frequently employed approach to personality measurement is with printed tests in which the individual is required to describe himself. A typical item, for which the subject is required to answer yes or no, is, "Do you usually lead the discussion in group situations?" Although such self-inventories have been used for a long time (Galton used one to measure individual differences in imagery), the first systematic effort to develop them is credited to Woodworth (1918). During World War I, the Army needed some means for weeding out emotionally unfit men before they were sent overseas. Previously such screening had been done by psychiatric interviewers, but there were not nearly enough interviewers to do the job. Woodworth's solution essentially was to have each man "interview himself." Questions were obtained from a search of the psychiatric literature and from conferences with psychiatrists. The questions were those that psychiatrists frequently used in interviews. Some of them were as follows:

1. Do you often have the feeling of suffocating?
2. Did you ever have convulsions?
3. Can you stand the sight of blood?
4. Did you have a happy childhood?
5. Have you ever had a vision?
6. Did you ever have a strong desire to commit suicide?

A list of 116 such questions constituted a printed form called the Personal Data Sheet. A neurotic-tendency score for each person was obtained by counting the number of problems marked by each man. A small amount of standardization research was performed with the instrument. Items were eliminated if the "neurotic" response was given by more than 25 percent of normal soldiers. Comparisons were made of responses given by unselected soldiers and by a small group of declared neurotic soldiers.

The Personal Data Sheet was considered not as a test, in the stricter meaning of the term, but as an aid to interviewing. Persons who gave numerous "neurotic" responses were called in for detailed psychiatric interviews. Although little direct evidence of validity was obtained, persons who worked with the Personal Data Sheet during World War II were generally pleased with it. After World War I, an interest developed in the development of tests of all kinds, personality self-inventories included. Many of the inventories were modeled after the Personal Data Sheet, to the extent of using some of the same items. Now there are literally hundreds of self-inventories employed for one purpose or another.

TYPES OF INVENTORIES In a discussion of inventories, it is important to make a distinction between self-inventories and other types of inventories, even though the distinction sometimes is not clear. By a self-inventory is meant one in which the individual describes his own traits, such as is the case in the Personal Data Sheet. Self-inventories essentially ask the individual: "What are you like as a person? Show us by responding frankly to the following items." Such self-inventories should be distinguished from inventories that do not require the subject to describe himself. It has been the custom to refer to any objective (as regards scoring) printed test as an inventory. (It is unfortunate to group tests in terms of whether they are printed forms or appear in some other guise, because there are better ways to classify tests.) An example of an inventory that does not concern self-description is one in which the individual answers multiple-choice questions concerning what the average person would do in certain social situations, e.g., whether the average person would return money which he found. As another example of an inventory which does not directly concern self-description, efforts have been made to develop measures of personality attributes from esthetic preferences among different types of geometric forms, e.g., choosing between regular and irregular forms. The reason for the importance of distinguishing self-inventories from other types of printed tests of personality is that self-inventories have their own logic and their own particular problems, ones that do not necessarily hold with other printed tests of personality. This section concerns self-inventories; other printed tests for measuring personality traits will be mentioned at various points in the remainder of the chapter.

TYPES OF SELF-INVENTORY ITEMS   There are numerous types of items that can be employed in self-inventories. Most typically, the subject is presented with a list of statements and asked to mark yes-no, true-false, or agree-disagree. Various types of rating scales can also be employed with such statements, such as seven-step scales of agreement-disagreement, percentage scales comparing the individual with people in general, and others. Instead of such absolute rating methods, various types of comparative ratings methods can be employed. These include forced-choice scales, ranking of statements, and Q sorts. Issues regarding the psychometric properties of these different ways of obtaining responses were discussed in Chapter Two. Special issues in the development and use of rating methods in the study of personality and in the study of attitudes will be discussed in the next chapter. Such technical considerations regarding how responses are elicited, however, are secondary to other problems in the measurement of personality traits. If it were not for the other problems discussed in this chapter, any and all of the rating methods probably could be successfully employed in the measurement of personality.

FACTORS IN SELF-INVENTORY ITEMS   There is an interesting parallel in the growth of knowledge about factors in self-inventories and the growth of knowledge about factors in tests of human abilities. At first only several factors were proposed, e.g., adjustment and introversion-extraversion. Then others were proposed, such as dominance and sociability; and the list grew and grew. In the attempt to make sense out of the increasing list of proposed factors, factor-analytic studies were undertaken. (Guilford, 1959, provides a comprehensive discussion of the history of this work, the many factors which have been proposed, and one man's view of the evidence.) Just as it was necessary to make yearly revisions of the number of factors of human ability that existed, it was necessary to make yearly revisions of the number of factors of personality that existed. At the present time, it is difficult to say how many factors have been found in self-inventories, because (1) the statistical evidence for some of the factors is so weak, (2) different investigators include different types of traits under the heading of personality, and (3) it is very difficult to compare factors reported by different investigators. The most conservative estimate, however, is that over 20 factors have been reported in self-inventories. Cattell (1957) reports over 45 factors of personality, and Guilford (1959) apparently thinks in terms of similar numbers (some of these factors being defined mainly by measurement methods other than self-inventories).

Typical of the factors which have been found in self-inventories are the following 10 factors from the Guilford-Zimmerman Temperament Survey (Guilford and Zimmerman, 1949):

General activity   High energy, quickness of action, liking for speed, and efficiency

Restraint   Deliberate, serious-minded, persistent

Ascendance   Leadership, initiative, persuasiveness

Sociability   Having many friends and liking social activities

Emotional stability   Composure, cheerfulness, evenness of moods

Objectivity   Freedom from suspiciousness, from hypersensitivity, and from getting into trouble

Friendliness   Respect for others, acceptance of domination, toleration of hostility

Thoughtfulness   Reflective, meditative, observing of self and others

Personal relations   Tolerance of people, faith in social institutions, freedom from fault finding and from self-pity

Masculinity   Interest in masculine activities, hard-bolled, not easily disgusted versus (for femininity) romantic and emotionally expressive

EVIDENCE FOR THE FACTORS   In spite of the many reported factors in self-inventories, there is serious doubt that more than several *important* factors are presently known (important in terms of the criteria discussed in the last chapter). Statistical evidence for most of the reported factors is rather weak. Because constructing tests before resorting to factor analysis has proved difficult, in many cases it has been necessary to perform factor analyses of items. Because of the low correlations typically found among such items and the small variance of such correlations in a matrix, the results typically have been unreliable. It has been difficult to tell when to stop factoring, and since many analyses have been highly exploratory, it has been difficult to tell how to rotate factors. Typically only a relatively small number of items load on each factor, and loadings frequently are tiny. As a result, some of the factors have very low reliabilities, and many of them are difficult to interpret.

Even in those instances where the factor-analytic results are reasonably "neat," the picture frequently is changed markedly by the way in which factor scores are estimated. (This issue was discussed in Chapter Ten.) Then, for example, even in those cases where factors are kept orthogonal, one frequently finds very high correlations among the groups of items used to define those factors in subsequent studies. This makes the original factor analysis somewhat meaningless.

These factor-analytic practices have resulted in a large number of groups of items, each supposedly relating to a different factor. Since the number of items relating to each factor usually is less than 20, reliabilities of factors usually are low. Usually there are substantial correlations among those groups of items, so high in some cases that nearly all the reliable variance in one group of items can be explained (by multiple regression) from other groups of items.

It probably is a mistake to interpret this statistical mess as meaningfully portraying the important factors in self-inventories; it would be better to employ one of three complementary approaches. One approach is to hypothesize whole tests relating to personality constructs (e.g., anxiety), develop homogeneous tests by methods discussed in previous chapters, and then submit those tests to factor analysis. If one does not attempt to analyze whole tests, but works with individual items instead, it is better to retain only the several strong factors that are obtained from methods of condensation (e.g., the centroid method). These can be rotated and their importance investigated in subsequent studies. A third approach is to intercorrelate the groups of items that have been found as factors in previous studies and submit those correlations to factor analysis. This is similar to second-order factoring, as it was described in Chapter Ten.

When any of these three approaches is tried, one comes to the conclusion that presently there is evidence for only several statistically strong factors in self-inventories. Careful analyses of these kinds led Peterson (1965) to the following conclusions:

Factor analyses of verbal personality measures have typically generated highly complex multidimensional structural systems. Available evidence now suggests that the most dependable dimensions drawn from conventional factor analyses of ratings and questionnaires are simple, familiar dimensions of broad scope. It also appears that most of the initially obscure, apparently more precise, more narrowly defined factors many investigators claim to have revealed are either trivial, artifactual, capricious, or all three. Verbal descriptions of personality were reduced to two factors, and the two factors were reduced to two ratings, one concerning perceived adjustment and the other related to introversion-extraversion.

As Peterson says, at the present time two factors explain much of the common variance among self-inventories: adjustment and introversion-extraversion, the former being much more prominent than the latter. This is essentially the same position as held by Eysenck (1953) for years, except that he interprets the opposite pole of adjustment and calls it "neuroticism," and also, he deals with a third major factor, one of "psychoticism." This author's inclination is to interpret the dominant factor as *the tendency to say good rather than bad things about one's self*, or as Edwards (1957b) refers to it, *social desirability*. The most obvious thing about the dominant factor is that people who are high on it mark "yes" on socially desirable traits and "no" on socially undesirable traits, and vice versa for persons who are low on the factor. To assume that the former type of person is "adjusted" and that the latter type of person is "neurotic" is a matter that needs proof.

The broadness of the factor of introversion-extraversion is a matter of dispute (Carrigan, 1960), but there is enough evidence for such a factor to encourage continued investigation. Eysenck's factor of "psychoticism" probably is statistically strong only in comparing hospitalized psychotics with supposedly normal people. In studies of college students, for example, most of the variance attributable to that factor probably would be explained by social desirability and introversion-extraversion.

SOCIAL DESIRABILITY   As was mentioned in the previous section, one of the present problems in employing self-inventories to measure personality traits is that such self-inventories are dominated by a general factor of social desirability. Although this fact was suspected for a long time, it remained for Edwards (1957b) and his colleagues to thoroughly explore the matter. In the first major study (Edwards, 1953), 152 subjects rated the social desirability of 140 self-inventory items. Each item was rated on a nine-point scale. The mean rating of each item represented the social desirability of the item as viewed by the subjects as a group. Next, Edwards placed the 140 items in a self-inventory and obtained yes-no responses from a group of subjects. He found a correlation (over items) of .87 between the mean desirability ratings and the proportion of people endorsing each item. This is strong evidence that the average person tends to describe himself in a socially desirable manner on self-inventories.

The above evidence regarding social desirability, however, said nothing directly about *individual differences* in the tendency to say good things about one's self; rather, it pointed to a bias in that regard for the average person. More recent evidence has made it quite clear that individual differences in that tendency do explain much of the variance on self-inventories. One type of circumstantial evidence comes from correlating the average social-desirability ratings of different inventories with loadings of those inventories on a general factor. (The logic of doing this is discussed by Tellegen, 1965.) Studies of this kind have been done with the numerous scales developed for the Minnesota Multiphasic Personality Inventory (MMPI). First, subjects rate the social desirability of each item in each scale, from which the average social desirability of each scale can be obtained. Next, the scales are administered as self-inventories, correlations among scales are computed, and a general factor (usually the first centroid factor) is computed. Loadings on the factor are then correlated with the average desirability ratings of the scales. Studies to date have found substantial correlations between the two indices.

A more direct type of evidence for the importance of individual differences in social desirability comes from the following type of study. Edwards (1957b) developed a self-inventory to measure the extent to which each individual rates himself as socially desirable rather than socially undesirable. Items were obtained from different scales of the MMPI on the basis of ratings of social desirability, by the method discussed previously. Each item so selected was rated as either definitely desirable or definitely undesirable. The items were selected in such a way that approximately half the items were keyed "no" for the desirable response, and the others were keyed "yes" for the desirable response. When the items are used in a self-inventory, scores should reflect individual differences in rated self-desirability (the tendency to say good things about one's self). Other psychologists have developed scales by similar methods for measuring individual differences in rated self-desirability. (These scales, and the evidence from employing them, are discussed by Holtzman, 1965.) It has been found that these scales correlate substantially with many different self-inventories, the directions of the correlations depending on whether the inventories are keyed for "good" or "bad" traits, e.g., adjustment versus maladjustment. In some cases the correlations are almost as high as the reliabilities of the self-inventories.

There no longer is room for argument about the statistical importance of scales constructed to measure self-desirability. They explain so much of the variance of individual differences in responses to self-inventories that statistical arguments concern whether or not there is enough independent variance in such inventories to continue investigating them. The major arguments now concern the psychological nature of self-desirability scores. Some speak of such scores as concerning only *response styles*, individual differences in test-taking habits which are unrelated to the purpose of the instruments. (Response styles will be discussed more fully in Chapter Fifteen.) Others have gone so far as to suggest that the variance in self-desirability ratings represents individual differences only in conscious faking, which in turn implies that self-inventories in general tend to measure only individual differences in the tendency to "fake good." At the other extreme, some argue that the correlations between self-desirability scores and scores on self-inventories do not invalidate the latter, but rather serve to show that adjustment and self-desirability (or self-esteem) are much the same thing. It could further be argued that, to picture one's self as socially desirable, one must know what is desirable in particular situations, and if an individual is unable to "fake good," it indicates that he has been subjected to highly unusual environmental influences. In other words, only a poorly adjusted person would be so unfamiliar with social expectations as to not know how to "fake good" on a self-inventory.

Admittedly the dominant factor in self-inventories (social desirability) is quite complex. It probably is neither a pure measure of adjustment nor a pure measure of faking, but rather a combination of those and other attributes. The major components of social desirability probably are (1) actual adjustment of the individual, (2) knowledge the individual has about his own traits, and (3) frankness of the individual in stating what he knows. An individual could be maladjusted (by popular standards) and not know it, and thus he might rate himself as being high in social desirability. In contrast, an individual could be maladjusted and know it but consciously distort his responses so as to appear socially desirable. Another possibility would be an individual who is highly adjusted, knows it, and frankly describes himself as being high in social desirability. Since each of these three component characteristics can be thought of as relatively continuous, the expressed self-desirability of each person can be thought of as some combination of the three.

Social desirability is an interesting variable that should be investigated in detail. There is enough circumstantial evidence to show that it is related to adjustment, but also there is enough circumstantial evidence to show that a large share of its variance concerns other traits, such as self-knowledge and frankness. Unfortunately, we do not know how to measure these components separately, but if we could learn to do so, it would constitute a major "breakthrough" in the use of self-inventories to measure personality traits.

OTHER PROBLEMS WITH SELF-INVENTORIES In addition to the problems that have been discussed so far in the use of self-inventories to measure personality traits, there are other problems that should be mentioned. Such inventories are beset with severe *semantic problems,* which occur both in communicating the meaning of items to subjects and in communicating the results of studies to researchers. The former type of problem can be illustrated with the following item: "Do you usually lead the discussion in group situations?" First, the individual must decide what is meant by "group situations." Does this pertain to family settings as well as to groups found outside the home? Does it pertain only to formal groups, such as clubs and business groups, or does it also apply to informal group situations? Second, the subject must decide what is meant by "lead." Does this mean to speak the most, make the best points, or to have the last say? Third, the subject must decide what is meant by "usually." Does that mean nearly all the time, most of the time, or at least half the time?

Anyone who works with self-inventories should, on at least one occasion, ask several subjects how they interpret each item on a typical inventory. When that is done, one is rather appalled by the differences in meanings held by different subjects and by the extent to which all subjects are somewhat confused by many of the items. For these reasons, it frequently is found that subjects give different responses to sizable percentages of the items when responding to the same self-inventory on two or more occasions. This, of course, relates only to the general confusion about the meanings of items. In contrast, if an individual has a definite, but erroneous, interpretation of an item, he will consistently respond erroneously to the item.

A second semantic problem occurs in communicating the results of studies with self-inventories to other researchers. Factor names and descriptions tend to be less clear than is the case for factors of human ability. This is partly because researchers employ terms in common parlance to describe factors, and people do not entirely agree about the meanings of such terms. For example, the factor that Guilford calls "thoughtfulness" might be misinterpreted by many as relating to "considerateness," whereas it relates to "contemplativeness." Admitting that it is difficult to find precise terms for communicating about personality traits, some investigators have gone out of their way to employ vague terms, e.g., "rhathymia" and "adventurous cyclothymia."

Another major problem with self-inventories is that scores are somewhat affected by situational factors. (Evidence for this is summarized by Guilford, 1959.) For example, if a self-inventory is used in personnel selection, individuals are likely to give somewhat different answers when applying for a job than they will sometime later when they are performing satisfactorily on the job. Numerous studies have shown that responses are somewhat different when the same subjects are required to take the same inventory under different instructions, e.g., under instructions to appear adjusted, appear maladjusted, and to be frank. Although there is not enough evidence to know for sure, it might be that self-inventories used in basic research are affected to some extent by the subject's conceptions of the intents and purposes of the research. For example, if the subject thinks the research concerns emotions, he might give somewhat different responses to an inventory than he would if he thought the research concerned learning.

Another problem with self-inventories is that they are beset with response styles, test-taking habits that are unrelated to the purpose of the instruments. This is a matter which will be discussed in greater detail in Chapter Fifteen. For example, there is some evidence regarding a response style of *acquiescence,* the tendency to say "yes" or to agree regardless of the item content. In most cases the variance attributable to such response styles is logically unrelated to the trait being measured.

For reasons which will be discussed in Chapter Fifteen, it has proved very difficult to remove such response styles from personality inventories.

DIRECTIONS FOR RESEARCH In spite of the severe problems with self-inventories, such inventories play a very important part in research today, and they probably will continue to do so for a long time to come. Even though there are mountains of circumstantial evidence to indicate that few self-inventories measure what they claim to measure with a high degree of validity, in most cases such inventories apparently are more valid than the measures provided by other approaches. For example, even though practically no one in psychology would claim that self-inventories to measure anxiety have more than a modest level of validity, they certainly are more valid than existing projective instruments, physiological indices, and other approaches. The problem is that we have few, if any, highly valid measures of personality traits provided by any approach, and the measures provided by self-inventories currently are the best of the lot.

Since individual differences in social desirability are so strongly represented in most self-inventories, plans for improving such inventories must consider what is to be done about that variable. As was mentioned previously, it is an interesting variable which merits investigation in its own right, but it is serving to cloud the measurement of other personality traits. It is hard to believe that there really are only several general traits of personality (such as Eysenck's triumvirate of neuroticism, psychoticism, and introversion-extraversion), but because of the strong influence of social desirability, the statistical evidence for other factors is rather weak. There are numerous "splinter" factors, where only a small number of items have loadings and those loadings frequently are not high, but there are only several broad, statistically strong factors in self-inventories.

Numerous suggestions have been made for ways to delete the social-desirability factor in self-report inventories, but none of these has proved very satisfactory. One suggestion is to measure social desirability separately and then partial such scores from the scores on self-inventories. There are two large problems in doing that. First, even if one were successful in that regard, it would markedly reduce the reliable variance in self-inventories. Such partialed scores would have reliabilities predictable from equations for the reliabilities of linear combinations (Chapter Seven). Since it is known that social desirability correlates substantially with most self-inventories, partialing social desirability would result in rather unreliable "corrected" self-inventory scores. Another way of looking at this matter is in terms of correlations among self-inventories. Since it is known that social desirability can explain much of the common variance among self-inventories (in factor analysis), correlations among self-inventories would be rather small if scores on social desirability were partialed. Then it would be very difficult to find statistically strong factors among such partialed scores.

The second major problem with attempting to partial social desirability from self-inventories is that, before this can be done, it is necessary to measure some components of social desirability. The problem with present measures of social desirability is that they lump together several underlying traits, i.e., adjustment, self-knowledge, and frankness. Rather than partialing these in conglomerate form from self-inventories, it would be better to partial only one or two of these, particularly frankness and/or self-knowledge. Before this can be done, it will be necessary to measure the different components of social desirability, but at the present time, there are no appealing suggestions as to how that could be done.

One possible way to deal with social desirability without encountering the problems mentioned above is to employ items that are neutral with respect to social desirability. Logically this is very difficult, because to varying degrees, personality traits are intrinsically related to social desirability. Thus dominance is considered more desirable than submissiveness, sociability is considered more desirable than nonsociability, energeticness is considered more desirable than laziness, and so on for other personality traits. For these reasons, it is very difficult to find neutral items that actually measure personality traits; however, by employing items that are not extreme with respect to social desirability, one should be able to obtain some reduction of the importance of that factor.

Rather than attempt to employ items that are neutral with respect to social desirability, another approach is to employ forced-choice items that are matched for social desirability. Two examples are:

Do you worry more about

_____ social problems

or _____ health problems

Most of your friends consider you as more

_____ frank

or _____ tender-hearted

Although the use of forced-choice self-inventories has stirred much interest, and considerable work has been done to develop such inventories, the forced-choice item by no means constitutes a panacea for the problems that beset self-inventories. (In a review of the literature on forced-choice inventories, Zavala, 1965, paints a much more sanguine picture of the effectiveness of forced-choice inventories than is being painted here.) One major problem is that it is very difficult to equate alternatives for social desirability. Even when the alternatives have almost identical ratings of social desirability when rated separately, they are not rated equal in social desirability when paired. This is probably because relative ratings are more precise in this instance, for reasons that were discussed in Chapter Two. For example, even if frankness and tender-heartedness receive the same mean rating of 6.0 on a seven-step social-desirability scale, 60 percent of the people may say that frankness is more desirable than tender-heartedness when they actually are paired. Apparently, in forced-choice inventories, people are able to detect fine differences in social desirability, which partly destroys the purpose of using such instruments.

Another problem with forced-choice inventories relates to public relations, particularly in applied settings. People tend to feel "trapped" by forced-choice inventories, and in many cases rightly so. As extreme examples, almost anyone would feel uncomfortable in responding to the following two items:

Are you more

_____ honest

or _____ intelligent

Are you more

_____ cowardly

or _____ cruel

The general public apparently already has a low opinion of self-inventories, and the wide use of forced-choice inventories would do little to improve the image.

In the long run it may prove that some traits are validly measured by self-inventories. In some cases self-inventories may be employed for the sake of economy because more valid methods prove to be laborious and expensive. Also, self-inventories surely will prove useful in developing better measures of personality traits, if they are forthcoming. It is hard to believe, however, that self-inventories will in the long run constitute the major method for the measurement of personality traits. Until better methods for measuring personality are developed, there is no choice but to rely heavily on self-inventories.

observational methods

Related to self-inventories are observational methods for the measurement of personality traits, the difference being that in the latter method an individual is asked to describe someone else rather than himself. In most observational methods, the interest is in the personality traits of the person being observed, and the intention is for the observer to be an impartial, accurate judge of the traits of the other person. In some observational methods, however, it is really the personality traits of the observer that are at issue, and the observer's observations are used to infer something about his personality. This is the case in studies of "person perception," to be discussed later.

In most observational methods, the validity of the measurements is completely at the mercy of the observers. They make judgments about the personality traits of other people, and such judgments can be accurate only if the experimenter asks the right questions of the observers and only if the observers know the correct answers. It is proper to say that observational methods of these kinds are "subjective," in that judgments necessarily flow from the silent intuitive processes of the observers. Such subjective judgments surely constitute the oldest approach to the understanding of personality traits. Men have always observed other men and tried to describe their characteristics with words relating to personality. What has been done in psychometric research on observational methods is to objectify the recording of impressions (e.g., with rating scales) and to objectify the analysis of results.

In contrast to most observational methods, which are based on subjective judgments of personality traits, some observational methods are quite objective, in that all the observer does is record what the subject actually does, e.g., how many questions a child asks in an interview situation. In other instances, observational methods are "almost" objective, in that the observer is required to make ratings that entail only a low level of inference, e.g., that a child is shy in an interview situation. What typically is found is that the more objective the behavior to be observed, the more molecular the trait involved. It is easy to be objective about traits at the level of simple "habits," e.g., number of questions asked, amount of time spent in different activities, and number of words of different kinds uttered by the person being observed. When observations are being made of more general personality traits, however, judgments usually are highly subjective, e.g., judging personality traits like anxiety, dominance, and achievement motivation. Thus efforts to make observational methods more objective usually result in narrowing the traits under investigation to the level of highly specific modes of response (or habits). Then there is a question of how to combine such highly specific responses into measures of more general personality traits. To do so requires a great deal of construct validation, very little of which has been done at the present time. If one goes to the other extreme and deals directly with general traits of personality, much credence must be placed in the accuracy of subjective judgments by observers.

Most observational methods employ rating scales to record impressions, e.g., a seven-step scale bounded by the adjectives "anxious" and "calm" to be used in rating psychiatric patients in an interview. Some psychometric properties of rating methods will be discussed in Chapter Fourteen; here will be considered the types of situations in which such rating scales are employed. There is a large literature on observational methods, so large that it is not possible here to summarize all the evidence with respect to the many approaches that have been explored. In this section will be mentioned only some of the outstanding properties of the major observational methods. (Guilford, 1959, provides a detailed summary of methods and results.)

OBSERVATIONS IN DAILY LIFE   Observation in daily life probably is employed more frequently than any other observational method for the measurement of personality traits. Examples are a teacher rating the personality traits of his students, parents rating the traits of their children, and students rating the personality traits of one another. Such observations are analogous to having one individual fill out a self-inventory for someone else, and consequently both methods tend to run into the same types of problems. Ratings of persons in daily life tend to be dominated by a general factor, not unlike the factor of social desirability found in self-inventories (Peterson, 1965). Such ratings tend to concern rather obviously good- and bad-sounding traits, e.g., anxious rather than calm, friendly rather than hostile. Although only moderate correlations typically are found among different rating scales, this is mainly because of only a moderate level of reliability. Much of the common variance among scales in a typical study can be accounted for by a general factor. This is particularly so in ratings of social traits and motives of normal people. Apparently there is less tendency for a general factor to prevail in studies of symptoms of maladjustment in groups of neurotics and psychotics. An example is the study by Grinker (1961) and his colleagues, which produced 15 factors relating to the symptoms of depressed patients.

The general factor that usually appears in self-inventories concerns self-desirability (or rated self-esteem). The general factor that appears in most ratings of normal people concerns *leniency,* the tendency to say good things or bad things about people in general. This might be thought of as other-desirability rather than self-desirability. Individual differences in the former tendency have been documented on numerous occasions, where it has been found that raters differ in their average ratings of other people.

The factor of other-desirability, in addition to making it difficult to document additional factors in ratings, also introduces a source of bias into ratings. Since the ratings of a person depend to some extent on the level of other-desirability held by the rater, this is a source of unreliability. Obviously this bias would lead to some faulty decisions about people in applied situations, e.g., in ratings of workers by foremen and in the rating of psychiatric patients by nurses.

Just as self-desirability in self-inventories is influenced by the frankness of the subject, the rated social desirability of other persons is influenced by personal prejudices. For example, parents are prone to give more favorable ratings to their children than to other peoples' children, and teachers are influenced in the ratings of students by their personal likes and dislikes.

Just as self-inventories are limited to what the individual knows about himself, ratings in daily life are limited to what the observer knows about the person being rated. Actually, this is more of a problem with observational methods than with self-inventories, because with the former it can at least be assumed that the individual "lives with himself," and whether or not he takes advantage of it, has myriad opportunities to observe himself in action. Frequently ratings are made by people who barely know the person being rated or have had opportunities to observe the person only in highly restricted settings. In this connection, the author once performed a study of ratings (unpublished) in a military setting, in which officers were asked to identify by name the photographs of men that they previously had rated. On the average, they could identify less than 50 percent of the men, and interestingly enough, the men identified were predominantly from the "good" and "bad" ends of the rating continuum rather than from the middle.

Even if the observer has had considerable opportunity to observe an individual in one type of situation, he may have had practically no opportunity to observe the individual in situations relevant to the traits being rated. This frequently occurs in university settings, where professors are asked to rate personality characteristics of students in applications for graduate work or for a particular position. The professor may have only the vaguest idea about some of the social traits of the student.

In spite of their problems, observations in daily life tend to be superior to the other types of observational methods. Although such ratings frequently suffer because the observer has not had sufficient opportunities to observe the individual in circumstances relevant to the traits being rated, the situation in this regard tends to be much worse with the other observational methods. Typically the latter methods permit the observer to witness only a tiny sample of the individual's behavior, and frequently that is done in highly artificial situations. If nothing else, observations in daily life provide a much more economical way of obtaining approximate information about personality characteristics than is provided by other observational methods.

INTERVIEWS   The interview is simply one type of observational situation. It is seldom used for observing personality traits in general; rather, it usually is restricted to "sizing up" an individual with respect to particular decisions about him, e.g., as in a job interview or a psychiatric interview. Usually the interviewer either has never previously met the person being interviewed or has known the person only casually. Because of the small amount of time to observe the individual (usually less than one hour), interviews make sense only if it can be assumed that (1) the interviewer is particularly talented at observing some important traits and (2) the interview is limited to obtaining information about only a small number of traits. Because the results of interviews naturally depend on the questions asked by the interviewers, efforts have been made to "structure" such interviews with standard lists of questions and other ways of establishing uniformity.

Even with the best efforts, ratings based on interviews tend to have only a low level of reliability and validity (Guilford, 1959; Ulrich and Trumbo, 1965). Since interviews usually are employed in making personnel decisions, validity is determined by correlating ratings with specific criteria. When that is done, it usually is found that ratings add little to the predictive validity that is obtainable from objective tests of ability, personality, and interest. In spite of this fact, interviews probably will continue to be used for some time, because in some instances there is nothing else that can be used, e.g., as is the case with psychiatric interviews. It is surprising, however, that some people who castigate standardized tests place inordinate faith in what can be obtained from a 30-minute interview. It is clear that the interview does not provide a valid general tool for the measurement of personality traits.

OBSERVATIONS IN CONTRIVED SITUATIONS   One approach to observation is to have the individual participate in a contrived situation, which is frequently spoken of as a *situational test*. One of the pioneering efforts of this kind was the screening program developed by the Office of Strategic Services during World War II. The purpose was to select men for military intelligence work, espionage, and other dangerous assignments. In addition to taking standardized tests of personality and ability, each candidate was given a series of situational tests, each situation involving a type of problem that might be encountered in actual duty. The candidate's performance was rated in terms of ability to think quickly and effectively and in terms of emotional stability and leadership. In one such situation, the candidate was told to imagine that he is caught in a government office going through files marked "secret," that he does not work in the building, and that he carries no identification papers. The candidate was given 12 minutes to construct an alibi for his presence in the suspicious circumstances. Then he was subjected to a harrowing interrogation, in which attempts were made to break his alibi and make his statements appear foolish. The candidate was rated on how convincing his story was and his ability to support it under interrogation.

A large-scale use of situational tests was in a study to develop selection instruments for clinical psychology trainees (Kelly and Fiske, 1951). In one such test, each candidate was required to express in pantomime the meaning of different emotions. In that study, situational tests added nothing to the prediction of success in clinical practice over what was provided by standardized tests of ability and personality (and the same was true for interviews).

By their nature, observations in contrived situations are not suited to the measurement of personality traits in general; rather, they are restricted to a very limited number of traits relating to the particular contrived situations. Also, since in many cases they are extremely laborious and time-consuming, they should not be employed unless they add something to simpler methods of measurement, and most of the evidence on that score is negative. Perhaps in some situations such observations are no more valid than they are because the situations are so obviously contrived. Some situations amount to "play acting," and it is reasonable to believe that such "play acting" is not entirely representative of behavior in real life. For example, the individual who shows leadership qualities in daily life might regard situational tests as silly and thus might appear to perform rather poorly.

Observations in contrived situations probably will continue to be used only with respect to applied problems of personnel selection. There is evidence (Guilford, 1959) that some of the approaches work reasonably well for that purpose, particularly when the situations are made "natural" for the persons to be observed. An example is the "leaderless group discussion," in which half a dozen persons are observed while they discuss some issue. Ratings of leadership qualities in such situations correlate reasonably well with actual performance in supervisory positions.

BEHAVIORAL TESTS   In some observational situations, directly observable aspects of the subject's behavior are used as measures of personality characteristics. Because the observations concern observable behavior, the situations in which such observations are made are usually referred to as _behavioral tests_. Like situational tests, behavioral tests also consist of contrived situations. One of the earliest and still the best-known use of behavioral tests was that of Hartshorne and May in the Character Educational Inquiry. They wanted to measure traits in schoolchildren such as honesty, truthfulness, cooperativeness, and self-control. Rather than use conventional tests or ratings to measure those characteristics, they chose to observe the actual behavior of children with respect to the traits. The observations were made in the normal routine of school activities—in athletics, recreation, and classroom work.

Observations were made so as to provide objective scores. For example, one of the measures of honesty was made by allowing students to grade their own papers; then a check was made as to the student's honesty in correctly scoring his paper. Since a duplicate copy of each paper had been prepared before it was given to the student, it was a simple matter to check the student's honesty in that situation. Another behavioral test in that study concerned the trait of "charity," in which children were first given an attractive kit of school supplies and were then allowed to donate some of the items to "less fortunate children." The donations appeared to be anonymous, but the experimenters had marked the items so as to be able to count the number of items donated by each child.

Another type of behavioral test is the Minimal Social Behavior Scale (Farina et al., 1957), in which mental patients are submitted to a structured interview. In one "item," the interviewer offers the patient a pencil, and the item is scored "correct" if the patient accepts the pencil or acknowledges the offer in some other way. In another item, the interviewer places a cigarette in his mouth and fumbles for a match, during which time a book of matches is in plain view of the patient but is not visible to the interviewer. The item is scored "correct" if the patient mentions the matches or offers a match from his own pocket.

When behavioral tests can be employed, they have a number of attractive advantages. The use of actual behavioral products frees the measurement methods from the subjectivity of rating scales. If observations can be made in natural settings where the subject is unaware that he is being tested in any sense, the results probably are more valid. There have, however, been so few systematic uses of behavioral tests that it is difficult to judge how useful they will be in the measurement of personality traits. They probably will continue to be used more with children than with adults. This is because it is easier to place children in the test situations without having them suspect an ulterior purpose. Also, the relevant behaviors of children are more easily observed than is the case in complex adult interactions.

For a number of reasons, it is doubtful that behavioral tests will occupy more than a modest place in the measurement of personality traits. Like all observations in contrived situations, they are expensive and time-consuming to apply. More important, it is very difficult to think of behavioral products that might relate to most personality traits. For example, what behavioral products in adults might relate to dominance or sociability? Behavioral tests will probably continue to be used only for rather special purposes, such as in the basic research of Hartshorne and May on character traits in children or for diagnosing rather specific traits in clinical populations.

PERSON PERCEPTION   As was mentioned previously, in some instances observational methods are employed in the effort to learn something about the personality of the observer rather than about the persons being observed. Such methods are said to concern person perception. For example, previously it was said that observers differ in other-desirability, as manifested in mean differences among observers in their ratings of the social desirability of persons in general. It might be thought that such differences in other-desirability would relate to the personalities of observers—that observers who generally rate all people as "positive" are accepting and friendly, and observers who tend to rate all people as "negative" are sullen grouches. If differences in mean favorableness ratings relate to personality characteristics of observers, convincing evidence is yet to be obtained. More likely, most of the variance among observers in that regard is because of "sets" regarding the use of rating scales. In most cases observers would probably change their mean ratings of other people if they learned that their ratings were well above or below the mean ratings given by other observers.

Another aspect of person perception concerns the ability to guess how another person will rate himself, which has been referred to as *empathy*. One attempt to measure this supposed trait is as follows. An individual responds to the items on a self-inventory; then a friend of the person attempts to guess how the person responded to each item. The percentage of correct guesses is taken as an empathy score. This approach has been used to investigate the amount of empathy of psychotherapists, in which case the therapist is required to guess the responses of his client. Unfortunately, accuracy scores tend to be rather specific to the "target" person. A person might have a rather high empathy score in guessing the responses of one person but a rather low empathy score in guessing the responses of another person. What consistency there is in such judgments has not found much construct validity for the measurement of a trait of empathy (Guilford, 1959).

A third aspect of person perception concerns *assumed similarity*, the degree to which a person rates other persons as much the same as one another or different from one another. One approach is as follows. An individual is asked to rate a person that he likes very much and a person that he dislikes on a list of rating scales, each rating scale being bounded by bipolar adjectives such as kind-cruel, friendly-unfriendly, wise-foolish, and strong-weak. An assumed similarity score is obtained from a comparison of the ratings given to the two persons. The D statistics discussed in Chapter Eleven have been used frequently for that purpose. One of the major problems with studies of assumed similarity is that they are beset with numerous artifacts that are very difficult to control (these are discussed by Cronbach, 1955). For example, the assumed similarity score obtained from comparing "most liked person" with "least liked person" depends on the persons that the rater has in mind, and thus it may be more of an indication of the wideness of the person's acquaintance with other people than an indication of the tendency to view others much the same as rather than different from one another. There are numerous statistical artifacts in measures of assumed similarity. For example, since most of the rating scales employed in such studies are heavily loaded with social desirability (e.g., wise-foolish and strong-weak), statistics relating to profile analysis, such as D, are largely superfluous. Most of the information in the differences in profiles for most liked and least liked persons is contained in the difference in mean favorableness ratings on the scales as a group. There is little convincing evidence that measures of assumed similarity are important measures of personality traits.

EVALUATION OF OBSERVATIONAL METHODS   As can be seen from the foregoing discussion, observational methods as a group have severe limitations as approaches to the measurement of personality traits. Individual methods tend to suffer from one or all of the problems of being (1) based on insufficient experience with the person being observed, (2) dependent on the subjective judgment of observers, (3) dominated by a general factor of other-desirability in ratings, (4) logically restricted to the measurement of only a limited range of traits, (5) possessing only modest to low interobserver reliability, and (6) in those instances where a particular criterion is to be predicted, having little predictive validity. As a general tool, the best of this lot is the method of obtaining ratings in daily life. If there is a truism in the use of observational methods, it is that the validity depends much more on the amount of experience the observer has had with the ratee in situations relative to the traits being rated than it does on the qualifications of the rater in other regards. For example, in military settings it is consistently found that trainees in officer candidate schools do a better job of rating one another than is done by officers rating the trainees. This probably is because the trainees know one another much better than their officers know them. As another example, in a study by Grinker (1961) and his colleagues, an *inverse* relationship was found between the years of experience of psychiatrists and the reliability of rating depressive patients in hospitals. They hypothesized that this was because the younger psychiatrists had much more direct experience with the patients, seeing them on numerous occasions on the ward, whereas the senior psychiatrists saw the patient only in an interview and briefly on other occasions.

Even when observers have approximately the same amount of information about persons being rated, there are individual differences in the ability of observers to make accurate ratings (Guilford, 1959), and the accuracy of the rater interacts with the type of person being rated. This is analogous to the case of intelligence testers who differ in their overall accuracy of administering tests and who do a better job with some types of persons than with others. This must happen to some extent with intelligence tests, but it surely happens to a much greater extent in ratings. To the extent that there are differences in accuracy of raters and these differences interact with the persons being rated, ratings simply are not standardized measures of personality traits. Ratings, and all observational methods presently employed, mostly are stopgap approaches that surely will be replaced one day by better methods for the measurement of personality traits.

projective techniques

Projective techniques are based on the principle that, when a situation is open to a variety of interpretations, interpretations sometimes differ in accordance with the personalities of people. There is a great deal of everyday experience to support the principle, which is evidenced, for example, in the individual who, while suppressing his own intense hostility, attributes hostile motives to other people. As another example, the principle is clearly evidenced in the writings of children, where children are given a few lines of a story and told to complete it. The achievement-oriented child writes about prizes and conquests; the highly anxious child writes about explosions and mayhem; and the child with harsh parents populates his story with unkind adults.

Whereas the techniques employed with respect to these phenomena are called "projective," in a strict sense projection is only one of the mechanisms involved. Projection refers to the tendency of a person to attribute his own unwanted motives and social traits to other people, as in the case of the hostile person mentioned above. Actually, projective techniques are used to measure numerous types of social traits, motives, and forms of maladjustment. Although it would be better to speak of the methods as concerning interpretation rather than projection, the name "projective techniques" is too well ingrained in psychology to allow the change.

It is frequently said that the essence of projective techniques is that they are *unstructured*, in contrast to self-inventories and rating methods, which are said to be *structured*. If there is an agreed-on public meaning for a stimulus configuration, it is said to be structured; but if there is no agreed-on public meaning, it is said to be unstructured. For example, a structured stimulus would be employed in the situation where an individual is shown an outline drawing of a house and asked to tell what he sees. Since there is an agreed-on public meaning for the stimulus configuration, nearly all subjects are likely to say that it is a house. In other words, there is little room for interpretation of a highly structured stimulus, and consequently individual differences in interpretation are not very important. In contrast, an unstructured stimulus would be employed if the individual were presented with some random smudges of color on a piece of paper and asked to tell what it is. Another example of an unstructured situation is that in which the individual is shown a drawing of a house and asked to tell what the people are like who live there. In both of these instances, there are no agreed-on ways of responding. The individual must make an interpretation rather than give an objective description, and it is reasonable to think that the nature of the interpretation will depend on the personality characteristics of the individual. Even if there is much truth in that principle, however, there still is the chore of turning such interpretive responses into valid measures of personality characteristics, which apparently is much easier said than done.

Since self-inventories and projective techniques are used more frequently than any other methods for the measurement of personality traits, it is important to make some comparisons between the two approaches. Whereas the essence of projective techniques is that they are unstructured, self-inventories are intended to be structured. That is, on a self-inventory, regardless of what motivates an individual to respond in one way or another to an item, he should clearly understand the item. Previously it was mentioned that this goal is only approximately achieved because of the language problems in the development of self-inventories.

It is sometimes said that projective techniques are subjective methods, whereas self-inventories are objective methods. Actually, both of them are subjective but in different ways. The objectivity in self-inventories is in the scoring, but the validity of the results depends on the subjective processes of the subjects. In contrast, the projective techniques do not depend on the subjective processes of subjects to describe their personalities, but most of these techniques depend very much on the subjective processes of test examiners to interpret the responses. Rather than speak of objectivity, it would be better to say that self-inventories are much more highly *standardized* than are projective techniques, a matter that will be discussed in more detail later.

The growth of projective techniques has paralleled the growth of self-inventories, but they have been nourished by somewhat different traditions. Projective techniques have been developed mainly in conjunction with psychiatry and clinical psychology, but to a large extent, self-inventories have been developed in conjunction with basic research on personality traits and with personnel selection programs in military and vocational settings. Because of the affiliation of projective techniques with clinical activities, they frequently are spoken of as "diagnostic instruments." In clinical settings, projective techniques are mainly used to specify what is particularly "sick" about an individual who, at the outset, is known to have serious problems.

Whereas self-inventories tend to be more concerned with social traits than with motives or specific forms of maladjustment, the reverse is true in most uses of projective techniques. Since motives must be inferred rather than observed directly, some people claim that projective techniques offer rich material for making such inferences. If so, projective techniques will be an improvement over self-inventories in the measurement of motives, because the social-desirability factor in self-inventories tends to obscure the valid measurement of motives.

TYPES OF PROJECTIVE TECHNIQUES The projective techniques do not fall into neat types with common properties, as do observational methods. Rather, the apparent differences among them mainly concern the physical characteristics of the stimulus materials. Some consist of pictures of nonhuman objects, others consist of written material, and others consist of three-dimensional materials of one type or another. Detailed descriptions of particular techniques are found in the Suggested Additional Readings at the end of this chapter.

The most widely used projective technique is the Rorschach Ink Blot Test, which, as almost everyone knows, consists of ten ink blots. The individual is asked to tell what he sees on each blot, and for this reason, the Rorschach is frequently called a perceptual test. The word "perception" in this context, however, is rather inappropriate, because other than for poor eyesight, everyone can see the blots, and what is at issue is the individual's interpretation of what he sees. Because of the wide use of the Rorschach, much of the evidence regarding the psychometic properties of projective techniques is based on research with that instrument.

The Thematic Apperception Test (TAT) is next in popularity to the Rorschach. It consists of pictures of people in different types of social situations. Perhaps more than any other instrument, it is directly concerned with motives. For this reason, the pictures that are used lend themselves to interpretations of motives of aggression, affiliation, security, achievement, and others. Whereas on the Rorschach the subjects are required to tell what they see, on the TAT they are asked to make up a story about each picture.

Probably third in popularity are tests consisting of incomplete sentences such as the following:

1 I dislike most to _____

2 I wish that I had never _____

3 The people I like most _____

In some cases, semiobjective scoring systems have been developed for tests employing incomplete sentences (e.g., Rotter et al., 1949).

In addition to the major methods discussed above, many other types of projective techniques have been developed. Various play activities of children have been used for that purpose, such as doll play, finger painting, and molding of clay.

VALIDITY   Apparently most projective techniques do a rather poor job of measuring personality traits. (Evidence regarding statements in this and following sections is found in the summaries of literature on projective techniques by Guilford, 1959, and Masling, 1960.) Most of the traits measured by projective techniques require construct validation, but there is little evidence to support the construct validity for such measures. For example, there is no convincing evidence that any projective technique validly measures the trait of anxiety.

In applied settings, the evidence is clear that projective techniques have, at most, only a low level of validity in predicting particular criteria. They tend to correlate very little with criteria of vocational success. Also, they do a poor job of differentiating normal people from people who are diagnosed as neurotic, and they do a poor job of differentiating different types of mentally ill persons. There are scattered findings that particular techniques are valid for particular purposes, but the total evidence points to the fact that, as a group, projective techniques do not provide very valid measures of personality traits. The following sections will consider some of the reasons for this state of affairs.

RELIABILITY   Although there are some exceptions to the rule, projective techniques tend to have unacceptably low reliabilities. Although there are arguments about how the reliability of projective techniques should be measured, however it is measured, the typical finding is a reliability around .60, and very few reliabilities as high as .80 are found.

Logically, the most appropriate measure of reliability with projective techniques is the correlation of alternative forms administered and scored by different examiners, but very few studies of that kind have been done. With projective techniques, it is particularly important to develop alternative forms, because with most of the techniques, it is difficult to define the domain of content. For example, what is the domain of content for the Rorschach test? Is it all possible inkblots, all ink-blots of particular kinds, or what? If an alternative form can be con-structed, and the two forms correlate highly, it gives one confidence that a definable domain of content is involved. With some of the projec-tive techniques (e.g., the original Rorschach inkblots), there is no al-ternative form, and consequently the alternative-form reliability is un-known. Alternative forms also would be useful for practical purposes, such as in testing the amount of improvement during psychotherapy.

In addition to the need for alternative forms in studying the reliabil-ity of projective techniques, it is necessary to investigate the measure-ment error because of examiners. The interpretation of most projective techniques is highly subjective, and in such instances one is likely to find considerable measurement error because of differences in interpreta-tions by different examiners.

In many cases the reliabilities of projective techniques are not too low to permit their use in research, but in most cases they are far too low to permit their use in those applied settings where important issues about people are at stake. For reasons which were discussed in Chapter Seven, one can tolerate a reliability of .60 in basic research; but when important decisions about people are based on psychological measures, even a reliability of .90 is not high enough. Since the typical reliability of trait measures from projective techniques is around .60, this means that the standard error of measurement is .63 times as large as the standard deviation of the trait. Such a large dose of mea-surement error cannot be tolerated in situations where measures have important impacts on the lives of people.

STANDARDIZATION As has been mentioned in a number of places previously in this book, the essence of measurement in science is that the measure-ment procedures be *standardized*. If measures are standardized, their results are repeatable—repeatable by the same individual employing different forms of the same instrument and repeatable by different indi-viduals. Because the results depend very much on the tester, most projective techniques are rather unstandardized. The tester influences the kinds of responses that the subject gives, and the interpretations of responses vary considerably with the tester. For example, studies with the Rorschach have found that different examiners tend to obtain different numbers of responses from subjects. Some examiners typically obtain only 20 responses, and others typically obtain 40 or more. Since many of the Rorschach scores correlate with the total number of re-sponses given, those scores depend to some extent on the person ad-ministering the test. Male examiners tend to obtain different types of responses than female examiners, and different examiners tend to elicit different types of responses in particular categories (Masling, 1960).

The examiner, in addition to his influence on the responses given to projective techniques, has an even more marked influence on the interpretation of results. With most projective techniques, the end result is not a set of trait scores, but a description of some aspects of the subject. On the Rorschach, for example, a semiobjective method is used for scoring individual responses, but those scores are only stepping stones to the interpretation, and the step from the scores to the interpretation is highly intuitive. Thus, after studying the responses given by a subject, the examiner might conclude, among other things, that the subject "is rigid, overintellectualizes, and has much free anxiety." There are, however, only rough guides as to how to make such interpretations, which is the major reason why some projective techniques are so unstandardized.

There is some evidence that projective techniques are projective both for the examiner and for the subject (Masling, 1960). For example, one study found that examiners who were rated by their colleagues as hostile tended to interpret the responses of psychiatric patients to a projective technique as being hostile. Aside from particular differences among examiners in the interpretation of responses, there surely are important differences among examiners in overall validity. One gets the impression that some examiners are very accurate in their interpretations and others tend to miss the mark entirely. This would be much like the situation where some meteorologists were very accurate in measuring humidity and others were very poor in that regard. Then the accuracy of weather forecasting would differ greatly from locality to locality, and the data obtained from such observations would not aid the science of meteorology.

Since the validity of most projective techniques depends on the interaction of examiner, subject, technique, situation, and trait being measured, these techniques are unstandardized and thus should not be called tests. (Some exceptions will be discussed later.) Since it obviously is impossible to determine the validity of these myriad possible interactions of examiners and other factors, it is not possible to know the validity with which projective techniques are employed in particular instances. It is better to think of most projective techniques as "aids to interviewing." Although it is not clear that they actually aid interviewing, they certainly cannot be classified as standardized measures of personality traits.

DIRECTIONS FOR RESEARCH   In spite of the weaknesses of most projective techniques, the concept of projective testing still is promising. This is because there is so much everyday experience to support the notion that people tend to interpret unstructured stimuli in ways that relate to their personalities. The problem is that most projective techniques are psychometrically unsound vehicles for measuring anything. Projective testing might be advanced considerably by efforts to develop homogeneous scales for particular traits, e.g., gathering responses to inkblots that are thought to measure anxiety, standardization of procedures of administration and scoring, factor analysis of correlations among scales, and construct validation of the obtained factors. This would not necessarily be more difficult than the other approaches to the measurement of personality traits, but it is surprising how little work has been done in this regard.

The good things that can be done with projective techniques are exemplified by the work of Holtzman (1961) and his colleagues on inkblot tests. After careful psychometric work, they constructed alternative forms of an inkblot test, each test consisting of 45 blots. Homogeneous scales were developed for scoring particular types of responses, e.g., the tendency to see "good forms" and the tendency to respond to colors. Each subject makes only one response to each blot, and consequently there is no possibility of variation in that regard influencing results. Instructions and scoring are well standardized, and alternative-form reliabilities of most trait measures are acceptable. Norms were obtained from diverse groups across the country, and comparisons were made of average scores given by normal, neurotic, and psychotic populations. Correlations were made between scales on the inkblot test and self-inventories (which, interestingly enough, were all nil). Similar efforts have been made to develop standardized versions of sentence-completion tests (discussed in Guilford, 1959).

In the development of standardized projective techniques, more attention should be given to the place of *structure* in such instruments. Projective techniques are founded on responses to unstructured stimuli, and that is good because it allows one to investigate interpretive responses. One can, however, push the concept of unstructuredness too far. Some projective testers apparently assume that *everything* in the situation should be unstructured. Consequently they do almost nothing to direct subjects' responses in one way or another, and they employ complex materials (e.g., TAT pictures of people in social situations) which permit subjects to go off in many different directions. A better approach is to have projective techniques entirely structured except for responses relating to a particular dimension, e.g., hostility. Materials should be of a kind that force all subjects to say something that relates to a single dimension. To do that requires simpler materials than sometimes are employed, materials that direct the subject toward responses that are related to the trait of interest, and/or instructions by the examiner that elicit relevant responses. For example, the subject can be shown a simple picture of two boys fighting. It is obvious that they are fighting, and there are no other persons or objects in the picture to elicit nonrelevant responses. To ensure that the subject gives responses that relate to hostility, the examiner could ask, "Why do you think they are fighting?"

The success that has been had in the standardization of sentence-completion tests probably is because such tests structure responses up to the point where lack of structure is called for. For example, even though the following sentences do not entirely structure the subject's responses, they do ensure that his responses will relate to guilt feelings:

1 I wish that I had never _____

2 I feel guilty when _____

3 When I hurt others _____

Because many projective techniques are so entirely unstructured, they do not obtain comparable information from subjects. One subject might give 10 responses that relate to anxiety, and another subject might not give any, but this may have nothing to do with the amount of that trait in the two subjects. If both subjects were required to give 20 responses structured so that they would provide information about anxiety, the latter person might prove to be more anxious. Also, because many of the techniques are so unstructured, the results must be influenced by incidental sets that subjects form. Most subjects, particularly adults, know that they are taking a personality test, and since the situation is so unstructured, they formulate hypotheses about how to respond. For example, on seeing an inkblot, an adult may think that it is a test of "childish imagination," since, after all, it is an inkblot and to call it anything else would be make-believe. Consequently the subject gives as few responses as possible, and the responses that he does give concern physical resemblances between parts of the blot and objects in daily life. College students, being on their mettle in this regard, might react to the inkblot as being an intellectual task, and consequently they might give many clever interpretations interspersed with classical references. One of the problems with such sets is that they frequently produce "pseudoreliability." Although the set may have been formulated quite capriciously when the subject first saw the testing materials and although it may have nothing to do with the traits under study, the subject may hold his set throughout the testing session, which will make the internal consistency high. Also, subjects may hold the same set when responding to an alternative form on another occasion. In both instances this leads to "pseudoreliability," the true reliability being obtainable only in the science-fiction circumstance where memory of each response is erased after it is made. (Pseudoreliability will be discussed in more detail in Chapter Fifteen.)

physiological measures of personality traits

This is a short section, because it does not take much space to summarize what is presently known about the possibilities of employing physiological variables as measures of personality traits. In spite of the fact that personality traits (if there are any general traits of personality) must have some type of physical representation inside the individual, to date there has been very little success in deriving measures of such traits from physiological processes. No physiological variable (or group of such variables) is known to correlate substantially with self-inventories, ratings, projective techniques, or other indicants of personality traits; and there are no physiological variables that are known to sharply distinguish mentally ill people from normal people or different types of mentally ill persons from one another. (Evidence for these and other assertions about relations between physiological variables and personality traits is summarized by Guilford, 1959, and by Stern and McDonald, 1965.)

PHYSIQUE For centuries it has been thought that different types of body builds are related to different patterns of temperament; e.g., the fat person is jolly, the thin person is contemplative and morose, and the muscular person is extraversive and dominant. Factor analyses of bodily measurements have produced half a dozen factors (discussed in Guilford, 1959), such as trunk length, trunk depth, and muscular thickness. There is little evidence that these factors relate to personality characteristics, and consequently the age-old assumption of relations between physique and personality is much in doubt.

BLOOD CHEMISTRY It is reasonable to hypothesize that some personality traits relate to some of the myriad chemical components of the blood stream. The numerous attempts to find such relations have, however, not yet met with success. Most of the efforts along these lines have been to find chemical differences between mentally ill persons and normal persons. Although there have been numerous suggestive findings (Stern and McDonald, 1965), the evidence so far for the importance of any one chemical substance is rather weak. Very little is known about relations between blood chemistry and personality traits in normal people.

AUTONOMIC FUNCTIONING Potentially one of the richest sources of personality correlates is in the functioning of the autonomic nervous system.

This system participates in the activation and deactivation of the organism. It might, for example, be thought that anxious persons would show a pattern of autonomic responses typical of activation and that certain types of lethargic neurotic and psychotic persons would show a pattern of autonomic responses typical of deactivation. There are some small correlations between measures of autonomic functioning and self-inventories; otherwise, few relations have been found between autonomic functioning and personality.

REGULATORY PROCESSES One might expect to find personality correlates in various regulatory processes, such as heart rate, blood pressure, breathing rate, typical amounts of sleep, fluid intake, and others. For example, one hears of the "hypertension syndrome," supposedly a type of individual whose psychological tension is manifested in heart rate, blood pressure, and other physiological variables. There is, however, very little evidence for these and other correlations between personality traits and regulatory processes. In an extensive review of the literature on studies relating blood pressure to personality traits (McGinn et al., 1964), for example, few consistent correlations, if any, could be reported.

BRAIN FUNCTIONING Since personality traits must be represented in some form in the brain, it is logical to hope that some day various aspects of brain functioning may be used as measures of personality traits. The problem, of course, is that it is so very hard to get at the brains of living people, and consequently, until better techniques are available, there is little that can be done to find measures of personality traits in terms of brain functioning. The most that has been done so far is to compare brain waves of normal people with those of groups of abnormal persons. Some suggestive small differences in that regard have been reported (Stern and McDonald, 1965), but few correlations, if any, have been found between brain waves and personality characteristics in normal people. Brain waves are such gross indicators of brain functioning that it is unlikely they will be very useful for the measurement of personality traits.

REACTIONS TO STRESS The studies of physiological variables discussed above concern measurements taken in normal states, for example, while the subject lies on a comfortable couch. Of equal interest are physiological reactions to stress. It has been hypothesized, for example, that anxious persons recover more slowly in their physiological reactions to stress than do nonanxious persons. Typical stressful situations that have been employed in these studies involve electric shock, sudden loud noises, and highly speeded, difficult tests of ability. What has been found in such studies is that different persons respond in terms of *different* physiological indicators. For example, whereas one person typically responds to different stressful situations with increased blood pressure but not with increased rate of breathing, the reverse is true for another person. This tells us something interesting about physiological responses to stress, but it provides little encouragement for the measurement of personality traits in terms of physiological variables.

PROBLEMS IN MEASURING PERSONALITY TRAITS WITH PHYSIOLOGICAL VARIABLES One of the major problems in searching for physiological correlates of personality traits is that people's somatic complaints frequently are not matched by actual somatic responses (Stern and McDonald, 1965). The person who complains of rapid heart beat frequently does not have a rapid heart rate. The person who complains of being tense frequently does not show tenseness of muscles. The person who complains of difficulty in breathing may show no abnormality in actual breathing. Consequently it is necessary to make a careful distinction between the labels that people employ for conscious states (e.g., "tension") and physical states that go by the same names. Apparently this semantic confusion has led us to expect that it would be rather easy to find physiological correlates of some personality traits (e.g., anxiety), but that certainly has not been the case.

A second problem in the use of physiological variables as measures of personality traits is that many of the measures have very low reliabilities. In a study by Wenger (1948) of 19 physiological variables which were repeated after one day, only one variable had a reliability as high as .80, numerous were below .50, and one was only .11 (sublingual temperature). Repeated measures after three months tended to show even lower reliabilities. The reliabilities of individual variables were not so low, however, that it would not be possible to obtain highly reliable linear combinations of them.

A third problem in the use of physiological variables as measures of personality is that, at the present time, we are sorely lacking in techniques for measuring many physiological variables. Physiological psychology has burgeoned in recent years partly because of the development of ingenious measurement techniques, e.g., the techniques for measuring electrical activity in single cells of the brain. Many of these techniques, however, either kill or maim the organism. Until comparable measurements can be taken without hurting people, they cannot, of course, be used in the search for measures of personality traits. Some of the physiological variables that might relate to personality traits (e.g., chemical changes at the synapses of neurons in the brain) are so microscopic in locus and so "delicate" that it may be some time before adequate measurement techniques are developed.

The fourth, and major, problem in employing physiological indices as measures of personality traits concerns the basic logic of such investigations. It is hard to disagree with the statement that if general traits of personality exist, they are entirely represented within the physical structure of the person. It is quite another thing, however, to assume that personality traits are manifested in the same ways in different people or that they are manifested in ways that will lend themselves to measurement. Present evidence suggests that many physiological variables do not obey general laws (e.g., as in the studies of reactions to stress mentioned previously); rather, they tend to behave idiographically. It is as though people developed largely different "styles" of responding to the same types of conscious states. For this reason, the "visceral" variables (those outside the central nervous system) may not be usable as measures of personality traits. If that is true, it means that one must search for measures of personality traits in the central nervous system, particularly in the brain. At the present time, however, the workings of the brain are so poorly understood, and techniques for learning more about those functions are so limited, that it is hard to know how to proceed. Also, personality may not be fully represented in gross structural or chemical differences among people, but rather may be represented in terms of what is "stored" as habits and memories in the brain. It is quite baffling to consider how one would ever recover those through measurements of brain processes in living humans. Even if that ever comes about, it may prove to be much more economical to measure personality traits in terms of overt behavior, as in the case of printed tests of personality. It obviously is worthwhile to continue exploring the possibilities of measuring some personality traits with physiological variables, but at the same time, it also is obviously worthwhile to continue trying to develop measures of personality traits in terms of overt behavior (including verbal responses).

note

personality traits in perception and judgment

One of the most hopeful places to find valid measures of personality traits is in terms of individual differences in laboratory investigations of perception and judgment. Of course, such studies have a long tradition in experimental psychology, but it has been only during the last 20 years that individual differences in those situations have been related to personality. Whereas such studies ostensibly concern *abilities*, it may be that individual differences actually relate to personality traits.

Although the evidence so far for measuring personality traits in terms of perception and judgment is only suggestive, the approach has a number of attractive features. In contrast to rating methods and projective techniques, measures of judgment and perception are not dependent on the subjective processes of observers and test examiners. In contrast to self-inventories, measures of perception and judgment are not dependent on what the individual knows about himself and is willing to relate. In contrast to physiological measures, measures of perception and judgment are not fraught with technical difficulties.

VISUAL ACUITY   Surprisingly enough, there is suggestive evidence that some aspects of visual acuity are related to personality traits. The most significant findings to date concern correlations between dark vision and self-inventory measures of neuroticism. In one study, Eysenck (1947) found a correlation of .60 between the two variables! It is hard to believe that correlations of that magnitude will generally be found between aspects of visual acuity and personality traits, but the evidence so far does suggest that, whereas visual acuity has been considered a passive perceptual function, it may, in part, be dynamically related to personality.

FIELD DEPENDENCE   One of the most encouraging lines of evidence for the measurement of personality variables with tasks concerning perception and judgment comes from studies of field dependence (these studies are summarized by Holtzman, 1965). The rod-and-frame test was first used as a measure of field dependence. In the test, a subject sits in a darkened room and looks at a luminous, square, wooden frame. The frame can be rotated to the left or to the right by the experimenter. In the center of the frame is a luminous rod which can be rotated with remote controls by the subject. With the frame tilted to the left or right at various angles, the subject tries to adjust the rod so that it is placed in vertical position. This is difficult for the subject to do without being influenced by the frame. The frame is spoken of as the *field,* and to the extent that the subject places the rod vertical with respect to the frame rather than the room, he is said to be *field-dependent.*

Field dependency scores on the rod-and-frame test correlate with other perceptual measures that also appear to concern field dependence. One of these is the embedded-figures test. On each item of the test, the subject tries to locate a simple geometrical form embedded in a complex form. The total figure constitutes the perceptual field, from which the subject must differentiate the embedded figure. Numerous studies have found substantial correlations between the rod-and-frame test and the embedded-figures test, and both tests tend to correlate with other perceptual measures that apparently concern field dependence (Holtzman, 1965). Suggestive correlations have been found between these measures and conventional measures of personality. The evidence is that the individual who appears "dependent" in tests of field dependence also tends to be dependent in his social behavior.

CATEGORIZING BEHAVIOR   Efforts have been made to develop personality measures from the ways in which people employ categories in tasks concerning judgment (this research is summarized in Holtzman, 1965). The task which has been used most frequently for that purpose is the object-sorting test. Typically the subject is presented with a miscellaneous collection of 50 or more objects (e.g., a spool, small rubber ball, paper clip, etc.) and told to sort them into groups of objects that "go together." It is left to the subject to judge how many categories should be used and what properties of objects should be used for forming categories. The measure which has been studied most often is simply the number of categories formed, which is thought to relate to *conceptual differentiation*. The person who employs many categories is thought to make fine conceptual differentiations, and the person who employs only a small number of categories is thought to make coarse conceptual differentiations.

Another task relating to categorizing behavior is the Category Width Scale (Pettigrew, 1958). The items concern judgments about the largest and smallest members of particular classes of objects, e.g., the lengths of the largest whale and the smallest whale. It has been hypothesized that the person who manifests "broad categories" on the Category Width Scale will also employ only a small number of categories. The evidence (Gardner and Schoen, 1962) is that these and other tests concerning conceptual differentiation tend to have positive correlations with one another, although the correlations tend to be modest. Also, suggestive correlations have been found between measures of conceptual differentiation and conventional measures of personality.

EYE MOVEMENTS   There is suggestive evidence that eye movements relate to personality variables. Gardner and his colleagues have investigated *scanning behavior* as measured by amount of eye movements of a subject when he is judging the size of one geometrical form in the context of distracting forms (summarized in Messick and Ross, 1962). Some subjects typically focus only on the relevant form, and the eyes of other subjects wander constantly about both the relevant form and irrelevant forms. There is suggestive evidence that extensive scanners tend to be obsessive or compulsive people, in contrast to restricted scanners, who tend to be the opposite.

In addition to studies directly concerned with personality correlates of eye movements, laboratory investigations of eye movements suggest that they might be fruitfully studied as measures of some personality traits. It has been found that eye movements of subjects tend to "approach" objects that are pleasant and to "avoid" objects that are neutral or negative (Nunnally, Stevens, and Hall, 1965). In a typical study, eye movements of children are photographed while they look at a display containing nonsense syllables that previously have been associated with reward, punishment, or neither. Children look most at reward syllables, next most at neutral syllables, and least at punishment syllables. Since so much of personality concerns individual differences in what people "approach" and "avoid," it is logical to think that eye movements in looking at visual displays of different kinds could provide information relating to personality traits.

PUPILLARY RESPONSE There is suggestive evidence that pupillary response might be used for the measurement of personality traits (Hess, 1965). There is pupillary dilation when an individual looks at anything that arouses him. Particularly it has been found that pupillary dilation occurs when the individual encounters any pleasant object, e.g., a picture of food for a hungry subject or a picture of a cool-looking drink for a thirsty subject. This response is involuntary, and since there is no feedback from the pupil, the subject is not directly aware of pupillary changes.

Since pupillary response is affected by the pleasantness of objects, individual differences in response might be related to the degree that different objects are pleasant to different persons. (The relationship here apparently is most clear-cut in comparing objects ranging from neutral to intensely pleasant. It may be that unpleasant objects also induce dilation.) It has been found, for example, that men dilate more to the picture of a seminude female than to the picture of a seminude male, and vice versa for pupillary response in female subjects. Homosexual males dilate more to the picture of a seminude male than to the picture of a seminude female. Women dilate to the picture of a baby, but men dilate little to the same picture. There is other evidence (Hess, 1965) that individual differences in pupillary response to different kinds of stimuli relate to motives and other aspects of personality. There is then the possibility of developing personality tests in which the "scores" consist of amount of dilation to different types of visual and auditory stimuli.

LOOKING TIME A perceptual variable that might be useful for the measurement of personality traits is the amount of time that individuals choose to look at different visual displays. A procedure that is employed for that purpose is as follows (Nunnally, Duchnowski, and Parker, 1965). The front face of a metal box has six windows. By pressing the proper button, the subject can turn on a light behind each window, which permits him to view a particular picture. The subject is allowed to press buttons at will to look at what he likes. The amount of time he spends looking at each picture is automatically recorded. Studies have found that children look at nonsense syllables and geometrical forms that have been associated with rewards more than at neutral stimuli, and they look at neutral stimuli more than at ones that have been associated with punishment. Also, it has been found that the amount of time the subject spends viewing real-life objects is related to the pleasantness of the object. For example, children spend more time looking at a picture of a quarter than at a picture of a dime, and more time looking at a picture of a dime than at a picture of a penny.

Although the author knows of no studies to date on the topic, looking time might be useful as a measure of motives in children. (Adults probably would not perform "naturally" in the situation, and consequently it is doubtful that the results would have any orderly relations with personality characteristics.) Looking time could be measured not only for material objects, but also for pictures of different kinds of persons in different types of situations. For this purpose, one could employ scenes concerning aggression, health, affection, and others. The amount of time children spend looking at such stimuli might be related to their motives, needs, and problems.

DIRECTIONS FOR RESEARCH So far the surface has only been scratched in the search for personality measures in situations involving perception and judgment. It would be best to summarize all of the research to date in that regard as being only suggestive. The methods which have been discussed in this section are illustrative only of what might be done, not of what has actually been accomplished.

A principle that should be kept in mind is that it is not likely that strong correlations will be found between personality traits and *accuracy* of perception and judgment. Accuracy would be involved, for example, in estimating the size of illusory geometrical forms or in the recognition threshold for emotionally toned words. In all psychophysical studies, individual differences in accuracy tend to be slight, and usually what reliable variance there is in that regard can be accounted for by factors other than personality traits. Richer ground for finding measures of personality traits is in selective attention and in the *style* with which an individual perceives and makes judgments. For example, scanning behavior, as discussed previously, concerns individual differences in style of inspecting visual displays rather than in accuracy of size estimation (although the two are not entirely unrelated). The previously discussed studies of eye movements with respect to displays of pleasant and unpleasant objects concerned selective attention to different objects, and accuracy of perception was not at issue. Also, accuracy is not involved in studies of pupillary response and looking time; rather, such studies are concerned with intensity of attention and selective attention, respectively.

other methods for the measurement of personality

In addition to the major approaches to the measurement of personality, there are numerous other approaches which do not fit any of the major classifications. A number of these will be illustrated here. More detailed accounts of the "other" approaches are given in the Suggested Additional Readings.

RESPONSE STYLES   Response styles are hypothesized to be reliable individual differences in test-taking habits. One of these is *acquiescence,* supposedly a tendency to say "yes" or to agree rather than the opposite when an issue is ambiguous or very difficult. Another response style is *cautiousness,* which supposedly concerns the tendency to leave items on ability tests blank when the correct answer is in doubt. A third response style is *extremeness,* which supposedly relates to the tendency to mark the extremes of rating scales rather than points toward the middle.

More about response styles will be said in Chapter Fifteen, but since they have frequently been mentioned as possible measures of personality, it is necessary to discuss them here. Unless one wants to call the social-desirability factor in self-inventories a response style (the author prefers not to), there is very little evidence that measures of response style relate to personality. This is not because of a lack of studies in that regard, but because the many studies that have been done generally failed to find positive evidence. This work is critically evaluated by Rorer (1965) in an article which is aptly entitled "The Great Response-style Myth."

The major problem in employing measures of response style as measures of personality is that response styles apparently are highly specific to the measuring instrument. For example, numerous measures of acquiescence have been proposed, all of which make sense in terms of appearances, but the correlations among the different measures are very low. As another example, in the effort to measure the extremeness tendency, it is found that correlations of extremeness scores in different rating tasks are very low. Reliabilities often are high in terms of internal consistency, repeated measures, and alternative forms; consequently each type of test tends to measure something consistently, but different measures of the same response style are inconsistent with one another. This suggests that the apparent reliability of individual instruments is largely "pseudoreliability," a matter which will be discussed in more detail in Chapter Fifteen.

PRODUCTS OF ABILITY TESTS   Tests that superficially concern abilities also can be used in the attempt to measure personality traits. Such tests frequently are spoken of as "objective" tests of personality. An example is as follows. One page of a test is filled with randomly ordered alphabetical letters. Subjects are told to circle each a and to mark an X through each b, and they are required to work quickly. On the next page of the test, subjects are told to reverse their method of operation, to mark an X through each a and circle each b. The extent to which the first task interferes with the second task is determined by subtracting the score on the first task from that on the second task. The amount of interference in that regard has been hypothesized as having relations with personality.

Another ability test that has been used as a personality test is the *color-word test*. The subject is given a stack of cards, on each of which is the name of a color. In each case the color name is printed in a different color, e.g., "blue" printed in red. The subject is required to say the words as rapidly as he can. Next he is asked to go back through the cards and state the color in which each word is printed. Supposedly the colors and names of colors will interfere with one another, and individual differences in the amount of this interference might be related to personality traits.

Products of ability tests have been used in the hope of measuring a trait of *rigidity*. A typical test is as follows. The subject is given a list of reasoning problems, all the same basic type. The first 10 problems are rather easily solved by the application of a simple principle. The remaining items can be solved by the same principle, but they are much more easily solved by a second principle. To the extent that a subject fails to switch from employing the first principle to employing the second principle, he is said to be rigid.

The possibility of obtaining measures of personality from the products of ability tests is quite attractive, because such tests are not beset with some of the unfortunate features of other approaches to the measurement of personality, e.g., logically they are not influenced by the social-desirability factor. The results to date with such measures, however, have not been very successful (evidence is summarized by Holtzman, 1965). Different tests intended to measure the same trait frequently do not correlate well with one another, and consequently the factor structures among such tests tend to be "weak." Also, personality measures obtained from ability tests correlate very little with other measures of personality, such as with ratings and self-inventories.

BIOGRAPHICAL INVENTORIES   Unlike self-inventories, biographical inventories ask the subject factual questions about his personal history, e.g., about ages of parents and siblings, types of schools attended, hobbies, health problems, and membership in organizations. Inventories of this type have been rather successful in selecting personnel for particular vocations, but very little has been done to form general measures of personality traits from them. For two reasons, however, the possibility is attractive. First, to the extent that the questions concern factual matters, test scores are not likely to be strongly influenced by social desirability. Second, information about personal history logically should be rich in information about personality. If it were possible to learn enough about what has happened to a person and how he has behaved in the past, it should be possible to make good predictions of his behavior in the future.

A major problem in employing biographical inventories is that people frequently do not know the answers to many important questions about themselves, e.g., behavior in early childhood or the amount of body weight at different ages. Another problem is that it is difficult to find a standard list of questions that will get at the important background characteristics of people in general. To a large extent these may be particular to the person. The construction of biographical inventories has been dominated by "shotgun empiricism," with little theory being used to guide the work. More careful thought about the background characteristics that theoretically should relate to personality traits might lead to biographical inventories that validly measure some aspects of personality.

VERBAL BEHAVIOR   Another possible approach to personality measurement is with respect to the words that individuals typically employ. It may prove to be the case that "words are the mark of a man," more so than clothes are. For example, by listening to the words that a person employs, we frequently judge him to be either an intellectual, a beatnik, a psychotic person, or a person in a particular profession. It may be that more subtle differences in word usage relate to personality characteristics.

One approach to investigating individual differences in word usage is with binary-choice measures of association (Nunnally and Hodges, 1965). Typical items are as follows:

1   Snake: _____ dangerous _____ long

2   Orange: _____ sweet _____ round

3   Coal: _____ burn _____ dirty

In each item the subject picks one of the two response words as forming the best associate for the stimulus word. The responses of each subject are scored in terms of the tendency to give associations in different categories, some of these categories being (1) positive evaluations, e.g., orange-sweet and priest-kind, (2) negative evaluations, e.g., snake-dangerous and knife-hurt, and (3) antonyms, e.g., night-day and fast-slow. Factor analyses of associations have produced six factors (Nunnally and Hodges, 1965). Some interesting differences have been found on the factors for different types of people (e.g., psychotic and normal persons), and some small correlations have been found with self-inventories. As is true of so many of the approaches to measuring personality discussed in this chapter, a great deal more research will have to be done on individual differences in verbal behavior to determine whether or not this approach can contribute to the measurement of personality traits.

SUGGESTED ADDITIONAL READINGS

Cattell, R. B. *Personality and motivation structure and measurement.* New York: Harcourt, Brace & World, 1957.

Eysenck, H. J. *The structure of personality.* New York: Wiley, 1953.

Guilford, J. P. *Personality.* New York: McGraw-Hill, 1959.

Nunnally, J. C. *Tests and measurements: Assessment and prediction.* New York: McGraw-Hill, 1959, chaps. 14, 16.

CHAPTER FOURTEEN

MEASUREMENT OF SENTIMENTS

Although the boundaries are not crystal clear, it is useful to distinguish sentiments from abilities and personality traits. In Chapter Two, it was said that "sentiment" is a generic term for all forms of likes and dislikes, and a distinction was made between psychophysical methods concerning judgments and those concerning sentiments. In this chapter will be discussed some methods for measuring various types of sentiments, and since rating methods are most frequently employed for measuring sentiments, the major consideration will be given to rating methods. Two widely used rating methods, the semantic differential and the Q sort, will be discussed in some detail.

TYPES OF SENTIMENTS: INTERESTS, VALUES, AND ATTITUDES The distinctions among different types of sentiments are less clear than those among sentiments, abilities, and personality traits. Sentiments usually are divided into three overlapping groups: interests, values, and attitudes. *Interests* are preferences for particular activities. Examples of statements relating to interests are as follows:

1 I would rather repair a clock than write a letter.

2 I like to supervise the work of others.

3 I would enjoy keeping a stamp collection.

4 I prefer outdoor work to work in an office.

Although investigations have been made of interests in many different types of activities, such as hobbies and reading habits, they are most frequently made of interests relating to vocational pursuits. Measures of vocational interests are used so widely for career planning in schools, industry, government agencies, and the armed forces that it is rare to find a person who has not "taken" at least one of the available inventories. (Interest inventories are discussed in detail in most introductory texts on psychological measurement, e.g., Cronbach, 1960; Nunnally, 1959.)

The evidence is that measures of vocational interests are valuable aids to vocational counseling and educational guidance. Starting in the late "teens," interests tend to stabilize and remain rather stable over periods of 10 or more years. Scores on interest scales are moderately predictive of what occupations people enter, satisfaction with occupations, and changes in occupations. Although interest inventories are primarily intended to predict how well people will like occupations rather than how well they will perform in them, positive correlations have been found between inventories and criteria of performance in some occupations. In contrast to the success of interest inventories in vocational and educational planning, they have met with only a small amount of success in personnel selection. (Evidence regarding the above assertions is summarized in Guilford, 1959.)

Values concern preferences for "life goals" and "ways of life," in contrast to interests, which concern preferences for particular activities. Examples of statements relating to values are as follows:

1 I consider it more important to have people respect me than to like me.

2 A man's duty to his family comes before his duty to society.

3 I do not think it is right for some people to have much more money than others.

4 Service to others is more important to me than personal ambition.

In contrast to measures of interests, measures of values are seldom employed in applied activities; instead, they usually are employed in basic research in sociology and social psychology. Also, in many cases the statements used in studies of values are similar to the statements employed in self-inventory measures of personality. Not nearly so much research has been done on values as has been done on interests and attitudes.

Attitudes concern feelings about particular social objects—physical objects, types of people, particular persons, social institutions, government policies, and others. Some statements relating to attitudes are as follows:

1 The United Nations is a constructive force in the world today.

2 Trade unions have too much effect on our economy.

3 All public schools should be fully integrated.

4 Fraternities and sororities do more harm than good.

The feature that distinguishes attitudes from interests and values is the fact that attitudes always concern a particular "target" or object. In contrast, interests and values concern numerous activities—specific activities in measures of interests and very broad categories of activities in measures of values.

For several reasons, more attention will be given in this chapter to the measurement of attitudes than to the measurement of the other two types of sentiments. There is not much need to discuss in detail the logic and methodology of the measurement of interests, because they are rather simple. In the measurement of interests, the purpose is to predict occupational choice and satisfaction in occupational endeavors. In other words, interest inventories are predictor instruments, and the logic of constructing and validating predictor instruments has been discussed in previous chapters. Other than for some indirect approaches to the measurement of interests (summarized in Guilford, 1959), interest inventories contain simple statements about preferences for activities relating to occupations. More attention will be given in this chapter to the measurement of attitudes than to the measurement of values because (1) there presently is a great deal more research activity concerning attitudes than there is concerning values and (2) the logic and methodology for the investigation of the two are essentially the same.

APPROACHES TO THE MEASUREMENT OF ATTITUDES   The most direct approach to the measurement of attitudes is to ask people, in one manner or another, what their attitudes are. For example, subjects are presented with a list containing favorable and unfavorable statements toward the United Nations and asked to agree or disagree with each. Such self-report inventories are called *attitude scales,* and much of the literature on the measurement of attitudes concerns different methods for developing such scales. In addition to self-report methods, numerous other methods have been explored as measures of attitudes (these are discussed in Campbell, 1950, and in Cook and Selltiz, 1964). One approach is with physiological measures. For example, physiological processes, such as the galvanic skin response or pupillary response, can be measured while an individual reads statements relating to a particular national group or while he looks at a picture of Negroes and whites in a social setting. Projective techniques have been employed for the measurement of attitudes, e.g., the use of TAT-type pictures showing Negroes and whites in various social situations. Real, or near-real, behavior with respect to attitudinal objects has in some cases been explored as a measure of attitudes. For example, individuals have been asked to indicate the degree to which they would be willing to participate in activities relating to desegregation of the races.

Although some of the indirect approaches to the measurement of attitudes seem promising, a great deal more research must be done before such measures are actually usable. At the present time, most measures of attitudes are based on self-report, and from what evidence there is concerning the validity of different approaches to the measurement of attitudes, it is an easy conclusion that self-report offers the most valid approach currently available.

VALIDITY OF SELF-REPORT MEASURES   Potentially, self-report measures of attitudes are susceptible to the same weaknesses as those that accompany self-description inventories. In particular, self-report measures of attitudes are limited to what the individual knows about his attitudes and is willing to relate. Both these limitations, however, probably are not so severe in self-report measures of attitudes as they are in self-description inventories. On self-description inventories, some of the items require the subject to make fairly complex judgments about his social behavior, e.g., "Do you usually lead the discussion in group situations?" In contrast, most self-report measures of attitudes concern items relating to direct feelings about a particular object, e.g., "I would not mind having a Japanese immigrant as a neighbor." In comparison to what is the case on self-description inventories, the items on self-report measures of attitudes usually are more understandable, and subjects feel more confident about their responses. (These assertions are based on informal experience with the two types of instruments, but not on any formal evidence.)

Self-report measures of attitudes probably have an advantage over self-description inventories in terms of the extent to which they are influenced by social desirability. Whereas all people tend to have the same concepts of social desirability of personality traits, people differ markedly in their concepts of social desirability of attitudes, e.g., regional differences in attitudes toward racial segregation. Frankness of responding on self-report measures of attitudes, then, frequently is lessened by pressures from social groups, e.g., the prevalent attitudes in a college fraternity toward intercollegiate athletics or the prevalent attitudes in a factory toward a particular trade union. To the extent to which anonymity of responses can be assured, however, self-report measures of attitudes logically should not be strongly influenced by lack of frankness on the part of subjects.

The validity of a self-report measure depends upon the way results are interpreted. At one extreme, there is nothing wrong with the investigator having a direct interest in reported attitudes, regardless of whether or not such reported attitudes relate to attitudes measured in any other way. It has been noted on numerous occasions that verbalized attitudes usually do not correlate highly with behavior pertaining to the attitude. (Some evidence on this point is summarized by Guilford, 1959.) This does not necessarily mean, however, that verbalized attitudes are invalid. In some cases they may be highly valid measures of *reported* attitudes, but not valid measures of attitudes measurable in other ways.

Actually, in many instances what people say is more predictive of the course of social action than what they may feel in any deeper sense. For example, if most of the people in a particular community *say* that they favor school integration, this might bring about rapid integration even if, "down deep," some of the people feel somewhat negative toward the idea. In some instances it is reasonable to believe that verbalized attitudes represent the "cutting edge" of changes in feelings. Thus a person may start saying that he is in favor of integration before his feeling catches up with his verbalized attitudes. Also, verbalized attitudes have powerful effects on courses of social action, as is evidenced by the extent to which government officials are strongly influenced by the results of opinion polls. So, then, one has a right to be directly interested in verbalized attitudes, without claiming that they have a high degree of correspondence with other attitude-related forms of behavior.

If one is mainly interested in verbalized attitudes for their own sake, *content validity* (Chapter Three) is the major issue. For that purpose, it must be ensured that a broad sample of item content is obtained, e.g., of statements relating to the United Nations or toward intercollegiate athletics. The broadness of the content must be judged by those who are involved in investigating the particular type of attitude. Next, the investigator must perform item analyses to determine the number and kinds of homogeneous scales that are implicit in the item pool. If a scale developed by this method is highly reliable and correlates highly with scales developed by other investigators using the same or different methods of scale construction, it can be said that the scale has a high degree of content validity for the measurement of verbalized attitudes.

Instead of being interested only in verbalized attitudes, one may be interested in explicating a particular type of attitude as a construct. Previously, an attitude was defined as a *feeling* toward a social object, but, of course, verbalized feelings provide only one indicant of such feelings. To explicate a particular attitude as a construct requires a multi-indicator approach (as discussed by Cook and Selltiz, 1964). For example, in the course of explicating a construct concerning attitudes toward Negroes, one might decide to investigate behavioral tests, projective techniques, and verbal report. If these correlate substantially, some combination of them could be said to have a measure of construct validity. Also, the construct validity of the combination of measures could be further evidenced in changes occurring in controlled experiments, e.g., in studies of attitude change involving persuasive communications or in structured group situations. To the extent that verbal report alone correlated highly with other measures related to the construct and faithfully mirrored changes in controlled experiments, it could be said to have a high degree of construct validity. Then it could be used alone, with some assurance that it was measuring more than verbal report. To the extent that a measure of verbal report had low correlations with other hypothesized indicants of the construct and only weakly differentiated differently treated groups in controlled experiments, it would not suffice as a sufficient measure of the construct.

Of course, it is far easier to talk about these complex approaches to explicating attitudes as constructs than it is to do anything about them. (For some attempts, see Campbell, 1950, and Cook and Selltiz, 1964.) At the present time, most investigations of attitudes in sociology and social psychology are undertaken with self-report measures, and although there is ample evidence that many of these validly measure verbalized attitudes, in most cases there is little or no evidence regarding the extent to which the instruments measure more than verbalized attitudes.

PSYCHOPHYSICAL METHODS   Many of the psychophysical methods discussed in Chapter Two can be used to measure verbalized attitudes. Various kinds of comparative responses (as distinct from absolute responses) can be investigated for that purpose. For example, the order of preference for different national groups could be obtained by the method of rank order or the method of pair comparisons. Since, however, the comparative-response methods provide no indication of overall level of response to the stimuli as a group, they are not frequently used in studies of attitudes. For example, no matter how much an individual liked or disliked foreigners as a group, this could not be told from his rank ordering of the names of national groups. Comparative methods are more useful for scaling stimuli with respect to sentiments than for scaling individuals with respect to sentiments. Thus the method of rank order would serve very well to develop a scale of preference for national groups, but it could not be directly employed to measure the attitude of one person toward, say, the Japanese. Since, as previously defined, an attitude concerns feelings about a particular social object rather than comparative differences in feelings among social objects, the comparative methods are not highly appropriate for the measurement of attitudes. Instead, it is more appropriate to employ an absolute-response method. The numerous possible particular approaches to obtaining such absolute responses are said to constitute *rating scales*. Because of the importance of rating scales in the scaling of attitudes, the next section will discuss rating scales in some detail.

properties of rating scales

This section will consider some of the major psychometric properties of rating scales without going into detail about how rating scales are

measurement of sentiments   **519**

constructed and employed in research. Guilford (1954) provides an excellent discussion of technical problems in using rating scales.

GRAPHIC AND NUMERICAL SCALES   We usually think of rating scales as being presented graphically, e.g., as follows:

Completely   Completely
disagree   ____:____:____:____:____:____   agree
                1   2   3   4   5   6

In some instances, however, the numbers are defined and written in spaces opposite the objects to be rated, instead of having the appropriate numbers marked on a graphic scale. It is customary to refer to these as *numerical scales* rather than as graphic scales. The issue, however, usually concerns whether there will be numbers employed with a graphic scale or without a graphic scale. Numbers are used as anchors in most rating scales. The numbers must first be defined, e.g.:

1 Completely disagree

2 Mostly disagree

3 Slightly disagree

4 Slightly agree

5 Mostly agree

6 Completely agree

Employing the above scheme with a so-called numerical scale, the subject would be given a list of statements (say, concerning attitudes toward the United Nations). Opposite each statement would be a blank space, in which the subject would write the number corresponding to his agreement or disagreement. In this instance a graphic scale would be employed as follows. First, as with the numerical scale, the numbers corresponding to scale steps would be defined. Then, rather than write the number in a blank space, the subject would mark a graphic scale, as illustrated above, to indicate his agreement or disagreement.

For several reasons, the graphic scale with numbers is preferable to the use of numbers without the graphic scale. First, because people frequently think of quantities as represented by degrees of physical extensions (e.g., the yardstick and the thermometer), the presence of a graphic scale probably helps to convey the idea of a rating continuum. Second, the graphic scale should lessen clerical errors in making ratings. If the meanings for numbers are defined only at the beginning of an inventory and subjects have to remember the meanings as they record the numbers in blank spaces, subjects are likely to forget the meanings of the numbers, e.g., to confuse ends of the scale or to assume that 4 means "mostly agree" when it was defined as "slightly agree." The presence of the graphic scale should lessen such errors, particularly if the ends of the scale are anchored by the extremes of the attribute being rated, e.g., "completely agree" and "completely disagree" as in the previous example. Third, if subjects write numbers in blank spaces, in some instances it will be difficult to decipher the numbers. For example, it might prove difficult to tell whether a particular number is 1, 7, or 9. Fewer errors in this regard are made in reading the points marked on graphic scales.

NUMBER OF SCALE STEPS   In most cases the experimenter has a choice of the number of scale steps. He might decide to use a two-step (or dichotomous) scale, as follows:

<u>_____   _____</u>
Disagree   Agree

Or he might choose to employ many steps, as in the following example:

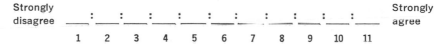

In terms of psychometric theory, the advantage always is with using more rather than fewer steps. This is demonstrated by the numerous studies showing that the reliability of individual rating scales is a monotonically increasing function of the number of steps (Guilford, 1954). Essentially the same principle is derivable from another body of evidence, that concerning relations between the number of scale steps and the *information* (or amount of discrimination) found in classical methods of psychophysical scaling (Garner, 1960). The amount of discrimination provided by psychophysical scales (e.g., obtained from the average ratings by a group of subjects for 20 stimuli) increases with the number of scale steps up to at least 20 steps.

As the number of scale steps is increased from 2 up through 20, the increase in reliability is very rapid at first. It tends to level off at about 7, and after about 11 steps, there is little gain in reliability from increasing the number of steps. To some extent, the monotonic relationship between scale reliability and number of scale steps may be at variance with common sense. It might, for example, be reasoned that, if there are numerous scale steps, the subject would have difficulty making up his mind and might mark a different point on a retest. It is true that, as the number of scale points increases, the error variance increases, but at the same time, the true-score variance increases at an even more rapid rate.

The only exception to the rule that reliability increases with the number of scale steps would occur in instances where a large number of steps confused subjects or irritated them to the point where they became careless. Then it would be possible to find the reliability coming back down with, say, as many as 20 steps. Isolated studies have reported such results (Guilford, 1954), but such findings are rare. By far the bulk of the studies report increasing reliabilities up to 20 steps (although the increase from about 11 to 20 usually is small).

Another issue regarding the number of steps on rating scales concerns whether an even number of steps or an odd number of steps generally is preferable. The argument for an odd number of steps is that it permits the use of a middle step meaning "neutral," "neither," or "neither agree nor disagree." This is thought to make subjects more "comfortable" in making ratings, and it can also be argued that subjects frequently have neutral reactions which should be measured. On the other hand, it can be argued that the use of a "neutral" step introduces response styles. Some subjects tend to use the "neutral" step more than others, and individual differences in that regard might not relate highly to the attitude in question. In looking through responses to attitude scales, one frequently sees the responses of a subject who made all his marks in the "neutral" step. This might represent a truly neutral attitude, but one has the suspicion that this is a way the subject took to say that he did not want to participate in the study. More to the point, in some studies it has been found that reliable differentiations can be made among persons who mark the "neutral" step. This can be done as follows. First, subjects are given five-step scales, each of which contains a "neutral" step. Later the scales are readministered to all subjects who marked the "neutral" step, except on the second occasion six steps are employed, with no neutral step present. The variance of ratings over subjects can then be shown to be reliable, indicating that there actually are reliable differences among subjects who marked the "neutral" step on the first administration of the scale. Although the issue is not highly important, in most cases there is a slight advantage in having an even number of steps rather than an odd number, as was illustrated previously in the 6-step scale ranging from "completely disagree" to "completely agree."

SUMMATED SCALES   The question of the number of steps on a rating scale is very important if one is dealing with only one scale, but it usually is less important if scores are summed over a number of scales. The former would be the case, for example, if attitudes toward the United Nations were measured by only one scale, as follows:

United Nations

Unfavorable ____:____:____:____:____:____ Favorable

       1   2   3   4   5   6

When only one scale is used to measure attitudes, it is wise to have at least 10 steps. In the usual case, however, one obtains an overall measure of attitudes by summing the rating given to at least half a dozen scales. One could do this in the example above by having scales for the adjective pairs valuable-worthless, efficient-inefficient, effective-ineffective, and others. As another example of summated ratings, agree-disagree ratings could be summed over a number of positive and negative statements about the United Nations.

The reliability of summated ratings is directly related to the correlations among scales (which, as was discussed in previous chapters, is so in all uses of the summative model for constructing measures). The numbers of steps on rating scales tend to place limits on the sizes of correlations among scales. In the case of a two-step (or dichotomous) scale, the correlations are phi coefficients, and the sizes of phi coefficients are limited by the differences in p values of items. Then, if there is a large standard deviation of p values over items, the average correlation of items with one another will tend to be low, and according to the logic of coefficient alpha, the reliability will tend to be low. When there are three rather than two steps on the scale, the restriction on correlations is less, and it tends to become less and less as the number of scale steps is further increased.

In addition to the effect of the average correlation among items, the reliability of summated scales also depends directly on the number of items. If there are only half a dozen items in the scale, the reliability obtained from two-step scales might be markedly increased by an increase in the number of scale steps. If, on the other hand, there are over 20 items in the summated scale, it seldom is the case that the reliability is materially increased by the addition of scale steps to the individual scales. Of course, in nearly all instances it is safer to have at least five or six steps than to hope that two-step scales will be sufficient. Also, there seldom are practical advantages in having only two steps.

Reliabilities of summated attitude scales tend to be higher (holding numbers of items constant) than those of summated scales of abilities and self-inventory measures of personality. This is true even when two-step scales are employed in the measurement of attitudes. Attitude scales tend to be highly reliable because the items tend to correlate rather highly with one another. This makes KR-20 high, which, for reasons discussed in previous chapters, usually is a good estimate of the alternative-form reliability measured over relatively short periods of time.

Individual scales on summated attitude scales tend to correlate substantially with one another because they obviously relate to the same thing. For example, in a summated scale to measure attitudes toward the United Nations, the separate statements obviously relate to the same thing. It is easy for the experimenter to intuit items that will correlate highly with one another, and it is easy for the subject to see the common core of meaning in the items. For these reasons, one often finds reliabilities in the nineties for summated scales containing 20 statements rated on a two-step scale of agreement-disagreement. Also, one frequently finds, for example, that a summated scale consisting of 6 eight-step ratings has a reliability above .80. Reliability, then, usually is not a serious problem in the construction of summated attitude scales. At least this is so for the reliability over moderate periods of time (e.g., up to six months); but depending on the attitude being measured, systematic changes might be expected to occur in attitudes over longer periods of time, e.g., in attitudes toward the Russians or toward contraceptives.

PHYSICAL APPEARANCE OF SCALES   One of the *least* important considerations regarding rating scales is physical appearance. One choice, for example, is whether to place the scale horizontally or vertically on the page. Some have argued that the vertical scale is more familiar to the average person, as in reading a thermometer. Another choice concerns whether the steps are connected or separated, as in the following examples:

Completely
disagree
. : : : : :
1 2 3 4 5 6
Completely
agree

Completely
disagree
___ ___ ___ ___ ___ ___
1 2 3 4 5 6
Completely
agree

The argument for the separation of steps is that it lowers the probability that subjects will mark between steps, which sometimes occurs when there are no breaks between steps. The preference for a continuous line frequently is based on the experimenter's superstition that, if ratings are made on a continuum, this somehow ensures that the scale numbers can be legitimately interpreted as forming an interval scale. Better arguments for making that assumption were given in Chapter One.

Another consideration is whether steps will be "open," as shown in previous examples, or "boxed," as follows:

Completely
disagree
1 2 3 4 5 6
Completely
agree

These and other variations on the physical appearance of rating scales apparently make little difference in the important psychometric properties of ratings. Such differences usually are based more on esthetic preferences than on psychometric considerations.

OBJECT RATED There are some important distinctions that should be made among the different types of objects rated on rating scales. In the previous chapter were discussed some of the properties of ratings made of the personality characteristics of people. It was said that such ratings are strongly influenced by (1) the knowledge the observer (or rater) has of the ratee and (2) the rater's tendency to be "lenient" or "severe" in rating other people in general. Numerous other artifacts have been shown to influence the ratings of people (Guilford, 1954). What is important to realize, however, is that, in many uses of rating scales, either ratings are not made of people, or if they are, they do not concern personality characteristics directly. In such cases many of the artifacts that plague ratings of personality characteristics of people either are logically not present at all or are present to a lesser extent.

In attitude scales, ratings frequently are made of agreement or disagreement with statements, e.g., "The United Nations is our best hope for permanent peace." In rating such statements, neither leniency nor lack of information influences ratings in the same way that they do in the ratings of the personality characteristics of people. Leniency in the case of attitude statements would be present only to the extent that the subject appeared to have either favorable or unfavorable attitudes regardless of what social object was being considered. The extent to which that actually occurs is largey unknown, but if it occurred, either it would represent genuine individual differences in the tendency to have favorable rather than unfavorable attitudes or it would represent social desirability. Lack of knowledge has a different effect in ratings of statements concerning attitudes than it does in ratings of people. In the latter, lack of information lowers the validity of ratings of people, but in the former, it may serve to explain *why* an individual has a particular attitude although it does not necessarily lead to invalid measurements of what his attitudes actually are.

Instead of ratings being made of statements relating to attitudes, in some attitude scales ratings are made of the attitudinal object itself, as would be the case, for example, in having United Nations rated on a six-point scale bounded by the adjectives "effective" and "ineffective." Other attitudinal objects that could be rated directly are labor unions, Japan, educational television, and intercollegiate athletics. When attitudinal objects are rated directly, leniency (as the term applies in ratings of people) would spring from the same sources as it would in ratings of statements. Individual differences in that regard would represent either differences in favorable attitudes toward social objects of all kinds (which is a rather farfetched notion) or differences in social desirability. Regarding the subject's information about attitudinal objects, the caliber of his information might help explain why he has developed the particular attitude, but it would not influence the validity of measurements of his attitudes at one point in time. A person can, for example, hold genuinely negative or positive attitudes toward the United Nations while entertaining either very little information or much misinformation.

The major point to be made in this section is that the many factors that have been shown to influence ratings of people (Guilford, 1954) do not necessarily have the same kinds and amounts of effects on ratings made for other purposes. The major factor limiting the validity of attitude ratings probably is social desirability, and as was mentioned previously, there are good logical grounds for thinking that social desirability plays less of a part in attitude scales than it does in self-inventory measures of personality.

TYPES OF ANCHORS   Before subjects can employ rating scales, steps on the scales must be defined. The definitions of scale steps are referred to as *anchors,* and there are different types of anchors that can be employed. Usually numerical anchors are employed in conjunction with other types of anchors. There is no harm in employing numbers on the scale, and they have several distinct advantages. If the meaning of each step on the scale is specified at the beginning of the rating form, as is usually the case, numbers provide an effective means of coordinating those definitions with the rating scales. A second advantage is that numbers on the rating scales constantly remind subjects of the meanings of scale steps. Another advantage of having numbers on the rating scales is that it facilitates the analysis of data, e.g., as in placing ratings on cards for computer analyses.

A special type of numerical anchor that is useful in some studies is found on *percentage scales.* On percentage scales, subjects rate themselves, or other people, on a continuum ranging from zero to 100 percent, either in comparison to people in general or in comparison to some special reference group, e.g., other students in a particular college. The scale usually is divided into 10 steps, corresponding to intervals of 10 percentage points. The subject can rate himself, or someone else, in terms of attributes such as intelligence and energy, or less frequently, the percentage scale can be used to measure sentiments. The latter would be the case, for example, if the individual were asked to rate how favorable he is toward labor unions in comparison to how people in general feel. Then, if he marked the step corresponding to the 70 to 80 percent level, this would mean that he considers himself more favorable than 70 percent of people in general. Where they can be employed, percentage scales usually are highly meaningful to subjects.

A second type of anchor which is widely employed in rating scales is that concerning degrees of agreement and disagreement, as has been amply illustrated previously in this chapter. Where they can be applied, agreement scales are easy to work with. They are easily understood by subjects, and the results obtained from them are rather easily interpreted by researchers. Whereas, superficially, agreement scales might seem to concern judgments rather than sentiments, in attitude scales this is not the case. What an individual does in responding to agreement scales is to indicate his sentiments by agreeing or disagreeing with favorable and unfavorable statements.

Adjectives constitute a third type of anchor for rating scales, as was illustrated previously for scales anchored by valuable-worthless, effective-ineffective, and other pairs of bipolar adjectives. Attitude scales employing bipolar adjectives as anchors are easily constructed and applied to many types of attitudinal objectives. Rating scales employing bipolar adjectives as anchors are said to form a semantic differential, a matter that will be discussed in detail later.

A fourth type of anchor for rating scales is in terms of actual behavior, this type of anchor being more useful for the rating of people than for the rating of attitudes and other types of sentiments. A numerical scale for that purpose concerning the tendency of mental patients to have hallucinations is as follows:

1   Shows no signs of having hallucinations.

2   Gestures and talks to self as having hallucinations on occasions, but does not verbalize hallucinations.

3   Verbalizes hallucinations only occasionally.

4   Actively hallucinates much of the time.

The rater would mark the one statement that best described each patient's tendency to hallucinate. There are three major difficulties with employing behavioral anchors. First, a different set of anchors is needed for each scale, which makes it difficult to construct inventories based on such scales. Second, in some cases it is not at all certain that the different behaviors used as anchors actually represent different levels of the trait in question. For example, in the illustrative four-step scale above for hallucinatory behavior, one might argue that step 2 represents more involvement with hallucinations than step 3. Third, it frequently is difficult to find discrete, easily specified forms of behavior that relate to more general traits. This point was discussed in detail in the previous chapter.

A fifth type of anchor for rating scales concerns comparison stimuli, or *product scales,* as they are called. A classic example is that of a product scale for the legibility of handwriting. A six-step scale is employed, with each of the numbers 1 through 6 being illustrated with samples of handwriting at different levels of legibility. The samples of handwriting appropriate for the different levels are obtained from prior research, in which experts are asked to make discriminations among samples of handwriting (with one or another of the psychophysical methods). Once the samples are chosen for each level of legibility, it is assumed that the samples (comparison stimuli) will be helpful in having ratings of handwriting made by people who are not highly expert in that regard. Usually verbal anchors are used in addition to comparison stimuli; e.g., in the six-step scale for handwriting, 6 equals "excellent" and 1 equals "very poor." In addition to scales for handwriting, product scales of this kind have been developed for artistic productions, but beyond that, few product scales are reported in the literature. Although they are attractive approaches to ratings when they can be developed, logically they are restricted to only a few types of ratings.

models for the scaling of verbalized attitudes

Except in the unusual case where attitudes are measured with only one item, some model must be employed to specify how responses to a collection of items will be translated into an attitude scale. In Chapter Two were discussed the various models that can be employed for the scaling of people with respect to all kinds of psychological traits, attitudes included. What will be done in this section is to summarize the considerations that lead to an acceptance of one of the models over the others for the scaling of verbalized attitudes in most situations.

DETERMINISTIC MODELS   Deterministic models are ones in which each item is assumed to have a perfect relationship, of one kind or another, with a hypothetical trait. In the scaling of attitudes, the trait in question is, of course, the set of true scores for subjects on the particular dimension of attitudes being investigated, e.g., verbalized attitudes toward the United Nations. The only deterministic model that has received wide attention for the scaling of verbalized attitudes is the monotone deterministic model, which is usually referred to as a Guttman scale. In this model, it is hypothesized that each dichotomous item has a perfect biserial (not point-biserial) correlation with the hypothetical trait.

A number of reasons were given in Chapter Two why the monotone deterministic model is unrealistic for the measurement of most human traits, and this applies with particular force to the scaling of verbalized attitudes. The model does not take account of the amount of unique variance in each item, and consequently it is very difficult to find items that fit the model. The scales that do partially fit the model nearly always have only a handful of items; thus only gross discriminations can be made among people. Also, the model leads only to an ordinal scaling of people with respect to attitudes. In Chapter One, it was argued that psychology has a legitimate claim to the measurement of human traits on at least interval scales, if not ratio scales. Other reasons were given in Chapter Two why the Guttman scale is an impractical approach to the measurement of most human traits. Aside from the few instances in which data do fit the models well, the deterministic models mainly are useful as theoretical reference points for the development of practicable models for the actual scaling of attitudes.

NONMONOTONE PROBABILITY MODELS   A nonmonotone model logically underlies what is called the Thurstone scale for the measurement of attitudes. Like the Guttman scale, the Thurstone scale also deals with dichotomous responses to statements concerning attitudes, e.g., agreeing or disagreeing with the statement, "I feel a need for religion but do not find what I want in any one church." Each item is intended to represent, in a statistical sense, one point on an attitude continuum. Only persons in a narrow zone about that point are expected to agree with the item; persons having either more positive or more negative attitudes are expected to disagree with the item. In the ideal case, then, one would expect the item trace line for each item (the curve showing the probability of agreeing to the item as a function of the underlying trait) to be a normal distribution, with the mode corresponding to the true point on the attitude continuum.

The Thurstone scaling method employs judges to establish the scale points for items. In a typical study, 100 judges would rate the attitude implied by each of 100 statements. The judgments could be made on an 11-step continuum ranging from "strong positive attitude" to "strong negative attitude." The mean rating by judges is taken as the scale point for each item. About 20 items are selected for the final scale such that (1) each item has a small standard deviation of ratings over judges and (2) the mean ratings spread evenly from one end of the rating continuum to the other. When the scale is used in subsequent studies to measure the attitudes of people, each subject is instructed to mark only those statements with which he agrees. (Some have advocated restricting subjects to marking the three statements with which they most agree.) The score for the subject is then the scale value of the median item endorsed or the average scale value of the items endorsed.

During the last 40 years, the Thurstone method of attitude scaling has been used very widely in psychology and sociology (this work is summarized by Edwards, 1957a). As was said in Chapter Two, however, there are better methods for the scaling of attitudes. The original as sumptions of the model are unrealistic for the scaling of attitude statements. It simply is very difficult to find items that have nonmonotone trace lines. One can find the approximate trace line in this regard by plotting the percentage of people who endorse an item as a function of scores on the total scale. In the effort to obtain nonmontone items, the investigators frequently produce doubled-barreled statements, as was illustrated in Chapter Two. This is evidenced by the fact that so many of the items on such scales are populated by and's, but's, or's, and other indicators of multiple ideas within statements.

Unless one assumes nonmonotone trace lines for items, it is rather difficult to see how the method of assigning scale scores makes much sense, e.g., taking the median scale point of three items marked as the attitude score for a person. In practice, however, few of the items on such scales have nonmonotone trace lines (Edwards, 1957a). Items on the extremes of the scale tend to have monotone trace lines, with the lines sloping downward for negative items and upward for positive items. Items near the middle of the scale tend to have flat trace lines, and thus they do a poor job of discriminating persons in terms of attitudes. The only items that might have distinctly nonmonotone trace lines would be ones that are moderately positive or moderately negative, and such items typically are double-barreled.

The major advantage assumed for Thurstone attitude scales over other types of scales is that they permit a direct interpretation of the attitude of an individual, or the average attitude of a group of people, without recourse to general norms for the attitude in question. In most studies in psychology and sociology, however, that really is not much of an advantage. In most studies, the researcher is interested in correlating individual differences in an attitude with other types of individual differences, or he is interested in the mean differences in attitudes of existing groups of people or of groups of people that are differently treated in controlled experiments. For those purposes, there is little need for a direct interpretation of the attitude of any one person, in an absolute sense. Also, in cases where such interpretations are important, they can be made with only modest precision from Thurstone scales. Even with the best of efforts to select items that judges agree on, the standard deviations of scale values over judges still are considerable. Also, it has been found that different types of judges give markedly different ratings to some of the statements employed in Thurstone scales (discussed in Edwards, 1957a). This is the case, for example, when judgments are made about attitudes toward Negroes by a group of Southern whites and by a group of Negroes. The rank ordering of statements on the scale tends to remain the same, but the absolute scale values shift markedly. Then, if a direct interpretation is made of the responses of one person, we must ask the question, "In whose eyes?"

In the next section it will be argued that summative scales do, in general, constitute the best approach to the scaling of verbalized attitudes. Aside from the numerous logical arguments that favor summative scales, it has repeatedly been found that summative scales are somewhat more reliable than Thurstone scales. Where the Thurstone scaling technique is very useful is in the scaling of stimuli, not in the scaling of people. For example, it is one of the best methods available for scaling the familiarity of words, the complexity of geometrical forms, and the pleasantness of pictures.

SUMMATIVE MODEL   As was said in Chapter Two, the summative model is the one that is most generally useful in the scaling of people with respect to psychological traits. It assumes only that individual items are monotonically related to underlying traits and that a summation of item scores is approximately linearly related to the trait. One obtains a total score by adding scores on individual items (reversing the scoring for statements that imply negative attitudes). This same logic is applied both to dichotomous items and to multipoint items.

Because summative scales for the measurement of attitudes were championed by Likert (1932), they sometimes are referred to as Likert scales. Summative scales have a number of attractive advantages over all other methods: they (1) follow from an appealing model, (2) are rather easy to construct, (3) usually are highly reliable, (4) can be adapted to the measurement of many different kinds of attitudes, and (5) have produced meaningful results in many studies to date.

construction of summative scales for verbalized attitudes

The construction of summative attitude scales is only a special case of the general method for constructing nonspeeded (power) measures which was discussed in Chapter Eight. In this section will be described a few of the particular features of constructing summative scales for attitudes. Aspects of scale construction will be illustrated with agree-disagree scales applied to statements concerning attitudes. The methods, however, are general to all summative scales. They apply, for example, to summative scales one obtains by adding responses to individual rating scales bounded by bipolar adjectives, and they apply to summative scales one obtains by adding responses to individual rating scales anchored by actual behaviors.

ITEM POOL   All the statements in the item pool should, of course, concern a particular attitudinal object, e.g., the United Nations or labor unions. Since it usually is easy to obtain a homogeneous scale for the measurement of attitudes, seldom are more than 40 items required in the item pool. Since the purpose of each item on a summative scale is to obtain reliable variance with respect to the attitude in question, most of the items should be either moderately positive or moderately negative. There is no place for truly neutral statements in summative scales. Statements that are very extreme in either direction tend to create less variance than statements that are less extreme. The pool of items should be about evenly divided between positive and negative statements.

DATA FOR ITEM ANALYSIS   The item pool should be administered to a group of subjects that is similar to the groups with which the final instrument will be used, e.g., samples of college students for a scale to be used in research on college students or a broad sample of the general population for a scale that will be used in national surveys. Because it usually is rather easy to develop homogeneous scales of verbalized attitudes, the number of subjects need be no more than five times the number of items, but if larger numbers of subjects are easily obtained, the more subjects the better.

     In the development of attitude scales, it is very important that the data for item analysis be obtained under circumstances very similar to those in which the final scale will be employed. For example, the data for an item analysis might be very misleading if they are obtained under conditions of anonymity for subjects but the final scale is intended for use in circumstances where responses of subjects will not be anonymous. Also, it is very important to think out carefully the instructions that will be used with the final instrument and use those instructions in obtaining data for item analysis.

ITEM ANALYSIS   Before correlating items with total scale scores, scoring should be reversed for negative statements. (The same result could be obtained by reversing the scoring for positive statements.) For dichotomous items, this would mean scoring 1 for agreement with positive statements and zero for disagreement, and vice versa for negative statements. One reverses scales for negative statements when multipoint items are employed by subtracting each scale position from the number of scale steps plus 1. For example, if a seven-step scale is applied to each statement and 7 means "completely agree," the rating made of each negative statement would be subtracted from 8. This would then treat complete disagreement with a negative statement like complete agreement with a positive statement, and vice versa.

As was mentioned in Chapter Eight, one of the difficulties in scoring responses in preparation for item analysis is that, with some item pools, the proper directions of scoring for many of the items are difficult to discern. This results in what was called "bipolar item pools." Iterative procedures were mentioned in Chapter Eight for dealing with this situation. In the development of attitude scales (and for the measurement of sentiments in general), however, these procedures are seldom necessary. If, as advised earlier, all the statements are either moderately positive or moderately negative, the proper direction for scoring each item usually is very easy to discern. After the directions of scoring are established, it is very rare to find any item that has a substantial negative correlation with total scale scores.

After the directions for scoring are established, one obtains total scores over all items in the item pool by simply summing scores over items. At that point one could compute coefficient alpha (KR-20, for dichotomous items), or since that usually is very high when computed over the total item pool, one could proceed to the correlation of each item with total scores. Correlations would be regular PM coefficients for multipoint scales and point-biserial coefficients for dichotomous scales. Separate rank orderings of the correlations should be made for positive and for negative statements. Then, working from the top of the rank orders downward, one would choose an equal number of positive and negative items for the final scale. Say, for example, that out of a total item pool of 40 items, 10 positive and 10 negative statements are selected. The 20 items would then be combined to form a trial scale, and coefficient alpha would be computed for the 20 items. This would require computing the variance of each item and obtaining total scores summed over the 20 items (reversing directions of scoring negative items as before). If coefficient alpha is sufficiently high, the 20 items could be accepted as the final scale. In the construction of summative scales of attitudes, usually 20 statements selected in that way will have a reliability above .80. As was mentioned previously, the size of the reliability relates to the number of scale steps for the rating scale used with each statement.

WEIGHTING OF INDIVIDUAL SCALES Numerous weighting schemes have been proposed for the items on summative scales. For example, scores on each item could be weighted by the correlation of the item with total scale scores. Other approaches to weighting items were discussed in

Chapter Eight. For two reasons, it usually is not necessary to apply differential weights to the items on summative scales of attitudes (other than to reverse the scoring for negative statements). First, it is difficult to defend any particular method of weighting over the method of simply summing unweighted ratings. Second, and more to the point, weighted and unweighted summative scores usually correlate very highly. A classic example was found in a study by Likert (1932), in which he compared unweighted scores with scores obtained by an elaborate method of weighting each item. The two sets of scores correlated .99.

FACTOR ANALYSIS OF ITEMS   In Chapter Eight it was advised that factor analysis of an item pool should be considered only as a last resort, after efforts to hypothesize homogeneous scales have led to naught. This is because the average correlation among items in the typical item pool is small, and the standard deviation of such correlations is small, this tending to be the case more with dichotomous items than with multipoint items. In these circumstances, the results of factor analyses tend to be very "messy." For two reasons, these conditions tend not to hold in item pools constructed for the measurement of attitudes. First, even if dichotomous items are employed for the measurement of attitudes, the correlations among them tend to be higher than is the case for measures of ability and personality characteristics. Second, the fact that multipoint scales are employed more frequently than dichotomous scales to measure attitudes tends to further increase the size of the average correlation among items. In addition to the size of the average correlation among items, there frequently is enough variance in the sizes of correlations to document "strong" factors.

If one hypothesizes a number of factors relating to a particular attitude, or lacking hypotheses, one suspects that an item pool harbors a number of "strong" factors, there is nothing wrong with factor analyzing the item pool initially rather than proceeding directly to the construction of a homogeneous scale as was outlined previously. The factor structures obtained from multipoint ratings of attitudes frequently are as "strong" as those obtained from factor structures for whole tests of ability and personality characteristics.

An example of a domain of content in which a number of factors might be expected would be in relation to labor unions. A person might feel that labor unions are worthwhile in terms of the national economy but have a stifling influence on cultural values, or a person might think that labor unions are "bad" in both these respects but have a constructive influence politically. Factor analysis could be used to test hypotheses about the major factors of attitudes toward labor unions and to construct scales for the measurement of those factors. The use of factor analysis with item pools relating to attitudes is the major exception to the principle stated in Chapter Eight that it usually is unwise to start an item analysis with factor analysis.

semantic-differential scales

A very useful type of scale is that which employs direct ratings of concepts with scales anchored on the extremes by bipolar adjectives:

United Nations

Ineffective	___ : ___ : ___ : ___ : ___ : ___	Effective
	1 2 3 4 5 6	
Foolish	___ : ___ : ___ : ___ : ___ : ___	Wise
	1 2 3 4 5 6	
Weak	___ : ___ : ___ : ___ : ___ : ___	Strong
	1 2 3 4 5 6	
Useless	___ : ___ : ___ : ___ : ___ : ___	Useful
	1 2 3 4 5 6	

A collection of scales such as those above is referred to as a semantic differential. Although it will be convenient here to speak of *the* semantic differential, the term is used in a generic sense to refer to any collection of rating scales anchored by bipolar adjectives. Rather than the semantic differential being a particular instrument (or test, as some have called it), it is a very flexible approach to obtaining measures of attitudes and other sentiments. The flexibility of the approach is one of its appealing features. The object that is rated is referred to as a *concept,* and anything that can be named can be rated, e.g., Winston Churchill, peach ice cream, labor unions, birth control, my best friend, and automobiles. Not only are bipolar adjectives easily adapted to a multitude of concepts, but it is easy to apply a list of scales to a number of different concepts in the same rating form. For example, if one is interested in examining attitudes toward a number of different political figures, institutions, and forms of policy, these can all be investigated in the same instrument. Subjects have no trouble in rating 20 concepts on 20 scales in an hour's time or less. The semantic differential is very flexible in another sense: it makes it easy to construct scales for the measurement of different facets of attitudes, a matter which will be discussed more fully later.

An impressive array of studies has been performed on semantic-differential scales by C. E. Osgood and his colleagues (Osgood, 1962; Osgood, Suci, and Tannenbaum, 1957). The semantic differential was mainly developed in relation to a mediational theory of learning (Osgood, 1962). Since in that theory the "meaning" of stimuli occupies a central role, some ways of measuring various facets of meaning are required to give the theory empirical implications. The semantic differential was developed as such a measure.

LOGIC OF THE SEMANTIC DIFFERENTIAL In spoken and written language, characteristics of ideas and real things are communicated largely by adjectives. Thus the characteristics of a particular person are communicated as being polite, urbane, timid, and intelligent; and a particular policy in foreign affairs is characterized as being outmoded, rigid, and discriminatory. If it is reasonable to assume that much of "meaning" can be, and usually is, communicated with adjectives, it is also reasonable to assume that adjectives can be used to measure various facets of meaning. Carrying this line of reasoning a step further, to obtain anchors for the ends of rating scales, it is useful to work with pairs of bipolar adjectives. Most adjectives have logical opposites, such as is evidenced in the pairs sweet-sour, dark-light, and tall-short. Where an opposing adjective is not obviously available, one can easily be generated with "in" or "un," e.g., sufficient-insufficient and satisfactory-unsatisfactory. All that remains, then, is to (1) generate a wide sample of such pairs of adjectives, (2) use them as anchors on rating scales, as illustrated previously, and (3) search for common factors among the scales. If strong factors are found and the factors appear in ratings of many different kinds of concepts, the factors can be used as general measures of different factors of meaning.

FACTORS IN SEMANTIC–DIFFERENTIAL SCALES Numerous factor analyses have been performed to date on semantic-differential scales (these are summarized by Osgood, 1962). Different studies have employed different types of concepts, e.g., names of prominent persons, geometrical forms, commercial products, persons with different types of physical or mental illness, different animals, and others. Studies have been performed of ratings made by people in different countries around the world and by different types of persons in our country. Also, many different adjective pairs have been employed in one or more of the studies.

The numerous factor-analytic studies of semantic-differential scales lead to the conclusion that there are three major factors of meaning involved. The factors do not always have exactly the same content in different studies, and in some studies more than three prominent factors are found. The remarkable fact, however, is that three factors with similar content have occurred in so many analyses under such varied conditions.

The most frequently found factor is *evaluation,* which is defined by pairs of adjectives like the following:

good–bad	honest–dishonest
pleasant–unpleasant	positive–negative
fair–unfair	sweet–sour
wise–foolish	valuable–worthless
successful–unsuccessful	clean–dirty

The evaluative factor is by far the strongest factor in semantic-differential scales. In some studies it is so strong that little common variance is left to define other factors. The evaluative factor is prominent because nearly all adjectives imply negative and positive characteristics. Actually it is difficult to think of bipolar pairs of adjectives that do not hint at evaluation. Even such pairs as wet-dry, long-short, and up-down hint of evaluation. The evaluative factor almost serves as a definition for the term "attitude," and consequently scales on the evaluative factor should serve well as measures of verbalized attitudes.

The second strongest factor that frequently appears in factor analyses of semantic-differential scales is *potency.* Some of the pairs of adjectives that usually load on that factor are as follows:

strong–weak	rugged–delicate
hard–soft	large–small
heavy–light	masculine–feminine
thick–thin	severe–lenient

The third strongest factor that frequently appears is *activity.* Some pairs of adjectives relating to that factor are as follows:

active–passive	quick–slow
tense–relaxed	hot–cold
excitable–calm	sharp–dull
impetuous–quiet	busy–lazy

In comparison to the factor of evaluation, the factors of potency and activity are not as strong statistically, and whereas one can easily think of many adjective pairs that relate to evaluation, it is difficult to find adjective pairs that clearly measure the other two factors. Typically it is found that even the best scales for measuring potency and activity also correlate with the factor of evaluation. This is particularly so for the potency factor, where one usually finds substantial positive correlations, e.g., between the scales good-bad and strong-weak and between effective-ineffective and rugged-delicate. Correlations also occur between scales to measure activity and scales to measure evaluation, e.g., between the scales valuable-worthless and active-passive and between the scales efficient-inefficient and quick-slow.

The sizes of correlations between scales used to define the three major factors vary considerably from scale to scale. For example, the scale strong-weak tends to have higher correlations with scales on the evaluative factor than do the scales hard-soft and heavy-light (also from the potency factor). As examples from the activity factor, the scale active-passive tends to have relatively high positive correlations with scales from the evaluative factor, but the scales tense-relaxed and excitable-calm do not.

Less important than the correlations between scales used to measure the different factors are correlations between estimates of factor scores on the three factors. Typically half a dozen scales from each of the factors are used to determine factor scores. For this purpose, ratings simply are summed over the scales in each factor. When that is done, one typically finds positive correlations between the three factors, i.e., considering the extremes, some concepts tend to be rated as good, strong, and active, and at the other extreme, some concepts tend to be rated as bad, weak, and inactive. Typically one finds an average correlation between measures of the three factors ranging from about .30 to about .50 in different studies, the size of the average correlation varying with the types of concepts being investigated.

In addition to these three factors that have appeared in numerous analyses, other prominent factors have been found in semantic-differential scales. Nunnally (1961) found a factor of *familiarity* (or *understandability*, as it was called), defined by scales like the following:

familiar—unfamiliar   understandable—mysterious

usual—unusual   predictable—unpredictable

clear—confusing   simple—complex

Potentially, the factor of familiarity is important for the scaling of stimuli to be used in controlled experiments. There are numerous instances in which actual familiarity and rated familiarity have proved to be important determiners of rate of verbal learning and rate of perceptual recognition.

Osgood (1962) reports a number of other factors that appear with particular types of scales and concepts. The factor structure tends to be more "diverse" when ratings are made of concepts relating to human personality, such as a good friend, a mother, and an athlete. With such concepts, one tends to find about eight factors, and partly because of the limited number of scales that can be employed in a study, only a few scales have substantial loadings on each factor. In several studies of concepts relating to personality, a factor of rationality has been found, which is defined by scales like logical-intuitive, objective-subjective, and rational-irrational. In the same studies, a factor of morality was found, with scales like moral-immoral, reputable-disreputable, and wholesome-unwholesome.

INTERACTIONS OF SCALES AND CONCEPTS   One caution in employing semantic-differential scales is that the meanings of scales sometimes depend on the concept being rated. For example, whereas "rugged" is positively evaluative when applied to men, it is not positively evaluative when applied to women. Whereas "sweet" is positively evaluative when applied to many concepts, it certainly is not positively evaluative when applied to the brand names for different beers. Whereas the scale tense-relaxed tends to measure the activity factor when applied to material objects, it tends to measure neurotic tendency when applied to persons. Whereas tough-tender would correlate positively with valuable-worthless in ratings of the photographs of men, the correlation obviously would be negative in rating the brand names of steaks, lamb chops, hams, and other meats. Many other examples could be given in which the meanings of scales differ with the concepts being studied and in which the size and directions of correlations among scales differ with the types of concepts.

The interaction of scales with concepts places a limit on the extent to which individual scales can be interpreted the same when applied to different concepts, and it also places a limit on the extent to which factors in semantic-differential scales can be employed as general yardsticks (e.g., to measure evaluation) regardless of the concepts in a particular study. There are several lessons to be learned from these points. First, less scale-concept interaction is likely to occur when all the concepts in a particular study are from the same domain of discourse. It would, for example, be better in most studies to have all the concepts be four-legged animals, all be types of persons, all be social institutions, rather than mix the three types of concepts in one study. There is no harm in having a mixed bag of concepts rated at the same time by the same people, but it usually makes more sense to perform separate analyses, and make separate interpretations, of the data for different types of concepts.

Second, it is wise to perform factor analyses for any type of concept which is to be investigated extensively. For example, if one intended to make extensive use of semantic-differential scales with many different types of geometrical designs, it would be wise to investigate the factor structure of such scales with that particular type of concept rather than depend entirely on the factor structures found with other types of concepts. In that instance one would expect the three major factors to have much the same content (e.g., it would be surprising not to find good-bad and pleasant-unpleasant loading substantially on a factor of evaluation), but some of the factor content might be different from that typically found in other studies.

Third, instead of relying blindly on the scales that usually define factors in semantic-differential scales, it is wise to think carefully about possible interactions of scales and concepts in particular studies. For example, whereas the scale beautiful-ugly usually measures evaluation, anyone would be foolish to employ it for that purpose in ratings of famous statesmen, e.g., Churchill, Napoleon, and Lincoln. In some instances a scale that usually does not load highly on a factor does have a high loading with a particular type of concept. This is the case for the scale effective-ineffective, which has only a moderate-sized loading on the evaluative factor with many types of concepts but has a high loading on that factor when the concepts concern professions, such as psychologist, psychiatrist, engineer, surgeon, and economist. Such concepts tend to "bunch together" on the high end of most scales commonly used to measure the evaluative factor (e.g., good-bad and fair-unfair), but they are drawn apart on the scale effective-ineffective. Though the final test of the wisdom of selecting particular scales to be used with particular concepts is made by factor analyzing the data, careful forethought can lead to a selection of scales that will manifest the desired factor structure.

WHAT THE SEMANTIC DIFFERENTIAL MEASURES   Previously it was said that the initial purpose of the semantic differential was to measure the meaning of concepts. Here we will go into more detail about the evidence regarding what is measured by semantic-differential scales. "Meaning" is a very global term: in the ultimate it includes all possible reactions that people have to words and things. There are, however, some facets of meaning that can be usefully discussed with respect to the semantic differential. It is useful to distinguish three overlapping facets of meaning: denotation, connotation, and association. *Denotation* concerns an objective description of an object in terms of its physical characteristics. Thus an orange is denoted as being a round, yellowish fruit, with a juicy interior containing seeds, etc. The United Nations is denoted as an international association of governments, with the purpose of furthering world peace, economic advancement, education, etc. Essentially, the denotative aspects of meaning are those that direct a person to a specific object to the exclusion of all other objects.

In addition to denotation, there is *connotation*, that is, what implications the object in question has for the particular person. Thus after an individual has completely denoted the object orange, he could say, "I like them very much," which would represent a connotation (or sentiment) for that person. Similarly, after an individual has completely denoted the United Nations, he could say, "I think that it is a rather ineffective organization," which again would represent a connotation or sentiment.

Overlapping with denotation and connotation is *association*. "Associations," as the term will be used here, consist of other objects that are brought to mind when an individual sees or hears about a particular object. Associations typically are obtained by the classical method of free association, in which the subject is presented with one word and told to write down an associate. Associations to orange would be fruit, seed, apple, and sweet. Associations to United Nations would be world, New York, peace, government, and Russians.

The semantic differential mainly measures *connotative* aspects of meaning, particularly the evaluative connotations of objects. For that purpose, it probably is the most valid measure of connotative meaning available. Because of the nature of the instrument, it cannot measure nonconnotative associations, e.g., from the instrument alone there is no way to learn that apple is associated with orange or that New York is associated with the United Nations. The evaluative factor on the semantic differential is almost purely connotative in character rather than denotative or associative (in the sense of object-object associations). This is why previously it was said that the evaluative factor should provide a good measure of attitudes.

Both the semantic differential and the classical method of free association are partly denotative in character, and this is where the three facets of meaning overlap. In the method of free association, denotative associations to orange would be fruit and round. Denotative aspects of the concept orange would be found in ratings on semantic-differential scales such as sweet-sour and angular-rounded. Both of these approaches, however, only incidentally provide evidence about the denotative meanings of concepts. The semantic differential is dominated by connotative meaning, particularly evaluation. Free association to nouns (concepts or attitudinal objects) is dominated by responses that also are nouns, or "object associates," as the term is used here.

Whereas the factors of potency and activity ostensibly concern denotative aspects of meaning, they do so only in part. First, even though scales on those factors ostensibly concern physical properties of objects (e.g., heavy, large, fast, and active), they also are partly evaluative in nature, and thus they partly relate to connotative as well as to denotative aspects of meaning. Second, ratings of potency and activity can be interpreted only with respect to classes of stimuli. To use an example provided by Osgood (1962), a baby would be rated as small and a railroad spike would be rated as large, but of course the former actually is much larger in physical size than the latter. Osgood suggests that this is because objects are rated in comparison to implicit classes of stimuli. Thus a baby is small in the class of all persons, and a railroad spike is large in the class of all nail-like objects. Actually, however, rather than this being a bad feature of the semantic differential, it is a good feature. If one really wanted to learn the physical properties of objects (e.g., their strength and speed), measuring those properties directly would be far better than having people guess at them. The potency and activity factors provide auxiliary information about evaluation beyond that provided by the scales specifically intended to measure evaluation, and they provide suggestions about conceptual classes of objects, e.g., persons and nail-like objects.

USE OF SEMANTIC-DIFFERENTIAL SCALES   In previous sections some general suggestions were made about the employment of semantic-differential scales in research; here, some additional points in that regard will be made. When scores are summed over a number of scales, as is usually the case, the logic of constructing summative measures is the same as that discussed previously for the construction of summative scales of verbalized attitudes. That is, by methods of item analysis, one seeks a homogeneous group of scales that meets requirements of reliability. It usually is not difficult to accomplish that goal. One frequently finds, for example, that half a dozen pairs of adjectives rated on eight-step scales have a coefficient alpha as high as .80.

It is well to employ numbers to designate the steps on semantic-differential scales, e.g., the numbers 1 through 8 to designate the steps of an eight-step scale. Also, the meanings of the numbers should be carefully defined and illustrated in the instructions to the inventory. For example, subjects can be told that, on the scale good-bad, 5 means "slightly good" rather than "bad," 4 means "slightly bad" rather than "good," and so on for the other steps on the scale.

In many studies it has been the practice to randomly, or systematically, alternate the polarities of scales. Thus, for the scale good-bad, "good" would be placed on the right, and "bad" would be placed on the left. Then, for the scale wise-foolish, the polarity would be reversed: "wise" would be placed on the left, and "foolish" would be placed on the right. The purpose of such reversals of polarity is to prevent subjects from being influenced from scale to scale by ratings made on previous scales. To the extent that this is accomplished by alternating directions of scales, however, the practice probably is not worth the price that is paid in measurement error. One frequently sees ratings where subjects apparently became confused by the numerous alternations of scale directions. For example, one frequently finds that a subject rates a concept as both "very good" and "very worthless," or "very active" and "very slow." The weight of the argument is for keeping the scales pertaining to any factor all pointing in the same direction, e.g., making the "good" pole of all evaluative scales either on the left or on the right, and making the "active" pole of all scales concerning the activity factor either on the left or on the right.

Rather than employing only the "standard" factors that have been found in studies of diverse concepts, there is nothing wrong with developing particular groups of scales for particular purposes. For example, the following scales would be useful in studying subjective feelings of anxiety in experiments concerning the effects of different types of stressful circumstances:

anxious–calm	afraid–unafraid
tense–relaxed	nervous–restful
disturbed–undisturbed	upset–quiet

Of course, the advantage of summing scores over a number of scales rather than relying on one scale alone (e.g., anxious-calm) is that it permits finer differentiations among persons. Even though such scales may, in general usage, have somewhat different patterns of factor loadings with the "usual" factors, in such special uses as that illustrated above, the scales may correlate highly. Numerous other special groups of scales can be employed in particular studies.

In addition to summing scores over groups of scales, in most studies it also is instructive to compare concepts on individual scales. Thus, as was mentioned previously, the scale effective-ineffective provides useful information about public attitudes toward professional groups, beyond that which is provided by other scales that typically have high loadings on the evaluative factor. As other examples, Nunnally (1961) found that the scale tense-relaxed served better than any other scale to differentiate public attitudes toward neurotic persons and normal persons and that the scale predictable-unpredictable served better than any other scale to differentiate public attitudes toward psychotic persons and normal persons. Such differences between concepts on individual scales provide many hints for subsequent investigations.

Numerous examples of studies employing the semantic differential are reported in the following sources: Nunnally (1961), Osgood (1962), and Osgood, Suci, and Tannenbaum (1957). A list of 99 scales employed in one or more studies is reported by Nunnally (1959). Sample instructions for inventories containing semantic-differential scales, and ratings on a variety of scales for a large number of person concepts, are reported by Nunnally (1961). As can be seen from the many studies mentioned in the above sources, and from the many particular studies not mentioned in those sources, during the last 10 years the semantic differential has become an important "workhorse" in psychology for the investigation of attitudes and other types of sentiments.

the Q sort

The Q sort and the semantic differential gained their fame at about the same time, in the early 1950s. Beyond that similarity, however, they are very different types of rating tasks. The Q sort grew out of a more general methodology developed by Stephenson (1953) for the study of verbalized attitudes, self-description, preferences, and other issues in social psychology, clinical psychology, and the study of personality. A salient principle in that methodology is that, for the advancement of psychology, it is more important to make comparisons among different responses (e.g., statements regarding preferences) within persons than between persons. In other words, basic to Stephenson's methodology is a reliance on *comparative* rating methods and on an analysis of comparative data within persons even when absolute rating methods are employed. The Q sort is a handy comparative rating method that has proved useful for the type of study that Stephenson envisaged. Also, it has been used widely to study numerous issues ranging from psychotherapy to advertising. Wittenborn (1961) surveyed studies employing the Q sort up to 1961. More detailed descriptions of studies employing the Q sort are given by Nunnally (1959) and Stephenson (1953).

AN ILLUSTRATIVE STUDY Before the psychometric properties of the Q sort are discussed, a simple example will illustrate the nature of the rating method. The study concerns preferences for statues, each of 100 statues appearing separately in a photograph. The statues are from many different cultures around the world and from many different historical periods. Rather than rate each photograph separately, as with an absolute rating method such as the rating scale, the subject is asked to make comparative preferences by "sorting" the photographs into a specified number of piles. The end piles are designated "prefer least" and "prefer most," respectively. The particular feature of the Q sort is that the subject is required to sort the stimuli in terms of a fixed distribution, usually an approximately normal distribution. A forced distribution that could be used for the study of 100 statues is as follows:

					Number of photographs					
2	4	8	12	14	20	14	12	8	4	2
Prefer least 0	1	2	3	4	5 Pile number	6	7	8	9	10 Prefer most

The number for each pile is written on a file card, and the cards are spread out in a line on a large table. To lessen order effects, the investigator shuffles the 100 photographs before giving them to the subject. Before sorting the photographs, the subject is instructed to look at them one at a time and then spread them out on the table to make comparisons among them. Preparatory to the actual sorting, the subject frequently is asked to place the photographs into three gross classes— ones that he definitely likes, ones that he definitely dislikes, and ones about which he is ambivalent. This is done only to facilitate the subsequent sorting, and judgments made at that time can be changed later.

In the actual sorting of the photographs, the subject is instructed to work from both ends of the continuum toward the middle. The extreme likes and dislikes usually are spotted quicker than less extreme preferences. Also, since in correlational studies so much depends on the extreme scores, it is important that the subject pay particular attention to the placements in the two or three extreme piles on each end of the continuum. In a study of preferences, the subject usually would be instructed to work from the most-prefer end toward the middle. He would be instructed to find the 2 most preferred statues and place them in pile 10. From the remaining 98 photographs, he would pick the 4 that are next most preferred and place them in pile 9. From the remaining 94 photographs, the subject would pick 8 for pile 8; and from the remaining photographs, 12 to go in pile 7. Then the subject would be instructed to switch to the least-prefer end of the continuum, pick the 2 statues least preferred and place these in pile zero, and work upward in that way through pile 3. The subject would then sort the remaining 48 photographs into piles 4, 5, and 6. Finally, the subject would be instructed to examine the entire ratings to make sure that photographs are not out of place, and if some are, to make rearrangements of positions of the photographs.

NATURE OF THE RATING TASK As was mentioned previously, the Q sort obviously is a comparative rating method rather than an absolute rating method. The task forces all subjects to have the same mean rating, and thus one learns nothing about level of response to the stimuli as a group. A subject could detest all the statues in the example above, or like them all very much, but no hint of that would be obtained from the Q sort. All comparative rating tasks (e.g., the method of rank order) force all subjects to have the same mean rating, and thus none of them are intended to provide information about absolute levels of response.

The Q sort also requires subjects to distribute their responses in terms of a fixed distribution, usually an approximately normal distribution. This forces all subjects not only to have the same mean rating, but also to have the same standard deviation of ratings and the same curve shape of ratings. The Q sort has been criticized on this score, because one could argue that subjects would employ different shapes of distributions if left to their own devices. For a number of reasons, such criticisms are not well justified.

If the intention is to obtain comparative ratings, as it is in employing the Q sort, it is necessary to stipulate the distribution mean, shape, and standard deviation in advance. This is exactly what is done in the method of rank order, which is the logical paradigm for all comparative methods. With the Q sort, if subjects are allowed to put as many stimuli as they like in a pile, the method begins to regress to the method of single stimuli (discussed in Chapter Two), a method for studying absolute responses. For example, a photograph would be placed in the top pile not only because it was liked *more* than others, but also because it was liked very much in an absolute sense. If one wants to have comparative responses made with respect to all the stimuli in a set, rather than with respect to two at a time as with the method of pair comparisons or in other subsets, the mean, standard deviation, and curve form must be fixed.

Thus arguments about the use of a forced distribution in the Q sort boil down to (1) whether a comparative rating method should be used in studies of the kinds where the Q sort is used and (2) if so, whether the Q sort should be used in preference to other comparative methods. The first point is well worth considering, and will be returned to later, but here let us consider the second point. The major reason for using the Q sort rather than some other comparative rating method is that it greatly conserves the time taken to make ratings. For example, a Q sort of 100 photographs would take no more than 30 minutes on the average; but a complete rank ordering would probably take well over an hour and would prove very tedious to subjects. Because of the time other comparative rating methods take, they would be almost out of the question. For example, if the method of pair comparisons were employed with 100 photographs and each subject judged each pair only once, the subject would have to make 4,950 comparisons. Obviously, most of the comparative rating methods are limited to rather small sets of stimuli. Even with the method of rank order, it is difficult to employ more than 50 stimuli. The Q sort then is a useful compromise between two needs: (1) the need to have precise differentiations made among the stimuli, as is done in the method of pair comparisons, and (2) the need to have comparisons made among the members of large sets of stimuli, which is the case in many studies in psychology.

It is best to regard the forced distribution in the Q sort as an approximation to rank order, a rank ordering in which the number of tied ranks at each point is specified for the subject. The use of an approximately normal distribution rather than some other fixed distribution (e.g., a rectangular distribution) is justified in the general case, because (1) so many things in nature are distributed approximately that way and (2) it fits in with the statistical methods applied to the data.

Another reason why criticisms of the forced Q-sort distribution are largely unjustified is that the exact distribution form has little effect on the kinds of analyses which are made of the data. Correlation coefficients, and the factors obtained from them, are largely insensitive to changes in distribution shapes. Of course, they are not affected at all by changes in means and standard deviations of raw scores. To the extent that it is meaningful to apply inferential statistics to Q-sort ratings (e.g., a t test of the mean preferences of one person for two types of statues), it is known that the results of such inferential statistics tend to be affected very little by changes in distribution form. For purposes of analysis, then, even if one allowed subjects to sort stimuli into any distribution form that they chose, differences in distribution forms among subjects would make little difference in the results of statistical analyses.

Actually, those who work extensively with Q sorts recommend that a relatively large number of piles be employed and the distribution be somewhat flatter than the normal distribution. This allows subjects to make rather fine discriminations among stimuli and tends to increase the reliability of ratings, the same as is done by increasing the number of steps on rating scales.

STIMULUS SAMPLES   It is to the credit of Stephenson and his colleagues that research with Q sorts has emphasized the importance of stimulus (or content) sampling. As was mentioned in Chapter One, psychology, and other disciplines as well, are faced with problems concerning two types of sampling—sampling of people and sampling of stimuli. While psychologists usually are careful to adequately sample people, at least to the point of obtaining sufficient numbers of subjects, and employ very elegant statistical methods for assessing the error associated with the sampling of people, less is usually done about the sampling of stimuli (or content). To take an oversimplified example, regardless of what type of rating method was employed, one would not learn much about food preferences unless a representative list of food names was sampled. The sample would be inadequate if it left out all meats, included desserts of only certain kinds, or contained numerous foreign dishes that the subjects had never heard of. In more subtle ways, biased samples of content lead to poor measurements, e.g., a vocabulary test for the general population which is loaded with technical terms relating to particular occupations, or a scale for verbalized attitudes toward the United Nations that contains statements about only restricted aspects of the organization.

The problem of sampling stimuli occurs in many types of ratings, but for good reasons, it has had to be faced more squarely in the use of Q sorts than in other rating methods. One reason for this is that the rating task makes sense only if all stimuli are from a specifiable universe of content. To understand why this is so, imagine that subjects are asked to rate the esthetic quality of 100 photographs, 50 of which are pictures of statues and 50 of which are pictures of automobiles. In sorting the pictures not only would the subject have to decide which statues were more esthetically pleasing and which automobiles were more esthetically pleasing, but in essence, he would have to decide whether statues as a group were more esthetically pleasing than automobiles as a group. Obviously, the results of such a study would be far more meaningful if separate Q sortings were made of statues and automobiles. Although surely no one would mix such different types of stimuli in a Q sort, to a lesser extent the use of Q sorts is constantly plagued by the need to ensure that all stimuli are from some common frame of reference.

The problem with ensuring that all stimuli are from a common frame of reference is that it is hard to define a common frame of reference. The counterpart in the sampling of people is the problem of defining the population which the sample is intended to represent. There are some problems there, e.g., generalizing from studies of college students to people in general or deciding whether American Indians will be included in a national sample for obtaining norms for intelligence tests. The problems in defining populations of people are small, however, in comparison to the problems of defining "populations" of stimuli. These problems are particularly severe with one type of content that has been used frequently with Q sorts—statements relating to personality traits, such as the following:

1 I have many friends.

2 Most people like me.

3 I am a nervous person.

4 I had an unhappy childhood.

5 I dread the future.

6 I enjoy physical exercise.

It is hard to see how a comparative rating method like the Q sort makes sense with such diverse content as illustrated in the six statements above. Samples of statements concerning personality used with Q sorts frequently fail to represent a common frame of reference because (1) they mix motives, social traits, and symptoms of maladjustment, (2) they contain statements relating to past, present, and future, (3) some statements concern self-description and others concern judgments about what other people think, and (4) some statements concern general traits (e.g., tendency to be anxious) and others concern rather specific habits (e.g., overeating). Even if none of these rather obvious failures to keep all stimuli in a common frame of reference occur, it frequently is difficult to stipulate what domain of content is intended to be covered or to justify the method employed to sample the domain.

TYPES OF STIMULUS SAMPLES   Two types of content samples are employed with the Q sort: *random* samples and *structured* samples. In both instances, it is important to realize that the so-called sampling is not done in the same way that one samples from populations of persons. Rather, in "sampling" material for a Q sort, one either constructs the materials himself or borrows them from some available source, e.g., a book containing many photographs of statues. The structured sample is one in which the experimenter stipulates the kinds of stimuli that will be included in the content sample in terms of an experimental design. An oversimplified example is as follows. In a study of photographs of statues, the experimenter decides to have some of the photographs be of oriental statues and others of occidental statues. Also, he decides to have some of the photographs concern abstract statues and others be representational. The structural sample then could be summarized in terms of the following design:

	ORIENTAL	OCCIDENTAL
REPRESENTATIONAL	25	25
ABSTRACT	25	25

The experimenter would employ 25 photographs depicting statues that are both representational and oriental in origin, 25 that are both abstract and occidental in origin, and so on for the other two cells of the design. If there are no other facets of the design, the 25 photographs in each cell should be "random," which the experimenter best approximates simply by ensuring that they are diversely representative of sculptors and subject matters.

So that any faith can be placed in a structured sample of content, two types of data must be obtained. First, prior to the use of the sample in Q sorts, judgments should be made by knowledgeable people of the appropriateness of the classifications of stimuli. In the example above, one could have five artists independently judge the relevance of each photograph for its classification, e.g., by giving each artist the 100 photographs and having him place each photograph in the cell where it belongs. Only those photographs would be retained that received high agreement among judges. The second type of assurance for the correctness of cell placements comes from analyzing the responses of subjects who make Q sortings of the stimuli. If the stimuli in a particular cell actually "hang together," it should be found that the variance of Q-sort ratings by each subject for the stimuli in any cell is considerably less than the variance of the Q-sort distribution. If that is not the case, it means that the stimuli that are assigned to a particular cell of the structured sample scatter all up and down the Q-sort continuum in the ratings made by each subject. Then, even if one could argue that there are good logical reasons for the placements of stimuli in a structured sample, it would be obvious that the design did very little to explain the actual ratings made by subjects.

In some cases, it is very difficult to generate a sensible structured sample for the stimuli to be used in a Q sort. This would be true, for example, in having psychotherapists make Q-sort ratings of the day-to-day progress of patients with statements like the following:

1 Spends much time expressing appreciation to me for my understanding.

2 Avoids talking about painful issues.

3 Seems more intent on the future than what the past was like.

4 Seems discouraged about the possibility of solving major problems.

With such statements, and with many other types of stimuli, the best that can be done is to "randomly sample" the desired number of "things" to be used in a Q sort. What this means is that one tries to obtain a highly diverse collection of materials of the kind to be investigated, e.g., photographs of many different types of statues drawn from a number of different sources, statements about important things to observe in psychotherapy taken from a number of prominent books on the topic, or symptoms of mental illness taken from case histories in the files of a number of different types of psychiatric institutions.

Where it can be employed, the structured sample has obvious advantages over the so-called random sample. The facets of the structure help in communicating the nature of the content to other investigators. One of the problems with many "random" samples of content is that it is very difficult to specify the domain that has been "sampled." Also, the "random" sample typically attempts to cover too much ground, and consequently it is frequently learned from analyses of Q sorts that insufficient numbers of stimuli of particular kinds were included in the sample. The structured sample serves to limit the content to manageable proportions, and it helps ensure that sufficient numbers of stimuli of the specified kinds are included. Also, as was mentioned previously, an analysis of the data obtained from investigating a structured sample will provide information about the adequacy of the placement of stimuli in the design. In sum, although the structured sample attempts to cover

the content areas

less ground than the "random" sample, it does a better job of specifying the ground to be covered, usually does a better job of covering that ground, and in addition, the internal checks possible with the structured sample provide evidence regarding the original assignment of stimuli to cells.

When it is not possible to construct a structured sample of content initially, that frequently becomes possible after some investigations are made with a "random" sample. The results of statistical analyses may indicate that there are homogeneous groups of items, i.e., a number of items that tend to be given similar placements in Q sorts, regardless of where they are placed as a group by different subjects. Results of these kinds could lead to asserting a structure for the sample. For the final structured sample, then, it probably would be necessary to discard some items that did not relate to the structured design and to add items in some cells to achieve equal numbers. Also, whether one achieves a structured sample initially or only after preliminary research, in continued research it frequently happens that additional facets are added to the design. This is because continued research teaches the investigator how to make important, new distinctions among the kinds of stimuli in his domain of interest.

ANALYSIS OF Q-SORT DATA   Many criticisms of research employing the Q sort pertain not so much to the Q sort itself but rather to methods of analysis that have been applied to Q-sort data. The most popular methods of analysis have concerned correlations, e.g., the correlation of two Q sorts of the same material by the same subject under different conditions or the correlation of Q sorts by different persons. An example of the former would be to have one person make "sorts" under two sets of instructions, such as a set pertaining to the subject's esthetic preferences for 100 statues and a set pertaining to the subject's estimate of what esthetic preferences would be made by the average six-year-old child. The PM correlation could then be computed between the two "sorts" by the same person. As an example of the latter approach to correlation, the PM correlation could be computed between the "sorts" made by two persons on a list of statements relating to personality traits. In addition to employing simple correlational methods with Q sorts, many studies have employed more complex methods of correlational analysis, including partial correlation, multiple correlation, and various methods of factor analysis.

In addition to correlational analysis, analysis of variance has also been employed with Q sorts, this having particular applicability to the data obtained from structured samples. For example, for the 2×2 factorial design mentioned previously for photographs of statues, one could employ the usual formula for analysis of variance to examine the statistical significance of each of the two facets of the design and of the interaction of those facets. To take an example at a simpler level of analysis, one could perform a t test between the mean placements in the Q sort for any two groups of items, regardless of whether or not those groups of items had been stipulated as part of a structured sample, e.g., a t test between the mean ratings by one person for statues of humans and for statues of lower animals.

Although there is not sufficient space here to go into the many questions concerning various methods of analysis applied to Q-sort data, some of the major issues will be discussed. In this regard, it is important to take separate looks at *inferential statistics* applied to Q-sort data and *descriptive statistics* applied to Q-sort data. Considering the former, it is somewhat difficult to interpret inferential statistics applied in those instances where the sampling unit is the stimulus rather than the person and in which "degrees of freedom" are determined by the number of stimuli (e.g., photographs) rather than the number of persons. This is done when the usual "test for significance" is applied to a correlation between two "sorts" by the same or different persons. Let us say that the correlation is .40 between two sorts by one person, and there are 100 stimuli in the content sample. As has frequently been done, one can find a standard error for the correlation coefficient, inserting 100 as the sample size in the customary formulas.

To compute a standard error for a correlation coefficient in the above way assumes that it is legitimate to define the sample size as the number of stimuli employed in the Q sort. Obviously, since the correlation is computed on the responses from only one subject, there is no basis at all for generalizing to other subjects. Logically, in such cases, inferential statistics concern probability statements about relations between samples of content and a hypothetical "population" (universe or domain) of content. If, by considering the sample size to be the number of stimuli, a correlation of .40 reached acceptable levels of statistical significance, this would provide some statistical confidence that the population correlation is different from zero. The population correlation would be that obtained if the Q sort contained every stimulus in a finite population of stimuli, or in the case of an infinite population of content, the hypothetical Q sort made with an infinite number of stimuli.

In all other uses of inferential statistics where the sample size is considered to be the number of stimuli rather than the number of persons, probability statements necessarily relate only to stimulus sampling, and thus they have no direct implications for the generality of results over populations of persons. This is true, for example, in the use of analysis of variance with structured samples of stimuli. It was mentioned previously how one might employ the usual F ratios to assess the main effects and interactions occurring in the placement of stimuli in one "sorting" by one person. If, then, one of the main effects proved to be "significant" in this way, what the experimenter would conclude is that the cell means would probably be different even if the Q sort contained all the stimuli in a domain of stimuli.

As has been mentioned and illustrated at numerous points in this book, the theory of psychological measurement is more intimately related to principles concerning the sampling of content than to principles concerning the sampling of people. That does not mean, however, that it is necessary or wise to translate inferential statistics concerning the sampling of people into inferential statistics concerning the sampling of content. One can develop most of the necessary principles in the theory of psychological measurement without considering inferential statistics relating to content sampling (one of the few exceptions being principles concerning the stability of reliability coefficients as a function of content sampling, a matter discussed in Chapter Six).

If one employs inferential statistics with respect to problems of content sampling, as is frequently done with Q-sort data, he must be aware that the assumptions for employing such statistics are much more difficult to justify than they are in sampling people. First, there must be a definable population (domain or universe), and it is difficult to define domains of content for Q sorts. Second, the sampling unit must be defined. This is obviously the individual person in the usual sampling of people, but it is not so obvious what the sampling unit is with certain types of content, e.g., statements about psychotherapy or statements relating to personality traits. Third, the stimuli must be either randomly sampled overall (the so-called random sample for Q sorts) or randomly sampled within specified categories (as in the structured sample for Q sorts). As was mentioned previously, it usually is uncertain that one is sampling at all when he is obtaining or constructing materials for a Q sort, and it is even less certain that he is sampling randomly.

It is best not to make fine interpretations of the probability values found in applying inferential statistics to problems concerning the sampling of content. One does better to consider them as rough guides to the probable generality of findings over large collections of stimuli of the same general kinds. As an example, assume that the correlation of Q-sort self-descriptions by two persons is .80, and the correlation with the same stimuli for two other persons is zero. By applying the usual formulas for inferential statistics and using the number of stimuli as the sample size, one finds that the difference in the two correlations is accompanied by an extremely high level of statistical confidence. Then, even if it usually is difficult to justify the assumptions necessary to employ inferential statistics with problems concerning the sampling of content, the level of statistical confidence provides some assurance that the difference in the two correlations is "real" and not entirely because of the fortuitous circumstances that led to the selection of some materials rather than others for the Q sort. In the same way, an informal use of analysis of variance and other inferential statistics with problems of content sampling is justified.

In most forms of analysis applied to Q-sort data, however, there is little need to make statistical inferences regarding the generality of results over hypothetical domains of content. Simple correlations, and more complex products of correlational analysis, can be used only as descriptive indices of degrees of relationship. Analysis of variance also can be used to provide descriptive indices, in contrast to the more customary probability statements. For example, the variance of means in any facet of a structured sample can be divided by the fixed variance of the Q-sort distribution, and that ratio would provide a direct index of the extent to which the facet has explanatory power for the variance of ratings. Other ratios of components of variance relating to the "sort" of one person for stimuli from a structured sample can be used as descriptive indices.

After descriptive indices are computed for each person, inferential statistics can be applied to the variabilities of such indices over a priori groups of persons (e.g., men versus women) or differences in differently treated groups in controlled experiments. An example of the former would be as follows. The purpose of the study is to compare the esthetic preferences of college students with those of professional artists. The mean placement of 25 abstract, oriental statues would be obtained for each person, resulting in a distribution of means for each of the two groups. The means and variances of those two distributions of means would be obtained, and this information would be used in a t test of the differences in grand means of the two groups. Another example is as follows. Patients entering psychotherapy could be asked to make Q-sort descriptions of themselves and how they would like to be ideally. The two "sorts" are correlated for each patient, giving a distribution of such correlations over the number of patients in the study. All patients would be asked to repeat the two "sorts" on the completion of psychotherapy. The tendency for the "after" correlations to be higher than the "before" correlations could be assessed by any of the methods of inferential statistics relating to repeated observations, e.g., the sign test. In many other ways, the results from studies employing Q sorts can be examined in terms of inferential statistics relating to the sampling of persons rather than to the sampling of stimuli.

SUMMARY REMARKS ABOUT THE Q SORT   There are advantages and disadvantages to employing the Q sort rather than other rating methods.

The chief advantage is in those instances where one is seeking relatively precise comparative responses among a rather large number of stimuli. As was mentioned previously, highly precise comparative methods such as pair comparisons are almost out of the question with large numbers of stimuli. At the other extreme of the continuum of precision, one could make comparative analyses of absolute responses obtained from rating scales. An example concerning ratings of the handsomeness of men will illustrate the possibilities. If the stimuli were 100 photographs of men, it would be almost out of the question to employ pair comparisons and difficult to employ rank order. Comparative ratings could be obtained quickly and easily with the Q sort.

Another way to obtain comparative information about the rated handsomeness of the men would be as follows. Instead of having comparisons made among the men with regard to handsomeness, each photograph is rated on an eight-step scale, anchored on the extremes by "very handsome" and "very ugly." Then one could make comparative analyses among the absolute ratings given by each person. A first step would be to convert all distributions of ratings by different raters to a common distribution form. One could do this by standardizing the distribution of 100 ratings for each person. Then all subjects would have the same mean and standard deviation of ratings, and the standard scores would provide comparative information about the ratings made by each person. These scores could then be treated in all the ways that scores obtained from Q sorts are treated.

If economy of time, effort, and money was the major consideration, it would pay to make comparative analyses of separate ratings rather than employ the Q sort. Subjects can make 100 separate ratings in less than half the time that they can perform a Q sort of 100 stimuli. In previous years, the Q sort had a marked advantage in statistical analyses over comparative analyses of separate ratings. This is because in the Q sort, all sets of comparative ratings have a fixed distribution, and consequently there is no need to make conversions to a common distribution, as must be done in order to make comparative analyses of absolute responses. Also, with only a desk calculator, it is much faster to compute correlations between Q sorts than between sets of absolute ratings (correlating over stimuli as is done in the Q sort). Those were very important considerations 15 years ago, but no longer. Most analyses these days are done on high-speed computers, and the difference in computer time to make analyses of Q sorts and similar comparative analyses of absolute responses is trivial.

What then are the advantages of using Q sorts over performing comparative analyses of absolute ratings? The major potential advantage is that one might obtain more precise comparative information from the Q sort. The Q sort explicitly requires the subject to make comparative responses, but this occurs only incidentally in making separate ratings. The various response styles that accompany absolute ratings (e.g., the tendency to make extreme ratings) could cloud the comparative information in such ratings. Also, the tendency of subjects to shift sets (e.g., to respond more favorably as they proceed from rating to rating) also would tend to cloud the comparative information in the ratings. Then, one would usually expect to find a higher reliability (e.g., retest) for comparative responses obtained from the Q sort than from comparative analyses of absolute ratings.

Aside from questions of reliability, it is also possible that the factor composition of Q sorts sometimes is somewhat different from comparatively analyzed ratings. In the latter, since the subject does not actually make comparative responses, it is an assumption on the part of the experimenter that a comparative analysis of those responses results in measurement of the same attributes that would be measured by actually obtaining comparative responses.

Even if the Q sort has certain advantages as a method of eliciting comparative responses, a more basic question concerns whether or not it is wise to obtain comparative responses with sets of stimuli of the kinds that frequently are employed with the Q sort. It can be strongly argued that comparative responses make sense only if all the stimuli in a set are from some common frame of reference. As was illustrated previously, it is hard to make a convincing case for this with some of the Q-sort samples that have been employed in studies to date.

In those cases where all stimuli are from a common frame of reference, whether one employs a comparative rating method or an absolute rating method is largely independent of the methods of analyzing the data. One can employ an R-technique or Q-technique logic with either (the difference was discussed in Chapter Ten). Data from the Q sort have usually been analyzed in terms of the logic of its namesake, Q technique. For example, one frequently correlates the "sorts" made by different persons and performs factor analyses of the correlations. In contrast, data obtained from absolute-response methods (e.g., rating scales) usually are analyzed in terms of the logic of R technique. For example, in studying the factor structure of ratings of attitude statements, one usually would correlate scales over persons (instead of persons over scales) and factor-analyze the obtained correlations.

It is possible, however, to employ an R-technique logic in the analysis of Q-sort data and a Q-technique logic in the analysis of data obtained from methods that elicit absolute responses, although neither is frequently done. The latter has already been illustrated, as in the situation where comparative analyses are made of separate ratings of the members of a set of stimuli. Correlations between persons could be analyzed in all the ways typically employed with Q sorts. Illustrating the other possibility, pairs of stimuli in Q sorts could be correlated over persons, and correlations among stimuli could be treated as they are in R technique.

The above considerations lead us to four major conclusions about the Q sort and related methods of analysis. First, if one is seeking comparative responses, the Q sort has certain advantages for that purpose. Second, before the Q sort is employed, it is important to ensure that sensible comparative responses can be made among the stimuli employed in a particular study. Third, if one elects to use the Q sort as a rating method, that does not necessarily tie him to the use of particular techniques of mathematical analysis rather than others. Fourth, choices among approaches to mathematical analysis (e.g., R technique versus Q technique) are mainly matters of taste and hunch. In the long run we shall learn which approaches are generally more fruitful, but at this early stage in the growth of our science, it is good that all the research eggs are not being placed in the same methodological basket.

scaling of stimuli

Most of the discussion in this chapter has concerned the use of rating methods for the scaling of persons with respect to psychological traits. Summative scales based on statements concerning attitudinal objects are used to scale people in terms of their attitudes, e.g., toward the United Nations. Semantic-differential scales are used to measure individual differences in the connotative meanings of concepts. The Q sort is used to measure individual differences in preferences for stimuli of different kinds.

In spite of the important place of rating methods in the scaling of people, it would be appropriate to close this chapter by reminding the reader that rating methods also are very useful for the scaling of stimuli. Numerous methods for scaling stimuli were discussed in Chapter Two, all of which, in essence, are "rating methods." The particular rating methods discussed in this chapter frequently are used for the scaling of stimuli. Summative scales of agree-disagree ratings of statements can be used, for example, to scale typical reactions to different levels of dosage of a particular drug or different levels of reaction to different levels of electric shock. The semantic differential has many uses in the scaling of stimuli, as was illustrated previously for the scaling of nonsense syllables in terms of degree of familiarity and the scaling of geometrical designs in terms of pleasantness, complexity, and other aspects of connotative meaning. The Q sort also has many applications to the scaling of stimuli. Words can be "sorted" in terms of emotionality; statements relating to personality traits can be "sorted" in terms of social desirability; and patches of gray paper can be "sorted" in terms of brightness.

When rating scales are used to scale stimuli rather than people, the major assumption is that individual differences are not important in judgments or preferences in relation to the particular set of stimuli. If that is a safe assumption, the experimenter can average over raters to obtain a scale for the stimuli. The assumption is safe with certain classes of stimuli (e.g., patches of gray paper) and not safe with other classes of stimuli (e.g., ratings of values). Whether or not the assumption seems safe a priori, the wisdom of making the assumption can be tested after the data are in hand. The extent to which subjects can be considered replicates of one another can be determined by an inspection of the correlations among subjects, or if necessary, by a factor analysis. Regardless of the details of constructing such scales, it is more important to keep in mind that the rating methods discussed in this chapter are important for the scaling of stimuli as well as for the scaling of people.

SUGGESTED ADDITIONAL READINGS

Edwards, A. L. *Techniques of attitude scale construction.* New York: Appleton-Century-Crofts, 1957.

Guilford, J. P. *Psychometric methods.* New York: McGraw-Hill, 1954, chap. 11.

Guilford, J. P. *Personality.* New York: McGraw-Hill, 1959, chaps. 7, 9.

Nunnally, J. C. *Tests and measurements: Assessment and prediction.* New York: McGraw-Hill, 1959, chaps. 14, 17.

CHAPTER FIFTEEN

CONTINGENT VARIABLES

Potentially, measurements of all human traits are affected by a host of contingent variables, such as speed, guessing, response styles, fatigue, motivation, and others. The purpose of this chapter is to discuss the available theory and evidence regarding some of the most important contingent variables. Specialists in psychological measurement often have been criticized for being concerned mainly with response-response relations, as is involved, for example, in correlating responses to a personality test with responses to a test of ability. Although differential psychology is rightly concerned with such response-response relations, it also is important to consider stimulus-response relations in the measurement of human traits. For example, it is important to investigate the effects on test performance of different types of items, different time limits, different opportunities for guessing the correct answer, different types of distractions, and others. Such stimulus-response relations are important to investigate for two reasons. First, they help put differential psychology on an experimental footing, rather than leaving it as a purely descriptive enterprise. That is, experiments concerning the effects of different approaches to measurement provide suggestions regarding how individual differences arise initially. Second, stimulus-response relations provide evidence about optimum methods of measurement. For example, if it is found that one time limit leads to more reliable measurement than another time limit, this offers information about the most effective approach to measurement. As another example, if a test administered under one type of instruction is more predictive of a particular criterion than is a test administered under another instruction, again this offers information about the most effective approach to measurement.

Some of the investigations of contingent variables discussed in this chapter are similar to the typical investigations of stimulus-response relations in controlled experiments. For example, the experimenter employs three different time limits with three different groups of subjects and examines the effects on reliability and other psychometric properties of test scores. Some of the other studies of contingent variables to be discussed are only indirectly similar to controlled experiments. In these, the subject supplies his own "stimulus," and individual differences in that regard are related to test performance. This is the case in studies of the effects of response styles on psychological measurement, e.g., the effect of the agreement tendency on results obtained from self-inventories. In such cases, the experimenter cannot literally control the contingent variable. If he can measure the contingent variables, however, he can, by forming groups on the basis of such measures, examine mean differences of those groups on measures of psychological traits.

There is no end to the contingent variables that potentially influence measures of psychological traits. Many of those variables have been almost entirely neglected, as is the case with the effects of motivation on test performance. Much of the evidence concerning some of the contingent variables has been incidentally obtained as part of studies performed for other purposes, which tends to be true of the evidence relating to the effects of time limits on tests of abilities.

effects of speed

Because of the theoretical and practical importance of the effects of speed on psychological measures, many investigations have been made in this regard. (The most comprehensive single source for this work is the report of a symposium, The effects of time limits on test scores, *Educ. psychol. Measmt*, 1960, **20**, 221–274.) There are two broad questions concerning speed, the first relating to psychological theories and the second relating to the methodology of measurement. The first question is, "Are speed of response and goodness of response interchangeable?" For example, would one expect a high correlation between the speed of solving very simple reasoning problems and the ability to solve difficult reasoning problems when no time limit is employed? Spearman (1927) claimed that speed of response and goodness of response are interchangeable concepts, and he mustered some evidence to support his point of view; but that point of view has been strongly challenged in the intervening years.

The second broad question is, "How do different time limits affect the psychometric properties of measurement methods?" For example, what would happen to the reliability of a particular test if the time limit were shortened from 50 to 30 minutes?

The problem with the two questions above is that they are far too broad to permit neat answers. In each case the answer is, "It depends." Each question must be broken down into a number of different questions relating to different types of instruments, different types of scoring, different methods of administration, different types of research designs, and different methods of analyzing the results. Some of the more important distinctions to be considered with respect to the effects of speed are discussed in this section.

TYPES OF INSTRUMENTS   Most of the practical and theoretical issues concerning speed relate only to measures of human ability rather than to measures of personality traits and sentiments. For example, almost no consideration has been given to the effects of speed on self-inventories, and most such instruments are administered under liberal time limits. In a test of ability, the hope is that the individual's ability will be directly manifested in the test score. Then, to the extent that the individual is made to hurry through the test, the score may represent somewhat different abilities than it would had the individual been given all the time he wanted. In contrast, in a self-inventory, the score is not thought to represent a direct measure of personality in action. In that case the most that is hoped for is that the subject will honestly relate how he usually behaves in daily life, and thus measurement is indirect. To force the subject to speed through the inventory would not necessarily measure an interaction of speed with personality traits; rather, it would serve only to make the subject describe himself faster. Restrictive time limits may have small effects on the results of self-inventories and other nonability measures, but if they do, very little is known about such effects.

In a discussion of effects of speed, it is important to distinguish among tests of ability that are intended to serve basically different purposes, i.e., those requiring content validity, predictive validity, and construct validity, respectively. Accompanying these three types of instruments are different issues concerning speed—different degrees of practical importance, different theoretical concepts, and different approaches to investigating the effects of speed. Some of these differences will be discussed later.

VARIABLES RELATING TO SPEED   One reason why the two questions posed at the beginning of this section are not sufficiently specific is that they ask only about the effects of speed, without specifying the variables to be considered. One aspect of speed concerns *speed instructions*. For example, in measures of word association, subjects are usually instructed to work quickly and respond with the first word that comes to mind. With speed instructions, however, subjects frequently are not forced to perform at any set speed, item per item, or to stop responding after any particular amount of time. Also, in such cases no measurement is made of how rapidly subjects actually respond. As a variable, then, speed instructions serve only to encourage rapid responses. They do not ensure rapid responses by the average subject; they do not prevent individual differences in rate of response; and they do not necessarily lead to measures of individual differences in rate of response.

Another variable relating to speed is *preferred rate* of response, which concerns how rapidly subjects like to respond. Preferred rate can be purely measured only in the situation where (1) responses are very easy (i.e., not mentally difficult or physically exhausting) and (2) the experimenter does not provide incentives for responding either quickly or slowly. There are very few tasks that meet those standards. An example is in the situation where a subject is told to tap a stylus on a table at any rate that he chooses, while the number of taps per unit of time is recorded. If a word-association test were given without speed instructions, the total time taken by each subject would be an almost pure measure of preferred rate in relation to that task. It would not be a completely pure measure of preferred rate, because there is a small amount of "mental strain" in forming associates, and individual differences in that regard would have different effects on preferred rate.

Preferred rate is the motivational component of the effects of speed on test scores. It concerns how rapidly the subject tries to work in a particular setting. Obviously, the purpose of speed instructions is to alter preferred rate, as in the example above concerning the use of speed instructions with a test of word association. There are two important unsolved questions concerning preferred rate. First, is it a general trait of personality or is it largely specific to the task at hand? Second, regardless of the generality of preferred rate, how does preferred rate interact with speed instructions? Even if the average person responds more quickly under speed instructions than without speed instructions, this still leaves open the question of whether or not changes in individual differences occur. If the correlation between scores in the two situations is 1.0, it means that speed instructions influence only the average rate of responding but do not alter individual differences in preferred rate. If the correlation is zero, it means that speed instructions erase individual differences in preferred rate.

One reason why we know so little about preferred rate is that it is very difficult to investigate preferred rate independently of other variables. In most tasks, the apparent preferred rate actually is a mixture of how quickly the subject would like to respond and how quickly he can respond. This is the case, for example, in a numerical computation test consisting of simple arithmetic problems. One person may take considerable time to complete the problems although he is making every effort to work quickly. Another person may feel no pressure to work quickly, but having superior ability for the type of problem, he completes the test in less time than the average person does.

Another distinction that must be made is between *time scores* and *accuracy scores*. With accuracy scores, the amount of time to complete a set of problems is held constant for all subjects, and the score for each subject consists of the number of problems correctly solved. This would be the case, for example, where subjects were given 20 minutes to solve as many arithmetic problems as they could out of a list of 30 problems. Time scores are employed in the situation where each subject is required to work until a problem is solved, or a list of problems is solved, and the score consists of the amount of time used. In studies of individual differences, accuracy scores are employed more frequently than time scores, e.g., in measures of perceptual speed, verbal fluency, reading speed, and speed of numerical computation. Time scores are used very widely in controlled experiments, e.g., reaction time of humans and time rats take to traverse a maze. In studies of individual differences, accuracy scores are used more frequently than time scores, because they have obvious practical advantages and they are influenced less by preferred rate, personality, age, and other extraneous variables.

A final distinction in this section must be made between speed evidenced under two types of restrictive time limits. One type of time limit is that in which all subjects are given a set amount of time to respond to each item, which is referred to as a *paced* condition. This would be the case, for example, where subjects were given one minute to solve each of 20 arithmetic problems. After the time is up for one problem, subjects are required to hand their written answers to the experimenter. Next, another problem is handed to subjects, and they are given one minute to find the answer. The paced condition is seldom employed in studies of individual differences, because it obviously has practical disadvantages. It has some important uses, however, in basic research concerning the effects of speed on test scores. In the more frequently employed *time-limit* method, subjects are given a set amount of time for completing a whole test. With the time-limit method, the subject has to pace himself. He might work slowly and strive for accuracy on the problems that he attempts, or he might work rapidly and sacrifice accuracy to attempt every item. He might work slowly on the first half of the problems, but seeing that the time is running out, make wild guesses on the remaining problems. Also, to the extent that there are individual differences in motivational characteristics relating to preferred rate, logically these should have a more pronounced influence on time-limit tests than on paced tests.

The major issues concerning speed relate to the psychometric characteristics of accuracy scores on time-limit tests. Such tests are used very widely, and it is in such tests that (1) special factors of ability concerning speed might occur and (2) individual differences in preferred rate and other response styles might strongly influence scores.

DIFFICULTY OF ITEMS It is important here to refresh the reader's memory about the types of items that are employed on pure speed tests and on pure power tests. On a pure speed test, the items are so easy that nearly all subjects would obtain perfect scores if they were allowed to take as much time as they liked. Such items are said to be of *trivial difficulty*. If one actually computed the difficulty levels for such items, by definition they would range upward from p values of .95. With such items, the only way to obtain a reliable dispersion of scores is to employ highly restrictive time limits. There is no question, then, of whether or not restrictive time limits should be employed. Also, a good argument can be made that in most cases the ideal time limit is the one that produces the most reliable distribution of scores.

In contrast to a pure speed test, a pure power test is one in which subjects are allowed to take as much time as they like. In such tests, the items cannot be of trivial difficulty, because that would not produce a desirable distribution of scores. A test composed of items having p values of .95 or higher would probably not be highly reliable (a matter discussed in Chapter Eight), and the distribution of scores would be highly skewed. In Chapter Eight it was said that it is best to select test items not in terms of p values, but rather in terms of item-test correlations. As was mentioned, however, the latter method tends to reject items with extreme p values, e.g., those below .2 or above .8.

The discussion of pure speed tests and pure power tests becomes somewhat complex when it must be considered that two types of combinations of these tests are frequently found in practice. The first occurs when restrictive time limits are placed on what was previously almost a pure power test, as in the following example. The power test is constructed from data obtained under very liberal time limits, and subsequently, the same liberal time limits are employed with the test. Later, someone decides to reduce the time limit, say, shortening it from one hour to 40 minutes. This type of mixture of speed and power will be referred to as a *timed-power* test. A major question to be considered later is whether or not the psychometric properties of timed-power tests usually are different from pure power tests.

A second type of mixture of speed and power occurs in the case where the items are not completely trivial in difficulty when given under power conditions, but most of them are very easy—say, the p values range from .8 to 1.0. To obtain a symmetrical, reliable distribution of scores, then, the experimenter investigates restrictive time limits for the test. This type of mixture of speed and power can be referred to as a speed and difficulty test, or more simply, as a *speed-difficulty* test. It is important to distinguish between timed-power tests and speed-difficulty tests, because the issues are simpler with respect to the former and the practical problems are more severe with respect to the latter. These matters will be discussed in a later section.

TYPES OF TIME LIMITS   Instead of speaking only of power conditions and restrictive time limits, one must make finer distinctions between these conditions. Because of the practical problems involved, it is very rare that a pure power condition is employed. There usually is a time limit, no matter how liberal it might be. Typically, when persons are allowed to take as much time as they like on tests of ability, the distribution of working times is highly skewed. For example, in a test that most persons complete in one hour, a small percentage of persons will remain for two hours, and one person will want to remain for four hours. In that case the experimenter naturally considers the possibility of saving himself a great deal of time on the next use of the test by requiring all subjects to finish in 90 minutes.

It is useful to think in terms of a *comfortable-time limit*, which will be defined as the amount of time required for 90 percent of the persons to complete a test under power conditions. To determine the comfortable-time limit in that way would, of course, require that the test be administered to an initial group of persons under power conditions. In some cases it is not feasible to make such a study, as in the case of classroom examinations that must be completed in 50 minutes. In these cases a check can be made of whether or not a comfortable-time limit is being employed. At the end of the test, each person is asked to indicate whether or not he had sufficient time for completing the test. If at least 90 percent of the persons mark "yes," it can be said that a comfortable-time limit is being employed. Of course, the comfortable-time limit is related to the type of person being tested. It might be markedly different, for example, for high school students and college students or for younger persons and older persons.

The comfortable-time limit offers a basis for scaling all levels of restrictive time limits. Thus one could investigate the effects of employing only 75 percent of the comfortable-time, 50 percent of the comfortable-time, and so on. Also, the comfortable-time offers a basis for comparing the effects of differences in restrictive time limits on different tests. For example, it would be meaningful to compare changes in mean scores on two tests as a function of varying fractions of the comfortable-time limit, e.g., from 25 percent up to 200 percent of the comfortable-time.

In most investigations of the effects of speed on test performance, no index comparable to the comfortable-time has been obtained. Consequently one can only guess at the extent to which different time limits are actually restrictive. For example, cutting the usual time limit for a test in half might still provide more time than the comfortable-time or might reduce the time to only a small fraction of the comfortable-time. The lack of a uniform base for comparing the effects of different time limits (such as that provided by the comfortable-time) is one of the major reasons it is so difficult to interpret the many, scattered studies that have been performed on the effects of different time limits on test performance.

POTENTIAL EFECTS OF TIME LIMITS Here we shall consider the potential effects of different time limits in relation to the comfortable-time. The results from any measurement method are defined entirely in terms of a limited number of psychometric properties, these being the mean, standard deviation, distribution shape, reliability, and validity. Restrictive time limits potentially influence all these.

The potential effects of restrictive time limits on the mean score are obvious. If there are any effects at all, the expectation is that the mean will increase with increasing fractions of the comfortable-time, with little increase being expected above 100 percent of the comfortable-time. There is, however, no strict relationship between the mean and reliability or validity. A mean near the center of the usable score range (e.g., half the number of items on a dichotomously scored free-response test) tends to favor high reliability, but the relationship holds in only a loose statistical way.

Effects of time limits on the standard deviation and distribution shape are important mainly to the extent that they relate to reliability. The time limit that produces the largest standard deviation of scores usually produces the most reliable set of scores (as determined by separately timed halves or by alternative forms). Effects of time limits on the distribution shape are important because they relate to differences in reliability at different score levels. For example, if a particular time limit produces a distribution that is markedly skewed toward the high-score end of the continuum, this indicates that more reliable discriminations are made among persons of high ability than among persons of low ability. This is so regardless of the overall reliability, which, as was said above, is highly related to the standard deviation. The overall reliability is related to the distribution shape only indirectly through relations between shape and standard deviation.

All the above considerations still leave open the question of effects of restrictive time limits on validity. Later we shall consider effects of time limits on instruments that require different kinds of evidence for validity. There is, however, one standard that can be employed to determine effects of restrictive time limits on instruments of all kinds. This standard is the change in factor composition under different time limits. In any particular investigation, one might not know the factor composition of a test given under comfortable-time limits, and one might not know whether changes in the factor composition under different time limits make the test more or less valid, but it is possible to tell whether or not the factor composition changes.

When the correlation between two sets of scores is corrected for attenuation, it is a direct index of the extent that the two instruments measure the same thing. The square of this is the common variance shared by the two measures. This leads to an approach for determining the effects of restrictive time limits on changes in the factor composition (and thus the validity) of different types of test materials. Alternative forms of a test can be constructed and administered to the same subjects on different days under different time limits. Assuming that previous studies have established the reliability of each test, the correlation between tests given under different time limits can be corrected for attenuation. The square of this result is then a measure of *shared common variance (SCV)*. A formula for obtaining this result is as follows:

(15-1)
$$SCV = \frac{r_{12}^2}{r_{11}r_{22}}$$

where r_{12} = PM correlation between scores in time limit 1 and scores in time limit 2

r_{11}, r_{22} = reliabilities of scores in the two time-limit conditions

An example of the use of Eq. (15-1) is where the reliability of scores under one time limit is .8, the reliability under a shorter time limit is .6, and the squared correlation between the two sets of scores is .48. In that case the *SCV* equals 1.0. Thus scores obtained under more restrictive time limits have the same factor composition as scores obtained under more generous time limits, but the former are more reliable.

To investigate changes in *SCV* as discussed above, one must be careful to counterbalance testing sessions so as to control for practice effects, and one must investigate each alternative form in each time-limit condition. Because of the labors of performing studies of these kinds, very few have been done. One of the most thorough studies of this kind was by Morrison (1960).

ONE-TRIAL MEASURES OF THE EFFECTS OF TIME LIMITS Computation of the *SCV*, as described above, is based on correlations among alternative forms administered under different time limits. Consequently, all subjects have to be administered a number of alternative forms. Proposals have been made for examining changes in factor structure because of varying time limits in terms of item statistics rather than in terms of correlations between alternative forms (these are discussed in detail by Gulliksen, 1950, and by Morrison, 1960). One such index can be developed through the following line of reasoning. A pure speed test could be defined as one in which (1) no subject has time to attempt all items and (2) all attempted items are correct. In other words, each subject attempts each item as he works through the test, and he makes correct responses on all items attempted up to the point that time is called. In this case there would be no attempted items that were not correct, and consequently the score for each person would equal the number of items attempted.

Logically, if a test is not a pure speed test, the above considerations will not hold exactly. If the test is a mixture of factors relating to power and speed, there will be some attempted items that are not correct. In this case the total number of incorrect responses given by each person can be decomposed in the following manner:

U = number of unattempted items

W = number of incorrect attempted items

X = total number of errors, $U + W$

A case in point would be where the individual attempts 30 items in a test containing 40 items, and of the 30 items attempted, three are responded to incorrectly, e.g., wrong answers on three arithmetic problems. In this case $U = 10$, $W = 3$, and $X = 13$.

To the extent that the variance of U is large with respect to variance of X, it could be argued that the test mainly concerns abilities relating to speed rather than abilities relating to power. Similarly, to the extent that the variance of W is large relative to the variance of X, it could be argued that the test mainly concerns abilities relating to power rather than abilities relating to speed. Considering the former possibility, the following index could be employed in experiments on the effects of different time limits on test performance:

(15-2)   Degree of speeding $= \dfrac{\sigma_U{}^2}{\sigma_X{}^2}$

One could develop more refined formulas by considering possible correlations between U and W, but Eq. (15-2) will serve to illustrate the logic of one-trial measures of the effects of speed. Formulas such as Eq. (15-2) could be employed with respect to data obtained from the following type of study. One test is administered to different samples of subjects under different time limits, and the degree of speeding is determined separately for each time period. To the extent that shorter time limits result in a higher index than do longer time limits, it could be argued that changes in time limits tend to alter the factor composition of scores. Also, for any one time limit considered separately, the size of the index could be considered a measure of the extent that scores relate to abilities concerning speed rather than to abilities concerning power.

One-trial indices of the effects of speed will not be discussed here in greater detail because they have rightly fallen into disrepute in recent years. They are appealing for practical reasons: they do not require the construction of alternative forms, and they do not require each group of subjects to take more than one test. Beyond these practical advantages, however, the one-trial measures have little to recommend them. They are founded on a number of unreasonable assumptions, the first of which is that the degree of speeding is intimately related to the number of unattempted items (U). In fact, the number of unattempted items is, in large measure, determined by the test instructions and the overall atmosphere in which the test is administered, regardless of the amount of time given to complete the test. Even if a very generous time limit is used for a power test, the experimenter can force the number of unattempted items to be large relative to the total number of errors simply by strongly warning the subjects to be sure to get all the answers correct as far as they go and not to guess when unsure. Conversely, even with a highly restrictive time limit applied to items of trivial difficulty, one can force a high ratio of incorrect attempted items W to total errors by strongly urging all subjects to answer all items in the allotted time, even if this requires wild guesses on some of the items.

Even if the basic assumptions of the one-trial formulas for the effects of speed were not arguable, the one-trial indices would still fail to provide some important information that is needed. Administering the same test to different groups under different time limits can produce direct information about effects on the mean, distribution shape, standard deviation, and reliability, but it cannot provide direct information about effects of time limits on the factor composition of scores. Investigations of factor composition necessarily are based on correlations of alternative forms (or the same test) administered to the same subjects under different time limits, which is the case with the SCV discussed previously.

TIMED-POWER TESTS   Here we shall begin to review the evidence regarding effects of speed on performance, first by discussing the effects of employing restrictive time limits on tests that are constructed under power conditions. Essentially, the issues concern the effects on psychometric properties of tests when testing time is varied as a function of the comfortable-time. As was mentioned previously, however, in most of the studies which have been conducted, no standard base (such as the comfortable-time) was employed. Instead, in most studies the experimenters have simply varied the time and examined effects of different time limits on performance. The evidence, then, must be considered circumstantial rather than direct. There is, however, a wealth of circumstantial evidence to indicate that *the comfortable-time can be decreased appreciably without seriously affecting any of the psychometric properties of tests.*

Examples of studies that support the above conclusion are reported by the following authors: Cronbach (1949), Kendall (1964), Lord (1956), Morrison (1960), Rimland (1960), Toops (1960), and Wesman (1960). Some studies have shown that doubling the usual time limit has little effect on performance, and other studies have shown that cutting the usual time limit in half has almost no effect. In some studies it has been found that even the mean performance is unaffected by cutting the usual time limit in half. Even in those cases where the mean was affected, the reliability tended to remain the same over broad ranges of time limits, e.g., time limits of 30, 40, and 50 minutes.

Obviously, there is a limit to the restrictive times that can be employed without affecting the reliability. For example, if the time limit were only one minute for a vocabulary test, the standard deviation of scores would be very small, and the reliability would be small also. The level at which time limits have a marked effect on the reliability has been surprisingly low in most studies, in comparison to the usual time limits employed for the tests and in comparison to the different time limits investigated.

Even in those studies where time limits were so restrictive as to materially influence the reliability, in most cases there was little evidence that the factor composition was materially influenced. An excellent study supporting this conclusion was performed by Morrison (1960). Even if restrictive time limits tend to increase or decrease the reliability, the reliable variance tends to relate to the same underlying factors, i.e., the *SCV* is high.

Not all of the evidence supports the above conclusions, as is shown in some of the studies summarized by Guilford (1954, pp. 366–370) and by Morrison (1960). In some cases the *SCV* was sufficiently low to indicate that somewhat different factors were being measured by tests given under different time limits. In some studies this may have been because the investigations concerned speed-difficulty tests rather than timed-power tests, i.e., the average p value of items under power conditions would be very high. Also, in many instances this may have been accounted for by the way items were ordered on the test. In many aptitude tests and achievement tests, there is a wide range of item difficulty, and the practice frequently is to order the items in terms of difficulty. Then the items at the beginning of the test are very easy, and the items near the end of the test are very difficult. By employing a very restrictive time limit for such a test, one could prevent most subjects from attempting more than half the items. Scores obtained under these conditions could then be compared with scores obtained from the same subjects on an alternative form of the test administered under a generous time limit. The SCV might be considerably less than 1.0, but that might be entirely because of the way items were ordered on the test. The second half of the items on such tests not only are more difficult than those in the first half, but also tend to measure different factors.

Easy items and difficult items often measure somewhat different factors, even when one would guess that they measured the same thing. For example, in the typical "quantitative" test employed along with a verbal test for the selection of college students, the easy items at the beginning of the test tend to measure numerical skills, but the difficult items near the end of the test tend to measure reasoning abilities. On some tests of spatial relations, the easy items at the beginning of the test tend to measure somewhat different spatial factors than those measured by the difficult items near the end of the test. In such cases it is no wonder that restrictive time limits affect the factor composition of scores. But that does not mean that speed, per se, introduces new factors of ability. What it means is that restrictive time limits force the subject to take a somewhat *different* test than would be taken if a more generous time limit were employed.

The SCV tends to remain high where items are *randomly* ordered on tests. In this case, even if the time limit is very restrictive, subjects still are taking the *same kind* of test as they would if a generous time limit were employed.

A good working rule is that, on a timed-power test, the comfortable-time can be cut by at least *one-third* without materially changing the standard deviation, reliability, or factor composition. It should be kept in mind that this rule applies to timed-power tests, ones that are constructed under power conditions. The definition of the comfortable-time also should be kept in mind—the amount of time required for 90 percent of the subjects to say that they have had ample time for completing the test. The rule applies better when the mean score in the comfortable-time is near the center of the effective range rather than near either extreme. That is the case in most tests constructed under power conditions (by methods discussed in Chapter Eight).

The above rule tends to hold because most subjects can perform effectively at a faster rate than their preferred rate. In many instances subjects are annoyed by having to work faster, and they frequently claim that restrictive time limits hurt their performance when that is not actually the case.

Since power tests are not grossly affected by mildly restrictive time limits (e.g., employing the comfortable-time rather than a more generous time limit), this offers an approach to a more efficient use of testing time. For example, this might permit one to give twice as many items on a multiple-choice achievement test, which in turn would permit a wider sampling of content. As another example, in basic research on human abilities, this might allow one to investigate more tests in a fixed amount of available testing time.

FACTORS MEASURED BY SPEED AND POWER TESTS One question to raise regarding effects of speed on factors of ability is whether the factors measured by power tests tend to be the same as those measured by speed tests. Since it can be concluded that moderately restrictive time limits on power tests do not markedly alter their psychometric properties, the question also can be phrased in terms of the factors typically measured by timed-power tests and pure speed tests. Regarding the latter type of test, the discussion in this section will be concerned only with tests composed of items of trivial difficulty. A later section will consider the psychometric properties of speed-difficulty tests, on which restrictive time limits are employed with items that range in p value from .8 to 1.0 when given under power conditions.

Although no general answer can be given to the question of differences in factor structure of power tests and speed tests, such tests tend to measure different factors. For example, speed tests concerning the production of simple words tend to measure a factor of verbal fluency, but power tests concerning the understanding of more difficult words tend to measure a factor of verbal comprehension. Simple items concerning perceptual judgment concern a factor of perceptual speed, but more difficult items concerning perceptual judgment tend to measure a factor of spatial visualization. And so it tends to be with the factors measured by the simple items on pure speed tests as contrasted with the factors measured by the moderately difficult items on pure power tests and timed-power tests. When the speed and power tests apparently concern the same types of mental operations (e.g., perceptual judgment), they typically correlate positively, but the SCV seldom is very high.

At the start of this section a question was raised regarding the interchangeability of speed of performance and goodness of performance. The question can now be rephrased as follows: Do items of trivial difficulty which are intended to measure the same thing as power items actually measure the same thing? The answer is that it depends on the type of ability being measured, but in general the two types of tests do not correlate highly. Thus the ability to perform very quickly on very simple problems is quite different from the ability to perform at a high level on difficult problems.

SPEED-DIFFICULTY TESTS   The issues regarding the effects of speed on performance would be simpler if all tests were either pure speed tests or power tests (including those with only moderately restrictive time limits). The issues become somewhat blurred, however, when the speed-difficulty type of test must be considered. The items in such tests are so easy that, without highly restrictive time limits, it would not be possible to obtain a highly reliable distribution of scores. With such items, it usually is necessary to employ a time limit that is only a small fraction of the comfortable-time. The author does not know of any studies directly relating to this point, but it is probably true that many speed difficulty tests are administered with less than one-quarter of the comfortable-time. Although previously it was stated with some assurance that the comfortable-time on timed-power tests can usually be cut by one-third without resulting in important changes in psychometric properties, it would not be safe to say that the time can be cut below one-half without having major changes occur.

Whereas considerable research has been done to compare pure speed tests with power tests (including timed-power tests), very little has been done to compare speed-difficulty tests with the former two. Logically one would expect speed-difficulty tests to be mixtures of the factors defined by pure speed tests and those defined by power tests, but that is mainly an untested hypothesis. If the hypothesis is correct, it may be that the mixture of factors in the speed-difficulty test varies with different time limits.

Perhaps the easiest way to escape the confusion caused by speed-difficulty tests is to use them less frequently. Because they are neither pure speed tests nor power tests, it is difficult to develop adequate psychometric theory for them. Also, in many cases they probably are not doing a good job of what they are intended to do. For practical reasons, they frequently are used to measure abilities that logically concern power rather than speed. For example, one sees numerous reasoning tests of this kind, such as items concerning letter series and number series. The average item is rather easy, and consequently one increases the difficulty by employing highly restrictive time limits. Items of these types are used because it is very time-consuming to make up large numbers of reasoning items that are moderately difficult when given in the comfortable-time. In most cases, however, it is doubtful that the speed-difficulty test measures exactly what the experimenter is trying to measure.

IMPLICATIONS FOR RESEARCH   Whether or not one wants to employ pure speed tests or power tests depends on the type of test. In most instances it is not desirable to use speed tests for measures that require content validity, e.g., standardized achievement tests. Most measures that require content validity are supposedly related to abilities concerning power rather than speed. Of course, there are exceptions, such as in classroom examinations for typing and shorthand.

It is with measures that require content validity that the most danger arises in placing restrictive time limits on power tests. For example, restrictive time limits on a classroom examination might lower the mean score. Changes in the mean, per se, are of only incidental importance in most measures that require predictive validity or construct validity. In a classroom examination, however, grades are based to some extent on the absolute score obtained by each student, e.g., the number of correct answers given to multiple-choice questions. Before giving an examination, the instructor may decide that anyone who gets fewer than half the items correct will fail the course. Then, to the extent that the number of test items permits ample time or causes students to work quickly, the mean score may be influenced, which in turn would determine the number of students who fail. In such cases, and in many other instances where measures require content validity, the intention is to test not speed of performance, but level of performance.

As was said previously, on most power tests, moderately restrictive time limits seldom materially influence the psychometric properties of tests. If anything is affected, however, it is most likely to be the mean score. Consequently one should be very careful in applying highly restrictive time limits on many measures that require content validity, particularly so with standardized achievement tests and classroom examinations. Even with such types of tests, however, it is safe to employ the comfortable-time, which frequently is less than half the total testing time required under pure power conditions.

With instruments used to predict specific criteria, the place of speed is a matter for research. In a particular instance, it may be that the abilities measured by pure speed tests are more predictive than the abilities measured by power tests, or vice versa. Also, with predictor instruments, it is an open question what effect there will be on validity of employing restrictive time limits on a power test. It might, for example, be found that a particular power test is more valid when the time limit is less than half the comfortable-time.

With measures that require construct validity, there are no simple rules to guide the experimenter in the choice of pure speed tests or power tests. Logically, which of these should be used is determined by the theory being investigated if the theory is specific enough to make the choice clear. If the choice is to employ power tests, it is safe to administer those tests at two-thirds of the comfortable-time. Testing time usually is at a premium in studies relating to construct validity, and consequently, even if there is a slight effect of employing a moderately restrictive time limit, it usually is more than offset by the practical advantages.

effects of guessing

An issue that occurs in many types of experiments in psychology is that of the effects of "guessing" on the statistical and psychometric properties of score distributions. This issue arises in any investigation where the subject is not free to respond in any way that he chooses but rather is required to select one response from a number of specified responses. The most obvious instance in which this occurs is in a multiple-choice test of ability, particularly so when subjects are required to attempt all items. Questions regarding the effects of guessing, however, are by no means restricted to multiple-choice tests of ability. Effects of guessing occur in many types of controlled experiments on learning, perception, and other topics. In a typical study of concept formation, the subject is shown a series of geometrical designs, half of which represent instances of a concept, and half of which do not represent instances of the concept. On each trial, then, the subject would have a 50-50 chance of being correct by guessing alone.

Another example involving a limited number of alternative responses occurs in certain types of studies of recognition thresholds. In the first phase of the study, one nonsense syllable is associated with a painful electric shock. Subjects are familiarized with a second nonsense syllable, but it is not associated with shock. In the visual recognition task, each syllable is shown for varying intervals of time, the intervals being gradually increased on each trial up to the point where the subject is correct on every trial. On each trial, the nonsense syllable appears in one of the four corners of a screen rather than in the center of the screen. Instead of being asked to state what he sees on each trial, the subject is asked to state the corner in which a syllable appears, regardless of what the syllable is. In this type of experiment, the subject has one chance in four of making the correct response on each trial by guessing alone.

Experimental procedures where guessing is a factor are employed in many different types of investigations, because they frequently allow one to investigate phenomena that would be difficult or impossible to investigate otherwise. Multiple-choice tests are used very widely, because they lend themselves to the measurement of many different traits and they have obvious practical advantages. In a study of concept formation, the subject must be asked to judge whether each stimulus does or does not fit the concept, and thus it is necessary to deal with only a limited number of alternative responses. In the study mentioned above concerning perception, the use of a multiple-choice procedure has some advantages over the use of a free-response procedure. For example, potentially it reduces response biases, such as the reluctance of subjects to verbalize a syllable that has been associated with shock, regardless of whether or not they actually see it.

Because of the obvious advantages of multiple-choice procedures in so many types of experiments, these procedures probably will continue to be used. Inherent in such procedures, however, is the problem of dealing with the effects of chance success (guessing).

A MODEL FOR RANDOM RESPONSES   Here we shall discuss a simple model for predicting effects of random responses (guesses) on the psychometric properties of score distributions. The model is based on the primary assumption that, in multiple-choice tasks, the probability of making a correct response on each trial (or test item) is either 1.0 or the reciprocal of the number of available choices. On an intuitive level, this means that the subject either makes the correct response on each trial with perfect certainty or guesses blindly. In the latter case, the a priori probability of a correct response would equal $1/A$, where A is the number of available choices. In a binary-choice test (e.g., a true-false test), the probability would be .5; in a test having four alternative answers for each question, the probability would be .25.

For reasons that will be discussed later, the above assumptions are seldom entirely realistic, and consequently predictions based on them seldom are precisely correct. Such predictions are, however, almost always correct with regard to the *direction* of effects on scores because of the use of multiple-choice procedures. For example, certain equations derivable from the above assumptions lead to predictions of the change in reliability expected if the number of alternative responses (A) is increased or decreased by any particular amount. Although such predictions are not borne out exactly, the general trend of results is predicted.

The predictions discussed here follow from the above assumptions. Later we shall discuss how realistic the assumptions are in particular kinds of tests and experimental procedures.

A special set of symbols will prove useful in the discussion of the model for random responses:

K = total number of test items

R = number of correct or "right" responses

W = number of incorrect or "wrong" responses

T = number of items attempted, $R + W$

A = number of alternatives for each item

R_c = number of items for a person for which probability of correct response is 1.0 rather than $1/A$

All the terms in the list except the last one are obvious—some explanations are required regarding the meaning of R_c. It can be thought of as the score a subject would obtain on a particular test if guessing played no part. Although the analogy is somewhat misleading, one can also think of R as the score a subject receives on a multiple-choice test, and R_c can be thought of as the score that a subject would receive on the same items cast in a free-response (fill-in) format. It also is useful to think of R_c as representing what the subject "really knows" and R as the score obtained when there is some part played by guessing.

Of course, it would be highly desirable to measure R_c directly, but that is not possible. All that can be done is to estimate R_c from the observable variables. The logic for that is as follows. It should be obvious that the number of observed correct scores R can be constituted as follows:

(15-3)
$$R = R_c + p(T - R_c)$$

where $p = 1/A$

The meaning of Eq. (15-3) can be clarified by a hypothetical case. In working through a test, the subject marks the items that he "really knows" (R_c). Then he attempts additional items ($T - R_c$). If all subjects attempt all items, the number of additional attempted items would be $K - R_c$. On each of those "guessed" items, the subject has a fixed probability p of making a correct response, which is $1/A$. The probability of making an incorrect response q equals $1 - p$, or $A - 1$ divided by A.

The following manipulations of Eq. (15-3) will show how an estimate of R_c is obtained:

$$R = R_c + pT - pR_c$$
$$= R_c - pR_c + pT$$
$$= R_c(1 - p) + pT$$

(15-4)
$$= qR_c + pT$$
$$qR_c = R - pT$$
$$R_c = \frac{R - pT}{q}$$

Equation (15-4) could be used directly to obtain estimates of R_c, but further manipulations of the equation lead to simpler computational approaches and provide some insights into the nature of the problem of estimation. Since the total number of items attempted (T) equals the total correct (R) plus the total incorrect (W), Eq. (15-4) can be transformed in the following steps:

$$R_c = \frac{R - p(R + W)}{q}$$

$$= \frac{R - pR - pW}{q}$$

$$= \frac{R(1 - p) - pW}{q}$$

$$= \frac{qR - pW}{q}$$

$$= R - \left(\frac{p}{q}\right) W$$

Examination of the ratio of p to q in terms of the numbers of alternative responses shows that the above equation can be expressed as follows:

(15-5) $\quad R_c = R - \dfrac{W}{A - 1}$

Equation (15-5) is the well-known *correction for guessing*. The model has led to the conclusion that one obtains an estimate of R_c by subtracting, from the actual number correct R, a fraction of the number of the attempted but incorrect responses W. Thus the model leads to the conclusion that the particular fraction equals the reciprocal of the number of alternatives minus 1.

An example of how Eq. (15-5) is applied can be given in the situation where (1) there are four alternatives for each question, (2) the subject attempts 32 items out of, say, 40, and (3) 20 of the responses are correct and 12 are incorrect. The computations would be as follows:

$$R_c = 20 - 12/3$$

$$R_c = 16$$

The estimate is that the subject "really knows" the answers to 16 items. Of course, it is something of a misnomer to refer to Eq. (15-5) as a "correction" for guessing, because all that it can do is *estimate* the effects of guessing. Whether or not it is an unbiased estimate depends on the correctness of the assumptions in the model. How well Eq. (15-5) actually estimates the effects of guessing will be considered later.

EFFECTS OF GUESSING ON TEST PARAMETERS   Here we shall continue to follow the logic of the model discussed above and examine some of

the effects of guessing on the psychometric properties of score distributions. First, it is obvious that if subjects do guess when in doubt, or
are forced to guess by the nature of the instructions, the estimate
is that the mean score will increase. The expected amount of the increase
is obtained by subtracting R_c from R.

A reinspection of Eq. (15-5) makes it obvious that the difference
between R_c and R for different people is directly related to W, the
number of attempted but incorrect responses. In other words, Eq. (15-5)
is based on the principle that the amount of guessing done by different
people is directly related to the number of W responses.

In the case where all subjects attempt all items, the expected gain
from guessing is inversely related to R_c. People who know the least guess
the most, and consequently they stand to gain most from guessing. Figure
15-1 shows the expected relationship between R and R_c for a test with

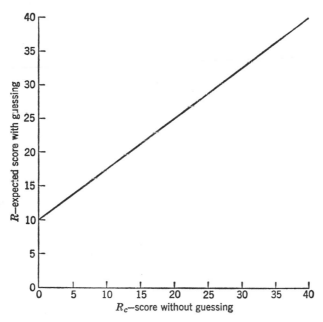

figure 15-1 *Expected scores when guessing is a factor* (R) *as a function of
scores when guessing is not a factor* (R_c). *The figure assumes that R is based
on a multiple-choice test with four alternatives for each item and that each
subject attempts all items.*

40 items and four alternatives for each item. People who "actually know"
the answers to all 40 items are expected to obtain a score of 40. People
who "actually know" the answers to none of the items are expected to
obtain a score of 10, purely from guessing. The fact that R_c and R are
linearly related is evidenced in Figure 15-1 by the straight line of relationship between the end points of R_c.

Regardless of the estimated effects of guessing in the general case, there obviously are individual differences in the effects of guessing. because of the amount of guessing. Also, for individuals who have the same R and W scores, the actual effects of guessing vary in terms of chance. If two people each guess at the answers for 10 true-false items, one person may get as many as 9 correct, and the other person may get only 1 correct. In a model for blind guessing, it is reasonable to assume that probabilities of correctly guessing on different items are independent, in which case the expected variance of the distribution of effects of guessing can be determined from the binomial theorem:

(15-6) $$\sigma_{eg}^2 = npq$$

where n = number of guesses made $(T - R_c)$

$\quad p$ = probability of making correct response by guessing $1/A$

$\quad q$ = probability of making incorrect response by guessing $(A - 1)/A$

$\quad \sigma_{eg}^2$ = expected variance of $R - R_c$ for people who guess on n items

The meaning of Eq. (15-6) can be illustrated by the hypothetical case depicted in Figure 15-1, in which there are 40 items, each item has four alternative answers, and R_c ranges from zero to 40. Also, in that example, each person is forced to respond to each item $(T = K)$. Persons who do not really know the answers to any of the items (for whom R_c is zero) guess on all items. Then, in Eq. (15-6), n is 40, p is .25, and q is .75. The expected variance of correct scores R is then 7.5 for that particular group of people, and the expected standard deviation of R for that group of people is the square root of 7.5 (2.74).

Persons who know the answers to all items do not guess on any of them. Then n is zero, the variance of actual scores R because of guessing is zero, and all persons in that group have the same score on R as on R_c. Since σ_{eg}^2 is a linear function of n (p and q being constant in a particular type of test), the amount of variance because of guessing is a linear function of the number of items on which subjects guess. In the case where subjects are required to respond to all items, the variance of errors because of guessing decreases linearly with R_c. The effect expected in this situation is illustrated in Figure 15-2.

What Figure 15-2 illustrates is the fact that, when subjects are required to attempt all items, the variance of errors because of guessing is largest for persons who know the least, and it steadily decreases with increasing levels of R_c. It should be kept in mind that these results hold exactly only for those situations where subjects are required to attempt all items, as with most multiple-choice methods used in controlled experiments and most measures of individual differences used in basic research. In some applied uses of measures of human ability, however, subjects are urged not to guess when they are unsure of the correct answer. These cases will be discussed later.

The variance of errors because of guessing represents a component of measurement error in addition to that of the other types of measurement error inherent in the particular measurement tool. As was shown in Figure 15-2, the amount of measurement error (unreliability) because of guessing is a decreasing function of actual ability. Then guessing serves not only to increase the scores more for people of low ability as compared to people of high ability, but also to make the scores of the former type of people less reliable. Since Eq. (15-6) involves the number of items on which guesses are made n, it is only of theoretical interest. Estimates of the variance of scores because of guessing

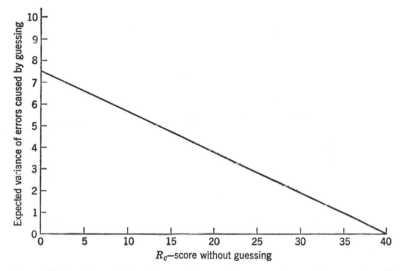

figure 15-2 *Expected variance of errors because of guessing as a function of R_c. The figure assumes that there are four alternatives for each item on the multiple-choice test and that each subject attempts all items.*

can, however, be obtained from actual data. Since p and q are known in any instance, all that is required is an estimate of n. By definition, n equals the total number of attempted items T minus the score that would be obtained if guessing were not involved R_c:

(15-7) $n = T - R_c$

Equation (15-5) can be used to estimate R_c. Then it is permissible to write the following equation for n:

$$n = T - \left(R - \frac{W}{A - 1} \right)$$

$$= T - R + \frac{W}{A - 1}$$

Since by definition $T - R$ equals the number of attempted but incorrect responses, it is permissible to rewrite the above equation as follows:

(15-8) $$n = W + \frac{W}{A - 1}$$

Equation (15-8) is an estimate of the number of items on which the individual guesses (n). When that is multiplied by the product of p and q, an estimate is obtained of the amount of measurement error because of guessing for people with the same number of attempted but incorrect responses W. This is stated in the form of an equation as follows:

(15-9) $$\sigma_{eg}^2 = pq\left(W + \frac{W}{A - 1}\right)$$

The use of Eq. (15-9) can be illustrated in the case where (1) a large number of people all have W scores of 8, (2) there are five alternatives for each item, and (3) all subjects have the same R_c score. The computations would be as follows:

$$\sigma_{eg}^2 = (.2)(.8)(8 + \tfrac{8}{4})$$
$$= (.16)(10)$$
$$\sigma_{eg}^2 = 1.6$$

Thus, in the above example, even though all subjects "know" the same amount, there is a variance of 1.6 in actual scores because of guessing.

EFFECTS ON OVERALL RELIABILITY   If a set of scores x had no error because of guessing (σ_{eg}^2), the variance of those scores could be depicted as follows:

$$\sigma_x^2 = \sigma_t^2 + \sigma_e^2$$

There would be some variance σ_e^2 resulting from errors because of factors other than guessing, but there would be no variance σ_{eg}^2 because of errors of guessing. Then if there were an opportunity for guessing and σ_{eg}^2 were not zero, σ_{eg}^2 would add to the variance attributable to true scores and errors because of factors other than guessing:

$$\sigma_{x'}^2 = \sigma_t^2 + \sigma_e^2 + \sigma_{eg}^2 + ?$$
$$= \sigma_x^2 + \sigma_{eg}^2 + ?$$

where $x' =$ scores in which guessing is a factor

In the foregoing expression, the question marks raise the issue of whether or not there would be other terms required, which is an issue that will be returned to later. First let us see how σ_{eg}^2 is estimated.

Equation (15-9) provides an estimate of σ_{eg}^2 for subjects with a constant number of W scores. What is needed for the formulation above is the *typical* error variance because of guessing for the group as a whole. This would be analogous to the squared standard error of measurement

the content areas

$\sigma_e{}^2$, which is the typical error variance for subjects as a group, regardless of whether or not all subjects have the same standard error. A modification of Eq. (15-9) leads to an estimate of the typical error variance because of guessing. It is obtained by replacing W with the average number of attempted but incorrect items $\bar{W}$ for all the subjects in an investigation:

(15-10) $$\sigma_{eg}{}^2 = pq \left(\bar{W} + \frac{\bar{W}}{A-1} \right)$$

Equation (15-10) could be applied to the test results obtained from any group of subjects. Imagine that 200 subjects have been administered a multiple-choice test and the subjects vary considerably in ability. There are 40 test items and five alternative answers for each item. The other item of information needed to compute $\sigma_{eg}{}^2$ is the average number of attempted but incorrect responses $\bar{W}$, which, let us say, is 8. The $\sigma_{eg}{}^2$ would be 1.6, which is the predicted typical error variance because of guessing for the subjects as a group. Some further considerations will indicate how Eq. (15-10) provides a means of estimating the effects of guessing on the overall test reliability.

Now we shall look at what was missing from the foregoing expression for the components of reliable and error variance in a set of scores where guessing is a factor. The complete equation is as follows:

(15-11) $$\sigma_{x'}{}^2 = \sigma_x{}^2 + \sigma_{eg}{}^2 + \sigma_g{}^2 + 2r_{gx}\sigma_g\sigma_x$$

where $\sigma_g{}^2$ = variance of expected score increments (gains) because of differences in amounts of guessing

r_{gx} = correlation of expected increments g with scores x on test where guessing is not a factor

An expected increment, or gain g, equals R minus the estimate of R_c. If there are individual differences in amount of guessing, as is usually the case, there are individual differences in the expected gains from guessing. Then $\sigma_g{}^2$ adds a *reliable* portion of variance to scores on x', which must be included in Eq. (15-11) for the components of variance in x'. The last term on the right of Eq. (15-11) is necessary because gains from guessing are likely to correlate with scores on x. Following from Eq. (15-11), one could develop general formulas for the relative reliabilities of tests with and without errors because of guessing. Although the general formulas are logically straightforward, they are complex in terms of details. Rather than go into those complexities, let us see what happens in an important special case. Where all persons attempted all items on x', there would be a perfect negative correlation between g and x, in which case Eq. (15-11) would reduce to the following expression:

(15-12) $$\sigma_{x'}{}^2 = \sigma_x{}^2 + \sigma_{eg}{}^2 + \sigma_g{}^2 - 2\sigma_g\sigma_x$$

contingent variables   **583**

An important point in these developments is that the variance of expected numbers of guesses on x' is the same as the variance of x. If there are K items on test x, the amount of guessing on x' for any particular subject should equal $K - x$ (which previously was symbolized as n). Then n should correlate -1.00 with x, and their standard deviations should be the same. The expected gain from guessing g equals pn, where p is the reciprocal of the number of alternative answers to items on x'. Then the standard deviation of g equals $p\sigma_n$. More important, $\sigma_g = p\sigma_x$, which leads to the following transformations of Eq. (15-12):

$$\sigma_{x'}{}^2 = \sigma_x{}^2 + \sigma_{eg}{}^2 + p^2\sigma_x{}^2 - 2p\sigma_x{}^2$$

(15-13)
$$= \sigma_x{}^2 + \sigma_{eg}{}^2 + \sigma_x{}^2(p^2 - 2p)$$
$$= \sigma_x{}^2(1 - 2p + p^2) + \sigma_{eg}{}^2$$
$$= \sigma_x{}^2(1 - p)^2 + \sigma_{eg}{}^2$$
$$= q^2\sigma_x{}^2 + \sigma_{eg}{}^2$$

Equation (15-13) opens the possibility of developing many formulas to estimate the effects of guessing on reliability and other parameters of score distributions (in those cases where all subjects attempt all items). Let us see how the reliability of x (with no error because of guessing) can be estimated from the reliability of a test x' where guessing is a factor. The reliability of x could be expressed as follows:

$$r_{xx} = 1 - \frac{\sigma_e{}^2}{\sigma_x{}^2}$$

The foregoing expression is hypothetical, because σ_e and σ_x are not known in the illustrative problem. First, let us see how σ_e can be estimated. It is the error variance of x, which is *not* the same as the error variance $\sigma_{e'}$ of x'. The latter equals $\sigma_e + \sigma_{eg}$; consequently $\sigma_e = \sigma_{e'} - \sigma_{eg}$. Next, σ_x is estimated by the following transformation of Eq. (15-13):

$$\sigma_{x'}{}^2 = q^2\sigma_x{}^2 + \sigma_{eg}{}^2$$

(15-14)
$$\sigma_x{}^2 = \frac{\sigma_{x'}{}^2 - \sigma_{eg}{}^2}{q^2}$$

Then the reliability of x can be estimated from parameters of x' as follows:

(15-15) $\quad r_{xx} = 1 - \dfrac{q^2(\sigma_{e'}{}^2 - \sigma_{eg}{}^2)}{\sigma_{x'}{}^2 - \sigma_{eg}{}^2}$

To employ Eq. (15-15), one must first obtain the reliability of x'. That is subtracted from 1.0, and the result is multiplied by $\sigma_{x'}{}^2$, which gives $\sigma_{e'}{}^2$. Then $\sigma_{eg}{}^2$ would be obtained from Eq. (15-10). The reciprocal of the number of alternatives on x' equals p, and $1 - p = q$. All that is left is to include the variance of x' in the formula, and an estimate is obtained of the reliability in the situation in which guessing is not a factor. This offers a general approach to investigating the losses in reliability because of guessing. A typical finding on a 40-item test with five alternatives for each item is that the reliability of scores x' is .80 and the reliability of x is .85. The estimate then is that measurement error because of guessing reduces the reliability by .05.

USE OF CORRECTIONS FOR GUESSING Although the model for random guessing discussed in the previous chapter leads to many important deductions about effects of guessing, it is proper to inquire about the accuracy of predictions from the model. Unfortunately, most of the evidence in this regard comes from a domain of data for which the model logically should be least accurate, that of aptitude and achievement testing in education. Many of the items on such tests concern the recognition of facts or simple principles, as in the following item:

The speed of sound is affected by

1 the loudness of the sound at its source

2 the medium in which it travels

3 the frequency, or pitch, of the sound

4 phases of the moon

To illustrate the nature of guessing on educational tests, a poor alternative was purposely included in the above item. Even a student who had no idea that 2 is the correct answer would be likely to recognize that alternative 4 is probably not the correct answer. In that case the student would rule out alternative 4 and make a wild guess among the remaining alternatives if he chose to guess under instructions that discourage guessing. Then, in effect, there are not four alternatives from which he guesses, but only three. Another student may be slightly better acquainted with the particular issue, and in addition to ruling out alternative 4, knows enough to rule out alternative 3 also. Then, if he guesses blindly, his chances of getting a correct answer would be .5 rather than the probability of .25 which would follow from the model for blind guessing.

Because in most educational tests there is some opportunity for "narrowing" alternatives before guessing, this tends to make the correction for guessing [Eq. (15-5)] an *underestimate* of the actual effects of guessing (evidence summarized by Price, 1964). One determines the amount of correction by dividing the number of attempted but incorrect responses W by the number of alternative answers minus 1 ($A - 1$).

Thus when A is large, the amount of correction is small, and vice versa when A is small. Because of the narrowing of alternatives before guessing, in effect the actual number of alternatives before guessing is smaller than that employed in the correction for guessing. Consequently there is a tendency in educational tests for the correction not to subtract enough.

In contrast to the effects of the narrowing of alternatives, the use of "misleads" as alternatives tends to make the correction for guessing [Eq. (15-5)] *overestimate* the effects of guessing. A mislead is a highly plausible but incorrect alternative. In some instances those misleads are so attractive that they "trap" even very knowledgeable students. An example of such a mislead would be in an item concerning a principle in physics that had been accepted as correct for many years but had recently been supplanted by a new principle. Then even some of the most knowledgeable students with regard to physics might be trapped by the mislead. If there are many such misleads on a test, the number of W responses is not directly related to the actual amount of guessing. A student may make a strenuous effort not to guess when in doubt, but because of misleads, make many W responses. It can be argued that it is poor practice to include such highly plausible misleads, and good methods of test construction tend to weed them out. Rather than employ highly plausible misleads, it is better to compose the alternatives so that they all sound plausible to the student who knows very little about the particular issue, but only one of them is plausible to the student who is quite knowledgeable about the issue. To the extent that there are misleads, however, the correction for guessing tends to over-correct.

The weight of the evidence (summarized by Price, 1964) is that the correction for guessing generally tends to undercorrect rather than overcorrect. This is because most tests have few highly plausible misleads, but there are ample opportunities for narrowing alternatives before guessing.

Because of the above considerations, it is appropriate to ask whether or not the correction for guessing should be used in practice. The choice to use the formula or not depends, among other things, on the nature of the test instructions. If subjects are instructed to attempt every item and they do so, in most cases there is no reason to make the correction for guessing. In that case W has a perfect negative correlation with R, and consequently corrected scores correlate perfectly with obtained scores. Then, for purposes of correlational analysis, obtained scores and corrected scores would produce identical results. In the analysis of the results of some types of controlled experiments, however, it might make important differences to use corrected scores rather than obtained scores. This would be the case, for example, in comparing the means of two differently treated groups. If the mean score for one group is high, the correction would tend to lower that mean only slightly. If the mean score for the other group is near the middle of the score range, the correction would tend to lower the mean of that group considerably. The correction would tend to pull the two means further apart, which would influence the interpretation of results.

In most tests of ability employed in basic research and in most measures employed in controlled experiments, it usually is preferable to instruct all subjects to attempt all items even if that requires some blind guessing. On some types of educational tests, however, there are two major reasons for not instructing all subjects to attempt all items. First, this tends to introduce some unreliability into test scores. The difference in reliability under instructions to attempt all items and under instructions to not guess tends to be no more than about .03 or .04 in the typical study (evidence summarized by Price, 1964). For reasons which were discussed in Chapter Seven, such small differences in reliability might be important on educational tests, but they would not be important in most instruments used in basic research. Also, for practical purposes, it frequently is better to increase the reliability by adding items rather than to incur the side effects of not having students attempt all items (a matter which will be discussed later).

A second major reason for not instructing all students to attempt all items on educational tests is that it might lead to poor attitudes on the part of students. It can be argued that, since students are not taught to guess blindly in daily schoolwork, but rather are taught to investigate facts and "think out" unsolved problems, forced guessing on multiple-choice tests would generate poor intellectual habits. The author personally considers it doubtful that multiple-choice tests have such far-reaching effects on the minds of students. Students may react somewhat negatively to guess-instructions *while taking a test*, but it is doubtful that study habits and thinking habits are materially influenced.

There are a number of major problems with employing instructions not to guess. First, it is hard to frame such instructions in a manner that students can understand and in a manner that does not actually penalize some students. The student frequently is told that it will not pay him to guess when in doubt, but usually that is not true. Students may be told that they will be penalized for guessing (e.g., the correction for guessing will be employed), but since most students would find the nature of the penalty too difficult to understand, no explanation of the penalty usually is given. Thus the penalty stands only as a shadowy threat, which may do more to disturb students than if they were forced to attempt all items.

A second major problem with the use of instructions that discourage guessing is that such instructions are responded to differently by different students. There are reliable individual differences in amount of guessing even when all students are urged not to guess. Partly this is because there are degrees of guessing, ranging from blind guessing to answering a question on the basis of partial knowledge. Thus the meaning of "guessing" is open to differences in interpretation by different students. Individual differences in the tendency to guess relate more to personality characteristics than to intelligence and knowledge of the particular subject matter (Price, 1964). Consequently individual differences in guessing usually serve to change the factor composition somewhat from that which would be obtained if all students were required to attempt all items. Thus, per unit of reliable variance, the latter type of instruction produces better results than do instructions that discourage guessing.

If instructions that discourage guessing are used, a decision must be made about using corrections for guessing. For reasons discussed previously, the correction based on a model for blind guessing is not highly precise, but the alternative of making no correction at all also poses difficulties. A very conscientious student might lower his score appreciably by taking too seriously the instructions not to guess. Other formulas have been proposed to correct for guessing (summarized by Price, 1964), but these tend to be no more precise in the general case than is the formula based on the model for blind guessing. Also, the models underlying these other corrections for guessing do not have the same power of explanation or practical advantages as afforded by the model for blind guessing.

The above considerations make it difficult to find an entirely satisfactory solution to the problem of correcting for guessing when instructions discourage blind guessing. Until a better solution is found, it probably is best to make the correction for guessing based on the model for blind guessing. The scores corrected for guessing typically have the same reliability as uncorrected scores on the same test, but there is considerable evidence that the predictive validity of the corrected scores is higher by about .03 (Guilford, 1954; Lord, 1963; Price, 1964). Unless there is some good reason, however, to employ instructions that discourage guessing, it is better to require all subjects to attempt all items. This is feasible in nearly all measures used in basic research, and in the author's opinion, it also is feasible with most educational tests.

USE OF THE MODEL FOR THE ESTIMATION OF TEST PARAMETERS   Even if the model for blind guessing leads to only moderately precise corrections for guessing, that does not necessarily destroy its general usefulness for predicting the effects of guessing on test reliability and other important psychometric properties of score distributions. We shall examine some of the evidence regarding how effectively the model for blind guessing is used for those purposes.

In a number of previous points in this book, it has been necessary to make a distinction between the possible score range and the *effective* score range. If the range is defined as the highest score minus the lowest score, the possible score range on a dichotomously scored test equals the number of test items. Of course, in any particular use of a test, it is not likely that scores will be so diverse as to fill up that range, but at least it is possible to have a range equal to the number of items. When guessing is a factor, however, it is necessary to think about an effective score range rather than a possible score range.

The effective score range is easily defined in the case where all subjects attempt all items. In that case the expected lower bound of the effective range equals the number of test items multiplied by the probability of guessing correctly by chance. Thus, on a 40-item test with four alternatives for each item, logically the effective score range is from scores of 10 to 40. If the model for blind guessing is correct, students who make scores of 10 "actually know" the answers to none of the questions, and consequently they guess on them all. Then it follows that scores of less than 10 occur only by chance. As a result of the variance of errors because of guessing (σ_{eg}^2), blind guessing would permit some scores to range below 10. If the model is accurate, however, the variance of scores below the chance level should be entirely because of chance, and consequently the scores should be totally unreliable. Although there is very little evidence to support the claim, this probably is the case with many types of measures that logically fit the model for blind guessing, e.g., in the use of multiple-choice procedures in studies of learning and perception. This is not always the case, however, in the use of educational tests. It has been found (Cliff, 1958) that in some instances scores below the chance level actually are not entirely because of chance. In such instances scores below the chance level on one test correlate significantly with scores below chance level on an alternative form. What this indicates is that, with some types of tests, the model for blind guessing leads to an underestimate of the effective score range.

Regardless of whether or not all subjects attempt all items, the effective score range can be discussed in terms of scores corrected for guessing R_c. The effective range of the corrected scores should equal the possible range of scores, the number of test items. Then one does not expect to find corrected scores below zero, and one should obtain negative corrected scores only as a result of the variance of errors because of guessing. In some instances, particularly in educational tests, this does not always occur, which is another form of evidence for the fact that the model for blind guessing sometimes leads to a small underestimate of the effective score range.

The presence of some reliable variance in scores below the estimated effective score range is probably because of several factors. First, this may be because of a highly restrictive time limit, a matter that will be discussed in a later section. Second, it probably occurs only for students who are low in ability and take very seriously the instructions not to guess. Third, even with such students, reliable variance below the predicted effective score range probably occurs only in those cases where there is not much opportunity for narrowing alternatives before guessing, but where there are highly plausible misleads for some of the items.

Previously some important deductions regarding the effects of guessing on test reliability were shown to follow from the model for blind guessing. Are those predictions accurate? Attempts have been made to answer the question by comparing the psychometric properties of multiple-choice tests with the psychometric properties of the same tests when presented in the form of completion (free-response) items. For example, subjects can be asked either to write in the correct solution to an algebraic problem or to select the correct answer from a number of alternative answers. If it is true that free-response tests are free from measurement error because of guessing, Eq. (15-15) should lead to predictions of the increase in reliability in going from a multiple-choice test to a free-response test. The evidence (Plumlee, 1952) is that Eq. (15-15) leads to an overestimate of the gain in reliability in that case. In other words, the free-response test is not as reliable as predicted, or looking at it the other way, the multiple-choice test is more reliable than predicted. The exact degree to which Eq. (15-15) overestimates in that case is not known, and it probably depends somewhat on the type of test. The available evidence suggests that the actual gain in reliability is between one-half and two-thirds that predicted by Eq. (15-15).

The above type of evidence would seem to suggest that the model based on blind guessing leads to poor estimates of the effects of guessing on test reliability, but that is not necessarily the case. The flaw in that line of reasoning is a hidden premise that the multiple-choice test is only a less reliable cousin of the free-response test. Actually, the model for blind guessing is not intended to estimate relations between a multiple-choice test and a free-response test of the same attribute. It is intended to estimate relations between a test with a particular number of alternatives for each item and a hypothetical test with an infinite number of alternatives for each item.

A free-response test is not the same as a test with an infinite number of alternative answers. Actually, free-response tests have some sources of measurement error that are not present in multiple-choice tests. Good multiple-choice items serve to "aim" knowledgeable students toward the correct answer. Items that are quite clear when presented in multiple-choice form sometimes are unclear when presented in free-response form. For example, the free-response form of an item is "An important product of Bolivia is ———." In the multiple-choice form, the "stem" of the item is followed by the names of four mining products—coal, tin, diamonds, and lead. When the question is presented in the multiple-choice form, all students will understand it, and knowledgeable students will know that the correct answer is "tin." If the same students were presented with the free-response item instead of the multiple-choice item, there would be some confusion regarding the meaning of the word "product." Students would wonder whether the term referred to farm products, manufacturing products, mining products, or some other type of product. The confusion in that regard would introduce a source of measurement error in the free-response form that would be present to a lesser degree in the multiple-choice form. Then, even if there is some measurement error in the multiple-choice form because of guessing, there is a different type of measurement error in the free-response form because of confusion. For this reason, Eq. (15-15) leads to an overestimate of the gain in reliability when going from one type of test to the other.

An actual test of the predictiveness of Eq. (15-15) relates to the concept of a test with an infinite number of alternatives. Of course, an infinite number of alternatives is only a handy fiction, but it is possible to investigate the extent to which the model for blind guessing predicts differences in reliability for different numbers of alternative answers to the same items. For example, if one of the incorrect alternatives is randomly removed from items having five alternatives, what would be the relative reliabilities of the four-alternative and five-alternative tests? Studies of this kind have been undertaken, and it has been found that reliability grows as a function of the number of alternative responses. As far as the author knows, however, such studies have not examined the predictiveness of changes in reliability following from the model for blind guessing.

How to estimate the influence on test reliability of varying the numbers of alternative responses can be seen by a reinspection of Eq. (15-8) for estimating the number of items on which subjects guess. Theoretically, that quantity n should remain the same regardless of the number of alternative answers, this being particularly so in the case where all subjects attempt all items. If a person guesses when there are four alternative answers for an item, logically he is expected to guess when there are five alternative answers for the item. Under the assumptions of the model for blind guessing, what would change would be the probability of selecting the correct alternative. Then, in Eq. (15-10) for σ_{eg}^2, only p and q would vary with changes in the number of alternative responses, and σ_{eg}^2 would decrease in a predictable manner with increases in the number of alternative responses. These assumptions are unreasonable with respect to the responses of each subject to each item, but they may be very reasonable with respect to the average responses of a group of subjects to a group of items.

By virtue of the predictable changes in σ_{eg}^2, there also are predictable changes in overall reliability as a function of different numbers of alternative responses. Not enough research has been done to determine how accurate such predictions are, which leaves open an important field of investigation.

SPEED TESTS   All the previous comments in this section regarding effects of guessing apply to power tests and power tests given under moderately restrictive time limits. On pure speed tests, the intention is for subjects to make correct responses as far as they can go until time is called. In that ideal situation, there would be no attempted but incorrect responses W, and according to the logic of the model for blind guessing, there would be no evidence of guessing and no correction to make. In many instances, however, there are appreciable numbers of W responses, which raises questions about guessing.

On pure speed tests, the burden of preventing appreciable numbers of W responses rests on the test instructions. Subjects must be warned that they will be penalized for guessing, but as was discussed previously, it is difficult to give a reasonable explanation of the nature of the penalty. Also, there are systematic individual differences in the way that subjects interpret and respond to such instructions.

In some instances it actually would behoove subjects to ignore instructions not to guess, particularly subjects who are very low in ability. This can be illustrated with speed items like the following:

wH6¢le ——— wH6¢le

'r4ItY ——— 'r4ItY

+glip? ——— +Glip?

The above items relate to the factor of *perceptual speed*, which is useful for, among other things, the selection of filing clerks. On each item, the subject makes a check mark in the space between the two letter groups if they are the same and leaves the space blank if the two letter groups are different in any way. Even under the usual instructions not to guess, it is obvious that some W responses would be given. If a subject were very low in perceptual speed, it would probably benefit him to hurriedly mark every item. If there actually were no penalty for guessing (e.g., if the correction for guessing were not employed), that strategy would, in most cases, give the person a score near the mean of the distribution rather than on the bottom tail of the distribution.

One cannot handle problems arising from guessing on speed tests by having all subjects attempt all items, because speed tests are standardized so that the average subject has time to attempt only about half the items. If many W responses are given in a particular type of speed test, it is wise to make the correction for guessing [Eq. (15-5)]. Also, in that case the model for blind guessing will specify the approximate effects of guessing on the psychometric properties of the instrument.

Whenever possible, speed items should be in a free-response format or in some other form that discourages guessing. An example of a speed item in free-response form is an arithmetic item on a test concerning the factor of numerical computation. The subject fills in the correct answer rather than marking one of a number of alternative answers. If it is not practical to employ free-response items, one can discourage guessing by having a relatively large number of alternatives rather than only two alternatives such as illustrated previously for marking or not marking pairs of letter groupings. One could do this with pairs of letter groupings, for example, by making one of the letters in the second grouping different from that in the first. Then either the subject would be required to mark the letter in the second grouping that is different from that in the first grouping or he would be required to write the "different" letter in a space provided for that purpose.

If a type of item that greatly restricts W responses is not employed, guessing can be a larger problem on speed tests than it is on power tests. In that case the reliability and factor composition of the scores depend too much on the test instructions and on individual differences in test-taking strategies.

response styles

Another important class of contingent variables concerns response styles, which also are frequently referred to as response sets and test-taking habits. As the term will be employed here, a *response style* is (1) a reliable source of variance in individual differences which (2) is an artifactual product of measurement methods and (3) is at least partially independent of the trait which the measurement methods are intended to measure. A careful look at the components of this definition will be necessary to clarify what is meant by response styles.

To illustrate the components of the definition above, an example of a simple type of response style will be used—the tendency to guess on multiple-choice tests when unsure. First, this tendency qualifies as a response style only if there are reliable individual differences in this respect. One could determine this, for example, by estimating the number of items on which subjects guess on alternative forms of tests [by Eq. (15-8)]. If the estimated guessing scores on the alternative forms correlate substantially, the tendency to guess is reliable, and thus it will fit the first component of the definition of a response style.

The second component of the definition of response styles states that they are artifactual products of measurement methods, and this is the most difficult component of the definition to express in operational terms. The idea is understandable, and it is easy to give numerous illustrations of such artifactual sources of variance, but it is difficult to say what is and what is not an artifactual source of variance. For an illustration, we can return to the example of reliable individual differences in amount of guessing. Such reliable individual differences occur only on certain types of measurement instruments employed in certain ways. Logically there are no reliable individual differences in the tendency to guess when in doubt on free-response tests. Also, there cannot be any reliable individual differences in this regard when all subjects are forced to respond to all items. In other words, then, reliable individual differences in the tendency to guess when in doubt are artifactually generated by the particular techniques of measurement.

Another example of an artifactual source of variance that qualifies as a response style is that of the reliable tendency to mark "true" rather than "false" when in doubt about the correct answer on a true-false test (which will be discussed in some detail in a later section). Since reliable individual differences in this regard logically cannot occur on multiple-choice tests or on other types of tests, these reliable individual differences are artifactually generated by the particular technique of measurement.

The third component of the definition of response styles states that they are at least partly independent of the traits which instruments are intended to measure. Reliable individual differences in the tendency to guess when in doubt fit this requirement. As was mentioned previously, such individual differences have been found to have only small correlations with scores corrected for guessing. One makes the real test of the partial independence of the response style and the trait by computing the shared common variance (SCV), which was previously defined as the ratio of the squared correlation between two measures divided by the product of their respective reliabilities. If that is less than 1.0, the response style and the trait are not totally dependent; and to the extent that the SCV is near zero, the two are nearly independent (in the correlational sense of the term "independent").

RESPONSE STYLES AND RESPONSE BIAS   Although the names frequently are used interchangeably in the literature, it is important to make a careful distinction between "response styles" and "response bias." In the definition given previously, it was said that a "response style" concerns reliable individual differences because of artifacts of measurement. As the term will be used here, a "response bias" does not necessarily concern reliable individual differences; rather, it concerns the effects of measurement artifacts on the *average responses* of a group of people.

An example of a response bias is the effect of guessing on the p values of items when subjects are required to attempt all items. The bias in that case is toward making the p values higher than would be the case if subjects were cautioned not to guess. As another example, there are numerous forms of semantic bias because of the wording of questions. For example, the use of extreme modifiers like "always" and "never" alters the average response from that which is obtained from the use of less extreme modifiers like "usually" and "seldom." There are numerous examples of response bias that occur in psychophysical scaling. This occurs, for example, in the *method of limits*, where the subject makes same-different comparisons of different weights with a standard. One approach is to start the series of comparisons with a weight which is the same, or very nearly the same, as the standard and then gradually increase the size of the comparison weights until the subject is accurate in his judgments 100 percent of the time. Another approach is to start the series of comparisons with a comparison weight which is clearly larger than the standard and then gradually decrease the size of the comparison weights until the subject is accurate in his judgments only 50 percent of the time. Typically it is found that sensory thresholds derived from these two approaches are not quite the same, which points to sources of bias in the measurement methods.

Response biases are so legion in psychology and so diverse in type that there are no general principles that apply. Rather, one can learn about the response biases in particular methods of measurement only by having firsthand acquaintance with the methods. In most cases there are ways of dealing with the response bias that occurs in a particular measurement method. For example, either the effect of guessing on the p value of items could be partly overcome with instructions not to guess or an approximate correction could be developed from the model for blind guessing. The bias that occurs in the method of limits, as illustrated above in a study of lifted weights, can be approximately offset if one averages the thresholds obtained from the ascending and descending series of judgments.

When a measurement artifact produces not only a change in the average response, but also reliable individual differences in that regard, it is referred to as a "response style." Only some of the response biases produce reliable individual differences in response style. For example, there is little evidence of reliable individual differences in effects of ascending versus descending approaches to the measurement of threshold by the method of limits. Whereas there are known to be many, many forms of response bias, so far only a few types of reliable individual differences because of measurement artifacts (response style) are known to exist.

Response biases are important mainly in psychophysical scaling, which is a small part of the total arena of psychological research. They are not very important in studies of individual differences or in controlled experiments, because in both instances the mean response of all subjects usually is only of incidental importance. The remainder of this section will be concerned with response styles only, not with response bias.

POTENTIAL IMPORTANCE OF RESPONSE STYLES There are three major reasons for investigating response styles. First, in some types of tests, they logically are correlated very little or even negatively with the trait in question. By definition stylistic variables are more like personality traits than like abilities. For example, the tendency to guess when unsure is not an ability in any obvious sense, and even though it might pay off in certain circumstances, it would serve only to cloud the measurement of a particular ability, e.g., spelling ability.

In some types of measures of personality and sentiment, it is arguable to what extent a response style adds to or detracts from the valid variance. These possibilities are illustrated in the measurement of "authoritarian attitudes," where there is some evidence of a tendency to agree rather than disagree with items regardless of their content. Some have claimed that this stylistic variance detracts from the validity of the instruments; others have claimed that the agreement tendency is part of the authoritarian attitude and thus that the stylistic variance tends to increase the validity of the instruments. The latter claim is doubtful in that case and even more doubtful in most other cases. With most instruments, it is hard to make a case that stylistic variables do anything other than make measurement instruments *less* valid. Thus in most cases the reason for investigating response styles is to learn how to remove their variance.

Even if stylistic variables usually lower the validity of instruments, this does not mean that they usually lower the reliability. In the oversimplified case where the reliable variance could be partitioned into additive components because of trait and style, the reliability of the sum could be estimated from the reliability of linear combinations (Chapter Seven). The reliability of the sum might be either higher or lower than the reliability of the trait (with the stylistic variance removed), depending on the correlation between trait and style and on the reliability of each. If the reliability of variance because of the trait is only moderately high and the reliability because of stylistic variance is higher, the reliability of the sum (the obtained scores) could be much higher than the reliability of the trait (stylistic variance partialed from obtained scores). Potentially, this is one of the deceptive things about some response styles: they can add to the reliable variance and thus give the investigator a false sense of security with his measurement tool.

The second major reason for investigating response styles is that they might prove to be important measures of personality. Some of the response styles that have been cataloged sound like important personality traits, e.g., cautiousness, acquiescence, and extremeness. To the extent that such stylistic variables can be measured independently of content relating to nonstylistic variables or to the extent that they can somehow be separated from the variance of other traits, they might prove useful as measures of personality traits. For reasons which will be discussed later, mountains of research on the development of personality measures from response styles have mainly met with failure. Most of the supposed measures of personality that have been developed from scores concerning response styles falter on logical or empirical grounds, or both.

As will be seen in particular instances later, the hope of deriving important measures of personality has been based in large part on a semantic problem, the tendency to give a name to a very limited type of response style that implies sweepingly general characteristics of people. For example, when the tendency to guess when in doubt was named (among other things) as the *willingness to gamble*, this suggested that guessing on multiple-choice tests is predictive of the willingness to take risks in many different types of situations. This vain hope has been crushed under the weight of much negative evidence, and such has also been the case for the other particular stylistic tendencies measured in other particular types of instruments. Those tendencies simply are not as general as their names would imply.

In addition to the semantic confusion, the effort to develop personality characteristics from response styles has suffered from some confusions about the nature of measurement. In some instances small correlations have been found between supposed measures of stylistic tendencies and supposed measures of particular personality traits, e.g., correlations between the agreement tendency and inventory measures of neuroticism.

Though such correlations are scientifically interesting, they do not provide evidence that the stylistic variable is an adequate measure of the personality trait. To do that requires construct validation, which in turn requires (1) finding a number of instruments that define a strong general factor relating to the construct and (2) determining that different measures relating to the construct are affected in similar manners in controlled experiments relating to the construct. On both these scores, attempts to develop measures of personality traits from response styles mainly have failed.

It should be obvious that the effort to measure response styles and validate them as measures of personality is at cross purposes with the effort to measure the nonstylistic variance in the same instruments. Thus, for example, it is illogical to expect the same instrument to be both a good measure of spelling ability and a good measure of the willingness to gamble. Also, it is illogical to expect an inventory to be both a good measure of extraversion and a good measure of the tendency to make extreme responses. Consequently, if one is interested in the trait supposedly measured by the instrument rather than in stylistic variance that creeps in the back door, he should do everything possible to rid the instrument of stylistic variance. If, on the other hand, the interest is in measuring the response style rather than the trait that supposedly is involved in the instrument, the experimenter should magnify the variance of the response style at the expense of the variance of the trait. For example, if one were interested in measuring the agreement tendency in agree-disagree dichotomous responses to attitude statements, he might promote the stylistic variance in that regard by making each item highly ambiguous, which is just the opposite of what he would do to obtain a reliable measurement of attitudes.

The third, final, and perhaps least important reason for investigating response styles is that some of them are scientifically interesting in their own right. For example, purely apart from any intention of developing a measure of personality, a researcher might be curious about the nature of people who tend to guess considerably when in doubt about correct answers on multiple-choice tests. Some small correlations have been found between this stylistic variable and measures of personality and ability, and the same is true for some of the other stylistic variables. Even though, as mentioned previously, this is far from sufficient evidence to show that any of the stylistic variables are adequate measures of personality traits, it does tell us something about the stylistic variables. Most stylistic variables, however, mainly are annoying things that are of scientific interest only for the first reason given in this section—to find ways of ridding instruments of their effects.

It is an understatement to say that the literature on response styles is voluminous. There have been not only a number of major reviews of the literature, but even reviews of the reviews. A key to this vast literature is the incisive critical review by Rorer (1965), the temper of which is easily detected from the title: "The great response-style myth." The review by Damarin and Messick (1965) is particularly pertinent to one of the three reasons given previously for the investigation of response styles, that of the use of measures of response styles as measures of personality traits. Unless specifically referenced otherwise, statements here regarding empirical evidence relating to response styles are supported by findings summarized in these two reviews. Following will be summarized in turn the issues and evidence relating to the types of response styles that have been investigated most extensively.

COMPONENTS OF EXPRESSED SELF-DESIRABILITY   In Chapter Thirteen the variable of social desirability was discussed, and it was said that much of the variance on all self-inventory measures of personality can be explained by a factor concerning the tendency to say good rather than bad things about one's self. (Evidence of the omnipresence and potency of this factor in self-inventories is summarized by Edwards, 1964.) This factor also is referred to as "social desirability," and perhaps more appropriately, as "expressed self-desirability." A good argument can be made that it is no more meaningful to speak of this factor as measuring expressed self-desirability than it is to speak of it as measuring expressed adjustment (or the other pole of the factor as measuring neuroticism), because (1) the two are logically related and (2) there are mountains of evidence to show that some self-inventories are at least moderately valid for the measurement of some personality traits. The position taken in this book is that, for the time being, it is better to use the term "expressed self-desirability," because that is close to an operational definition of what subjects actually do on self-inventories for the measurement of personality.

People who are high in the factor "say" many more good than bad things about themselves, and vice versa for people who are at the opposite extreme of the factor. The use of this terminology is not meant to prejudice the possibility that self-inventories measure personality, but it is intended to stick to known facts until more evidence is available. This is felt necessary because the general factor in self-inventories is given somewhat different names by different investigators, and these different names have different implications for psychological theories. For example, scales specifically intended to measure expressed self-desirability (called "social-desirability scales," or SD scales, by most persons who work with them) have very high positive correlations with scales intended to measure adjustment and very high negative correlations with scales intended to measure neuroticism and anxiety, respectively. The SD scales also have strong correlations with scales intended to measure the tendency to fake-good on self-inventories. If one takes the names for these supposed traits seriously, the web of relationships among them leads to confusion. For example, when the factor of expressed self-desirability is turned upside down, one can take his pick between those who refer to it as "neuroticism" and those who refer to it as "anxiety," but these two terms have very different implications for psychological theories. Neuroticism is not a trait dimension, but rather a collection of types of people, some of which are very different from others in terms of trait dimensions. In contrast, anxiety usually is thought of as a trait dimension. Calling the dominant factor in self-inventories "anxiety" implies that the factor has autonomic and other physiological correlates, but the evidence on this point is still very incomplete.

As can be seen, when the dominant factor in self-inventories is interpreted in terms of the supposed psychological processes involved, there is a tendency to go way beyond the available evidence, and the different interpretations that are made of the factor lead to confusion. Consequently, until much more research is done, it would be better to refer to the factor in terms of what it is on an operational level. It represents the tendency to say good rather than bad things about one's self, or expressed self-desirability (SD).

As was mentioned in Chapter Thirteen, it is meaningful to think of SD in terms of three hypothetical components: (1) the subject's actual state of adjustment, (2) his knowledge of his own personal characteristics, and (3) his frankness in telling what he knows. Some writers have gone to the extreme of interpreting SD only as conscious faking, or merely a response style, but this is a gross mistake. Only component 3 above, frankness, can be clearly classified either as faking or as a response style in self-inventories. No one would classify actual adjustment as a response style, for if he did, the term would be so global as to lose all meaning. In self-inventories, it also is not wise to think of component 2 above, self-knowledge, as a response style. Rather, it is best to think of self-knowledge as an inherent limitation to what can be learned about people from self-inventories.

Only component 3 above, frankness, clearly qualifies as a response style according to the definition of a response style given previously. Even if there is no way at present to clearly measure individual differences in frankness, much common sense and much circumstantial evidence suggest that there are reliable individual differences in that regard. Further support for speaking of frankness as a response style comes from numerous studies showing that scores on self-inventories are influenced somewhat by artifacts of measurement. Somewhat different scores are obtained depending on the test instructions, the institutional setting in which the test is used, uses that will be made of scores, and other situational variables. Also, the rank ordering of people is somewhat different with different types of items intended to measure adjustment. Since in these instances it is not meaningful to think that variations in measurement techniques affect either actual adjustment or self-knowledge, differences in scores in these circumstances logically should be because of differences in the extent to which frankness either can or does play a part.

Even if it is true that the lion's share of the variance on most self-inventories can be explained by SD, it does not necessarily mean that this is because of variance in frankness. Although self-inventories are not nearly as valid as one would like, there are mountains of evidence to testify that some of them have some validity. For example, if groups of subjects are selected from the extremes of a scale to measure anxiety, it will be found by many different standards that the groups differ on the average in expected ways. As another example, if one investigates the bottom 10 percent of people on an inventory intended to measure adjustment, he will find that as a group they show numerous signs of maladjustment. The problem is that these self-inventories are prevented from making fine distinctions among people as a result of the variance because of self-knowledge and frankness. Between these two, it is reasonable to hypothesize that the variance because of *self-knowledge is larger* than the variance because of *frankness.*

Evidence regarding the variance because of individual differences in frankness necessarily is indirect. Experiments have shown that to some extent people can make themselves appear more adjusted on self-inventories when they are instructed to fake-good, i.e., to be the opposite of frank. The changes in scores, however, are not as large as might be expected (evidence summarized by Guilford, 1961). Also, the fact that people can manipulate their scores somewhat by intentional faking does not mean that they actually do so in the usual testing situation. Further, mean differences under different instructions regarding frankness do not imply that the reliable variance because of frankness is large in any of the conditions. The mean score could shift without there being any reliable individual differences in frankness.

The fact that the rank ordering of people is changed somewhat because of different test instructions, types of items, and situational variables does argue for the importance of variance because of frankness under some conditions. Changes in the rank ordering of people under different experimental conditions relating to frankness, however, typically are not large, and consequently the correlations between scores in the different conditions tend to be high. If the correlation were low in that case, it could be argued that there is a large component of reliable variance because of frankness in one of the conditions. But if the correlations tend to be high, as is the case, the result could be interpreted with equal credibility as evidence either that frankness does not explain much of the variance on either occasion or that the effort to reduce variance because of frankness on one of the occasions was not successful. Thus, whereas this line of evidence provides little positive support for the contention that variance because of frankness plays a large part in self-inventories, it also does not rule out the possibility.

Efforts have been made to develop direct measures of individual differences in frankness, the products of which have frequently been referred to by the unfortunate term "lie" scales. Most of the scales to measure frankness are based on the same principle: if a person fails to admit common failings or lays claims to extraordinary virtues, he is lying. Examples of such items are as follows:

1 I never say anything bad about anyone.

2 I am always honest in everything I do.

3 There have been occasions on which I felt jealous of other people.

4 I can remember times when I was embarrassed.

If a person answers "yes" to the first two items and "no" to the second two, this would be taken as evidence that he is lying, faking good, or in the language being used here, not being frank in responding. Scales developed from items such as these are used to measure reliable individual differences in frankness.

The problem with scales to measure frankness developed in the manner described above is that they confound actual traits with frankness. It is entirely conceivable that some people have such sterling characteristics, or at least their self-knowledge leads them to think so, that they honestly respond in the direction taken to indicate conscious faking. Also, if there were no variance because of frankness, one would expect the probability of a person's responding in one way rather than another to be related to the trait itself. In that case, the person who actually is highly honest would have a higher probability of responding "yes" to item 2 above than would a person who actually is lower in honesty. For these reasons, the persons who obtain high scores on lie scales probably represent a mixture of people who actually are not being frank and people who either have sterling qualities or have misinformation about their own personal characteristics. To the extent that the variance in lie scales is caused by variance in self-knowledge rather variance in frankness, it is inappropriate to refer to such scales as lie scales. Rather, insofar as such scales actually measure anything other than the trait in question, they measure a mixture of reliable sources of invalidity, including self-knowledge, frankness, and perhaps other variables not currently known.

Another approach to the independent measurement of individual differences in frankness is to key items empirically so as to differentiate groups that are given different instructions regarding frankness. One can do this, for example, by comparing the responses of subjects under instructions to be as frank as possible with the responses of the same subjects to the same items under instructions to fake-good, i.e., to appear as well adjusted as possible. The items on which p values shift the most are taken to be items that are sensitive to degrees of frankness. For example, if most people disagree with an item under instructions to be frank and agree with it under instructions to fake-good, it is assumed that agreeing with that item under the usual instructions to be frank also is an indicator of the tendency to fake-good. Not only is it unusual to find items that are so markedly affected by instructions, but the whole approach has a severe logical problem.

As was mentioned previously, a shift in mean response (p value on individual items) is no guarantee that individual differences are affected or that such shifts point to ways to measure individual differences in the variable that produced the shift. It may be that different instructions relating to frankness result in large changes in p values on some items, but that is only weak circumstantial evidence that individual differences in response to those items in any circumstance actually relate to degrees of frankness.

Another severe logical problem with the above-mentioned method for deriving independent measures of individual differences in frankness is that it inevitably confounds measures of stylistic variables with measures of nonstylistic traits. If the scale for measuring frankness is derived from a scale intended to measure, say, dominance, the scoring key for the stylistic tendency probably will overlap the scoring key for the nonstylistic variable (which, as we shall see later, is a severe problem in all efforts to measure stylistic variables from items intended to measure nonstylistic traits). Then, even if the experimenter filled in at random the test responses on 100 test blanks, he probably would find a substantial correlation between the two sets of "scores." Thus it is obvious that the so-called measure of the stylistic variable is confounded with the measurement of the trait. Even if one employs a hodgepodge of item content, this still does not overcome the difficulty. By this means it is possible to make the measure of stylistic tendency relatively pure of particular personality traits (e.g., dominance), but it is very difficult to prevent it from being confounded with expressed self-desirability. This is because almost all items usable for self-inventories tend to measure SD, even if items vary considerably in that regard. Unless the scale to measure a response style has equal amounts of variance from items keyed in a socially desirable and socially undesirable direction, which is a very difficult condition to obtain exactly, the measure of the stylistic tendency is artifactually confounded with actual adjustment. That logically follows if, as previously hypothesized, one component of SD actually is adjustment.

contingent variables

Still another logical problem with empirically keyed measures of stylistic tendencies is they do not cleanly distinguish between frankness and self-knowledge, and even at best, they probably incorporate only a small portion of the variance because of self-knowledge. Scales to measure stylistic tendencies become confounded with individual differences in self-knowledge in the same ways that they become confounded with actual adjustment. If one knew how to score a set of items so as to measure self-knowledge rather than frankness or actual adjustment, it would be the sheerest of accidents if the scoring keys for frankness and self-knowledge were not artifactually related.

One can argue that it is all right if a so-called lie scale actually measures a combination of frankness and self-knowledge, because both are systematic sources of invalidity. No one has even suggested, however, that the procedures for deriving such scales could lead to an adequate measurement of individual differences in self-knowledge. The procedures do that only incidentally, because of the above-mentioned difficulties of preventing the two from being artifactually related. Logically, however, measures of frankness developed from empirically keyed items still would tap only a portion of the variance because of self-knowledge.

Another approach to the development of empirically keyed scales for the measurement of stylistic variables is by the comparison of responses of two groups of subjects that are presumed to differ in terms of the stylistic variable. An example is the K scale on the Minnesota Multiphasic Personality Inventory (MMPI). The scale was developed by a comparison of the item responses of hospitalized psychotic patients who gave normal score profiles with the responses of normal persons. The assumption was that psychotics who have normal score profiles either are not being frank or are lacking in self-knowledge. Even though the overall profiles of the two groups were not very different, it was possible to find individual items where they differed, and a scoring key was based on those items. This approach to the measurement of stylistic variables probably does a better job of measuring both frankness and self-knowledge (the latter, strictly speaking, does not fit the definition of a response style, but it is a systematic source of invalidity). This approach is, however, subject to all the above-mentioned criticisms of empirically keyed measures of response styles developed so far, and it is subject to some special problems of its own. Obviously a scale developed by this approach is no better than the primary assumption on which it is based——that either patients hospitalized as being psychotic show profiles different from normal persons or their responses are invalidated by lack of frankness, lack of self-knowledge, or both. Another possibility is that the particular patients either are not psychotic at all, or if they are, have a pattern of psychosis that is not adequately measured by the usual scales employed for the measurement of mental illness on the MMPI.

From the above discussion it can be seen that the components of expressed self-desirability are complex, and presently there are no means for neatly unraveling them. Regardless of what the validity of self-inventories would be if the variance of both variables could be removed, in most cases the variance because of self-knowledge probably is greater than the variance because of frankness. Even if, on the average, people are not very frank in responding to self-inventories, it is yet to be convincingly demonstrated that *individual differences* in that regard explain a major portion of the variance of scores. It is more reasonable to think that a larger portion of the total variance is because of individual differences in self-knowledge.

When discussing self-knowledge, one must consider not only the lack of knowledge, but also mistaken conceptions the subject has of himself. In addition, it is necessary to consider not only individual differences in overall amount of self-knowledge, but also differences in self-knowledge relating to different types of traits.

There are many ways in which people can lack knowledge about their own characteristics as mirrored in the items employed in self-inventories. They may have not been in many situations that permitted them to observe themselves in action or to observe the responses of other people to them; or when in such situations, they may have selectively attended to cues that supported an idealized self-concept. To some extent, we learn what we are like from important people in our lives, and in many cases these people are not correct about our actual characteristics. Also, there is some selective "forgetting" of our own actions and the ways in which we have been responded to by other people, and those memories that remain active frequently are reshaped in one way or another. To the extent that questionnaire items concern typical behavior over a long period of time or behavior in an earlier stage of life, an individual may be deficient in self-knowledge purely because he cannot accurately recall how he performed or how he was responded to by other people, e.g., as might be the case regarding the responses of adults to factual questions about forms of discipline in the home during childhood days.

Even if none of the above variables were at work to attenuate self-knowledge about personality characteristics, the individual might still find it difficult to express what self-knowledge he has in terms of the items typically employed on self-inventories. Some of the semantic problems with such items were discussed in Chapter Thirteen. The individual might not understand exactly what information the item is seeking, he might have different meanings for some of the key words than those intended by the test constructor, or he might feel that the item "lumps together" traits that he had always considered separately. For these and other reasons, semantic problems tend to put a veil between self-knowledge and the picturing of that self-knowledge on self-inventories.

In addition to the above limitations concerning self-knowledge, apparently there is a tendency in people to form general attitudes toward themselves based on their history of experience with other people and self-observation. Inconsistencies in the pattern tend to be ignored, rationalized, forgotten, or reshaped in memory. Thus there is an interaction of self-knowledge with self-esteem, by which is meant expressed desirability when bereft of the stylistic variance because of frankness. In the formative years, self-knowledge serves to influence self-esteem, and self-esteem in turn influences the way that new self-knowledge is gathered and characterized. Later in life, the level of self-esteem tends to reshape and color the interpretation of events earlier in life.

Even if the above hypotheses about the nature of self-knowledge and the interaction of self-knowledge with self-esteem are correct, that still leaves open the question of whether or not variance in self-knowledge is prominent in self-inventories. Everyday experience suggests that there are important individual differences in self-knowledge, but if this is so, there is presently no way of knowing how much variance such individual differences account for on self-inventories. Although there are possible ways to investigate variance because of frankness and to reduce that variance in self-inventories, presently there are no hints as to how either could be done for the variable of self-knowledge. Individual differences in self-knowledge may be an inherent limitation to the validity of self-inventory measures of personality.

TENDENCY TO GUESS WHEN IN DOUBT   A response style which was considered previously in this chapter was the tendency to guess when in doubt about the correct answers on multiple-choice tests. There are reliable individual differences in that regard on particular types of tests (e.g., tests of word meaning and tests concerning history). Only a very small portion of the variance of scores, however, can be accounted for by that stylistic tendency.

In the early stages of research, the tendency to guess when in doubt was referred to as the "willingness to gamble," and the opposite of it was referred to as "cautiousness." Continued research with the guessing tendency has shown that these broad trait names are entirely unjustified. The tendency is limited to true-false and multiple-choice tests of ability, particularly educational tests, and it is not even very consistent over tests in different areas of subject matter. It does not correlate with the willingness to gamble in other types of situations, e.g., simulated betting situations in research on risk taking. There are some small correlations between the tendency to guess and personality variables (Price, 1964). For example, one study reported that maladjusted children tended to guess less than normal children. These correlations are so few, and so small in size, that there is little indication that the tendency to guess can be employed as an important measure of personality.

Most of the reliable variance of the tendency to guess when in doubt probably relates to specific strategies for taking tests. It obviously is desirable to limit the variance from this source as much as possible. To some extent that variance can be reduced by instructions that discourage blind guessing. In this case the correction for guessing also serves to further reduce the variance because of the guessing tendency. One can remove that variance altogether by requiring all subjects to attempt all items, in which case there cannot possibly be any variance in the tendency to guess when in doubt.

TENDENCY TO GUESS "TRUE"   One of the findings that kindled the interest in response styles is that on true-false tests there are reliable individual differences in the tendency to guess "true" rather than "false." A measure of this tendency is simply the percentage of wrong answers marked "true." For example, if an individual has 10 incorrect answers, 3 of which are marked "false" and 7 are marked "true," his score on the stylistic variable would be 70. Not only is this tendency reliable within particular tests, but also there are modest correlations between this tendency on true-false tests in different subject areas.

The above finding led to the postulation of a very general personality trait, which has variously been referred to as the "agreement tendency," "acquiescence," and "yeasaying" as opposed to "naysaying." There are mountains of negative evidence now to show that these broad trait names are unjustified. The tendency to guess "true" on educational tests is not very general even over different types of educational tests, and there is no firm evidence at all that it correlates with the agreement tendency in measures of personality and sentiment. Also, there is no evidence that the tendency to guess "true" correlates with acquiescence, or yeasaying, in social situations.

As is true of the tendency to guess when in doubt, the tendency to guess "true" on true-false tests apparently is a highly special form of test-taking strategy. Students have different conceptions of the probable number of items that are keyed "true" and "false." This is understandable, because teachers vary in the extent to which they balance the numbers of "true" and "false" items, with the average teacher tending to include more of the former than the latter. Correctly or incorrectly, students develop hunches about the probable payoff from guessing "true" rather than "false," and there is some generality of this tendency from test to test.

The best solution to the problem of stylistic variance because of guessing "true" on true-false tests is to not use true-false tests. Variance in that tendency obviously cannot occur on multiple-choice tests or free-response tests. Even if it were not for some variance because of guessing "true," most true-false tests suffer from other problems, such as the amount of measurement error from guessing and the difficulty in composing statements on some topics that are unambiguously true or false.

THE AGREEMENT TENDENCY   Above it was said that the tendency to guess "true" is not a broad trait concerning the agreement tendency, but this does not rule out the possibility that such a trait exists in self-inventories and measures of sentiments. In the early stages of research on response styles, some investigators thought they had found evidence of the presence of such a trait in a measure of attitudes, the California F scale for the measurement of "authoritarian attitudes." A special form of the scale was constructed, in which each item was rewritten so as to make the meaning the reverse of that in the original scale. Ordinarily one would expect a high negative correlation between scores obtained from the customary scale and the reversed scale, but a substantial positive correlation was found instead. This led investigators to think that the scale mainly measured a tendency to agree rather than disagree, or *acquiescence* as it was called. This hypothesis led to volumes of research to measure a general trait of acquiescence, which so far has met mainly with failure (evidence summarized by McGee, 1962).

The hypothesis behind the search for a general trait of acquiescence is that there are important individual differences in the extent to which people will agree with the opinions and decisions of other people rather than curry their disfavor. Logically, variance in such a trait should occur only when there is some room for doubt about the correctness of a point of view, because no matter how much an individual wants to please others, he is not likely to agree that $2 + 2 = 13$ or that it is only 6 miles from New York to Chicago.

Maybe there is a broad general trait of social acquiescence, but if there is, it has not been measured so far by the methods employed for that purpose. This can be said because (1) basically different types of instruments for measuring acquiescence have either zero correlations with one another or correlations no higher than .20 on the average and (2) none of them correlate with behavioral measures of acquiescence. A discussion of some of the particulars relating to these two conclusions will be instructive regarding future efforts to measure response styles.

If there were some way to conclusively reverse the meaning of statements relating to attitudes, it would be possible to derive measures of the agreement tendency. One approach would be to subtract the number of unchanged "disagree" responses from the number of un-changed "agree" responses. The extreme of the agreement tendency would be represented by the person who agreed to all items on both the original statements and their reversals. The opposite extreme of the agreement tendency would be represented by the person who dis-agreed with all items on both forms. The difference between these two types of unchanged responses could serve as a measure of the agreement tendency for persons who are between the extremes of the trait.

Unfortunately it is very difficult to know when the meaning of an item actually has been reversed. Consequently the different reversed scales for the same trait correlate very little with one another, most of the evidence in this regard coming from different efforts to reverse items on the F scale. Also, correlations of those reversed scales with the original scale range all the way from high positive to as negative as the reliabilities of the scales will permit.

Rorer (1965) presents numerous examples of attempted reversals of items that, on close inspection, really are not reversals. An example is the following pair of statements, in which the second statement is intended to be a reversal of the meaning of the first statement:

Item Obedience and respect for authority are the most important virtues that children should learn.

Reversal A love of freedom and complete independence are the most important virtues children should learn.

Regardless of the agreement tendency, a person could realistically agree with both these statements or disagree with both. He might, for example, disagree with both because he is reluctant to say that any one thing is most important for children to learn, or he might disagree with both because he thinks that something else is more important, e.g., religious devotion. Both the weight of the evidence and logical considerations indicate that it is not feasible to measure an agreement tendency with reversed scales.

Another approach to the measurement of the agreement tendency is with either highly ambiguous or very abstruse statements such as the following:

1 The International Monetary Fund should adopt a fiscal policy that fulfills a need for rapid balancing of reciprocal tariff obligations.

2 The orbit of the planet Saturn is more elliptical than that of Neptune.

The first statement above is only a jumble of words that add up to nothing, and the second statement concerns matters with which very few persons are familiar. Logically, then, one might think that the ten-dency to agree rather than disagree with statements like these would represent acquiescence, this following from the notion that people agree with such statements because they are "pushed along" by the force of the statement itself. The evidence, however, is that such abstruse and ambiguous statements do not measure a trait of acquiescence. Scales based on such statements typically do not provide highly reliable individual differences among subjects. It is very rare, for example, to find persons who agree with as many as 90 percent of the statements on such scales or who disagree with 90 percent of the statements. Probably this is because subjects actually form opinions about such statements even when such statements are intended to be nonsense. For example, the statement above about the International Monetary Fund "sounds" like a good thing to do, because it speaks of "fulfilling a need." On the statement concerning orbits of two planets, the subject might not actually know the answer, but he might feel that he has a faint idea about the matter. For these and other reasons, scales composed of such statements are not entirely "contentless," and consequently the real or apparent content of the statements partly determines the responses of subjects.

Even if it were not for the above logical considerations that pose problems for the use of abstruse and ambiguous statements to measure acquiescence, the evidence indicates that the approach does not produce valid measurements. What little reliable variance there is on such scales is not related to other types of measures of acquiescence (e.g., measures derived from reversed scales), and such scales do not correlate with more behavioral measures of acquiescence (e.g., scores on conformity in group situations).

Another approach to the measurement of acquiescence is with "mish-mash" scales composed of items on so many different topics that they logically do not add up to anything. For such purposes, one could obtain items pertaining to many different personality traits and sentiments. Then it could be argued that the tendency to agree rather than disagree with such a wide collection of material would relate to acquiescence. To prevent the number of agreements from measuring expressed social desirability, one could either (1) search for a collection of items that correlate near zero with SD scales, (2) employ items that are near neutral with respect to SD, or (3) partial SD scores from the scores intended to measure acquiescence. But in spite of the appealing sound of these approaches, they have not led to measures of acquiescence. Different scales developed by these approaches do tend to correlate substantially with one another, but apparently the correlations are not because of acquiescence, but because of artifacts of measurement. This can safely be said because scales developed by these approaches do not correlate substantially with measures of acquiescence developed by other approaches, and they do not correlate substantially with more behavioral measures of acquiescence in social situations.

One of the major reasons why "mish-mash" scales do not measure acquiescence well is that, in spite of the best efforts, they inevitably measure traits other than acquiescence. No matter how diverse the content which is employed in such scales, it still tends to relate to nonstylistic dimensions of personality and sentiment. If nothing else, the content usually relates to expressed self-desirability.

What is deceiving about the "mish-mash" scales is that they do have substantial correlations with inventory measures of personality traits, and consequently they give the appearance of successfully measuring a trait of social acquiescence. That, however, is most reasonably attributed to the artifacts described above, because the "mish-mash" scales do not correlate with basically different types of scales to measure acquiescence (e.g., ambiguous statements), and they do not correlate substantially with more behavioral measures of social conformity and acquiescence.

Another approach to the measurement of acquiescence is with "contentless" scales. For example, a method devised by Husek (1961) centers around a mock experiment in extrasensory perception. Subjects are asked to mark their agreement with each of 100 statements being read silently by the experimenter. Actually, the experimenter is not reading statements, and consequently subjects are agreeing and disagreeing with perfectly nothing. Another contentless measure is that developed by Nunnally and Husek (1958), which is posed as a test of ability to guess the meanings of German words. Randomly chosen abstruse German nouns are substituted for the subject and predicate of English sentences. Even if one spoke German fluently, the sentences would be nonsense. Thus subjects are agreeing or disagreeing with meaningless statements.

Both the contentless measures above have reliable variance, the reliability of the ESP testing being almost .90. The reliable variance in these and other contentless measures, however, apparently is not related to social acquiescence or any other personality trait, because the contentless instruments (1) correlate very little with one another, (2) correlate very little with measures of acquiescence derived from other approaches, and (3) do not correlate at all with behavioral indices of social acquiescence and other traits.

The overwhelming weight of the evidence now points to the fact that the agreement tendency is of very little importance either as a measure of personality or as a source of systematic invalidity in measures of personality and sentiments. What little stylistic variance there is because of that tendency, if any, can be mostly eliminated by ensuring that an instrument is constructed so that there is a balance of items keyed "agree" and "disagree" with respect to the trait in question.

THE EXTREME-RESPONSE TENDENCY   Another stylistic variable is the tendency to give extreme responses, which has been investigated mostly on rating scales used for the measurement of attitudes and other sentiments. The hypothesis is that, regardless of the content, people differ in the tendency to mark the extremes of rating scales rather than points near the middle of the scale. This hypothesis grew out of findings that there are small correlations between degrees of extremeness of ratings made by subjects on different rating tasks, e.g., on ratings of esthetic preferences for pictures and ratings of attitudes toward minority groups.

The extremeness tendency logically should be evidenced in the sum of absolute differences of ratings from the midpoint of the scale. For example, on a seven-step scale of agreement and disagreement, a rating of 7 is scored 3, and a rating of 3 is scored 1. The sum of such deviations is taken as a score on the tendency to give extreme responses.

As is true of attempts to measure other stylistic variables, it is very difficult to prevent measures of extremeness from being confounded with actual attitudes or other sentiments. For example, if a person had either a strongly positive or a strongly negative attitude toward the United Nations, he would obtain a high sum of deviations from the center of the scale, but that could be entirely because of his attitude as validly reflected in his ratings rather than because of the tendency to give extreme responses.

Before concluding that there is reliable variance because of the extremeness tendency in a particular set of ratings, one must first score the responses in two ways: (1) as indicated above in terms of the sum of deviations and (2) in terms of the sum of dichotomized scores for the trait in question. For the latter, any rating to the left or to the right of the midpoint would be scored either as an "agree" or "disagree" response, regardless of how extreme the rating. This could then be considered a measure of the trait in which the extremeness tendency logically is not present. The squared correlation between the two sets of scores should then be divided by the product of their internal-consistency reliabilities (coefficient alpha), the result being the shared common variance discussed previously. If that is considerably less than 1.0 (e.g., as low as .80), it can reasonably be concluded that the extremeness tendency is present to some degree. Then, by partialing the sum of dichotomous responses from the sum of midpoint deviations, one might obtain a relatively pure measure of the extremeness tendency. So little research of this kind has been done, however, that at the present time it is difficult to know how much reliable variance because of the extremeness tendency is present in particular instruments or to what extent the reliable variance of that kind correlates with the reliable variance of the same kind in other instruments.

What circumstantial evidence there is suggests that there is a small amount of reliable variance on some instruments because of the extremeness tendency, particularly on measures of attitudes. Also, some suggestive small correlations have been found between measures of the extremeness tendency and measures of intelligence (negative correlations) and measures of various personality attributes. Although the evidence does not point to extremeness tendency as being either very general across basically different types of instruments or an important measure of personality, it does suggest that stylistic variance because of the extremeness tendency may be a small source of systematic invalidity in some uses of rating scales. Of course, the usual way to score multipoint ratings is not dichotomously, but in terms of the sum of ratings (reversing scores of items that imply negative attitudes). When that is done, there is a danger of permitting stylistic variance because of the extremeness tendency to confound the actual measurement of attitudes. One can determine whether or not that occurs in particular instruments by computing the shared common variance between the dichotomously scored and continuously scored versions of the instrument. If that is not very high (e.g., less than .90), it might be wise to employ the dichotomous scoring rather than the continuous scoring in future uses of the instrument. This may result in a loss of reliabilty, but if it is feasible to increase the number of items, the reliability usually can be restored to satisfactory levels.

DEVIANT-RESPONSE TENDENCY   The deviant-response tendency concerns individual differences in making uncommon responses. For example, if 80 percent of the people agree with a statement, anyone who disagrees with the statement is said to give a deviant response. It has been hypothesized (Berg, 1961) that the deviant-response tendency is very general across many different types of instruments and that it is an important dimension of personality.

There is some evidence that the deviant-response tendency is rather general across self-inventories, but mainly this can be shown to be more parsimoniously explained in terms of conventional psychometric concepts rather than in terms of a new construct of deviant-response tendency. On inventories to measure adjustment, frequently most of the items indicative of maladjustment are keyed in terms of deviant responses. Following are two examples:

1 I feel that I am as mentally healthy as the average person.

2 I sometimes think that someone is following me.

More than half the people will agree with the first statement, and far more than half the people will disagree with the second statement. Consequently anyone who gives different responses from those of the majority of the people certainly is, in one sense, giving deviant responses; but that does not mean that it is necessary to invoke a special construct concerning a dimension of personality to explain that behavior. It is more parsimonious to interpret such responses in terms of the traits which the instruments are intended to measure, including the components of expressed self-desirability.

Efforts have been made to develop scales of deviant responding by comparing the responses of normal persons with the responses of patients in mental hospitals. As might be expected, the responses of the hospital patients are deviant on the average with respect to the average responses of normal people. This is not very surprising, because highly deviant people are expected to give deviant responses in many different types of situations. Actually, it is hard to find a test of ability or measure of personality or sentiment on which the average responses of hospitalized mental patients are not different on the average from normal people. Partly, however, that may be because of test-taking behavior rather than because of the traits supposedly measured by the particular instruments. For example, many mental patients are so confused and out of touch with reality that they give nearly random responses to tests and inventories. For reasons which will be discussed later, a person who gives random, or careless, responses will also give many deviant responses. This is evidenced, for example, in what would happen if a person flipped a coin to decide whether to agree or disagree with each of the following statements:

1 I sometimes think that I am God.

2 There is a squirrel in my head.

3 I am glass from the waist down.

The concept of deviant responding is potentially useful only in considering differences between very deviant people and normal people. If it were a general trait in normal people one would expect to find substantial positive correlations between deviant responding on basically different types of instruments, e.g., ratings of esthetic preferences for designs and ratings of attitudes toward the United Nations. There is very little evidence that substantial correlations of that kind exist (evidence summarized by Rorer, 1965). Just because a number of different instruments differentiate normal people from obviously deviant people, that does not necessarily mean that there are substantial correlations among the instruments within either group.

It should be apparent that although the deviant-response tendency has frequently been discussed as a response style, it is not a response style according to the definition given earlier. It is not an artifact of measurement; rather, it comes from a special way of analyzing the valid variance. Consequently it is neither desirable nor logically possible to construct instruments so that variance because of deviant responding will not be present.

The problem with the construct of deviant responding is not so much that it is lacking in empirical support as that it is an overly global, nonanalytic construct that makes little contribution to psychological theories or programs of research. Just to say that a person is deviant on the average in his responses does not tell whether he is deviantly "good" or deviantly "bad," e.g., deviantly well adjusted rather than maladjusted or deviantly high in intelligence rather than low in intelligence. Also, if one is to understand human traits, it is necessary to measure the particular ways in which some people are different from others rather than to lump deviant responses from instruments concerning many different factors of ability, personality characteristics, and sentiments. To understand human traits, one must employ concepts concerning measures of different traits and factors among those traits, and one adds very little to those concepts by postulating a deviant-response tendency. Doing so would be like abandoning techniques for diagnosing particular forms of illness in favor of a global technique that would determine only whether people are sick or well.

summary of research on response styles

As can be seen from the preceding discussion, hindsight makes it clear that the research on response styles was mainly built on false hopes and methodological flaws. Unless one wants to speak of some of the components of expressed self-desirability as being response styles, there is little evidence that any of the response styles (1) explain more than a small fraction of the variance in any instrument intended to measure nonstylistic traits, (2) are highly general across basically different types of instruments, or (3) correlate substantially with experimentally independent measures of personality or ability.

The intensive research on response styles that began about 1950 probably was spurred primarily by suggestions that a broad trait of acquiescence is evidenced in agree-disagree responses to many different kinds of items. Since that time, the bulk of the research on response styles has centered on the effort to measure and investigate a trait of acquiescence. Probably the reason for the emphasis on acquiescence rather than on other stylistic variables is that, intuitively, there are objective inroads into the measurement of acquiescence. Logically, if a trait of acquiescence is present in an instrument, it should be manifested as some function of the number and kinds of agree responses in relation to the number and kinds of disagree responses.

In spite of the appealing (at the time) hypotheses about the existence of a trait of acquiescence and in spite of the possible inroads into the measurement of the trait, the evidence now overwhelmingly indicates that no more than a small fraction of the variance in any instrument springs from that source. Also, there is no convincing evidence that the small variance of that kind which can be isolated strongly relates to social acquiescence or any other personality trait. This weight of negative evidence with respect to acquiescence has spurred a more careful look at the evidence with respect to other potential forms of response style, and as can be seen from recent critical reviews (e.g., McGee, 1962; Rorer, 1965), the weight of the evidence is mainly negative with respect to the importance of all the response styles that have been postulated to date. Although some researchers are doggedly persisting in the search for measures of important forms of response style and their fortitude in that regard is admirable, most specialists in psychological measurement apparently are becoming very discouraged with this line of reasearch. Although one need not agree entirely with Rorer (1965) in speaking of "the great response-style myth," it must be admitted that most of the evidence shows either that (1) very little variance is explained by response styles in most tests and inventories or (2) efforts to measure personality traits with variance relating to response styles has mainly been unsuccessful.

Perhaps the most fruitful products of the research on response styles have been new methodological principles relating to all forms of measurement, some of which were discussed previously in the section on response styles. One of these principles concerns a concept mentioned in previous chapters, that of *pseudo reliability*. The need for such a concept is evidenced in the contentless measures of response styles, particularly those used in the attempt to measure acquiescence. A particular case in point is the mock ESP test described previously. As was mentioned, the number of agreements to nonexistent statements is highly reliable, and this makes one wonder about the nature of the reliable variance. Since scores on the different contentless measures correlate very little with one another, it means that there are highly reliable specific traits relating to each measurement technique. But how did such traits arise? The testing materials are so novel that there has been no previous opportunity for differences in learning to produce reliable individual differences. Also, it is unreasonable to think that inherited traits would be so highly specific that they would appear only on a highly novel instrument contrived for a particular study.

Findings such as the above suggest that in some cases there may be pseudo reliability, because when faced with novel material, subjects develop a set for responding and consistently follow the set throughout the testing session. Also, when faced with the same or highly similar materials on other occasions, they may follow the same set. If there are individual differences in such sets (e.g., to agree rather than disagree with most of the items), the pseudo reliability would be manifested in high coefficients of internal consistency and high retest correlations. One can speak of the reliability in that case as being "pseudo," because it is reasonable to believe that the sets that people happen to adopt are nearly randomly related to their abilities and personality characteristics. If that were not so, one would expect to find high correlations between different contentless measures of the same stylistic tendency.

An alternative way of considering the matter is to think of a "splinter" trait being generated on the spot in response to the test materials. The trait has not existed previously and will not be manifested in other situations in the future, but it is reliable then and there and may even remain reliable over a period of time. If it were possible to erase the memory of the first set of responses to the contentless measure and administer the measure again, it might be found that the sets developed on the second occasion were randomly related to the sets formed on the first occasion.

Pseudo reliability may be a problem in studying responses to any type of highly novel test materials, contentless measures being only the extreme case. In such instances, when the subject is very unsure of how to respond to the test as a whole, he may decide just to "do something" and do it consistently throughout the test. The pseudo reliability arising from such sets misleadingly indicates that traits are present, whereas in the more proper meaning of the term, no traits are present at all.

effects of carelessness and confusion

Another important class of contingent variables concerns carelessness and confusion in relation to the purpose of the test, the test instructions, the item content, or other aspects of the testing situation. Carelessness and confusion are considered jointly because the expected effect is the same—they introduce a source of randomness into test responses. Of course, any particular person who is careless or confused might not act randomly, but that is the expected result for a group of persons who are either careless or confused. Since the effects of individual differences in motivation, fatigue, and physical health should relate to carelessness and confusion, what will be said in this section has some relevance for the former three variables also.

One sees ample evidence of the effects of carelessness and confusion in the responses to many different types of psychological measures.

For example, on semantic-differential scales, one frequently sees the same concept rated as "highly useful" and "highly worthless." On a set of rating scales for the measurement of attitudes, one sometimes finds that the subject has marked both ends of all scales. One frequently sees "pattern" responding on rating scales, such as progressively marking the next higher step on each scale, marking all scales in the neutral category, or alternately marking the extreme ends of scales to form an illogical set of ratings. One sometimes finds other evidence regarding the effects of carelessness and confusion in comparing the responses of abnormal subjects with those of normal subjects. This would be the case, for example, if it were found that the mean evaluation scores for the concepts "devil" and "God" were not well separated in the abnormal group, because they always are well separated in normal groups.

The most danger from carelessness and confusion is when the purpose of the research is to compare mean responses by different types of people, e.g., children and adults. This is because carelessness and confusion can artifactually produce large apparent mean differences if one group is more careless or confused than the other. It is reasonable to expect that more carelessness or confusion will be found in some groups than in others when they are responding to particular kinds of testing materials. Thus one would expect more carelessness or confusion in hospitalized psychotics than in normal people, in children than in adults, and in deaf children than in normal children. When such groups are compared, there is a real danger that artifactual differences in mean scores may be only because of differences between groups in amount of carelessness or confusion. This actually may have been the case in many studies reported in the literature.

EFFECTS ON TEST PARAMETERS   Carelessness and confusion are expected to have two major effects: They introduce a source of measurement error in addition to that from guessing and other components of measurement error, and they serve to bias scores toward the *chance level*. The effects of carelessness and confusion are directly analogous to the effects of guessing on true-false and multiple-choice tests, but the effects of both are somewhat different from other sources of measurement error. To the extent that carelessness and confusion introduce some randomness into responses, it should be obvious that such randomness will introduce measurement error. The classical theory of measurement error (Chapter Six) assumes that measurement error results in a symmetrical distribution of obtained (fallible) scores about the true score for each person. The errors because of carelessness and confusion, however, not only lower the precision of obtained scores, but also serve to *bias* obtained scores toward the chance level.

The chance level is the score that a person would be expected to obtain if he responded randomly to all items, a matter which was discussed previously with respect to guessing. If a person responds randomly to 20 agree-disagree statements concerning attitudes toward the United Nations, the best a priori estimate is that he will agree with 10 of the statements and disagree with 10. If agreement with each statement is keyed as a positive attitude and the total score equals the number of agreements on positive statements, the expected score is 10. If half the statements are keyed "agree" for a positive attitude and half are keyed "disagree," and the total score equals the number of agreements on the former plus the number of disagreements on the latter, again the expected score from complete confusion or carelessness will be 10.

On an instrument in which the total score consists of the sum of ratings on multipoint scales, complete confusion or carelessness would be expected to lead to a total score equaling the number of scales multiplied by the midpoint of the scales. For example, with a seven-step scale ranging from 1 to 7, the midpoint is 4. Thus, with 20 items, the expected score would be 80. With an eight-step scale, the midpoint would be 4.5 and the expected score with 20 items would be 90.

Whereas on tests of ability, scores are not expected below the chance level, that, of course, is not the case on nonability measures such as measures of attitudes. For example, a person with a very negative attitude might disagree with 20 positive statements. If the scoring is in terms of the number of agreements to positive statements, that person will receive a score of zero rather than the score of 10 expected by chance. Regardless of whether the person's true score is above or below the chance level, the effect of carelessness and confusion is to regress the score toward the chance level.

If all members of a group are careless or confused to the same extent, the rank order of obtained scores is expected to be the rank order of true scores, except for some random shifting about because of measurement error. Very high true scores and true scores far below the chance level would be expected to regress more than would true scores nearer the chance level, but the rank order would be expected to remain the same. The net effect would be to shrink the distribution and shift the mean of true scores toward the chance level. In that case there would be some unreliability because of carelessness and confusion, but there would be no systematic source of invalidity.

If, however, there are individual differences in amount of carelessness or confusion, systematic sources of invalidity can be generated. Suppose, for example, that people with negative attitudes tend to be much more careless than people with mildly negative or positive attitudes. In this case the chance level might be indicative of a neutral attitude, and consequently the people with very negative attitudes would obtain less negative scores than would persons with mildly negative attitudes. Just what happens to scores when there are systematic individual differences in amount of carelessness or confusion is complexly interwoven with the type of item, the scoring key, and the correlation of the amount of carelessness and confusion with the trait in question. Whatever the specific effects, however, individual differences in amount of carelessness and confusion can be expected to add not only a component of measurement error, but also a component of systematic invalidity.

EFFECTS ON DIFFERENT TYPES OF INSTRUMENTS   Effects of carelessness and confusion are interestingly different in terms of different types of instruments and different types of scoring keys. On tests of ability, the expectation is that scores will be lower, but that is not always the case on some tests of personality. If, as mentioned previously, the keyed responses on measures of maladjustment are deviant responses (p values well removed from .5 in either direction for dichotomous items), carelessness and confusion will lead to scores indicative of a high level of maladjustment. On an interest inventory, carelessness and confusion could produce high interest scores on some scales (e.g., for engineers) and low scores on other scales, depending on the p values of the items keyed for those scales.

Although it is expected that carelessness and confusion will regress scores toward the chance level, the relative standing of such scores depends on the mean and standard deviation of responses of persons who are not careless or confused. If the mean of the total group were well above the chance level on a scale of attitudes, persons who were careless or confused would appear to have negative attitudes; but the reverse would be true if the mean of the total group were well below the chance level. For these reasons, the effects of carelessness or confusion will be interpreted quite differently depending on the way in which an instrument is keyed and the distribution of scores of persons who are not suffering from carelessness or confusion.

EFFECTS ON CORRELATIONS   If there is about the same amount of carelessness or confusion among the members of a group, the expectation is that correlations among different measures will be less than they otherwise would be. This is because of the measurement error introduced by carelessness and confusion. However, if there are systematic differences in carelessness or confusion, the effects on correlations among measures will depend on the correlation of amounts of carelessness and confusion with the traits in question. In rare instances the correlations could be inflated. That, however, is a result which is hardly to be expected, the more usual case being a lowering of correlations.

COMPARISONS OF GROUPS   As was mentioned previously, the major danger from carelessness and confusion is in comparing mean responses from different types of groups of people. An example will suffice to show how spurious results can be obtained in that case. In a hypothetical study, comparisons are made of the semantic-differential ratings by psychotics and normal persons of role concepts such as "father," "mother," "policeman," and others. Ratings are made on a seven-step scale, the midpoint being 4. It is found that normal subjects have an average evaluative rating for "father" of 5.5, and psychotic patients have an average rating for "father" of 4.0. It is found that the mean difference is highly significant statistically. It is tempting to interpret this finding as indicating that psychotic patients have less regard for their fathers than normal persons do. It is equally plausible, however, that the difference is because of much more confusion or carelessness on the part of the psychotic patients than on the part of normal subjects. It may be that the mean true score of psychotics is also 5.5, but because of carelessness or confusion, the mean obtained score is regressed to 4.0.

The possibility of obtaining statistically significant mean differences because of differences in amount of carelessness or confusion is an ever-present danger in research. The danger is most prominent when responses from different types of people are compared, but potentially it is also present when subjects are randomly assigned to different experimental treatments. To the extent that the different treatments incidentally lead to different amounts of carelessness or confusion, mean differences might be entirely because of those factors. For example, if one group of subjects makes self-ratings under constant threat of a painful electric shock, they might be more careless or confused than a group which makes ratings under less threatening conditions.

DETECTION OF CARELESSNESS AND CONFUSION   As mentioned previously, there are some forms of circumstantial evidence regarding the presence of carelessness and confusion, and such evidence can be sought when those factors seem to be important. On tests of ability, one form of evidence concerns the number of easy and difficult questions properly answered by the subjects. To take an extreme case, if a college student could not add $2 + 2$ in one part of a test, but could correctly solve a calculus problem in another part of the test, there would be some evidence of carelessness or confusion. In more subtle cases, a comparison of responses on rather easy items with those on rather difficult items will provide circumstantial evidence regarding carelessness or confusion.

contingent variables

On ratings of agreement and disagreement or on semantic-differential scales, circumstantial evidence regarding carelessness and confusion can be obtained from the number of incompatible responses, e.g., rating the same concept as "useful" and "worthless." These and other methods for detecting carelessness and confusion, however, provide only circumstantial evidence, because they are based on the assumption that, when people are not careless or confused, their behavior with respect to the items is perfectly uniform. Since the correlations among items usually are not large, many inconsistencies in responses from item to item are to be expected. Differences between groups in these regards, however, should provide useful suggestions about carelessness and confusion.

CONTROL OF CARELESSNESS AND CONFUSION Of course, rather than looking for evidence of carlessness or confusion after it has occurred, it is far better to do everything possible to reduce those factors before data are gathered. One can do this by experimenting with the instructions to ensure that they are understandable, employing very simple language in items, employing simpler types of items (e.g., binary-choice agree-disagree items rather than multipoint rating scales), and cross-checking the results from one instrument with those from another instrument. After large amounts of measurement error and bias have been introduced because of carelessness or confusion, there are no sensible "correction procedures" that can be applied; attempting to do so would be as feasible as attempting to unscramble an egg.

SUGGESTED ADDITIONAL READINGS

Edwards, A. L. Social desirability and performance on the MMPI. *Psychometrika,* 1964, **29,** 295–308.

Guilford, J. P. *Psychometric methods.* New York: McGraw-Hill, 1954, chap. 15.

Morrison, E. J. On test variance and the dimensions of the measurement situation. *Educ. psychol. Measmt,* 1960, **20,** 231–250.

Price, Dorothy B. A group approach to the analysis of individual differences in the randomness of guessing behavior on multiple-choice tests and the development of scoring methods to take such differences into account. *Res. Bull.* No. 64-59. Princeton, N.J.: Educational Testing Service, 1964.

Rorer, L. G. The great response-style myth. *Psychol. Bull.,* 1965, **63,** 129–156.

Anderson, T. W. *An introduction to multivariate statistical analysis.* New York: Wiley, 1958.

Bechtoldt, H. P. Construct validity: A critique. *Amer. Psychologist,* 1959, **14,** 619–629.

Berg, I. A. Measuring deviant behavior by means of deviant response sets. In I. A. Berg and B. M. Bass (Eds.), *Conformity and deviation.* New York: Harper & Row, 1961. Pp. 328–379.

Binet, A., and Simon, T. Méthodes nouvelles pour le diagnostic du niveau intellectuel des anormaux. *Année psychol.,* 1905, **11,** 191–244.

Burt, C. *The factors of the mind: An introduction to factor analysis in psychology.* New York: Macmillan, 1941.

Burt, C. Tests of significance in factor analysis. *Brit. J. Psychol.,* Statist. Section, 1952, **5,** 109–133.

Campbell, D. T. The indirect assessment of social attitudes. *Psychol. Bull.,* 1950, **47,** 15–38.

Campbell, D. T. Recommendations for APA test standards regarding construct, trait, and discriminant validity. *Amer. Psychologist,* 1960, **15,** 546–553.

Carrigan, Patricia M. Extraversion-introversion as a dimension of personality: A reappraisal. *Psychol. Bull.,* 1960, **57,** 329–360.

Cattell, R. B. The three basic factor-analytic research designs—their interrelations and derivatives. *Psychol. Bull.,* 1952, **49,** 499–520.

Cattell, R. B. *Personality and motivation structure and measurement.* New York: Harcourt, Brace & World, 1957.

Cliff, Rosemary. The predictive value of chance-level scores. *Educ. psychol. Measmt,* 1958, **18,** 607–616.

Cook, S. W., and Selltiz, Claire. A multiple-indicator approach to attitude measurement. *Psychol. Bull.,* 1964, **62,** 36–55.

Coombs, C. H. A theory of data. *Psychol. Rev.*, 1960, **67**, 143–159.

Cronbach, L. J. *Essentials of psychological testing*. New York: Harper & Row, 1949.

Cronbach, L. J. Coefficient alpha and the internal structure of tests. *Psychometrika*, 1951, **16**, 297–334.

Cronbach, L. J. Processes affecting scores on "understanding of others" and "assumed similarity." *Psychol. Bull.*, 1955, **52**, 177–193.

Cronbach, L. J. *Essentials of psychological testing*. (Revised.) New York: Harper & Row, 1960.

Cronbach, L. J., and Azuma, H. Internal-consistency reliability formulas applied to randomly sampled single-factor tests: An empirical comparison. *Educ. psychol. Measmt*, 1962, **22**, 645–666.

Cronbach, L. J., and Gleser, Goldine C. Assessing similarity between profiles. *Psychol. Bull.*, 1953, **50**, 456–473.

Cronbach, L. J., and Meehl, P. E. Construct validity in psychological tests. *Psychol. Bull.*, 1955, **52**, 281–302.

Damarin, F. L., and Messick, S. J. Response styles as personality variables: A theoretical integration of multivariate research. *Res. Bull.* No. 65-10. Princeton, N.J.: Educational Testing Service, 1965.

Davis, F. B. Item analysis in relation to educational and psychological testing. *Psychol. Bull.*, 1952, **49**, 97–121.

Edwards, A. L. The relationship between the judged desirability of a trait and the probability that the trait will be endorsed. *J. appl. Psychol.*, 1953, **37**, 90–93.

Edwards, A. L. *Techniques of attitude scale construction*. New York: Appleton-Century-Crofts, 1957. (a)

Edwards, A. L. *The social desirability variable in personality assessment and research.* New York: Holt, 1957. (b)

Edwards, A. L. Social desirability and performance on the MMPI. *Psychometrika*, 1964, **29**, 295–308.

Eysenck, H. J. *Dimensions of personality*. London: Routledge, 1947.

Eysenck, H. J. *The structure of personality*. New York: Wiley, 1953.

Farina, A., Arenberg, D., and Guskin, S. L. A scale for measuring minimal social behavior. *J. consult. Psychol.*, 1957, **21**, 265–268.

Ferguson, G. A. On learning and human ability. *Canad. J. Psychol.*, 1954, **8**, 95–112.

Fiedler, F. E. A comparison of the therapeutic relationships in psychoanalytic, non-directive, and Adlerian therapy. *J. consult. Psychol.*, 1950, **14**, 436–445.

Fisher, R. A. The use of multiple measurements in taxonomic problems. *Ann. Eugenics*, 1936, **7**, 179–188.

Fleishman, E. A., and Hempel, W. E. Changes in factor structure of a complex psychomotor test as a function of practice. *Psychometrika*, 1954, **19**, 239–252.

French, J. W. The description of aptitude and achievement tests in terms of rotated factors. *Psychometr. Monogr.*, No. 5. Chicago: Univer. Chicago Press, 1951.

Fruchter, B. *Introduction to factor analysis*. Princeton, N.J.: Van Nostrand, 1954.

Gardner, R. W., and Schoen, R. A. Differentiation and abstraction in concept formation. *Psychol. Monogr.*, 1962, **76**, No. 560.

Garner, W. R. Rating scales, discriminability, and information transmission. *Psychol. Rev.*, 1960, **67**, 343–352.

Gerberich, J. R. *Specimen objective test items: A guide to achievement test construction*. New York: Longmans, 1956.

Grinker, R. R., Miller, J., Sabshin, M., Nunn, R., and Nunnally, J. C. *The phenomena of depressions*. New York: Hoeber-Harper, 1961.

Guilford, J. P. *Psychometric methods*. New York: McGraw-Hill, 1954.

Guilford, J. P. The structure of intellect. *Psychol. Bull.*, 1956, **53**, 267–293.

Guilford, J. P. *Personality*. New York: McGraw-Hill, 1959.

Guilford, J. P. Factorial angles to psychology. *Psychol. Rev.*, 1961, **68**, 1–20.

Guilford, J. P. *Fundamental statistics in psychology and education*. New York: McGraw-Hill, 1965.

Guilford, J. P., and Zimmerman, W. S. *The Guilford-Zimmerman Temperament Survey: Manual*. Beverly Hills, Calif.: Sheridan Supply Co., 1949.

Gulliksen, H. *Theory of mental tests*. New York: Wiley, 1950.

Gulliksen, H., and Messick, S. (Eds.) *Psychological scaling: Theory and applications*. New York: Wiley, 1960.

Guttman, L. Image theory for the structure of quantitative variates. *Psychometrika*, 1953, **18**, 277–296.

Guttman, L. Best possible systematic estimates of communalities. *Psychometrika*, 1956, **21**, 273–285.

Guttman, L. To what extent can communalities reduce rank? *Psychometrika*, 1958, **23**, 297–308.

Harman, H. H. *Modern factor analysis*. Chicago: Univer. Chicago Press, 1960.

Hays, W. L. *Statistics for psychologists*. New York: Holt, 1963.

Helmstadter, G. C. An empirical comparison of methods for estimating profile similarity. *Educ. psychol. Measmt*, 1957, **18**, 71–82.

Hess, E. H. Attitude and pupil size. *Scient. Amer.*, 1965, **212**, 46–65.

Holtzman, W. H. Personality structure. In P. R. Farnsworth, Olga McNemar, and Q. McNemar (Eds.), *Annual review of psychology*. Palo Alto, Calif.: Annual Reviews, 1965. Pp. 119–156.

Holtzman, W. H., Thorpe, J. S., Swartz, J. D., and Herron, E. W. *Inkblot perception and personality*. Austin, Tex.: Univer. Texas Press, 1961.

Holzinger, K. *Factor analysis*. Chicago: Univer. Chicago Press, 1941.

Horst, P. *Factor analysis of data matrices*. New York: Holt, 1965.

Hotelling, H. The generalization of Student's ratio. *Ann. math. Statist.*, 1931, **2**, 360–378.

Hull, C. L. *A behavior system*. New Haven, Conn.: Yale Univer. Press, 1952.

Humphreys, L. G. The organization of human abilities. *Amer. Psychologist*, 1962, **17**, 475–483.

Husek, T. R. Acquiescence as a response set and as a personality characteristic. *Educ. psychol. Measmt*, 1961, **21**, 295–307.

Kaiser, H. F. The varimax criterion for analytic rotation in factor analysis. *Psychometrika*, 1958, **23**, 187–200.

Kelly, E. L., and Fiske, D. W. *The prediction of performance in clinical psychology*. Ann Arbor, Mich.: Univer. Michigan Press, 1951.

Kendall, L. M. The effects of varying time limits on test validity. *Educ. psychol. Measmt*, 1964, **24**, 801–806.

Kendall, M. G. *Rank correlation methods*. London: Griffin, 1948.

Kristof, W. Statistical inferences about the error variance. *Psychometrika*, 1963, **28**, 129–144.

Kruskal, J. B. Multidimensional scaling by optimizing goodness of fit to a nonmetric hypothesis. *Psychometrika*, 1964, **29**, 1–28.

Lennon, R. T. Assumptions underlying the use of content validity. *Educ. psychol. Measmt*, 1956, **16**, 294–304.

Lewis, D. *Quantitative methods in psychology.* New York: McGraw-Hill, 1960.

Likert, R. A technique for the measurement of attitudes. *Arch. Psychol.,* 1932, No. 140.

Lindquist, E. F. (Ed.) *Educational measurement.* Washington: American Council on Education, 1951.

Loevinger, Jane. Objective tests as instruments of psychological theory. *Psychol. Rep.,* 1957, **3**, 635–694.

Lohnes, P. R. Test space and discriminant space classification models and related significance tests. *Educ. psychol. Measmt,* 1961, **21**, 559–574.

Lord, F. M. The relation of the reliability of multiple-choice tests to the distribution of item difficulties. *Psychometrika,* 1952, **17**, 181–194. (a)

Lord, F. M. A theory of test scores. *Psychometr. Monogr.,* 1952, No. 7. (b)

Lord, F. M. A study of speed factors in tests and academic grades. *Psychometrika,* 1956, **21**, 31–50.

Lord, F. M. An approach to mental test theory. *Psychometrika,* 1959, **24**, 283–302.

Lord, F. M. *The negative hypergeometric distribution with practical application to mental test scores.* Princeton, N.J.: Educational Testing Service, 1960.

Lord, F. M. Formula scoring and validity. *Educ. psychol. Measmt,* 1963, **23**, 663–672.

McGee, R. K. Response style as a personality variable: By what criterion? *Psychol. Bull.,* 1962, **59**, 284–295.

McGinn, N. F., Harburg, E., Julius, S., and McLeod, J. M. Psychological correlates of blood pressure. *Psychol. Bull.,* 1964, **61**, 209–219.

McNemar, Q. *Psychological statistics.* New York: Wiley, 1962.

McQuitty, L. L. Typal analysis. *Educ. psychol. Measmt,* 1961, **22**, 677–696.

Masling, J. The influences of situational and interpersonal variables in projective testing. *Psychol. Bull.,* 1960, **57**, 65–85.

Maxwell, A. E. Statistical methods in factor analysis. *Psychol. Bull.,* 1959, **56**, 228–235.

Maxwell, A. E. Canonical variate analysis when the variables are dichotomous. *Educ. psychol. Measmt,* 1961, **21**, 259–272.

Messick, S. J. The additive constant problem in multidimensional scaling. *Psychometrika,* 1956, **21**, 1–15.

Messick, S., and Ross, J. (Eds.) *Measurement in personality and cognition.* New York: Wiley, 1962.

Morrison, E. J. On test variance and the dimensions of the measurement situation. *Educ. psychol. Measmt*, 1960, **22**, 231–250.

Muldoon, J. F., and Ray, O. S. A comparison of pattern similarity as measured by six statistical techniques and eleven clinicians. *Educ. psychol. Measmt*, 1958, **18**, 775–782.

Neuhaus, J. O., and Wrigley, C. The Quartimax Method: An analytical approach to orthogonal simple structure. *Brit. J. statist. Psychol.*, 1954, **7**, 81–91.

Nunnally, J. C. An investigation of some propositions of self-conception: The case of Miss Sun. *J. abnorm. soc. Psychol.*, 1955, **50**, 87–92.

Nunnally, J. C. *Tests and measurements: Assessment and prediction.* New York: McGraw-Hill, 1959.

Nunnally, J. C. *Popular conceptions of mental health: Their development and change.* New York: Holt, 1961.

Nunnally, J. C. The analysis of profile data. *Psychol. Bull.*, 1962, **59**, 311–319.

Nunnally, J. C. *Educational measurement and evaluation.* New York: McGraw-Hill, 1964.

Nunnally, J. C., Duchnowski, A. J., and Parker, R. K. Association of neutral objects with rewards: Effect on verbal evaluation, reward expectancy, and selective attention. *J. pers. soc. Psychol.*, 1965, **1**, 270–274.

Nunnally, J. C., and Hodges, W. F. Some dimensions of individual differences in word association. *J. verb. Learn. verb. Behav.*, 1965, **4**, 82–88.

Nunnally, J. C., and Husek, T. R. The phony language examination: An approach to the measurement of response bias. *Educ. psychol. Measmt*, 1958, **18**, 275–282.

Nunnally, J. C., Stevens, D. A., and Hall, G. F. Association of neutral objects with rewards. *J. exp. child Psychol.*, 1965, **2**, 44–57.

Osgood, C. E. Studies on the generality of affective meaning systems. *Amer. Psychologist*, 1962, **17**, 10–28.

Osgood, C. E., and Suci, G. J. A measure of relation determined by both mean differences and profile information. *Psychol. Bull.*, 1952, **49**, 251–262.

Osgood, C. E., Suci, G. J., and Tannenbaum, P. H. *The measurement of meaning.* Urbana, Ill.: Univer. Illinois Press, 1957.

Peters, C. C., and Van Voorhis, W. R. *Statistical procedures and their mathematical bases.* New York: McGraw-Hill, 1940.

Peterson, D. R. Scope and generality of verbally defined personality factors. *Psychol. Rev.*, 1965, **72**, 48–59.

Pettigrew, T. F. The measurement and correlates of category width as a cognitive variable. *J. Pers.*, 1958, **26**, 532–544.

Pinneau, S. R., and Newhouse, A. Measures of invariance and comparability in factor analysis for fixed variables. *Psychometrika*, 1964, **29**, 271–282.

Plumlee, L. B. The effect of difficulty and chance success on item-test correlation and on test reliability. *Psychometrika*, 1952, **17**, 69–86.

Price, Dorothy B. A group approach to the analysis of individual differences in the randomness of guessing behavior on multiple-choice tests and the development of scoring methods to take such differences into account. *Res. Bull.* No. 64-59. Princeton, N.J.: Educational Testing Service, 1964.

Rimland, B. The effects of varying time limits and of using "right answer not given" in experimental forms of the U.S. Navy Arithmetic Test. *Educ. psychol. Measmt*, 1960, **20**, 533–540.

Rorer, L. G. The great response-style myth. *Psychol. Bull.*, 1965, **63**, 129–156.

Rotter, J. B., Rafferty, Janet E., and Schachtitz, E. Validation of the Rotter Incomplete Sentences Blank for college screening. *J. consult. Psychol.*, 1949, **13**, 348–356.

Rulon, P. J. Distinctions between discriminant analysis and regression analysis and a geometric interpretation of the discriminant function. *Harvard Educ. Rev.*, 1951, **21**, 80–90.

Sawrey, W. L., Keller, L., and Conger, J. J. An objective method of grouping profiles by distance functions and its relation to factor analysis. *Educ. psychol. Measmt*, 1960, **20**, 651–673.

Shepard, R. N. The analysis of proximities: Multidimensional scaling with an unknown distance function. II. *Psychometrika*, 1962, **27**, 125–140.

Shure, G. H., and Miles, R. S. Note of caution on the factor analysis of the MMPI. *Psychol. Bull.*, 1965, **63**, 14–18.

Sokal, B. R. A comparison of five tests for completeness of factor extraction. *Trans. Kans. Acad. Sci.*, 1959, **62**, 141–152.

Spearman, C. "General intelligence" objectively determined and measured. *Amer. J. Psychol.*, 1904, **15**, 201–293.

Spearman, C. *The abilities of man.* New York: Macmillan, 1927.

Spearman, C., and Holzinger, K. J. The sampling error in the theory of two factors. *Brit. J. Psychol.*, 1924, **15**, 17–19.

Stephenson, W. *The study of behavior.* Chicago: Univer. Chicago Press, 1953.

Stern, J. A., and McDonald, D. G. Physiological correlates of mental disease. In P. R. Farnsworth, Olga McNemar, and Q. McNemar (Eds.), *Annual review of psychology*. Palo Alto, Calif.: Annual Reviews, 1965. Pp. 225–264.

Stevens, S. S. (Ed.) *Handbook of experimental psychology*. New York: Wiley, 1951.

Stevens, S. S. Problems and methods of psychophysics. *Psychol. Bull.*, 1958, **55**, 177–196.

Taylor, Janet A. A personality scale of manifest anxiety. *J. abnorm. soc. Psychol.*, 1953, **48**, 285–290.

Tellegen, A. Direction of measurement: A source of misinterpretation. *Psychol. Bull.*, 1965, **63**, 233–243.

Thorndike, R. L. Reliability. In E. F. Lindquist (Ed.), *Educational measurement*. Washington: American Council on Education, 1951. Pp. 560–620.

Thorndike, R. L., and Hagen, Elizabeth. *Ten thousand careers*. New York: Wiley, 1959.

Thorndike, R. L., and Hagen, Elizabeth. *Measurement and evaluation in psychology and education*. New York: Wiley, 1961.

Thurstone, L. L. A law of comparative judgment. *Psychol. Rev.*, 1927, **34**, 273–286.

Thurstone, L. L. *Multiple-factor analysis*. Chicago: Univer. Chicago Press, 1947.

Thurstone, L. L., and Chave, E. J. *The measurement of attitude*. Chicago: Univer. Chicago Press, 1929.

Tiedeman, D. V., Bryan, J. G., and Rulon, P. J. An application of the multiple discriminant function to data from the airman classification battery. *Res. Bull.* No. 52–37. San Antonio, Tex.: Lackland Air Force Base, 1952.

Toops, H. A. A comparison, by work limit and time limit, of item analysis indices for practical test construction. *Educ. psychol. Measmt*, 1960, **20**, 251–266.

Torgerson, W. *Theory and methods of scaling*. New York: Wiley, 1958.

Tyler, F., and Michael, W. B. An empirical study of the comparability of factor structure when unities and communality estimates are used. *Educ. psychol. Measmt*, 1958, **18**, 347–354.

Ulrich, Lynn, and Trumbo, D. The selection interview since 1949. *Psychol. Bull.*, 1965, **63**, 100–116.

Wenger, M. A. Studies of autonomic balance in Army Air Forces personnel. *Comp. Psychol. Monogr.*, 1948, **19**, No. 101.

Wesman, A. G. Some effects of speed in test use. *Educ. psychol. Measmt*, 1960, **20**, 267–274.

Wittenborn, J. R. Contributions and current status of Q-methodology. *Psychol. Bull.*, 1961, **58**, 132–142.

Wood, Dorothy A. *Test construction: Development and interpretation of achievement tests.* Columbus, Ohio: Merrill, 1960.

Woodworth, R. S. *Personal data sheet.* Chicago: Stoelting, 1918.

Wrigley, C. The case against communalities. *Res. Rep.* No. 19. Berkeley, Calif.: Univer. California Press, 1957.

Zavala, A. Development of the forced-choice rating scale technique. *Psychol. Bull.*, 1965, **63**, 117–124.

INDEX